PROTESTANT THEOLOGY
IN THE NINETEENTH CENTURY

Protestant Theology in the Nineteenth Century

Its Background & History

KARL BARTH

JUDSON PRESS
Valley Forge

Library of Congress Cataloging in Publication Data

Barth, Karl, 1886–1968.
    Protestant theology in the nineteenth century.

    "The first complete translation of Die protestantische
Theologie im 19. Jahrhundert."
        1. Theology, Doctrinal—History—Germany.
        2. Theology, Doctrinal—History—18th century.
        3. Theology, Doctrinal—History—19th century.
        4. Theology, Protestant—Germany. I. Title.
BT30.G3B13   1972   230'.09'034   72–1956
ISBN 0–8170–0572–2

Judson Press edition, 1973
Second Printing 1976
© SCM Press Ltd 1959, 1972
Printed in Great Britain

CONTENTS

Preface to the First Complete English Edition   7
Foreword   11

1 THE TASK OF A HISTORY OF MODERN
PROTESTANT THEOLOGY   15

PART 1 · BACKGROUND

2 MAN IN THE EIGHTEENTH CENTURY   33
3 THE PROBLEM OF THEOLOGY IN THE
EIGHTEENTH CENTURY   80
4 PROTESTANT THEOLOGY IN THE EIGHTEENTH
CENTURY   136
5 ROUSSEAU   174
6 LESSING   234
7 KANT   266
8 HERDER   313
9 NOVALIS   341
10 HEGEL   384

PART 2 · HISTORY

11 SCHLEIERMACHER   425
12 WEGSCHEIDER   474
13 DE WETTE   482
14 MARHEINEKE   491
15 BAUR   499

CONTENTS

16 THOLUCK   508

17 MENKEN   519

18 FEUERBACH   534

19 STRAUSS   541

20 SCHWEIZER   569

21 DORNER   577

22 MÜLLER   588

23 ROTHE   597

24 HOFMANN   607

25 BECK   616

26 VILMAR   625

27 KOHLBRÜGGE   634

28 BLUMHARDT   643

29 RITSCHL   654

Index of Names   663

PREFACE TO THE
FIRST COMPLETE ENGLISH EDITION

IN 1959, a translation of eleven chapters of Barth's great book *Protestant Theology in the Nineteenth Century* was published by the SCM Press under the title *From Rousseau to Ritschl*. The appearance of some of the book in this form was a compromise solution to a number of difficult problems, but it was a solution that had its critics right from the beginning, and certainly did not win the approval of Barth himself. To a request for a Foreword to the English translation he wrote as follows:

> I have recently pondered in vain what I should say in the Foreword to my history book which you wish from me, and have come to the conclusion that it is better if you or one of your friends write it. Reason: it appears now in a form for which *you* have assumed responsibility that you must bear *vis-à-vis* English readers. I cannot alter the fact that I see the whole affair with a certain amount of head-shaking. I have looked at the book again recently and am more than ever convinced that the whole is indeed a fragment— but, as a fragment, nevertheless a unity, in which the two chief parts (Background and History) form unities. The reasons which have moved you to present this united fragment in still more fragments, you will have to explain to the English reader yourself: I cannot, because I just do not understand it. You know, of course, that there is also a shorter selection in French. But for that, too, I wrote no foreword, for the selection was not my responsibility. Please do not be angry with me. I neither can nor will hold up this matter, after your judgment and appraisal; but to give my blessing is *not* possible.

Confronted with the vast bulk of Barth's work, one can sympathize with the decision to abbreviate it; but a comparison of the present volume with *From Rousseau to Ritschl* will immediately indicate how

much the English reader has previously been missing and how right
Barth was in his reactions. As he says in his preface to the original
German, the book *is* a torso. Moreover, as he tried to explain in discussion of the book, despite its title it is neither a coherent history
of theology nor a collection of the biographies of leading theologians.
In a history of theology he would have had to mention more men,
tendencies and movements than he actually does. Moreover, the single
essays about the life and work of various theologians are no biographies
of the men concerned; they are always only about one single aspect
of their life and work. When Barth prepared the lectures which developed into the book, and which Hitler prevented him from finishing,
it was his intention to find out what answers there were to various
theological questions, what contributions there were towards the understanding of the main topics of dogmatic theology in the age about
which he had to speak. One cannot even call the book a theological
history of ideas, because it does not depict the history of all theological
ideas, but only of some of them.

Still, as Barth published it, the torso makes sense. It has a clear
structure, with introductory chapter and twofold division, of which
the first part relates to the eighteenth century and the second to the
nineteenth. For Barth, the nineteenth century cannot be understood
without the century that preceded it; for us, Barth cannot be understood without the men of the century which preceded him—even if
they are so often no more than names to us now. The links which
hold the book together are tenuous; misplaced surgery can all too
easily sever them.

It is because Barth's original book is a torso of this kind that an
alteration in his selection of figures can put them in an unintended
perspective. Barth took the chapter on Julius Müller as an example
of this problem. This chapter is not a description of Müller's life and
work as a whole. Anyone who wants to know anything about Müller
has to consult other sources. Nor can it be regarded as a history of
the doctrine of sin in the nineteenth century. The optimistic nineteenth century more or less ignored sin and neglected the doctrine of
sin. Barth wrote about Müller because Müller was concerned with the
doctrine of sin, but Müller had no essential influence upon the theological thought of his age, and he had no adherents or successors. If
the essay on Müller were to be published in isolation the reader would
get a wrong impression both of the man and of his age. He would get
the impression that Müller was only concerned with the doctrine of
sin, and that the age in which he lived had followed him—which was

not the case. Consequently, Barth believed that the selection of parts
of the book would lead to a false picture of the people described in
it and to a wrong impression of his own intentions.

The arguments, therefore, for publishing a complete English version
are overwhelming. That this is one of Barth's greatest achievements,
few will doubt. Paul Tillich, whose work at a similar task for a rather
later period can be seen in his *Perspectives on Nineteenth and Twentieth
Century Protestant Theology*, claimed that it was his favourite among
Barth's books. 'It shows clearly,' he remarked, 'how inadequate is the
image of Karl Barth in the English-speaking world, how much greater
Barth is than the "Barthians" have made him appear. It evaluates with
fairness and appreciation those men again whose theological influence
Barth fought all his life.' His verdict has been echoed time and again.

FOREWORD

THIS is not a new book. Indeed, it is a relatively old work. During my time in Basle I was unable to continue and improve the lectures on the history of modern Protestant theology that I gave in Münster and Bonn, though I have continually been preoccupied with the theme and even with some of the material. Their last form was a course that I gave in Bonn during the winter semester of 1932-3 and the summer semester of 1933 in which I examined first the 'background' and then the 'history' of Protestant theology from the time of Schleiermacher. (When the Hitler régime dawned, I happened to be occupied with Rousseau!) Both parts remain torsos. The 'background' was intended to end in a study of Goethe, for which at that time I was not completely unprepared and to which I was particularly looking forward. I had planned to take the 'history' as far as the time of Troeltsch. The limits of the academic semester prevented both parts from reaching their intended conclusions.

The reader is invited to reflect on the omissions. He will find all sorts of gaps that I would not leave open today, and accents which I would now place differently. He will also see where I have worked more with secondary than with primary sources. And he will probably stumble on one or other error of interpretation or judgment, caused by the haste in which I had to work and, at a deeper level, by limits to my vision. Let him remember that while I love history and have my own quite definite ideas about its role in a theological context, I am not a professional historian, and ultimately can only make suggestions and drop hints.

The reasons why despite this I am having the two sets of lectures published as I wrote them are twofold. First, they are in any case circulating in incomplete as well as complete copies and are constantly asked after, so that the demand must be satisfied in a legitimate way. Some sections (Schleiermacher, Menken, Feuerbach, Strauss) have already been published here and there. Since the lectures were given, considerable treatments of the same subject-matter have appeared: H. R. Mackintosh, *Types of Modern Theology* (1937) and Horst Stephan, *Geschichte der evangelischen Theologie seit dem deutschen Idealismus* (History of Protestant Theology from the period of German Idealism) (1938).

Secondly, and more profoundly, I have allowed publication because I have constantly had occasion to wish and suggest that the attitude and approach of the younger generations of Protestant theologians to the period of the Church that is just past might be rather different from that which they now often seem to regard, somewhat impetuously, as the norm—misunderstanding the guidance they have received from me. I would be very pleased if they were (to put it simply) to show a little more love towards those who have gone before us, despite the degree of alienation they feel from them. I made a few remarks to this effect in 1932-3, when I introduced the lectures. I hope that my own approach here will make clear to one and all that the better exegesis and dogmatic theology for which we are striving again today must prove itself by the way in which its advocates acquire not only a sharper but also a more impartial eye for the historical reality of their fellow-theologians of yesterday and the day before. We need openness towards and interest in particular figures with their individual characteristics, an understanding of the circumstances in which they worked, much patience and also much humour in the face of their obvious limitations and weaknesses, a little grace in expressing even the most profound criticism and finally, even in the worst cases, a certain tranquil delight that they were as they were. *Que voulez-vous? Le bon Dieu l'a fait comme cela*, remarked a Moroccan soldier to me about a human fellow-creature with whom he was not exactly pleased. And after all this, perhaps we ourselves will be portrayed, discussed and assessed by a posterity that is better instructed than ourselves! Above all, such an approach is in accord with the knowledge of the divine judgment on all that is called the flesh, which has rightly and necessarily come alive among us in such a different way. Whence comes historical rectitude, if not from here? I would venture to make the exaggerated claim that it is possible and necessary to portray someone like Schleiermacher in a very different way against the background of my *Church Dogmatics*, necessary to show him in a much more attractive and much more impressive light than does, say, Horst Stephan, against the background of his theology. I will allow the objection that in this respect my lectures fall far short of the demands of the task to stand as witness to an understanding of what I would really like to see and strive for in this field. And I hope all the more that in this respect the new generation reaching maturity will not fall short, but surpass me.

Basle, September 1946

I

THE TASK OF A HISTORY OF
MODERN PROTESTANT THEOLOGY

THE course and the destination of the work that lies before us are by no means obvious. So at the beginning, it may be worth while making a brief attempt to reach some degree of understanding about them.

I. To describe and understand the history of Protestant theology from the time of Schleiermacher onwards is a *theological* task. Even as an object of historical consideration, theology demands theological perception, theological thought and theological involvement. Of course, there is no method, not even a theological one, by means of which we can be certain of catching sight of theology. In this way, too, it can escape us, because we are inadequate to the task it poses. Nevertheless, it is a *conditio sine qua non* of the success of our undertaking that it should be approached theologically, in accordance with its subject-matter. This subject-matter will certainly escape us to the degree that we want to deny it this special participation. Here we come up against the universal rule of historical understanding about which Luther, two days before his death, wrote on a scrap of paper these famous words: 'No one can understand Virgil in his Bucolics and Georgics unless he has been a shepherd or a farmer for fifty years. No one can understand Cicero in his letters unless he has been involved for twenty years in the life of a powerful state. Let no one think that he has tasted Holy Scripture unless he has for a century *ecclesias gubernarit* and has been responsible for the Church.' We know history only when and in that something happens in us and for us, perhaps even happens against us; we know it only when and in that an event concerns us, so concerns us that we are there, that we participate in it. Any knowledge of history that proved to be merely seeing, observing, establishing, is a contradiction in itself. Certainly the knowledge of human action—and that is what history is about—involves seeing, observing, establishing, but not in isolated theory. The theory of practice is the only possible theory where history is concerned. It is a seeing, observing, establishing where we ourselves are taken up in a particular movement, taken up in an action of our own which somehow encounters, corresponds to or even contradicts the action of another. We know history in that another's action somehow becomes a question to which our own action has to give some sort of answer. Without this responsible reaction to being questioned, our knowledge of history would be knowledge of facts, but not of living people; it would not be history but a form of science.

The subject-matter of history, the historical fact, is living man. His actions become evident to us in their relationship to our actions. So no one can understand the theology of the nineteenth century or of any other century unless in some way he has himself taken upon himself the burden of theological work. By this is meant not merely assuming the status of a theologian, but actively participating in his problems. This participation need not exclude critical, negative, sceptical attitudes within and even towards theology, provided that it is itself theological, provided that it does not represent an abandonment of the problem of theology, a μετάβασις εἰς ἄλλο γένος, provided that the presupposition remains, even here, a readiness for one's own responsible involvement, practical reason. Neither the misguided theologian nor even the opponent of theology are excluded as incompetent —it is impossible to be an opponent of theology without being a theologian oneself—but only the idle onlooker who thinks that he can see and talk about something that does not concern him. Here, as anywhere, this onlooker sees nothing at all of history as such, of the event, no matter how carefully and widely the net of things that have happened is spread before him. If his eyes are to be opened and he is to be entitled to join in the discussion, he must be involved in the matter.

Now the matter, theology, is critical and systematic reflection on the presupposition of the Church's ministry of witness. The servant of the Word of God must be a theologian because he has to testify to that Word by his speaking in preaching, instruction and pastoral care. It is not the Word of God that is conditioned by human knowledge and requires critical, systematic reflection, but his own service to the Word of God, this particular service to the Word of God by the testimony of his own speaking. What is involved is always the hearing of the Word of God, documented in the Bible, in any given present, since that necessarily precedes any speaking. Because the present is continually changing, the theologian cannot be content with establishing and communicating the results obtained by some classical period; his reflection must be renewed constantly. For this reason, serious theological work is forced, again and again, to begin from the beginning. However, as this is done, the theology of past periods, classical and less classical, also plays a part and demands a hearing. It demands a hearing as surely as it occupies a place with us in the context of the Church. The Church does not stand in a vacuum. Beginning from the beginning, however necessary, cannot be a matter of beginning off one's own bat. We have to remember the communion of saints, bearing and being borne by each other, asking and being asked, having to take mutual responsibility for and among the sinners gathered together in Christ. As regards theology, also, we cannot be in the Church without taking as much responsibility for the theology of the past as for the theology of our present. Augustine, Thomas Aquinas, Luther, Schleiermacher and all the rest are not dead, but living. They still speak and demand a hearing as living voices, as surely as we know that they and we belong together in the Church. They made in their time the same contribution to the task of the Church that is required of us today. As we make our contribution, they join in with theirs, and we cannot play our part today without allowing them to play theirs. Our responsibility is not only to God, to ourselves, to the men of today, to other living theologians, but to them. There is no past in the Church, so there is no past in theology. 'In him they all live.' Only the heretic, indeed only the arch-heretic, the one who is totally lost even for God's invisible Church, could really belong to the past and have nothing more to say to us. And we are in no position to identify such arch-heresy. Not even among avowed pagans, much less among Jews or suspect, even very suspect, Christians. All heretics are relatively heretical, so even those who have been branded heretics at one time or another and condemned for their avowed folly and wickedness must be allowed their say in theology. The theology of any period must be strong and free enough to give a calm, attentive and open hearing not only to the voices of the Church Fathers, not only to favourite voices, not only to the voices of the classical past, but to all the voices of the past. God is the Lord of the Church. He is also the Lord of theology. We cannot anticipate which of our fellow-workers from the past are welcome in our own work and which are not. It may always be that we have especial need of quite unsuspected (and among these, of quite unwelcome) voices in one sense or another. So history, the history of the Church, of doctrine and of theology, enters the theological workshop and becomes a theological task.

We shall be concerned here with the history of more recent Protestant theology, Protestant theology in the nineteenth and twentieth centuries. In other words, we are concerned with that theology which lies closest to us (the present excepted) and therefore makes the most urgent contribution to our time, the theology of our fathers, grandfathers and great-grandfathers. It has often been said that to understand and describe a piece of history that lies so close to us is a difficult, even impossible task. This comment is right in that it is easier to understand and describe such a piece of history if it confronts us as to some degree a rounded whole than if it is all too evidently in the course of development; it is easier, because seeing, observing and establishing are so much easier. But make no mistake, there are in reality no completely closed periods of history that are not in the course of development; this only seems to be the case when, as a result of adequate source material, living men cease to play any part as subjects of history and therefore fail to gain a hearing and fall from view. Where that is the case, where we have only objective facts as the subject-matter of our knowledge, of a kind that bear no relationship to our own actions, where seeing, observing, establishing are made all too easy, history must inevitably turn into science. If we are really concerned with what makes history different from science, we shall find no ideal conditions for historical knowledge in the immobility with which this or that distant event stands before us, nor shall we lament the degree of incompleteness, the topical urgency of the history that stands closest to us and so hampers our vision. The more difficult it is to see, observe, establish, the more urgently history asks questions of us and demands an answer, thus leaving no time for being a mere spectator, the more we have to do with real history.

It is clear that this is the situation in which we find ourselves in connection with our present task. The time of Schleiermacher and his followers is all too pressingly related to our own time; their problems, questions and answers reach all too openly into our own. We are all too conscious of the familiar gaze of our fathers, grandfathers and great-grandfathers to be able to see, observe, establish as we would like to—as a matter of convenience, but to the detriment of the true historicity of our subject-matter and our knowledge of it. We cannot consider them as we feel we can consider the history of distant times, countries and cultures. The way in which the proximity of the subject-matter disturbs us is a sign of its eminent historicity. Theological Philistines—but only theological Philistines, and perhaps very learned

Philistines at that—may manage to face the Trinitarian and Christo-logical disputes of the fourth and fifth centuries, or even the eucharistic dispute of the sixteenth century, in the mood of the man who sees 'the nations fighting far away in distant Turkey', but it might be good for precisely these Philistines if such a mood were disrupted. Here the theology of the earlier period presses us hard, so hard that Hausrath seems to be right in ending his biography of Richard Rothe with the words: *mutato nomine de te fabula narratur*. Or, if that seems to be saying too much, we cannot fail to feel the demand for a sense of mutual responsibility, which church theology now has to meet. To this degree, concern with this particular period of the history of theology might be a specially salutary practice in learning the tranquil, attentive and open hearing of the involved participant which we cannot fail to give to the history of theology if we want to do theology in the Church, that is, in the only possible sphere for this undertaking.

II. The moment of one's own theological knowledge is always to some extent an intoxicating one, not only when a student in his middle or later years has the experience, through the guidance of his teacher or through his own initiative, of having discovered what is going on behind the sphinx-like expression of theology, but still more when many an argument has been held and half, or even the whole, of a life devoted to scholarship lies in the past. The intoxication of such a moment represents a temptation which must now be mentioned. It is by no means the case that one's hearing of the voices of the past is correct and that it remains correct, however much that may have been the case to begin with.

In this respect, the moment of one's own theological recognition represents a crisis. Will it remain clear to us at this moment that while the present can always be right over against the past, we can give no satisfactory answer to the question whether it is right in actual fact? If that is forgotten, if in the intoxication of the moment the conscious-ness of being able to be right turns into the consciousness of actually being right, then our hearing of the voices of the past will be objectively wrong, however much it may be subjectively right. The one who is all too sure, illegitimately sure, that 'we have brought it to so glorious a conclusion' cannot and may not notice carefully 'what a wise man thought before us'. When that happens, he is no longer on the same level as this wise man from the past, he is no longer responsible to him, but has clearly made him responsible to himself. That man now in some way stands before his throne of judgment. He must be his own witness, either in his wisdom or in his folly. He now belongs either to the sheep, who will be put on the right hand, or the goats, who will be put on the left, both to the greater glory of the theological judge of the world presiding at that particular session. He is now no longer allowed to have his own say, but has to play a role corresponding with my point of view. He becomes a black or a white piece on my chessboard, and I am the man who plays both black and white together, and so, interestingly, plays for himself against himself.

The description of the history of theology, and more particularly of recent theology, has largely been dominated by this pattern. I can think of a whole series of accounts where it is all too evident that the authors are not guiding us in a shared investigation of what the men of the past may be saying to us; rather, the one who has already made his discovery, who has done with listening, directs us with vigorous gestures to the position where he is now standing (not to say, sitting!). There is no question of being on the way. It is all too obvious that the figures of the past are to be explained to us only as positive or negative forerunners of the messiah of the time, however modestly he may be hiding his own appearance, his own knowledge (in this case his own *Dogmatics*) under the ample garb of the 'historian'. This is clearly the case with the first volume, the historical survey, of E. Schaeder, *Theozentrische Theologie* (first published 1909), in which the author is concerned to trace through the entire history of the previous century the scarlet thread of the right approach, which has somehow been 'snarled up' or 'broken'; he then develops this approach and brings it to a triumphant conclusion in the second volume. Troeltsch's article 'Rückblick auf ein halbes Jahrhundert der theologischen Wissenschaft'[1] is a brilliant example of its kind, but his procedure is precisely the same when he elaborates two or three problems as the riddle of the century and develops them just to the point at which, in a comforting way, the historian's own systematic solution begins. Again, Herrmann, under the title of *A History of Protestant Dogmatics*,[2] has produced a plain and simple history of the infection of all theology by a legalistic view of Christianity and of the dawning triumph of the pure *fides qua creditur*, a triumph as a result of which, at the conclusion of Herrmann's account, positive and liberal dogmatics are literally 'thrown into the same grave'. Similarly, the Erlangen theologian Frank could take up Schiller's statement 'World history is the world's judgment' on the

[1] First published 1908; *Gesammelte Schriften* II, pp. 193ff.
[2] *Geschichte der protestantischen Dogmatik*, in Hinnenberg, *Kultur der Gegenwart* I, 4, 2, first published 1906.

very first page of his *Geschichte und Kritik der neueren Theologie* (History and Criticism of Modern Theology) (first published 1894) and consequently give himself the task of demonstrating the 'self-corrupting process of sin and the lie' over against 'the preservative, self-renewing and victorious powers of the positive Christian life' from a 'standpoint of the faith of the Church', knowledge of which he can take for granted. W. Elert, *Der Kampf um das Christentum seit Schleiermacher und Hegel* (The Struggle over Christianity from the time of Schleiermacher and Hegel) (1921) is a unique and very valuable collection of material and literature, but it carries on the tradition of Erlangen only too faithfully in presupposing that Christianity and Christendom are given and known entities and that the change from the synthesis of Christian and profane consciousness to the diastasis between them can be used as a historical criterion of value. Brunner, in his *Mysticism and the Word* (first published 1924), armed with the standards of Reformation theology, brings Schleiermacher to a trial from which he has to depart condemned before it has even begun. Again, F. K. Schumann, in the second, historical part of his book *Der christliche Gottesgedanke und der Zerfall der Moderne* (The Christian Notion of God and the Collapse of Modernity) (1929), undertakes to pursue what he considers to be the arch-enemy, idealistic 'non-objectivity', right through most recent theology to its most secret lair in books by Karl Heim and myself. However, the unchallenged master of the above-mentioned art of directing all water to one's mill in a refined combination of eirenism and polemic is not a Protestant at all, but the Catholic theologian Erich Przywara, whose historical analyses as given in his *Religions-philosophie katholische Theologie* (1926) and his articles in *Stimmen der Zeit* (now collected in two volumes, *Ringen der Gegenwart*, 1929) cannot go unmentioned here. He is one of the few Catholics who also know Protestant literature and can evaluate the problems with which it deals appropriately. His method of approach is uncommonly instructive for the point under discussion here. It is not surprising that all his roads in the end lead to Rome, but it is surprising that the same thing happens, *mutatis mutandis*, with so many Protestant writers, though not so artistically and without so attractive a prospect as the view of Rome now presents.

The perspective by which all these writers have been approached is not meant to be an attack on the material content of their polemic; I have mentioned only good books of this kind, from which one can continually draw instruction and stimulation. I would, however, like, to issue a warning against a book that is definitely not a good one,

T. Odenwald, *Protestantische Theologie. Überblick und Einführung* (Protestant Theology. Survey and Introduction) (1928). It is bad not just because there is a naïve commendation of everything on a line from Luther to Wobbermin through Schleiermacher and Ritschl, but because the work is so tedious, formalistic and lacking in deeper insight; because one can find only slogans, and not ideas in it. The accounts mentioned above are to be objected to, not as evidence of the often very fruitful and promising preoccupation of their authors with particular problems, but in so far as they set out more or less explicitly to be at the same time historical accounts. In this capacity, they share the common feature that in their accounts, after a long day of storm and tempest (represented by the bad or incomplete theology of the others, from earlier times) there is a very bright evening (namely, when the theology of the author announces itself as the point of reference for his historical study): *post tenebras lux!* 'What the shadow prefigured has now taken place!' But this mode of procedure cannot be allowed where knowledge of history is honestly sought as a presupposition of one's own position and does not serve merely as a pretext for the subsequent strengthening of a position that has already been adopted. I hope that anyone who feels from these lectures how good it is, after a long detour from Schleiermacher via Ritschl to Troeltsch, Seeberg and Holl, to arrive at 'dialectical theology' as the long-suspected and awaited salvation from all distress which has so far evaded everyone's grasp, will have made a mistake. I would fail by my own standards if I took such a course of action. History is not a paint-box at the disposal of anyone who thinks he knows something and has a need to make his knowledge more impressive by an appropriate account of history.

To repeat the point, history is made up of living men whose work is handed over defenceless to our understanding and appreciation upon their death. Precisely because of this, they have a claim on our courtesy, a claim that their own concerns should be heard and that they should not be used simply as a means to our ends. History is meant to bear witness to the truth of God, not to our achievements, so that we must avoid any thought that we already know what they have to say and be prepared to hear something new. Of course world history is the world's judgment, but this principle is an eschatological one: world history is the world's judgment in God's eyes, not in ours. We cannot be forbidden, rather, we are enjoined at particular times to say yes or no on our own responsibility to the work of the past by our own personal decisions and actions. We hear the voices of the ancients in order to give an answer by our own attitude and decision. But we do that for or against ourselves, not for or against them. With our own personal decisions we cannot associate judgments upon our forefathers, whether it is a case of pronouncing canonizations or settling accounts and carrying out funerals. For instance, if we were occupied here with the theology of the century of the Reformation, the desire to canonize would be the danger against which a warning needed to be issued. Anyone who is occupied today with the theology of the nineteenth century, on the other hand, needs to be warned not to suppose that he can settle it and be rid of it, as people always tend to be particularly blind and perhaps ungrateful to the period that went immediately before. An explicit judgment, the feeling that for better or for worse we can be 'finished' with this or that, always means the closing of a door that ought to remain open, the silencing of a voice that ought to continue to speak, and that is not only to our detriment, but also to the detriment of the Church. By transgressing the prohibition once formulated by Overbeck, to the effect that men are not called to hold the Last Judgment on one another[1], people violate the mystery of the body of Christ and at the least cut themselves off from a source of life.

We should not allow ourselves to be led astray here by the sophistic distinction that such judgments are directed merely at the subject-matter and not at the person. Frank, in particular, often comforted himself with this thought when passing judgment, and Brunner retreated to it with a somewhat hasty explanation at the end of his book on Schleiermacher (p. 361). A man can and must decide between Creator and creature where the Creator is God. But to distinguish between man and his work, between the sinner and his sinful action, is an impossible abstraction, which does not become more possible as a result of the frequency with which it is attempted. To the degree to which one commends or rejects a work, one also condemns or rejects a man. That must be stopped. The decisiveness of one's own thought, where we cannot but leave others explicitly to right or left behind us, is another matter—to decide about them oneself, to judge their otherness, their peculiarities, their narrowness, the limitations of their concern is another matter again. History writing cannot be a proclamation of judgment. In that case, it would seem that prophetic inspiration warranted us to presuppose not only that our age could be right, but that it was right. We shall do well not to claim this possibility too hastily or too often. It is appropriate for us to leave on one side what the Son of Man will do in his future, namely, to divide the good from the evil.

[1] *Christentum und Kultur*, p. 250.

The condition for a legitimate concern with the theology of the past is rather that we should escape again from the unavoidable intoxication of the moment of our own theological recognition as quickly as possible and with the utmost speed meet up again with our fathers, with those whose voices we think that we have heard often enough before. To say it again, we are with them in the Church. If perhaps they are not with us, if their voice is only the warning voice of total heresy, then precisely by being and remaining completely open to it, we shall experience its salutary effect upon us, which in that case is all that it can bring about. But the decision is not ours. To hear someone else always means to suspend one's own concern, to be open to the concern of the other. Care will always be taken that this openness is not too wide. But the demand directed towards us, that we must know and may not evade, here or elsewhere, by qualifying it and weakening it, is for openness. The success of our preoccupation with the theology of the nineteenth century will depend on the degree to which we can bring this openness to our particular concern.

To end these observations, I shall mention some books which, while in other respects less pioneering and fruitful than those already mentioned, deserve to be given an honourable mention before them because of the absence of theological concern for world judgment and the presence of genuine openness in their thought. First, two older works, the four-volume *Geschichte der protestantischen Dogmatik* (History of Protestant Dogmatics) by W. Gass (1854-67) and the *Geschichte der protestantischen Theologie* (History of Protestant Theology) by J. A Dorner (1867). Neither author, of course, conceals that for them in this sphere Schleiermacher represents the provisional end of the road to God, though Dorner is more independent, and more critical towards the master than Gass. But this orientation is not a hindrance; it does not arouse any unfavourable prejudgments in favour of Schleiermacher. On the contrary, it leads them to wait patiently, listen carefully and report appropriately, all along the line. The same thing can be said about F. Kattenbusch, *Die deutsche evangelische Theologie seit Schleiermacher* (German Protestant Theology from the time of Schleiermacher) (1926). Here, too, there is no lack of a clear tendency. Kattenbusch is one of those many theologians who want to be rid of all Scholasticism and Greekness in theology and who look for salvation from a return to Luther, of course as they understand him. As a result, he feels free to follow the tortuous paths of nineteenth-century theology with close and equitable attention, without making his master Ritschl the measure of all things. The way in which this scholar, now seventy-eight

years old, manages really to come to grips, albeit critically, with
spirits as alien to him and his kind as our present generation, calls
for unqualified respect. I would not commend his book to beginners,
as it presupposes too much and is written in somewhat unattractive
language. However, anyone who has some knowledge of its content
will be grateful for many stimulating observations. In this context,
mention ought also to be made of a book which appeared this summer
(1932): F. Spemann, *Theologische Bekenntnisse* (Theological Confessions).
It, too, is concerned with a survey and interpretation of the theology
of the nineteenth century, not in the form of a thorough-going investigation but rather by communicating all kinds of impressions, dominated by moods and biographical considerations, and often described
in an abundance of slogans. The author describes his account as one
'in disturbed movement' (p. 43), and under cover of this title the
reader has to put up with many all to naïve and superficial
instances of 'it seems to me'. A trace of partisan resentment against
the whole left wing of theology can be detected here, but the book
also deserves consideration for its attempts at a kind of ecumenical
breadth and openness for many, astonishingly many, one might
even say terrifyingly many possibilities on the other side, and the
seriousness with which it puts the question of special immediacy to
God, that cannot be denied even to the theology of the nineteenth
century.

While we are dealing with books, it is worth mentioning a practical
means of orienting ourselves towards the material which occupies us:
R. Grützmacher, *Textbuch zur Systematische Theologie* (Book of texts on
Systematic Theology) (²1923), a collection of source material. Of
course, I would recommend that the study of extracts made by someone else should be accompanied right from the start by one's own systematic study of a fairly short text like Schleiermacher's *Addresses* or
Ritschl's *Unterricht in der christlichen Religion* (Instruction in the Christian
Religion) or Harnack's *What is Christianity?* In any case, it is most
desirable to begin (whether in excerpts or in the original) with a few
sources and only to take up one or other of the accounts mentioned
when one has some first-hand idea of the atmosphere, the trends and
the feel of the time. And while I am giving advice, might I suggest to
everyone who might be interested in work by themselves that they
should make a synchronous chart for every single year of the period
with which we are occupied? It should have five columns: the first
for entering the most important dates of world history in general; the
second for the most noteworthy events in the history of culture, art

and literature; the third for church history in general; the fourth for the dates of birth and death of the most prominent theologians of the period; and the fifth for the years in which their most important books were published. Anyone who does this will see a mass of connexions which I shall rarely be able to go into here; this will also save us time, as I shall be able to leave out details of dates and the like as far as possible.

III. I must follow the remarks made in the second section with a few specific remarks about the procedure to be adopted in the present investigation.

I originally entitled this series of lectures 'The history of Protestant theology from the time of Schleiermacher'. This title implies, without giving grounds for the assumption, that this piece of history is a period, i.e. a complex of historical events that are connected in a particular way. Proof that the history of Protestant theology from the time of Schleiermacher is in fact such a complex, a meaningful period of history, can only be given in the course of the account itself. In historical knowledge, periodization is always the announcement of a hypothesis the proof of which is to be given afterwards, and this proof can only be given if one works with it and in this way allows it to speak for itself. Even then it is qualified by a last provision. To use Lessing's terms, a piece of history taken by itself and separated from the rest cannot be understood δογματικῶς, but only γυμναστικῶς. However, if this practice is carried out correctly, the result must be that not only this part of history will become visible, but somehow at the same time the whole of the history of theology in this part. There is a theory about the history of dogma, once impressively put forward by Thomasius of Erlangen and Vilmar of Marburg, but now generally abandoned as obsolete, according to which each period of history is to be compared with a particular stage in the development of a living organism. Each age seems to have, so to speak, thrust upon itself and suggested to itself in a certain necessary sequence the special knowledge and the special confession of a quite definite side of revealed truth. For example, the second and third centuries are entrusted with the knowledge of God the Creator in their struggle with early Gnosticism, the fourth century with the dogma of the Trinity, the fifth with the mystery of the Incarnation, the sixteenth with the doctrine of justification as forgiveness, etc. These theological philosophers of history ascribe to their own time, the nineteenth century, the special illumination of the doctrine of the Church. This theory might easily lead to constructive musings as soon as one tries to take it beyond a couple of illuminating examples, and one can do more than put a question mark against the statement that the nineteenth century was really the century of the Church (as is well known, our own century has already been proclaimed to be such once again). Nevertheless, the following points may certainly be maintained.

Every *period* of the Church does in fact want to be understood as a period of the *Church*, that is, as a time of revelation, knowledge and confession of the one Christian truth, indeed as a special time, as *this* time of such revelation, knowledge and confession. By being aware that we stand alongside theologians of the past in the Church, we are with them, even before we know them more closely, by knowing that in the last resort they are vitally concerned with the answer to a question which poses itself decisively to them also, a question which is raised for men by the Christian revelation that is the foundation of the Church. They are in search of the answer to a question that concerns us, too. Of course it is clear that they are concerned about something else before that; they are concerned with something that is only indirectly connected with that fundamental point, concerned, namely, to find an answer to the question in a language appropriate to their time, a particular answer that can be understood by their fellow-men, just as we in our time are without doubt concerned to find a language in which to give our answer. There are differences. But over and above the differences a unity can continually be seen, a unity of perplexity and disquiet, but also a unity of richness and hope, which in the end binds us to the theologians of the past. It would be slighting on both theology and on the Church if we were not to approach a particular period on this presupposition, or were to put it in question.

In view of a mood which is widespread in theological circles today, it is necessary to remind ourselves that it has in no way been revealed to us that the nineteenth century was in whole or in part a time in which God withdrew his hand from the Church. We cannot assume that the theologians of the period were in the end, ultimately and decisively, concerned with anything other than knowledge and confession of the Christian revelation. Whatever objections we may have, rightly or wrongly, to Schleiermacher and Ritschl, we are quite unjustified in ascribing to them any other theme, understanding them in the light of any other theme than that which we—to put it cautiously—would like ultimately and decisively to be our own, in the light of which we ourselves would like to be understood. The question 'Are you with Christ or with Wegscheider? . . . Is there still a word of God or not?', which the revivalist theologian Friedrich Sander hurled in the face of his liberal opponents during the Halle dispute of 1830[1] was understandable and perhaps necessary in the heat of battle. But if we are being honest with history, we may not make use of such antitheses. The Christian faith is not an authority which we are in a position to quote against others. That it is the basis for the mutual conversation between them and us may not be doubted for a moment, much less denied, no matter if we have a thousand reasons for such a verdict. Nor may we ascribe alien motives to others, as has happened so often from Frank to Brunner. *Credo unam sanctam catholicam et apostolicam ecclesiam* is the reason for this, and if I am to pay serious attention to a theologian of the past, whether he is called Schleiermacher or Ritschl or anyone else, then I must be deadly serious about this credo, unless I have been dispensed from it by individual inspiration to the conrary. In other words, regardless of my thousand reasons, I have to count all these people as members of the Christian Church and, remembering that I and my theological work are in the Christian Church only on the ground of forgiveness, I have neither to dispute nor even to doubt that, like me, they were ultimately concerned with the Christian faith. Were things in reality otherwise and I had still acted as though this were the case, that would certainly not be to my detriment: their partial and total errors and shortcomings will certainly come to light on the basis of this 'as if', and will not be in a position to lead me astray. But it could be to my detriment, and not only to mine, if it were the case and I acted towards them on the basis of my thousand reasons as though things were otherwise. In that case I would not have heard the Church in them as I should.

Now, however, on the basis of our unity with our predecessors, we must also take quite seriously the difference between them and ourselves. Even when we give full weight to the *credo ecclesiam* and take it specifically, we cannot mistake the fact that they obviously speak quite a different language from us. It is not only grammatically, syntactically and stylistically different, though there, of course, we can see significant distinctions. Its content, too, is different, in that the common vocabulary of the Christian Church which we both share is stressed, evaluated, used, classified and interpreted in quite another way. We may, indeed we must grant that in the end their intentions were not different from our own. Nevertheless, we cannot ignore the fact that they set out to do the same thing in quite a different way. They were involved in the same perplexity and disquiet, the same richness and

[1] Biography of Hengstenberg, II, p. 272.

hope towards the divine revelation that are also ours, in quite a different way. They translated and interpreted the same text in a particular way that is quite different from ours. In this encounter they were troubled in quite a different way from us. The Church means that the eternal revelation entered not only into time but also into the sequence and the changes of time. That the peculiarities and varying characteristics of this sequence of time can be surveyed as a whole and be understood as part of a process of organic growth, as Thomasius and Vilmar argued, was a consequence of this insight that we would prefer to leave alone as being all too naturalistic. The same thing applies to the insight that so to speak all the *loci* of classical dogma had their day and had to find their place in the timetable of church history. Nevertheless, it cannot be disputed that beyond the basis of unity, the various periods of the Church are different and do have their peculiarities, so that real historical knowledge of another period must consist in an awareness of its peculiarity and otherness, of its subsidiary themes, as well as of the main theme which it shares with us. In theology, we have beyond question not only the right but even the duty to be clear about the degree and manner in which our own particular approach was already present in an earlier time; we have to see how the peculiar theological concern of our own historical context was already seen and developed at an earlier date, or how far it was overlooked and neglected. It is quite legitimate for us to carry on a controversy, both positively and negatively, with the past in this way. But if we are to be dealing with history—and before we pursue our own concerns and while we do so, as theologians, we must also be occupied with history—this controversy originating in our own time must not be allowed to dominate the proceedings. We must always—under the presupposition of the unity of the Church—investigate the particular context and concern of the past and understand this from its own relative centre and not from ours. That is the concern with which we must enter upon the task that lies before us. . . .

PART ONE

BACKGROUND

2

MAN IN THE EIGHTEENTH CENTURY

IN 1720 there appeared the famous work *Vernünfftige Gedancken von Gott, der Welt und der Seele des Menschen auch allen Dingen überhaupt den Liebhabern der Wahrheit mitgetheilet von Christian Wolffen*.[1] Its frontispiece shows a sun whose powerful rays pierce a mass of black clouds, and spread light upon mountains, forests, towns and villages. The aureole of this sun is obviously not considered to be insupportable to the human gaze, for it takes the form of an exceedingly friendly and pleasantly smiling human face, whose owner seems to be extremely pleased to see the clouds in the heavens and the shadows on the earth dissipate everywhere.

In view of the logic, psychology, cosmology and theology which this book expounds, it is very understandable, and largely in harmony with the author's spirit, that the spiritual movement, whose document the book is, should be termed the Enlightenment, that Enlightenment has been understood to mean man's optimistic effort to master life by means of his understanding ('thoughts'), and finally that the age of that movement, the eighteenth century, has been classified, praised or blamed *a parte potiori* as the age of Enlightenment and that of this kind of Enlightenment. The man of the eighteenth century would then be the champion against prejudices and passions, against vice and hypocrisy, ignorance and superstition, intolerance, partiality and fanaticism; he would honour wisdom and virtue, reason and nature; he would seek his 'pleasure' by finding 'happiness' in the fulfilment of duty, and he would seem to see the supreme goal of the understanding (and therefore of man) as 'utility', personal and general 'welfare', and the supreme spiritual gift as the possession of 'taste' and 'wit', and to see man also as a somewhat tepid, but always very assured and busy believer in God, freedom and immortality.

The man of the eighteenth century would then be such as Gottsched, Nicolai and Basedow, as they lived on in the memory of the men of

[1] *Reasonable Thoughts on God, the World and the Human Soul, and All things in General, communicated to the Lovers of Truth by Christian Wolff.*

the *Sturm und Drang*, and as indeed they were, in large measure. He would be like Wagner, the familiar in Goethe's *Faust* who was so severely judged by his master ('That this dry creeping fellow should disturb this wealth of visions!'), the enemy of all history, enthusiasm, poetry, mystery, as Novalis described him in *Die Christenheit oder Europa* (Christendom or Europe). Or even he would be like that 'divinely Chinese optimist' to whom Kierkegaard in *Begriff der Ironie* (The Concept of Irony) has raised a frightening little monument.

What are we to say of all this? Certainly, that kind of man did exist in the eighteenth century, and perhaps every more or less typical eighteenth-century man in his own way had something of him in himself. But we must not forget that the likeness even of Christian Wolff and his successors is only partially caught in these pictures or caricatures and in the slogans of optimism, moralism, intellectualism and so on. And, moreover, Christian Wolff and his like were not the only bearers of Enlightenment. Voltaire, who was assuredly one, was at any rate no Wagner. Alongside Wagner, Goethe, as Korff justly points out,[1] set Mephistopheles, a figure of Enlightenment, who was not very optimistic, a sceptic—think of the resignation in which Frederick the Great ended—in whom the Enlightenment doubts itself, or at least reaches enlightenment about itself.

But even Mephistopheles is not the only alternative to Wagner. Mozart's *Magic Flute*, first performed in 1791, is certainly also a classic document of the Enlightenment. Here too the group of symbols, sun, light, darkness, plays a decisive part. But who would think of Nicolai or Voltaire in connexion with its mysticism of initiation and its message of the power of music to lead man triumphantly through the night of death? Or what have the architecture and the park of Brühl castle to do with the spirit of Wagner and Mephistopheles? And has not, as again Korff points out, Faust himself, the man of Goethe's time, by a partially almost insensible transition emerged from the man of the Enlightenment, so that we must give the latter the credit for having after all contained his successor in embryo? We shall come to this in our discussion of Rousseau, Lessing and Kant.

But if this is so, what would become of the definition which has been indefatigably repeated by the historians of theology (Stephan, Hoffmann and others), and even maintained by Korff (I, 24), of the Enlightenment as 'culture of the understanding', as 'rationalism', a rationalism to be happily replaced in Goethe's time by a new 'irrationalism'? And how could this pattern fit the great Leibnitz, called 'the

---

[1] *Geist der Goethezeit* (The Spirit of the Age of Goethe), I, 31.

father of the Enlightenment'? Would it not show a very poor understanding of him, to appeal to an irrational completion of his rationalism? As if he of all people did not understand this dialectic very well!
For it was the problem of his whole thought and life to overcome that
pattern. However when we call Leibnitz the pre-eminent representative
of his century, must we not continue to ask whether the whole concept
of 'Enlightenment', the whole picture of the sun piercing the clouds, is
enough to characterize one aspect of the century—even on the widest
possible interpretation. Could we not with almost as much justice call
it the century of mystery? Is it not one of the remarkable characteristics of that century that the darkness, that is, the spirit, the order and
disorder of the Middle Ages, to which on the one hand it so eagerly
opposed the light of reason and virtue, was something which on the
other hand it both desired and confirmed? Did it not seek freedom and,
in the very search for what it understood by freedom, again and again
re-create the old unfreedom? How could one reduce without remainder
say, the will of Frederick the Great to the denominator 'Enlightenment'? Even in Goethe's time, beside the learned student of Göttingen,
and the worldly-wise student of Leipzig, there was still to be found the
unbroken rowdy and drunkard of Jena, whom the poet and minister
had sometimes to call to order in the theatre at Weimar, in a voice of
thunder and with the threat of the Hussars. All three types are true
children of the age.

But even apart from these connexions with the past, what is the
significance for the Enlightenment that an institution so characteristic
of its spirit as the order of Freemasons, founded in 1717, should assume
the form of an introduction to a mystery religion? One must in fact say
that, on closer inspection, the century possessed, somewhere in the
midst of its consciousness, in spite of and besides its cult of light, but
also in the end in relation to it a peculiar and widespread and various
knowledge and pursuit of the mysterious. The century did not only
have its philosophers (in the traditional sense as well as in its own
special understanding of the word), its historians and naturalists, its
princely and its commoner philanthropists, its schoolmasters and
journalists, but also (entirely out of its own peculiar genius) its mystics
and enthusiasts and pietists, its Rosicrucians and *illuminati*, its al-
chemists and quacks, its Swedenborg and Cagliostro and Casanova.
Count Zinzendorf read and treasured his Pierre Bayle, but this obviously did not in the least hinder him from singing and spreading the
praise of the Lamb. The most eminent scientists of the time, such as
the biologist Albrecht von Haller and the mathematician Leonhard

Euler, were also serious and convinced defenders of traditional Christianity. In the struggle which was fought out at the end of the seventeenth century in the closest entourage of Louis XIV about Quietism, with Madame de Guyon and Fénelon on the one side and Bossuet on the other, typical tendencies of our very age were found on both sides. But what did either of them have to do with 'Enlightenment'? Of course, this expression does have and retains its interpretive significance. But if we really want to see and understand the time from Louis XIV to the French Revolution in its totality, then we must not designate the period as a whole as 'the Enlightenment', but rather interpret it in a more comprehensive way. It is and remains a fact which we cannot ignore that the *Sturm und Drang*, idealism and romanticism, and above all Goethe himself, in dealing with that time, understood it as 'Enlightenment', and that predominantly in the narrower sense of the term. But I do not see how we can understand that discussion by simply appropriating its own terms; rather we must grasp the background and the circumstances in which they have their relative importance. Above all, I do not see how we can reach a theological understanding of the whole situation except by such a procedure.

The sixth volume of Walter Goetz's *Propyläen-Weltgeschichte* (Propyläen—Universal History, 1931), which deals with this period, is entitled *Das Zeitalter des Absolutismus* (The Age of Absolutism). This description probably refers to the well-known structure of the political order of that period, so characteristic of Louis XIV as well as of Frederick the Great and Joseph II. But political structure is at all times and was therefore also at that time no more than an expression of the order of life, the ideal of life in general. 'Absolutism' in general can obviously mean a system of life based upon the belief in the omnipotence of human powers. Man, who discovers his own power and ability, the potentiality dormant in his humanity, that is, his human being as such, and looks upon it as the final, the real and absolute, I mean as something 'detached', self-justifying, with its own authority and power, which he can therefore set in motion in all directions and without any restraint—this man is absolute man. And this absolute man, whether he is called Louis XIV or Frederick the Great or Voltaire, whether he lives the obscure life of a philistine with secret revolutionary thoughts or of a friend of letters with liberal religious or even sceptical tendencies, or of a lady in her castle devoted to the mysticism of Tersteegen, or whether he sails the seas with James Cook or is a watchmaker in Geneva making tiny but useful improvements in the products of his handiwork—for the nature and the degree of the expression he gives to his life is not what matters, nor the extent of his knowledge of how much he shares in the general movement of the time, all that matters is the thing itself—this absolute man is eighteenth-century man, who appears to us more or less distinctly, more or less open or veiled in conventional drapings, in all the human faces of that century which are so different amongst themselves.

We can see this man even in Leibnitz, to some extent. He can be a man of the Enlightenment, but not necessarily, and above all not necessarily in the narrower sense of the term. He is primarily the discoverer, the believer, and the exploiter of the miracle of human power. As such he can be a man of the Enlightenment, but he can also—for he does not need instruction from us about the necessity and beauty of the 'irrational'—become something quite different: Wagner and Mephistopheles and Faust in one, not forgetting: also Nathan and Saladin, Goetz and Egmont, and a 'sensitive soul', Moor the Robber, Don Carlos, and many others. We shall speak in following chapters of the Christianity of this man, of the form which theology takes in his world. For the moment he interests us for his own sake, for his sheer humanity. 'Absolutism': this comprehensive key-word which we are now going to enquire into clearly indicates a programme. But where there is a programme, there is also a problem. And where there is a problem we find ourselves recalled, in one way or another, to a reality beyond the scope of programmes. A problem means limits and contradiction, perhaps self-contradiction. This is certainly what we find when we try to come to closer grips with the material which we have provisionally described as 'absolutism'.

Let us begin with some external facts. Eighteenth-century man was the man who could no longer remain ignorant of the significance of the fact that Copernicus and Galileo were right, that this vast and rich earth of his, the theatre of his deeds was not the centre of the universe, but a grain of dust amid countless others in this universe, and who clearly saw the consequences of all this. What did this really apocalyptic revolution in his picture of the universe mean for man? An unprecedented and boundless humiliation of man? No, said the man of the eighteenth century, who was not the first to gain this knowledge, but certainly the first to realize it fully and completely; no, man is all the greater for this, man is in the centre of all things, in a quite different sense, too, for he was able to discover this revolutionary truth by his own resources and to think it abstractly, again to consider and penetrate a world which had expanded overnight into infinity—and without anything else having changed, without his having to pay for it in any

way: clearly now the world was even more and properly so *his* world!
It is paradoxical and yet it is a fact that the answer to his humiliation
was those philosophical systems of rationalism, empiricism and scepticism which made men even more self-confident. The geocentric picture
of the universe was replaced as a matter of course by the anthropocentric.

And European man of the eighteenth century was also, in relation
to the old earth, one whose world had become immeasurably greater
and who nevertheless claimed this world too, even more as a matter of
course, as *his* world. As with Copernicus's discovery, so too he became
fully conscious of the discovery of Columbus and all that followed it in
west and east and south. Atlases and travel books became an indispensable part of the more serious literature, even in bourgeois houses,
afterwards in the world outside—and that already in the seventeenth century there had been a continuous succession of seizures of new territories
following the example of the Spaniards and Portuguese (stimulated
by the rising capitalist trade); these new possessions were ceaselessly
expanded, defended, consolidated, and exploited, making ever fresh
demands on the mother countries, and though with recessions and
disappointments in individual instances yet leading on the whole to
ever fresh successes. Holland—to whom still in 1669 belonged two-
thirds of all seafaring vessels—though gradually being overtaken by
England, led this enterprise in the company of France, while from
1683 to 1717 the Electorate of Brandenburg possessed a colony on the
Gold Coast, and from 1720 to 1727 there was also an Austrian East
India Company in Ostend. Nothing is more characteristic of this
extension of the European horizon and power than the fact that the
attraction of oversea possessions, and what indeed made them possible,
was primarily the slave trade and the possession of slaves. Moral
scruples, let alone Christian ones, were so little in evidence that it was
even possible to say without contradiction of the flourishing town of
Liverpool that it was built on the skulls of negroes.

It was in that same England—though Dutchmen and Frenchmen did
not behave differently—that Milton wrote his *Paradise Lost* and Bunyan
his *Pilgrim's Progress*, and Lord Shaftesbury, on the other hand, developed
the heroic-aesthetic idealism of his *Virtuoso*. The absolute man can and
does do both. One must see the significance of this double activity:
while Gellert was writing his Odes and Kant his *Critique of Pure
Reason*, while Goethe was writing his letters to Frau von Stein, and even
later, the two things were actually being done simultaneously by
absolute man: piety was practised at home, reason was criticized, truth

made into poetry and poetry into truth, while abroad slaves were being hunted and sold. The absolute man can really do both. But even within Europe space had both enlarged and diminished. It had enlarged, in the sense that from the time of Peter the Great Russia, from being an unknown entity, had become one which was at least approximately known. It had diminished, in the sense that ever-increasing trade had brought nations and lands perceptibly nearer to one another, and that travel had become a part of education and even a truly 'irrational' necessity for many people. 'One' must have been to Paris at least once. 'One' begins to wish to see Italy. Not everyone, but some daring spirits make for the extreme north, or for Alpine peaks. Mutual visits among like-minded people living far away from each other become one of the most important means of intellectual exchange. Pietists and Moravians led the way in that respect, showing themselves in this detail as well as in other ways to be very modern men. But even without leaving one's own town the entirely new possibility was discovered of meeting in a *salon*, with tea and tobacco acquiring a by no means negligible sociological significance. Lastly, the rise of the printed newspaper, and of the most beloved journals of philosophy, art, literature, and culture of all kinds, meant the spread from place to place of new thoughts, which were none the less effective because they were conveyed in an impersonal way. So Europe, its countries and its cities, became smaller, more easily seen as a whole, more easily penetrated. And so man too grew in this space in the sense that he unmistakably became more and more master of his existence, though the space too grew larger and larger.

Further, eighteenth-century man began to become conscious of his power for science, and of his power through science. The development at the Renaissance, which had been hindered and reduced for almost one hundred and fifty years through the period of religious wars, now began to make immense strides. Once again man, led by a philosophy, which was only apparently disunited but was in essentials united, began to be conscious—and more forcibly than before—of a capacity for thinking which was responsible to no other authority than himself. This free thought he once more finds related to nature which was just as freely observed. Mathematics were once more discovered by him to be the bridge which carried him across in both directions, from concept to intuition, from intuition to concept. Logic, observation and mathematics were the three decisive elements of the absolute power now disclosed in science. This absoluteness is symbolized in the undeniable separation of these elements from the universities, which had hitherto

ranked as the places of science. There did not exist a court with any
pretensions which did not at this time found an academy to be the
nursery of free research. Even the smallest courts supported at least a
local historian, and established a library, a museum of coins and
natural history. This free pursuit of science was also followed by the
well-to-do bourgeois families in the towns, and in many a manor house
and manse in the country. The ideal of a science of history and of
natural science, without presuppositions and possessing supreme intellectual dignity in virtue of this very absence of presuppositions, was so
firmly established in the minds of that century that it is hard for us to
imagine the intensity with which they pursued their activities under
the spell of that idea: reading, collecting, observing, experimenting
and also perhaps indulging in many a scientific fantasy. And all this
went on in circles which long since have learned to spend their leisure
again in very different ways.

I take as one example for many the Würtemberg parson Philipp
Mattaeus Hahn, a good theologian, in his way, of the school of Bengel
and Oetinger. He contrived an astronomical machine of the universe
which was much admired, and even respectfully examined by the
emperor Joseph II. It also contained a device for stopping it in the
year 1836, when, according to Bengel's calculations, the return of Christ
and the beginning of the millennium was expected. It is characteristic
of the time that alongside the study of the natural world the favourite
scientific objects were primarily the study of the nature and activity of
the human soul, human customs, and habits new and old, among
savages as well as civilized peoples, the 'spirit of laws', as in the title of
Montesquieu's famous book, and the various historical possibilities
of education, culture, government and society. 'The proper study
of mankind is man', said Pope, expressing the conscious or unconscious idea of the whole century in its pursuit of science. The desire to
know was so serious that men understood only too well what the old
sophists meant, and the best minds understood Socrates and Plato as
well. Those who deplore the 'intellectualism' of that time should at
least be clear that the human capacity for acquiring knowledge, which
had been so long neglected, now began to spread in every sphere like a
stream running along dry beds, and produced a movement from whose
influence no clear mind could withdraw. And that the achievements of
the time were considerable is seen in the fact that even now every
science, without exception, has its historical foundations in the
eighteenth century. But the amazing scientific spirit of that time which
confronts us here was unquestionably one of the manifestations of

all-conquering, absolute man, who expressed himself also and with special effect in this field of human activity.

Here we may also suitably call to mind the achievements of modern technique which also come from this time. The curve of progress in this field has not yet risen as steeply as it was to do in the nineteenth century. Here are some dates. In 1684 Hooke invented the optical telegraph, in 1690 Papin, a Frenchman, invented the steam cylinder with which, in 1707, he attempted, though without success, to sail a steam-boat on the river Fulda. The invention of springs for coaches in 1706 made the popular activity of travelling more comfortable. In 1714 Fahrenheit constructed his mercury thermometer. In 1718 Lady Mary Wortley Montagu tried to introduce the practice of inoculation for smallpox, and in the same year Leopold von Dessau invented the iron loading-rod for guns. Metal-boring machines appeared in 1720, accurate spinning machines in 1738. The idea of steam heat appears in 1745. In 1747 sugar was produced from beets. In 1751 the Frenchman Chamette invented a gun which was loaded from the rear, in 1764 James Watt invented the steam engine. In 1770 Priestley discovered oxygen. In 1780 Galvani made his decisive discoveries in electricity. In 1782 the brothers Montgolfier offered Paris the sight of the first balloon flight. In 1786 gas for lighting purposes was first made.

In almost every case we are seeing the first efforts of individual bold pioneers who were followed by the rest of the world only with hesitation, and whose efforts to a large extent were only properly applied much later. And Germany, in this as in the matter of colonies, was obviously a laggard. If we are to understand the feeling of life which surged through the whole of Europe, we must not underestimate the significance of the hopeful excitement which was also stirred by these discoveries too; here too is manifested the existence of the absolute man, the man almost capable of anything.

Yet more significant than science and technique was undoubtedly the political experience of the period. Perhaps eighteenth-century man is in this respect best described negatively: he is the man who no longer has an emperor. Of course, it was not till 1803 that the old empire actually broke up, in the external sense. But inwardly it had already broken up, we can even say, during the Thirty Years War and certainly clearly in the wars with Louis XIV, in which it showed its powerlessness. The image of the Holy Roman Empire which impressed itself on the mind of the young Goethe at the imperial coronation of Joseph II in 1765, and later in a practical form during his work at the imperial supreme law court in Wetzlar, was clearly that of an interesting, honourable, but entirely outdated old age, incapable of any action. The French Revolution was not necessary in order to destroy the real old order in Europe. It was already destroyed long before this Revolution, which was a revolution from below, took place. The Revolution was not the cause but the necessary effect of the destruction. For the Empire had been, ideally, the guarantee, as the means of cohesion and order among the large and small political units of which it was composed, of the hierarchy of relationships which had grown up between these various units. The guarantee of this hierarchy was not a one-way matter, it was not only the guarantee of the might of the higher classes against the lower, but also the guarantee of the right of the lower against the higher. The Empire was the concrete veto on any kind of political absolutism. It represented—imperfectly enough, but still, it did represent, while spanning the oppositions of higher and lower in the individual political units—a third factor, which excluded encroachments within these orders. That is why it was the *Holy* Roman Empire. So the end of the Empire necessarily meant the beginning of absolutism. That was shown both in the separation, in 1648, of the aristocratic republics of Switzerland from the Empire, and in the German principalities. The beginning of absolutism in France also coincides with the practical end of the Empire in Germany. The old French kingdom had corresponded exactly to the German Empire, with its supreme authority both respecting and guaranteeing the existing distances and competences and relationships in a political world with manifold forms. With the extinction of the imperial ideal this French kingdom also came to an end. Only after that was a monarch like Louis XIV possible. He was one type of the politically absolute man. Politically, absolutism means the determination of law by that class in the state which in contrast to the others possesses the effective power. The first type of this absolutism was created when the highest class after the effective elimination of the emperor, namely, that of the princes or the city oligarchs, used their actual power to identify with their own will the law of the political unit which had been entrusted to their leadership. When the king, against the background of this identification, calls himself king 'by the grace of God', no personal religious uprightness or humility which may reside in this kind of confession regarding the origin of his office can alter the fact that he is in effect made to be like God. 'By the grace of God' should mean that he bears the power in common submission with the people before a power which is superior to them both, and therefore that he also recognizes the rights of the people. The concrete form of that superior power had been the Empire. With its fall the prince became absolute and the people were deprived of their rights, while 'by the grace of God' simply masked the prince's resemblance to God. That is the meaning of Louis XIV's famous remark '*L'état c'est moi!*' It is the declaration of the prince, needing no other grounds than those of his actual power to assume the status of law, that right in the state, and the freedom guaranteed by it, are the right established by *me*, and the freedom guaranteed by *me*. The first party to suffer from this was the nobility. It was against their power, that is, against their ancient good right, that the new 'revolution from above' which now started was first directed. This was the meaning of the home policy of Richelieu, of Mazarin and of Louis XIV, and in Germany, in a specially classic form, of the Great Elector of Brandenburg.

Besides this, of course, princely absolutism struck also at the middle classes, who had been steadily rising since the end of the Middle Ages, and at the peasants, who in the sixteenth century had demanded their rights in vain—the first serious sign of the decay of the imperial idea. But it is significant in every respect that there could also on occasion be manifested a certain agreement, a deep community of interests between the absolute prince and the citizens, the class which nourished the rest of society. It is at any rate a fact that this age saw not only the rise of the princes but also—though on a different plane, that of economics and education—the rise of the citizens on an unprecedented scale. 'For reasons of state the princes conceived the idea of a productive bourgeois class . . . and gradually brought them up.'[1] Why did the absolute prince need the power of the unitary state for whose sake he had first to destroy the rights of the nobility? The first answer can only be that he needed this power because—wishing to be an absolute prince, and having in effect no emperor over him—he needed more power. He needed the unitary state, and in it a relatively prosperous bourgeoisie which could provide a regular flow of money to him. He needed money because he needed a standing army which was always at his disposal. He needed the army because his power was 'territorial', as we now say, with other territories alongside it. The existence of other territories openly contradicts the idea of an absolute prince, but this state of affairs could be improved by inheritance, by marriage, by acquisition and—the *ultima ratio*—by wars of conquest. And because the other means had their strict limitations, wars of conquest were the natural method.

War became, therefore, a latent principle. It is not surprising that open war again and again broke out. What is surprising is that it did

[1] *Propyläen-Weltgeschichte*, 6, p. 277.

not happen more frequently. Absolute politics of this kind are out-wardly dynastic, cabinet politics; but by an inward necessity, sooner or later they lead to a policy of conquest. This is the way—the securing of internal power, that is, a unitary state by revolution from above, with a view to external power—which was followed by the king of France in the eighteenth century, as well as by the aristocrats of Berne and the great and petty potentates of Germany, among whom the emperor was now only one among the rest, later to be called—logically, though absurdly—emperor of Austria. Only the clever English—per-haps one of the few nations really gifted politically—foresaw in time the folly of this development, though they were just as penetrated by the spirit of absolutism as the rest, and introduced checks which spared them the catastrophe to which the system by its nature must lead.

This political absolutism from above has, as is known, two variants. They have in fact crossed and mingled in many ways; their roots are one, but they may be clearly distinguished. The principle 'through power to power' had of course also a non-military aspect. This could consist in the princely display of splendour and pomp at which Louis XIV was so inventive, even creative, setting a baleful example which was widely followed. The name of Versailles has thrice had great historical significance resulting in grave consequences. The first time it was as the prototype and symbol of a princely attitude to life and form of life, based on unqualified power. From this life there flowed a brilliance, like the glory of a god, into architecture, the gardens and parks, the decoration in the houses, into comforts and enjoyments of every kind, but above all into the transitory but all the more intoxi-cating splendour of the festivities. Far beyond the boundaries of France there arose small and miniature imitations of Versailles whose princely and noble inhabitants attempted, with more or less luck and dignity and taste, to emulate Louis XIV.

After his death the Regent Philip of Orléans, then Louis' grandson, Louis XV, in Germany Augustus the Strong of Saxony, Eberhard Ludwig, Karl Alexander, and Karl Eugen of Würtemberg, Max Emanuel and Karl Theodor of Bavaria, Ludwig IX of Hesse, and many others, were absolute princes of this kind. The notorious immor-ality, even debauchery, the just as notorious financial transactions, and the scandalous arbitrariness of justice at all these courts, was perhaps not the necessary, but as has happened in all similar phenomena in history the practical, consequence of the representation which one thought to be owing—and that not without some logic—to the conception of the prince by divine right.

The idea inevitably presupposed great demands upon the economy of the country, which were made with an astonishing unconcern—not to speak of the sons of Hesse and Brunswick who were sold out of hand to America! And ironically enough the command was in fact often not in the hands of its true possessor, but largely and for all to see in those of a woman—sometimes, admittedly, in those of a woman far from unfitted for such an office, but only in a derivative sense can her rule ever have been described as 'by the grace of God'. But all these things cannot and must not blind us to the tremendous stimulus imparted to economic and artistic life by the fantastic burgeoning of absolutism. Neither must we forget that the luxury these potentates cultivated, though so dubious in many respects, acted in practice as a safety valve and corrective against the possibility of a universal state of war, which should really have been the logical consequence of the general principle 'through power to power' and of dynastic cabinet politics. If it had not been for the Sun-king's notion of the unfolding of power and the relative enervation which was involved herein, Louis himself and all the other God-kings might well with the absolute power they had arrogated have reduced Europe to even greater disasters than those they did in fact cause. Lastly it should be added that anyone who failed to sense not only the pathos imparted by lavishness of ideas, space and materials, but the underlying, unending and truly insatiable yearning in the midst of sensual delight which emanates from every line and form of the art of the age would be guilty of badly misunderstanding those artistic and architectural monuments of that time which still hold a meaning for us. It is this eternal yearning which is the style's inmost beauty, a beauty peculiarly moving for all the horror which is sometimes apt to seize the beholder.

Besides this kind of political absolutism there was another, going by the name of enlightened absolutism. It is possible for the 'through power to power' principle to manifest itself in depth rather than in extent, rationally rather than aesthetically. In that case it takes the form of experiments in social reform—in the technical advance of civilization, in agriculture, industry and in the economic sphere in general, in health measures and policies designed to benefit the population as a whole. There are attempts to improve the state of the law, but also to advance the arts and sciences, to raise the general standard of education—in short all sorts of measures tending to the so-called 'welfare' of the subjects of the state. In chastising a Jew, Frederick William I says: 'You should love me rather than fear me, love me, I say!' As Frederick the Great's famous remark shows, the absolute monarch can also cherish the wish to be 'the first servant of the state'. 'It is our duty to sacrifice ourselves for the public good'—this was a *mot* of Louis XIV already, and as proof that it was not just a *bon mot* one might point to the extensive official activities in the cultural field of his minister Jean Baptiste Colbert, who is too easily overlooked beside the more eye-catching figures of a Louvois or of the various great ladies of Louis' court. Circumstances permitting the absolute monarch might then, in startling contrast to his princely contemporaries, assume the rough aspect of a king of ancient Rome or Sparta, as did Frederick William I of Prussia, or like Joseph II epitomize affability at all costs and an idealism verging upon folly; or, as in Joseph Emmerich, elector of Mayence, he might take the astonishing form of a wise prince of an ecclesiastical state, at once open-minded enough to accept progress in every form; or, finally, as with Frederick the Great he might be that almost legendary figure, the 'Sage of Sans Souci', seeming to have his whole existence centred upon a philosophy stripped of illusion yet rigid upon certain moral points, its purpose being to enable him to be all the more detached in attending to the business of providing, maintaining and furthering law, order and progress among the people he happened to be governing. Sarastro, Mozart's strange character in *The Magic Flute*, combines elements from all these figures. And we need only be reminded of Karl August of Saxe-Weimar-Eisenach, the sovereign who was served by Goethe, to see how sometimes the entire zest for life of the one kind of prince could be reconciled with the earnest zeal of the second. It is needless to state that this second interpretation of the art of kingship at this time and the achievements which sprang from it command great respect. But let us not forget that although there may be absolutists in the performing of good they are absolutists for all that. It is thus with the 'enlightened' absolutism of which we have been speaking.

We must appreciate this particularly in the classic case of Frederick the Great. In the preface to his *Histoire de mon temps* he wrote in reflective mood: 'I trust that posterity will do me justice and understand how to distinguish the king in me from the philosopher, the decent from the political man.' Indeed: as king he is no less a 'soldier king' than his father, and no less a dynastic cabinet politician than Louis XIV, although and in that he wants to be king and philosopher and a decent man simultaneously. Temper as one may Lessing's harsh judgment that the Prussia of Frederick the Great was 'the most slavish country in Europe' and that 'Berlin freedom' consisted solely in the right 'to hawk as many anti-religious imbecilities as one wishes', there is still no escaping the fact that the enlightenment which Frederick desired had absolutely nothing to do with freedom—as freedom of the press, for example, it was a hollow pretence, and it was a foregone conclusion that freedom was not applied to the army or anything connected with the army, e.g. the administration of justice in the army. There is no blinking the fact, either, that Frederick's state had to be a welfare state—a Frederick naturally sees farther than the usual run of despots—in order to be—precisely as welfare state—a state worshipping power, an absolute state. The fact remains that the measure of wisdom and rectitude with which the king happened to be endowed, together with the limitations imposed upon these qualities by his highly individual character, his taste and his whims—limitations common to every mortal—had the significance of destiny for his people, his country and for every individual within his realms—a destiny which like God could bless or punish, might cherish or destroy, and could do so without let of appeal to any higher law. Lessing certainly had nothing to thank King Frederick for, nor did his loyal subject Immanuel Kant, nor did Leonhard Euler, and they were all misjudged for reasons which they and all the people they lived among had to accept as if these reasons represented the impenetrable will of God. The things he found uninteresting just didn't interest him, and the things he didn't like he just didn't like. The remark about 'the first servant of the state' is good, but what practical significance has it if this very first servant is alone from first to last in decreeing every policy of state, if every counsellor, be wise as he may, must ever fear him like a slave? The same might equally be said of Joseph II and his entirely well-intentioned and frequently beneficial innovations. He did much for his people and had in mind to do much more. But once again the highly personal limits of his circumspection and temperament were, like those of fate, the limits of the goodness and usefulness of the things his radicalism had created. His achievements stood with him. It was inevitable that with him they should also fall—to make way for the will of his equally absolutist successor, which chanced to have different objects. In short 'enlightened' absolutism also consisted essentially in 'revolution from above', and could provide no substitute for what the imperial idea had once stood for, or had been intended to stand for: the policy, which not only exercises dominion, but bestows freedom, which not only dispenses favours, but establishes justice, and establishes it by means of justice, a policy whereby the best possible is done for the people with the people, and therefore as a matter of principle just as much through the people as through the king; a policy therefore in whose eyes as a matter of principle no person is merely an object; again, a policy subject not only to an abstract responsibility, but to a concrete one—a policy therefore which might well deserve the title, 'by the grace of God'. Those who do not happen to be in power, who are subjected to an absolute monarch, whether he be enlightened or unenlightened, are bound to look upon him with that rather distant and nervous awe exemplified in the form of the great prayer of the Church at Basle to be found in the liturgy of 1752, a prayer to be offered for 'the wise and worshipful first citizens, counsellors, judges and officials of our Christian town and district of Basle': 'Guide them, O Lord, with the spirit of wisdom and understanding, with good counsel and courage, with the knowledge and fear of thy holy name, that in their care we may lead a peaceful and quiet life in all honour and righteousness.'

It is of course possible to question whether that other policy, pursued in the Middle Ages in the name of the imperial ideal, ever became a reality anywhere. But there was at least a chance that it might be realized while it was still at least an active point of reference (questionable in itself but at least fairly well-defined) within the framework of the imperial ideal. It was when this fell away that the realization of such a policy became impossible. For when the prince's power was made absolute, a step which brought with it the death of the imperial ideal, the prerequisite of such a policy, the very notion of a concrete responsibility, of a higher authority, was removed also, and in its place there arose the state without a master, or alternatively the state governed by an arbitrary master, beneath whose sway, even if he were the best of all possible monarchs, justice was a matter of pure chance.

We have taken the one kind of political absolutist, the absolute prince, as the first for discussion. The second kind, his perfectly legitimate brother, his *alter ego*, following in his footsteps as inevitably as the darkness following the light, as the thunder following the lightning, is the absolute revolutionary—or perhaps it would be better to say, since his predecessor was already a revolutionary—the revolutionary from below, the representative of the lower class, who conceiving those above him to have injured him in his rights, and even to have deprived him of them, takes steps to defend himself by snatching the power lying in the hands of the governing princes in order that he might now determine without let of appeal what is right and just, because he in his turn has the power in his hands. The *rôles* are reversed. Whereas before it had been the prince who had declared himself to be identical with the state, it was now the people, the 'nation', as it at this time began to be called, who assumed the title by means of a simple inversion of

Louis XIV's dictum. This happened true to type in Paris on the 17th June, 1789. The representatives of the so-called third estate, who were, be it remembered, the delegates of that section of the population of France which was in the overwhelming majority, formed themselves into a 'National Assembly' and three days later declared with a collective oath, that they were determined in the teeth of all opposition never to disband until they had given the state a new constitution. Everything that happened afterwards, up to the execution of Louis XVI and beyond, was a direct result of this event. Its inner logic is, however, as follows. (We shall restrict ourselves in the following to the two classic revolutionary documents, the Declaration of Independence of the United States of America of June 1776 and the Statement of Human and Civil Rights ratified by the French National Assembly in August 1789.) According to the revolutionary doctrine there exists a self-evident truth which can and must be recognized and announced *en présence et sous les auspices de l'être suprême*:

1. All men are equal, i.e. created with equal rights (Am.), or alternatively (as in the Fr.), born with equal rights.

2. These equal rights are of nature, inalienable, sacred (Fr.), endowed by their creator (Am.).

3. Their names are freedom, property, security and the right to protect oneself from violence (Fr.) or: life, liberty and the pursuit of happiness (Am.). The French statement goes on to make a special point of saying that freedom consists in being able to do anything which does not harm anybody and is not as such forbidden by law. And it also considers the right to property important enough to describe it in a special last article as *inviolable et sacré*.

4. It is in order to protect these rights that *governments are instituted among men* (Am.). *Le but de toute association publique est la conservation des droits . . . de l'homme* (Fr.).

5. Governments *derive* their just authority from *the consent* of the governed. *Le principe de toute souveraineté réside essentiellement dans la nation.* All authority exercised by individuals or corporate bodies stems expressly from the people (*en émane expressément*).

6. The law is *l'expression de la volonté générale* so all must have a part in making it, all are equal in its eyes and every office and honour for which it provides are as a matter of principle open to all.

7. Whenever a form of government becomes injurious to the aims of the state, i.e. to the upholding of the rights aforementioned, it is the people's right to remove it and replace it by a government more conducive to their *safety and happiness*. It will be advisable not to proceed too

hastily in such an event, but once it has become plain that a government is seeking to establish *absolute despotism* it is not only the citizen's right but his duty to free himself of its yoke.

The subtle differences of emphasis revealed by a comparison of these two documents are of considerable interest: the French version is clearly distinctive by virtue of the fact that, apart from the mention of the *être suprême* in the preamble, the theological note has entirely disappeared, together with the implicit notion still to be found in the American document that at least in the beginning there could have been a 'government among men' that was not created by the will of the people; a notion that the revolution itself was not only the exercising of a right, but something like the fulfilment of a duty; that this right and duty was of a transitory nature, and that while the authority of a government might rest upon the consent of a people, this was not quite the same thing as the people's will. In contrast to this the French statement is explicit in taking the state to be an *association*, its sovereignty to be the sovereignty of the nation as a whole, and the authority of its laws to be contained in the will of all, i.e. in the generality of the individual possessors of the human rights. The Calvinism gone to seed of the American document still distinguishes itself favourably from the Catholicism gone to seed of the French one. But these fine variations of meaning only reveal the sources and aims common to both versions. They both think of the state in terms of the individual, or the sum of the individuals forming a nation. Both of them show that those who drew them up imagined that they were standing before an ultimate reality, and indeed before a reality beyond which no man would ever see. Face to face with the supreme Being, or self-evidently, man knows according to both documents that he has a right to life, liberty, property and so on. For the sake of these universal rights it is necessary to have a state, and this state comes into being and subsists by virtue of general recognition of these universal rights, and in case of need, should it be found that this right is in effect being suppressed, by the strength of the majority it is actively called into being. It is this which forms the revolution. Such was the line of thought upon which the third estate in 1789 based its declaration that it was identical with the 'nation', and resolved come what might to undertake the transformation of the state.

This then is the essentially unanimous confession of faith of the second kind of absolutist in politics, diametrically opposed to the first kind, the enlightened or unenlightened princely absolutist. Diametrically opposed? Indeed he is, and yet he is himself confined within the same vicious circle. The *Déclaration des droits de l'homme*, in the form in which it was first printed and sold in Paris in 1789, bears over its title a picture of the radiant eye of God, enclosed within the usual triangle, which even here calls to mind the Trinity. At the foot of the page, admittedly, there are to be found the words, *L'œil suprême de la raison qui vient de dissiper les nuages qui l'obscurcissaient*. But beneath the title there is the ingenious symbol of a snake biting its own tail. The snake, unfortunately, is not explained: but it can hardly have any other meaning but that the time was ripe for doing the same as the princely absolutist had done though in reverse: *L'état c'est moi!* That section of society which holds the power (or that which at the moment is striving to acquire it) determines according to its own particular standards what is right for society as a whole. He knows what is right! Why shouldn't he? And why, if he knows, shouldn't he determine for the whole? He needs only to overcome his diffidence to place his conception of freedom, life, property, etc., on the absolute plane with the greatest of ease: and what is there then left to him but to place his will also on a level with them? All this the *ancien régime* had also done, the only difference being that it employed the phrase 'by the grace of God', whereas the revolutionary spoke rather more badly of the Creator, or simply maintained that everything relating to the subject was *naturel*, *inviolable*, *sacré*, and *self-evident*. Thus on both sides the same thing happens: the same usurpation and entry into the same vicious circle.

There are as we saw fine distinctions of attitude also within this new kind of absolutism; it is possible within the revolution from below to adhere more to the conservative or more to the radical side. It is possible to place the individual as such, who forms the state, more in the centre of things, or the nation which unites within itself all individuals: this means that there will now be a liberal movement with a nationalist movement as its antagonist, and a liberal-nationalist movement at any point between the two. In short, the nineteenth century can now begin. Occasionally, as in the time of the restoration, and as was perhaps inevitable in any monarchy—it has also been known to happen in a modern republic—a feeling of repugnance against the whole state of things created by the French Revolution, a romantic nostalgia for monarchical absolutism and for the glorious days before 1789 might spring to life and begin to take effect over against both liberalism and nationalism, and in their efforts to combat this reactionary tendency both the liberals and the nationalists would find themselves compelled to invoke ever more and anew the exalted spirit of 1776 and 1789, and oppose reaction by being themselves reactionary. And so one way or the other, whether people prefer the 'Marseillaise' or the 'March of Hohenfriedberg', or even if they wish to combine both in one anthem, the snake is for ever biting its own tail. One way or another, either as individuals or, taken collectively, as a nation, the men who assume that they have 'rights' and experience the desire to assert them by violence stand, almost like God, very much alone, thrown upon themselves in a way for which, with due regard for the imperfections of the human state, there was never any true necessity. The empire, it is true, was a concrete political authority, but its authority was higher than the state, and therefore had once made the absolute state impossible in any form; again, it had once in spite of all its political ambiguity not been completely without eschatological significance, drawing attention to the existence of a law that neither princes nor peoples could give themselves, and that therefore they could not play off one against the other; all this, however, is completely foreign to the political world of the eighteenth century. Has man, either as a prince or as man generally, really such a right as the political absolutist thinks he is justified in assuming, whether he tends to the left or the right? Is it really 'right' which they seize in each particular case? Does not right cease to be right whenever it is seized? Is not right possible only in a relationship which presupposes peace and excludes the thought of revolution because its basis is a commandment? Is it not this relationship which alone forms the basis for distinguishing the bearer of office just as it alone forms the basis for the equality of all men? It is of course a relationship which, when destroyed, makes revolution and counterrevolution an absolute necessity, because when it is destroyed everything is bound to become absolute and abstract, and all things fall together like a pile of skittles. It was in fact the destruction of this relationship in the eighteenth century which made inevitable the appearance of the two kinds of political absolutism, the appearance, that is, of the possibility of taking the law into one's own hand and making the state omnipotent. The first kind and the last! And what is more—the consternation and the lamentings of the legitimists were very much misplaced—the second kind was brought about by the first. For political man as he appeared upon the scene in 1789 had been the same man for a long time before, albeit in a different guise. The whole century in fact thought as he did; and so did even the circles which were to fall victim to the revolution. The tyrant will secretly always be a conspirator against himself. If this is not realized the lightning outbreak of this upheaval and its tremendous repercussions throughout Europe will never be understood. By virtue of the same fiction of the contract which constitutes the state whereby the kings of Europe had justified their rule, they now found that rule had been snatched from them again. They themselves, as we saw, had encouraged the growth of the bourgeois, not because they loved him, but because they needed him. And now he was there, just as they had wanted him and shaped him to be, except that at this point he suddenly found that he could do with a little more of the *liberté, propriété*, happiness, etc., which the others accorded themselves in such generous measure—more than the others were in fact ready to grant him—and except for the fact that the bourgeois now suddenly discovered that he was in the majority, and that he had only to reach out and seize the power to achieve what he wanted forthwith. Upon which, of course, it became immediately apparent that he who invokes death to tyrants is also always something of a tyrant himself and will reveal himself to be one soon enough.

To show not only the connexion, but the essential unity of the things we have been discussing it will be significant if in conclusion we cast a glance at the political philosophy which first of all nourished the princely absolutist and then provided an equal delight to the palate of the bourgeois. It was truly not without good cause that their tastes were similar. It is the political philosophy of Thomas Hobbes, which stems, it is true, from well back in the seventeenth, but is in effect standard for the whole of the eighteenth century. According to his teaching in *de cive*—part of *Leviathan*—the significance of the state is as follows: the ultimate reality to be reckoned with in man is his instinct to preserve himself and enjoy his life accordingly. He follows this instinct in everything he does, and he is perfectly right to do so. Nature has in actual fact given to all men the same claim to all things, the only restraining factor being that to bring this instinct into play indiscriminately would benefit no one, as its necessary consequence would be universal war. Reason, therefore, backed by the fear of death and the desire for rest, will counsel man to adopt self-imposed restrictions. Thus subjective right in itself seeks an objective kind of right, which is created by way of a transference of law (*translatio iuris*). Agreement is reached and each one of the parties transfers a part of his rights to the state. The state, however, is a *persona civilis*, representing the unity of the general will and possessing power over all: *persona una, unius voluntas ex pactis plurium hominum pro voluntate habenda est ipsorum omnium*. In return this single person affords all men protection, and with it promises to each his own: *Suum cuique!* and in so doing provides the first possibility for all to live a truly human life. Who is this single person? According to Hobbes he can just as easily be represented by monarchy as by an aristocracy or a democracy. (His personal choice was for a monarchy.) The only essential thing is that he should be understood as being one person, whose will is law subject to no condition, and who is alone in determining and sanctioning what is good and what is bad. There exists nothing either good or bad in itself apart from the state, but the public law is the citizen's conscience, just as originally it emerged thence. Free thought exists only in respect to the Church, i.e. in respect to the question that remains of the inevitable fear of the unseen powers. But, while the subject is permitted to adopt what attitude he pleases to the Church, there *is* a fear of invisible powers which is officially sanctioned by the state, and from which, as from the faith which is right in all circumstances, it is superstitious to deviate—from which to deviate would not only mean superstition, but revolution, and which therefore cannot be tolerated. Thus speaks Hobbes.

It is usual in this context to make mention of John Locke's *Two Treatises on Civil Government* (1690). But his political philosophy would seem to be of less significance than Hobbes', because in it the philosophy of revolution from below, the doctrine that force has its source in the people, already preponderates and makes his work one-sided. Hobbes' political philosophy is great by virtue of the fact that it rises above this antithesis and is therefore capable of presenting a comprehensive view of the ideology of politics obtaining in his time.

Hobbes' train of thought leads like a corridor to princely or to bourgeois absolutism, to the arrogation of God-like powers in politics by the individual or by the community, as Hobbes himself says: to the omnipotent monarchy or to the omnipotent republic. Either way it is essentially the same process. In actual fact the eighteenth century took both courses, and it is this which is characteristic for the political experience it gathered.

We have considered the political problem presented by the eighteenth century in particular detail because it is from the political angle that the eighteenth century can be seen most clearly as a whole. Let us now proceed to the attempt to comprehend it under two other aspects which present a less definite picture—the inner and outer forms imparted to life by man as he lived at that time.

By that external form which life has in any age I mean that particular element in its cultural aims and achievements which is evinced fairly consistently throughout its various expressions. Consequently it is possible to identify, with some precision, from the documents of any one of the expressions of this element, the tendency, nature and spirit of its other expressions, and so of the culture of the time as a whole. If there is such an external cast for the eighteenth century, and one that we can identify, it is perhaps most allowable to comprehend it in terms of a striving to reduce everything to an absolute form. Inanimate nature especially, in all its realms, but man's somatic existence too, the sound that could be spontaneously called forth, with all the possibilities for coloration and different rhythmic patterns which it presented, human language in all its adaptability as a means of expression, social intercourse, individual development and the individual in relation to society—all this abundance of things provided is in the eyes of eighteenth-century man a mass of raw material, of which he believes himself to be the master. This material he confronts as he who has all the knowledge: knowledge of the form, the intrinsically right, fitting, worthy, beautiful form for which all the things provided are clearly intended to be the material, for which they are obviously crying out, and into which, as is plain, they must be brought with all the speed, artistry and energy man has at his command. It is easy to become ironical about this, but we must fight against the temptation if we wish to understand the true irony contained in such an attitude.

Eighteenth-century man, at least at the higher levels of society, had very close ties with nature, and they were far from being simply of the kind which lead man to study nature scientifically and exploit it for gain; they could also be felt and enjoyed aesthetically. It is however— let it not be said too quickly—a rationalized, but rather a humanized nature, a nature which has been put to rights and formed in accordance with man's sensibility and enjoyment, an idealized, and most preferably a visibly idealized nature, which is meant: the stream as a fountain, the lake as a clean and tidy pond, the wood as a park reduced to visible order, the field and the bushes and flowers as a garden, the tree shaped with the garden-shears, all these things reduced to harmony, which inevitably means to geometry, more or less; the tamed, groomed and trained animals, shepherds and shepherdesses whose nice prettiness and grace really left them no alternative but to turn eventually into those little porcelain figures; a nature which even after the grooming it has had to endure is really beautiful only when there is a Greek temple, a statue or a bust somewhere about which quite unequivocally serves as a reminder of the lords of creation. It was the time of Goethe which brought about a decisive inner change here, but the external change took much longer and was slower in asserting itself: it would seem, as we can see from the *Elective Affinities*, for instance, that the game of 'creating' nature in the eighteenth-century sense was indulged in for a long time and on a grand scale in Weimar too. The man who expresses an attitude to nature such as this must be unusually conscious and certain that he knows how he feels and that his feeling is valid in the sense that it is the true feeling.

The same determined and absolute will for form is conveyed by the architecture of the time. The domineering way in which building materials were handled is evidenced in works like the stairway of Brühl castle. Stone may no longer be stone, nor iron, iron, nor wood, wood. Every material must be transposed (hence the particular fondness that arose at this time for plaster, so obedient to the forming hand!) according to the imaginative though lucid and logical form, which man felt he ought to impose upon space. This form was that of the perception which he held significant and valuable enough to justify its projection into the materials, regardless of everything in them contrary to its own nature. Think too of the way they dared to build whole cities in those days—not with the help of a natural rise in the ground or following the course of a river, as the builder of the older towns had built them, but as in Karlsruhe, Mannheim and Ludwigsburg, with a fully deliberate use of the ruler and compasses and with a mathematical and to that extent harmonious form in mind, absolute enough to be capable of taking shape not only in one building or group of buildings, but on occasion in complete towns. And in this there is as little true contrast in the attitude to life between the relative immoderacy of the so-called Baroque style, with its almost wildly sweeping and intersecting lines, its exuberant ornamentation, and its human and angel statuary imbued with the whole gamut of the human passions, and the Rococo moderation which tended to revert to a kind of tranquil cheerfulness or cheerful tranquillity, as there is contrast in the attitude to life of the ordinary absolutist and his enlightened counterpart, as there is for that matter between pietism and rationalism. The buildings which are most characteristic of that time are precisely those which represent the transitional period between the two styles, and it is only from them that either can begin to be understood. It is just as irrelevant to condemn the one on the grounds that it is bombastic and overladen as to condemn the other for being stiff and affected, unless we have first appreciated in both the boldness of feeling behind them—feeling which took itself entirely seriously and whose entire striving was therefore for an adequate means of expression. What other age has dared to make architecture of its inmost heart to the extent that this one did? But this was an age which simply had to, for its inmost heart *was* precisely this idea of man as one taking hold of everything about him and subjecting it to his will. It is an idea so big and so ill-starred that we do better, especially when confronted by the art it bodied forth, to see and hear and stay silent, instead of saying the all-too obvious things which might well come to mind.

It must also be granted to eighteenth-century man that he did not, still in accordance with the same absolute will for form, spare himself his own personal outer appearance, either. We have only to think of the fashion of the eighteenth century. There is no need for me here to describe the dress, the coiffure, both for men and for women, the forms of intercourse, sociability, play and dancing. One cannot look too attentively at the portraits of the time, the contemporary illustrations of historical and social life, and also at the caricatures, if one is bent upon finding out what it was exactly that these people who thus adorned and comported themselves were trying to express (unconsciously, and therefore all the more revealingly, as is always the case with fashion). What they were certainly not trying to say was that like the lilies of the field we should not care for our attire. And they were certainly not saying that no man can increase his height by an ell. What they were expressing the whole time, from top to toe in actual fact, was this: that man carries in his soul an image of himself which in comparison with his actual figure is still much more noble, much more graceful and much more perfect, and that he is not at a loss for means to externalize this image and render it visible. No age, perhaps, has made this confession of faith so systematically as man of the eighteenth century. As to its results, they need not concern us here. We need only note the following: when man, as happened at that time, proceeded to take himself (that is to say, his idea of himself) seriously, in the grand manner, without humour, but with a certain logic, all the things emerged which now cause us astonishment in the matter of men's and women's dress and in the manners of the age. Man felt bound to weigh himself down in these respects with all the burdens and discomforts which an absolute will for form apparently demands—but at the same time he was able to achieve all the dignity and charm to which eighteenth-century man did without doubt achieve.

Man in the eighteenth century affirms his attitude to nature and to material objects in his relationship to history, and the world of much more profound contrasts inherent in it. H. Hoffmann is quite right to protest against the habit of describing the time of the Enlightenment as deficient in a sense of history, and to refute it by pointing out what close attention the eighteenth century in particular bestowed upon the near and the distant past, the industry and care with which it pursued researches in these fields. But in one important sense the accusation is true, and not disprovable by a reminder of the historical research done in the eighteenth century, a reminder which far from discrediting the accusation in fact corroborates it. H. Hoffmann says it himself: in that century began that highly problematical affair which we call 'critical study of history'. But what else can this mean but that it was in the eighteenth century that man began axiomatically to credit himself with being superior to the past, and assumed a standpoint in relation to it whence he found it possible to set himself up as a judge over past events according to fixed principles, as well as to describe its deeds and to substantiate history's own report? And the yardstick of these fixed principles, at least as applied by the typical observer of history living at that age, has the inevitable effect of turning that judgment of the past into an extremely radical one. For the yardstick is quite simply the man of the present with his complete trust in his own powers of discernment and judgment, with his feeling for freedom, his desire for intellectual conquest, his urge to form and his supreme moral self-confidence. What historical facts, even, can be true except those which to the man of the age seem psychologically and physiologically probable, or at any rate not improbable? How, in face of such a firm certainty about what was psychologically and physiologically probable and improbable could eighteenth-century man conceive of the existence of historical riddles and secrets? And what else in fact could the past consist of than either of light, in so far as it reveals itself to be a preparation and mount for the ever-better present 'You'll pardon me—it is my great diversion, to steep myself in ages long since past; to see how prudent men did think before us, and how much further since we have advanced'—or simply of darkness—a warning counter-example and as such, if you like, a welcome counter-example—in so far as the past had not yet sensed the right road to the future, or had even actively opposed it. The third thing which this attitude precluded was that the historian should take history seriously as a force outside himself, which had it in its power to contradict him and which spoke to him with authority. One way or another the historian himself said that which he considered history might seriously be allowed to say, and, being his own advocate, he dared to set forth both aspects of what he alleged history to have said, its admonitory and its encouraging aspect.

What was the inevitable effect of this criterion when it was applied to antiquity, to the Middle Ages, and also to the time of the Reformation, and indeed to the immediate past? An answer is to be found in

Gottfried Arnold's *Unparteiische Kirchen- und Ketzerhistorie* (Unbiased History of Churches and Heresies). The author, according to the preface, 'wishes most heartily that love might settle my spirits in this work to a sweet harmony and tranquillity, so that all my sentiments might be held as far as is possible in perfect balance and that every requisite of a proper, true historian might be conferred upon me'. It was Arnold's wish to maintain an attitude of detachment towards the view of history held in earlier times, which had been dictated by church dogma, and he was in fact thoroughly successful. It was this which made him all the more certain and unconditional in elevating to the measure of all things his own and his sympathizers' mystically inclined Christian belief, whence he arrived very naturally at the conclusion that the whole history of the Church after the time of the 'first Love', that is, after the end of the first century, was with very few exceptions one single, monstrous decline: 'a hotchpotch of violence and error', as Goethe quite rightly later put it when describing his impressions of the book. It is fundamentally the same evil eye with which not only the Encyclopaedists and Voltaire (in his history of Louis XIV, for instance), but also the German disciples of the Enlightenment later saw and mastered history, the only difference between them being in the distribution of light and shade. And this way of mastering history was also axiomatic in cases where the modern consciousness gave the beholder of history a wider scope than was possible for Arnold or Voltaire, for example. It was employed whenever historians found it fitting to abstract from the past all sorts of exemplary heroic tales; in particular from classical antiquity, preferably for instance, from the history of Sparta, but also from Reformation history. It must be said of this race of historians, those who seemed to dismiss the past either in whole or in part as one whole night of wickedness and folly, as well as those who lavished all their love and praise upon one particular aspect of it, that although as a race they were very learned in historical matters, they were at the same time singularly uninstructed, simply because their modern self-consciousness as such made them basically unteachable. But they were far from imagining themselves impoverished by this attitude, by the abandonment of all attempt at historical objectivity. On the contrary; they felt themselves to be enriched and powerful. It was again the sovereign will for form that looked upon history, as it did upon nature, as just so much raw material; which was therefore not at all 'unhistorical' but simply found only raw material, only light and shade, which obviously were the light and shade of its own deeds and aspirations.

If we remember this we cannot be surprised that the eighteenth century was most emphatically also a century of educational theories. The new educational points of view which distinguished it decisively from the preceding age gradually asserted themselves in this century. All those who were active in this field in the manner of their age, the long line from A. H. Francke on the one hand to J. B. Basedow on the other, were agreed about these ideas. They can be summarized as follows:

1. There was now an ever-growing conviction that education is a business resting upon a possibility over which mankind has been given complete command. It follows that it can and must be made the subject of particular thought. There is now a belief in teaching the teacher, so that it was this age which saw the beginnings of a real literature on the theory of education and the beginnings of a real education for teachers: the first teachers' training colleges.

2. There was now the conviction that the young person can be introduced to actual life through the medium of a comprehensive education. He can be brought to 'true godliness and Christian wisdom' (A. H. Francke). Thus the study of ancient languages and of antiquity in general, which had been the alpha and omega of the teaching of previous times, had now to give place to the study of the mother-tongue, of modern languages and of French in particular, and even more to technical studies including manual and physical training of all kinds—only to be deliberately taken up again in the course of a later development from a completely new point of view—a development similarly characteristic of our own time. This was that the classical writers were, after all, 'the greatest people and the noblest spirits who have ever lived' and from them could be learned criteria for both art and ethics, facility in expression and a host of good maxims which improve both the will and the understanding (Matthias Gesner, 1691-1761). As to what precisely was meant by the 'real life' to which the children were to be introduced; this was a point concerning which there was a divergence of opinion between the educators of the pietistic and those of the enlightened school. They did however agree that this introduction was a matter over which they were quite capable of taking control.

3. There was now also the conviction that a communicable method of correct education exists. Hence—mirroring the two philosophic doctrines that dominated the age—on the one hand the more or less correctly understood Socratic method, that of imparting the desired knowledge by skilfully eliciting it from the children themselves through questioning, and on the other the principle of demonstration and

handicrafts-teaching, were now discovered and made to bear fruit in many ways.

4. The faith of educators in the possibility of teaching was now such that they believed—just as it was believed possible to take man generally as a completely explicable object of study—that they, as adults, have it in their power to see the child as a child, and to understand and treat it as such. Hence the spate of methods and experiments designed to enable the teacher to approach the child in a childlike way carefully suited to the child in its various ages, to bring it to the desired goal by a wise descent to its own thought and feeling, as these were then understood, by all sorts of ingenious punishments and amiably enticing rewards, by disguising the dire process of learning as a merry game, by bringing home to it as unobtrusively as possible, and therefore all the more effectively, the 'moral of the story' both in theory and in practice. Thus the eighteenth century really was, in this sense at least, already the 'century of the child'. This is perhaps one of the most noteworthy manifestations of its absolute will for form: that it so confidently believes that it understands that greatest of mysteries presented to man, the child.

5. People were now so completely convinced that the attempt to educate is both feasible and worth while that they wanted no one to be without its benefits. This is shown by the fact that the state now began to take some interest in schools. The enlightened of the absolute princes, Frederick II and Joseph II chiefly, but their predecessors Frederick William I and Maria Theresa too, included schools in their programmes for the betterment of the state, making them one of their most important points and providing very extensively for them. It was Fénelon (*De l'éducation des filles*) who had for the first time in 1687 pointed out in principle the importance of education for the female sex too, and in 1698 it was A. H. Francke once again who was the first to advance to the founding of a '*Gynaeceum*'. In 1717 Frederick William I introduced compulsory schooling for all in Prussia, and during his reign two thousand new schools came into being. Thus the government school now became an accepted principle. It now came to be regarded as being an essential general part in a person that he can be educated, and therefore that it is every person's duty (a duty which must be imposed if need be) that he should allow himself to be educated.

6. Finally, the sense of conviction concerning aims, possibilities and achievements in this field was so strong that education progressively dared to esteem itself more and more independent of, nay even superior to, the revealed gospel; the school, in fact, felt superior to the Church.

'What's more exalted than the teacher?' At first for a long time humbly, but then with mounting self-assurance, and finally turning the tables and attempting to snatch the highest honour himself, the schoolmaster now steps up beside the parish priest as one who has something of his own, something special—something different and indeed much better —to say and offer to all the world: his immortal prototype, this very J. B. Basedow, who not for nothing looked upon the doctrine of the Holy Trinity as his personal enemy. And if all the other convictions of the age about education are valid then it must in fact be admitted that education is a task in itself. This does then prompt the question whether it might not in fact be the superior task: as opposed to the proclamation of the Gospel, the real and true one of the two, and whether it might not be as well for the Church first to make room for the school next to it, then to regard it with respect, and then to look up to it even more respectfully before finally, conscious of its own superfluity, allowing itself to be completely merged with it, or alternatively itself becoming a school, just one more educational establishment among many others.

The commanding way the age took up the problem of education has its equivalent in the freedom with which it treated the problem of the forming of associations. Let us bear in mind that all the associations that had existed until then might be described as associations formed by necessity, such as the natural communion of marriage and family life, the professional association of the guild and the corporation, and the associations, partly geographical, partly political, of the village, the township and the state. Embracing all the others, and not so much formed as instituted, the community of the Church, and that of the empire too, which found its ultimate sanction in the Church, united in the *Corpus Christianum*, stood guarantor for the necessity and sanctity of all those other associations which had come into being by necessity. And the sole voluntary institution which the Church did actually create, the Catholic men's and women's orders, by virtue of its integration in the Church, as a deliberately sanctioned exception hedged about with every imaginable proviso, could ultimately serve only to prove the rule. Its purport was that while there might well be *ordines* there was in fact no such thing as a *societas*. The fact that the Jesuit order specifically assumed the title *Societas Jesu* and not that of an *ordo*, and showed itself to be a *societas* by its whole form and conduct, was one of the seeds of a course of development which found its full fruition in the eighteenth century. The discovery had been made that association could be created, and indeed that association in its true and really living sense had to be created. The old obligatory institutions, the Church included, now began to lose their influence in a way most peculiarly their own—and who would claim to be able to give the final reasons? Imperceptibly but irresistibly they began to sink in the esteem of ever more numerous groups of people to the point where they came to be looked upon as the simple product of nature and history with which one must of course comply, but which could not be sufficient; to the point where they were regarded as the mere visible sign of community—all too visible, in fact—and for this very reason not worthy to be considered its true expression. Within, beyond and beside the old institutions, it was felt, one must seek to find the proper, true, living, invisible community, and right through them all discover, work and build that proper community. Once again it is the expression of the age's absolute will for form, a will to which all the things we find existing about us are mere material to be moulded by man. The meaning of a *societas*, as distinct from an *ordo*, is *Gesellschaft*, that is to say it is an association of companions who meet by their own free choice, independently of the old institutions, seeming to respect them, but inwardly, in some way and at some point doing quite the reverse—united by some common feeling, and for the achievement of some common aim. This feeling, it was thought, did not pulse, or at any rate only feebly pulsed, in the members of the old institutions, and men no longer expected—or little expected—the old institutions to strive after and achieve that aim, whereas in the new, free associations they were in good heart and full of confidence on both counts. It is now that we hear 'He is a prince—but more, he is man!' in *The Magic Flute*. And it is now that the name 'Brother' becomes a freely conferred title of honour.

What does this mean? It means that an entirely new dividing principle, an entirely new way of distinguishing between the lower and higher orders of men, between those who should be taken seriously and those it is safe to ignore, was now coming into effect whereby the old distinctions became relative. The man who does not belong to the same family, class, state or Church could now become an associate and hence a friend, and hence a brother, as and when he belongs to the sacred circle of common views and common aims; and the man belonging to the same family, class, state, and Church can be reduced to one of the anonymous herd, the ignorant masses, as and when he is not included, but shut out from the new, free society's point of view. We have already seen how significantly the theory of man's right to form free associations had affected his conception of the state, and how, once it had taken effect, the political development which led either to monarchical or to liberal-national absolutism was possible. Or was it rather that absolutism formed the root for the new theory of association? Be that as it may, it *was* absolutism, which expressed itself in the idea that association could be created in the form of a community of feeling and aims, and that this community was the true, real and living one. It was a completely non-political manifestation of absolutism, and indeed deliberately non-political—a belief in the limitless nature of man's capacities, and in this, as it were, personal and private form absolutism experienced in the forming of associations now began in all manner of ways to underpin (or shall we say rather, undermine?) the ramparts of the old social institutions.

Suffice it to say that this new, free form of association now existed, and was to prove itself characteristic of man in the eighteenth century. It established itself at every point within the old institutions and, if the truth be known, set them their limits. It provided at least a temporary refuge against a feeling that the old institutions were inadequate—it was available whenever the outside world became too cold and desolate. But within it one could await better times, and in expectation of a better future do many things in the company of fellow-conspirators, and make many preparations against the day. It was a complete world within the world, in which, in contrast to those living outside, men confronted whatever else might happen, God or destiny or the future —face to face, directly and not indirectly—directly by virtue of the fact that the place for the encounter had been freely chosen, a place which after all was invested with the entire strength of human community.

It was this course of development that gave birth, or rebirth, to a counterpart of the Society of Jesus, secular, but only too similar to it in kind. That counterpart originated from a body scarcely distinguishable from the regular orders, the 'Bauhütten' (the corporation of the builders) of the Middle Ages; the order of Freemasons, all bathed in the splendour of the invisible, and for this very reason, the real and true Church, the veritable Church of mankind. Here long before the revolution, the enlightened of the absolute princes, Frederick the Great at their head, had begun to join with their bourgeois antagonists in the peaceful building of temples. 'The search for truth, a life of virtue, heartfelt love for God and man; let these our watchword be!' the masons' song declaims. And again, in *The Magic Flute*, 'be steadfast, patient and discreet!' is the cry to the adept. And what other comment is there than that contained in the same work: 'Who finds no joy in this our plan, does but demean the name of man!'? But the uniting influence and momentum of the esoteric doctrines imbuing the lodges of the eighteenth century must be construed as greater and more widespread than may appear from such professions of faith, whose purpose was after all to pave the way and dispel the general disquiet. Let us hear what Goethe was already saying on the subject (in his *Symbolum* of 1815):

The mason's searching
Is life's whole mirror;
The aims he strives for
The perfect seeming
Of human behaviour.

The times imparting
Their joy and sorrow
Are slow to follow,
But not desisting
We hasten onward.

In awesome distance
A veil hangs gleaming;
Above the beaming
Soft stars' insistence,
And tombs are beneath.

Regard them closer,
And see! they invest
The heroes' breast
With stealthy terror
And solemn feeling.

But beyond are sounding
The phantom voices,
The masters' voices:
Delay not in aiding
The powers of good!

Here crowns are woven
In endless silence,
A gift of abundance
To garland the chosen!
We conjure you, hope![1]

This was the heart of the matter. And why should it surprise us? It must have been utterly exhilarating to countless people to know that this *was* in fact the matter, and that it could now be contemplated regardless of state boundaries, church precincts or any class distinctions, in an association which had arisen freely and stood freely; that

[1] Cf. Appendix p. 399.

is to say, in a league of free men, and therefore in a league which was genuinely fraternal. Anyone, however, who sought still stronger forms of communal secrecy or secret community could find what he was looking for by joining with the Rosicrucians, just as anyone who had determined upon a more energetic offensive against the existing powers of Church and state could find an answer to his needs in the society of the Illuminati. If, on the other hand, he desired less mysticism, something a little less potent and inspired by more practical feeling and aims, he could engage in what appealed to him in one of the numerous societies for the furtherance of knowledge and the common good which were springing up. A further point to notice in this connexion is that the old universities now found new rivals as centres of research in the academies instituted in accordance with social theory. Neither must we forget that the eighteenth century was the time which saw the formation of the student associations in the ideological and sociological form which still characterizes them today. 'He who guides the stars in the canopy of the heavens' now had many banners to hold. And of course we must on no account overlook here the pietistic movements and especially the founding of the Moravian brethren. Surely the end of all things—for the first time, at any rate on German soil but with a universality unprecedented even elsewhere, they implemented the idea of a free connexion between all the churches, based on their common 'love of the Saviour'. This notion was the all-absorbing interest of Count Zinzendorf. Especially in the first half of the century, everyone who seriously wished to be a Christian, whether or not he was one of the Moravian brotherhood, felt himself a little at home, not in Wittenberg, not in Geneva, but in the invisible *Philadelphia* which was yet everywhere assuming tangible form. In spite of all the diversity of their forms it is impossible not to recognize the single unifying intention, spirit and conviction underlying all this building of free associations of feeling and aim: the conviction that it is possible to create community. This is the exact parallel to the conviction that it is possible to educate. It is this freely formed community, not that already known and in existence, which is alone in possession of the truth, and therefore of the future—or of the joyful, assured prospect of the future. We might well ask ourselves whether the French Revolution would not have broken out very much sooner, had not these convictions and the numerous bodies they created satisfied for a time so many desires tending towards an absolutist sociology, and in so doing temporarily tied up—or engaged—so many energies in relatively harmless activities.

A quick glance at the field of eighteenth-century language, literature and poetry will show us that it too was subject to the absolutism of the will for form as the phenomenon which did most to shape the picture presented by the life of the time. The decisive event here—we are of course speaking of the time before Goethe—was, I suppose, the all-embracing claim made on behalf of the mother tongue in opposition to the language of antiquity which had dominated the cultural life in the Middle Ages and continued to do so even well into the seventeenth century. It was now the mother tongue which was explored, given literary and poetic form, moulded and developed in all its possibilities. This also started happening at first simply because people had become aware that in this sphere there was an enormous mass of raw material to hand, which was clearly inviting conquest, mastery and the imposition of form. They had become aware of an unknown land in the closest proximity and the fact that it had up to then been untouched tempted a generation of such expansive sensibilities simply by virtue of the law of the *horror vacui*. The wildness and barbaric lack of form of this land now gradually became a source of shame, but its rich possibilities at the hands of those with the impulse to activity seemed to give promise of limitlessly fruitful fields.

It is well known that it was France in the great era of Louis XIV which preceded the other nations in transforming the vernacular with all its possibilities into a classical language. The fact that the measure and model of the classical style which the great French formal masters took as their weapon in the task was none other than that provided by antiquity, is a subject apart. They were in something of a hurry and took up the rules of form where they found them. The inner relationship of the French genius with the Latin genius in particular made this form the choice that seemed by far the most natural and obvious one. And the energy of the highly original and peculiar French will to impose form did ultimately prove strong enough to produce a classicism which, even by the aid of a borrowed instrument, succeeded in emerging as something new and peculiarly French, a structure now in its turn impressive enough to serve as a model for the same development to which the German language was subjected at a somewhat later date.

There are no doubt profound reasons, which this is not the place to discuss, why German literature in the first half of the eighteenth century produced no classical literature but only works imitating classical forms: why it produced no Racine, Corneille or Molière, but only a Johann Christian Gottsched, who in spite of the noteworthy collaboration of his spouse Luise Adelgunde Viktoria, née Kulmus, found it quite impossible to achieve fame as a poet, and was only of note as a professor of the German language. But it was not, as it happened, his sterile subservience to French models which in the new period beginning with Klopstock and Lessing gave rise to the violent reaction against the aims he pursued and the works he wrote. It was, on the contrary, the very thing French classicism, so ingenious in its own way, and the patently uninspired German classical style had in common which made his work significant, and later an object of hatred; the conviction, that the language should and could be mastered, the will to achieve a German 'art of language' (grammar), 'art of speaking' (rhetoric) and 'art of composition' (poetics), as the titles of Gottsched's chief works typically indicated. Gottsched wanted to make Leipzig, of all places, for Germany what Paris was to France: a central forum in questions of good taste relating to German language, literature and poetry. The fact that it only managed to become a 'little Paris', as we may still learn among other things from Goethe's *Faust*, does not, however unfortunate this may have been, seriously affect the issue. The true issue was Gottsched's supreme and all-too supreme confidence in the German artistic will as such; and it was this that first called J. J. Breitinger of Zürich—another professor—and then the entire body of inspired youth, into the lists against him. It was his misfortune even if it was certainly no accident that he was doomed to compromise his cause by an all-too conspicuous personal vanity, which led him to play the dictator in his Paris on the river Pleisse, that he was plunged all-too deeply into the shadow of the Titans who were following after him, and that he was therefore doomed even at the height of his fame, to be transformed into a kind of comic figure. But his widely-ranging endeavours on behalf of the early and earliest language and literature of the Germans can bear witness, in a way that commands a certain respect, to the professorial but sincere earnestness with which he furthered his cause. We have mentioned Gottsched here as the typical exponent of the German classical style, which together with French classicism, provides evidence of the dictatorial manner that eighteenth-century man was bold enough to adopt also in his approach to work in the literary sphere.

Let us now conclude our survey of the external form imparted to the life of the age by a few reflections upon its music. Here we touch upon a region which we have to confess is extraordinarily difficult to com prehend even a little, either historically or in any other kind of thought. It is, however, the fact that, with everything else, this century was musical as well and perhaps above all else; more musical certainly than any age that had gone before and perhaps than any since. And

there is something in the way in which it was musical which is so characteristic of the whole spirit of the age, that if we wish to understand this
spirit we simply cannot escape making some reference to it. We can
study the history of a past age, we can contemplate its architectural
and other works of art, its portraits and its dress, and we can read the
books it gave us, but we cannot hear the voices of the people then
living—and this imposes a tremendous limitation upon our understanding—except as they are transcribed and laid before us in their
music in so far as it has been handed down to us. Is not this form of
communication perhaps the most intimate we can hope for from a
past age? How many extraordinary generalizations and judgments on
the eighteenth century would have been quite out of the question if
only those who made them had recalled that this was also the century
of Bach and Handel, Gluck and Haydn, and had remembered just a
few notes from the works of any one of them before once again setting
pen to paper with their diffusions on the 'one-sided intellectual
civilization' of that age and various other catchwords. For Frederick
the Great was not only the victor of the battle of Leuthen or the
friend of Voltaire, and not only the intellectual author of the Prussian national code of laws. All this is no doubt very important, but
Frederick was also an ardent flute player and we may at least ask
whether there should not be intensive historical study with the task of
investigating whether he might not have been more truly himself in
this than in anything else he did. How intently, nay devotedly, people
practised music at this time, and—what may show even more clearly
how intensely musical they were—how intently they listened. But in the
attempt to see them in this aspect of their nature, we must be careful
to concede them their own kind of musicality. This discussion is barred
to anyone who is familiar only with the modern world and will therefore brook no argument in taking as his yardstick the lyricism of Beethoven or Schubert who simply *are* part of this completely different
modern world; to anyone whose ideas in assessing J. S. Bach are like
those of Richard Wagner: 'Bach is like the sphinx. The noble head
struggling forth from the periwig resembles the human face in its first
emergence from the animal body.' On the other hand it is barred too to
anyone who thinks Bach should be revered as a true saint of Protestantism, and immediately imagines that he hears in the Passions and
Cantatas a complete expression of Luther's theology, and then again to
anyone who applies to him the saying, in itself unanswerable, that like
all great music Bach's is truly human and therefore timeless. It is moreover debatable whether a true modern feeling for music, would treat the

true musicality of a former age in this way. Would it not rather seek to discover and honour its timelessness within and not outside the very qualities which made it a part of its age?

If we hold this to be the true way then the problems which present themselves are such that we can only briefly touch upon them. I would consider it suitable to take as our starting point the fact that all the minor musicians of the eighteenth century *and* the great ones, and perhaps especially the great ones, were not either in their own sight or in that of their contemporaries what we today describe as artists or composers, but quite simply craftsmen of the profession concerned with honouring God and delighting the heart of man: a profession which primarily consisted in the mastery of one or of several musical instruments. And the significant fact we must realize is that the musician of the eighteenth century preferred these instruments to be the piano or its predecessors current at that time, and the organ; the instruments, which were polyphonic in intention. Art was in those days still most definitely the product of technical ability. Art was proficiency. It was this proficiency which first made Bach famous, and kept him famous right up to the time when, as 'old Bach' he was the object of Frederick the Great's admiration. It was this proficiency which made the young Mozart the wonder of Europe. But at that time the art of composing was looked upon by great and small merely as a means of applying, of widening and deepening the scope of the art of professional musicianship, as a means of proving the perfected skill which, in this as in all things, reveals the master. Not sensibility, not experience, not mystique and not Protestantism, but art as a skill, as proficiency in the manipulation of the most exacting rules—not without 'invention', certainly, as it was then called, but invention continually inventing a new necessity, invention in the expression not so much of what the composer himself found personally stimulating, but rather of general laws—this was needed to write a fugue. And the quality which distinguished a good fugue from a bad one in composition and performance was, in the opinion of no less a man than Bach himself, the art which was revealed in the craftsman's skill. The beautiful, so to speak, had to follow as a matter of course (unsought and not to be sought in the abstract) from that which was properly done from the craftsman's point of view. Inspiration on the composer's part was also essential. What emerged would certainly be 'beautiful' too. But an informed admirer like Frederick the Great would admire only the beauty of the skill and style which the work causes to become audible, and not, specifically not, the beauty of the piece in itself. The steadfast conviction that art, understood in this way, would of itself result in the glory of God and the delight of the soul was the first quality peculiar to the typical music of the time.

But what was the mastery which these musicians sought and practised? I should say that it consisted of the sovereign attitude which they had first of all towards the instrument producing the sounds and then to the abundance of possibilities inherent in these sounds. It was the full and joyous awareness of this sovereignty which made them prefer the polyphonic instruments and polyphonic composition. It was for them a question of humanizing, so to speak, the rough amorphous mass of possible sounds—of forcing, imposing and stamping upon it not any individual style as such, but rather the law known to each individual human being, the order of sounds which he 'invents', i.e. finds already within himself as an objectively valid order—until there is no longer merely sound, but sound existing as musical tone. Further, it was for them a question of evolving harmony from the confused mass of possible combinations of sounds and, from the equally confused mass of possible sequences of sounds, something that was henceforth to be a singing cosmos, put forth by man and penetrating space. The man who can do that, who knows the law involved in doing it, and also knows how to handle them in spite of their deep secrecy and bewildering diversity, is a *maestro*. Bach did not consider himself a genius, nor did his contemporaries, as is well known, treat him as one. But both he and they were united in the awareness that he was a master of his art in the sense we have just described, and it was this which they appreciated in him. Making music means subjecting the sound to the laws. That is the second peculiarity of the music of the time: the straightforward way its practitioners believed as a matter of course in the existence of these laws, in the possibility of their being recognized and applied; and the absolutely impartial way they applied them.

We can then go on to ask in what way we can understand this way of making music as serving the glory of God and the delight of the soul in the spirit of the age, and what precisely we should take to be its whole aim and extent? My answer would be that the whole aim and extent of this music was really immaculate playing, not in spite of, but because of the virtuosity expected both in the art of composition and the art of execution. This cannot be said in the same way of the music of any other century. Once this mastery of the world of sound had been achieved, eighteenth-century music-making, with its background of exacting labour, seemed to assume a form which enabled it to attain in an even more unqualified way a totally superior and at the same time totally disinterested ability to deal with the possibilities of that world. *Res severa verum gaudium!* It was only on the basis of this craftsman's mastery of the art of transforming the world of sounds into music that the game of making music could be played. But on the basis of this transformation and re-creation it could be played with assurance and in accordance with the laws of necessity. And it was this playing which was looked upon as the be-all and end-all of the entire process. Here and only here the beauty of the music as such was accorded any place. For its beauty consisted in the freedom founded upon subjection to the law, the freedom upon which we hear the musician embark. It was Goethe who said perhaps the profoundest thing it is possible to say about Bach's music: 'As if the eternal harmony were discoursing with itself, as might perhaps have happened in the bosom of the Lord just before the Creation; so I was moved inwardly and felt that I no longer needed ears, nor eyes the least of all, nor any other senses.' Let the words: 'just *before* the Creation' be noted. There is as we know a passage in the Bible according to which something like a conversation of the eternal harmony with itself takes place, just before the Creation, with a similar reference to playing, i.e. Prov. 8.27-31: 'When he prepared the heavens, I was there: when he set a compass upon the face of the depth: when he established the clouds above: when he strengthened the fountains of the deep: when he gave to the sea his decree, that the waters should not pass his commandment: when he appointed the foundations of the earth: then was I by him, as a master workman: and had delight continually, playing always before him; playing in the habitable part of his earth; and my delights were with the sons of men.' Would it not be the revelation of a supreme will for form, a will for form manifesting perhaps only in this sphere its utmost absolutism, if the music of the eighteenth century sought to emulate the wisdom even of the Creator in its results and in the abandonment and superiority which cause us to forget all the craftsmanship behind it? Be that as it may, all earlier music is still too much involved in the struggle to subdue the raw material of musical sound, and it must be said that the later music, from Beethoven onwards, desired and loved the world of sound too little for its own sake, to be capable of looking upon it in the same unequivocal way as a game. The music of the eighteenth century, the music of absolutism, plays, and for this reason it is in a peculiar way beautiful and that not only in its great exponents but in its minor ones too. Something of the glow of freedom which is peculiar to this age in this particular sphere rests upon all who come to our mind, be they German, Italian or French.

There is something else in the realm of music which is still greater, or at any rate more eloquent than this freedom. It makes its appearance whenever the riddle of human existence appears over against full musical freedom; for it is impossible to explore and resolve this riddle completely by any earthly play. When this happens the play of the sounds which have become entirely transformed into musical tone, which have been quite humanized, breaks like the sea against a rocky shore. It is still the sea, not the infinite sea, which after all only seems infinite, but the sea bounded, as it truly is. If my view—or hearing—of the matter is correct, this cannot be said either of Bach or Handel, or of Gluck or Haydn. As musicians they were naïve children of their century. Their music is like the sea at a point where no shore is in sight. There was one musician who had all the things which distinguished the musicians of the eighteenth century from all those who had gone before and from all those who came after, but who had in addition something entirely personal to himself: the sadness or horror inherent in the knowledge of the border before which absolutist man, even and particularly when cutting his finest figure, stands in blissful unawareness. Like his Don Giovanni, he heard the footfall of the visitor of stone. But, also like Don Giovanni, he did not allow himself to be betrayed into simply forgetting to go on playing in the stony visitor's presence. He still fully belonged to the eighteenth century and was nevertheless already one of the men of the time of transition of whom it will be our chief task to speak in this survey of the antecedents to our story proper. I am referring to Wolfgang Amadeus Mozart.

Before we proceed, almost at once, to the subject of our next chapter we shall discuss the form of the inner life of eighteenth-century man. I mean the thing which is regularly recurrent in the make-up of the great number of individuals of that time who are known to us, and which is therefore characteristic in the attitude they ultimately seem to adopt towards themselves, the world, and the Deity. I do not think we shall be guilty of being too schematic if we surmise that such a common denominator, let us say a psychological common denominators, exists in visible and comprehensible form in every epoch of human events that is recognizable as a unity, such as the eighteenth century, and to which the existence of all those who shared in such a time can in some sense ultimately be reduced, in spite of the abundance of variety and contradiction that may exist. It is an inner analogue to the form of their outward life. With both of them together we can find no actual explanation, certainly, but an instructive light upon the historical experiences (of which we have spoken in the first half of our chapter) of man at this time. Let us first try to state in simple terms what there is still left to see:

1. All the people who are truly representative of the eighteenth century have a naïvely strong conviction that their self-awareness as human beings is superior to the totality of those things which differ from it, which are in some way outside it. They know that the things outside can certainly be got at in some way by means of human apprehension, willing and feeling. Their relation to them is a free one and they, the men, are the masters. It was not for nothing that one of the favourite figures in the literature of the time was Robinson Crusoe, the man thrown completely upon his own resources, who in spite of this and for this very reason was able to take care of himself so triumphantly.

2. Corresponding to this subjective conviction there is the objective one, that this outside world of things is in itself suited and even planned, and appointed—in a manner which cannot be sufficiently wondered at —to become the object and scene of this expansion of human self-awareness. 'The world is good' means it is good as the object and scene of the deeds of men.

3. In view of this admirable concordance between the inner and the outer world the man of the eighteenth century believed (with few exceptions) in a God who is common lord of both of them, but who of course stands nearer to man and the human world. God is the quintessence, the perfection, unapproached and unapproachable, of that wisdom and goodness with which man is confident enough to approach the world, and which clearly meets him in the world. God is the highest *motive*—as regards the degree of reasonableness which man and the world can produce, for what is possible in the advancement of knowledge, the extension of the sphere of the will and a deepening of the feelings' on man's part, and further revelations on the part of the universe. And at the same time God is the highest *quietive* in respect to the effective limits of human self-consciousness which are to be conceded: these limits are as much a part of it in itself as imposed by the mysteries of the universe which are as yet unsolved or might prove altogether insoluble.

4. Man knows that he is linked with, and ultimately of the same substance as, the God significant for him in this double function. God is spirit, man is spirit too. God is mighty and so is man. God is wise and benevolent, and so is man. But he is all these things, of course, infinitely less perfectly than God. Man's way of being these things is confused

and fragmentary, but it *is* the same way. Hence that which outside in the world man finds already imbued with reason, or makes reasonable by the exercise of his will, is also, in all its imperfection, of one substance with God.

5. The conviction that God exists thus justified and ensured the conviction that human self-awareness is superior both in the valiant enthusiasm which is necessary to it and in its equally necessary humble acquiescence. This conviction concerning man rests firmly on the conviction about God. The latter, it is true, does not in itself rest firmly upon anything, and it must for this reason from time to time be reaffirmed, if only for the sake of the other conviction. The conviction that God exists and holds sway must from time to time be justified and guaranteed anew. How is this to be done? The proof will be conveyed by a renewed confirmation of the existence of this wonderful concordance between man and the world he inhabits. It is by this means that man will once again be fired with a belief in God, and it is this renewed confirmation which must serve as instrument of the theodicy.

6. The theodicy—that is, the renewed confirmation of this concordance, which is necessary for the sake of the anthropodicy—can indeed also be established theoretically, but the decisive factor will always be that man actually experiences it. But he experiences it in taking up the normal position which he must take up in relation to the world at large, i.e. in acting virtuously. For he can act thus, and in doing so he experiences and apprehends this concordance and in it God, and in God the necessary motive and quietive governing his own mode of existence. The theoretical theodicy is only a paraphrasing of this practical one.

7. But what is meant by acting virtuously? Fulfilling the will of God? Certainly, but what is the will of God that must be fulfilled? Clearly a correct understanding of ourselves and a correct understanding of the world is bound to tell us what virtuous conduct is, as surely as both the world and we ourselves are sprung from God. The correct understanding, will, however, be the natural way of understanding, that is to say, the understanding of ourselves and of the world in their quality as sprung from God. We must therefore allow Nature (and this is within our power) to tell us what is good. We need only allow ourselves to be told by subjective reason, as the elemental voice within every man, and by objective reason, as the elemental voice speaking to every man. For the right understanding of these voices we have only, if at all—for they are assuredly plain to us—to talk of them or alternatively be instructed about them in order to realize that we are quite able to remember what they say. He who hears the voice of reason and

obeys it is acting virtuously and thus finds the theodicy he was seeking and together with it the anthropodicy he was more truly seeking.

But has not man in fact asked himself and himself given the answer he apparently really wished to hear from some other source? This is the question of which, thus expressed, man in the eighteenth century was not aware. This was the absolutism also inherent in his inner attitude to life; he assumed it to be self-evident that in taking himself to account, and himself answering the account, and then acting in obedience to it he was also showing the existence of God, justifying and guaranteeing anew his relationship with God and thereby affirming that his own existence was possible. He believed—even in this inmost place we find him a prey to a strange vicious circle—that by virtue of the reality of his own existence he could vouch for God and in so doing for the possible existence of God. This may have been the secret of his inward attitude in outline.

We can now call to mind a historical connexion. The eighteenth century was without doubt a revival (a very peculiar one, admittedly) of the sixteenth-century Renaissance, or, if you would rather, a recrudescence of that Renaissance. The nature of this Renaissance is however explained by the idea of humanism, the latter to be understood in its widest sense. And the idea of humanism was that the perfect life consisted in the complete autarchy of rational man in a rational world on the basis of the existence and dominion of a Deity guaranteeing this association and thus too man's complete autarchy. It was transplanted from antiquity into the soil of Northern Europe in the late middle ages and became the ideal of England, France and Germany: from antiquity—we should say, from late antiquity, and more precisely still, from that spiritual world which had found its philosophical exponents in the schools—which were in conflict and yet only too united —of the so-called Stoics and the so-called Epicureans. This humanism had been thrust into the background at first by the Reformation and the upheavals which followed it, but it had always remained alive, especially in England. And in Germany too it had only, so to speak, hibernated. For it was a fact which was bound to have some effect eventually, so that—only too faithfully in accordance with the instructions of Melanchthon himself—a whole series of generations of future theologians, philosophers, lawyers, scientists and statesmen and other educated men had been fed at the most impressionable age on Cicero and Plutarch, and then again on Plutarch and Cicero, *ad infinitum*. This seed was now sprouting. There are no doubt deeper reasons why it chose this particular time to sprout, but there is no disputing the fact that the inner attitude to life of the eighteenth century, reduced to its simplest formula, ultimately consisted only of the fact that Cicero and Plutarch were now taken seriously. The attitude of mind of eighteenth-century man makes it quite clear that the man, the citizen, the hero, the sage, the virtuous and the pious man he held before his mind's eye as his model and his measure, as the frame into which he set his own picture, was the man of late pre-Christian or extra-Christian antiquity of quite a definite stamp: the Stoic with a dash and sometimes with a lot more than just a dash of Epicureanism in his make-up. If it is to make sense, the title 'the philosophical century' which has been applied to the eighteenth century can only mean that at this time there were hundreds and thousands of people everywhere to whom philosophy was what it had been to countless numbers of people in the time of the emperors of Rome, namely a practical teaching of life, nay more: a whole attitude to life based on this complete authority of rational man in a rational world with a religious background. In the 'philosopher of Sans Souci' this historical connexion, his place in philosophy some-where in the middle between Zeno and Epicurus, is quite plain for all to see. But it is also possible to recognize immediately a successor to Seneca and Epictetus in a man as devout and pious in his way as Gellert. And the young Goethe was still firmly rooted in this same soil, and on his own confession started from there for the rest of his way. And strangely enough it continually reappears, either in hidden or in patent form, in the utterances of many a pietist.

The purest form to which this new humanism rose already is in the early eighteenth century—its transfigured form, so to speak—was embodied in the personality and philosophy of Gottfried Wilhelm Leibnitz. This is not the place even to attempt to represent and assess it. Throughout the outline I have just given, I have continually had the thought of this man in mind. It is the thought of a man who was at the same time one of the most typical and one of the most individual men of his age. His life's work represents as in a microcosm all the tendencies of his time, showing how numerous and yet at the same time how similar they were. If we prefer to put it another way, he was in a great manner and most comprehensively what nearly all his contemporaries were capable of being only in a small way and in particular. He was philosopher, theologian, lawyer, politician, courtier, mathematician, naturalist, historian and linguist in one, and was fairly well possessed of the same detailed knowledge, and achieved the same success, in all of them. At one moment he was planning to lay before Louis XIV the Napoleonic idea of a conquest of Egypt, the so-called *consilium Aegyptiacum*; and at another conducting a violent political pamphlet war in the defence of the German emperor and empire against this very same king. At one moment he invented a calculating machine and at another he was at least the co-inventor of the modern infinitesimal calculus. For years he was concerned with the problem of whether it would not be better to drive the pumps in the Hanoverian mines in the Harz Mountains by windmills instead of with water. He then wrote a history of the Guelphs based on the widest possible research into the historical sources. At one moment he formed a plan for the conversion of the heathen and at another he conceived one, and brought about negotiations based upon it, for the reunion of the Catholic and Protestant Churches, or at least of the Lutheran and Reformed Churches. At one moment he was able to write a pre-history of the Earth, and at the next to found, together with many others, the Prussian Academy of the Sciences which is still in existence today. As a most genuine philosopher of the age, he never presented his philosophical teaching in the form of a system, but only in fragments of information quickly and surely set down while actually at grips with one or other of his contemporaries or, as with his theodicy, at the personal wish of a woman of enquiring mind, Queen Sophia Charlotte of Prussia. But it was in this philosophical teaching that, in pursuing lines of thought which were highly original and endowed with a splendour all of their own, he at the same time most perfectly revealed the ideal of the inner attitude to life which prevailed in his time. Or are we mistaken in thinking that we can recognize eighteenth-century man in Leibnitz' teaching of the monad, for instance? This simple and utterly individual, indeed unique spiritual substance is the fountain-head of all reality. The utterly self-sufficient monad is an emanation, an image, a mirror of God himself and is therefore nowhere limited by things outside it, but only in its own being; which has no windows, and changes only by its inner principle, its own most peculiar striving; which is always the best it is possible for it to be, and which can therefore transform itself by the tendency of its own most peculiar nature; but it cannot be destroyed, cannot perish, and is immortal like God himself who created it? And do we not meet again that wonderful concordance of man with the world surrounding him when we hear from Leibnitz that between the monads themselves, but also between the monads and the bodies together with which they are effected, there exists a pre-established harmony (*harmonie préétablie*)? That there is a pre-established harmony between body and soul, between form and extension, between the purposive and effective cause, between the dynamic and the mathematical principle, between *vérités de raison* and *vérités de fait*, between chance and necessity, between the sphere of wisdom and the sphere of energy, and between grace and nature? That this is like the harmony between two synchronized clocks constructed in the most artificial manner imaginable for this very purpose; that therefore the relationship of the monads to one another and to the physical world is a piece of work worthy of God, and of God alone? Do we not meet God again, God who guarantees and justifies that concordance and therefore man in the teaching that it is in fact God who is the creator of this best of all possible worlds as a whole, but that he allows each monad to be the best it possibly can and should be, whose world is the best possible one because it is the most suited to the building of his kingdom? Surely this kingdom is the kingdom of the spirit, and that means of the spirits of which each individual one is summoned to be, after his fashion in his particular place, the whole, and the king of this whole? And is not the converse question which inevitably arises here, namely the question concerning the truth of the existence and dominion of God, who vouches for the whole and for the single parts in the whole, answered by way of referring man to himself? Do we not find a theodicy here which decisively refers man to himself? I mean, a converse question and a theodicy in the form of the direct call to man to accept both freely and humbly his individuality and the position it occupies in the plan of the whole, to fill this position as if only God and the soul existed (the soul willed by God precisely in its self-determination and autonomy), and thus to discover that the physical and the moral evil in the world which he imagines to be actively opposed to him contain in truth nothing positive, but are, so to speak, only a shadow fleeing before the light; an inevitable result of the term of life imposed upon all things which are not God, but as such a determining factor also for the harmony of the whole which God created? And may we not ask, to return to the historical connexion, whether all this does not represent Stoicism in its most sublime form, in a form more sublime than ever existed in ancient Greece and Rome; a Stoicism which is a triumph of humanism, which can itself find the answer to every question and seems not to know of a question which might be posed to it? The shape which Christianity was bound to take in this world, which spiritually perhaps found its liveliest and most eloquent embodiment in Leibnitz, we shall have to discuss.

3

THE PROBLEM OF THEOLOGY
IN THE EIGHTEENTH CENTURY

BY THE phrase 'problem of theology' I mean the subject-matter of theology, the reality that occupies theology, taking the word 'problem' in its old and proper sense. It may be sufficient at this point to recall a few key-phrases which characterize this reality. It is a matter of God and his revelation, his communication of himself and his claim on man, his Gospel and his law, or, in other words, of his covenant concluded with man in the name of Jesus Christ, of the Holy Spirit as his presence among men promised in this covenant, of the justification and sanctification of man that takes place in this covenant, of man understood as God's creature, but as God's fallen creature, a sinner. It is a matter of this man being in the Church as the place or organ of the covenant, of the action of this Church in word and sacrament, of the faith and obedience of man in the covenant with God and therefore in the community of the Church, of the redemption to be expected in this covenant and therefore in the Church, beyond the bounds of his natural and historical existence set by death. It is a matter of a book, the Bible, in which everything is documented and told to us. That is the subject-matter of theology, the reality with which it is concerned. That is so-called Christianity. I mention these key-phrases here only as pointers. Of course, they paraphrase the Christian confession, but they are meant to be heard here primarily without any theological filling, without any systematic stress or conjunction. They simply indicate the subjects with which all theology has dealt and will deal in one way or another; they point to the empty page (of course a very special empty page!) which even the eighteenth century, in which we are interested here, inscribed in its own way. They show the x which even the eighteenth century, in its own way, resolved into a particular number. We are not concerned here with the correct solution of the equation, but only with the solution that was given to it at that time. Nor do we presuppose any correct solution to this equation by which we shall measure the answer given then. Rather, we shall attempt to see and understand the earlier solution in its own way, to let it speak for or against itself.

Thus the title 'The Problem of Theology in the Eighteenth Century' simply indicates the question: what was the attitude of the man of the eighteenth century to the subject-matter of theology? What did it mean for him? What place, what character, what *rôle* did it have in his consciousness and his life? We can also put the question in this way: what did men make of this subject-matter? What form did it take under their hands? What became of Christianity in the eighteenth century? Thus we are not yet concerned with the theology of the eighteenth century as such, but with its foundation, with the reflection of its subject-matter in the general consciousness and life of the time. We may certainly expect that theology will be, for its part, a repetition of this general reflection. But it could be, and probably will be the case that theology will not simply coincide with this reflection but will also differ from the general consciousness of the time, at least in part, and may even, at least in part, be in conflict with it. At any rate, it would be imprudent to identify the two from the start. So to begin with we shall pose the wider question of eighteenth-century man's view and conception of the subject-matter of theology. Then, in the fourth section, we shall raise the particular question: how does eighteenth-century theology deal with this general view and conception of the time, and what is its relationship to its subject-matter?

It seems to me that the answer to the first general question must be given as follows: we see eighteenth-century man at first preserving the characteristic *absolutism* with which he masters all problems, even here. His attitude towards Christianity at first proves to be just one further instance of his attitude to life in general, as we have already seen it. On the other hand, we see how he does not handle this problem, and his absolutism, in the same way and with the same success as elsewhere. In his attempt to come to grips with Christianity in his own way, we see him hesitate and stumble at various points. He succeeds only partially in what was evidently his original purpose. Of course, even in this hesitation and stumbling and partial failure he remains true to himself. The way in which here, in contrast to his attitude elsewhere, he seems to see and to respect certain boundaries, confirms something decisive in his attitude elsewhere. Even here he thinks and acts as the absolutist that he is. It is a new development when this attitude itself is called in question later. Nevertheless, the picture that emerges here is not as uniform as that which confronted us hitherto. There is a break, an ambivalence, an ambiguity, a contradiction in it. It must be seen if we are to understand how the problem of theology in the new period following the typical eighteenth century could take such a different form and significance from that which it had previously. Our task in the following sections will therefore be to show: 1. how eighteenth-century man attempted to master even the problem of theology in his customary absolutist manner; 2. how this problem proved, even in the absolutist treatment accorded to it, a less than soluble problem, which could not be completely encompassed in a traditional form—in other words, how it proved to be a geniune problem.

I believe that the dualism which is to be observed here (within the historical picture which is homogeneous even at this point) is in fact to be observed only here, in relation to the problem of theology. With regard to science, philosophy, politics and art in the eighteenth century, one might well say that the account balances. With regard to theology, or rather the problem of theology, this cannot be said. And were one to ask, might there not be a hidden imbalance in the other areas, the answer would have to be the counter-question whether the hidden imbalance in the accounts which might in fact be discovered in every area could not be connected with the fact that even in this time there might have been a genuine problem that could not be solved and thus a definite account that did not balance, the shadow of which inevitably fell on the totality. In that case, might this genuine problem not have been the problem of theology?

So to begin with, we simply have to enlarge the lines of the picture that we have achieved so far and to note that the grandiose attempt of the eighteenth century, undertaken with a grandiose self-confidence, to treat everything given and handed down in nature and in history as the property of man, to be assimilated to him and thus to be humanized—this attempt extended not least to the subject-matter of theology, to Christianity. To put it cautiously, the tints of this century shade all the phrases with which we described this subject-matter earlier, the substantiations, associations and emphases with which they had been taken over from the past, the whole structure of other words needed to explain the key-phrases. They also shade the approach by which the reality designated by these key-phrases is accessible to men, the formal authority and material significance that it has for them and ultimately the manner in which man himself has to react, the way in which he interprets his own existence in the face of this reality. They shade the face and form of the visible Church alongside and in the state, society, its relation to culture. The serpent makes an attempt even at this morsel. Perhaps this is the most profound significance of the whole historical process, perhaps everything else is merely pre-liminary or incidental to it: that it first and last and above all has to make an attempt at this morsel. Be this as it may, the man of the eighteenth century approaches even Christianity with belief in the omnipotence of human capability. Now he believes he can experience and know even the essence of Christianity as the omnipotence of human capability. His approach was not to expunge the theological problem. At this time, as at any time, direct denials of the truth of Christianity, explicit paganism or explicit atheism, were marginal instances, phenomena not to be taken seriously. The eighteenth cen-tury was as pious as any other century. Like every century before it, like the nineteenth century after it (and as even the twentieth century will have to do), the eighteenth century recognized the problem of theology, the need to adopt an attitude towards the reality designated by those key-phrases, to be responsible for it in some way. But it subjected—or rather attempted to subject—this problem to a particular transformation in its own particular climate. It framed the question posed to it by Christianity in such a way that it fitted the answer which it, in the train of its particular genius, could or would give. It made the question into a topical one. And by doing this, in faith in the omnipotence of human capability for even this question, in faith that man had the power and the right to reshape this question in a deliberate way, it inevitably made the very question into a further expression of man's omnipotence. The peculiar importance and urgency of this way of overcoming the problem is obvious. The reality with which theology is occupied seems to raise the claim to be a final and quite superior authority, no matter how few and how qualified are the key-phrases in which it is expressed. One need only say words like creation, sin, gospel, law, grace, faith at least to hear this claim as such. This reality seems to be an authority that is set over against men, an authority that is different from men: at least one of these key-phrases, albeit the most central and least dispensable, the name of Jesus Christ, in his contingency which stands out from the universal name of God, seems to say this, and in conjunction with the name, the fact of the equally contingent documentation of the reality in the Bible. If humanization had to present any problem, then this was evidently the one. Did not the man of the eighteenth century, the man who believed in the omnipotence of human capability, for whom there could be no subject-matter of this kind in the last resort, find himself confronted

here *in nuce* with the problem of the nature of his subject-matter? Was
not the attack which he had carried out so victoriously on all fronts
against his subject-matter a failure if it was a failure here? On this
decisive front humanization had to mean the experience and knowledge of that superior authority, as a reality that was not ultimately
and absolutely, but only provisionally and relatively different from
man himself or his capability in the widest sense. Humanization had
to mean, if not the abolition, at least the incorporation of God into the
sphere of sovereign human self-awareness, the transformation of the
reality that came and was to be perceived from outside into a reality
that was experienced and understood inwardly. Experienced and
understood inwardly, but that meant appropriate for man, incorporated into human capabilities, comprehended as such a reality as can
be begotten of man's capability and must so be begotten to count as
reality. Experienced and understood, but that meant comprehended
as material whose form man was in a position to treat in the same way
that he was able to impose himself upon nature and history. Was not
the reality designated by Christianity the key position? If man was
unable to occupy it, then his possession of all other positions had to
appear doubtful, but if he could occupy it he had so to speak covered
himself against doubts in all other respects. No wonder, then, that the
treatment of the religious, Christian, theological problem plays so
important a *rôle* within the whole intellectual structure and movement
of the eighteenth century, In the midst of the great controversies by
which the century was moved, all along the line it had at least to keep
in mind its open or latent controversy with Christianity, which took
place under a variety of forms and gave the struggles of the time their
real passion.

With respect to the humanization of the problem of theology in the
eighteenth century it is possible with some degree of clarity to distinguish four developments, not following each other but rather running alongside each other, sometimes parallel, sometimes merging
into each other, occasionally crossing over each other, i.e. contradicting each other and yet forming a coherent whole. In passing, I should
mention here that I regard as misguided the view put forward by
Troeltsch, H. Stephan, H. Hoffmann and in part, among others, by
Wernle, that so-called Pietism is to be understood essentially as an
independent, retrogressive movement, taking up the impetus of the
Reformation and continuing the Reformation where possible, whereas
the so-called Enlightenment is an independent movement opposed to
Pietism, forward-looking and therefore to be regarded as particularly

characteristic of the eighteenth century. On the contrary, I follow the views of F. C. Baur on the one side and A. Ritschl on the other, according to whom all stress is to be placed on the fact that the origins and culminations of both Pietism and the Enlightenment lie close together. This makes possible the judgment that in them we find two forms of the one essence, of Christianity as shaped by the spirit of the eighteenth century, two forms which are equally close to the Reformation and equally distant from it. In what follows, therefore, I would prefer not to make these forms the framework of my account but to keep to a few fundamental perspectives, that is, perspectives clearly provided by the intellectual movement of the time. Of course, as these are discussed, there will be opportunity enough to mention the two forms of the one essence with which we are concerned here, different, but more so outwardly than inwardly. The four series of phenomena I have in mind are these: we are concerned with the attempt of the eighteenth century to humanize the problem of theology by its incorporation into (1) the state; (2) morality and the bourgeoisie; (3) science and philosophy; (4) inwardness and the individual. Consideration of a figure like Leibnitz, so representative of the eighteenth century at its best, will show that these four perspectives have not been chosen arbitrarily.

1. We begin at the point at which the humanization of the problem of theology emerges so to speak in tangible form, in politics. The eighteenth century was the classical century of the state Church or of Caesaro-papism. True, this phenomenon goes back as far as the sixteenth century, indeed to the Middle Ages. In Protestant and in loyally Catholic areas, the spirit of the Renaissance not only refused to be suppressed in this respect, but continued to exercise its influence further in a straight-line development. The eighteenth century marks the climax of this development. Caesaro-papism, the existence of the state Church, is a situation where man, giving his own law an absolute status in the power of a territorial or national state, whether monarchy, aristocracy or democracy, also understands the Christianity preached and represented by the Church as a concern of its own law and thus as an instrument of state sovereignty, in other words, where he 'nationalizes' the Church and the Church allows this nationalization, whether deliberately or *de facto*. When at the time of the Reformation political rulers usurped the supreme power of the Church, this was originally regarded as an emergency measure, but the doctrine of the supreme episcopacy of the ruler, devised at the beginning of the seventeenth

century, which raised the emergency measure to the status of a theory, and still more the corresponding Calvinistic theory and practice according to which the authorities collaborated in church affairs through their representatives in the framework of an independent church government—all this did not necessarily threaten the independence of the Church and on the whole did not in fact do so.

Things changed with the shift in the actual situation which was expressed in church law by the suppression of the episcopalist theory in favour of the mutually related and mutually complementary theories of territorialism and collegialism. According to the terrorialist theory, represented in Germany by Samuel von Pufendorf (1632-94), Christoph Thomasius (1655-1728) and Justus Henning Böhme (1674-1749), the church government (*ius sacrum*), standing over the individual communities and guaranteeing them relative freedom, is an emanation, an application of state government (*ius publicum*), one political function alongside others. According to the collegialist theory, represented in Germany by Christoph Matthias Pfaff (1686-1760) and Johannes Lorenz von Mosheim (1693-1755), the sovereignty of the state over the Church rests on a *pactum vel tacitum vel expressum*, in which the *collegia*, i.e. the individuals, similarly thought of as relatively free associations of believers, have transferred the *iura in sacra* relating to the matters that mutually concern them to the secular authority. It can be seen that these two theories, the originators of which were more or less in sympathy with Pietism and at the same time, as theologians and jurists, had a background of natural law or Hobbes' theory of contract, were devised to justify the same state of affairs and therefore necessarily came to the same result, despite the difference in their starting points: in any event, the Church as a whole has no independence over against politics. The outward government of it is thus as much a matter of state as any other function of public life. There is a crude demonstration of the fact that the sovereignty of the ruler over the Church lays no ecclesiastical obligations upon him in the feature that the *summus episcopus*, who has, for instance, to appoint and depose ministers, can also be of another confession from that of his own Church. Indeed, he could be like Augustus the Strong of Saxony in 1697, who changed his confession and became a Catholic because he wanted to take the crown of Poland, without ceasing to be *summus episcopus* of the Lutheran Church of Saxony. It can happen that the absolute state, which is now also the absolute Church (as first happened in England and the Netherlands), sets itself impartially—though it claims to have the *ius in sacra* over a particular Church—over the confessions and declares that the supreme religious principle is that each may gain salvation in his own fashion. In this way it elevates the idea of the relativity of all confessions to the status of a universally valid truth with the full weight of political power long before the theologians succeeded in struggling towards this or a similar wisdom. Alternatively, if one prefers to put it that way, a comprehensive third or fourth confession, the religion of the good of the state, is established as the only efficacious religion, and one that is in practice indispensable to all. On the other hand, if religious uniformity is more in the line of the purpose and will of the state, it can take up the interest of one particular confession with doubtful zeal, make the practice of one particular brand of churchmanship virtually a civic duty and brutally persecute the practice of others—as did Louis XIV with the Huguenots and the Quietists and as did the Berne government at the beginning of the century with the Baptists. Such a persecution must necessarily, in the popular judgment of contemporaries and posterity, be attributed to the intolerance of the Church which is apparently being protected in this way. Again, where an absolute state recognizing another confession is affable enough to people persecuted in this way because of their economic usefulness—as were e.g. the Prince Bishop of Basle to the Baptists of Berne, the Elector of Brandenburg to the Huguenots or, later, Prussia to the people of Salzburg—and accepts them in its midst, it can also take advantage of the Christian lustre of this broadminded gesture. Here the absolute state can take proceedings against the Jesuits, as happened in the second half of the century almost everywhere: with such success that in the end even the Pope (Clement XIV Ganganelli) was forced to yield and to suppress the order in 1773 (though of course in the last resort for internal ecclesiastical reasons!). On the other hand, another absolute state—Frederick the Great in Silesia—welcomed the same Jesuits into his territory because they were useful to it! Because Frederick William I of Prussia thought that the teaching of the philosopher Christian Wolff was a danger to faith, he required him to leave the university and city of Halle within twenty-four hours or risk hanging; the son and successor of Frederick William, Frederick the Great, had the same man brought back to Halle in a carriage and four, preceded by six postillions with trumpets and fifty students on horseback. In turn, however, Frederick's successor, Frederick William II, one of the least sophisticated of the absolute princes, had his minister, the Freemason and Rosicrucian Johann Christoph Wöllner, publish and carry through an edict in 1788 to protect belief 'in the mysteries of revealed religion in general and principally in the mystery of the redemptive work and satisfaction of the Redeemer of the world'. In 1792 he was still inexorably hostile to pastor Schulz at Geilsdorf in the Mark, who was such a free-thinker that he wore pigtails in the pulpit instead of the wig prescribed!

What has all this to do with the Church and its message, with Christianity? Of course, it has a great deal to do with the will of the state that has governed the Church at particular times. Two instances show how this will of the state could even infringe conditions and laws established by history in dealing with the Church. In 1721 Peter the Great, the all too apt pupil of Western European absolutism, arbitrarily set the Holy Synod over the Orthodox Church as an organ of state power; in his church politics, Joseph II dissolved monasteries and intervened in the election of bishops. One might add the Pope's deal-ings with the Church in Austria and even the forms of the Catholic liturgy, and finally, the farce of the introduction of the cult of reason in 1793 during the French Revolution, outwardly doomed to failure, but neverthless a very telling instance of the whole spirit of absolutism. But we need not recall such extraordinary events. The decisive factor was what was taken for granted and done in an orderly fashion calmly and publicly: all along the line the Church was led and claimed by the state in such a way that the state was primarily concerned for itself and for the Church only to the degree that this concern matched its own interests, put, with the utmost naïvety, in the foreground. Just consider the significance of the following rulings by the council of Berne. To prevent the emergence of any independent will on the part of the Church, it refused permission for any general assembly of ministers within its territory. On the other hand, it not only expected pastors and parishes continually to burden services with endless read-ings of official orders of every possible kind purely relating to police business, but also prescribed that within its territory all male partici-pants in the eucharist should appear at the feast with side arms! Or imagine the significance of the scene, harmless in itself, which took place at Weimar in 1775/6. The *serenissimus* Karl August, at that time barely nineteen years old, and his privy councillor Goethe, aged twenty-six, were looking for a man for the vacant post of a General Superintendent and found him in the person of the thirty-one-year-old Consistory Councillor Herder in Bückeburg, a matter which, as can be seen from Goethe's letters, they could not celebrate openly enough as an extremely successful stroke of genius: Herder as the messiah entering Jerusalem, but riding on one hundred and fifty asses instead of one! A jolly business, but after all, this was the governing of the Church, and it is a strange system, to say the least, under which church government can be carried on so merrily by three such cheerful young men. Again, consider what it meant that Leibnitz envisaged an undertaking like that of his confessional reunions (hardly without ecclesiastical relevance!), not in the interest of the Churches, but, apart from its general cultural interest, above all in the interest of his notional future German state. Moreover, he did not intend to carry this plan through by means of the Churches or by theologians, but by lawyers and diplomats.

And now it must also be noted that the Churches, the parishes as well as the theologians, the orthodox as well as the Pietists and the men of the Enlightenment, finding themselves in this situation and being treated in this way, indicated by more than a sign that they found this situation and this treatment in order. This Caesaro-papism cannot therefore be understood one-sidedly, say, as an expression of princely arrogance; at the same time, it must surely be understood as the expression of a sense of law and order that was also shared even by conscious and earnest church members and Christians. Parishes and churchmen, theologians and lawyers, orthodox, Pietists and men of the Enlightenment seemed united in the conviction that in this respect everything had to be as it was. We shall see how people looked for compensation in other areas, a fact which is as significant in its own way for the spirit of the time as is what had to be compensated for here. In this sphere men first allowed the principle of absolutism to have unlimited effect, interpreted it as a Christian demand or as something to be accepted with Christian humility, worked to develop or apply it, or *de facto* occupied the same ground without protest. This sense of law and order does not go either necessarily or in principle with an underestimation of the problem of theology, a denial of the transcendence and eternity of God, of the extraordinariness of revelation and of the foundation of the Church, of the authority of Holy Scripture, of the spiritual dignity of the office of preaching and the administration of the sacrament, of the validity of the dogmas of christology and soteriology. In precisely such a person as Leibnitz, it is remarkable to see how the immanent substance and form of the Christian totality is not attacked from this side, from Caesaro-papism, but is at least respected for what it is. The incursions into this totality which took place at the same time come from another side; they have nothing to do with the incorporation of Christianity in the state as such. This 'as such' merely (*merely!*) means that this totality is bracketed off as such by the political will, which sets its secular aims *de facto* not in deliberate opposition to Christianity, but *de facto* in an absolute fashion. This bracketing off did not always have to happen with the free-thinking irony that we see, for example, in the case of Frederick the Great. It never represented an explicit and fundamental hostility to the Church, not even in the revolutionary politics of France after 1789. The absolute monarchies, aristocracies and democracies simply could not dare to attempt that, even if on occasion it matched the inclinations dominant in their leading circles. Rather, the incorporation of Christianity in the state could very well be associated with the highest personal and material estimation of the totality in its immanence, with faith and the fear of God, and indeed with deepest mysticism, among both leaders and those whom they led. Leaving aside the American and French revolutions, it might indeed be said that this unprecedented modernization of the problem took a form that we would be inclined —wrongly, of course—to feel and claim to be typically conservative. In principle, secularization consisted merely (*merely!*) in setting the key: the man who places himself in an absolute position in the state (whether it is represented by absolute princes or as a sovereign people makes no material difference) affirms, administers and uses even this totality in the authority which he ascribes to himself as a matter of patriotic concern or true obedience or, later, as a matter of the free will of the people or the free duty of the citizen. Whatever else may be said of them, the Church and Christianity are *in the state* and receive their outward form and movement entirely *from the state*, and not from their own being and laws. Their outward aspect was indeed a valid one, significant in itself, but it was incorporated into that greater whole and was a factor of life that was subordinate to it. In one state or another a man can and may be saved in a particular way or 'each after his own fashion': that is the political statement of the problem of theology at this period.

Would there not almost have to be a miracle if it could still be seen that this problem, the concepts of faith, hope and love, could be the designation of a free power, the most sovereign power, indeed the only sovereign polity? Could anything be reasonably expected other than that this picture of the state Church, simple and impressive as it now was, should stamp on whole generations, in an indelible way which could not be made good again by all the other forms of impressions and instructions, the conviction that the Church and the cause represented by this Church belonged among the things which, in and despite their character, were given over into the hand of omnipotent man?

2. We termed the second form of the attempt at humanization to which Christianity was subjected in the eighteenth century its incorporation into *morality* and the *bourgeoisie*. But this aspect of the matter must at any rate also be understood in its sociological sense: in the eighteenth century, active interest in the Church, in religion and Christianity—here, too, taking up again a tendency that had already been expressed in the sixteenth century—was explicitly a concern of the bourgeoisie who were flourishing again after the terrors of the Thirty Years' War in the independent states or under the gentle treatment of the absolute princes, at least in certain areas. Their interest in possessions and status, their view of life and morality conditioned by their needs and the demands made upon them, the perspectives and ideals of the craftsman and merchant, their aspirations to education, now become increasingly the formative influences which make themselves felt in the religious and ecclesiastical questions which come into their hands. It was a typical middle-class ideology that, leaving aside their Christian content, gave shape to the liturgies and hymn books, and even the sermons, of the time. We can see its sterling, but somewhat limited horizon, its modest but self-centred confidence, its sage compliance with superiors and its condescension towards inferiors, its inclination towards the practical and the tangible and its justified desire for outward peace and inward tranquillity, its need to be elevated above the cares of everyday life and its sober disinclination for incomprehensible paradoxes. The very un-bourgeois hinterland, the vistas of and the detours into the realm of mysticism and speculation are contrasting effects that are not to be excluded, but the sphere within which the lives of Christians and the Church were played out was primarily the sphere of the bourgeois world, even for the Pietists, and still more for the men of the Enlightenment. On some special occasions it could acquire a note of more than bourgeois distinction, particularly among the Pietists, by the participation of certain groups of the lower and at times the middle nobility. More important than the outward aspect of this development, however, is its inward side. The effect of the bourgeoisie and their morality on the problem of theology in the eighteenth century consists essentially in the terms in which people sought to understand the problem at the time. It was regarded as the problem of altering and shaping life in a visible and tangible way, that could be experienced and established concretely

and directly, inwardly and outwardly, accomplished by man in particular thoughts, actions and modes of action. The identification of Christianity with this alteration and shaping of human life is, from this perspective, the great attempt of the time at humanizing.

When the Christian citizen or the bourgeois Christian of the time hears the great words of the Christian creed founded upon the Bible as the fundamental record of divine revelation, he feels as well and honestly and seriously as Christians of all times that he is confronted here with the announcement of things which are very new and very shattering, which at the same time claim him with supreme authority and power. But he can also see a past, in the sixteenth and seventeenth centuries, disturbed by a series of devastating, repulsive and extremely terrifying wars of a spiritual and political nature which at their climax, in the Thirty Years' War, made Germany into a wilderness and cost Europe not only rivers of blood but also whole rivers of ink and printers' ink poured out in a highly questionable fashion. He also knows of the damnable moral brutalization of the upper classes on the one hand and of the great mass of the lower classes on the other, which followed the wars of religion. He knows that these wars were all waged in a more or less honest or hypocritical way over this very Christian creed, over the new, shattering, demanding things which the men of this desolate, sorry past thought that they could find in the Christian creed. And now he also knows and sees that the Christian creed, as the men of this dark past thought they understood it, had insufficient power to combat the brutalization. As a man with a historical horizon, he knows further that a similar understanding of the Christian creed in other, more distant times, has caused similar wars and has equally failed the moral demands made upon it. But the Christian citizen of the eighteenth century certainly does not wish such wars and such moral brutalization to be repeated or continued in any way, and therefore rejects the view of the Christian creed that caused such wars and did not prevent such brutalization. He thinks that he can see the mistake which crept in during all those dark times: the way in which people understood the Christian creed then was wrong, perverse and evil. Understanding in those dark times was theoretical and only theoretical; Christianity was made into a collection of conflicting doctrines and precepts, dialectic subtleties which merely occupied the mind and heated the head, but left the heart empty and the conscience in perplexity. The supreme verities of faith had been robbed of their real content and had been changed into barren theological maxims whose contradictions inevitably aroused the direst passions. Proclaiming and accepting them could help no one, because he either failed to understand them, as being too scholarly and learned, or, if he did understand them, could not understand them for his salvation. In short, the Christian citizen of the time invented—and it was a truly significant and momentous discovery—the theory of the barrenness, indeed the danger of theological theory. With by no means unjustified resentment and an imagination which was certainly not devoid of specific substance, he brought into being the ghost of 'dead orthodoxy', which—as is well known—has been on the prowl ever since, giving grown-ups and children a real fright, to take responsibility for the evil which had befallen the history of the Christian Church in general and the sixteenth and seventeenth centuries in particular. The Christian citizen of the eighteenth century is in a position of being able to point to a thousand greater or lesser abominations in the life of the Church and theology; to the arrogance of princes and the disputatious spirit of the orthodox watchmen of Zion, and the writers of folios in the theological faculties, to the slovenliness of their students crying out to heaven, to the crass worldliness of the preaching and life of the greater part of the clergy, to the ignorance and rawness of the lower classes, to the corrupt relaxation of all morality among the nobility and in the courts, in short, to the sorry state of the allegedly Christian communities—and finally, to the fact that all this went hand in hand with, and was not least affected by, the way in which Christianity was understood by preachers and their audience, by professors of theology and simple Christians, as teaching and not as life.

For that is the great positive side of the discovery which the Christian citizen of this time made: Christianity is not teaching, but life; its teaching is only teaching for living. The Christian creed, those new, shattering, demanding things of which it speaks, means life. It demands of us a changed, a transformed life, and that alone can be the 'true' faith with which we are to respond if we are really to be called Christians. It is expected to make the evil brought about by dead faith in words impossible in the future and to introduce the improvement prevented by that evil. So while the first stage in the process of the adaptation of Christianity to bourgeois life consists in a general attack against reasoning, against subtleties, dialectic, the controversy in past theology and the life of the Church, the second consists in the presentation of the positive demand that the right, i.e. the practical use of the Christian creed shall take the place of this perverted theoretical understanding. Note that even here, to begin with, there is no intention of any attack on the Christian creed as such. Even from this perspective, the old is maintained. There is still an affirmation of the Church, of dogma, in all its previous state. No one, apart from a few extravagant figures, wishes at first to forego the good reputation of his orthodoxy; men simply refuse, for the world, to have any responsibility for 'dead' orthodoxy! However, through all the pores of orthodoxy there begins to seep the conviction that the change and transformation of life that is so desired is the real meaning of Christianity, the true mystery of revelation, which has only now been understood correctly. For this purpose God was born man in Christ, the Holy Scriptures were given to us as the Word of God, and the Church was founded. In this respect, too, the attempt of the eighteenth century at humanization consisted primarily in an embrace from outside, in the application of the self-evident presupposition that Christianity, rightly understood, must necessarily match the needs and hopes of the time, in the freedom with which it was now thought possible to place all the emphasis on these needs and hopes. But what did that mean? How was Christian practice understood, if these were the emphases?

At this point we must distinguish so to speak an inner and an outer line of development, though of course at some points they come together so closely that they are indistinguishable and in any case belong materially together. On so to speak the inner line, the Church, dogma, the cult as such seem to be the point of departure, and the principle of the transformation of life merely forms the hermeneutical principle for the right understanding of the text. Here we find the well-known biblical ideas of the rebirth, conversion and sanctification of the true Christian, of faith which is active in love, namely in love of God and the brethren, of the necessary fruits of the Holy Spirit, of honest repentance, of striving for a good conscience and a truly living testimony to the experience of grace, the dying of the old man, a way of life in light and before God achieved by fighting against sin and the world. This, expressed simply and rather abruptly, is of course the pietistic side of the new bourgeois Christianity which we find if we pay attention.

On the other, so to speak outer, line, the starting point seems rather to be what the modern man thinks that he may expect of the Church, dogma and the cult. Here the planned transformation of life is the text that is read, and the concern will be to understand it in some way that is related to the principles of interpretation given in the Bible, dogma and the Church. Thus on this side we find that the right reverence of God consists, or must necessarily show itself, in the improvement of life, in sincere, i.e. active love of God, in struggles against

unreason and depravity, in the steady practice of the Christian duties
and virtues. The following such Christian duties and virtues are
enumerated, for example, in J. J. Spalding's hymn book of 1778:
self-knowledge:

> Who am I? That I have to know.
> God grant that I may understand.
> Help me myself the truth to show
> And place its mirror in my hand.
> Who from himself this truth doth hide
> With wisdom never can abide;

humility and well ordered love of self:

> It is thy will, O Lord,
> That I myself should love;
> O may my conscience heed
> Thy precepts from above.
> Guard thou thyself the wish
> that I should happy be;
> Keep it within the bounds
> That thou hast given me;

care of the soul, but also appropriate care of the body:

> Creator, I am bound
> To guard and tend my frame
> Let no misuse be found
> That might profane thy name.
> With wisdom stand by me
> That I may holy be;

industry and faithfulness in a man's temporal calling:

> Lord, thou hast said
> That we must work
> And from our labour
> Must not shirk.
> The idle man
> His God offends;
> Vice is a snare
> That traps our friends;

right conduct in suffering and readiness for death, love of one's neighbour, righteousness, peace and gentleness, readiness for service and
mercy, sincerity and truth:

Malice, gossip, cheating, lies
Are not pleasing in thine eyes.
Honest make my mind and heart,
Give me truth in every part.

This line could be pursued still further. In 1792, Traugott Günther Röller, pastor of Schonfels in Kür-Saxony, dedicated to Archduke Karl August of Weimar his *Dorfpredigten für gemeine Leute, bes. Handwerksleute und Bauern, daraus sie lernen sollen, wie sie verständiger, besser und frommer und glücklicher werden können* (Village Sermons for Common People, especially Craftsmen and Farmers, from which They may Learn how They may become More Learned, Better, Happier and More Pious). This collection shows that its author, who does not seem to have been the only man of his kind, interpreted the concept of self-improvement so extensively, so existentially, that he was in a position to choose as his theme for a sermon on Christmas Day that while the day was indeed a great festival of the Church, the authorities were not wrong in doing away with the so-called lesser feasts, saints' days, etc. (his motto was: 'A Christian's faith is not abated, if some feasts are not celebrated'). On the Fourth Sunday after Epiphany he preached on 'The Duties of a Christian Congregation saved from a Grave Risk of Fire', and at Easter on 'Reasonable Rules for the Christian Burial of Corpses' (motto: 'Ne'er speed the body underground, in case within some life be found'). On Whit Sunday he gave a detailed report on his own fortunate recovery from smallpox, with appropriate advice and words of consolation for others, and on the same festival another year discussed 'How to keep Faithful and Safe during Thunderstorms'. The sermon on Trinity Sunday was devoted entirely to commending a pocket book 'giving help to those in distress' composed by the preacher, which evidently contained further advice for health and prosperity (motto: 'The careless man who does not know, is often caught by need and woe'). Finally, on the First Sunday after Trinity he castigated the 'Horrific Sin of Premeditated Murder', on the occasion of a murder which had taken place in the community (motto: 'Doom hangs o'er the murderer's head, since he human blood has shed').

It would be unfair to such climaxes in the tendencies of the century with which we are concerned here, not to mention the mild moralism of a Spalding or a Jerusalem, if we were to see them as no more than a crass secularization, a manifest denial of the Gospel of the Bible and the Reformers, and so on. Pastors who preached in this or a similar fashion and their congregations certainly did not think that they were in any way apostasizing from the Gospel; rather, in all good faith, though obviously on many occasions with little spirit or taste, they thought that by going on this road, or at least in this direction, they were preaching and perceiving true, i.e. at any rate a living, Christianity. Even aversion to miracle or a rejection of dogma based on some other rationalistic ground is not the normative motive here. People did not preach like this because as critical rationalists they did not know any other way of preaching, but because they regarded what they preached as being both necessary and good. It would be easy to find a faithful presentation of almost all orthodox dogma, albeit in muted form, alongside all the moralizing contained in Spalding's hymn book, and even a man like pastor Röller, mentioned above, sometimes mentions at the beginning of his sermon the saving facts due to be mentioned on the day in question. His style may be somewhat dry, but he is honest and uncritical. The only thing is, that the desire is to put all the emphasis, not on the saving facts as such, but on the improvement of life that is associated with them and understood in a more or less concrete way. Still, the undermining of the Christian creed that we can clearly see at work here was, at any rate from the perspective of the moralizing that is occupying us at present, merely so to speak an invisible undermining, and not a piece of demolition. The creed as such remained essentially intact. Moreover, people believed that far from undermining the creed, by understanding Christianity in such moralistic, and often such utilitarian terms, they were rightly filling a gap that they felt had been left open. The pastor of this kind—the so-called rationalist kind—stands among his congregation like a wise and kindly father among his children, concerned for the best in everyone and concerned, too, not to be an intolerant controversialist, a remote theoretician or a rigid pillar of orthodoxy; he will be quite innocent of wars of religion and abominations of such kinds. If there have nevertheless been profligacy, idiocy, wild customs and, apparently, even murder and homicide in his community, this has certainly not been the fault of the pastor: he did all that was humanly possible to set high standards in this direction, so that the Church is really above all criticism in this respect.

At this point it is important to note that despite the great differences in the structure of the preaching of Pietists and rationalists, in their devotion and way of life, despite the fierce battles that they waged against each other, and despite the difference in their language, attitude and taste, they were not in the last resort in two minds about the direction which had now been taken. Rather, they were quite agreed over the aim of their understanding of Christianity, in which their time was so far removed from the whole of the past, and over the way in which the accents should be placed within the Christian creed that they both affirmed in common. The attention of both was focussed on the practical life that was to be changed, on the Christian works that came from faith, but the Pietists were more concerned with inner works (though not without all kinds of very outward regulation and determination) and the rationalists more with outward works (though this did not prevent them from speaking most earnestly about the renewal of the heart, the conscience and the disposition, and from laying weight on the appropriate feelings). Each felt that they should issue a warning against what they felt to be the quietistic misunderstanding of the Reformers' doctrine of justification which had crept in during the seventeenth century. Here they were both also to a great extent in unconscious or even very conscious opposition to the correct understanding of the Reformers' doctrine of justification and unavoidably found themselves in the midst of the world of the Tridentine doctrine of justification. In the question of good, which occupied so important a position in their general approach, both sides oriented themselves, whether tacitly or openly, on Stoic natural law and not on Holy Scripture. In practice (though they diverged in theory), both sides believed that it was within the power of man, man in general or at least converted man, to experience a new and better life and to give it visible expression. Both in fact, at least relatively, devalued the objective elements in the Christian creed over against its subjective elements. Both in fact, at least relatively, furthered an obscuring of the concept of the sacrament, which points towards those objective elements. Together, they could not but fail to force into the background, at least relatively, the significance of the creed as such in contrast to the significance of what they felt should happen in men on the basis of the creed. In their understanding and treatment of Christianity, both sides were really true children of the century. For whether as Pietists they interpreted the Bible and dogma by means of the leading concept of the improvement of life, the *praxis pietatis*, or whether with the rationalists they first affirmed and used this concept as such and later read it into the Bible with more or less success, despite the very different types of preaching, piety and conduct and despite the deep-seated differences between them which can be seen here beyond all denying, at heart both were the same: both Pietists and rationalists were modern men and, more particularly, modern citizens, who applied to traditional Christianity a particular presupposition, namely the presupposition, the idea, the systematic principle that in all circumstances Christianity must serve to improve life. This was the presupposition which determined the way in which they dealt with Christianity.

Once again, the absolutist desire of the man of this century for form, which we have already seen at work in so many areas, comes to the fore here. Now form means morality in the most comprehensive sense of the concept, ranging from the almost unconscious inward work of 'conversion', by its nature to be interpreted as a work of the Holy Spirit, to the decision, to be wrung from the avaricious peasant with every argument of natural and revealed religion, to have a fire engine installed, a matter whose secular character was there for all to see. Form means the dignified and therefore divinely willed—or divinely willed and therefore dignified—and on both grounds the better, happier pattern that real life, human life in towns and villages, must achieve, outwardly and inwardly, inwardly and outwardly. Form is the opposite to the wilderness of the seventeenth century from which people had emerged and to which they did not want to return. This form was what was wanted, and the substance was the Church and Christianity, which, if they were to continue to be affirmed, had, whatever happened, to acquire and assume this form. If we are to understand the position, we may not join the Pietists in censuring the rationalists for the intolerable superficiality with which they regarded Christianity because of their external conception of santification, nor may we join the rationalists in censuring the Pietists for their enthusiastic persistence in the depths of the circle of inward, psychological problems of the great work of improvement. We must not get excited about the obvious and unmistakable misfortunes in which both sides became involved. Nor, in view of the exaggerations and distortions which crept in on both sides, and the degree of narrowness in the approach that they had in common, may we follow Schleiermacher in adopting a position set over and above the two which sees them both *sub specie aeternitatis*, or any other standpoint of today. The moralism and the bourgeois character of Christianity in the eighteenth century should certainly not be despised unless one has first paid respectful attention to its absolutist will for form in this area, too. If we had lived as Christians and as theologians in that century, what other alternative would we have had than to base ourselves, also, on that presupposition, arm ourselves with that form, and then take that form as seriously as did the best men of the time on the two wings of the movement that was in essentials a single one? At any rate, it says a great deal for the force and value of their idea that with it they achieved a success which long outlasted the particular intellectual limitations of the time. It has had a tenacity, unaffected by all that has happened in the meantime, right down to our own day, with which it has left a mark on a whole series of generations: Christianity means moralistic, bourgeois Christianity, or it does not mean Christianity at all. It can have a pietistic or a rationalistic colouring, but whatever happens it must be a *praxis pietatis*. We need not investigate here whether this matter-of-fact assumption is as obvious as it might have seemed then and still seems today, when we are supposed to be so far removed from this old-fashioned Pietism and rationalism. Perhaps Christianity is not really suited to being treated as the substance of the human will for form, like the elements of nature and history, of music and language, even if this will is as historically comprehensible and materially significant as that with which we have to deal at the end of the seventeenth and beginning of the eighteenth centuries. Perhaps Christianity, in view of what its creed understands by sanctification and obedience, sets out to be a free, really spiritual power, set over against all human morality. But even if the legacy bequeathed by Christianity at that time is in the last resort an illegitimate connexion, we should not withhold human admiration at the historical force of the idea underlying it.

3. It is quite paradoxical, but historically mandatory, that after what has just been said we should speak in the same breath of the academic and philosophical transformation of Christianity in the eighteenth century. A widespread and indeed dominant view of the problem of theology in the eighteenth century tends to put this point in the foreground and make it the key issue. For this approach, the eighteenth century, above all in its relationship to Christianity, is the century of religious Enlightenment, of the dawn and even the widespread triumph of rational criticism of the Bible, Church and dogma, of the shattering of the historic basis of their validity, of the reinterpretation and relativizing, the doubting and open denial of the truths of revelation that they proclaimed on the basis of the insights of modern philosophy and science. It is the time of the reduction of the teaching of Christianity to the contents of a doctrine of so-called natural or rational religion or morality. In fact, the eighteenth century was concerned with all this, as we shall see in a moment. But it does seem important to me that all this should be seen in a wider historical context. We caricature the Christian man of the eighteenth century if we put these things, either the affirmation of them or the struggle against

them or the compromises reached over them, in the foreground of his consciousness. He was primarily a citizen and a moralist and then, as a consequence, a philosopher, doubter, critic, inventor of a new type of Christian teaching, purified by academic study. And his philosophizing, doubting, criticizing must not be understood as an expression of an independent concern but as a particular expression of the concern which was peculiar to his whole being.

I remarked that it was paradoxical that the very period which, as we saw, strove so energetically to free itself from the view of Christianity thought to be held or really held by its predecessors, and wanted to understand Christianity simply as life and action, now felt that it should take such an active part in forming a new theory of Christianity, so active, indeed, that it has gone down in history with the reputation of being a quite specially intellectual time. In this activity, however, it was simply following a rhythm that can be observed in the development of the problem of theology in every age. Christian intellectualism, triumphal dogmatics and polemics, theological pedagogy like that with which the seventeenth century can in fact rightly be charged, usually has to be paid for by a sudden cry, perhaps even from the heart of one and the same person, a cry which is raised in protest, not only for ethics but for life, for reality. Here is a manifest indication that something must be wrong with the pedagogy. In turn, the price for this Christian moralism is that it has itself to be given a theoretical foundation and justification. Probably because it does not completely succeed in reaching the reality for which it longs so much, it must in turn manage to confirm that it is at least the truth. Thereupon there arises the new, critical, philosophical theory of Christianity. Psychologically speaking, abstract theories of Christianity, whether they are positive or critical, traditional or neological, are always a compensation for an actual (albeit at times very hidden) deficiency in Christian practice. Unless we see this connexion, we shall look in vain for the real pathos of the eighteenth century's criticism of Bible and dogma, its philosophizing of Christianity. It was not necessary in principle that the cry for ethics, or for life, should have brought with it all the dogmatic restrictions and negations which arose at this time. Indeed, we saw that the original intention was, in theory, merely a shifting of emphasis within traditional teaching in favour of the subjective side of Christian truth and a heightening of the ethical theory that was provided for and developed even in orthodox dogmatics, and that in the midst of high rationalism there was still a care at least to go on marking the objective side, however much it had been undermined.

Despite the great stress that has been placed on the significance of the change in the picture of the world and the rise of scientific and mathematical thought, it should not be over-estimated here: a man like Leibnitz, who occupies so exalted a place in modern intellectual history and who incorporates its results so consistently into his system, shows that it was quite possible to know everything that could be known of philosophy and science at that time without the necessity of taking the offensive even against dogma, let alone the Bible. He was able without a struggle in his own way to combine the traditional church doctrine of the Trinity and even the specifically Protestant dogmas of predestination and justification with his theory of monads and of prestabilized harmony. Things did not *necessarily* (from that point, at any rate) have to come out differently. That they did come out differently was only a matter of fact, or rather, was governed by a necessity which had its grounds elsewhere.

In its pietistic or rationalistic form, however carefully it was introduced, the Christian moralism of which we have been speaking was in nucleus as much a usurpation of the human subject as the Caesaropapism of the same century. It was, however, directed towards an object whose usurpation was not so obvious a matter as some other expressions of the same will for usurpation. It is not immediately obvious that man can only experience, realize and confirm Christianity in the way that was desired at that time. Perhaps it is in fact quite impossible. If one wants to make Christianity the object of such a concern, perhaps one finds oneself suddenly not only inadequate, incomplete, but confronted by and involved in a complete impossibility. And then, if one still wants to maintain the same course, does not one find oneself suddenly in another world outside Christianity, outside the Christianity for which this willing and action is perhaps in fact an impossibility which one cannot affirm without denying Christianity? But if one does not want to deny Christianity nor, on the other hand, to renounce the willing and action, what remains but to come to an arrangement with Christianity through criticism in such a way that to experience it, realize it and confirm it nevertheless becomes a possible object of human concern? In this way, opposition, which first gave rise to this concern, might be lessened or even removed. Hence there are three things which did in fact happen in the eighteenth century:

(*a*) It must have been evident soon enough that in undertaking not only an integral realization of Christianity, but this particular realization as such, an impossible venture had been begun. Certainly, under the pressure of the will for form, the man of the eighteenth century had become gradually and partially—though only very gradually and partially—a rather more civilized creature than the man of the seventeenth or sixteenth centuries, or even of the dark Middle Ages. But had he therefore become more Christian? Few, even among the optimists of the eighteenth century, were optimistic enough to think that what had in any event been achieved and could further be achieved was in fact a realization of Christianity. Evidence for this insight—this resigned insight—is on the one hand the twofold issue of Pietism into the mysticism of men like Tersteegen, far removed from the ideals of Spener and Francke, and into the *Brüdergemeinde*, marked out by the revival of certain integral features of earlier Lutheranism and everywhere in sharp conflict with the older Pietism, where in the end all that was left of the pietistic realization was the work of common love for the crucified saviour, and on the other hand the transition of the Christian men of the Enlightenment to a moralism understood increasingly in a more external way, increasingly centred on the concepts of duty and virtue, passing over into manifest utilitarianism. What was all this but evasion, retreat, flight—flight from the Christian renewal of life which men had really wanted and could not achieve, flight into what they could do or thought that they could do? Composedly to follow the footsteps of Madame de Guyon towards God, to rush to Herrnhut or Herrnhag and—'heart and heart together joined' —worship the saviour and surrender oneself to his guidance, still more to what, say, Pastor Röller set as a goal—all this people could do or thought that they could do. But what they could not in fact do in the eighteenth century, what they saw with reasonable clarity that they could not do, was what they had originally thought and intended to do: they could not present either themselves or others as converted and sanctified men, and they could not realize Christianity.

(*b*) This result first confronted men with the necessity of revising their relationship to Christianity as such. If it in fact proved impossible to realize Christianity, then the question inevitably arose whether Christianity could be realized at all in the manner intended or whether the intention of such a realization was not in fact a misunderstanding. The relationship not only of Zinzendorf, but also of earlier Pietists like Zinzendorf's friend Samuel Lutz of Berne, to Luther is an extremely significant indication of the rise of this question. Was not the proscribed seventeenth century perhaps right in thinking that even on the subjective side the meaning of the Christian creed is not that we ourselves and others should and could set ourselves up as those who have been converted and sanctified? Anyone who could not evade this question—

and in one way or another it must have oppressed the whole Christian consciousness of the time—evidently had three possibilities. He could avoid it either to the right or to the left in the way described, retreat so to speak to a minimum of Christian realization, into a mystical, enthusiastic or common moralism, and from there affirm the Lutheran understanding (or the supposed Lutheran understanding) of the Christian creed without giving up the moralistic principle altogether. Or he had to give up the moralistic principle. Or he had to give up the Christian creed. In short, he had either to make a compromise (this was the course taken by mystical Pietism and the Pietism of the Herrnhutters and by the thoroughgoing rationalists), or he had to choose.

(c) In fact, only relatively restricted circles compromised. And by and large nobody made a choice. There was still a fourth possibility. This was seized upon, and explains the solemnity of the philosophically scientific criticism of Christianity which took place in the eighteenth century. The question could be asked whether the error might not lie in Christianity, i.e. in the whole understanding of Christianity laid down in the creed itself. Was there not another, genuine, original, true Christianity, which did not involve a man in such a dilemma, a Christianity which could be realized as well as other possibilities, a Christianity which in that case would not, of course, be identical with Christian dogma nor even, without qualification, with that of the Bible? It would still be Christianity, but a Christianity that simply needed to be dug out from the debris of centuries and millennia, debris which included, from this perspective, both dogma and the Bible. These questions could be asked in the eighteenth century, since men, as we saw, were no longer in fact bound by dogma and the Bible. They were bound by their systematic principle, their own will for renewing and transforming life, by their moralism and their civic principles. The relationship between this principle and the Bible and dogma was like that of an axiom to the tenet grounded on it. Both are valid, but the certainty of the one is absolute, whereas the certainty of the other is only relative.

This was the relationship that now emerged. And so did something more profound. The man who was bound by the Bible and dogma only in a relative way was also bound by Christianity only in that same way. He only felt himself bound by Christianity to the degree that he bound himself to it in a particular way, i.e. morally. He regarded it as something that can be looked at in a variety of ways, one or other of whose features can be treasured and preferred, depending on the insight of the onlooker. It need not be taken precisely as it presents itself. Christianity was affirmed, but men affirmed it with a secret sovereignty which already seemed to make it questionable whether what was being affirmed was still Christianity. Perhaps Christianity cannot be affirmed in this way. Perhaps those who made the attempt were already secretly denying it.

Because this was the case, even within the creed the accents could be shifted to match the approach which was believed to be the right one. And because this was the case, if need be—and need there was— criticism could even be extended to the creed itself. This criticism *had* to be undertaken, because while there was no desire to abandon Christianity as such at any price, there was still less desire to abandon its moral principle! And when it became evident that the two could not be reconciled, the decision was made (not lightly, but reluctantly, though with a resolute heart) to make such modifications and altera- tions to the previous understanding of Christianity as would allow it to be united with the principle. In concrete terms, the renewal of life possible to men was to be understood as the realization of Christianity, or the realization of Christianity was to be understood as a renewal of life possible to men.

But what sort of a Christianity was it that people needed and sought and therefore also found to fulfil this purpose? Now we can under- stand the great slogans: they needed, sought and found a *natural* or (and it amounts to the same thing) a *reasonable* Christianity. The decisive contrast that explains the choice of these slogans is not, say, with revealed or miraculous Christianity: even in the realm of 'natural' or 'reasonable' Christianity there were possibilities enough of affirming that Christianity was revealed or miraculous. No, the contrast was rather with what man could not realize, what was not the object of his willing and his action, material that could not be shaped by his will for form. For the man of the eighteenth century, 'nature' was the embodiment of what was at the disposal of himself, his spirit, his understanding, his will and his feeling, what was left for him to shape, what could be reached by his will for form. And 'reason', reason was the embodiment of his capacity, his superiority over matter, his ability to comprehend it and appropriate it for himself. Thus naturally Christianity simply means a Christianity that presents itself to man in a manner appropriate to his capacity, and reasonable Christianity means a Christianity that is understood and affirmed by man in accordance with his capacity. The meaning of both statements is obvi- ously the same. The fervour with which such a Christianity was sought was the fervour of the citizen who on the one hand could not leave

the sphere of the Christian Church, but on the other hand perceived
within this sphere all manner of things which seemed to him to indicate
that the cause of this Church could not be natural or reasonable in
the sense indicated. In other words, he inevitably longed for a purification of the sphere of the Church from the elements which disturbed it. Only now does criticism of the Bible and dogma begin,
a criticism which takes what is natural or reasonable as its criterion
for judging what Christianity must be if it is to be the Christianity
of the bourgeois man. The primary attack of this criticism is simply
directed against those elements of the understanding of Christianity
laid down in the creed which showed themselves to be unnatural
or unreasonable by diverging from the moralism that was desider-
ated, which stood out as alien bodies in the *corpus doctrinae moralis*
that Christianity was expected to be, perhaps even conflicting and
hostile alien bodies. It is difficult and even impossible to relate the
patristic doctrine of the Trinity to the improvement of life that is
to be brought about by man himself in the heart or in the moral
attitude of man. That doctrine clearly draws attention, rather, to a
being and action of God in himself. For that reason it is contestable.
The doctrine of the two natures in Christ cannot be put in this context. It does not talk of Christ as one who can be a teacher and a
model and therefore an instrument of the improvement of life that
we are to bring about by ourselves. It only speaks in an extremely
indirect way of what man as a moralist can understand by the *beneficia
Christi*. It is therefore suspect. As for the doctrine of Christ's vicarious
satisfaction and, in connexion with this, the doctrine of the justification
of men before God which comes about through faith in the righteousness of Christ which is alien to us and merely reckoned to our account,
it not only cannot be introduced in this context, but even contradicts
the presupposition that we have to show ourselves to be true reverers
and lovers of God and therefore as worthy objects of his love through
our own actions. It makes men rotten and wanton. It is therefore
not only suspect, but reprehensible. In the same way, the doctrine of
the once-for-allness of God's revealing and reconciling act in man can
only be felt as a contradiction to what the moralist has to think and
say: that what can really be termed the revelation of God or the reconciliation of the world with him takes place in individual experiences,
circumstances and actions among men of all possible times. It is therefore to be rejected. The doctrine of a word of God coming to man
with an external authority and of a testimony of the Holy Spirit which
comes to meet it with an inward force can no longer be understood,

since authority and force are manifestly most immoral concepts, and since the doctrine says precisely the opposite to what man himself thinks: that everything depends on one becoming one's own authority, one's own force, with the support of God. Therefore this doctrine can no longer be used. In particular, one can no longer start from the normativeness of all Holy Scripture, for—you dear, dear time—this book evidently contains so much that is merely historical and, among these historical elements, especially in the Old Testament, so much that is clearly morally offensive and painfully reminiscent of the seventeenth century and the dark Middle Ages, and besides, so many mysteries after the fashion of later dogma which, whatever they may once have meant and however venerable they may be to us now, obviously cannot be the Word of God in the strict sense, because they do not say anything about what we lack, about our religious needs— in other words, because they are impracticable. So despite the high value attached to certain parts of the Bible, this doctrine, too, cannot be given credit. In short, the traditional understanding of Christianity was felt to be not quite along the right lines or not quite reasonable in the sense mentioned above. So with a serious face and with profound disquiet, or with frivolous mockery, people began to doubt it, to undermine it here and there, and finally to fight against it openly.

This was the inward road, the real, essential concern of the modern biblical criticism and criticism of dogma that began in the eighteenth century, of the liberalism and modernism which now—though not without a variety of preparations going back to the spiritualists and humanists of the period of the Reformation—began to dominate the problem of theology. It is primarily a concern of the bourgeoisie, that does not want to be without Christianity, that finds the old Christianity too crude, and therefore wants to knock all the corners off it to make it accessible, i.e. fit for society. The last great breakthrough of this original and authentic feature of theological liberalism was the theology of Albrecht Ritschl and his pupils, as late as the middle of the nine-teenth century. In none of his contributions should one lose sight of this, his original and authentic concern, if one is to evaluate properly his historical importance and at the same time his quite unintentional humour.

Only at this point can we now also understand that the consequence of the special character of this criticism of the Bible and dogma and above all the character of the positive possibilities of understanding Christianity which emerge from the fire of this criticism had to be the transformation of Christianity into a science or a philosophy. Only now do the new picture of the world, mathematically scientific thought, anthropocentric, autonomous philosophy, the virtue of 'historical truth-fulness' and with it the distaste for miracle in the strict sense of the term become significant. All this is not a foundation and a cause, but an instrument, indeed one might go so far as to say a garb, for the criticism. Fine and impressive reasons are given so that men in the modern world *can* no longer believe the teaching of Christianity in its traditional form, without a deliberate intention to deceive, but in fact because people no longer *want* to believe it. Man makes the opposition to older Christianity which had come about through his new moralism into a contrast between the modern and the obsolete presuppositions for cosmology and epistemology—in order to justify himself.

People now began to think that it was extremely significant that Athanasius and Augustine, Luther and Calvin, despite all their other admirable characteristics, were children of earlier, less enlightened times, still standing on the ground of the Ptolemaic system of the world and ignorant of the concept of natural law as now administered at the University of Göttingen and in other places of the true light. The whole of the Christian past was now fondly imagined as that of a rather credulous, naïve mythology which had fallen victim to a quite brutal authoritarian way of thinking, a blind literalism which ignored all intellectual difficulties. And as modern men, people felt themselves justified in making the necessary (necessary, of course, from other grounds) criticism of this legacy from the past—and armed to do so. And it was so easy to seize the requisite authority and weapons. One and the same man of the eighteenth century was simultaneously the intellectual conqueror of the new view of the world, the inventor of the new science of nature and history, the anthropocentric philosopher, the impartial seeker after the truth and the modern citizen who was moralistic at any price. So attacks were now mounted on the Trinity again; with solemn faces, as though this had never occurred to anyone before, it was objected that three cannot be one and one cannot be three. Against the doctrine of the two natures in Christ it was asked whether the essential difference between the divine nature and the creaturely, human nature allowed, even conceptually, the kind of unity that dogma asserted. Not only the vote of a purified jurisprudence, but also the history of dogma was set against the doctrine of representation and the corresponding doctrine of justification, and attempts were made to prove that this had not been the original understanding of the death of Christ. Now, against the doctrine of the once-for-allness of revelation, was raised the objection of a way of thought that surveyed apparently infinite space and time, but to which it no longer occurred that really and literally everything happened in the One and through the One. Now there arose the historical question, how the alleged word of God in the one Christ and the one Holy Scripture could be differentiated from the many other alleged words of God in the mouths of other wise men and founders of religion. Psychological questions were asked about the claim to have the *testimonium spiritus sancti internum*, and people felt very honest when they could declare that they had never perceived it. Now people objected to the all too many miracle stories in the Bible because of their manifest conflict with the known laws of nature, as well as to the philosophical impossibility of accepting instruction about God, man and the world without qualification from only one book, and this particular book. From the juxtaposition it can be clearly seen that these are not the real, primary and pioneering reasons for the criticism, but very plausible, secondary, useful aids to that criticism, which were well worth thinking about. By means of these second-order reasons one could proceed against the old doctrine on the basis of that doctrine itself, and set a new doctrine in the place of the old, with reference to it. By means of all this—in a way which would have been impossible with the real reasons—it was possible to show that the old conceptions of Bible and dogma were contradictory and impossible in themselves, and by referring to them men could believe that they were entitled, indeed called, to go forward to the construction of a better edifice.

This new edifice could, however, be built up in very different ways. There was a conservative possibility, in which the offensive points in Bible and dogma were not so much denied as carefully diluted and explained away, or respectfully moved into the background as mysteries —even fondly called to remembrance in the liturgy and the hymn book in the luxuriant loquacity of the time, but avoided as far as possible in preaching, instruction and pastoral care. And there was a radical possibility, which amounted to open rectifications which were not afraid of scandal, to more or less sparing or totally unsparing negations and rejections. We shall return to these possibilities in the account of the theology of the period. Here we are merely interested in one thing: what was positive and undisputed, what was in one way or another finally asserted as true, salutary and necessary, was a construction of those religious principles which were capable of representing Christianity as something that could be realized by man and which presented to him that will for form, that will for morality, as something that he could achieve; and at the same time, they were capable of doing away with the conflict over the general theoretical presuppositions in which it was believed that the old conception of Christianity was trapped. The second was there for the sake of the first; intellectual honesty for the sake of practical usefulness. So God now becomes, in accordance with modern man's theoretical knowledge of the world and so to speak as his objective counterpart, the infinitely wise builder of the world, and in accordance with his moralistic will and as his exact counterpart, the infinitely gracious giver of the moral law. In accordance with the continuing theoretical and technical penetration of the world by man, God's action is now seen to be identical with the principle of 'providence', which accompanies and directs every event in the same way, and within which revelation, reconciliation, etc. are simply particular 'forms', i.e. particular modes of appearance of his one all-embracing action. In accordance with the equally continuing practical presupposition of men it becomes the moral truth that guides, directs, illuminates and redeems each individual, in the last instance, in his reason. As a result of the theoretical basis that has been advanced, Christ now no longer falls into the category of the God-man, but—and this was the real, moral concern of the men of the time—into the category of the en-lightened and enlightening teacher and the powerful model of wisdom and virtue, categories in which he could still be praised at Christmas, Easter and Ascension, in sincerity and in the loftiest tones, and possibly even in the language of ancient dogma. In accordance with the mani-fest juxtaposition of confessions and religions in history, and above all because of what men in fact wanted to find, the Church becomes a religious society, that is, the society, founded by Jesus Christ for our salvation, of the sincere worshippers of the true, i.e. the wise and gracious God, with all the goods and gifts that such a society could not fail to have. In accordance with the subtler philosophy of the time, and above all, in accordance with present expectations of the nature of salvation, the *ordo salutis* becomes the way from imperfection (and, indeed, even in imperfection) to a perfection in living which at least is clearly envisaged as a goal and is therefore conceived of as being attainable in principle. In accordance with the new picture of the world, without the resurrection of the flesh, and above all in accordance with the new morality, without the eternal punishment of hell, eschato-logy becomes the doctrine of the immortality of the soul in a purely spiritual Beyond. These negations and these positions would not have been necessary purely for the sake of theoretical philosophy; they were, however, necessary—and as a result the help of theoretical philosophy or modern science and history had to be enlisted—because of the practical philosophy presupposed, or rather, because of the particular will for life whose expression this practical philosophy was. The one dictated and the other wrote.

This, then, is how Christianity was intellectualized or made a philosophy in the period. The intentions were not as evil as they may probably sometimes seem. The Christianity of this time by no means desired to deny God, nor did it even seek to deny revelation or miracle. It made a neat enough distinction between Creator and creature. It proved the existence of God. It wondered at the glory of his works. It could praise him loudly and sincerely. It could justify his wisdom and goodness against all suspicions to the contrary. It even affirmed his revelation, whether by understanding it as the communication of those of course rather problematical mysteries, or by thinking of it as the work of the moral education of the human race, in the course of which there might be extraordinary climaxes which might even be characterized by miracle. This Christianity need not necessarily be rationalistic; it could also be supranaturalistic and was, in fact, largely so: even when it was rationalistic, one would do it an injustice if one were to term it totally impious (there were, of course, irreligious and frivolous individuals in this as in any time).

It should be realized quite clearly that Pietism did not fail to play a part, even on this side of the great process. We know of the Basle hymn-writer, Hieronymus Annoni, a very sympathetic Pietist, who was a zealous Philadelphian sympathizer and a spiritual kinsman of Hiller of Württemberg, that all his life he had to struggle in the stillness with the severest doubts *de veritate religionis christianae*. Ludwig von Muralt of Berne was a remarkable combination of the noble humanism of a man of the world and an almost adventurous faith in inspiration and inspired men of all kinds. Johann Christian Edelmann (1698-1767) began as a Pietist, but ended with the even more 'inspired' knowledge that the interpretation of John 1.1 is 'God is reason', with the discovery of Spinoza and the biblical criticism of the English deists. And the Pietism of Johann Konrad Dippel (1673-1734) came to a climax in a vigorous contestation of the orthodox doctrines of sin, satisfaction and justification. Paul Wernle, while seeing Pietism in contrast to the Enlightenment as one of the two offshoots of old post-Reformation Christianity, has to assert: 'The first radical attacks on dogma came from the pietistic side' (II, 35).

So we may certainly say that this period should not be thought of as impious because of its negations or the inadequacy of its position. Who knows whether in its own way it was not more religious than other

periods which were less radical in this field? However, in view of the
decisive negations and doctrinal positions to which it had reduced
Christianity, it must be said that it had reduced Christian doctrine
to the teaching of a religiously determined philosophy, a philosophy
which, historically speaking, might be said to coincide approximately
in its view of the world and of morality with the better Stoa of the
Roman period, which has already been mentioned. Certainly, its
doctrine also contains non-Stoic, even non-philosophical elements. But
it should be noted that the elements which it stresses, with which its
heart beats, which it not merely concedes, but desires and affirms
with its inmost being, are not those other elements, but rather the
Stoic, philosophical ones—and here the poems of Christian Fürchtegott
Gellert may be indicated as a typical instance. These are absolutely
certain; all else is only relatively so. These are the substance; all else
is accidental. These are the standard by which all else is measured—
perhaps, as Gellert and so many others found with the Christmas and
Easter miracles, to be accepted joyfully—but to be measured by the
creed of the Stoa. It was this by which men lived, or wanted to live,
or thought that they lived.

This is the third form of the attempt at humanization to which
Christianity was subjected in the eighteenth century. It could also be
termed the secondary form of the second. At any rate, it belongs very
closely with it. We need only point briefly to the immense historical
effect of this side of the proceedings also. The delusion over the normative influences to which unconscious surrender had been made, the
insidiousness of the idea which manifested itself in this self-deception,
was so strong that posterity largely thought that underneath all this
it had to see the reduction of Christianity to what was understandable
in intellectually natural or reasonable terms as an independent, even
as the real concern of the time. Countless people since then have
welcomed and affirmed this intellectualist reduction of Christian
doctrine in one or other of its many possible garbs and have joined
with it under the impression that they were sharing in a great act of
spiritual freedom, of intellectual honesty, of the science that is indispensable to modern man. They should have taken a look at the face
of the petty bourgeois of the eighteenth century, showing simple concern but not perhaps the highest possible interest, who for the first
time had covered his nakedness with this fig-leaf, to escape the gaze
of the society in which he found himself, on the presumption that this
action was by no means one of ultimate concern. But again, in the
context of this historical treatment we would do better to conclude

with a recognition of the astonishing vitality displayed by this petty bourgeois in respect of the great *quid pro quo* that he had accomplished. Here, too, he is truly the absolutist that we have already come to know elsewhere.

4. The eighteenth century is the century of the attempt, or rather of the beginning of the attempt, to make Christianity a more *individual*, more *inward* matter. It was not—I need only mention the name of Leibnitz—the time of Goethe or of the Romantics that first discovered, or rather rediscovered, the individual. In this respect, too, our period simply took further the subterranean but uninterrupted developments from the Renaissance. If man recognizes himself as an *in-dividuum*, as undivided and indivisible, that means that he recognizes himself as a being who is at least similar, at least related to the ultimate reality of God. He finds himself, or he finds in himself—however he may imagine that relationship to God—something eternal, almighty, wise, good, glorious, whose presence—however he then takes account of God as the origin and embodiment of all these divine qualities—at any rate allows and even requires him first to take himself seriously over against everything outside God that is different from him and, from that point, also to take seriously everything outside God that is different from him. Individualization means the enthronement of man—not of humanity, but of man, of the man experiencing himself here and now as the secret, yet for himself supremely real king of at least the sub-lunar world. Individualization means that this man, the man who I feel myself to be, is given authority to be the secret judge, the secret authority over all things outside God. Individualization means making inward, the making inward of what is external, objective to man, by which it is robbed of its objectivity, so to speak eaten up and digested, made into something within man. Of course one could conversely speak of externalization, in so far as it is a question of man projecting what is within him externally in such a way that it is now also quite outside him, so that he obtrudes himself upon the object, identifies himself with it. Individualization means appropriation of the object to be the purpose of his domination. One can immediately see that here, so to speak, we have the pure form of the general tendency of the time, that here we are confronted as it were with the common root of both the incorporation of Christianity into the state and of its trans-formation into a matter of religion and morality. But the individualiza-tion of Christianity also means something special in addition to this; in the eighteenth century it appears in historical forms in which it is

not a matter of morality or the intellect, and even seems to be completely contrary to involvement in the state.

Here we must think particularly of the original and most authentic motive for what is termed *Pietism*. In its basic form, Pietism is identical with the pure form of what later had so many modes of expression in Christianity. But in its basic form it is neither moralism nor intellectualism, and it even seems to be sharply opposed to Caesaro-papism. In its basic form, in so to speak the original Pietist, it is *individualism*. 'The original Pietist' does not mean the earliest Pietist. The earliest Pietism only shows some of his characteristics and, on the other hand, he also lives on in the later forms of Pietism. What is meant is therefore the authentic, original Pietist who represents the essence of this matter. This Pietist is to be seen as a fighter, a conqueror. The one who fights and conquers here is the man who has discovered himself or in himself that ultimate reality, related to God; who thus knows no object which is not in the first place really within him and which must therefore, if he sets himself against it, be brought in, be made inward, be transposed to where it originally and authentically belongs. The fight here is over Christianity as a Church, a creed, a historical force, as a guide to life, a help in life, a power in life, against the whole possibility of an encounter with God and communion with God, as it now confronts man in Christianity for the first time. The fight of the original Pietist is the fight against this confrontation: he wants to have Christianity, he wants to believe, but belief—living belief, as he puts it—for him means taking Christianity seriously from the perspective and by the criterion of taking himself seriously, incorporating it into the kingdom of man, and consequently means the interiorization and resultant abolition of the confrontation between man and Christianity, the taking in of all those elements of Christianity which seem to represent an outwardness, a contrast. The sought-for goal is the appropriation of Christianity, which is regarded as complete when all that is not one's own as such is dissolved and made one's own.

One element in Christianity which the original Pietist does not regard as his own and wants to transform into something that he can make his own is the central fact of the Christian Church and its creed, the incarnation of the word of God in Jesus Christ. This central fact is intolerable to the individualist, an external object in that it stands over against us in the form of temporal distance, the distance between our time and the period AD 1-30, as an *illic et tunc*. This is something he has to do away with. In this respect, to interiorize it means to make it present, to transpose it to one's own present. This means not only

to have it transposed into one's own present after the manner of the
Reformation doctrine of the Holy Spirit, which did not of course do
away with the temporal distance, but also to experience it in one's
own present, indeed as one's own present, in a different way from the
presence of the Holy Spirit, which is still an objective presence. The
experience of the incarnation of the word does away with the temporal
distance. What happened in the distant past has now faded away as
such, and is less significant. Extreme Pietists were the first to say that
it was meaningless as such. Temporal distance is now disqualified and
means the mere past. The real birth of Christ is in our hearts; his real
and saving death is that which we see accomplished in ourselves, that
which we have to accomplish ourselves; his real resurrection is his
triumph in us as those who believe in him. Accordingly, original
Pietism can be and often was (say in Tersteegen and his spiritual kins-
men) a revival of much earlier historical mysticism. The interiorization
can, of course, also be understood merely as a parallel to the history
of Christ which is to be drawn here today by us. But sometimes there
can also be the further development that the history of Christ is seen
as simply the outward expression, inessential in itself, of the history
that takes place today, here and in us. A somewhat strange expression
of this desire to make Christ present may in that case be seen in so
unmystical an action as Zinzendorf's allowing himself to call the
saviour the supreme elder of his community of brethren.

One may even go on to ask whether one of the most famous undertakings of late orthodoxy, the proclamation of the so-called 'verbal
inspiration' of Holy Scripture, does not in fact belong here. What is
it, in effect, but an extremely effective making present of the incarnation of the word, a very convenient and easily understandable codifica-
tion, for the possession of and at the disposal of the man alive today?
At almost the same time as this final culmination of the old system
(though it should be seen much more as one of the beginnings of the
new), a pietistic biblicism set in which was as different from that of the
Reformation as grasping is from being grasped. The earnestness and
zeal of the study now quite newly devoted to the Bible hardly needs
stressing; it should, however, also be noted that it was not so much a
case of man being open to the Bible as of the Bible having to be open
to men at any price; man did not so much allow the Bible to be master
as think that he should and could obtain quite definite instructions,
powers and blessings from it. In short, this biblicism also—indeed,
precisely this biblicism—was an act of the concern for relationship to the
present, a development which already bore within itself the dangerous

seeds of later biblical criticism. Anyone who thinks that he can approach the Bible so certain of what he wants, with such sovereignty as was characteristic of the time, will undoubtedly have to wake up one day to the fact that he cannot be as content with the Bible as he used to be. Indeed, he may not be satisfied with it at all.

A second element in Christianity that was hard to appropriate was the fact that while Christianity is directed towards the individual man, it is not directed towards individual man in the abstract, but to the particular individual man, the man in the Church who is related to his fellow man. In this respect, the appropriation of Christianity necessarily meant assimilation, the removal or at least the neutralization of the alien character of one's fellow man. The neighbour, the brother in Christ, is now in principle to be no more than the other man. He is now to be my own: in other words, in the first place he is no longer to disturb me by his otherness, and in the second place, where possible he is to be the sort of man that I can find again in myself. Community is not to disquieten me, but to strengthen me. This external element is also to be internalized. After that, and on that presupposition, the individualist can and will love, have brothers, be in the Church. This is the context of the antipathy of the original Pietists to the national Church and the worldly Church, an antipathy which was often muted, often displayed in an acute form, but in every case was quite fundamental. It was particularly outspoken against the celebration of the eucharist, in which there was a feeling that Cherethites and Pelethites were being made untried brothers and sisters. This, too, is the context of the decline in the significance of baptism in favour of real conversion, taking place later, or confirmation administered within the framework of the Church. (We have to thank the Pietists not so much for the invention of this institution as for its establishment within the Church. The Enlightenment took it over with enthusiasm. It was first in the eighteenth century that confirmation gained the significance which it now has, to the incalculable detriment of the Church.) Pietism could lead to separation, though on the whole it sought to avoid it. Its primary desire was toleration within the Church, freedom to be able to lead one's own (i.e. more intensive, more lively, more authentic) life of faith, in contrast to the great mass of other church members. As a result of its own need, Pietism became one of the most effective proponents of the idea of tolerance. What the Pietist wants, albeit with a rather different emphasis, is what Frederick the Great proclaimed as the religious right of every man; he wants to seek his own salvation in his own way without trouble or hindrance, and as a result he can understand that other people want to do the same thing. But he wants even more than this: he wants not only to be undisturbed by his neighbour but also to have him, i.e. to have him as he himself is, to find him again in his own self. And he cannot do this with the neighbour that he finds in the national Church as it is. He can, however, with the neighbour who is also the man of his time.

At this point the general tendency towards free community, towards a community of choice, also extends to the Christian sphere. There would have been no Pietism without inner separation, i.e. without private assemblies (albeit in the context of the Church of the land), without the formation of an élite (however much it felt itself to be the élite of the poor in spirit), without *Philadelphia*, the visible yet invisible brotherly covenant of the 'elect aliens here and there' who feel that they belong together in a special way in the same place as in all the rest of the world, without the formation of groups, around the continually new, free centre of one or several, male or female, leading personalities. The community of brethren then attempted to make cross-connexions not only between the great Protestant churches but also between the various Pietist separatist groups inside and outside the churches, thus making of necessity, with their own peculiar spirit, one great, all-embracing separatist group which in an almost miraculous way represented for many contemporaries the world-wide Church. Here, in Pietism, was the origin of the transformation of the concept of the Church in Germany, following the pattern of English and Dutch models, into that of a free and voluntary religious assembly. It was not the Enlightenment, but Pietism, from the depths of its being, that pioneered this second concept. The freely-formed, chosen community is what is left of the community once it has been in effect assaulted and overcome by the individual, King Man.

The third element in Christianity that could not be appropriated is indicated by the concept of authority. Individualism does not mean a denial of authority, but the supersession of all alien external authority in favour of the inner, personal authority of the man whose ultimate foundation as an individual is in himself, an authority close to and indeed related to the authority of God in a way that could sometimes be clarified in particular details. Christian individualism had, in this respect also, to mean the incorporation of the external authority of the Church, dogma, in the last resort even the Bible, into a unity with the authority which the Christian man has, in the last resort, as his own. In this respect also, original Pietism made powerful preparations not only for the idea of tolerance, but positively, for the ideal of religious freedom. True, it also knew the authority of the word of Scripture, but that had to be the authority of the word of Scripture experienced in a vivid, personal way—or, in objective terms, of the word of Scripture so to speak made fluid by a living personal testimony. But in the last resort was not this living, personal element more than the word of Scripture to which *de facto* authority was ascribed? It also recognized the authority of the Church's ministry, but laid down the condition that the pastor had to be truly converted in order to exercise it properly. Was this, however, not to ascribe authority to the ministerial brother in the pulpit for himself, and not to his office? Be this as it may, the authority of the Bible and of ministry had their limited, clearly visible bounds. And both could be by-passed. Beyond them was at all events the authority of a voice that could no longer be distinguished clearly from the voice of the pious individual: the so-called 'inner voice'. This primarily denotes the gifted leader, but can also at least catch the overtones of something that corresponds in the one who is led: it has ultimately quite uncontrollable insights into heavenly and earthly things, into the will of God and into human circumstances and relationships, from prophecy via the destinies of entire nations to supremely bourgeois marriage counselling; it gives admonitions and warnings, announcements of judgment and promises of grace in quite general and also quite particular situations. Inspiration like that of the biblical witnesses is now understood as a possibility the repeated realization of which cannot be ruled out. It seized the saddler Johann Friedrich Rock (1678-1749) and made him a seer and a prophet: half, and even all pietistic Germany listened to his strange messages, and even a Bengel, an Oetinger, a Tersteegen and a Jung-Stilling reverently sought him out. As 'It seems to me', inspiration even played a decisive role with Zinzendorf. To live in obedience now means, as the life of Jung-Stilling so vividly puts it, to listen to guidance. It can be perceived in one's own heart; it can also be received from a believing brother. Either way, it is characterized by its immediacy.

The authority which is heard in it is authentic, in contrast to that of the letter of Scripture or even that of the Church, because it is inner authority. It illuminates, i.e. it can, since and in that it has become inward, also be understood as man's own deepest conviction, and obedience towards it can be understood as man's own inner necessity, that is no longer different from the supreme freedom. I recognize that God himself is speaking to me in the fact that he is speaking in me. Consequently man now can and must on occasion go against and work against merely external authority, either directly or indirectly. Not all Pietism thought that it had to fight against what amounted to the whore of Babylon within the Church. But there was not and cannot be Pietism without resentment against the Church on the basis of the new, inward concept of authority, without a more or less perceptible call to repentance in addressing the pastors and theologians of the Church. And it is remarkable that on occasions Pietism—as in the case of Major Davel of the Canton of Vaud, executed for rebellion in 1723—could also express itself as political liberalism. What is meant by this inner authority of the original Pietist? The *lumen internum supernaturale* of the Quakers and their spiritual brethren in Germany? Or a misunderstanding of the *testimonium spiritus sancti* of Reformation doctrine? Or, quite simply, the *lumen naturale*, the divine spark, which man has before any revelation? It can glitter in all these colours. The one thing that is certain is that it claims to be living, direct authority, because and in that it is an authority adopted inwardly by man and appropriated by him. Hence it may be said that the actual significance of modern philosophy with its commendations of the 'thinking self' was perhaps child's play in the rise of the dogma of the religious autonomy of the individual in comparison with the living power effective in the self-glorification of the original Pietists about this idea, a self-glorification now mild, now violent, both taught and experienced. Here it was, here it existed: the monad without windows! To put the matter in an exaggerated way, perhaps the saddler Rock did more to proclaim it than the great Leibnitz.

The fourth thing in Christianity that could not be appropriated is indicated by the concept of the divine command. In the Christian, or at any rate the Protestant Christian view, the divine command is not the prescription of a general rule which then has to be interpreted and applied in particular cases. The command, rather, tells man what special thing is required of him by God on a particular occasion. Nothing needs to be interpreted; all that is necessary is either obedience or disobedience. The individualist treats the command as a general rule which he has to interpret, to which he has to give form by applying it. In this way he internalizes even the law. God's property becomes his own. That this is so is evident from the striking accumulation of what is extraordinary, of what is noticeably different from the actions of his surroundings, of what marks out his action. All this he regards as being enjoined on him. Is he really commanded to set up clear signs, as it were, by his actions? Is it not rather that he himself wants to do something of his own, something special, at the very point where obedience is required? Be that as it may, the original pietistic ethic, in contrast to that of early Lutheranism and Calvinism, is characterized by a demand for quite extraordinary actions and modes of life. It is important for it that the converted man should distinguish himself from the unconverted by avoiding dancing and visits to the theatre. The whole sexual sphere becomes for it a zone of quite particular decisions, dangers, occasions for sin, trials and sanctifications. Again, it commends all kinds of practices of outward and inward asceticism so that a higher degree of perfection may be reached. It can indicate the narrow way, in contrast to the wide road, with remarkably exact psychological and moral topography. In Pietism, the great truth that the way of the Christian is always his own way before God takes the form that the way of the Christian, in his own eyes and in those of his surroundings, i.e. even as seen from below, must be his own particular, original way. For that reason Pietism, even on a large scale, could be and had to be very active, and indeed active in its own, original way. It busied itself in hitherto neglected areas, in ventures like the famous foundation of the orphanage at Halle, and later in taking up the mission to the heathen, and—something quite different from earlier Protestantism—produced new saints, heroes of purity, of the life of prayer, of love and fervent faith, regarding them of course in the same way in which Catholicism regards its saints: these men are what they are through the grace of God, but they can be recognized for what they are directly from their works, their way of life, their attitude and the personal impression which they made. Moreover, they can be described as such in their biographies and can be celebrated in the same way as heroes in other spheres. The fact of the exceptional action and the exceptional personality can certainly be understood as obedience to God's special command or as a sign set up by God himself. The stress on the work or the personality of the individual and its evaluation in Pietism might in fact indicate that interest in a man's special characteristics played a decisive rôle in this matter. This stress and evaluation make it necessary to understand Pietism, too, as a piece of individualism, at least in this case.

The fifth element in Christianity that proved impossible to appropriate is denoted by the concept of mystery, or of the sacrament. The Protestantism of the Reformation, no different from Catholicism, but rather united with it in this respect, had always gathered the Church together around preaching, baptism and eucharist, understood in Augustinian terms as a 'visible sign of invisible grace', i.e. as a sacrament. The Christianity of the eighteenth century was not so alien from life and reality as to have wanted to deny or abolish the concept of mystery. In its own way, its feelings and thoughts were no less sacramental than at any other period of the Christian Church. It, too, sought and found 'visible signs of invisible grace'. But it interiorized this concept, also. In this direction, individualism meant that man discovered the mystery within himself: he himself becomes the visible sign of the invisible grace.

We have seen again and again that one must be very careful in defining and applying the concept of 'reason' as the normative concept characteristic of this time. On the one hand, the title may not be used to make the man of the eighteenth century a mere man of the understanding and the will—he certainly was not that. On the other hand, it is impossible to overlook the fact that precisely in those manifestations in which he shows himself to be rather different from a man of will and understanding, he is nevertheless the complete man of reason. He sees very clearly the limitations of his understanding and his will, but he also sees what is beyond these boundaries as being within the boundaries of his capacity to understand, to shape, to possess and to command, i.e. within the bounds of his reason.

Into this expanded inner room, beyond *ratio* in the narrower sense but within it in the wider sense, he introduces and transplants even the concept of mystery. He discovers that he is capable not only of understanding and willing, but also of feeling, experiencing and undergoing. He now translates and transforms the Christian mystery into a mystery in this sense, an accessible, not incomprehensible but comprehensible mystery. In this sense, now he himself can become the sacrament. Thus Pietism, in particular, is inconceivable without the undercurrent of mysticism, enthusiasm, ecstasy, inspiration and occasionally of theosophy and occultism of every kind. The undercurrent is sometimes more visible, sometimes less, but it is broad and deep. From this perspective, the phenomenon of the 'inner voice' as a substitute for previous authority, discussed above, is to be taken as only one element among many. The substitute for authority has its basis in the much more important substitute for the sacrament: because there can be felt, undergone, experienced an inner baptism of the spirit, an inner, spiritual eucharist, an inner perception of the word, because there can be a direct personal converse of the soul with God, because there are more things in heaven and earth than your philosophy can dream of, things which must not remain hidden from the deeper penetration of human wisdom since along with mystery in general one can also take the Christian mystery into that expanded inner room—because of all this, there is that prophecy, that 'It seems to me' with its immediate authority as a final resort. True, at this point everything was really in a flux: there was a down-to-earth Pietism, as embodied in a J. A. Bengel, who in his biblicism approximated to the attitude of orthodoxy and in his moralism to that of the Christian Enlightenment. Within Pietism there was a gentle or even an anxious repudiation of the extremes not only of the inspired separatist groups or of Swedenborgianism but even of the wonders and arbitrarinesses, say, of the Zinzendorf community. However, even with Bengel one need only think of those concepts that were so important to him, the concepts of the real and of the power to think, and of the compensations which he deliberately made in the field of biblical exposition—always in the direction of a religion of immediacy; one need only think of his pupil F. C. Oetinger, with the heavenly physics and chemistry by means of which he thought that he could defeat the spiritualism of the Leibnitzians directly on their own ground; one need only think of the whole strange connexion with natural philosophy by which the pietistic 'theology of power' was carried on in Württemberg—in a remarkable affinity to certain chthonic peculiarities of this area—right into the nineteenth century (J. T. Beck!) to see how even that 'South German original', so valued right down to our time, and rightly valued, was connected with the undercurrent of individualism.

One could say similar things about other apparently down-to-earth forms of Pietism in the eighteenth century: everywhere one sees the threads which bind it to the depths of that mystery which now is not completely the Christian mystery, but rather a domesticated mystery. Certainly it is no argument against the individualistic character of the undercurrent that the Christian and non-Christian Enlightenment dissociated themselves on occasions in very strong words from mysticism, enthusiasm and theosophy as against expressions of the irrationality that they so hated. One can see from more than one biography of typical people of the Enlightenment (e.g. Marie Huber of Geneva, but also the notorious K. F. Bahrdt) that this dissociation was more the expression of a disappointed love than of an opposition in principle. On the one hand there could be a very understandable fear of the depths and abysses of the *humanum* which soon open up before a man once he has undertaken to leave the relatively firm ground of *ratio* in the narrower sense. The obscurity, the confusion, the wildnesses of the area or the areas which are then entered might make it seem advisable to wise temperaments to turn back at the appropriate time, as was then the custom even for bold mountaineers when they reached the foot of the Gletscher. It might seem to be wise—and some of this wisdom (albeit in a very changed form) lived on in the new individualism of Goethe—to limit oneself to becoming and remaining master. On the other hand, it might be realized that even the best-domesticated mystery is still too strongly reminiscent of the real mystery that cannot be tamed, and that a resolute and far-seeing individualist could not do better than to have no truck with this guest, deciding boldly, though somewhat abruptly, that reason only begins with *ratio* in the narrower sense.

There is also a supremely sacramental pathos of the boundary. It is the pathos of the anti-pietistic man of the Enlightenment, which is clearly visible behind the mask of so many writers of the time who seem to be so sceptical and indeed to express themselves in so frivolous a way. It is this pathos that binds them to their opponents who have overstepped the boundary. They are distinct from the mystics, enthusiasts and theosophists of their time in the same way as the fox for whom the grapes are too sour is distinguished from his more fortunate (whether supposedly or in reality) fellow-creatures. He, too, does not lack the intent towards irrational individualism. But it has so to speak gone to earth, has become fused with the enthusiasm (which as such is ultimately also irrational) that he has for remaining within the bounds of *ratio* in the narrower sense. So precisely at this point, where the opposition between rationalism and Pietism seems to be at its greatest, we must recognize one of those places where they are both in reality very closely connected.

If one keeps together the five elements that we have cited under the concepts of temporal distance, the fellow-man, authority, the divine command and mystery, it may be possible to see the walls stormed by the Christian individualist in order to make everything his own: the walls of the external, that he wants to interiorize, the walls of the encounter that he wants to take within himself. The Pietist is the classical figure in whom one can see embodied this fourth effort of the eighteenth century, the attempt to make Christianity a matter for the individual. In view of the later, new individualism of the time of Goethe and of Romanticism, one cannot take Pietism seriously enough as a historical prelude. As individualism, Pietism was not only the far more original form of Christianity in the eighteenth century; it was also much more modern, and had in it much more of the future. But it is again important to be clear, on the line that we have attempted, how secretly even the non-pietistic eighteenth century had a part in its individualism.

We bring these paragraphs to a close with the comment that the attempt described above to humanize Christianity was undertaken with considerable force, but did not reach its goal. True, it endowed the Christian Church of this time with its historical features. But only the Church of *this* time. Granted, it has found all manner of continuations and repetitions down to our own time; it is impossible to say that we have even remotely finished with the legacy of the eighteenth century. We all still have alive in us somewhere the man of the eighteenth century in his attitude to the problem of theology. Nevertheless, it has long been evident that the attempt was one among many others. The eighteenth century, with its particular treatment of the problem of theology, went as it came. It did not have the catastrophic significance that people sometimes wanted to ascribe to it. Furthermore, even to that time the attempt depicted here presented only its historical *surface*. That is certainly no small matter, but it is far from being the whole. We must remember that when we understand the eighteenth century as moralistic, intellectualistic, individualistic, etc., however right we may be with this understanding, there is still an element in the reckoning that cannot be overlooked. It is impossible to read its documents without having to say that Christianity as it was really lived always went beyond the sphere marked out by all these categories. All this, therefore, means that the attempt depicted was only a partial success; it remained an attempt. We must keep in mind the intra-historical grounds or circumstances for this failure:

1. All along the line we have to note that the attempt at humanizing was carried on energetically, but without that last burst of energy, without radical means. The man of the eighteenth century was earnest enough in his wishes, but not so earnest as to bring them to a really victorious conclusion.

Why did the absolute princes and absolute democracy not sweep the board in their obvious intention to make the Church an instrument of the State? Why, in all their Caesaro-papistical encroachments, did they call a halt at the teaching and the worship of the Church? Did they overlook the fact that it was here that the real power of the Church rested, however much it had been weakened for other reasons, and that at this point it could avoid their attack at any time? Or did they not have the vitality to offer the necessary substitute in the form of a state religion in the right direction, along the lines of the emperor cult of antiquity? Under the influence of Voltaire, Frederick the Great seems to have considered for a moment the introduction of such a substitute.

Why did the harmless intention to found a colony of philosophers on the western boundary of Prussia never come about? Why—at the best possible moment for such a thing—did the attempt by the French revolutionaries to introduce a cult of reason die of ridicule? Was it that here even the most absolute state had something to fear if it ventured too far? It is enough to note that the attempt to incorporate Christianity into the state was in fact only carried out within certain, very modest bounds: despite all its ignominious external dependence, the Church was free and in fact remained free. Its inner possibilities were not attacked, however little use it may have made of them.

Thus the trees of Christian moralism and intellectualism in the eighteenth century grew—but not as far as heaven. Not even the bourgeoisie, for who this side of the development was so significant, reached as gladly and as naturally for these triumphs as one might, from a psychological or a sociological point of view, have expected. Here and there might be a secular ideal of life and a different picture of the world, but the basis for preaching and worship that was taken for granted remained, as before, orthodox dogma with its very different presuppositions. Why did the new men go so carefully, with so many accommodations and concessions? Why did Pietism stumble in the middle of the century, when it had originally been felt and seen to be so timely as an attempt to improve life? Why were the great masses in the cities so suspicious of the Christian Enlightenment until well into the second half of the century? Why did the Enlightenment have the feeling that it was an *ecclesia pressa*? Why did orthodox dogmatics dominate pulpits and cathedras until the end of the century, even if it had become broken and rather unsure of itself? Why did the Christian Enlightenment hardly produce a real martyr for its new faith? Why did it only really make an impact in wider circles when it was already too late, when it was already done for, when the feet of those who were to carry it out were already in the house? How was it possible that such prompt and annihilating laughter could break out first over Pietism and then even more, and in quite a different way, over the Christian Enlightenment? Whether one considers it from its moralistic or its philosophical, its pietistic or its rationalistic aspect, this movement does not look to be the kind that makes its way with really superior means, as did the Reformation.

Typically, however, even in the case of the individualism that has just been discussed, it offers the picture of an offensive that has ground to a standstill: to interiorize, to take in the distance in time, the alienation of one's fellow man, authority, prayer, the sacrament, to change all heteronomy into autonomy—yes, that of course is what people wanted! But were not those who in fact achieved something of this kind to a degree worth mentioning a very shallow stratum of those who were then alive, or rather, of those who were then aroused? Did they not, those who perhaps represented the most profound, the strongest element to be found here, in fact do far less to change and influence the attitude and influence of the Church than the much less profound, much less lively preachers of moral, rational Christianity? Why were they the ones who so soon seemed to be sealed off from the rest, the real movement of the time, as particular outsiders, with whom no rationalist and indeed no 'sound' Pietist wanted to declare his solidarity? What is the significance for the whole movement of this exclusion of the outspoken mystics and enthusiasts, if they were in fact the most genuine representatives of the whole? If the humanizing of Christianity was really to work, the man of the eighteenth century had to understand himself and take himself seriously to a much greater degree than was evidently the case. He undertook great things *à propos* of Christianity. The leverage that he applied seems to have been very impressive, powerful and threatening. Anyone who looks only at that may, with Troeltsch and other cultural historians, get himself drunk on the conception of a tremendous upheaval of everything, that is supposed to have taken place at that time. In fact, as far as success is concerned, one cannot but pass the historical judgment that the food was not as hot as the cooking. Quite a different kind of self-confidence would have been needed on the part of modern man to make his absolutism effective to any degree on this object, on Christianity. He does not seem to have had this necessary, greater self-confidence. Certainly he did not demonstrate it.

2. Quite apart from the faint-heartedness with which it was undertaken, the attempt at humanization in the eighteenth century came to grief on its manifold internal contradictions. It cannot be denied that the tendency towards a state Church and the individualism of the time were the children of one and the same thing, an absolutist spirit and will. It is a quite different question, however, how these children got on with each other, or rather, whether the two forms of the same absolutism did not overlap so much that their effects inevitably threatened each other, indeed cancelled each other out? How could the absolutist state tolerate religious individualism as it did, if it knew what it was dealing with? Did it not notice that the principle of individualism represented a dangerous threat alongside which tangible

political resistance, with which it had to deal, was paltry? Or did it notice, and yet hid under the generous gesture of tolerance from itself and from the world, the fact that it felt helpless in the face of this principle? One may certainly credit Frederick the Great with having noticed the fact; it was to a great degree resignation when he showed his much-praised tolerance to Tersteegen and his followers. But at this point individualism in its turn has its limitations. Is the mere inwardness of its religion not also a sign of a retreat on every side? What is the meaning of the autonomy of conscience, of feeling, of faith, if in the last resort they may only be lived out inwardly, in ideologies, in mystical experiences, in a distinctive private way of life, in ecstatic confessions, in the mystery of pastoral activity, in all kinds of poetry and prose, printed and unprinted? Was this not also resignation? Do not so many of the cramped manifestations in this sphere betray pressure from outside, from the absolutist rule over society, the fundamentally quite involuntary restraint with which men submitted to this pressure by way of compensation for being on extremely dangerous ground? Might not even the absolute state say that it did not have too much to fear from this quite individualistic world, that it could leave the restless children to their games without too much danger? Is there not a false relationship between the intensity of the feeling of freedom which made up the inward life of this group, the eschatological expectations on which it lived, and the lassitude with which it left the real external world more and more to itself, as though inward and outward, present and future, this-worldly and other-worldly could be separated so abstractly? In this way the two legitimate children of absolutism evidently marked out their own territory, to the inevitable detriment of each other.

We can see a similar contradictory relationship between the state Church and eighteenth-century moralism. There is no doubt that the absolute prince and later the absolute democrat of the eighteenth century on the one hand, and the citizen of the same period, reverencing virtue and duty for the sake of peace and quiet, belong inwardly together: both represent the same sovereignty of man over his fate. But we need not even enter the Christian sphere to have occasion to ask the sad question, how long will these two get along with each other? What could Augustus the Strong and his young subject C. F. Gellert have had in common? What heartfelt anxiety is there in the confirmation address which J. F. W. Jerusalem, that pious man of the Enlightenment, delivered to the crown prince of Brunswick! What concern must Frederick the Great's Silesian politics have caused the

Christian who was morally upright as the eighteenth century understood those terms! How many concessions this morality had to make
in an upward direction if it was to achieve its desire, not to be unloyal
at any price! But in that case, how could it be administered down-
wards with an entirely clear conscience? Was there something here
other than a relationship of mutual good-humoured tolerance? The
fathers of the country left the Churches their moral preaching and
praised them because they wanted to see their subjects kept virtuous.
The Churches left the fathers of the country their courtly life, their
financial activity and their political warfare, closing both eyes to this
manifest evil and piously ascribing to the inscrutable ways of providence
the fact that the laws for the *summus episcopus* seemed to be so different
from those of the Spalding hymn book. But could the Church in fact
do anything with its moral preaching other than open up a treasury
of disarmament in the face of the ruling immorality which would
inevitably explode one day—if only gradually, as in Germany—and
make the honest sense of subordination from the old days impossible
once and for all?

There was also, inevitably, a relationship of contradiction between
the moralism of the eighteenth century and its individualism. No
wonder that the Pietists and rationalists on the one hand, and the 'sound'
and less 'sound' Pietists on the other, felt so mutually aggrieved. No
wonder that the charges now of constricting legalism, the pressure of
conscience, externalism, now of free-thinking, worldliness, fleshly
security, flew between the different camps of the modern opposition
in such a way that the 'inspired' found it impossible to get on with
Spener's Pietists, and both with the Community of Brethren, and all
with the moralists of the Enlightenment, who for their part could not
bear all the divisions of Pietism. And yet all these were filled with
and driven by the same, essentially unproblematical absolutism of
the time. Goethe and his time were so to speak inwardly finished
with all this. Evidently, that was once they had worn each other out
with it all!

Again, the relationship between the moralism and the intellectualism
of the century should not be conceived of as simply as it has been presented here for the sake of comprehensibility. The most earnest
protests were made in the very name of morality against the translation
of Christianity into the insights and languages of the time. It could not
be, nor was it the case, that the relativism of the modern scientific
and historical approach called a halt with its criticism of early Christianity: rather, it became a powerful objection against the apparently

moral substance of the modern awareness of life. Here there slumbered
contradictions which only became acute in the period that followed,
but which were at least felt during the time that we are now
considering.

In short, when we consider the single intellectual development of
the eighteenth century in its relationship to the problem of theology,
apparently and in fact so much of a piece, we are dealing with a house
that was certainly not at unity in itself and that from that point of
view certainly did not have too promising a future.

3. In this connexion, without departing from our purely historical
treatment, we must point to a very simple and quite incalculable, yet
quite tangible element that represented an unparalleled resistance to
the trend of the time. Beneath and alongside all the books on philosophy,
psychology, aesthetics, history and morals, beneath and alongside all
the books by Pietists and men of the Enlightenment, at this time the
Bible, too, was read. Certainly from every possible perspective, with
every possible prejudgment and purpose. The Basle theologian Samuel
Werenfels was not far wrong when he said in his famous couplet about
the Bible:

> *Hic liber est in quo sua quaerit dogmata quisque*
> *Invenit et pariter dogmata quisque sua.*

There were real differences between the reflections of the biblical
message in the heads of the believers in reason, on the one hand, and
in those of the Pietists, on the other. Moreover, the emphatic way in
which appeals were made to it from every side could only serve to
bring this difference more clearly to light. Nevertheless, it was one
and the same Bible which lay on the tables in the homes of the disputing parties and which was read by them: an authority not only beyond
the opposition of the parties, but also beyond that on which the parties
were united, for better or for worse. The systems and compendia of
the seventeenth century may have acquired a very bad reputation and
finally, when no one would read them, may have found their way into
the lumber rooms to enter upon what is by now a two-hundred-year
sleep. In eighteenth-century Geneva, people may have preferred to
read the smooth apologetics of J. A. Turrettini rather than the
Institutio of his father Franz, who had been the last pillar of Calvinist
orthodoxy—indeed, they may have preferred it to Calvin's *Institutes*
themselves. In Germany the hymns of Luther and his time may have
been replaced by the sweet songs of the Pietists and bowdlerized by

the insipid efforts of the rationalists; the reading of the 'Heavenly' or the 'Earthly Contentment of the Soul in God' may have been on the increase—but over all this, whether with understanding or incomprehension, the reading of the Bible went on, of that Bible which had also been the Bible of the seventeenth century and the sixteenth, of the Catholic Middle Ages, and even of Athanasius and Augustine. And in view of this fact, we must not only see and stress what that gloomy man of Basle stressed: the relativity in which even the Bible, like all human things, was entangled during that time as at any other, and which at that time, as at any other, made it possible for any fool to shape it in any way that he liked, in the same way as a wax nose. Nevertheless, the Old and New Testaments were not conceived in the spirit of the eighteenth century, and if man felt obliged on all sides to present his own view where possible as the true view of this book, or read it into this book, how could it fail to happen that men continually had to struggle with an element of rebellion against their own modern views, with an element of continuity from early Christianity? Why did people not escape this contradiction and continuity as they escaped Chemnitz and Quenstedt and largely even the Reformers, by simply not reading the Bible any more? It was read with a great deal of historical criticism and a great deal of criticism of its content—but it was still read. People read it in extracts; they did not want to know too much about the Old Testament or, in the New Testament, about the Epistles, especially those of Paul; but if the view of the early Church was right, that the whole of the Bible is contained and recognizable in each individual part, then did they not read the Old Testament willy-nilly in the New, the whole in the extracts? They tried the theology of chthonic power, but how did it come about that they knew of no other—or better—way of doing it than in the very garb of biblicism, which in itself had so little power? They preached morality, but at least they did not do away with biblical readings in services, and throughout the century these will have spoken for themselves, despite all the mischief that may have been done in the pulpit. The fact that this book was not only not left on one side, but was even, in a sense, open everywhere is, in the last resort, however one may interpret it, a historical fact like any other, and when one considers why the eighteenth-century attempt to humanize Christianity did not completely succeed, one has to think of more than the weaknesses and the inner contradictions with which it was undertaken. This fact, too, must be kept in mind, and one must ask whether the attempt could succeed as long as men kept an enemy in the house in the shape of the

Bible and not only tolerated it in this respectable position but, despite everything, fostered and cherished it.

4. This formal fact is also matched by some matters of material substance. The great process of assimilation, which is what the eighteenth-century preoccupation with the problem of theology proved to be, was clearly unable to finish with some elements of early Christianity. They were like islands in a flooded landscape, which contradicted the rest of the picture and yet showed that the scene presented by the picture could only be an inundation.

I am thinking here primarily of the concept of God held by the rational belief of the eighteenth century. It has been characterized and censured as being deistic. People have taken up Goethe's question: 'What kind of a God would it be who only intervened from outside and allowed the universe to run round his finger in a circle?' We ourselves have understood the Creator and Sustainer God of this Christianity as an evident counterpart to the sovereign man of the period and must therefore, in contrast to Goethe, cast doubt on his real extra-worldliness and thus his divinity. But there is something apt in Goethe's objection, which notes the tendency of the eighteenth century, very different from his own, not to allow God and the world, God and man, to be fused together or to be brought deliberately under a common denominator. The real enthronement of Spinoza was a concern of the more sublime humanism of the period of Goethe; it was not typical of the eighteenth century. For the eighteenth century, the views of Spinoza were synonymous with atheism. And yet one would have expected that this century would have recognized in Spinoza's doctrine of God an expression of its own most absolutist tendency achieved at the most decisive point, and would have welcomed it as such! Why did it not do so? Why did it press forward in certain French masterpieces of materialism to a relatively authentic atheism, in Wolff to the conception of a mechanical world, resting and moving in itself, but not to pantheism or panentheism? Why was this progress only possible on the higher level of humanism that followed? All this surely cannot be understood as an expression of the spirit of the time; it is simply an expression of the constriction of this spirit, as the counter-activity of a factor that is alien to it. This counter-activity means at any rate that the conception of an encounter between God and man, the conception of a God who speaks and a man who listens, of God as a Lord and of man as his servant, or of God as a father and man as his child, remains at the least possible and open in a serious and not

merely symbolic, but real sense (however threatened it all may be).
But in so far as this conception remained bound up with the concept of
God, the eighteenth century had not carried through its programme at
this decisive point.

I am thinking, secondly, of the doctrine of justification in eighteenth-
century Pietism. Certainly, the rôle that it played here was extremely
ambiguous and equivocal. In the first beginnings of this movement it
had simply been pushed into the background in favour of the doctrine
of conversion and sanctification, in opposition to the orthodoxy that
seemed to stress it—or actually did stress it—in a false way; it then
vanished for a while almost without trace in the comprehensive
doctrine of rebirth and the communication of the Spirit. However, in
old Pietism itself—Lutz of Berne has already been mentioned—there
was no lack of counter-tendencies, and the Community of Brethren
must at any rate be seen as an attempt at a reform of Pietism in the
direction of the Lutheran doctrine of justification. Wherever Pietism
was seriously biblical, as it was, say, in Württemberg, it could not fail
to feel inward pressures in this direction. Of course, men read the
Bible and the Reformers, even in this respect, too much with their own
eyes, i.e. in the spirit of the eighteenth century, and thus read their own
moralism or their own mysticism into Paul as well as Luther. It says
much for the originality of Zinzendorf that he gave pride of place
among the confessional writings of the Reformation period to the
Synodus of Berne, composed by Capito of Strasbourg and therefore not
unconnected with sixteenth-century enthusiasm. On the whole, the
line of a cruder or more refined Osianderism, i.e. the view decisively
inaugurated by Augustine of justification as a gradual making righteous
of man by means of the outpouring of the Spirit that followed the
decisive act of forgiveness, was never crossed. It left its traces deep into
the Revival movement and in the pietistic biblicism of the nineteenth
century down to the present, so that men, in good faith, believed that
they had rediscovered the old Gospel in what was really a doctrine
that hardly differed in essentials from that of the Council of Trent.
At this point, however, we should perhaps be observant and patient
enough to recognize once again the concern for the authentic doctrine
of justification to be found in Paul and the Reformers in an element
of Pietism that took most visible form perhaps in the Community of
Brethren and that showed its strangest, most abstruse, indeed most
repulsive side not only to contemporaries and to the period of Goethe
that followed, but also to many men of later times, down to and
including our own: in what has disapprovingly and mockingly been

called its 'blood and wounds theology'. This refers to the way in which reference was made in pietistic preaching, hymns and books of instruction of every trend, to Jesus Christ, to the crucified, to the blood and wounds of his suffering on the cross as the sole place, origin and source of the help, power and renewal needed by all men and promised to them, as the decisive cause of their temporal and eternal blessedness. Now if the blood and wounds of Christ were stressed in this striking way, it was obviously in the balance whether redemption in Christ was not now—since the blood and wounds stressed the human side of the suffering and dying of Christ—to be understood as a pouring out of divine life into the soul of believers that takes place continuously in a moral or mystical way, and is to be perceived in certain movements and states of the soul, a pouring out in which the majesty of the 'for us' must necessarily issue in the familiarities of the 'in us' (in this instance again cultivated by Zinzendorf with brilliant understanding). This, perhaps, was largely the intention, and, in so far as it was the intention, we of course find ourselves at precisely this point in the middle of the authentic eighteenth century. Yet the scandal that the children of the world found here—including the stumbling-block prepared here by Lavater for the great Goethe—may well indicate that something different could have been and in fact was meant. The emphasis could lie on Jesus Christ instead of on the blood and wounds, and blood and wounds could simply point to his death as the final form of his intervention for us in our lowliness, to the objective reconciliation that has taken place in our flesh. Blood and wounds could, as the blood and wounds of the Lord, designate that point of free grace which men cannot reach or experience, that grace which intervenes for us as a grace that is and remains the grace of Jesus Christ, in such a way that neither divine outpouring nor human appropriation is necessary for its realization. It is grace for sinners, and the communication of the Holy Spirit is and remains the recognition of this grace for sinners. The eighteenth century made flourishes at a number of points. It probably would not have taken offence even at the pietistic 'blood and wounds' theology, as it did, had it not at some point sensed this second element, that was now completely alien to it. The sin against the spirit of the time, of which men accused the Pietists—and largely so unjustly!— was not the first factor, which was primary for Pietism itself, but the second factor, none the less effective because it was hidden. In so far as this second element was also effective in Pietism, this Pietism was, despite everything (and, of course, along with the rest of old orthodoxy), like Noah's ark, in which the doctrine of justification through faith

alone was able to be saved from the flood of pious and rational Pelagianism. Here we can see a second decisive point at which the Christianity of the eighteenth century evidently did not achieve its
programme.

The third point to be mentioned here is eschatology. First, we must
again credit Pietism not only with having noticed the problem of the
last things as a real problem, but also on the whole with having been
the first to rediscover them. True, at first they were seen only in the
form of a chiliasm which corresponded all too closely with the spirit
of the time, a supranatural, this-worldly expectation of the future. But
it should perhaps be said, despite section XVIII of the Augsburg
Confession, that there cannot be any Christian hope at all without a
drop of chiliasm. And it must certainly be said that more than once in
church history chiliasm has been the inevitable transitionary stage
towards an understanding of authentic redemption, which not only
crowns history, but also makes all things new. The chiliastic Pietism of
the eighteenth century, of which e.g. J. A. Bengel is also to be reckoned
a representative, did once again, despite its limitations, and yet in a
way pointing beyond itself, put the eschatological question, the question of Christ as the one who is to come again, and thus in fact restored
to life an insight which had had little effect on the orthodox seventeenth century and even on the Reformers, to their detriment. Thus it
can be said that at this point one side of the problem of theology not
only remained visible, but even became visible again for the first time,
albeit with somewhat blurred outlines—as a warning against the conception that this century was only a *saeculum obscurum*, and did not have
its own immediacy to God. However, at precisely this point, we must
not do an injustice to belief in reason. Granted, its faith in immortality
seems to be an all too flimsy, all too spiritual, all too eudaemonistic
matter. But remember what it is trying to say, that alongside God
and freedom, immortality makes up the three articles of the faith of
rational Christianity, articles that also made up the modest remnants
of the rational Christianity of a man like Voltaire. Even the men of
this time had in the last resort death, the grave and corruption as
frequently and as clearly before their eyes as the men of any other
time. That despite this fact they were not resigned, but looked forward
to an eternity that overcame it, may have been expressed in the form
of their never-failing absolutist optimism—but they believed in something which, contrary to their intellect, they could not see, could not
touch, could not possess, could not conquer: something in which they
could only believe. They may have understood eternal blessedness,

with Gellert, as a price granted to virtue as a reward for its industry, in a eudaemonistic way—but what does eudaemonism ultimately mean if the expected reward is really one which is to be expected in heaven, and that means beyond the impenetrable barrier of death, the grave and corruption? When the same Gellert wrote:

> Then in the brightness I shall gaze
>   At what on earth was dark and drear,
> Regard with wonder and amaze
>   What cannot now be fathomed here.
>   At last my mind will comprehend
>   With praise and thanks my journey's end,

one may well ask whether this thought of comprehension may be anything but that harmony in the divine perspective which Leibnitz had taught the century so finely to be its own view; we must, however, also notice that the pious men of this century expressly wanted to transfer the realization of the thought of this harmony to a point to which they could not see themselves as being able to go, a point that it was not within their power to touch. We can and must include even the idea of immortality held by this time among those elements in which its spirit was at least held back, and had at least to make a relative capitulation.

We should not say more than this, that the absolutism of the eighteenth century had its clear inward and outward limits in its treatment of the problem of theology. It is not for us to judge how much or how little this meant for the men of the time. One thing, though, is certain, that the result was that the problem of theology was not solved even in this time, but remained open, so that its history could go and had to go further.

4

PROTESTANT THEOLOGY
IN THE EIGHTEENTH CENTURY

THE general form and treatment of the problem of theology in the Church and Christendom is one thing, its particular discussion by the theologians of a period is another. We shall now deal with the theology of the eighteenth century in this special sense—of necessity with the utmost brevity.

A first generalization may be made. It did not have a simple effect on the trends of the time, i.e. its influence was not immediate, so that we can infer with some confidence the state of theological scholarship from the general character of the religious movements of the time. Nor did it guide the religious movement of the time in being the source of a stream of new ideas, no matter how they were to be judged. Rather, the theology of the eighteenth century—and perhaps the same thing will also be true of the nineteenth—follows the general form and treatment of the problem of theology. It sees itself confronted with particular facts in the Church, or rather in the Christianity of its time: with new interests, aims and attitudes, with obvious changes in disposition, thought and taste, with new convictions and new doctrines. It feels that both it and the concerns it represents by virtue of its office are isolated over against this new situation, and feels threatened in its isolation. On the one hand it would like to break through the isolation and yet on the other it recognizes that there may be all sorts of good things in the changes that have come about without it. It feels competent, indeed obliged, and technically capable of bringing about corresponding changes in its own sphere also, and so, rather late, there is theological progress.

Thus the theology of the eighteenth century moved in the general direction of its time, though rather behind that time, so that while in an absolute sense its movement was very vigorous, theology was always in a relative sense rather obsolete and old-fashioned, presenting to the general consciousness the appearance of a guardian of who knows what kind of ancient tradition, whereas its condition at any one time simply indicated that now, in faithful pursuit, it had reached an earlier stage of the general development. When Pietism was enjoying its spring and summer at the end of the seventeenth century, theology was experiencing the last late fruits of high orthodoxy (among which, of course, there were also some very sour apples). Then, when in the first decades of the eighteenth century theology in the shape of its most progressive men began to appropriate the results of Pietism in what was a very thorough way, Wolff's theology had already made an appearance on the one hand and Zinzendorfianism on the other. When theology assimilated even Wolffianism, i.e. when it brought more or less radical neology, reason and revelation into a new relationship that promised permanency, rationalism proper, with its pure reasonable Christianity, was already at the door. And by the time rationalism had triumphed in theology, Lessing, the men of the *Sturm und Drang*, Goethe and his followers, had long since appeared. We could continue: when the theologians became Idealist, Romanticism and the Revival movement reigned outside; when they turned to Romanticism, the great empiricist positivist reaction broke out in the middle of the nineteenth century, and when the theological positivist A. Ritschl celebrated his triumph, Nietzsche had long since made his appearance, to destroy even this kingdom.

But let us remain with the eighteenth century. From what has already been said we have to conclude that the theology with which we are concerned here did not have an explicitly heroic character. It produced a whole series of men who, whether by their piety, their dialectical acuteness, their biblical and historical learning, did it every honour and of whom one can only speak with the greatest personal respect. But with all respect, on the whole one cannot say that this theology guided the Church, that its teaching office was also that of guardians and prophets, that it could be heard to utter a perceptible and effective 'Forward!' or 'Back!' or 'Another way!'. And when we reflect that the same thing may be said of the nineteenth century also, we have to concede that on a purely historical level we have hit on one of the hardest and most grievous problems in the history of recent theology. One can certainly say even of Luther and Calvin that with their message they answered the needs and the questions of the Church of their time and to this degree followed its movement. But there can be no question—thinking of their attitude to humanism and the Baptists —that they were at the same time leaders of this movement. Indeed, I would think that one must concede that even the orthodoxy of the sixteenth and seventeenth century, whatever other mistakes it may have made, guided the Church of its time, and did not simply let go of the reins, handing them over to the movements, religious and otherwise, of the time. Only from the end of orthodoxy, that is, from the beginning of the eighteenth century, onwards did the wagon begin to skid, in that while theology was indeed involved in a vigorous forward movement, the cause of this progress did not lie in itself or its subject-matter but somewhere outside. Moreover, this progress was always lame, so that theology was never able to enjoy its modernity in peace, but willy-nilly went on becoming more out of date.

Be this as it may, we are now unfortunately not in a position to put alongside the picture of the man and the Christian of the eighteenth century a picture of the theologian of the time that is governed by such dramatic inner movement. The theologian of the period is (and we now know for the most part why) a very earnest, fluent and clever man, but at the same time he is evidently gloomy, worried, not to say oppressed and desperate. This is so even when, as often happened, he pretended to be very cheerful and self-confident. One can see that everywhere he is on the retreat, that he is vexed and sorry that things are so and that he cannot change them. He obviously fears that he will not long remain free from attack in any of the positions that he has chosen. He sees that he will constantly have to deal with new opponents. He is not certain where his retreat will take him in the end. His is rather the mood of a general staff which feels that the initiative has been taken out of its hands and lies with the enemy, not to mention that of an Indian tribe slowly dying out in the territory that has been provisionally allotted to it. All this can be seen in the attitude and remarks of these theologians, and one cannot help feeling that the most perceptive and the best of them are those who at least have a clear idea of their situation and do not seek to comfort themselves with all kinds of optimistic thoughts in an attempt to get over the inferiority complex which is inevitable in such a situation. Externally, however, there is one notable fact: perhaps in no century have theologians— from country pastors to those holding the highest offices—applied themselves with such zeal and intensity to all kinds of academic and non-academic matters instead of to theology.[1] All the earnestness and vigour with which they devote themselves to their task cannot alter the fact that in the last resort they have little or nothing to say about the real course of human and Christian affairs, because the decisive matters always happen or indeed have already happened elsewhere

---

[1] Stolzenburg, *Die Theologie des J. F. Buddeus und C. M. Pfaff*, 1926, 22f.

than in their lectures, sermons and books, in which they continually seek to express their cause again in a new contemporary form. They always adopt an attitude to those things that happen completely without them and always in some way against them *after* the event, and regroup in order to be able to send a few mournful or even angry words after the departing train. From the eighteenth century onwards, Protestant theology has acquired that obvious habit of looking round outside, at the circumstances and movements in the Church and the world, before venturing to speak, so as to be able to speak in a timely way, appropriate to reality and to the situation. Recent Protestant theology has deservedly earned the thanks of the House of Austria in that it has been increasingly ignored as time has gone on. But such a course of action must do harm, not just theology to itself and its prestige, but to its substance, if it was so forced into a corner when something could be done about it. Even the theology of the eighteenth century was concerned enough about its prestige. There was no lack of vigorous efforts, imitating the absolutist features of the men of the time, to be in the scene, too, to take a position against philosophers, politicians, historians and scientists by becoming in turn or alternately everything to everyone. Only one thing always seems to be missing. There was no life in the question whether the cause theology had to represent to Church and world in such a particularly responsible way did not have its own, inner movement which did not allow it to orient itself by outward movements and to devote all its concern to justifying itself outside, thus perhaps asserting itself with more or less good fortune, setting its own authentic right to existence at risk in such a way. In these circumstances—leaving aside other questions—could theology even be just modern? In order to be modern, had it not completely to renounce the desire to be modern? If only it had pursued its theme in the absolute way in which the men of its time pursued theirs! But the children of the world are probably at all times wiser in their generation than the children of light.

We begin our short survey with mention of a name the bearer of which does not, at least for the most part, fall under the general characterization given above: Valentin Ernst Löscher (1673-1749), professor in Wittenberg and from 1709 superintendent in Dresden. He won renown for enhancing the ministry of the Church, for furthering the life of the Church and for research, above all into the history of the Reformation. He deserves mentioning in the history of theology because it was he who in 1701 founded the first theological journal under the title *Unschuldige Nachrichten von alten und neuen theologischen Sachen* (Innocent News of Old and New Theological Matters). He is also noteworthy as the last significant representative of Lutheran orthodoxy because he knew and said what was afoot in the suppression of orthodoxy by Pietism and the Enlightenment which went even beyond him, and explained why he would not fall in with this movement of the time. Löscher was still aware of the war which Luther once waged on two fronts against humanism and enthusiasm, and believed that in the twofold movement of his time, in its naturalism and enthusiasm, its fanaticism and atheism, he could see none other than Pilate and Herod, who had become friends once again to the detriment of the Church. The polemic and the resolute 'No!' of this otherwise positively oriented theologian was directed to these opponents on left and right and to their alliance. He attacked his opponents in 1708 in his *Praenotiones theologicae*, Pietism in particular in 1718-22 in his *Timotheus Verinus*, and finally Wolffianism in 1735 in a work with the significant title *Quo ruitis?* It is at any rate an indication of the freedom and the thoroughness of his criticism that it began with none other than Luther himself, whom he found guilty of being too preoccupied with mystical writers, of overestimating the *Theologia Deutsch*, Tauler and Thomas à Kempis and even being troubled by Augustine and Scholasticism, which were now proving to be the source of unhealthy renewal in his Church.

As an example of Löscher's polemic I shall give his thirteen objections to Pietism, the *malum pietisticum*, as he used to call it, avoiding the word heresy. According to Löscher, the characteristics of Pietism are:

1. Indifference to the truth of the Gospel, boasting that Christianity is a Christianity of power;
2. Devaluation of the means of grace by their association with human piety;
3. Weakening of the ministry of the Church by the denial of the objective grace of the ministry (to be affirmed not for the benefit of godless pastors but by virtue of the matter itself);
4. The confusion of the righteousness of faith with works, the understanding of justification as a process which in the last resort takes place within man;
5. A tendency towards chiliasm;
6. The limitation of repentance to a particular time of life;
7. Preciousness, that is, the suppression of all natural pleasure and the so-called intermediates;

8. A mystical confusion of nature and grace in the conception of an essential part of man which is pure and good in itself even before rebirth;

9. The annihilation of the so-called *subsidia religionis*, i.e. the outward and visible Church, by devaluation of its symbols and ordinances, by the contestation of theological systems;

10. The fostering and acquittal of manifest enthusiasts;

11. The conception of an absolute perfection that is both possible and necessary, which leads to pride or despair;

12. The undertaking to improve not only people but the Church itself, that is, the desire to alter it;

13. The causing of manifest schisms.

All this may have been more or less accurately observed and rightly assessed; it is certain that points are seen here which should at any rate have been submitted to discussion before Pietism was simply accepted. Löscher presented them to his time for discussion in vain. He had a year-long feud on the matter with the Pietist faculty of Halle, especially with Professor Joachim Lange, in which human courtesy and indeed intellectual superiority were on his side. One of the gravest charges laid against him by the Pietist side in this dispute was that while he did not want to condemn Spener, he did not want to call him 'blessed' Spener. Still more significant is the fact that his standpoint was contested by Lange under the title of 'barbarism'. Löscher's *Quo ruitis?* was in vain; his standing in the Church and theology that of a lost position. But in the history of theology it is not success, but the superiority of a viewpoint, that is decisive. And one certainly cannot deny that to Löscher.

We enter a line more typical of the period with the rather older Johannes Franz Buddeus (1660-1727), professor in Jena from 1705. All the good properties of the theologian of this period must have been united in this man: warm personal piety, broad historical erudition, an open mind for the needs of practical theology, pedagogy and pastoral care, a resolute will to do them justice in any circumstances. It was primarily Pietism, the form of the spirit of the new time, to which Buddeus proved himself to be open—in contrast to Löscher, in a fundamentally uncritical way. Polemic against the theoretical subtleties of the old controversial theology, warnings against the separation of life and doctrine, *credenda* and *agenda*, admonitions to the *praxis pietatis* permeate the whole of his dogmatics (*Institutiones Theologiae dogmaticae*, 1724). If Hollaz had still concluded the treatment of each individual *locus* with a prayer, Buddeus has in the same place an admonition to grasp the particular Christian truth vigorously and make it fruitful. There is a quite essential theoretical background to this emphasis in his writings. In his view, the Christian truth as a whole and in its individual details is necessary to faith not as a revealed truth, but as one which leads to our salvation. The reality of the salvation that has been received, the reality of the man who is to be renewed through faith, is the centre towards which the attention of this theologian is directed, and it also, in his view, forms the criterion for the greater or lesser worth of the revealed truth.

With this approach, the decisive step into the new time has been taken. Its revolutionary significance hardly appears with Buddeus. He is conservative in background and by inclination, and externally his dogmatics seldom cross the line of orthodoxy, and even then only with care. But behind the recognition of the reality of the religious man which is so characteristic of him, there is no mistaking his insight into the possibilities of man in general. So in Buddeus there is at least no failure to note that the introduction of the new criterion involves a new assessment not only of human reason under grace, but also of natural human reason. He may declare with the severity of old orthodoxy that no so-called natural knowledge of God can help a man towards his salvation. But he also thinks that it, and therefore human reason, is capable of distinguishing between true and false revelation. Does that not evidently mean the recognition that reason has a character that not only serves, but controls faith or revelation? Is this not secretly to introduce a general religious truth that is perceptible by all men, by virtue of which man can distinguish between revelation and non-revelation and therefore by virtue of which he is in principle in control of revelation? Do not reason and revelation stand side by side, as a result, as competing sources of knowledge? Can the possibility be avoided that others will come who will make more energetic use than Buddeus feels to be right of this discriminatory capacity assigned to reason and of the exalted position consequently ascribed to men? One can see the root and the significance of the shift in theological epistemology that takes place here. With the Pietists, Buddeus allows justification to issue in a work that takes place within man and thinks that in conversion he can establish certain '*actus paedagogici*' independent of the work of the Holy Spirit. Against the background of such a doctrine of grace his epistemology must become what it did become.

Buddeus—'the good Buddeus' (Gass III, 125) thought that he must join the side of the Pietists in their dispute with Wolff. In so doing he won no laurels. Could it be otherwise? And can one be surprised to meet soon afterwards, on the side of and in the steps of his opponent Wolff, men of a habitus and concern scarcely different from his own? In the dispute of the Pietists with Löscher, too, Buddeus was essentially on the side of the Pietists. Here he certainly could not have taken any other course. But in the dispute with Wolff he could without doubt have taken other action. For the juxtaposition of reason and revelation on the same level, which can already clearly be seen in his writings, and the concealed advantage which is given to the former as judge of the latter, later became typical of the attitude of the theologians who no longer fought against Wolff, but joined his side, most of whom were no less concerned for orthodoxy than Buddeus. In the same way, the Pietists were misunderstanding themselves when they thought that they had to fight against Wolff.

Close to Buddeus stands his friend Christoph Matthias Pfaff (1686-1760), professor and chancellor in Tübingen from 1714 to 1756, who spent the end of his life in Giessen. We have already considered him in discussing the question of Church and state in his time. He was one of the great travellers of his day and a historian of wide learning; from a human point of view, however, his figure does not stand out as clearly as that of Buddeus (the forged Irenaeus fragments!). United with Buddeus in his negations of old orthodoxy and in his practical concerns, he differed from him in that his interest was directed more towards the enlightened than the pietistic elements of the Christian teaching of his time. One can certainly feel onself in the presence of a theologian who still wants to be orthodox but who also has an affinity with the Pietists when one hears Pfaff's praise of his own time: 'The supreme blessedness and excellence of the times in which we live consists in the fact that the prejudices which arise from an excessive reverence for human authority have been removed and the free arts and sciences, with the help of excellent people, who accept the truth into their hearts and are thus endowed with special insight and learning, are clothed in a new dress. All of philosophy and the so-called superior faculties, and criticism, morality, history, all learning, all science, has thrown off its old dress and presents itself now in a finer and more excellent state.' 'As we see, we live in a time that is distinguished by a special divine guidance of the human understanding and of all the sciences, as the old pattern and the inherited prejudices are thrown aside and everywhere men buy eye-salve so that they can see the truth plainly and clearly before their face, indeed as within twenty or thirty

years there has been so much improvement even in religious understanding.'[1] Again, one seems already to be hearing Lessing and Kant
when Pfaff can give the instruction:'Open your eyes and see whether
the matter is as it is presented to you, and see that you plant such a
love of truth in your heart that you value this above all things and do
not exchange it for all the goods in the world' (p. 29). His doctrine of
the control of reason over revelation is therefore this: 'The light of
nature goes still further. It also discloses to me the true characteristics
of this revelation. No revelation is true unless it accords with the light
of nature and extends it. No revelation is true which conflicts with
itself. A true revelation must glorify my God and all his properties, his
wisdom, his omnipotence, his holiness, his righteousness, his goodness,
etc., and show me a true and certain way which will tear me away from
the curse and the servitude of sin and implant in my soul a divine power
to do good and unite me with God, my highest good. Accordingly a
true revelation must prove itself to be such in my heart by a divine
power and conviction that I clearly feel. And if this is still further
confirmed as being divine by infallible wonders and by prophecies of
the future which are clearly fulfilled, and by other such characteristics,
there is no further challenging its truth. They are clear truths that the
light of nature teaches and in so doing leads me on and makes me curious
to seek and search out such a revelation and accordingly to prove the
true religion' (p. 219). Here everything is said in a more original way
and with more involvement and therefore more plainly and clearly
than in Buddeus, and if even in Pfaff there is no breakthrough beyond
the carefully conservative position of Buddeus and a similar relationship to Pietism, it was not only the greater awareness that this man had
of the world and his broader horizons which kept him from joining
his friend's imperceptive and necessary struggle against Wolff. The
only question to be put to him is why he did not go a few steps further.
But one can ask this question of all these theologians in vain. They
wanted to be 'reasonably orthodox', and they were, as they have
rightly been termed, 'theologians of transition'.

Before we pursue the sequence of German Lutheran theologians
further, we include at this point three Reformed theologians, also a
group of Swiss friends, contemporaries of Buddeus and Pfaff and
therefore very much akin to them.

Samuel Werenfels (1657-1740), professor in Basle, is to be regarded
above all as a monumental exponent of that esoteric tradition of the

[1] Cf. also 'S. Werenfels und die Theologie seiner Zeit', *EvTh* III, 1936, 180–203.

spirit, conditioned equally chthonically, in which theology was almost always done in the Basle of Erasmus and Oecolampadius, and probably will continue to be done until the Last Judgment. The Basle theologian who represents this spirit is from the start and in all essentials conservative, a basically shy man of the *quieta non movere*, and that will always emerge somewhere in his person. At the same time, however, he has his secret, almost sympathetic delight in the radicalism and the extravagances of others, e.g. of all kinds of excited foreigners, whom from David Joris to Nietzsche and Overbeck he has far from reluctantly welcomed within his walls for the contrast they provide. While finding them frightfully interesting, however, he will hesitate to make them his own. A so to speak inborn, mildly humanistic scepticism inoculates him against Catholicism and too strict an orthodoxy. A practical wisdom acquired by careful perception protects him from too great digressions to the left. So he will settle somewhere in the middle of these extremes, perhaps quietly devoting himself to a little freethinking, perhaps equally quietly indulging in a little pious enthusiasm, while outwardly in all circumstances presenting the picture of a sound union of freedom and moderation, outwardly in all circumstances affirming and striving for nothing impractical, assuming ironically the presence of eccentricity in instances of excessive insistence on principle, always inclined to seek the heart of all discussions in a mere dispute about words, victorious in the method of always leaving the first and last words to others and thus thinking one's own thoughts without having openly compromised oneself in action.

Thus, too, was Samuel Werenfels. He was an excellent representative of the sort of theologian a man naturally is in Basle, so to speak predestined for the theological movement that occupies us here. He seems to have inherited from his father, the distinguished Peter Werenfels, a fear of the Helvetic Formula of Consensus of 1675 which in Basle was shaken off again after a short interval, and thus of the orthodoxy of the old school—from which he could never detach himself. We recall his wise couplet about the Bible, of which every man is accustomed to make what seems best to him. This jest, however, did not of course have anything to do with his natural respect for the holy book. He, too, accepted dogma as valid, at least on the whole, in its principal concern, and around it he wanted to gather theologians and the community. But what was this principal concern? That part of the Bible and of dogma, of course, which related to practice and could be translated into practice. For him, practice was the fulfilling of the will of God, which is easy because, in his commandments, God requires no more of us than is possible. This is where his heart beat. In him one feels that existing dogma, like the pillars of a not very good piece of architecture, certainly seems to be bearing something, but is in reality bearing nothing, while wanting to be a sort of necessary, honourable requisite. No wonder, then, that he could talk so freely and energetically about the empty logomachy, the verbal quarrelling of past theological epochs; for him, what was struggled over so vigorously was really nothing but a verbal quarrel. No wonder, too, that he could imperceptibly manage to bring the controversy in the early Church over the Trinity into this category. No wonder that he could say, to urge men to exert their own strength, that they should not be afraid of seeming to encourage Pelagianism. His doctrine of grace, which of course he wanted to be regarded as anything but Pelagianism—he conceived of it and developed it as an offer of union to Lutheran theology—looked somewhat like this: grace is certainly an independent power which man can neither enlarge nor constrict, the effective principle of penitence and faith. But by divine ordinance certain preparatory means precede its working, which man can use in better or worse ways. And God can and will, as a rule, take account of this distinction in his apportioning of grace, remaining equally true to his righteousness and his freedom. In this way Werenfels could assert in one breath both the unconditioned character of grace and the conditions attached to it.

He understood the *testimonium spiritus sancti* to be the perception by the reason of the outward and inward criteria of the truth of Holy Scripture. To this day it is not clear how this man also came to be actively involved during 1729-30 in a heresy trial which caused a considerable stir in the Basle of his time and in a wider Protestant public, the proceedings against the biblical textual critic J. J. Wettstein. It is equally remarkable that Zinzendorf, who often travelled to Basle at that time, believed that he could count Werenfels more or less among his followers, rhymed Werenfelsis with *Deo Gloria in Excelsis* and dedicated a memorial to him after his death: 'Dr Samuel Werenfels, sometime *Summus theologus* in Basle, a most respected and blessed man, was remembered with some sorrow by Ludwig von Zinzendorf, *Fratrum episcopus*, who bore witness at his grave to the place that belongs to the Lamb in theology.' It is certain that at sixty years of age and concerned for the salvation of his soul, Werenfels withdrew from his profession and his ministry and in so doing, without doubt through real personal necessity, performed an act which could only be understood in the light of the Pietism of the time. What he really was, orthodox, Pietist, man of the Enlightenment, or something of all of them, even all of them at the same time, is a mystery that he took with him into the grave, like more than one citizen of Basle. 'They became modern as though in their sleep', said Wernle of Werenfels and his like. One might also say that, measured by the theological wakefulness of the Reformation and even the seventeenth century, they slept and in so doing had become modern as a matter of course.[1]

Alongside Werenfels belongs the figure of Jean Frédéric Osterwald (1663-1747), which has more distinct outlines. He was pastor in Neuenburg, which called him its second Reformer after Farel. Above all he was a churchman of such great style that, as often happens to men of this type, he appeared quite soon to posterity as a churchman of the old style, though he was no more such a man than any of the other theologians who occupy us here. With his considerable interest in liturgy, he gave his church and French-speaking Protestantism in general a new and enriched liturgical order. He re-established and reordered church discipline. The foundation of the theological faculty at Neuenburg goes back to him. He was the author of a new and widely circulated French translation of the Bible. As a result of this and his writing *Traité des sources de la corruption*, together with his catechism which appeared in 1702 and was also translated into German, and finally his *Compendium Theologiae Christianae* which appeared in 1739, he won a reputation which went far beyond the boundaries of his homeland.

We can best get some idea of who he was and where he stood from some of the details of his catechism. He, too, presents the strange phenomenon that while the hands are the hands of Esau, the voice is that of Jacob; in other words, the dogma stands and is held to be valid essentially in its old extent and wording, yet it is presented in a context and with a stress that tend to make its meaning questionable and therefore its validity dubious. Merely from its external appearance, everything seems to want to fall apart in this catechism: as an introduction we have an outline of the biblical story from creation to the content of the Christian religion as it was taught by the apostles. There then follow a first part consisting of the doctrines of the Christian religion and a second, very much larger, part presenting the duties of life, which are made to include—among other things (but only among other things: one can see clearly how the traditional form is not able to embrace the fullness of what the author has to say here)— the Ten Commandments, the Lord's Prayer and the sacraments. The

---

[1] J. G. Walch, *Historische und theologische Einleitung in die religiösen Streitigkeiten welche sonderlich ausser der evangelisch-lutherisch Kirche entstanden*, 1733-6, I, 549.

first section, leading up to an explanation of the creed, takes the following form. First there is a discussion of 'religion in general', how it is the most necessary subject of knowledge because it is the only one that can make us completely happy by comforting us in tribulation, redeeming us from sin and the anguish of death, and assuring us eternal blessedness. But knowledge of religion would not make us happy if it did not bring the fear of God and piety about in us. Its basis is faith in the one God, i.e. in an infinite and perfect Spirit who created the world and on whom all depends. We know of him (1) through the light of reason (in that it indicates to us the necessity for a first cause of all things and, in view of the construction of the world, an infinite power, wisdom and goodness); (2) through the promptings of conscience, which point us to a supreme and most powerful judge; (3) through Holy Scripture, of which Osterwald, however, can only say that God has given himself to be known 'most clearly and most perfectly' in it—though we are not given any principle on the basis of which this third source is so far superior to the two others. The author tells us that Holy Scripture is necessary for us because of human ignorance and corruption. That is all that we are told. We have to believe that Holy Scripture is true and that God is its author. The proof for this is the fact that things—especially miracles and predictions that are fulfilled later—are to be found in it which evidently cannot come from man, but only from God. Holy Scripture, recognized as an authority by such an insight, is the guideline of what we must believe and do for blessedness. The Christian religion which it presents teaches us faith in the true God and in the Lord Jesus Christ. In a remarkable fashion, Osterwald now remarks that the Christian religion has two main parts, faith and duties. Faith, of which the first part of the catechism is to treat, is the firm conviction of those truths which God has revealed to us in his word. The foremost of these truths is that Jesus Christ is the Son of God and the saviour of the world, that he died for our sins and thus has obtained eternal life for those who have true faith. But it is most clearly to be seen whether a man has true faith from his performance of good works.

These examples may suffice. It should also be mentioned that the second moral part of this catechism bears witness in all manner of ways to the experience and common sense of the author, as to his warm feeling for the Church. But the firmer the ground one feels under one's feet, the more one notices how in the exposition of the creed and in that remarkable apologetic that precedes it one is walking on sheer snow bridges; in other words, one is repeatedly getting answers which are given with great assurance and which sound quite respectable at first hearing, but to which one cannot pose any counter-question unless one wants to fall into the abyss. While one recognizes the serious and the admirable disposition which is expressed in this catechism, it seems almost incredible that such a textbook could acquire almost canonical status in its sphere for decades, as the supreme practical instruction in Christianity—in comparison with the supposedly intellectual catechisms of Geneva and Heidelberg. A second surprising thing is that it was the church of Neuenburg, teaching and being governed in the spirit of Osterwald, that came to hold to regular heresy trials shortly after his death: one in 1760 against Ferdinand Olivier Petitpierre, pastor in La Chaux-de-Fonds, who denied that the torments of hell were eternal (in connexion with this trial Frederick the Great, whose governor had to yield to the clergy and citizens of Neuenburg and have Petitpierre condemned, uttered the *bon mot*: 'If his subjects in Neuenburg were so anxious to be damned eternally, they could be as far as he was concerned'); the other against no less an opponent than Jean-Jacques Rousseau, who had settled in Motiers (Val de Travers) in 1762, for his attacks on the proof from miracle which was still indispensable for rationalist orthodoxy. It is really hard to see the inner legitimation of the church of Osterwald for introducing these trials. No wonder, then, that after a few decades the Osterwald catechism and the whole approach of Osterwald was felt to be much too orthodox and that for its own part it took on the character of a good old time of the fathers, whose ideals could no longer be maintained.

The third member of the alliance to be mentioned here is Jean Alphonse Turrettini (1671-1737), professor in Geneva. He is different from his friends and from other men of this disposition in being clearly less directly and less positively interested in the moralistic side of concern for or understanding of Christianity. As a consequence, with him there emerge even more clearly two formal concerns that might be put under the headings of apologetic and tolerance. One can and one must (this is the common element designated by these two terms) describe Christianity (which for Turrettini, too, is made up of two parts, principles of faith and of life) in such a way that it seems to modern man to be true. For apologetic to be possible there must be tolerance. And because tolerance is possible, apologetic, too, can be possible. For Turrettini the two things are very closely connected: eagerness to demonstrate that Christianity commends itself to human reason and the degree to which this is so, and eagerness for a reduction of the

articles of faith to those statements that reason, whether it has discovered them itself or received them from revelation, cannot properly
refute. It is again the spirit of a humanity that is in its way fine, lively
and sensitive that we see at work in Turrettini's writings. In this spirit
we see him active now as a liberator of the church of Calvin from the
exclusiveness of Calvinistic scholasticism as cultivated even by his
father, now as an advocate of the same church in the forum of modern
education and morality. Again there is in fact hardly any perceptible
break from dogma, even from Calvin's dogma of predestination, except
that what is in fact a completely different theological attitude is betrayed in a certain blunting and softening of its cutting edge. This
attitude manifestly consists in the fact that dogma is regarded and
treated as a venerable form of doctrine, but one that is no longer
binding on the theologian. Therefore the theologian or the Church
can and must defend dogma. And therefore the theologian or the
Church can and must be tolerant and advocate tolerance. Doctrinal
views even about the loftiest questions can and must be defended like
all human opinions; they cannot and may not be taken as absolutes.

If dogma, and in dogma Christianity, is really an academic opinion,
then one cannot do otherwise than regard the concerns of a Turrettini
on both fronts as very appropriate and praiseworthy. But the strange
thing is that he does not seem to have noticed that between himself
and his father and the whole of the past there is a quite fundamental
difference of opinion about this presupposition, and perhaps more than
a difference of opinion. On the one hand the inability for apologetic
and on the other hand the notorious intolerance of earlier times had
their root in constraints imposed by the subject-matter, in a quite
different conception of the relationship between reason and revelation
or their nature, and not just in an aberration of the seventeenth century. Once these constraints had fallen away it was easy for the younger
Turrettini to deliver his defensive addresses against atheists, naturalists
and sceptics and, as he did, to demonstrate on a couple of pages that
the dissent between Reformed and Lutherans over eucharist, Christology and elective grace was so superficial and easy to remove that the
union was really no more than a matter of good will. As though through
a miracle, with Turrettini theology seems all at once to have become
a business which would be very easy to settle on all sides if men would
only condescend to use the intellectual instruments to hand with moral
insight and goodwill, both of which were equally attainable. The
characteristics of the fundamental articles of Christianity are that they
are quite definitely manifest to us through reason and grace and are

completely adapted to our capacity for receiving them. They are *clara, popularia a scholae tricis salebrisque aliena: in simplicitate fides*, as Hilary had already put it. Moreover they are not numerous: *numero pauca*. They can be recognized by the fact that they necessarily strike us in Holy Scripture through their regular occurrence. And they all have a direct *usus ad pietatem*. How then could they not be defended, and how could intolerance be a Christian possibility? If Christianity is really such a simple matter, then in fact it must be evident to every man, so a man cannot refuse a brotherly hand because of secondary differences of opinion. It is really all so simple, if the theologian, i.e. man, is entitled to make it simple. That he is so entitled is the great discovery that was made by Turrettini and his learned colleagues near and far as true children of their time. That they by-passed dogma as a whole without having to dispute it is, in view of this discovery, a fortuitous and historically comprehensible piece of leeway that the following period made up soon enough.

Returning to Germany, we must first make brief mention of Johann Georg Walch (1693-1775), professor in Jena, a worthy man in his way. He was the son-in-law of Buddeus and like him was not averse from Pietism, but perhaps a little more restrained towards it. For him, too, it was characteristic to combine teaching and life, revelation and reason, but a greater hesitation in the application and the mutual correlation of these concepts is unmistakable when we set him along-side the three Swiss whom we have just been considering. This may have something to do with the direction of his interest, which is purely historical. Walch is one of the fathers of modern church-history writing, author of a well-known edition of Luther which has been much used right up to a recent German-American new impression, author of an account of the 'religious disputes' from the Reformation down to his own time and editor of a whole series of other sources and pieces of research. In contrast to Turrettini his account of the Lutheran-Reformed controversy ends with the words: 'If it is true that the differ-ence in doctrine between us and the Reformed is a fundamental one, it follows that there is no chance of establishing a church peace between the Protestants, because the best ground on which it might be estab-lished is absent, and without it no other means are adequate.'[3] There was no lack of attacks against Walch from the Pietists. One can perhaps say no more of him than that with his strivings that were so sym-pathetic in human terms, to do justice to everyone and to damp down the passions of past struggles as much as possible, he furthered the relativism against which he fought in principle. This could be said in even stronger terms of his son, Christian Wilhelm Franz Walch (1726-84), who was a church historian in Göttingen.

Much more characteristic of the course of development is the figure of the famous Johann Lorenz von Mosheim (1694-1755), professor in Helmstedt and from 1747 chancellor and professor in the newly-founded University of Göttingen. He, too, owes his reputation primarily to his concern with church history. Unlike the two Walchs, however, he went beyond exact and complete assembling of material to historical synthesis, to the demonstration of lines and connexions. Does not something of what was later called 'historical vision' appear in what Mosheim said on one occasion in a sermon: 'The history of mankind might almost be called a history of the struggle between the love of God and the aberration of man, and this world a battlefield on which the mercy of the Most Highest and the selfishness of man, the faithfulness of God and the unfaithfulness of his children, seek to wear out and conquer each other' (Gass III, 210)? And if, according to the older Walch, history-writing still maintained a clear, albeit loose, connexion with the traditional task of theological polemic, with the defence of the Lutheran Church against Papists, Reformed, heretics and atheists, we are unmistakably led up to a higher point of view when Mosheim's *Kirchengeschichte des Neuen Testamentes* (Church History of the New Testament) (1726) begins with the definition that church history is 'a clear and correct narration of the external and internal events in the society of Christians, presented in such a connexion of what has happened with its causes that we can see divine providence in its foundation and sustenance, and can become wiser and more pious.' Three things are worth noticing here for the progress that they reveal:

1. The information that church history is to be concerned with the 'society of Christians' founded and sustained by divine providence, and therefore not with the confessional Church or the 'true' Church in Arnold's sense;

2. The announcement that by means of a pragmatic combination of the traditional historical facts as causes and effects the foundation and sustaining of this society by 'divine providence' is to be made clear;

3. The announcement of aim: such insight is so that 'we may become wiser and more pious'.

Who is a man and where does he stand if he is in a position to regard the history of the Church at a stroke as the history of a 'society' and is in a position to investigate it? If he feels capable of demonstrating the working of divine providence in this society by means of a wise synthesis? If he is confident that the result of this work is capable of making us wiser and more pious? Of course Mosheim also knows and acknowledges revelation, but what is the meaning of revelation if it now seems to be taken up and drowned in the more comprehensive concept of a providence which is in the direct view of the historian (i.e. not in the Church, in hearing what the Church hears, but in contemplating the Church)? And what can the heralded wisdom and piety have to do with revelation if it is notoriously such 'insight' that is capable of making men wise and pious? Is not the superior unitary view of Christian matters that clearly wins the field with Mosheim purchased at too high a price in that the concepts of revelation, Church, faith, which belonged together for the old theologians and even for Walch—because they all derived from God—threaten here to fall apart so wretchedly, as we see revelation and reason, faith and life fall apart with others and, of course, with Mosheim himself?

We should note as a symptom of this new beginning of historical theology that what had already been heralded with C. M. Pfaff takes up the greatest space in Mosheim: the discovery that since then and up to our own day has blinded so many eyes, the discovery of Hellenism and Greek speculation in the church fathers and in the dogma of the third and fourth centuries. Its presence was rightly detected and its significance seen by Mosheim and still more in the nineteenth century, but it was also senselessly misunderstood. Things could not be otherwise: when a man was in fact philosophizing where he intended to theologize, he could no longer grasp and understand that others had perhaps in essence been theologizing where they seemed only to be philosophizing.

As a control we shall also take a look at Mosheim's ethics, which he began to publish in 1737 under the title *Sittenlehre der heiligen Schrift* (The Moral Doctrine of Christian Scripture). The spirit of this extensive work, completed by Mosheim's pupil Johann Peter Miller (1725-89), already says much about his disposition. Its first part deals with the inner holiness of the soul, specifically with: (1) the state of the nature, i.e. the natural corruption, of man; (2) the means of moving from the state of nature to the state of grace, i.e. of repentance; (3) the state of grace. The second part deals with the external sanctification of life and specifically with: (1) the general duties of all Christians: towards God, towards the neighbour and towards themselves; (2) the duties incurred by the Christian in his particular situation in marriage,

family, home, state and church. One can see that here, too, almost
everything is abstracted that can be abstracted and has repeatedly
been extracted in subsequent ethics: inner holiness and outward sanctification, man as sinner and man under grace, the Christian as himself
and the Christian in his situation (individual and social ethics, as it
would be termed today), and finally God, the neighbour and the self.
But can things be otherwise when Mosheim has assured us in the very
first paragraphs of his work that the 'moral doctrine of Holy Scripture'
is a 'collection made in the light of Scripture and of reason of those
doctrines and truths of Holy Scripture that instruct men how they can
move from the state of sin and natural unrighteousness into the state
of grace and peace with God and must accordingly prove and bring
to light their indwelling faith and renewal through outward good
works'? The internal collapse of the Christian principle that is visible
in this formula can evidently only draw other collapses after it. What
does 'made in the light of Scripture and of reason' mean? Mosheim
explains it in the following way (I, §3). Holy Scripture is the source of
all moral doctrine. Sound reason is certainly not excluded, but one
must be careful that spiritual moral doctrine does not become a sort
of reasonable wisdom. By reason, Mosheim understands partly the
capacity of man's own soul to seek truths and pass judgment on supposed truths, partly the embodiment of what man has already found
to be real and unassailable truth by means of this capacity. Now it is
not the task of reason in moral doctrine to attempt of its own accord
an outline of life and its duties or to identify the natural law and the
precepts of Holy Scripture without further ado, so that the one could
be explained from the other. Nor is it to qualify the divine laws in
accordance with human capability or to regard innate or acquired
natural virtues straightaway as Christian, or to want to improve the
soul with its own reasons and proofs. The place of this reason is rather
to serve to explain Holy Scripture by means of its rules, to describe
the duties, virtues and vices enumerated in Holy Scripture exactly,
clearly and plainly. The Spirit of the Lord has 'not allowed all and
every truth to be presented in Scripture which a reasonable man
can recognize without obscurity through his own reflection from the
light of nature' (Preface). Especially is it 'the occupation and the work
of sound reason' to derive specific duties from the general laws of God,
'to interpret what he has said in general with specific reference to itself
and others'. It also has light enough to demonstrate and to prove the
righteousness, the fairness, the wisdom, the excellence, the usefulness
of the laws of the Lord. It teaches us about the psychological nature

of man and, finally, it is the competent judge for distinguishing weaknesses of the understanding from true illumination, selfish practices from the true fear of God, day dreams from the power of God, changes of nature from the effects of grace.

The purpose with which we see Mosheim here loading the two pans of his scales carefully enough is tolerably clear: he entrusts a great deal to revelation and rather less to reason, but always something, and in proportion to this quantitative relationship he wants to present a believing rational or a rationally believing doctrine. But which of the qualifications on the one hand would not be apt to come into collision with one or more of the qualifications on the other? What hindrance can there be to reversing the quantitative relationship in favour of reason? And will much remain of faith for long once it is on the decline contrary to Mosheim's purpose? These questions recur in a sharper form once one considers Mosheim's hermeneutical rules (I, §4). In exegesis, we hear, we must never lose sight of the basic truths of the Christian teaching of sin, grace, Christ, etc. But we can and must often make use of sound reason as a guideline. And such an explanation of Holy Scripture could by no means be right and true if it ran counter to the concepts held by sound reason of the duties of man, if for example it represented an attack on the security of legitimately owned property or a questioning of the law of self-defence. Should it not become painfully clear that precisely this third rule, despite of and in its negativity, is the only unequivocal element in this instruction? What if someone were now to come who in addition to the right of property and self-defence also counted the autonomy of thought and conscience among the reasonable duties of man and thus made the second rule an exclusive 'must' instead of a 'can and must', thus deleting and removing the basic truths to which the first rule refers? Finally, when Mosheim (I, §9) suggests that the advantage of a spiritual moral doctrine over a merely reasonable one is that while it recognizes the natural law, by virtue of revelation it gives it a clearer and more certain basis, that it also gives a more complete description of the content of the good, that it can show more effective motives and reassurances—how many people, and for how long, will feel that these comparative 'advantages' are credible and acknowledge them? Cannot one already hear cracks all over this structure? Will it be possible to stop a collapse once it becomes clear from one side or the other that a teaching that lays claims to divinity, whether it has the credentials of revelation or reason, may not in any event raise such a claim, whether with more or less earnestness and power, against another which is to be assessed in merely quantitative terms? And will this recognition not inevitably break through, the recognition that revelation and reason, cannot be set off against one another without damage being done to one or the other, despite the attempts in this earlier theology of the eighteenth century, from Buddeus to Mosheim?

The philosophy and theology of Christian Wolff (1679-1754), which we must now consider as a clear turning-point in the development that we are examining, both held up and prepared for the change that had to come. For Wolff, too—and this is the delaying factor—knowledge from reason and knowledge from revelation formed one quantum set alongside another, except that now instead of being related as a narrower sphere to a wider, they are related as two spheres of equal size, mutually overlapping at a particular point. Two spheres of equal size—this prepares for the turning-point. For this means that the two require and supplement one another so that fundamentally the one knowledge is completely and totally also that of the other: reason is also revealed in its own way and revelation is rational in its way, the only difference being that each has its own character. From the point of view of reason some things, namely the whole field of mathematics and the natural sciences, are only to be known through reason itself, albeit understood as divine revelation; some things are to be known through both reason and revelation, among them the knowledge of God as the creator and ruler of the world (developed by philosophers from the principle of the sufficient cause and the idea of the most perfect being, and therefore to be proved cosmologically and teleologically), together with moral freedom and the immortality of the soul, things which are also to be understood by theologians as scriptural truth; finally, some things are beyond reason (though not therefore unreasonable or even contrary to reason) and can be proved only by revelation: to these belong the particular mysteries of the Christian faith, the Trinity, Christology, the doctrine of grace, the working out of which is the special task of the theologian.

From a theological point of view, what was this but a great contemporary repristination of the outline of the approach of Thomas Aquinas? It is really no coincidence that the possibility of a transition to Catholicism does not seem to have been completely out of the question for this philosopher, who was one of the most influential, if not one of the greatest, philosophers of the Enlightenment. And one would have thought that this affinity, the picture of this complete stabilization of the relationship of reason and revelation, which was quite impossible from the perspective of Reformation thought, must have awoken Protestant theology from its sleep and shown it the direction in which it was steering with such confused treatment of the relationship. But of course, after what we have heard, we could not expect this generation to have seen the enemy with which it was confronted in the modern garb of Wolffianism. Its spirit, and thus also the spirit of the age-old enemy, which took new shape in it, was far too much the spirit of the generation. This generation must have felt far too much that Wolff's system was a fortunate solution to its innermost difficulties, the problems with which it was plagued in this time of transition. And so it happened that there came about a useless war and a still more useless peace between theology and Wolffianism, both useless because they were both at a point where nothing essential was to be gained by either peace or war, whereas the real problem that one might feel to have been clearly displayed by Wolff remained unnoticed. As a result, it must be said that the only notable theological contribution of the whole of the period of Wolff was that the fever of Protestant theology rose a degree, with the inevitable prospect of a further rise, but that no crisis came about either for good or for ill.

The part of Wolff's system in which Protestant theology was interested both negatively and positively was, of course, that remarkable intermediary zone in which, according to Wolff, both reason and revelation may speak at the same time, saying the same thing with different words. Here, from the part of theology, one could either—and this was the significance of the dispute over Wolff that became so notorious and that at times took such a dramatic turn—take offence at certain philosophical positions of Wolff's and declare that they could never be reconcilable with those statements of revelation and the Christian faith that were supposed to be identical in content to them. In particular it was the treatment of the problem of freedom by Leibnitz and Wolff that was at issue here, together with the assertion made by Wolff (in accord with Thomas) of the impossibility of a proof for temporal beginning to the world and also with his doctrine of the relationship between body and soul explained by Leibnitz' example of two equal clocks wound up at the same time. The attacks which the theologians, Pietists to the fore, made against Wolff here did not run a victorious course and finally just faded out, evidently because in all these questions they were too much in harmony with their opponent. Furthermore, they were on a ground that *a priori* was unsuitable for theological argument, in that here partial success was only remotely within the realm of the possible. The only possibility would have been to attack the heart of Wolff's system as such, that is, his attempt to create a balance between revelation and reason. But if people could not, or would not, do this, it would probably have been wiser not to attack at all, for on the basis of this balance the theological concern that may have lain behind individual attacks could not be expressed or brought into effect.

Once again we have to pay our respects to V. E. Löscher, who not only criticized Wolff's system from within but also declared that it was very difficult for revealed religion to ally itself with any philosophy at all, least of all with one which claimed to be adequate to erect a construction of knowledge *a priori* or to understand everything from the principle of the sufficient ground (Gass III, 162). His voice rang out unheard. The merely internal criticism of the others had to come to nothing. Once men have sold their rights as firstborn for a mess of pottage, which is what the Pietists and the good Buddeus had done, they cannot expect still to enter upon the firstborn's inheritance. Those theologians therefore acted more wisely (unconsciously and, of course, only relatively so)—though they brought theology into still greater danger—who resolved not to go further into the problem of the smaller heresies of Wolff within that middle zone, but to rejoice that in all events: 1. in that middle zone, whatever doubts philosophy might introduce, it was clear that some statements might be asserted by both philosophy and theology without debate, which as a result seemed to gain for theology the significance of an assured minimum for existence or of a storm-free citadel; 2. beyond that middle zone there remained a sphere that was marked out and reserved by Wolff especially for revelation and thus for theology, for the investigation and presentation of which one could gratefully accept the help of the formal weapon of Wolff's logic.

The first of these two joys which Protestant theology allowed Wolff to prepare for itself resulted in a powerful resurgence of natural theology, which in orthodoxy and even in the earlier types of more modern theology had been forced into the narrowest limits and had in effect been made insignificant. Whatever might be the significance for salvation of the knowledge of God that was to be gained from pure reason—was it not something if the principal philosopher of Germany was heard to say so explicitly and to prove so consistently that there was indeed such a knowledge of God on the basis of pure reason? And how did the humanism of the time feel about the fact that it was the teleological argument, the proof of God from the relative perfection of the world, from its purposefulness, that together with the more abstract cosmological proof played the decisive *rôle* with Wolff! Here in particular the theologians and all kinds of theologically interested laity made their start, and here at the hands of well-meaning friends of God and nature began an astro-, pyro-, hydro- and litho-theology, together with a petino-, insecto- and even testazeo-theology, all with the aim of understanding the world as a great work of art and as the best-chosen expression of the necessary and the absolute, and therefore as the most perfect creation of the God who was perfect in himself, with an eternal omnipotence, wisdom and goodness.

As a sample here is a less well-known passage from *Irdisches Vergnügen in Gott* (Earthly Contentment in God) by the Hamburg senator Brockes, on the chamois:

> God has in the chamois' body
> given such facility,
> That they fear not fall or stumble
> and are glad where'er they be.
> For consumption is their tallow
> For the face their gall is good;
> Chamois' flesh is fine for eating,
> Cured is faintness by their blood.
> All their skin has many uses—
> From this beast does there not shine
> By the Almighty's power and goodness
> Something of his love divine?   (Wernle II, 227)

This is the way in which people took pleasure in the common alliance of philosophy and theology at that time, speaking in an existential way, speaking *ad hominem*, with the simple aim of removing prejudice. Why should that be described as apologetic in a derogatory sense? Why should it not also have been eristics in its own way?

The second joy prepared for theology by Wolff was the tranquil prospect to be enjoyed from his basic principle of the third area reserved for revelation which was not contrary to reason but was above reason, that of the specific Christian doctrine of salvation, of dogmatics in the narrower sense. This area, too, must have seemed desirably secure simply as a result of its obvious connexion with the ground common to philosophy and theology. In respect of this area, too, for example, the canon of purposefulness was valid in principle, so that it could be said not only that the statement 'There is a God' was a supremely necessary and useful truth in the world but also of the Christian revelation that it seemed desirable and beneficent on countless grounds (Gass III, 164). So theology applied itself to this its innermost sphere with new courage and new energy. There were now orthodox Wolffians, i.e. theologians who in the third area marked out by Wolff's system and by means of Wolff's logic set out to find a place for the dogmatics of the seventeenth century and to develop it afresh. We shall mention and describe some of the most important figures in this connexion.

There is a place here for Israel Gottlieb Canz (1690-1753), professor in Tübingen, who was particularly involved in a controversy with the scepticism of Pierre Bayle, above all in connexion with the thesis of the rationality even of revelation and the consequent insight that reason and revelation are equally bound up together and that as a result of this theology has relative independence. In 1728 he wrote the book *De usu Philosophiae Leibnitianae et Wolffianae in Theologia*.

There is also a place for Jakob Carpov (1699-1768), Rector of the *gymnasium* in Weimar, the real dogmatic theologian of the school— 'a new Quenstedt' (Gass III, 169). He was author of a *Theologia revelata methodo scientifica adornata* (1737-65), in which, as the title shows, he was able to demonstrate the whole of ancient dogma on the basis of revelation as clearly as the secular Wolffians by their attempts and achievements in their spheres with their principles and subject-matter. The only thing is that, as the title *Theologia revelata* shows, alongside revealed theology—but in the spirit of this school the fact is not a discredit but rather a support—there is also a *theologia naturalis*, with which it is in competition, and this competition sooner or later inevitably had to lead to further complications in a situation which for the moment seemed to have been clarified so well.

Here also belongs Siegmund Jakob Baumgarten (1706-57), from 1734 professor in Halle. The fundamental swing towards the Enlightenment, which seems to have held unbounded sway in what was once a citadel of Pietism for almost exactly a century (up to the call of Tholuck), can be dated from him. Baumgarten was also the dogmatic theologian (as far as I know the first) who gave this discipline the new name *Glaubenslehre* (Doctrine of Faith), though of course without the content that Schleiermacher gave to the term. Unlike Canz and Carpov he had wide historical interests and became the teacher of J. S. Semler, who edited his works after his early death. One need only read a few pages of this man to be transposed into the quite remarkable situation in which theology found itself after its peace—or its alliance —with Wolffianism. Baumgarten, too, is an orthodox Wolffian, i.e. in his writings there is hardly a perceptible trace of any criticism of dogma.

He is also said to have been a man of considerable personal piety. The Pietists lamented that his lectures and books were too much lacking in 'edification' and were full of cold 'subtleties', and the charge cannot be wholly rejected on the ground that this movement was content only with 'confused, indefinite, mystic and doleful' discourses and writings. In these outlines there are signs of a problem that even the present-day reader of Baumgarten cannot escape and that has a certain critical significance for the whole of this type of theological Wolffianism. Other enthusiastic hearers of Baumgarten—and there was no lack of these— praised him especially for the fact that his lectures could be written down so literally. This was what people liked: the sort of systematic definition, historical breadth, conceptual precision, didactic skill, sober matter-of-factness that can be found in the theological works of this man were certainly not found very often at an earlier stage, and perhaps ceased to be there later.

What is one to think of this matter-of-factness? Is it a credit to Wolffianism that it once more produced theology as a discipline in the old and venerable sense of the term? Or is this matter-of-factness, the freedom from all (and that means all) demonism, the tidiness with which so to speak a theological machine can be seen to work and to produce orthodox dogmatics point for point in a reasonably correct and yet reasonably contemporary form—is this not already something uncanny? Is it not strange that now something of the same thing is happening as was the subject of that passionate charge made by the eighteenth century against the seventeenth in this sphere: theology is being viewed as in essence an operation of understanding, necessarily developing on the basis of an exact knowledge of all orthodox authorities and heterodox counter-claims, on the presupposition of a dialectical key that would open every door? Was it not a disastrous consequence of Wolff's basic thesis about reason and revelation that with Baumgarten one catches sight of the possibility—in the subject-matter and not in the man himself—that theology could be done from revelation and allegedly on the basis of revelation, yet quite divorced from the event that bears this designation. There are also early orthodox dogmatic theologians, not Quenstedt, but for example J. F. König, of whose writings one can occasionally ask whether they really know what they are saying or whether some ghostly machine is not at work. But it can in no case be said of the old orthodox theologians that this possibility had a basis in their system. If one wanted to suppose that this was the case, one would have to accuse them of occasionally failing completely to understand their own principle. Here, however, the possibility lay in the system: if reason and revelation are set side by side in this stable and harmonious relationship, and revelation is still understood as an event, is it not in principle possible that revelation can be understood and interpreted completely on the analogy of reason: as the object of an *a priori* ability to know and a clearly defined *a posteriori* knowledge, an object which the person who is considering and interpreting need not approach in any different way from any other object? And is what can be considered and interpreted in this totally detached and cold-blooded, not to say frosty way, however orthodox the procedure, still to be called revelation? Will it be possible to carry through such a conception and interpretation? Dogma presented 'in a refrigerated state' (Gass III, 187) is perhaps no longer the dogma it sets out to be, however strict the presentation may be. Baumgartner died relatively young; through Semler we know that in private conversations he sometimes took a freer view than that presented in his writings (Gass III, 203). There is no mistaking that his matter-of-factness, which is so fine in itself, in a material and impersonal perspective, is connected with a loosening of the relationship between the theologian and theology, with a desperate rationalization of orthodoxy, as a result of which the latter could not continue for long. Wolff's orthodoxy was a colossus on feet of clay.

We also have to add that even the splendid optimism about the teleological proof for God and the confidence about the capacity of the middle zone had to have their natural limits. The optimism was, as is well known, shattered at the time of the Lisbon earthquake of 1755, which did not so much bring about the collapse of confidence throughout Christian Europe as bring it to light—in his *Poetry and Truth*, Goethe vividly described how this event destroyed his childhood religious feelings. So the Church found itself gradually faced with the necessity of protecting God in view of the imperfection of his world rather than praising him because of its perfection, a kind of apologetic for apologetic. From all this it seems that good Protestant theology had prescribed for itself a doctor whose treatment could prove impossible in the long run. From Wolff it had learnt—and this was certainly a good thing—that the claims of reason and of revelation were not two relative claims to be weighed up against each other, but claims which on either side are total and absolute. It had thought—and this was not a good thing—that it could combine these two absolute claims with one another by means of the usual trivial misunderstanding of the words of the Gospel: Render to Caesar that which is Caesar's and to God that which is God's. But the question had to be put, and was in fact put, whether the choice that had to be made was not to understand one of these claims as absolute and the other as relative. What has been said so far will have prepared us for the fact that if the question was put in this way, it could only be answered resolutely and still more resolutely in favour of reason.

The group of theologians with which we have to close our survey are known as 'neologists', the new men. It is, of course, no testimony to the profundity and acuteness of the historical self-understanding of the eighteenth century that this was the first point at which it believed an innovation was to be seen. And even in the well-known more modern accounts of the history of this period, like those of Troeltsch, Stephan, Hoffmann, Wernle and above all K. Aner,[4] there has in my view been insufficient awareness of the fact that the neology which is found so sympathetic does not stand out like an angel of light from the uniform darkness of the orthodoxy that preceded it, but developed in a very gradual way as a transition from earlier types of theology, types which one can only call rational or Wolffian 'orthodoxy' in jest. Did not Buddeus do more for the innovation with which we are concerned than the men who are now to be described in the usual way as neologists, whose merit (if it can be called that) ultimately was that they went a few more steps—though not very long steps—along the road opened up by Buddeus' dogmatics, which ascribed to reason the significance of a material criterion for revelation? True, even Buddeus did not invent it; he was simply drawing the systematic consequence of what, as we saw in chapter 3, was the new humanistic way of understanding the problem of theology as it presented itself to the whole of the eighteenth century. But was there not need of much more acuteness and courage at the beginning of the century than was required for the half-hearted pursuit of the same question which now, in the middle of the century (leaving aside the interlude with Wolff), bore the heretical or (in the judgment of those more recent writers) the honorific name of neology? How little have both the contemporary Pietists, orthodox rationalists and Wolffians, who used this name as a heretical name, and the present descendants of the so-called neologists, understood themselves in such a periodization!

In what does the progress of this 'neology' consist? I will answer the question with Aner's own words: 'The period of Wolffian conservatism, which applied the newly-won primacy of reason for the benefit of the traditional complex of revelation, was past. A new age was beginning

[1] K. Aner, *Die Theologie der Lessingszeit*, 1929.

that was not content with the logically mathematical possibility of conceiving of the content of revelation, but pushed this content on one side as contrary to reason' (pp. 245f.). The saga of neology, which Aner then goes on to tell, consists in the fact that its representatives now at last set to work not to deny revelation as such (that was a further step along the same course), but to attack the dogma handed down as revelation in a number of places and then ultimately to cut it down to the point at which what was still recognized as revelation had approximately reached the extent of what was thought to be secured as the rational truth of religion, namely to the ideas of God, of freedom or morality, and of immortality. For example, in striking battles more or less victorious struggles had been waged against the New Testament concept of demon-possession, against the Lutheran doctrine of the eucharist, against the authority of the symbolic books, against the eternity of the punishments in hell, against the devil, against satisfaction through the death of Christ, against supernatural grace and against predestination. And without public battles of any note, partly through silence, partly through denials, partly through reinterpretation, people had done away more or less energetically and completely with the inspiration of Holy Scripture, with the Trinity and particularly with the doctrine of the divinity of Christ, with original sin, with justification by faith alone, and of course with the virgin birth, the descent into hell, the resurrection and ascension of Christ and the rest of the biblical miracles, the Second Coming and the resurrection of the body. Augustine now had to be called 'the black-biled Augustine', because he had so little understood that man is fundamentally good (p. 162), and Irenaeus and Tertullian 'brainless chatterboxes and incorrigible sophists' (p. 229), while Christian antiquity and the Middle Ages had to be called 'dark ages' in toto, where 'ignorance, superstition and the restraint of conscience' obscured the divine form of religion (p. 296).

Now, what was fearful and what was heroic about that, once the older generation had made the main breach in asserting the right for 'reason' to have its say and after the Wolffians had made their own bold, but naturally unsuccessful, attempt for a while to keep the scales balanced. It was really no great matter—in the sphere of Protestantism where, unlike the equally neological Catholic system, there was no teaching office of the Church to keep this fatal balance artificially in equilibrium—to 'storm' (p. 270) positions in which no man could survive for long after what had happened earlier, i.e. because they could no longer be held after what Buddeus and his colleagues had conceded and surrendered.

Nor do we find anything extraordinary when we go on to consider the motives and the means of the neological criticism of dogma. What was it that made this generation think that those things which the Wolffians placidly designated as merely supra-rational, but not contrary to reason, were now in fact contrary to reason? It would be quite wrong to assume that now a generation had grown up that acted more strongly, more coolly, more logically and more consistently in applying the concept of modern science than Canz, Carpov and Baumgarten, and therefore found their way by intellectual means and on intellectual grounds to an insight into the impossibility of the Wolffian peace treaty. There is no question of that: Canz, Carpov and Baumgarten were the cold mathematical spirits, in this sense truly incisive modern spirits, who—the spiritual sons of Wolff and grandsons of Leibnitz—really had thought what was to be thought about theoretical questions of the world and their relationship to dogma, and yet wanted to be orthodox and were orthodox in their way. On the other hand, among the neologists, while there was more than one great scholar, remarkably enough, there was not a single systematic theologian who was remotely in the same class as the three Wolffians. J. F. W. Jerusalem, the man discovered and presented by Aner himself as the most representative figure in this movement, was a preacher and a writer of popular books on the philosopher of religion, to whom Gass, who was concerned simply with the history of theology, hardly devoted more than a couple of lines. The activity of J. J. Spalding and several other theologians who are named most often belongs in the same practical genus. In practice, perhaps their most effective man was a theological layman, albeit a widely read one, the bookseller, journalist and novelist F. Nicolai. Of course one finds strictly modern scholarship with the historians J. S. Semler, J. A. Ernesti, J. D. Michaelis, but remarkably enough, in their basic points of view these men are to be included among the neologists only with considerable qualifications and in Aner they do not get very good marks. In that case, however, what was the real motive force of neologistic criticism? To what gods had nine-tenths of the confessions of Luther and Calvin now all at once to be sacrificed? Why did Augustine now have to be 'black-biled', Irenaeus a chatterbox and Tertullian a sophist? It is easiest to answer this question with Aner's own words: 'It is typical of the neological stage of the German Enlightenment that it is determined by the needs of the soul. One cannot understand neology if one characterizes it in a predominantly intellectualistic way. Its criticism of dogma is not born of reason, but of ethical and personal needs.

Doubt is raised not by the compulsion to know in the searcher for truth but by the question of the value of traditional doctrines for practical piety. The questions of the time have now become what is needed for bringing up children and coping with distress, what leads to the moral transformation of life, what finds an echo in the religious sensibility of the man of the time. The strongest offence is taken to anything that does not seem to correspond with belief in the goodness of God, anything that is suspicious in its moral consequences, anything that does not satisfy the self-awareness of the growing generation' (p. 151). ' "Virtue", by which was understood a good-hearted, pure, active disposition, had become the object of general enthusiasm . . . in its rays a generation basked that was conscious of its moral powers. People reverenced it in others with tears of wonderment and praised themselves in that sublime hour' (p. 164). 'Neology comes from the same root as the "storm and stress". Long before the fever of Werther and the tears of Siegwart the genuine man of the Enlightenment had a superabundance of feeling aroused by Klopstock, similar to Pietism, partially deriving from it, yet different in nature from it' (p. 165). 'From the sphere of the eighteenth-century humanities deriving from psychologism was born the rejection of inherited dogmas, and significantly, first of all, of those dogmas that seemed to impair the value of man and the strivings upwards of morality' (p. 172). What is meant is the dogma of original sin. Of this in particular Aner says: 'Though they may have gone very different ways, all the spirits of the time from Goethe to Nicolai, from Herder to the simple country pastor, were agreed on condemning pessimism about sin and united in their optimistic faith' (p. 163).

Hinc illae lacrymae! So the neologists are by no means to be regarded as heroes of modern truthfulness in thought and knowledge. And if their transition to a material disputation of orthodoxy is to be reckoned a significant fact, then it is surely not to be termed a breakthrough of mathematical and scientific thought in a new way. If anything modern does break through—and that does happen here—it is the tears of the modern citizen touched by himself and his great, great morality, who now holds out this morality somewhat energetically as a principle of Christian faith and life. If this breakthrough is a serious matter, then, and only then, is the criticism of dogma by neology that broke through in the eighteenth century: this criticism of dogma which was taken over by the period of Goethe that followed, and also by Schleiermacher and more recent Protestant piety and theology down to our own days. What I mean is that precisely if one is told by a historian who is evidently as delighted over the matter as is Aner, how things really were at that time, one loses all pleasures in taking this matter seriously. What took place at the end of the seventeenth century and the beginning of the eighteenth was important, although at that point we are not dealing with either a Luther or a Copernicus. The Wolffian interlude is still more interesting and significant. But this third act is profoundly uninteresting, as in the end its sole significance is to have brought to light the real motives that were operative. If on this ground and in this sense people want to call it 'neology', innovation, then we may agree with them in so doing.

To conclude I shall now give an account of some of the characteristic individual figures in this theological trend.

Johannes Friedrich Wilhelm Jerusalem (1709-89), court preacher and abbot at Wolfenbüttel (father of the Karl Wilhelm Jerusalem whose tragic fate Goethe expressed poetically in his Werther), must have been a person in whom religious warmth, intellectual vigour and worldly assurance were combined in a way that made him not only suitable to be a much-admired spiritual adviser and pastor of the house of the Prince of Brunswick (he was the confirmation director of Karl Wilhelm Ferdinand of Brunswick, later renowned as a soldier), but also to be a spiritual centre and resting place for the rest of the neological movement in which in his later years he seems to have enjoyed the regard given to a patriarch. Interests in pedagogy and the national economy which he had brought back from a lengthy stay in England meant that he was also successfully active in this sphere. His best-known works are his collections of sermons which appeared in 1745 and his *Betrachtungen über die vornehmsten Wahrheiten der Religion* (Considerations on the Principal Truths of Religion) which appeared in 1768. For him revelation is a confirmation of natural religion, i.e. of the faith in one God that underlies all religions, a faith also in a providence at work in natural laws and in a more perfect life following our present existence. Revelation is related to this rational faith as a statement in physics is related to a mathematical statement, i.e. it is to be understood as being only relatively necessary, and has its sufficient ground not in itself but in God. From this there followed, for Jerusalem, the conception that became famous through Lessing, of a historical development of revelation by means of a divine plan of education which allowed the truth to become clearer stage by stage (*Vornehmste Wahrheiten* II, 623). From here it is again understandable that he could be seriously preoccupied with what he himself found to be the 'heretical' idea of a history of dogma with the purpose of demonstrating historically the 'true' statements of the Christian religion (Aner, pp. 145, 223). Wilhelm Münscher (1766-1814), professor in Marburg, was in fact the first of many to have written such a history of dogma. Starting from a criticism of the doctrine of original sin, Jerusalem seems only in his old age to have progressed to decisive christological negations: Jesus the redeemer as the teacher of the idea of the all-loving Father in place of the angry Jewish national god, his death as the presentation of sin in all its magnitude and as a proof of the supreme holiness and love of God—these tones, which have not died down even today, are those which took the place of the old dogma. His princess, the Dowager Countess Philippine Charlotte of Brunswick, set up a memorial for him in the convent church of Riddaghaus with the inscription: 'He laid out the first ground for the Enlightenment'.

We set alongside this very worthy and very serious man a very unworthy one, the notorious Karl Friedrich Bahrdt (1741-92), professor in Leipzig, Erfurt and Giessen, then Director of the *Philanthropinum* in Marschlins, then general superintendent in Durckheim a.d. Hard, then deposed and banished for heresy by the state High Court, then *Dozent* in Halle and finally an innkeeper there. Because of his not exactly exemplary way of life he has been called the Thersites, the Asasel, the *enfant terrible* of the Enlightenment. But on the other hand he was not a completely depraved subject; the one thing that one can disapprove of in him was the unquenchable and unquenchably self-conscious and optimistic cheerfulness with which he managed to meander through life as an unsurpassable artist, despite incessant, self-incurred drawbacks, and as a theologian to wage a hand-to-hand struggle against dogma and the Bible with the most primitive dialectic. On the other hand, one might ask of today's friends of neology, who would not regard him as a typical man of the Enlightenment: why now so moral? From a personal point of view it was certainly better that this man finally went over to the profession of refreshment. But in his cheerfulness, even as a caricature, was he not rather typical of the whole movement? In 1769 Bahrdt wrote a *Biblische Dogmatik*, in 1772-5 the *Neuesten Offenbarungen Gottes* (Newest Revelations of God), a paraphrase of the New Testament at which even Goethe laughed, in 1782 *Briefe über die Bibel im Volkston* (Letters about the Bible in a Popular Style), and in 1784 *Ausführung des Planes und Zwecks Jesu* (The Accomplishment of the Plan and Purpose of Jesus), a writing which nevertheless shows him to have been one of the first on the track of the so-called historical Jesus. As a taste of his style, I quote some of his New Testament paraphrases. Matthew 3.2: 'Improve yourselves! For

God is in the process of bringing into being a new religious society!';
Matt. 5.3: 'All is well for those who have little wish for this earth. For
them is the religion that comforts those who confess it for ever'; Matt.
5.4: 'All is well for those who prefer the sweet melancholy of virtue to
the teeming delights of vice' (Aner, p. 206).

In locating the persons and views of those who make up the main
body of the neologists, we must look somewhere in the centre between
Jerusalem and Bahrdt. We go on to mention some further representatives of this movement who in some way distinguish themselves from
the rest.

Johann Salomon Semler (1725-91), professor in Halle, proves to be
the most significant of the neologists because on the one hand his
desire for what they all want is perhaps the most profound and far-
reaching of them all, while on the other hand he wants the same thing
in quite a different way and consequently is to be reckoned among
them only dialectically, and with qualifications. Semler was completely
a Christian of his century—and this is made very plain indeed in his
work—in that he was resolved to unite Christianity with his own conception of morality. Again and again in his writings one comes across
the presupposition, taken for granted, of an 'essence' of Christianity,
which consists in an alteration of disposition, active improvement, the
confidence of faith and the welfare that derives from this, all coming
to men through Christ and the Holy Spirit. Salvation means moral
possession. But this modernistic religious pathos is held in check in
Semler by the still stronger pathos of the scientific historian of Christianity. In theory he wanted to know nothing of a natural, normal
religion, but in theory we can already find in him a conception that
was later taken up by Herder and Schleiermacher and then by the
whole of the nineteenth century, in contrast to the Enlightenment:
Christianity is a definite factor of history that has a definite effect. As
such, Christianity, with its historical concreteness, multiplicity and
inner variety interested him, although he personally understood by it
a quite definite moral possession. Theology is free critical investigation
of the total mass of traditional Christian material from the viewpoint
of divine bliss.

In that Semler's conception of this bliss is no different from that
of the other neologists and thus none other than the conception that
these had of a so-called natural religion, he doubtless belongs among
them. With them he moves on to criticism of traditional dogma which,
as a historian, he can understand as only one possible form of expression
of the one Christian faith. But at this very point he differs from them:

their criticism of dogma was dogmatic or systematic; it meant excision, rejection, repudiation of the statements under attack. For Semler the only consequence is that dogma is made relative: he does not criticize it without conceding that at other times and in other circumstances it may have had its value for salvation and that it may still do for many people today—Semler knows an 'infinite content of the Christian religion' (Gass IV, 41)—but he himself cannot share in this verdict. One looks in vain in Semler for the solemn earnestness with which a Jerusalem proceeded against dogma, or for the furiousness of a Bahrdt, although in fact his position is not so different from theirs. From here we can understand the real historian's insight which made Semler's picture of church history somewhat variable: his distinction between a free private religion of the individual, moral religion, in which of course the real essence of Christianity was to be seen, and a religion of society with an order of teaching to be guaranteed through the state, with a dogmatic church language resting on mutual agreement, with a particular form of worship, etc. Semler was not the first or the last historian who thought that he had to favour this proposal. There can be no doubt where he wanted to place himself. If only he had stated a little more clearly how the relationship of these two religions to one another was to be conceived!

Be this as it may; by making this distinction it could come about that in the dispute over the Wolfenbüttel fragments Semler could find himself among the opponents of Reimarus, that with a decisiveness for which he has been widely blamed he turned against the unfortunate Bahrdt, and that finally he even came out most emphatically for Wöllner's Edict of Religion. Paradoxical as all this may be—once one has understood that in practice Semler was for neological divine bliss and therefore for natural religion, but that (like Harnack later!) he regarded this as the historical essence of Christianity, which as such must indicate the necessity of a law of society as well as the freedom of the individual—once one has understood this, one will see that it is not exactly a sign of superior historical art when Aner can do no better than chide Semler for these things with the harsh word 'dishonesty' (p. 111). Semler's contribution to neology lies entirely in the sphere of historical methodology. With well-known historical means, but also armed with the criterion of moral usefulness, he attacked the authority of the biblical canon, the equation of the two Testaments, the inspiration of the text of the Bible and the identification of Scripture and revelation. And as a church historian he attacked the dogmas of Christology and soteriology. Particularly in relation to the complex of questions centred on the concept of the canon, 'liberal theology'—a designation first coined by Semler (or by Bahrdt?)—has lived off his legacy down to the present day. Remarkably, at the end of his life, disgusted with the fights against his neological colleagues, he turned right away from theology and devoted himself to natural history and then even to Hermetic philosophy, theosophy, Rosicrucianism, mystical chemistry, belief in a vanished but real light world 'and for some time with complete conviction fabricated air and stink-gold and Hermetic medicines'.[1] The somewhat demonic end of Semler's career will surely not make us more unsympathetic to this man whom his contemporaries and their like today find so difficult to take.

Similarly, Johann August Ernesti (1708-81), professor and exegete of the New Testament in Leipzig, though predominantly to be regarded as a philosophical academic, is to be counted among the neologists only with qualifications. He was not orthodox, but only conservative, as someone splendidly remarked about him (Gass IV, 69). That means that in true neological fashion he believed that he could see a derivation of the principles of religion from the nature of the Godhead and of humanity, but in practice he had too much respect for the positive nature of Christianity to be able to keep up with most neologians in their great strides in criticizing tradition. His best-known critical action is his attack on the orthodox doctrine of the threefold ministry of Christ. But the motive of this attack is directed more against all dogma as such than against orthodoxy. Ernesti was one of the first spokesmen for the discomforts of the exegete and the historian in connexion with the dogmatic theologian: he complained that the latter held all too lightly to the biblical material or to the facts as they were. Just as philosophy must adhere to reason, so theology must adhere to Holy Scripture understood in a historical and grammatical way. Ernesti's criticism was thus directed less towards the results of theology than towards its traditional procedure, and by indicating the most important principles of a legitimate hermeneutical method he attempted to bring about positive improvements in this procedure. One thing that is clearly characteristic of the neologians in this man is perhaps his absolute faith in the adequacy of the historical and grammatical exegesis that he commended. With his stress on the positive element in Christianity he already towered well beyond his time.

An Old Testament scholar of similar disposition to Ernesti may be mentioned alongside him, Johann David Michaelis (1717-91), professor in Göttingen. As well as writing all kinds of *Orientalia*, he produced a

[1] J. G. Eichhorn, quoted in Aner, op. cit., 102.

Compendium theologiae dogmaticae, with which he did not make many
friends in Hannover, although it hardly contains any striking attacks
on dogma. He, too, is concerned with the method of theology, and
specially with the freeing of biblical theology from dogmatic theology
and its consequent independence. Michaelis was one of the first to
strike that note, so well-known today, that the Old Testament has an
oriental spirit very different from our own and that as a result a great
many, if not all, of the usual biblical proof-texts for dogmatic statements are useless. He therefore counsels dogmatics to free itself from
biblical language and to stand on its own feet. More clearly than other
neologists, Michaelis also saw that the truth of Christianity could not
so easily be demonstrated by means of feeling. This was the by no
means bad sense of his famous saying about the *testimonium spiritus
sancti*, namely that although he was firmly convinced of the truth of
revelation and had sought every possible assurance of that truth,
throughout his life he had never felt such a testimony of the Holy
Spirit, nor did he find any word about it in the Bible. It was the historicism and psychologism from which the scriptural view of later
orthodoxy was not free and which had run riot still more in Pietism
and the Enlightenment, against which such criticism had to lead the
unavoidable counter-attack.

Johann Joachim Spalding (1717-1804), Provost and Chief Consistory Councillor in Berlin, deserves mention as a representative of
those churchmen who were neologists. Natural religion and the revelation that confirms it and therefore is to be measured by it stand intact,
side by side, in his writings. In practice that meant (as Spalding put
it in his writing of 1772, *Über die Nutzbarkeit des Predigtamtes und deren
Beförderung* (On the Usefulness of the Preaching Office and its Continuity)) that the Church had only to purge itself thoroughly from the
dogmas of original sin, the Trinity, the atonement, etc., or to reject
these dogmas energetically, to be able to commend itself to the state
and society in its true, i.e. moral, usefulness.

We conclude with Johann Gottlieb Töllner (1724-74), professor in
Frankfurt a.d. Oder. Like Semler, he was a pupil of Baumgarten and
like Semler also advocated a liberal, i.e. not dogmatic and absolute,
but historical and relative, criticism of dogma. He is interesting because,
like Jerusalem, he was without doubt an upright and honestly pious
person—'divine grace' was one of his favourite terms—yet he, too,
pressed forward in that series of negations, with no originality in
detail, but as it were under the pressure of a higher necessity, until all
that was left was what he expressed as a last confession of faith on his

deathbed (as Schleiermacher did later at a last eucharist): 'I am convinced of the divine mission of Jesus and of the truth of his story, which cannot have been invented. I am convinced of the divinity of his teaching, in which I find three things above all: a fine morality that can make men good and blessed in connexion with the redeeming death of Jesus, which is the most important motive for following it; God's attitude towards us as a reconciling Father, which is proved to us, made effective and communicated to us in the death of Jesus; and finally the doctrine of immortality and a better life to come. I know the probability of all this, which is provided by reason, but the word of Jesus alone gives me certainty: I live, and so you shall live. Now I see what is truly essential in religion, quite apart from the subtleties which do nothing to quieten me. To strengthen me in my faith, to establish me by the comparison of my small sufferings with the suffering of my Jesus, to give me living joy in my immortality, I now take the eucharist of the Lord' (Aner, 84).

5

ROUSSEAU

WITH Jean-Jacques Rousseau, in the middle of the eighteenth century, the new age begins which we call the age of Goethe, the age which presented Protestant theology after Schleiermacher with the problem with which it chose to concern itself, and which also largely supplied the answer it thought fit to give. The new age in the middle of the eighteenth century! There are two things implied here from which follow significant principles which must be borne in mind in interpreting Rousseau. Not to understand him as a child of his century, who for all his individuality could not help but participate very energetically—after his own fashion—in its general and characteristic trends, would be to understand him falsely. But we would be understanding him even less if we failed to realize that it was precisely as a child of his century that he fought, passionately and radically, against its most typical tendencies, and consummated a completely different new movement in opposition to them. We must be so careful in assessing him because as an event he contains a paradox. He was not merely incidentally a man of the eighteenth century. He was one very definitely, in a way which made him both bolder and more consistent than almost all those about him, and it was precisely in this way that he contradicted and rose above eighteenth-century man and, on the other hand, he contradicted and rose above eighteenth-century man in no other way than this that it was in Rousseau himself that eighteenth-century man achieved fulfilment. There are similar things which we shall have to say later of Lessing and Kant. They must be stated with particular emphasis in the case of Rousseau because as a historical figure he is attacked much more from both sides; and indeed he is much more open to attack.

It is very easy to see Rousseau almost involuntarily from the standpoint and according to the standards of his own age. For this age lives on in us, and Rousseau contradicted it so flatly that it is still possible for us simply to take his contemporaries' idea of him and assessment of him for our own. And what then remains but Rousseau the dreamer, Rousseau the idler, the subjectivist, the barren critic of civilization, the author of a voluminous treatise on education who consigned his five illegitimate children to the Foundlings' Home without ever seeing or wishing to see them again, the author of the *Contrat Social* who had not the faintest notion of how to fit himself to be a citizen or a member of any society and who even in private life was quite incapable of keeping on good terms for any length of time with anyone, however well-intentioned towards him he might be? Anyone who is inclined to dismiss Rousseau lightly for these and other similar obvious reasons, for these moral reasons, let us say, is in a position to claim that he has indeed understood the eighteenth century perfectly. But he has completely failed to understand Rousseau. For it was just in this way that all his typical contemporaries understood him; the only thing they did not understand was that Rousseau was still ultimately and at the deepest level at one with them in—and in spite of—this deviation of his from all they held most holy, and for which they condemned him. He was in fact at one with them as the man in whom all they held most holy was given a future; he had experienced their inmost feelings, the spirit of the old time, in a completely new way, had reproduced it in a new form and was proclaiming it in a new language; he was the man in whose deviation the time should have been able to recognize, for all its astonishing nature, the embodiment of its own hopes. He was recognized as such in and in spite of his deviation by those of his contemporaries who were not merely typical, but who as contemporaries also bore within them the restlessness of a coming era. In and in spite of his deviation they recognized him as the best exponent of their age.

On the other hand it is very easy to assess Rousseau from the standpoint and according to the standards of our own time, for instance, in so far as our time now in many ways presents a complete contrast to the eighteenth century. For Rousseau was so completely a man of the eighteenth century! What is easier for us than to see in his teaching that human nature was fundamentally good, the height and apotheosis of the Pelagian humanism which was triumphant in the eighteenth century; in the educational teaching of his *Emile*, which ultimately consisted simply in liberating the child in the right way and was the last word of that optimism in educational theory which distinguished that century before all others; and in his teaching of the social contract, above all the individualism and rationalism which knew of no history, i.e. boldly wished to make history solely and alone, and accordingly to which there was nothing given, no destiny, and hence no inequality, and no authority because in the last resort there exists neither sin nor grace? What is easier than to dismiss Rousseau on the grounds that we have dismissed the ideals of the French Revolution, of which, as we well know, he was thought to be the chief expounder? What is easier than to regard him as the really classic example of absolutist man, who belongs for us to the past, to the eighteenth-century past? But if we did this we would only show that while we might have understood ourselves we had once again completely failed to understand Rousseau. For we would be overlooking the fact that Rousseau's humanism had the significance of a revolutionary attack upon that which had been esteemed and cultivated as humanism since the Renaissance; that the man's final dislike, which again and again rises to the surface, was reserved for precisely the spirit of his time which was incorporated in the philosophy of men like Voltaire, Diderot, d'Alembert and Hume; that both his political and educational theories were not intended to be a continuation of, but a radical challenge to the political and educational theories of his time and were indeed understood in this sense; that there is something lyrical behind his theories of politics and education, and at the back of this an attitude to life and a feeling for life which surely have their place in the line of development leading from Louis XIV to the French Revolution only in so far as they represent a breakthrough, or an attempt, at least, to break through it. While Rousseau had the same aims as those who followed this line of development he was also developing in quite another direction. From that position he then actually rejected the aims of the line of development from Louis XIV to the French Revolution. He is the first of those men of whom it must be said that the nature of eighteenth-century man, which they did not completely discard, which indeed they perhaps brought to the point where it could be truly honoured, had been reduced in them to nothing but a loose outer garment. Anyone who embarks upon an attack upon Rousseau's individualism and rationalism must realize that this involves attacking all these men, including Hegel and Goethe. A criticism of Rousseau from this point of view which was not on principle also relevant to Hegel and Goethe could hardly touch Rousseau either. If he was an individualist and a rationalist then he was these things in exactly the same sense as they were and it was not the eighteenth-century sense. Rousseau was already a man of the new era, in eighteenth-century garb.

I can make plain the paradoxical conjunction of both these ages in Rousseau by means of an example which should be all the more convincing because it is fairly far removed from the subject of our chief question, the theological problem, and from the other favourite fields of those who engage in research into Rousseau. Rousseau once wrote the following on the nature of genius in music: 'Do not, young artist, ask what genius is! If you have it then you will sense what it is within yourself. And if you have not genius you will never understand it. Musical genius subjects the whole universe to its art. It paints in harmonious sounds all the pictures that it sees. It makes even silence eloquent. It conveys ideas in the form of feeling, feeling by means of accent. And in giving expression to passions it awakens them in the depths of the heart. Through it desire itself acquires new charms; the sadness it awakens calls forth cries of anguish. It burns unceasingly yet never consumes itself. It can burningly express the frost and ice; even in depicting the horrors of death it sustains within its soul that sense of life which never forsakes it, and communicates it to the hearts which are capable of feeling it. But alas! it can say nothing to those who have not its seed within them, and its wonders do little to impress those who cannot emulate them. You want to know whether some spark of this consuming fire glows within you? Hasten then, fly, to Naples and hear the masterpieces of Leo, Durante, Jommelli and Pergolesi. If your eyes fill with tears, if you feel your heart violently beat, if you are shaken by sobs and breathless with delight, then find yourself a poet and set to work; his genius will fire yours and you will create by his example: that is what the genius does, and soon other eyes will pay you the tribute of the tears the masters have caused yours to shed. But if the charms of this great art leave you unmoved, if you feel no ecstasy nor delight, if you find merely beautiful that which should move you to the depths of your being, how dare you ask the meaning of genius? The sacred name should not so much as pass your lips, low creature that you are. What possible concern of yours to know it? You would be incapable of feeling it: confine yourself to—French music.' The passage is to be found in Rousseau's *Dictionnaire de musique*, which he published in 1764, a book of instructive articles under the headings of the technical and scientific musical terms. For Rousseau's profession, in so far as he can be said to have had one in regard to society, might best be described as that of musician, in the craftsmanlike meaning of the word which was typical of the eighteenth century. He acquired a certain significance in the history of French opera through his *Le Devin du Village*, which was actually given a performance before Louis XV in 1752. His chief occupation as a musician, outwardly at least, was quite simply that of copying scores, and it was thus that he earned or supplemented his living during whole periods of his life. As a young man he invented a new musical orthography and urged its acceptance publicly, albeit in vain. And we know that until he was well advanced in years he was fond of singing for his own amusement, accompanying himself on the spinet. And then there was the technical and scientific aspect of the matter which the dictionary presents. So far nothing in Rousseau's musicality exceeds the limits which we have come to know were characteristic in this field of the old time. But then suddenly in the middle of this dictionary we find this article *Génie s.m.* (substantive masculine!), of which there is only one thing to be said: this is not the eighteenth century any more, it is not the genius of Bach nor the genius of Haydn (quite apart from the fact that a book of instruction in accordance with their way of making music could scarcely have contained an article on 'genius' at all), it is not Mozart either, but it *is* unmistakably Beethoven, Schubert and Mendelssohn, line for line. Music which holds the universe in thrall, which reflects ideas in the form of feeling, which aims at expressing and awakening the passions, which as feeling for life addresses itself in a mysterious way to the feeling for life, music which does not wish to be understood as beautiful, but as enchanting and only in a delirium, music which according to whether it moves one or not, reveals a kind of predestination to blessedness or damnation—all that might very well be found in Schleiermacher's *Speeches on Religion*, but not in any book previous to the age of Goethe, nor in any heart or head either. Anyone who read this article in those days was immediately called upon in the field of music to decide whether to receive the new message, that art is prophetic of feeling, as something rich with new promise or as something in the nature of a declaration of war; and whether he should welcome or hate it accordingly. Anyone who found himself in a position to agree perfectly with Rousseau must, like him, have belonged to both the old and to the new age.

I should like now to give a short account of Rousseau's life, as some knowledge of it is indispensable if we are to understand his work and its significance. Jean-Jacques Rousseau was born the son of a clockmaker in Geneva on 28th June 1712. His early education was pietistic in spirit. The first things he read were Plutarch and the heroic novels of the seventeenth century. At the age of sixteen he ran away from the engraver to whom he had been apprenticed and also abandoned his native city. He became a Roman Catholic in Turin in order to live, but not without having gained his knowledge of the Roman Catholic Church through people who made a great impression upon him; and shortly afterwards he came under the influence of Françoise Louise de Warens, née de la Tour, from the Canton of Vaud. She was twelve years older than he, and influenced him over a long period, and to a certain extent throughout his whole life. Like him rooted in Pietism, and like him a convert, she seems to have presented an extraordinary mixture of theoretical free-thought and practical devotion—she fled across the lake from Vevey taking with her—Bayle's *Dictionnaire*! She also combined the highest degree of spirituality and deep moral feeling with an almost incomprehensible thoughtlessness in erotic matters— in any case, an amazing personality. In the last lines which Rousseau ever set on paper, shortly before his death, he still thought of her as *la meilleure des femmes* and dedicated moving words to her memory. From 1728 to 1741 he kept abandoning all sorts of positions (as house-servant, music teacher, private tutor and government employee) in order to return to her. The last three years formed the climax of this period. He spent them with Madame de Warens on her estate, Les Charmettes, near Chambéry. It was these years also which seem to have been most truly those of his education, using the word in its narrower sense. It was at this time and at this time only that he was fully himself, as he puts it in that last description of his association with Madame de Warens: doing in perfect freedom only those things which he enjoyed doing, in the quiet of solitude, in the close proximity to nature afforded by country life, and in the presence and possession of a woman after his own heart. *J'ai joui d'un siècle de vie*.[1] The year 1741 saw the end of this idyll. Rousseau moved to Paris. He made the acquaintance and even won the friendship of several of the men who were most influential in the intellectual life of Paris at that time: Voltaire, Diderot, Grimm, Holbach and Buffon. It was during these years that he was probably in closest touch with the spirit of the age. But this close association did not last. A stay in Venice as secretary to the French Ambassador there ended unhappily. The year 1745 saw the beginning of his association with Thérèse Le Vasseur, which forms a remarkable parallel to that between Goethe and Christiane Vulpius, in particular also in this respect that he also raised it later to the status of a legitimate marriage. The decisive turning-point in Rousseau's life was in fact the year of Goethe's birth, 1749.

It was in that year that the Dijon academy set the question for a prize dissertation: 'Has the advance of the sciences and the arts helped to destroy or to purify moral standards?' Rousseau later described the effect the question alone had upon him in a style which bears all the hall-marks of an account of a religious conversion: he

---

[1] *Rêveries du promeneur solitaire, Xme. promenade. Œuvres complètes de J.-J. Rousseau*, Basle 1793-95, Vol. 20, p. 341.

read the announcement of the question for a prize competition in a newspaper while he was on the way to visit his friend Diderot, who was at that time in prison in Vincennes. 'If ever anything resembled a sudden inspiration it was the emotion which arose in me as I read this: all at once my mind seemed dazzled by a thousand lights, a throng of fertile ideas presented themselves there at the same instant with a force and a confusion which plunged me into a state of inexpressible excitement; my head swam with a dizziness akin to drunkenness. I was oppressed by the violence of my beating heart and by a swelling of my breast; being unable to draw breath any more while walking, I threw myself down beneath one of the trees beside the avenue, and lay there for half an hour so agitated that on picking myself up again I found my whole shirt-front wet with the tears I had not even noticed shedding.'[1] Diderot has given us a slightly different account of the event, maintaining not only that he made Rousseau acquainted with the question which had been set, but that he also suggested the answer which Rousseau afterwards gave. But however it came about it was not in Diderot's life that the question was seized upon and the answer provided, but in Rousseau's. He himself said of his answer that it gave the lie to everything which was an object of wonder to his age and that he was therefore prepared for its universal rejection. The answer ran: the sciences and the arts have always been harmful to morality because they have always decomposed and destroyed the natural virtue of the human heart, and also the virtues of the good citizen which spring from it. Rousseau's expectations were at first disappointed. Or rather: the expected disavowal of the man who dared to outrage his own time in such a manner, then, as at all times, first took the form of admiration and enthusiastic applause of the novelty of the thing he had produced, and of the brilliance with which, like all those who have something really new to say, he had been able to say it. The dissertation received the prize in 1750 and its author was famous at a blow, although, or perhaps directly because, his work found no lack of distinguished opponents. But he nevertheless demonstrated that he took his own thesis seriously by giving up the bourgeois employment in which he was then engaged in order henceforth to procure by copying scores both the inner peace and the economic freedom necessary to further reflection and literary production, and signalizing his entrance upon a monk-like existence in his outward appearance too, by laying aside the usual sword, white stockings and wig, and above all his watch—he could not rejoice

---

[1] *Letters to Malesherbes*, 12. I. 1762, Basle edition, Vol. 16, p. 245.

enough later in the liberating effect upon his soul which just this act had brought him—and assuming a 'good coarse, coat of cloth'. Later, for reasons of health, or rather of illness, he exchanged this garment for the dress of an Armenian, and it was thus clad that he busied the tongues and eyes of his contemporaries and has lived on in history. 'A great revolution took place within me, a different moral world revealed itself to my gaze, and caused me to see the absurdity of human prejudice.'[1] Solitude now became a necessity of life for him which could not be denied, because it was the quintessence of that which had been revealed to him as the one necessary thing, and which he now believed he should announce to his time at large. For solitude means a retreat into the original, simple and natural form of human existence in obedience to the dictates of the heart, such as he himself had come blissfully and unforgettably to know, in approximation at least, in Madame de Warens' orchard, and such as he thought he would surmise to be the lost *status integritatis*, the essential thing underlying the forms of human culture and society which are never anything but hidden.

In 1754 he once again answered a prize question set by the Dijon academy: *Concerning the origins and reasons of inequality among men.*[2] The answer, more radical than his first one, was as follows: The natural state of man (*qui n'existe plus, qui n'a peut-être point existé et qui probablement n'existera jamais*) is the state in which no man has need of any other, neither for good nor for bad purposes, neither in friendship nor enmity, because, sitting peacefully beneath an oak and drinking water from a spring, he is outwardly free of all tools and inwardly free of all reflection. It is with tools and reflection, with property and the cultivation of the soil that he becomes a social being. 'The first man who staked out a piece of land and dared to say: this belongs to me! and found people foolish enough to believe him—was the founder of bourgeois society.' It is precisely at this point and thus with society itself that inequality begins, but inequality means the possibility of unfreedom, tyranny and slavery, the possibility of the fateful *amour propre* in opposition to the neutral, and for this reason innocent, natural and good *amour de soi-même*; it means greed, and evil passion. Presupposing the inequality which has now obtruded there is now no other way of protecting each man from his neighbour except by the second-best possibility, which is only a second-best possibility, of the contract of the state, which by the establishment of positive law tries to a certain extent at least to make

---

[1] *Rêv. 3me. prom.*, Basle ed., Vol. 20, p. 202.
[2] *Œuvres de J.-J. Rousseau*, Amsterdam 1769, Vol. 2.

amends for what has been lost for ever by man's abandonment of natural law of that *véritable jeunesse du monde*. Voltaire's well-known mocking phrase, that Rousseau made him feel like going down on all fours, while supplying the most obvious comment there is to make to all this, completely fails as an attack upon Rousseau's position. Where *is* the famous *Revenons à la nature!*? I have never been able to find it in any of Rousseau's writings. It was not the return to this natural law which was the sense of what Rousseau considered to be his insight here and the conclusion he drew from it, but rather the necessity of basing positive law upon the natural law, that is to say, of keeping the natural law in view as an ideal when establishing the positive law and not starting from a natural law which was no true natural law at all, the right of the strongest, for instance. Hence there was no contradiction involved in Rousseau's dedicating the work in question to the municipal council of Geneva, his native town, of which he says that its political constitution was still the best of all those in existence, so that if he were not a citizen of Geneva already it would certainly be his wish to be allowed to become one.

His next work, the *Discours sur l'économie politique*,[1] in 1755, shows us that he has quite logically taken the next step by advancing to a discussion of the positive doctrine of the state: he now expressly presupposes man's sociability and the right to property. But man's original equality and freedom should not be lost sight of. The state is thus to be understood as arising out of and being sustained by and on behalf of the general will (*volonté générale*), in which one stands for all, but all also stand for one, and in which therefore it is the law that establishes and ensures freedom just as freedom establishes and guarantees the law. The wisdom of a government consists in its (1) teaching the people to love the state, i.e. the law as something which is their most personal concern; (2) making it clear to the citizen that the state with its laws is his mother, who wants only what is best for him. His own existence is a part of the existence of his native country; indeed correctly understood the two are identical. Thus he may and indeed must love it as in the best sense he loves himself; (3) the government must take care that the burdens which the state imposes upon the individual truly do not exceed the extent of the sacrifice which it is fitting each should make for his participation in the general will. This is to be accomplished by means of a just financial and taxation policy, which, especially, must be enforceable among the higher members of the society.

[1] Amsterdam ed., Vol. 2.

Incidentally, Rousseau had returned to Geneva in 1754 and had renounced his conversion. He would have stayed there but that his sojourn in his native town was marred for him by the proximity in Ferney of Voltaire and the prospect of the conflicts to which this might give rise. He therefore returned to Paris. The time from the day of his return until 1762 was on the one hand the period of his most important literary labours and on the other a time of difficult personal entanglements from which, in spite of his principles, he found it impossible to free himself. Their effect was to make his belief in his principles still stronger. Two more feminine influences came into his life: Madame d'Epinay, who probably loved him but whom he was not in a position to love, pressed him with the gift of a home which she intended to prepare for him in a country house which she called a hermitage, as well as with the duty she made conditional upon it that he should participate in the social and intellectual life she cultivated. In her house he came to know her sister-in-law, Madame d'Houdetot, and in her, already bound by another love as she was, the great love of his life. He not only respected the other bond, but in admiration of the love which he encountered in it, loved Madame d'Houdetot as one who was so bound and thus denied to him. But his connexion with his circle, one of whose chief members, unhappily for Rousseau, was the German Friedrich Melchior Grimm, was terminated by an open break, and Rousseau moved to Montmorency castle, owned by the Duke of Luxembourg and his wife, where he was permitted to live as he liked.

It was here in 1758 that he wrote the great Open Letter to d'Alembert.[1] D'Alembert, in the Encyclopaedia article 'Geneva', had proposed to the citizens of that town that the introduction of a theatre might be desirable, a suggestion which at once made Rousseau espouse the cause of the Calvinist tradition which in this matter was still unbroken in his native town. The necessary occasions for a people's pleasure should also be presented in union with the infallible voice of Nature, and Rousseau thought he could show that this was better achieved by a continuance and development of the old Genevan customs and behaviour than by that useless and corrupting modern institution, the theatre. Voltaire, who perfectly agreed with d'Alembert, treated Rousseau from then on as if he were a madman, and found a way of annoying both him and the old city of Geneva by opening a theatre just outside the town boundaries, which did then in fact contribute to the death of the tradition originated by Calvin and defended by Rousseau.

In 1760 Rousseau published his 'Proposal for a lasting peace'[2]

[1] Amsterdam ed., Vol. 3.   [2] Amsterdam ed., Vol. 2.

which was in fact written rather earlier, and had been inspired by the writings of the Abbé de Saint Pierre. This political work too reckons quite realistically with the existence of the state based on power politics and with the likelihood of rivalry between such states. It was however Rousseau's aim to confine this rivalry within its proper limits, and he points to the *Droit public germanique*, to the Holy Roman Empire, that is, which was still an active force in Germany, he says, and a far more important idea than the Germans themselves realized. What was needed to avoid further war was a way of making war impossible by rendering it useless. And this could be achieved by establishing a confederation—what he had in mind was without doubt the very idea of a Pan-Europe or United States of Europe which we have in mind today—a confederation including all the sovereign states of Europe, from the Holy Roman Empire to the Republic of Venice, from the Tsar to the Pope, with a central government presided over in turn by each member of the league, with its Supreme Court of Law, with a common army to oppose the Turk or any other external or for that matter internal enemy of the Union, which was above the state, with a guarantee to each member state that its borders and sovereignty within them, and its freedom of movement within them, would be respected on the basis of the Peace of Westphalia, together with a strict prohibition of an armed attack by one member state upon another. All that was required to allow the implementation of the project was the consent of the sovereigns concerned and in demanding this, Rousseau says, he is not imagining that they would have to be good, noble and selfless men, intent upon the general well-being for humanitarian reasons. Thus the usual observation that it is the sinfulness of human nature which makes the realization of such a plan impossible does not apply to Rousseau. He only presupposes, he says, the kind of man who is sensible enough to wish for something that will be useful for him. If, however, his project should prove incapable of fulfilment, let it not be said that it was merely fanciful: *c'est que les hommes sont insensés et que c'est une sorte de folie d'être sage au milieu des fous.*

The first of the three great literary ventures upon which Rousseau embarked during these years was the epistolary novel *Julie ou la nouvelle Héloïse*, which was written between 1757 and 1759 and carried the sub-title: *Lettres de deux amans, habitans d'une petite ville au pied des Alpes.*[1] The little town is Vevey, home of Madame de Warens. But even if the true hero of the story, Saint Preux, the lover, at first happy then unhappy and finally resigned is, as is doubtless the case, Rousseau

[1] Amsterdam ed., Vols. 4-6.

himself, Julie is not Madame d' Houdetot, as was widely assumed at the time, but a pure invention of Rousseau's heart and imagination, the quintessence of his dreams in regard to the woman he desired, in whom he believed without possessing or even knowing her. So we find Rousseau, in this as in no other of his works, thrown on his own resources as the lyric poet who inwardly torn can yet find satisfaction by putting into poetry what his suffering meant to him before, when he was inconsolable—a God had given him the power to tell what he had suffered—and this is the way by which he guards himself against this sorrow.

The opening words of the preface are as follows: 'Big cities need theatres and corrupted nations need novels. I know the moral habits of my time, and therefore I have published these letters. Why did I not live in an era when I would have had to throw them into the fire?' Here also then we are well involved in the complex of problems which we also encounter in Rousseau's political writings. We have to take note here of a dialectic both of form and content. It is without doubt his intention to give expression in these love-letters to the voice of the heart, that is to say, here, to the power of love which is absolutely free and strong, and which binds and frees not only as a force of nature, but by virtue of the whole dignity owned by the original human nature. And thus in the first part of the work we see the two lovers, who, because of their station in society, love without hope, drawn to one another in defiance of the world like steel to the magnet, like the magnet to the steel. But Rousseau is aware that here, as in other things, the state in which complete obedience to the voice of the heart is the normal thing, has been lost and that it is therefore no longer the sole determining factor. Here too his desire is not for a return or advance to a state of nature, which would in this case perhaps be the sphere of free-love. The laws of society are valid and continue to be recognized even if they are on occasion infringed. Hence in fact the free motions of the power of love are, even in this first part of the novel, everywhere interrupted and held in check by insights and principles which are also those of the lovers themselves, and especially of the women involved, and which are put forward with due emphasis by both. And when Julie subsequently becomes the wife of another this is not only accepted by both as their fate, albeit in the course of a severe inner conflict, but honoured as a new inevitable law to which their love (which is, however, undiminished) is now subject. Rousseau has his hero respect this law so much that the second half of the book becomes a very hymn to the praise of marriage and the family, these states, of course, representing not the fulfilment but the limit of the power of erotic love. We are reminded of the tendency which moved Goethe too in writing the *Elective Affinities*. It is just that the death of Julie, with which the work closes, and the energetic denial of the possibility that Saint Preux, reduced now to solitude, might himself marry, make it quite clear that an honest outward recognition of the social order is not capable of reducing by one iota the strength contained in the inner truth of the power of love, which is outwardly condemned as impossible.

The second dialectic of the book, that of form, arises directly from the dialectic of content. Why does Rousseau think that in a better time than his own he would have had to burn the book instead of being able to publish it? Why does he even go on to say in his preface that a chaste girl should abstain from reading it at sight of the title alone? If she did not do this, but read only one page, she would be showing by this act that she was not chaste, but *une fille perdue*, in which case she might just as well read the whole thing straight through. What does this mean? It apparently means that the representation of this broken power of love—broken by the necessary recognition of the law—is the only way in which it can be written about in that century, that is to say, within modern European society, and cannot be a pure comment upon love, as it should really be presented to a young girl and as Rousseau would really like to write it. Just as he would like to withhold the theatre from the good city of Geneva, so he would like to withhold from a girl who perhaps still has a belief in love the only novel, *rebus sic stantibus*, which it was possible for him to write. The novel cannot be chaste precisely because it must allow the conventions to triumph outwardly over love and can therefore show love only as it is inhibited by convention. Rousseau's contemporaries positively devoured the *Nouvelle Héloïse*. He once told the story of a lady who, while engaged in reading it, was due to attend a function to which she had been invited. She let the coach wait for hours before her door and finally read on in the coach until four o'clock in the morning, finishing the book only at daybreak. How did the people of Rousseau's time interpret and misinterpret the dual dialectic which the work contained? It must be admitted that of all Rousseau's works the *Nouvelle Héloïse* is the obscurest in its intention, and yet we feel bound to say that of all his works it is the one which it was most necessary for him to write and which most directly reveals his personal dialectic. And about this work in particular we can most definitely say that neither those people who were outraged at its sublime lasciviousness nor—much less—those who revelled in it succeeded in understanding what was actually taking place there: the rapturous shout of the man who had discovered himself deep down beneath all the human contrivance in which the age believed with such a passionate ardour, and the same man's cry of despair at finding that he cannot and does not wish to escape human contrivance, and is thus at a loss to know what to do with himself, simply because beyond all human contrivance he had only discovered himself. Such was the new Héloïse. And such was the complete Rousseau.

The second work of this period was the great treatise *Du contrat social ou Principes du droit politique*,[1] 1762, which was divided into four parts. This work in particular which today is perhaps relatively the best-known of Rousseau's writings, could not have become the political ogre it in fact was for many people, on the strength of its title alone, if only they had taken the trouble to read it in its place within the scheme of Rousseau's work as a whole and with an understanding of his peculiar position in relation to his own age. It is not true to say that its author makes the mistake of deducing the state from the abstract principles of the liberty and equality of the individual, while ignoring the realities of human history. Indeed the very first lines of the book, which are there for all to read, state that it is Rousseau's aim to understand man as he is, and the laws as they can be. The demand for political justice arises from the insight into the original freedom and equality of individual men, but this demand itself constitutes in Rousseau's doctrine of state only the weft introduced into the warp of the undeniably very 'historical' factor which he calls here 'interest' or 'advantage': in man's present no longer natural state (*l'homme est né libre, et par-tout il est dans les fers*, at once master and slave) which here also Rousseau presupposes as only the second-best state, his survival demands a *convention*, a means of regulating the mutual relationship between the lordly slaves or slavish masters. This convention is fundamentally and generally that which Rousseau calls the force exerted by society (*Contrat social*), and the point which he is trying to make in his doctrine of the state is this: that this convention, which he admits is necessary, things being as they are, should not be arrived at without due consideration for the demands of justice, i.e. without any thought being given to man's original state of freedom and equality. 'I seek to unite what the law allows with that which interest prescribes, so that justice and what is expedient might not ever remain divided.' It is thus nonsensical to say, as P. Wernle says,[2] that we find ourselves transferred in the *Contrat social* from the atmosphere of freedom, the pure inwardness and lyrical

[1] Amsterdam ed., Vol. 2. [2] Vol. 2, 63.

subjectivity of the *Nouvelle Héloïse* into a completely different world, that, namely, of the Jacobin state governed by compulsion. For the *Nouvelle Héloïse* does not simply convey the 'atmosphere of freedom' any more than the *Contrat social* is simply an account of the 'state with compulsory rule'. The theory and practice of the form of government arising from the French Revolution—the theory as laid down, for instance, in the Declaration of the Rights of Man of 1789—although later in time (*post hoc non propter hoc!*) belonged just as much to the time before Rousseau as did the theory and practice of the absolute monarchy of his time. Likewise in the opening pages Rousseau presents, in opposition to force from above and the force from below which repels it, the social order (*l'ordre social*) as a superior order whose right, although not a 'natural' one, is nevertheless 'holy'. Might, while it may very well be able to create facts, can never create right. Even the power which is ordained of God is, in so far as it is in fact only might, not necessarily right. And an agreement such as Hobbes had in mind, in which nothing but authority is given to the one side and nothing but the will to obey to the other, would not be an agreement at all and would destroy the idea of man as one capable of political action, and indeed the idea of man altogether.[1] The problem of the state is rather how to bring about a union between men which by its corporate might shields every individual in such a manner that he is at once one with the whole and yet free, and free—i.e. obeying himself alone—by virtue of this very consent. The basic act which represents the answer to this problem is an act of submission, the complete transference by the individual of all his rights to the community as such. It is precisely by everyone giving himself completely—not to somebody but to all and not to all as the sum of every individual, but to all as the public person which has arisen by their union—it is precisely by this act that the weft of justice is introduced into the warp of interest, which, *rebus sic stantibus*, is what is needed to make an agreement possible: for it is by the one giving himself to all that the only possible form of freedom and equality, *rebus sic stantibus*, is preserved by him and by all. Participation in the *volonté générale* which arises in this way thus essentially consists in an act of submission and distinguishes the *citoyen*, *civis*, πολίτης from the mere *bourgeois*. And the presence of such a general will distinguishes the *cité*, *civitas*, πόλις, the *république* or the *corps politique* from the mere *ville*: understood in the passive sense it is identical with the concept of the state, in the active sense it is identical with the idea of the sovereign, and understood in its relation to its

[1] I, 3-4.

equals it is identical with the idea of power, *puissance*. The whole
body of those who as individuals are united in the state or as sovereign
in their own right is the people, and individuals as such are *citoyens*
because they share in the sovereignty and *sujets* because they are subject
to the laws of the state.[1] The sovereign can therefore by his nature
never act in a way which would be harmful to his subjects, but only in
their favour, just as the citizen by his nature can never be against his
sovereign, but only for him, and, moreover, if he understands his freedom rightly, can imagine the constraint which the sovereign imposes only
as leading to his, the citizen's, own freedom.[2] For: 'Freedom consists in
an obedience to the law which has been self-imposed.' The citizen will
therefore subordinate himself, both in the rights to which he is entitled as
regards his own person and in his property rights as a landowner, to the
right of the generality. He will, that is to say, regard himself only as a
guardian and trustee appointed by the generality, and in this way he is the
legitimate owner of these rights, *possesseur* of his person and property.[3]

The sovereignty which is based on such precepts is essentially non-
transferable, i.e. it can be exercised by certain individuals but cannot
be irrevocably conferred upon certain individuals.[4] And it is essentially
indivisible, i.e. it cannot be split into a legislative power and an
executive power effectively separate from it.[5] According to Rousseau
the formation of political parties constitutes an injury to the rights of
the sovereign or state.[6] The sovereign power over the individual is
limited because while the sovereign can command the services of the
individual in every respect—even the sacrifice of his life (capital
punishment and war!) he can command them only as a sovereign, i.e.
on behalf of the generality.[7] The way in which these services can be
commanded is regulated by the law, whereby a people lays down its
rules for itself.[8] We would, of course have to be gods and not men in
order to recognize the laws which are best in all circumstances, since
the law which was to be imposed upon a man and which was at the
same time to proceed from him would have to be powerful enough to
bring about nothing more nor less than his transformation from a mere
individual into a social being. The *esprit social* which was the law's
intention must have been in effect even while the law was being set up.
Blessed are the peoples to whom it was granted, like Israel, to hear a
Moses, or, like Geneva, to hear a Calvin![9] It is necessary when engaged in legislating for a particular people to take into most careful
consideration the special nature of the people and country, and to

[1] I, 6.   [2] I, 7.   [3] I, 8-9.   [4] II, 1.   [5] II, 2.   [6] II, 3.
              [7] II, 4-5.   [8] II, 6.   [9] II, 7.

appreciate what exactly is its state of historical development. It is this appreciation which distinguishes the true legislator from the tyrant.[1] In any case it is essential that the legislative power, the power, that is, which brings a certain law into force, should, as a matter of principle, be the people, whether it be for constitutional, civil, or criminal law.[2]

Concerning government as such the situation is somewhat different. The government, it is true, is not sovereign either, but derives from the sovereign, i.e. from the people. But it is truly thus derived, i.e. as servant of the sovereign it is a link endowed with its own real existence and its own will between the people as the generality of citizens and the people as the generality of subjects. It receives from the people as representing the sovereign the commands which it has to pass on to the people as representing the state; but it is precisely in its quality of receiving and imparting spontaneously that it is for its own part a subject—not indeed of the sovereign power, but in exercising the sovereign power as the sovereign intends.[3] As to the form which the exercise of this power should take, this according to Rousseau depends most of all upon the size of the state in question and upon the material resources at its disposal: a large and prosperous state requires a strong form of government and therefore one where all the power resides in the hands of one person, the monarchical form in other words; in a state more limited in means and extent the exercise of power can safely be placed in the hands of several people, so that an aristocracy would be found suitable; the affairs of a small and impoverished state can be conducted more or less directly by the people itself, and so could be a democracy. In historical reality the form of government will inevitably be some sort of mixture of these three.[4] But Rousseau's inclination, quite apart from this practical distinction, was never for a more or less pure democracy: *Il n'a jamais existé de véritable démocratie et il n'en existera jamais*, he states very definitely; it is only very seldom that the right conditions for it exist, and the dangers of constant internal unrest are far too great with this form of government. *S'il y avoit un peuple de dieux, il se gouverneroit démocratiquement. Un gouvernement si parfait ne convient pas à des hommes.*[5] But the Jacobins and the modern exponents of political liberalism evidently thought otherwise. Rousseau it is true, also finds several objections to the aristocratic system and a great many to the system of monarchy. For it will not be in the personal interest of a king to regard the plenitude of power with which he is entrusted as merely expressive of the *volonté générale* as he ought to. Another evil is

---

[1] II, 8-11.   [2] II, 12.   [3] III, 1.   [4] III, 2-3.   [5] III, 4.

that he will not actually rule personally, but through his ministers; and yet another the fatal fact that the monarchy is hereditary, which means that it is possible for a child, a monster or an idiot suddenly to become king. And lastly there is the fact that the continuity of government is in no way ensured every time the throne changes hands. Rousseau would like to see this better preserved, as it is with a senate like that of Venice or Berne.[1] How is a good government to be recognized? Not by the form of government, for the same form of government can be the best possible for one people and the worst possible for another. By the magnificence of the government then, perhaps, or the prosperity of the people? Or by the preservation of peace at home and abroad?—No, says Rousseau in all sincerity, not by these things, but quite simply by the increase in population of the territory in question: it is this which will show that men have achieved what they intended in forsaking the state of nature for the social state, namely the collective preservation of their life, even if it should perhaps be attained in circumstances of the utmost general wretchedness and possibly of great violence and bloodshed.[2] The abuse of government and subsequent death of the state always occurs at the point where the state loses its meaning because the convention upon which it is based has been mangled by the establishment of some kind of tyranny.[3] But tyrannical also is the conception of the legislative power which causes a people's chosen emissaries to feel and behave like representatives (*représentants*) of the people, instead of feeling and behaving—just like the wielders of the executive power—like their delegates (*commissionaires*). The instant a people appoints representatives for itself it is no longer free; it is no longer even a people. For the instant a man, thinking of his representative in parliament, can say, politics are nothing to do with me, the state as such is doomed. Rousseau also very logically maintained that the institution of taxes was a more than dubious substitute for its underlying institution of co-operative labour (*la corvée*), which was alone worthy of a true *cité*.[4] Thus we can hardly defend or attack what we know today as the parliamentary system as something towards which Rousseau's ideas might have been tending. If a people adopts a system of government embracing a legislative and an executive power, then this does not, according to Rousseau, signify the concluding of a second social contract (just as on the other hand the social contract as such did not for him, as Hobbes thought, simply mean the appointment of a government), but the execution of the first and only contract, beside which there can be no other. In the course of that execution

[1] III, 5-6.   [2] III, 9.   [3] III, 10-11.   [4] III, 14-15.

the people, far from retiring into inactivity, is and remains as active as it possibly can be.[1]

From this it follows that it is impossible for the sovereign to determine by an irrevocable act either the form of government or which people are to be entrusted with it. These things must again and again be made the subject of his free decision. The instance of the general will which has again and again to be consulted, i.e. the will of the body politic or of the people as such, is proof against destruction by any attempt of the government to seize excessive power or any attempt by individual citizens to set up a state within the state.[2] This general will is by no means the will of the majority; the only purpose served by the majority is to determine what the general will actually is on a given point. The purpose of the vote is not to ask the citizen whether he is in agreement with a certain law or not, but to ask him whether in his opinion this law is in accordance with the general will. The healthier the political life of a country is the more its political decisions will come under the sign of unanimity. But anyone who has entered into the social contract has thereby expressed his readiness to accept in advance also those decisions which are not passed unanimously or which run counter to his convictions or interest. In this event he will not say to himself that he has perhaps erred in his convictions or in his judgment of the matter in question, but that he has probably erred in his assessment of the general will, and he will not wish, for the sake of his own freedom, which, properly understood, is based upon the true general will, for the result to be different. Rousseau at this point applauds the custom of the old republic of Genoa, which was to inscribe the very word *libertas* over the gates of prisons and on the chains of those condemned to service in the galleys. '*Cette application de la devise est belle et juste.*' It is precisely for freedom's sake, and for the sake of his own freedom, that the citizen who has encountered the severity of the law makes his way to the prison or the galley![3] As for elections, Rousseau is inclined to prefer the method of electing by lot, so that it may be quite clear that appointment to an official post is not a distinction, but signifies the imposition of a special burden for the citizen concerned, an imposition which in any case in a complete democracy—if such a thing existed— it would be best to leave to pure chance.[4] Finally, in accordance with strict logic, Rousseau finds it possible to attribute a good significance even to the two very illiberal political institutions of dictatorship and censorship. It is the will of the people to preserve the life of the state in all circumstances. But it is possible for circumstances to arise in which

[1] III, 16.   [2] IV, 1.   [3] IV, 2.   [4] IV, 3.

the existing laws, which cannot perhaps be changed immediately, become a danger to the state. In such cases the people's sovereignty must in its own interest be suspended, or alternatively suspend itself for a moment, by being temporarily placed in the hands of one or more persons, a state of affairs which can of course only be transitional if it is not to degenerate into a form of tyranny. And according to Rousseau the formation and cultivation of public opinion (*opinion publique*) in questions of morals and taste is no less a political matter and thus the government's task, than the formation and protection of the laws. The task of a wise censorship in the way in which it has always been exercised by princes and magistrates of note, would be not to create, sway and determine public opinion in these matters, but certainly to ascertain it and give it expression, and by thus propounding the laws which are unwritten constantly provide the written laws with the support they need.[1]

Rousseau ends the book with a strange disquisition on *la religion civile*, which is, it must be admitted, also remarkable for its inconsistencies and lack of careful thought. According to him religion and politics originally went hand in hand; every people had its gods in having its state, and lost them when its state was lost. The message of Jesus about the kingdom which is part of another world dispelled this unity. The pagan persecutors of the early Christians were not completely wrong in scenting political rebellion in the proclamation of this kingdom. With the Roman Papacy it actually became rebellion. The Church managed to establish itself as a political body in its own right, independent of the state, setting up a new social contract based on the benefit of communion and the threat of excommunication (*un chef d'œuvre en politique!*) whose power has proved itself to be greater even than that of the civil contract. We are faced with the two interrelated facts that the state has always had need of some religious basis, and that Christianity has in effect always been more harmful than beneficial to the state. We should really, thinks Rousseau, distinguish, first, *human religion*, which he describes as the purely inward cult of the highest God, which has no visible manifestation in a Church, which is bound up with the recognition of the eternal duties imposed by morality, and which he thinks he may identify with the 'pure and simple religion of the Gospel' or with the 'true theism' or with the 'natural religious right' (*droit divin naturel*); and, secondly, the *national religion* of pre-Christian times, the positive religious right (*droit divin civil ou positif*) whose dogma and cult were prescribed by the law and made the duty of the

[1] IV, 6-7.

citizen; and, thirdly, *priestly religion*, which demands of a man that he
should recognize two separate sources of law, two governments and
two fatherlands, and thus makes it difficult for him to be believer and
citizen at once; a religious right for which, according to Rousseau, there
is no name whatsoever (he expressly states that he is referring to Roman
Catholicism) and which he therefore declines to discuss further.
'Anything which shatters social unity is worthless. Every institution
which sets a man at loggerheads with himself is worthless.' It seems at
first that there are all sorts of things to be said in favour of national
religion, of the theocracy, from the political point of view. But it is
based upon a lie, makes peoples as such intolerant in matters of
religion, and places in the hands of those thus incensed the dreadful
weapons at the disposal of the power-state. Thus we must dismiss it
also from its place in the discussion. There remains human religion,
'Christianity, not that current today, but the quite different Christianity of the Gospel', the 'holy, sublime and true religion'. If only it
were not for its one bad failing: that it is incapable, without being
essentially connected with a state on earth, of lending strength to the
laws of a state on earth, but must rather loose the hearts of the citizens
from their state as it does from all earthly things. It is said, that a people
composed of true Christians would form the most perfect society. But
should it not be borne in mind that a society of true Christians would
no longer be a human society at all? And even assuming the possibility of such a society, would not that 'deep indifference' with which
it is alone possible for a Christian, whose homeland is not upon
this earth, to discharge his duties in the state, would not the ease,
with which he can accept bad conditions too, would not his fear of
becoming intoxicated with the glory of his country, would not his
readiness to bow beneath the hard yoke of God, would not all these
things be bound eventually to constitute a danger to the state in spite
of all the good political results which they may have as well? Will not
Christian soldiers believe not in victory but in God, and will they
then achieve what the pagan Romans achieved? Is it not inevitable
that they should fare badly in face of so inspired an enemy? Is there
in fact any such thing as a 'Christian soldier'? Is not a 'holy war' an
impossibility from the Christian standpoint? Is there a 'Christian
state' (*une république chrétienne*)? Or does not each of these words exclude
the other? Is not Christianity with its teaching of submission and
dependence an all-too favourable prerequisite for tyranny, which has
in fact never neglected to exploit it accordingly? Thus, according to
Rousseau, this third possibility, that of human religion, must also be

ruled out of the discussion. But the fact remains, that the state needs a religion, in order that its citizens might love their duties. It thus demands of them a civil profession of faith (*une profession de foi purement civile*), to be formulated by the state itself, containing the *sentiments de sociabilité* (the convictions on whose account a general will is necessary) without which it is not possible either to be a good citizen or a loyal subject. It demands a dogma concerning the existence of a mighty, wise, beneficent guiding and providing Deity, a future life with rewards and punishments, the sacred nature of the social contract and the Laws; its articles are to be few, simple and clear but—in order not to give rise to theological dispute—on no account too closely defined or even provided with a commentary. All else is conjecture (*opinions*) and this is no concern of the state or of the citizen of the state as such, and the individual should be left to ponder it freely. Anyone who does not accept this civil religion is to be banished; anyone who, after he has accepted it, behaves in a manner contrary to it commits the crime of giving the lie to the law and is to be punished by death. And every intolerant religious form is excluded at the outset, for wherever the principle 'without the Church there is no salvation' is thought valid, an alien sovereign power is in fact set up within the state in worldly political affairs (in questions concerning contracts of marriage, for example), which is set higher than the state, and constitutes an attack which the state can meet only by being for its own part intolerant. The only course for every honest man (*tout honnête homme*) is to renounce the Roman Catholic Church. Such are the last words in this book of the former convert Rousseau.[1]

Rousseau's third chief work of this period, a novel tracing its hero's mental growth and development and entitled *Emile ou De l'education* (1762),[2] is also an answer to the problem of how human life should be moulded in spite of and in its quality of being far removed from its original and natural state. But now the problem is presented in individual microcosmic form. It is now the moulding of a single life which is in question. Rousseau had been approached by a worried mother for advice in matters affecting education: the few short precepts he originally gave then grew into the now famous work which embraces five whole books. It begins with the words: 'All things are good as they proceed from the hands of the Author of all things; all things degenerate in the hands of man. . . . Man wants nothing to be as nature has made it, not even man. Because this is the present state of all things the child and the adolescent cannot simply be left alone, but are in

[1] IV, 8.   [2] Amsterdam ed., Vols. 7-8.

need of education. But the significance of this education must then be, in contrast to all the demands of society, class and future profession which are meant to influence the young, and in contrast to the existing customs and prevailing ideas of the adults surrounding the child: educating him to be a man, and indeed an *homme abstrait*,[1] a man, that is, who is as free as possible, and as far as possible acts in accordance with his true nature.

The first lesson which we learn from the book is that mothers should feed their infants themselves and not wrap them in swaddling clothes! The child's education is meant to provide him with room for himself, for the way of life which the child himself must shape and bring to perfection. *Vivre est le métier que je lui veux apprendre.*[2] Such an education will therefore have to consist in taking care that the child is allowed to develop as freely as possible those potentialities lying dormant within him which are quite distinct from the external factors which help to determine and influence it, in ensuring that he can acquire his own experience as freely as possible, and ensuring finally that he should be allowed to come to terms in the most natural way possible with the historical factors conditioning his existence. That is why Emile, the model Rousseau uses to present his ideas, is brought up far removed from society, in the country, and indeed he is educated from infancy not by his parents, but by a tutor. The first aim of education is to free the child of fear, commanding greed and bad behaviour by disposing of the false attitude to the things which can awaken such feelings. The child should be made aware automatically, so to speak, of the moral concepts of obedience, duty and obligation and further of virtue by himself experiencing his own strength and weakness, and necessity and compulsion. Learning and reading should be allowed to proceed from the child's interest in things around it, which is to be aroused first, and on no account should this sequence be reversed. Thus the development and exercise of the five senses is far more important at first than book learning. Instruction proper then follows quite simply upon the child's curiosity and its growing desire for knowledge, and therefore takes as its subject the things by which the child is surrounded, the house, the garden and the stars in the sky, and only finally the books, the first and most important of these being Robinson Crusoe, because like Crusoe the child should arrive at the point where he can decide his requirements for himself and be able to set about procuring them. It is to encourage him in this that Emile is given handicraft lessons even while he is still very young. Only when he is past fifteen is it time to introduce him to

[1] I, p. 12.   [2] I, p. 11.

foreign languages, and to history also, with the aim of paving the way for him to form an independent moral judgment on the basis not of the false speech, but of the deeds of men. And similarly his religious instruction is not to introduce him to the catechism of one particular faith but to enable him to choose that religion to which the best use of his reason must necessarily lead him. The purpose of a stay in the city is to allow the pupil to clarify and establish—in opposition to the bad taste prevailing there, be it understood—his own feeling for the truly beautiful. And then he is to be made acquainted with classical literature too. But the time when he becomes engaged and the first years of his marriage, are also part of the period of his education, a fact rather surprising in retrospect as we learn in the fifth book that Rousseau did not think a corresponding education, far from the parental home and society, necessary for the female sex, but considered the instilling at home, of a little knowledge of music, housekeeping and sewing, the virtue of cleanliness and an unfeigned propriety, sufficient for a girl. The essential things to be demanded of a wife are that she should please her husband and have learnt how to make life pleasant for him.

The part of the book which really determined its reception was the *Confession of faith of a Vicar of Savoy*,[1] which was interpolated in the fourth section. The Vicar is a cleric of the type which Rousseau had encountered in Savoy during his stormy youth, and into whose mouth he now put his own theology, or philosophy of religion. Some *bon sens*, a love of truth and a simple heart, in short *la bonne foi*, i.e. an opinion honestly held, seem to him to be the sufficient prerequisites of such an undertaking: he is confident that even any error into which he might fall could not be attributed to him as a crime provided he has adhered to these principles. Neither the Church's call to faith nor any philosophy, be it systematic or sceptical, the confession begins, can allay the mistrust of all truth in the heart for the immediate reason that those representing the Church or a philosophy are far too zealous and fundamentally lacking in objectivity in wishing others to accept their own opinions as the right ones. I must therefore begin at the very beginning. I start by establishing my own existence and with the fact that I am related to a being distinct from myself by virtue of the twofold, the passive and the active power of feeling and judging. Judgment is something other than feeling: in judging I am not passive but active in relation to the things about me. In judging I attribute something to them: existence, size, number, relationship, etc., something which I know not only by awareness of the object concerned but from within

[1] Amsterdam ed., Vol. 8, pp. 13ff.

myself. But I must now attribute exactly the same activity to the objects themselves: it is freedom and not only necessity in the movement by which I apprehend them. How do I know this? I know it from direct experience. *Je vous dirai, que je le sais, parce que je le sens.* It is of my own free will that I make this present motion of my arm. No artifice of reasoning can destroy this certainty within me. It is *plus fort que tout évidence; autant vaudroit me prouver que je n'existe pas* (p. 28). But if now, as I suppose, the universe is not, like myself, a living being, and if movement does not reside in the world as a whole and is even less a property of matter, then I am provided with my first dogma or article of faith, in explanation of the movement in the world, as: the recognition of a will which moves the world from outside. And from my insight into the causal and teleological connexion between all forms of movement, by virtue of which each single movement can at any time be considered as central to every other, I am given to recognize that this will is endowed with intelligence and wisdom. The Being which is possessed of this highest will and therefore, as is apparent, of this highest ability, and which therefore exists in itself—this Being I call God. *Pénétré de mon insuffisance* (note what theological principle comes to light here—) *je ne raisonnerai jamais sur la nature de Dieu, que je n'y sois forcé par le sentiment de ses rapports avec moi* (p. 39). We are evidently taught by nature herself to marvel at him, to worship and love him: a feeling of thankfulness towards him is the consequence of our love for ourselves which suggests itself first of all. But what a contrast there is, in the world created by God, between the peace and happiness of nature and the chaos of the world of men! For man is the slave of his senses and passions. But he is not only that. He is also free, capable, that is, of elevating himself to the level of the 'eternal truths'. Just as he can judge of what is true, so he can also, he who was created in the image of God, judge of what is good, and experience the desire to live up to this judgment. Thus moral evil and the physical evil which follows it stem from us, not from God, and not from our God-created nature. Take away our calamitous progress, take away our mistakes and our vices, take away the work of man, and all is good! *Sois juste et tu seras heureux!* (p. 51). And if in spite of this I see the wicked triumph and the just man suffer? It is precisely this which affords me proof of the immortality of the soul, of man's thinking nature, the dissolution of which is inconceivable to me, and whose preservation God owes less (!) to the deserts of man than to his own goodness (one senses none the less in this fateful sentence something like a lingering echo of the theology of old Geneva, in Rousseau's recalling here Psalm 115, verse 1: 'Not unto us, O Lord, not unto us, but unto thy name give glory!' p. 55). But Hell, the punishment of the wicked which corresponds to the heavenly reward of the good, I should not be inclined to seek in some everlasting Beyond, but in the hearts of the wicked, and then—for is not the wicked man also my brother?—rather hope for peace for them too in the world to come. I should consider spirituality, eternity, wisdom, goodness and righteousness, as qualities of God, to be absolute and attributable only to him as the Creator and therefore not think that they are to be comprehended by means of my corresponding notions of them. I shall say to him: 'Being of all beings, I am, because thou art; in thinking of thee without cease I understand also my own origin. And that is the noblest use to which my faculty of reason can be put, in recognizing that beside thee I am as nothing.' But to what else shall I now devote my life? Nature has inscribed it in indelible characters upon my heart: *Tout ce que je sens être bien est bien; tout ce que je sens être mal est mal* (p. 60). For if good is really good, then it must dwell within us for ever and cannot be lost. To be good, then, must simply mean to be healthy, i.e. to be in a state corresponding to the nature of goodness. How could admiration for good deeds and men, and revulsion at the sight of evil, be possible for all of us, how could pity be possible even for the criminal, if we were wicked in the depths of our nature, if we did not stem from goodness? Thus the form of the moral imperative can only be: *obéissons à la Nature!* (p. 65). In the depths of our souls (*au fond des âmes*) over and beyond all our principles, there dwells always an agent which passes judgment: the conscience, not as a prejudice, and not as an idea we have had grafted on to us by education and custom, but as an evidently innate *a priori* of all moral ideas which has manifested itself in the manners and history of every people at every time. *Nous sentons avant de connaître . . . Quoique toutes nos idées nous viennent du dehors, les sentimens, qui les apprécient sont au-dedans de nous. . . . Exister pour nous c'est sentir. . . . Nous avons eu des sentiments avant des idées* (p. 69). This *sentiment*, however, which is innate and thus inseparable from our existence, and which enables us to recognize good, and spurn evil, is in fact the conscience. 'Conscience! Conscience! Divine instinct; immortal and celestial voice; assured guide of a being who is ignorant and pressed hard, but intelligent and free; infallible judge of good and evil, it is you who make man resemble God; it is you who are responsible for the excellence of his nature and the morality of his actions; without you I sense nothing within me which raises me above brute creation, except the unhappy privilege of straying from error to error by means of a gift of perception which is unregulated, and a gift of reason which has no principle.

Heaven be praised, we are now delivered from all the terrifying apparatus of philosophy. We can be men without being scholars!' (p. 71). Why then are there so few men who heed this guide? This is simply because it speaks the language of nature, which the whole world conspires to have us forget. But does the man exist who has not at least once in his life yielded to the tug of the heart which is so natural and sweet and not in doing this found virtue lovable in spite of the difficulties it presents?

But what is virtue? What is goodness? It is placing oneself in relation to the whole, instead of placing the whole in relation to oneself, as the wicked do. The wicked man makes himself the centre of all things, the good man fits himself into an order where God is the centre of all created things, and these form the periphery about him. I put myself of my own free will at God's disposal as his work and as his instrument to the fulfilment of his will, and it is in this legitimate use of my freedom that I have at once my desert and my reward (p. 76). If a man chooses evil instead of goodness, that is attributable to the man himself, and most certainly not to God. But in this event the choice of good also depends upon myself alone. I shall be fortified and held in this good choice by contemplating and meditating upon the universe, not with the aim of idly systematizing, but of worshipping and marvelling at its author. I have nothing to ask of him. What, even, should I ask for? For miracles on my behalf?—I, who yet love his order of things as it is immutable? Such a prayer would merit punishment! Or am I to pray for strength to desire the good and to do it? How should I ask for something he has given me already: namely conscience, reason and freedom! *He* demands of *me* that my will should be otherwise than it is— it is not I who have to demand it of him! 'O good and merciful God, fount of justice and truth! In my trust in thee my heart's supreme desire is that thy will be done. In allying my will to thine I am doing as thou dost, and acquiescing in thy goodness; I feel that I am partaking in advance of the supreme joy which is the reward of such a will' (p. 79). I certainly have cause to doubt myself. Certainly I am not infallible. Certainly all the views I hold could be so many lies. But I have done what I could; how could I be held guilty for not having achieved more?

But how is all this now in relation to revelation, Scripture and dogma? It is certain that the answer to this must also be determined by the reasoning power of each individual: *cherchez la vérité vous-même!* Is any other religion but the natural religion, which has just been developed, really necessary? Am I likely to incur guilt in simply following the light which God himself has given me in my reason and conscience? What truth or injunction which is important to the glory of God, the good of society or my own advantage could I possibly miss in following this course? 'Our most sublime notions of the Deity come to us through our reason alone. Gaze upon the spectacle of nature, give heed to the inner voice. Has not God said everything to our eyes, our conscience and our judgment? What is there left for men to tell us?' (p. 82). What purpose will their revelations serve but to reduce God to an all-too human form? What purpose their dogmas but to create new obscurity? They have made man haughty, intolerant and cruel, and brought war instead of peace to the earth. *Je me demande à quoi bon tout cela sans savoir me répondre.* If we had only ever heeded what God says in the heart of man there would only be *one* religion on earth, the religion, namely, of the heart. But now every man, when asked which is the true religion, answers—mine! And how does he know that?—God has said so! he replies. And how does he know that God has said that?—My parson told me, and he should know.

But have we not a right to demand that the true religion should be distinguished by means of some quite unmistakable criterion? How can I be expected to believe on the authority of a man, who after all is in exactly the same position as myself? 'When I believe what he says, I don't believe it because he says it, but because he proves it. The evidence provided by men is therefore fundamentally nothing but that given me by my own reason and adds nothing to the natural means of recognizing the truth which God has given me.' *Apôtre de la vérité, qu'avez vous donc à me dire dont je ne reste pas le juge?* God has spoken to man, you say. Bold words, indeed! But why then have I not heard him? Why has he apparently spoken only to certain other men? Why must I above all else believe again in the miracles which are to attest that these men are speaking the truth? And why before all else in the books in which these miracles have—by men!— been handed down to us? *Quoi! toujours des témoignages humains? toujours des hommes, qui me rapportent ce que d'autres hommes ont rapporté? Que d'hommes entre Dieu et moi!* (p. 88). Must I now ponder, compare and verify? Could God really not spare me this labour? How learned I must be to seek through the whole of antiquity, nay through the entire world for the truth of the prophecies, revelations and miraculous events which are claimed! What critical abilities I must possess to distinguish the true documents from the false, to weigh the theses and counter-theses against each other, the originals and translations, the reliable and not so reliable historical witnesses! And all this as a mere preliminary to deciding whether the reported miracles are really miracles, the reported prophecies really prophecies. For there are also seeming miracles and prophecies which have some natural explanation. And when I have found the confirmation of their authenticity, then that in its turn is but a preliminary to the question: just why did God select such means for the confirmation of his word, as if he were purposely avoiding the simplest method, means which are themselves so much in need of confirmation? Is it credible that God should have given such signs to this or that particular man, and in so doing have made all the rest of mankind dependent upon them? Is it not too strange that every sect ultimately calls such signs to witness, so that all things considered—if all things were correct—there must have been more miraculous events than natural ones! And so that we should regard it as the greatest wonder of all if somewhere at some time no miracle should come to pass among some group of persecuted fanatics! No, I believe in God too much to believe in so many miracles unworthy of him (p. 90). Why do they not happen now in the broad light of day? Why did they all take place somewhere in a dark corner? Why are such and such a number of eye-witnesses necessary to make them credible? And even if they were credible to us, has not the Devil also worked miracles, according to the Bible itself? Is the true doctrine not once again necessary to prove the true miracle, which we were told should for its own part prove the true doctrine? The latter must, however, in any event be recognizable by bearing the 'sacred character of the divine', i.e. by the fact that it at the very least does not contradict the basic concepts of natural religion which it has brought with it. A wrathful, jealous, vengeful, factious God I could not acknowledge as being my God: He is not the good, gentle God my reason has already revealed to me. Further I would beg leave to demand of the dogmas of a revealed religion that they should be clearer, simpler and easier to comprehend than those of natural religion, and not perhaps even more mysterious and contradictory. 'The God whom I worship does not dwell in the shadows; he has not given me understanding to forbid me to use it. To demand of me that I should subject my reason is to insult its Author. A servant of truth would not tyrannize over my reason but enlighten it' (p. 93).

These then are my principles in testing a revealed religion. But would it then be enough to test one of the revealed religions in this manner? To be fair should we not have to look into all of them, and into every religious faction, comparing and weighing them one against the other, and not only by means of their literature but in our own person? Have we, for instance, done justice to the Jews and the arguments they advance for their religion? Have Christian and Mohammedan ever listened quietly to what the other has to say? How in justice can we regard as damned the millions of the heathen, whom no mission has yet reached? What guilt has the heathen incurred who happens to die on the evening before the arrival of the first mission to his district? What fault is it of his that he knew nothing of what is supposed to have happened in Jerusalem on the other side of the globe eighteen hundred years ago? That same Jerusalem, incidentally, where the people even today seem no better placed as regards that event than he himself! And what allegedly revealed religion is there to which the same objections could not be raised! (p. 108). If there were really only one religion which alone is able to grant salvation then, since everyone must test for himself in this matter, it would be everyone's first duty, regardless of age or sex, to ask all these questions and institute the enquiries necessary to answer them. The earth would be swarming with pilgrims wandering in all directions at vast expense and under the greatest difficulties in order to test their religions and find the true one. Then farewell to craftsmanship, art and science, and every social employment. There would then be no striving except for the true religion. And the best that could happen would be that the healthiest, the most zealous, the shrewdest and oldest man will get far enough to discover in his old age in retrospect which religion he *should* have taken as his guide in life. Anyone rejecting this method must grant the son of the Turk the right he concedes to the son of the Christian: the right to abide by his father's religion without being threatened with perdition. So far as I myself am concerned, I can reject this method because I have decided to take as my one and only guide the book of Nature which lies open before the eyes of all men, that is at my disposal come what may as a source for the recognition of God, and from which I learn more than all men can teach me (p. 110).

My attitude to the allegedly revealed religions is, however, neither approving nor disapproving, but one of respectful doubt: I see that there is much to be said for the various religions, but also that there is much to be said against them. Once again, I do not consider myself infallible. But I must think for myself. It may be that someone who can declare himself for a particular religion is gifted with better powers of judgment than I. Thus I certainly condemn no man, but I can imitate no man either: it is just that his judgment, superlative as it may be in itself, is not my judgment. This must be also my attitude in relation to Christianity. 'I gladly confess that the majesty of the Bible evokes my admiration, that the sanctity of the Gospel speaks to my heart. Philosophers for all their splendour are small beside it. Can a book at once so sublime and so simple be the work of men? Can he whom it describes be a mere man? Is his speech that of the enthusiast or of the ambitious founder of a sect? How sweet, how pure his ways! (*quelle douceur, quelle pureté dans ses mœurs!*) What moving grace (*quelle grâce touchante*) in his teachings! How noble his maxims! (*quelle élévation dans ses maximes!*) How wise his discourses! What aptness, finesse and justice in his answers! What command of his passions! What strength and self-denial in his sufferings!' (p. 112). Socrates cannot be compared with him, for just as certainly as his morality was something quite new in his surroundings—whereas Socrates' was but the affirmation of familiar Greek virtues—so his death was incomparably much harder than Socrates' death. *Si la vie et la mort de Socrate sont d'un Sage, la vie et la mort de Jésus sont d'un Dieu.* His story cannot have been invented. In that event its inventors would have had to be more astonishing than their invention. But it must be admitted that this Gospel is also full of things not worthy of belief, contrary to reason, and unacceptable. As far as these are concerned one can only withdraw to the attitude of silent but non-committal respect. This also holds good for the dogmas in so far as they are not relevant to life or to morality. 'I look upon all the individual religions as salutary institutions in so far as they are in each country the uniform means of public worship. Their reasons for being as they are may be in the climate, in the government, in the spirit of the people (*génie du peuple*) or in some other local cause which might make the one preferable to the other, according to the time and the place. I believe they are all good provided they allow God to be worshipped in a fitting manner, that is to say by rendering God the essential service of the heart' (p. 114).

God will certainly not reject any service rendered unto him, whatever its outward form. And now, the Vicar of Savoy declares, I shall make it my task to discharge my duties as a Roman Catholic priest, and especially those of the Mass, which formerly I took lightly, with all the inner conviction and outward punctiliousness I can muster, exactly as the Church prescribes, and to invest the words of the sacraments with all my belief in the highest Being. 'Whatever there is about this inconceivable mystery (the sacrament), I am not afraid that I shall be punished at the day of judgment for having profaned it in my heart.' And for the rest I shall obey the spirit of the Gospel more than the spirit of the Church, and therefore preach virtue to men, and dogma only in so far as it is of help to them in that respect. But one dogma I shall keep from them altogether, namely that of intolerance, which is cruel and immoral. Thus I shall play no part in attempts to convert people who hold another faith (pp. 116f.). The Protestant who has become a Roman Catholic is to be advised to return to the religion of his forefathers—we do not know if Rousseau was in fact so advised by a Roman Catholic priest—if only because it is morally still the purest and intellectually still the most modest of religions. In any case the true duties of religion are independent of the human religious institutions. The only essential thing is the *culte intérieur*, and it is in this sense that the saying 'no virtue without faith' may well be valid (p. 122). The teachings of philosophical scepticism and atheism which threaten us are just as bad as the teaching which we have to expect from the Churches. As they are even more dogmatic in their approach than the Church, they deprive man of everything he finds worthy of reverence, and thus rob the unhappy of their last comfort, the happy of their only warning, the criminal of the chance that he will repent, and the virtuous of hope. Fanaticism is at least a great passion, whereas this philosophy is tolerant only because of its indifference to good, and creates a state of quiet which can only be called the quiet of death. Both extremes of superstition and unbelief are therefore to be avoided (p. 126). 'Dare to profess a belief in God to the philosophers; dare to preach humanity to the intolerant!'—such is the confession of faith of the Vicar of Savoy and the confession of faith of J.-J. Rousseau.

It was this part of *Emile* which was to prove disastrous for the life of its author. Both Church and State found cause to take action with some speed after the book had appeared, particularly because of this section. Christophe de Beaumont, Archbishop of Paris, promulgated a severe pastoral letter against *Emile*. As a result of a decision and order by the Parliamentary Court of Justice in Paris the book was publicly burned on 11th June 1762 and an order was made for the arrest of its author. The latter step, however, was a vain one, for Rousseau's influential friends had caused him to flee in good time. At first he wanted to return to his native land, but on reaching Swiss soil he was horrified to learn that his book had been condemned and burned in his Protestant native city, Geneva, as well, and that he was threatened with arrest there too.

These events were a turning-point in Rousseau's inner life. From then dates the decline in his inward frame of mind and attitude which threw him on to the defensive, breeding pessimism, misanthropy and even persecution mania. Rousseau was never, even in his early youth, what might be called well-balanced. Judging by his own account of his life one can distinctly see the beginnings of a mental crisis already in his personal experiences between 1756 and 1762. From 1762 onwards he became in his own eyes increasingly the misunderstood, persecuted and suffering Jean-Jacques. He now imagined all the dishonesty and prevarication, all the harshness and cruelty, all the injustice, intolerance and spite of which he had so often accused man in his fall from the state of nature, to be an attack directed against himself personally. In the beginning it was of course a real attack to which he was subjected, an actual attempt at injury, which occupied his mind for some time— an attack by the Catholic and Protestant Churches, which had after all themselves been assailed by the remarks of the Vicar of Savoy, with the aim of defending themselves against his ideas. But he became progressively less conscious of this, so that he did not, as might have been expected, become specifically anti-clerical. He lost sight, so to speak, of this particular foe, that is to say, of the Church, in the ranks of the general front which he imagined was aligned against him, consisting of philosophers, academicians, literary men, politicians, the educated and uneducated public in general, and in short man as he was at that time, the same in all these varied forms. Contemporary man did not understand him because he understood him only too well, because he felt that Rousseau was arraigning him, and for this reason hated and persecuted the arraigner. That is why Jean-Jacques was now, at every turn and no matter with whom, a prey to a passionate mistrust which was likely to flare up at every second, a suspicion that he was being victimized, that he was faced by a general conspiracy, systematically conducted from the highest places and employing the most cunning methods. That is why from now until the end of his life he worked himself more and more into the *rôle* of the righteous sufferer, indeed into a kind of Christ-character, a *rôle* in which it would doubtless not have been possible for him to suffer subjectively more severely than he did if it had not been a merely assumed *rôle*. And indeed it was not entirely assumed—what Rousseau had to endure in the years immediately after 1762 was in fact hard and harsh. It was just that he insisted on investing his experiences with the character of a myth and suffering them accordingly, whereas the conditions of life he had to endure—taken by themselves—were not in fact of an unprecedently dreadful kind, as compared with those of other genuine martyrs.

This inner development is not of significance merely as a source of clinical biographical data, but constitutes together with the problems it presents the background without which we should fail to understand the man who is seemingly so optimistic in the things he wrote from 1756 to 1762, so completely in accord with his age, even hastening

impetuously before it along the path it was treading. This was the man
who saw himself as the hated and hating enemy of this age. But it was
only gradually that this came to light, under the weight of the blows of
fate which later fell upon him. It was with the feeling that with the
confession of faith of the Vicar of Savoy, of all things, he had written
the best and most worthwhile book of the century[1] that he fled from
Paris. Indeed he then felt he was the only man in France who believed
in God.[2] But he also had then the feeling: *ma carrière est finie*. Prevented
from returning to the town of his birth, and banished also from the
Bernese territory, where he had at first set foot at Yverdon, he turned
to the principality of Neuenburg, which was at that time Prussian. He
sent a letter to Frederick the Great beginning with the words: 'Sire, I
have said many bad things about you and shall probably say more',
and shortly afterwards thanked him in a second letter for the asylum
which had been granted him by bluntly demanding that he should
put an end to the Seven Years War.[3] He did in fact find at first at
Neuenburg that the Prussian governor, Field-Marshal von Keith, was
well disposed towards him, and found a lodging at Môtiers in the Val
de Travers. It was from here that he settled his score with his opponents in Paris, in the letter to Monseigneur de Beaumont[4] which
appeared in November 1762, and with those in Geneva in the Letters
from the Mountain in 1764[5]. The core of the charges made against
him by both sides had been that he denied revelation in favour of
natural religion, or in favour of human reason. It is obvious that
Rousseau was in the stronger position polemically not only with the
Archbishop but with the theologians of Geneva, because they were
both, the former with his Thomistic 'reason just as much as revelation',
and the latter, the pupils of one J. A. Turrettini, with their rational
orthodoxy, treading the same path which he had after all only naïvely
and logically trodden to its end in his *profession de foi,* and because it
was fairly easy for him to show—taking into account the moral enthusiasm of his age—that he, with his untroubled rationalism and
Pelagianism was only doing honestly, completely and logically what
they were doing half-heartedly and certainly not for any good reason.
It was he—he, the true, simple, truth-and-virtue-loving Christian
and disciple of Jesus—who retorted to the Archbishop,[6] and who said
to the Genevans that he understood what the Reformation was:

[1] Letter to Beaumont, Amsterdam ed., Vol. 9, p. 53.
[2] Letter of 7th June, 1762, Basle ed., Vol. 26, pp.1f.
[3] Letters of September and October 1762, Basle ed., Vol. 27, pp. 47f.
[4] Amsterdam ed., Vol. 9.   [5] Vol. 9, second half.
[6] Vol. 9, first half, p. 54.

namely the interpretation of the Bible on the sole basis of free conscience and free reason.[1] As for the things both the Roman Catholic and the Protestant sides complained about in his attitude to revelation but also to the doctrine of original sin, to Christ and miracles, his position was unassailable, not because he was right, but because his opponents were not so right in all these things as to be entitled and able to put him in the wrong. The triumph of the answer this logical rationalist and Pelagian was capable of giving especially to the Genevans was payment for the course which Protestant theology had pursued since the beginning of the century. It was in fact only by acting hypo-critically or in great self-deception that the Geneva of the younger Turrettini could find cause for the burning of *Emile*. We can understand to some extent the anger with which Rousseau, applying his teaching that in an emergency it was possible to contract out of the social contract, informed Geneva in 1763 that he intended henceforth to renounce his rights as its citizen.[2]

But this counter-offensive now made Neuchâtel too attentive to his person and heresies. The local priest at Môtiers, F. G. de Montmollin, with whom Rousseau had at first been on good terms, and who had even at his own request allowed him to take Holy Communion, turned from him and became his opponent. Behind him there was the assembled clergy of Neuchâtel as a class, behind them again the theologians of Geneva and Berne, and behind them the mighty arm of these two states. And remarkably enough it is most probable that among others Voltaire, of all people, had a hand from Ferney in the hounding of Rousseau which was now to be resumed. In the night of 6th to 7th September, 1765, the irate villagers of Môtiers bombarded his lodging with stones and he had to take flight again. He thought he had already found a new sanctuary on St Peter's Island, which belonged to the town of Berne, in the Lake of Biel. The two months of autumn which he spent there must once again have been a climax, reminiscent of the time at Chambéry in his remarkably intimate relationship to plants, animals, landscape and atmosphere. The winter was just beginning when the high bailiff of the neighbouring district of Nidau informed him that the Council of Berne had evicted him from here also. And only a day later he was disappointed once again in thinking that he had found a refuge, at least for the winter, in the town of Biel. He left Switzerland on 31st October, 1765.

The fate that was prepared for him in that year by Geneva, Neuchâtel and Berne can in no way be described as a glorious page in the

[1] Vol. 9, second half, pp. 42f.   [2] Amsterdam ed., Vol. 26, p. 58.

history of the Reformed Churches there. Rousseau was invited by Frederick the Great to come to Prussia, but preferred, to his great subsequent regret, to go to England. The philosopher David Hume had encouraged him to do so, and introduced him into English society, found somewhere for him to live in Wootton in Derbyshire and even managed to procure for him a fairly generous pension from the King. It was at this time that the disturbance of his mental balance was to become visible in an unmistakable way. For he suddenly rounded on Hume himself, without any justification whatsoever as far as can be seen, and accused him of being the one who was the worst-disposed of all towards him, and of being engaged on behalf of his extensive league of enemies in making his mental and physical life utterly impossible. At last he broke with Hume, an action which, judged by anything like normal standards, made no sense at all. Rousseau abruptly rejected the offer of the royal pension. From afar his friends in France pleaded with him in vain. The only thing they achieved was to fall within the sphere of his mistrust themselves; Rousseau thought they were probably involved in the general conspiracy against him too.

Nevertheless, it was during his stay in England that he wrote the first part of his famous *Confessions*, an autobiography which had in common with Augustine's work of the same name an utter frankness and a very deliberate method of presentation. Strangely enough this first part, the history of Rousseau's life until 1741, until the parting with Madame Warens, gives us in content and mood a perfect picture of one reconciled and content with God and the world, and above all with himself. Engrossed in this period of his past its author seems to have forgotten all the unpleasantness and hallucinations of his present. There he finds himself once again in a state of nature, so to speak, before entering into society and thus in innocence of all wickedness and evil. Thus we are surprised, and yet we should not really be at all surprised when we read later on, at the beginning of the second part, that he wrote the first in a state of most tranquil and happy composure. This could not be said of the second part if only because its subject was the years of activity and conflict which brought him towards all the sufferings of the present.

Rousseau returned to France in 1767, where for the last eleven years of his life, afflicted by bodily ills as well, he was scarcely heeded by those about him, much less menaced, but was inwardly condemned to the most painful instability and torment. In 1768 he married his Thérèse Le Vasseur, prompted probably more by gratitude for her loyalty than by love. He lived first at one place and then at another, maintaining himself by the proceeds from his books and by the score-copying which was the strange object of his affection, at the same time pursuing the tranquil pleasure he received from dabbling in botany, and generally going for walks and yet more walks, a pastime of which he never tired. But inwardly he was still—and now more than ever—a volcano. He could not be kept in any one place for long, for everywhere he lived in fear of snares. At the same time he was charged to bursting point with the indictment against a humanity which he imagined he had seen through to the very depths of its stupidity and wickedness, and he could not but conceive of himself, his own existence, as its quite special victim.

Apart from completing his *Confessions* in the manner just alluded to— one very contrary to their beginning—and writing a book on botany, he also composed at this time the strange dialogues *Rousseau juge de Jean-Jacques* in which he talks with a third party about himself, his sad and disputed position, his character and his works: always with the intention of pointing out this general conspiracy against him, its cruelty and senselessness, and of making protest upon protest against the society which thus misused him, and of begging over and beyond this for the right to his own existence and for the right to have room to move and be heard—which it implied. He has done this in a way which, in spite of all its overtones of vanity and self-pity and all the head-shakings it calls forth, instinctively moves the reader. He had the fantastic plan of placing this work on the high altar of Notre Dame, entrusting it to 'Eternal Providence', together with a letter to the same, so that it would be sure to be passed on to posterity, but he found himself—it was 24th February, 1776—forestalled in some mysterious manner. He eventually entrusted it to the care of a travelling English-man, who made its existence publicly known after his death. It would not be true to say of this manifestly pathological piece of writing either, that it is solely of biographical interest. How often have the *Contrat Social* and *Emile* been misconstrued by people who understood nothing of the vibrant sensitiveness or of the tensed-up bitterness or of the con-suming longing for peace and yet for love, too, as they were in this man, and which he expressed in so defenceless and exposed and therefore in so concrete a form perhaps only in this impossible polemic of his old age. But above all it must not be forgotten that this was not his last work, and that the mood in which he wrote it was not the one in which he departed this life. The idea that Rousseau committed suicide, which was believed for some time in the eighteenth century, has long since been proved to be without foundation.

It may only have been a relatively short time before his death, but yet it came: a time in which the state of conflict and tension he had experienced for fifteen years (he himself states this figure several times) was eased somewhat at least, and when at least something of the inner peace of which he had so often defiantly boasted and to which he had at once given the lie by the unrest in which he lived, seemed somehow to have become a reality after all. This last time saw the writing of *Les rêveries du promeneur solitaire*, in which he endeavours once again, for the third time now since the *Confessions*, to look back upon his life and to see and understand himself. In form, language and content these reveries may well be described as Rousseau's most beautiful piece of writing. They have this quality for the simple reason perhaps, if not for any other, that he did not write them with the idea of publishing them, but only for himself, and thus dispensed with all, or nearly all, rhetoric. It is certainly the most moving of all his works. Once again and now in a somehow still truer and more tangible form than in the *Confessions* we seem to catch in these calmer observations of the old man something like a reflection or echo of the young days at Chambéry that had had such a singular significance for him. Or did they only now assume the quite specific glow which his words about them emanate even now? Did he only now endow them with this splendour in a kind of creative act of remembrance? Be that as it may one is tempted to say that it is these reveries that bring his life full circle. The great struggle lies behind him, not done away with, not settled, it is true, but unforgotten, still alive within him, still part of the present, still capable at every moment of stinging him into pain or anger—and yet rumbling only in the distance like a receding thunderstorm, settled into its place in his life as a whole. Was it not his wish to be alone with nature in those days around 1740? The man of 1778 was alone with nature; he had achieved this very differently, and by way of quite different sufferings and disappointments from those he then imagined were in store for him. In the meantime he had also paid his due to life in society, to life in its unnatural form. He paid it in daring and because he had dared to challenge this life, in obedience to a highly necessary but also highly dangerous impulse, because he had dared to oppose to it as a corrective, and indeed as a secret court of judgment, the other life, the life of nature and solitude, and had dared, as a missionary coming from the true homeland of all life, to direct it into another course, namely that leading back to its origins. He had failed in this mission. He himself had been plunged into the condition he had wished to destroy, had been caught in the bonds from which he had sought to set society free. He let himself be infected to the point of madness by the thing he said we should on no account allow to infect us. But he let himself be infected so thoroughly, he took the perverted life of society and its unnaturalness so bitterly and radically to heart, that of necessity he yet found himself in the end back where he had started. He had only to lay down the weapons of the battle with society, the weapons which, after all, it pained him grievously to use, to find that, as in a re-awakening, he was once again thrown back upon solitude, upon himself and into the realm of nature. From here he now made no more warlike excursions. Now he only dreamed of his quarrel. The reality was peace—the peace following defeat, but peace all the same. Thus he let all his experiences pass before his mind's eye once again, but he could linger only upon those which were of ineffable beauty: those at Chambéry, on St Peter's Island, and a few in the neighbourhood of Paris. We should not wonder at finding everything which gives us cause for astonishment in Rousseau contained once more in this last work of his. His childish vanity, naïve egotism, downright ruthless moral optimism, his desire to have people tell him he is right, his rationalism and Pelagianism; all these are still there and bear new fruit on nearly every page of this his final work. There is no trace of heightened religious feeling or of anything like it. Rousseau never reformed or even improved. He is unmistakably the old sinner Jean-Jacques even in this his finest piece of writing, and there could be every reason to find this calm after the storm, this lonely peace, with himself and nature his sole companions, which formed the final tenor of his days, more suspect from a theological point of view than all the rest of his life. But it might be more fitting for us not to brandish any theological weapons at this point. Rousseau stands too rounded and complete before us—rounded and complete precisely in the complete vulnerability of his attitude and teaching—for us not to be glad to remain silent. If we understand what Rousseau seems never to have understood; that no one can live from anything but forgiveness, then we cannot be interested in establishing a fact which it is all too easy to establish; namely that this man was certainly a sinner of a quite unusual order. Nobody commands us to follow in his footsteps. It might in fact be advisable not to. All the less reason for us to feel that it is our duty to throw a stone at him. It might even seriously be doubted, whether the man who does not feel impelled to hail him as a figure lovable for all its tragi-comic doubtful quality—being somehow moved by the things which moved him so violently—is doing him any kind of justice. Rousseau died in Erménonville on 2nd July, 1778.

We shall now turn to a brief consideration of the significance of the phenomenon of Rousseau, for the question which here concerns us. If we are to see all that is to be seen on this subject, it is essential above all that we should choose our point of departure correctly. Even judging simply by what we have heard of his life it could not possibly be right to level the charge against him that his great literary fight, the fight which was to affect his life so much, was a fight against the Catholic and Protestant theologians—the orthodox ones from his point of view, that is. The Rousseau of the Vicar of Savoy, the letter to Beaumont, and the *Letters from the Mountain* is—and this is in itself significant enough— the fulfiller of the religion and theology of the human heart and under- standing, the man who boldly trod the path of eighteenth-century theology to its end in advance of all the orthodox. As such the things he says are final, and it is because of this that in this respect too the world strains to catch every word he says, and that in this respect too he evokes such passionate applause and opposition. But he does not say any first things, any new things. It is certainly inherent in the one uttering the new word that he should at the same time be the one uttering the last old word, but if we now wish to hear Rousseau as the speaker of the new word we must not persist in listening to him in his *rôle* as a fighter for religious progress and freedom. For we have seen how this matter did not play the commanding part in his own mind which the theologian viewing his work is tempted to ascribe to it. Further, we must certainly not have as points of departure the political and educational structures he planned in the *Contract* and in *Emile*, and what might be called the morality of the *Nouvelle Héloïse*. It was, to be sure, an inner necessity for Rousseau to dare to erect these struc- tures. They were more directly connected with what he essentially had to say and with what was new in him, because they were more positively connected with it than was his opposition to the old denomi¬ational Churches. In them he used his new and essential charac.eristics to contribute as far as ever they could to the striving of his own time. It is no wonder that with such a basis they com- pletely dwarfed the contributions of most of his contemporaries, and that, even taking into account the nature of his age, they had the effect of a revelation. But they were in fact his contribution to the striving of his time and as such did not represent the dawning of a new era or the essential thing he had to say. They were, as we saw, sugges- tions as to how a second-best solution might be reached, which Rousseau had become resigned to making. It is precisely the resignation behind them which is without doubt part of the secret of their effect. But it also directs our gaze to things beyond it. In this respect too Rousseau, seen from the point of view of his own time, might well have uttered conclusive words, but it was precisely because they were the last words that they were not yet, or perhaps no longer, the first, the new word which he meant by them and which he actually wanted to utter.

We might now feel tempted to make our point of departure the lyricism of immediate feeling for himself and the world about him which sounds especially in Rousseau's autobiographical works, but also in the *Nouvelle Héloïse*; man's lonely communion with nature which formed the beginning and ending of Rousseau's course in life. Fairly shrewd commentators have often stopped there. Why should this not prove to be the gateway leading directly to his secret? Why should it not be the vantage-point which yields a clear view forward to Goethe, Idealism and Romanticism? This side of his life and work must certainly be understood and appreciated before one can understand and appreciate how he could yet write the *Contract* and *Emile* and become a pioneer of the new human religion. But this side too of Rousseau's life and work can still be interpreted as a last word of the old time, of the age of absolutism, which in point of fact it was. We have constantly stressed the point that the age of Goethe, of which Rousseau was the first great representative, was also the peak of eighteenth-century absolutism. But it was not only its peak but also its end. There is not only continuity between it and the eighteenth century but also discontinuity, a break, and I am inclined to think that it is this break, as it was completed, in the last assessment, simply in Rousseau's biography, in his more or less pathological method of existing as such, which is the essential thing we have to consider in him. I think that this is the point of departure from which everything else about him which singled him out from his contemporaries first becomes clear, clear as something new which was already contained in this age as a coming age—an age struggling to be born.

From the point of view of Rousseau's biography, of his own idea of himself, it would be completely impossible—he himself felt the contrast so violently—to conceive of his being the culmination and last word of the era of absolutism. This need not, however, deceive us into thinking that he was not that as well. It does compel us however to think of him from another angle at the same time. It was not just an impudent lout who fled from his apprenticeship in Geneva in 1728, but at the same time someone who was quite aware of what he wanted, whose intention it was to escape from the bourgeois moral world of his century. It was not merely from some form of ethical chaos,

but from an inner world which was strange and new to the accustomed
behaviour and ideals of his time that Rousseau returned from Madame
de Warens' orchard to Paris society in 1741; he returned not merely
as a somewhat useless and unpractical dreamer, but at the same time
as the apostle of a new kind of historical reality, which, admittedly,
could not at first find any place in his time. It was not only a delight
in a cleverly discovered and pointed antithesis which led him in the
answer to the prize dissertation question of the Dijon academy in 1750
to begin his impetuous onslaught upon the value of art and science.
It was a force which was actually alive within him, sharply opposing
the things which his time most greatly and highly esteemed. It is not
only by listening to the psychologists and psychiatrists that we shall
reach an understanding of the fifteen years' persecution mania which
followed 1762; it is not just a case of someone with a grudge against
life on whom we must bestow our pity: no matter how delusory
Rousseau's grounds for hating and for thinking he was hated were in
these years, it was a delusion which had some meaning in so far as it
represented a protest in him against the entire inner and outer structure
of life in his time, a protest which made itself very definitely felt, and
one which within this structure had perhaps inevitably first to make
itself felt as a delusion. It is just from here that we cast an involuntary
glance in the direction of Goethe. In the first days of December 1777,
six months, that is, before Rousseau's death, Goethe made his 'Winter
journey in the Harz', and amongst the verses in which he poetically
described it, there are to be found the following:[1]

> Easy following Fortune's
> Carriage; one of that
> Leisurely train on the
> Re-made highway concluding
> The monarch's entry.
>
> O, how cure his torments
> To whom balm is now poison?
> Who drank in his hatred
> In fulsome delight!
> First spurned, now despising,
> Consuming in secret
> His own true merit
> In tortured self-love.
> But who walks there apart?
> His path is lost in the bushes,
> The foliage noiselessly
> Closes behind him,

[1] For original see Appendix, p. 400.

The grasses unbend,
The void engulfs him.

If, Father of Love, there be
One note of Thy psaltery
To his ear attuned
Then cheer his heart!
Clear his clouded gaze
That thirsting he may see
The thousand springs
In the desert!

Every word could not only refer and be addressed to Friedrich Plessing, who was its actual subject, but to Rousseau. But would it not also have been relevant to Goethe's Werther, and to his Faust, the man who no longer knew what to make of art and science, as he reached for the phial of poison early on the morning of Easter day? And therefore relevant to Goethe himself in his early days—and perhaps not only as he was in his early days? What else are his Götz von Berlichingen and Schiller's Karl Moor but Rousseau translated into manly, and heroic terms with a capacity for action, a transformation of the protesting, the deluded Rousseau? To be sure, Goethe and his age stand at a point beyond the conflict and tension in which Rousseau was involved. Anyone who can thus take him as a poetic subject has absorbed him and his protest and delusion, his 'Storm and Stress'; they are no longer something vital, but something which has been overcome. But Goethe would not have been Goethe if he had not passed through the period of storm and stress himself, if he had not carried it within him all the days of his life as a protest which, although no longer vital to him, was yet part of him and had taken shape within him; as a madness which had found rest and peace—if Goethe had not himself been a Rousseau, albeit a victorious and comforted Rousseau, but a Rousseau none the less and if Goethe had not been the man who, while he brought the eighteenth century to its culmination, was yet its most embittered opponent. Indeed, we have seen that at the very time when Goethe was writing those lines Rousseau himself was at least on the way to achieving for his part the comfort they offered. The contrast between the two men, which must certainly not be overlooked, is a contrast within a homogeneity which is more important and more powerful than the contrast, and they belong together at any rate also in their contrast with the eighteenth century. Thus the days of bitterness which Rousseau tasted to their end, his illness, were not even in themselves matters of pure chance. The time he lived in was his disease, and the fact that the age that was to come had not yet arrived, the time of which Goethe then became the master not *only* in a sick fashion but much more in a healthy fashion: the master in whom the sickness was overcome by good health. Without Rousseau's negation the affirmation of this new time would not have been possible. Rousseau's cups of bitterness had something of the nature of birth-pangs and it is for this reason that they are the primary and essential thing to which we should devote our attention in studying him, especially if it is our aim to understand him in relation to his time, and to approach his time through him.

The break indicated by the broken quality of Rousseau's own personal life represents, however, the breaking of the absolutist will for form which came to pass in him. This is, first of all, the significance of Rousseau as a phenomenon: here was a man who could not share the general joy which inspired his age, the joy in man's intellectual, technical and moral capacities. A man who could not produce the general unquestioning confidence in all that European society had so far achieved, but who on the contrary dissociated himself from it, so to speak, instead of naïvely taking part in these achievements. A man who measured the whole of these achievements against another Whole, and who from that angle was in a position to regard it with feelings of estrangement, bewilderment, disquiet and revulsion. A man who looking at it from that angle was not only not impressed by this world, who not only had objections to certain of its features, but who regarded this whole world as such as the cause of his suffering, and as such felt compelled to reject it wholly. He felt all this and yet at the same time he felt that he was the advocate, protector and avenger of his fellow-man, this very man who finds cause for triumph in the sum of his achievements and in the possession of the capacities which made them possible, who rejoiced so heartily in them and was so sure that he was on the right path and should go further and further along it.

Rousseau's protest reveals how self-contradictory the attitude of his fellow-man was. Driven by a demoniac or foolish spirit arising out of some depth of his being which was at first completely inexplicable he hurled his impeachment at society—but no, it was not his charge, but society's own, which it had drowned and not heeded. It was that the life of society, ruled as it was by this capacity for civilization and this will for form, was no real human life at all, no life in accordance with man's essential quality and nature, but signified rather its complete perversion and destruction; that it was not the heaven it pretended and told itself it was, but a hell. He could see no way of accepting any compromise. His only possible course was radically to deny the spiritual and intellectual, the moral and social forms which, unshaken by the Lisbon earthquake, held sway in Europe from 1750 to 1760. From the world in which Voltaire was a great man Rousseau, shaken to the depths of his being, could only withdraw, depart into the wilderness, into madness, put on fanciful Armenian clothing, marry Thérèse Le Vasseur, copy scores and go plant-gathering. Anyone who was a friend of this world could be no friend of his, even if his name was David Hume, and were he ever so well-disposed, or what passes for well-disposed, towards him. Let all his contemporaries reject him— indeed they must reject him, it cannot be otherwise. The time would come when he would be understood—in his last years Rousseau continually consoled himself with this, his prophecy.

And in considering all this we must always bear in mind that, no matter how often it seemed so to Rousseau himself, he was not fighting against any particular abuses of his time, any particular signs of decadence, folly or vice, not against those aspects of its spirit which were wrong, but against its spirit as a whole, not against the weaknesses of its civilization but against its civilization as such, not against its negative aspects but against the positive ones. That is why it was a struggle which was at once so embittered and so completely hopeless, and precisely why he could not remain hidden from his time, could not be ignored by it as though he were some eccentric of the kind we have always had with us. It was for this reason that his time took such an interest in him—whether this interest took the form of scorn and derision or was manifested as a friendly and sympathetic attention to what he had to say is another question. But his time could not dissociate itself from him, for the simple reason that he belonged to it. He spoke to it from its heart, just because he explained to it its own inner conflict. If Rousseau had been willing and able, he could have brought about a quite different, tranquil, honourable and harmonious end to his life as a respected, nay revered critic and fighter within society with a critical but somehow regulated relationship to the cultural beliefs of his time. It is worth remembering that he did not seek and did not accept any such formal outward kind of truce. He was not drawn by interest in what he was saying, no matter how warmly this interest might be expressed, but treated those who showed friendship towards him like enemies, maintaining his solitariness and therefore his protest not only in substance but also in form. His sense and interpretation of the contrast between himself and his time was as sharp as that. It was in this that his madness consisted. All things considered we cannot help admitting that in its own way it was at least a pertinent madness.

In face of this it might now seem rather remarkable that Rousseau's literary life-work should chiefly consist in the great structures we have mentioned: a political theory in the *Contract*, an educational programme in *Emile*, an interpretation of love and marriage in the *Nouvelle Héloïse*. And I presume we can and must add, a construction of his own life in the *Confessions* and other autobiographical works. In all these undertakings in themselves, and in the most important features of the way in which they were executed, we certainly can and must interpret him from the trends of his time, as being at one with it and as intending and desiring the same things which it wanted and intended. Or was it not the case that also here, in an even bolder and more consequential form than existed at the average cultural level of his time, the contemporary absolutist will for form was at work, whose enemy Rousseau had yet appointed and declared himself to be? Has he not fallen in—and well and truly fallen in—with the Philistines in spite of all things?

There are three primary arguments to discount this:

1. Rousseau betrays the fact that he is a thoroughgoing critic of his age in his literary work as well as in his life by the manifest unity of the anthropological theme running through all his writings. He was obviously never tempted to enter the fields of applied science or historical research. The things which did tempt him were art and natural science. But the thing which really cried out to him was man. The never-ending subject of his meditations was man, and, moreover —in this respect Rousseau is not unlike Socrates—man in relation to the problems he has to face in moulding his own peculiar existence. The results of these meditations he expressed at the very point where his time believed it had already essentially grasped and accordingly could handle everything.

2. Rousseau, in setting his contributions to the human problem beside those of his contemporaries, said things in all three or four spheres which stood out in such a way as to seem, at least relatively, still rather new, strange, Utopian, and indeed revolutionary. While he formally undertook something that could also be and was in fact done by others, he nevertheless drew patterns and created figures—think especially of the figure he presented as his own—which stood out in a sufficiently bizarre way when they were compared with what the others usually intended and achieved. It is true that the *Contract* and *Emile*, and the *Nouvelle Héloïse* too in its way are genuine eighteenth-century

creations, but it is also true that they are infused with an ardour which the rest of contemporary political, educational and erotic literature did not know in this degree, nor in this kind.

3. In contributing with these works to the achievements of his time and sharing through them his time's will to shape and mould, Rousseau made no secret of the fact that he intended even his boldest proposals to be regarded only as suggestions as to how second-best solutions might be reached. The typical man of the eighteenth century, while he was ready to admit that his insight and strength were imperfect, assumed as a matter of principle that he could yet want and achieve the best. He saw in principle only the one dimension of the possible, even when he knew that in practice he could not achieve all that it contains. Rousseau saw the second dimension, composed of the things it is not possible for man to achieve *hic et nunc*, and which therefore could not be taken as part of the programme. The man of whom Rousseau was speaking, whom he wished to help mould his life, was not the man in a state of nature whom he really has in mind, but man in society. Rousseau, as we have shown, was already resigned to this fact before he started to write the *Contract*, *Emile* and the *Nouvelle Héloïse*, but least perhaps in the *Confessions*, without trying to conceal the fact that he was nevertheless not resigned the whole time; that is, ultimately, after all, he has man in a state of nature in mind and only from this standpoint does he speak on the problem of man in society. Truly it is this extraordinary kind of resignation, resting as it does upon a most determined non-resignation, that lends his work the fire and impetus which distinguish it from everything else that was written in his time. It is precisely this kind of writing, where the author consciously refrains from giving of his best, which often has an electrifying effect which is absent from the works of many writers when they are in fact earnestly and passionately trying to write at their best. These then are the arguments against simply ranging Rousseau's works alongside those typical of the eighteenth century.

All the same, it must be maintained here that such a classification is possible. The same Rousseau who raised the anthropological problem in its ethical aspects, as a forerunner of Kant, in a situation when nobody had seen a problem there at all; the same Rousseau whose undertakings were so revolutionary in their effect for the very reason that behind them there is the recognition of a realm to which the only answer can be one of resignation; the same Rousseau said the last word concerning eighteenth-century absolutism. It is precisely in Rousseau that we see that clearly and how this absolutism, to be true, is now being restricted and broken by a new insight, only finally to assume another form in which it would continue to survive and enter the spirit of the new age, the age of Goethe. The two dimensions of Rousseau's anthropology come about only in this way, that he distinguishes between man in nature and man in society. According to Rousseau it was man's transition from this one to the other which constituted what might be called the Fall. And it is because Rousseau was aware of this irrevocable transition, yet declared himself by his suggestion for fallen man, i.e. man in society, and yet on the other hand never lost sight for one moment of the significance of the lost state before the Fall, which he saw as being condemnatory but at the same time indicative of the way we ought to go, that his doctrines of politics and education acquired this fire, this weight and impetus. But the word 'fall' in the biblical sense is not really the right one to describe this transition, however sharply Rousseau felt the contrast it implies, and however sharply this feeling distinguished him from his intellectual environment, whose way of thinking was one-dimensional. Rousseau very seriously takes it to be a transition from a good state to one less good, but not—however severely he may condemn and describe this state—a transition from good to evil.

But where in actual fact do these things have their source and domain, the possibilities of lying, tyranny, injustice, cruelty, intolerance, the effects of which Rousseau had found to be so powerful in human society, as it really is, which made him suffer so, and which caused him to attack society so radically? Wherever they may be, they are not in man, is the answer we must give, to be in agreement with him. They seem rather to be something with which man is faced, mere possibilities existing somewhere outside him. Man's downfall and misfortune consisted in his reaching within and becoming obsessed with them, so to speak, as they became real, at the moment when he went over from the individual, natural state to the social, historical one.

But this reaching within and becoming obsessed in no way alters the fact that man is fundamentally, essentially and naturally good, and has remained so. It is certainly true that his natural goodness does not prevent him from becoming less good. But even while he is deteriorating his natural goodness remains. In common with the whole of the eighteenth century Rousseau was a confirmed Pelagian, a declared opponent of the Church doctrine of original sin and no free will: man can in fact be wicked and is wicked times without number; but he is never essentially wicked and need not be so. He may well do

evil but he is not evil. The charge to be brought against man is relevant
only in a certain connexion, namely to his existence in society, which
brings with it all the evil possibilities we have mentioned. More precisely, it is relevant only to this connexion as such, or more particularly,
to society as such. The charge is levelled against the community at
large. When applied to the individual the charge loses its force and
becomes a warning against the community at large. It does not apply
to man himself, man as such. In him it encounters rather a natural
goodness, to which an appeal can be made. Thus it must not be taken
literally if we describe this transition from man in nature to man in
society in Rousseau's sense, as a fall brought about by sin. His man
neither sins when he undergoes this transition, nor is he fallen when he
has undergone it. He has merely changed in a regrettable way. He has
merely acquired a new, lamentable characteristic while remaining
substantially unchanged. He does evil, it is true, but he is still free to do
good. Rousseau was so energetic in pursuing this idea, so naïve in
taking it as his constant premise and in declaiming it, that he drew
unwelcome attention to himself even in his own Pelagian century, and
became a kind of martyr to Pelagianism, persecuted by a Roman
Catholic and Protestant Church both of which, however—they had
both been on the slippery slope for some time themselves in this
respect—had little enough to show him either as an example or as a
defence. Rousseau distinguished himself so much in this respect
particularly that it might well seem to us that he, the great opponent
of the optimism of his century, was the most optimistic of all its
optimists. While he is challenging the customs, institutions, ideals and
philosophical dicta of his time, its entire will for form and all its results.
he yet is all the more consistently able to affirm his belief in man
himself, who after all is the subject, the creator and master of all these
things.

That is why he is able to construct so boldly, and to make such
ruthlessly logical and thoroughly optimistic proposals in the fields of
politics and education. It is true that the second-best possibilities to
which he devoted himself here were different from the impossible
best ones, but even his discussion of the second-best possibilities consistently conveys an underlying faith in man as one who is fundamentally good, to whom one need only appeal, who has only to be
provided with the necessary scope, who has only to be freed as far as
possible from the temptations and burdens of society, to see appear in
him forthwith the natural miracle of virtue, even on his present plane
in the midst of society as it actually is.

The tension which is peculiar to Rousseau's teaching, in virtue of his distinction between two dimensions, consists only however of the difference, native to man himself, between the possibility and its particular realization at any time, between man as he is in his heart of hearts and his actual inner life, between what is truly human and man as he is in practice. It was this distinction which Rousseau discovered, and with it the great problem of critical idealism as it was later seen and developed by Kant, less passionately, but on the other hand with far greater precision and insight. And Rousseau's teaching operates with the tension designated by this distinction. But since his teaching recognizes this distinction only in man himself, since man's capacity for doing good is not affected by it, the end-effect of his teaching—and we shall have to say the same of Kant later—is none the less like an augmented and heightened triumph of man, or triumph of man's capacities, which to this extent makes it a solemn repetition and confirmation of the great eighteenth-century thesis. Rousseau believed that in politics we can count upon the *volonté générale* of which he speaks being actually present and active in the consciousness of the individual citizen. He believed that his Emile, having completed his education, will actually have become his own educator. He believed that a conflict such as he described in the *Nouvelle Héloïse* can really be solved in the manner he suggests. Why does he believe that all these things are possible? Because his citizen, his Emile, and his pair of lovers, St Preux and Julie, are fundamentally good human beings, even in the *status corruptionis*, simply because the corruption of this state is only relative corruption.

Rousseau expressed all this in its plainest and most comprehensible form in his autobiographical works. He was in no doubt about his faults and bad habits, and the candour with which he confessed them really leaves nothing to be desired. He made no bones of accusing himself of extreme weakness where his inclinations were concerned, of a laziness to which he again and again succumbed, of frivolity, and even of downright viciousness. As an old man he was still in all seriousness concerned about an act of meanness he had committed in his youth.[1] If it were really the recognition and confession of sin in concrete form which was all-important, then we should have to grant that his *Confessions* are a perfect model. But the other side to the matter is that Rousseau, at the same time as he was confessing his sins, scarcely ever neglected to point out to us that in the midst of and in spite of everything he had a good heart, to enumerate and vaunt the excellent

---

[1] *Rêv. 4me. promenade*, Basle ed., Vol. 20, pp. 219, 232.

qualities of his true character, the qualities of his inner nature which
people did not understand, to emphasize the good intentions which had
been behind nearly everything he had done, and either to present his
failings as merely negative aspects of his virtues (e.g. his indolence
as a manifestation of his great love of freedom, which would have him
act always only in response to his very own most deeply personal
impulses) or to trace them as regrettable reactions to even more regrettable behaviour prevalent in the world about him. It is scarcely
possible to find in these confessions an example of a truly undialectical
piece of self-accusation, apart from the memory of his youth we have
just mentioned. Another exception may be the fact that he did not tell
Madame de Warens the whole truth about his faithfulness to her, at a
meeting with her in later years.[1] On the other hand it is quite possible
to find more than one passage where he declares that it was always his
pride that his misfortune had been undeserved.[2] And there is more
than one passage where he quite openly declares that by and large, all
his faults, etc., considered, he could not help considering himself the
best of all men.[3] Bearing all this in mind, is it not perhaps possible
after all to interpret his delusion, his persecution mania, as expressing
the only too complete correspondence of his spirit with the spirit of
his age? Be that as it may, the church doctrine of original sin has
seldom, I believe, been denied with such disconcerting candour and
force and in so directly personal a way. The secret that man is good,
blurted out so expansively and with such assurance, was bound to
appear suspicious even to the many just men of the time who by and
large were as hard-boiled as Rousseau himself. But the people who
became angry with him in that respect branded themselves by the
very fact of their anger as backward, as lacking in understanding of
their own time. Anyone who was moving with the times was bound to
be thankful to Rousseau, and was thankful to him because he had
finally said the last word, because he had so ruthlessly lent such
momentum and language to that which they all felt and wanted
after all.

Seen from this aspect Rousseau, in the constructions of his main
works was not so much a critic and reformer of his time as its leader, its
most eloquent tongue, its most perfect culmination. And in so far as
the whole new age which made its appearance with him would follow
him in this, would not get beyond the distinction between man in his
heart of hearts and his actual inner life, between human possibility

---

[1] *Conf.* Basle ed., Vol. 21, p. 198.   [2] *Conf.* 21, 252.
[3] *Conf.* 22, 74; *Rêv.* 20, 265.

and actuality, in so far as the doctrine of original sin would be as a red rag to it too, in so far as it too would believe that man is good, and believe it perhaps in a way which was still far more comprehensive, far more logical and far more suited to genius; thus far this new age too would only be a culmination of the old one in spite of all the break with what had gone before. Is there any difference between Rousseau's *Confessions* and Goethe's *Dichtung und Wahrheit* except that in Goethe all the opposition of good and evil, which in Rousseau still seems to be indicating something like two worlds, is dissolved into the progression of a single development which is both inwardly and outwardly not accidental but necessary, so that all the self-justification which still rings through so naïvely in Rousseau can disappear in Goethe, to be replaced by a self-representation which is almost, but not quite, self-satisfied? Is there any difference except that the same good man who in Rousseau was seeking himself has in Goethe joyfully found himself? It is the fact that this seeking and finding should become a problem at all which is the new thing distinguishing the age of Goethe from the eighteenth century. For the eighteenth century, rejoicing in its command of all things, had *not* asked after this, after man himself, for all the importance man had assumed for it. But did the new quality of the age of Goethe signify anything except that man's command was now regarded as much wider: as including man's command over himself? Within this new element Rousseau's Pelagianism would then be to Goethe's as promise is to fulfilment. And we could then certainly interpret this new spirit as a whole as that of the eighteenth century reborn, and for the first time assuming classic stature, risen like the phoenix from the ashes.

But we would be failing to understand Rousseau's—or Goethe's—Pelagianism if we simply ascribed it, as theologians have so often done, to a lightness of conscience, and therefore judged it, so to speak, as a moral deficiency. The decisive factor we must take into account in considering Rousseau's belief in the goodness of man, held with a firmness astonishing even to such a time as his, and the wholehearted support for this view which the age of Goethe then lent him all along, is the fact that this new age, and Rousseau as one of the first within it, had made a completely new discovery in the realm of anthropology, and that it was this same discovery which underlay its contention that man was good, its rejection of the dogma of original sin, and such self-appreciations as those of Rousseau, so moving to us now in their *naïveté*; but which also underlay Goethe's glorified vision of his own existence and development. From this fact it follows also that what we might

call optimism of the new age was not only incomparably more powerful, but essentially different from what might strike us as being optimism in those belonging to the age which was then drawing to its close.
The natural goodness of man which Rousseau claimed exists is definitely not in any simple or direct sense that which we are in the habit of
calling moral goodness, freedom from evil impulses, freedom from
all kinds of temptation, and freedom to respect the feelings of our
fellow-men. And hence his self-praise is not in any simple or direct
sense moral self-praise. The goodness of which he speaks is of course
moral goodness too: Rousseau imagined that he was good-hearted truly
and particularly also in this respect. But his kind of goodness was not
primarily moral goodness. If Rousseau believed that his heart was good
he did so because he imagined that in the midst of a society whose whole
striving and interest were directed outwards, he had discovered quite
anew that man has a heart, and what the human heart actually is. The
heart is simply the man himself, discounting everything he produces or
which confronts him as an alien existence or as the work of alien hands.
This is what Rousseau has found: himself. And this is what he holds to
be good and even precious: the fact that he exists and does not not-
exist, precisely as the man he is, situated precisely as he is in fact
situated. A whole world revealed itself to him when he gazed into
himself. He did not do this in the manner of the individualism of his
time, which looked within in order to go out again at once into the
outside world, desiring to apprehend, form and conquer. Rousseau
intended to linger there because he had recognized that in it he
possessed his own unique world full of unique forms of truth and beauty.
Existence was not just a predicate, not entirely a matter of how I
conduct myself towards the outerworld. It was definitely not just
acting and suffering. Existence was a beautiful, rich and lively inner
life of its own, so beautiful, rich and lively that anyone who has once
discovered it no longer attributes any worth to any life which differs
from it, and can only have and love anything different from it as it is
connected with this life; but he really could have and love it now in
this connexion. Existence was, so to speak, the realm of the middle, the
mean. It was the paradise of the happy and at the same time the secure
haven of the unhappy. It was the dependable norm for all the distinctions and choices that are necessary in life, and a norm which functioned as it were automatically. Man existing, being himself as Rousseau
more than once said, was in God's presence and like him. If a state
exists where the soul can find a secure place which can contain it whole,
a place secure enough that it can find complete rest in it and can

collect again the forces of its being in it, without needing to recall the past, nor encroach upon the future, a place where time is as nothing to the soul and the present lasts for ever, without making its duration noticeable and without leaving any after-effects, a place where the soul is without any other feeling, be it privation or pleasure, joy or pain, fear or desire, except for that of existence, if there is such a state and if this feeling can fill the soul utterly, while it lasts he who is enjoying it can call himself happy. It would not be an imperfect, poor and relative happiness, like that found in the pleasures of life, but a happiness which is sufficient, perfect and full, leaving no void in the soul which the soul experiences the need to fill. Such is the state in which I often found myself on St Peter's Island during my solitary day-dreams, sitting sometimes in my boat, which I simply let drift as the waters took it, or sitting sometimes on the shore of the troubled lake, or beside a river murmuring over the pebbles. What does one enjoy in such a moment? One enjoys nothing exterior to oneself, nothing except oneself and one's own existence; while it lasts one is self-sufficient, like God. The feeling of existing stripped of all other emotions is in itself a precious feeling of peace and security, which would alone be quite enough to make one's existence sweet and dear.[1]

This then is the new world which Rousseau discovered, and it was because he discovered it, unlike the outside world, in *himself*, or rather discovered it as himself, and found it *good*, once again unlike the outside world, that he says that man is good naturally, in and in spite of all things. Nature, which Rousseau so often pointed out as the true source and eternal law of human life, is very simply man himself, as distinct from man as he is in his circumstances, as he is in his works, as he is determined by other people. That is why at the end of his life Rousseau is able to speak thankfully even of the hard fate which befell him in the shape of the persecution he imagined was being meted out to him. It was this fate, he said, which in sundering him violently from the outside world, had forced him to withdraw into himself still more intensively and now even more than ever before.[2] On St Peter's Island he even felt able to wish he were prisoner,[3] indeed it seemed to him that a stay in the Bastille, in a dungeon where there were no objects to catch the eye, might not be at all unpleasant.[4]

But this renunciation of things external particularly, must be interpreted as very dialectic in intention, if we wish to gain a true picture of the realm of anthropology as discovered by Rousseau. Terms like subjectivism and solipsism would describe badly what Rousseau means.

[1] *Rêv.* 20, 255f.   [2] *Rêv.* 20, 203f.   [3] *Rêv.* 20, 246.   [4] *Rêv.* 20, 257.

He was, as we saw in the confession just quoted, not in a dungeon at all, but surrounded by the delights of nature, and he knows and admits that in effect he cannot do without this partner, the object, at least in this form. No, even the most insignificant object has the power to rouse his imagination and thereby to move him to the depths of his being (*Conf.* 19, 158). He calls himself *une âme expansive*, a soul which simply will and must influence other beings by its feelings and existence.[1] He actually goes so far as to say that it was only in withdrawing into himself and precisely thereby that he first learned to appreciate and absorb external Nature, which previously he had allowed to affect him only in its entirety, in its concrete form, in the diversity of its scents, colours and forms.[2] That is why in old age he took up his botanical studies again after he had for a time given them up because he had tired of them. He started right from the beginning again long after he had given away all his herbaria and sold all his books.[3] It was, to be sure, only botany he took up again. He rejected with horror the suggestion that he should engage also in mineralogy or zoology, explaining that man can approach the study of earth and animals only in such an unpleasant way that this was in itself proof enough that in these sciences man was much too far removed from the will of nature, and therefore from himself. It was only the plant world, he said, which had any immediate contact with man as he truly is. But it is by no means his desire to practise botany systematically and still less with any practical end in view; he just wants to indulge in it as a quietly loving friend of the trees, flowers and grasses, to rejoice without any desire or object in nature's system, of which man cannot become the master because he at once feels himself identical with it, with the whole of Nature, accordingly as he gazes and accordingly as he directly absorbs its reality. To the very attentive, very loyal observer the actual contours of the various single things out there which only just now had been concrete merge into one another again. They cease for him to be single things. Nature becomes a whole again, and man cannot help but feel himself at one with the whole. Thus the single object makes an appearance certainly, but only to disappear again.[4] It is thus that Rousseau can still say that he feels as if he were *brûlant d'amour sans objet*.[5] He yearns for a kind of happiness *sans en savoir démêler l'objet*.[6] He thinks it is again the limitation imposed upon him to the feelings of his own heart which alone enables him to taste the sweetness of existence[7] and believes he can draw nourishment from his personal substance which seems to him inexhaustible.[8] *M'y*

[1] *Rêv.* 20, 287.   [2] 20, 280f.   [3] 20, 277f.   [4] 20, 257, 281, 287.
[5] *Conf.* 20, 75.   [6] *Rêv.* 20, 201.   [7] 20, 300.   [8] 20, 302.

voilà tranquille au fond de l'abyme, pauvre mortel infortuné, mais impassible comme Dieu même.[1]

It would certainly not be right to play off the one group of these remarks about the object against the other. Rousseau needs and does not need the object, he affirms the object and denies it. Both attitudes are equally essential to the 'ecstasy' of his sense of existing. It is a question with this sense of existing of there being a complete cycle, which must on principle be uninterrupted. It is this very cycle from the ego to the object and back again, in which, however, the ego gives to the motion its direction, force and measure, which forms the life of the inner world discovered by Rousseau. We must surely call it ultimately an inner world, an anthropological province: that province in which man, before he takes up any attitude to anything, and before he knows and acts, is immediately aware both of himself and of his relation to an outer world, in such a manner that he is just as able to absorb the second awareness, that of the object, in the awareness of self, as he is to allow the awareness of the object to proceed from the awareness of self in the first place. He is capable here, in his heart, in his sense of existing, of being non-identical with the outside world, and yet again identical with it. It is because the world Rousseau discovered is the world of this human capacity that we must ultimately call it an inner world, an anthropological province.

It is usual in the history of literature and ideas to find this circumstance expressed by means of the assertion that Rousseau, and the age of Goethe which followed him, had looked beyond knowledge and action and discovered their common source, feeling, which they also considered to be the true central organ of the human mind. But he must realize that by 'feeling' is meant the capacity to project consciously, the capacity to assume this dialectical relationship with the outside world, with the object. While feeling, man enjoys himself passively, and rejoices even in an existence which, while different from his own, is yet in contact with it. But in feeling he also has the desire to extend his own existence to include this other existence, and it is thus especially when he is feeling that man becomes and remains truly himself. There is absolutely no question of his perhaps allowing the objects to approach him indiscriminately, allowing himself to be affected and dominated by them without restraint. Nor certainly will he allow himself to fall into that kind of activist individualism, in which man attempts to become the master of the object. With feeling—and it is this which makes for the intoxicating grandeur of the human capacity which has

[1] *Rêv.* 20, 176.

been discovered here, and for the mature wisdom of him who is aware
of it—it is always a question of the superior freedom inherent in being able
to make contact with objects and yet being able to part from them again,
to be separate from them and yet able to make contact with them again
and again. The man who is feeling has respect for the object, does not,
that is, attempt to interfere with it in its quality as an object. He does
not allow it to approach too near, and keeps his distance from it in his
turn.

But this respect is nothing but respect for his own existence, which
is experienced by the same feeling, the existence which may enrich
itself from the object, but may not become submerged in it, and that
is why this respect cannot prevent man, in passing from the diastole
to the systole, from completely equating the object with himself again.
'To tend nature in oneself, oneself in nature' as Goethe later put it,
signifies the revolution of an eccentric wheel, in which the apparent
distance of the periphery from the centre is all the more decisively
transformed with the next half-turn into the closest proximity.

Goethe was destined to do more honour to the object than Rousseau,
engaging not only in botany, but in mineralogy and zoology too, and
many other kinds of natural science, without Rousseau's fear, seemingly so childish of offending nature and thereby himself. Goethe
would also once again bring historical man into the sphere of the objective world in which he showed interest, the sphere from which he had in
the end completely vanished, with Rousseau at least. And Goethe would
listen to what the world of objects has to say in a manner incomparably
more composed, more earnest and more patient, would be incomparably more receptive and more cautious in the attempt to extend his
own existence to include other beings. But for all that Goethe's world
would not be different from the inner world discovered by Rousseau,
the world containing the simultaneous capacity to take the object
completely seriously and not take it seriously at all, the world containing a sovereignty beside which the achievement of the eighteenth
century in mastering the object might well seem a lamentably half-
hearted attempt, simply because it did not yet have this freedom. It is
only when man is capable of controlling his capacity to influence
objects, capable of employing or of not employing it, when he is in fact
impassible comme Dieu même, unaffected by the claims of the object upon
him and unaffected by his feelings towards it, that he stands for the
first time invested with a true power in the world of things. In this too
Rousseau and Goethe were in accord, but whereas Rousseau seems
like a novice, agitated, spasmodic and confused, Goethe was calm,

superior, composed and lucid. And yet there was a certain selective, reserved and chance quality about Rousseau's attitude to the object which is characteristic of Goethe too: there were certain things in nature even, let alone in history and in life, which Goethe also did not wish to see or know, because they did not accord with his essential being. He did not wish to offend nature either, if only so that nature should not offend him. He also moved through the world of things, not coyly like Rousseau, but *impassible comme Dieu même*, with a supreme refinement, preserving the formalities. And this is how and why he was occasionally free to overlook and forget the non-identity between it and himself. It is not simply in an awareness of identity that Goethe's secret consists; it is just as little true of Goethe as it is of Rousseau— there had been monists long before their lifetime; monism just as much as the dualism of spirit and nature is from the point of view of Rousseau and Goethe a stupidly one-sided view. Their secret is in fact a much greater one, consisting in the freedom to alternate between the awareness of identity and the awareness of non-identity, or in being able to experience both as a unity in their own spirit-nature. There can be no doubt that Rousseau already knew about this spirit-nature. There is already something of the great peace imparted by this Goethean concept in Rousseau's confusion. Thus what Rousseau referred to ambiguously and confusingly enough as 'nature' is really spirit-nature. It was the one positive thing which threw him, as the only one with any knowledge of this matter, into his conflict with his age: twenty or thirty years later he would have been able to find a thousand people who shared his knowledge. He was referring to human spirit-nature when he said that man is good and therefore capable of the fantastic things we have just heard about. The eighteenth century did not understand itself for as long as it failed to understand what a splendid, radiant and at the same time profound Pelagianism Rousseau was offering it. But to a great extent it understood itself and equally Rousseau much better than Rousseau himself imagined in his prophetic solitude. At the points where this happened the new age had already dawned in the middle of the old.

We can now go on to state, in the briefest manner possible, what effect all this was to have upon the theological problem as it existed at this time. Rousseau's attack upon the absolutism of his age could also have signified a protest against his age's peculiar absolutist, i.e. moralizing, intellectualizing, individualizing treatment of the Christian question, and thus against the way theology had developed in his time. The opening up of this second dimension, which is so characteristic of his thinking, could have signified the opening up of a new understanding of sin, grace, revelation and reconciliation. Rousseau opposed his time in a way revolutionary enough to make us wonder whether this solitary fighter and sufferer might not in the last assessment simply have been someone in whose ears the word 'God' rang in quite an unprecedented way. Or are we wrong in being tempted to see in Rousseau, as he was when he made his first public appearance in Paris back in 1749-50, one inspired by a touch of the hem of the mantle of the prophet Amos? Not even the vision which called him was missing, nor persecution, nor the prophet's vicarious suffering. Even at the time of his madness everything had something of the quality of a call being answered, of revelation, inspiration and the inescapable earnestness of the Divine. Even his contemporaries observed this very clearly and he certainly was not lacking in supporters who acknowledged reverently and enthusiastically—quite apart from the fact that this was his own opinion—that he had rediscovered and proclaimed once again the true Christianity.

It is not for us either to confirm or deny that his was the true Christianity. We must however establish that in the very way he understood Christianity he did not deviate from the typical thought of his time, but here also he was merely the man who—putting the famous neologians of his time well and truly in the shade—pursued this thought to its conclusion in a highly radical way. That was what was theologically new about Rousseau: the fact that he broke completely with the doctrine of original sin, which had long been under fire from all sides, and with the conception of revelation also generally threatened for a long time, as an event which was something apart from the inherent development of humanity. Rousseau took both, sin and grace, as being relative movements within human reality, movements in which man, naturally good and persisting in this state of natural goodness, remains assured of his freedom. Rousseau's new gift to theology ultimately consists in this very widening of the concept of reason by means of the discovery of man's spirit-nature, for which objectivity and non-objectivity, non-identity and identity become reciprocal and interchangeable ideas. The theological significance of this discovery was nothing less than the settlement of the conflict between reason and revelation, since by it man was encouraged to look upon himself alternately now as reason and now as revelation. For this it was not first necessary that the word 'God' should take on a new sound. It was enough that the word 'Man' had now for the first time acquired its full, whole tone. Far from contradicting the theological absolutism of its time, Rousseau's doctrine was meant to convey a demand that this theology should at last understand itself rightly, i.e. truly understand man as one who in his true humanity can also command the true God.

Eighteenth-century theology was always thirty years behind the times. This was borne out also in the case of Rousseau. It accounts for the grotesque fact that Rousseau was martyred by an 'orthodoxy' not half so sinister as it seemed to him and to his other secular contemporaries. We must not allow ourselves to be blinded by this spectacle into not realizing that Rousseau did not actually oppose the theology of his time, but only rushed on far ahead of it. He himself prophesied that the theology of his Vicar of Savoy would rise again to a great future. From what we know of the development of the theology of the schools at that time no gift of prophecy was necessary to predict this fact. The theology of the Vicar of Savoy was, of course, like Rousseau's doctrine, still capable of being enriched, deepened and improved in many ways. Simply in the form he first gave it it did not win through. But taking it as it then was we can say in advance that it was indeed bound to have a great future. It is from Rousseau onwards and originating from Rousseau that the thing called theological rationalism, in the full sense of the term, exists: a theology for which the Christian spirit is identical with the truly humane spirit, as it is inalienably and tangibly present to us in that depth of the *ratio* in that inmost anthropological province. Such is the significance of Rousseau for the history of theology—but of Rousseau only as the first harbinger of the age of Goethe: he represented the invitation extended to theology to join forces in determined fashion with this determined rationalism.

6

LESSING

THE two things we had to say as a preliminary to discussing Rousseau we must also emphasize of Lessing: he was on the one hand a perfect and perfecting man of the eighteenth century and on the other a complete stranger to his age. There are none of the century's peculiarities of interest and desire which we cannot find again in Lessing. So far as theology especially is concerned, we find, just as with Rousseau, only conclusions which are rather forcibly drawn, and insights and attempts at expression which are terminated abruptly, and hang in the air, as it were, just waiting for some completely wise, completely free-minded person to pronounce and formulate them, to rank henceforth as definite achievements in the history of human thought. The philosophy of the Enlightenment, with its unconditional will for form in morality, and resulting respect for the all-embracing power of natural logic, its unquestioning acceptance of the view of life built up on this logic and on natural experience, Lessing effortlessly understood and was able to take as his standpoint without the slightest difficulty, as a self-evident point of departure for every advance. It was right to draw a parallel between the character and achievement of Lessing, and that of Frederick the Great. No one, in Germany in the second half of the eighteenth century, at any rate, afforded so classic an example of the spirit of the age as these two men.

But whilst Lessing represented this age in its most mature form, he also left it behind him. The course of his life, subject to frequent change, outwardly so unrewarding, so often beset by disaster, and no less violent in its way than Rousseau's, already shows that fundamentally he also could not find himself within the limitations imposed by the order, the customs and possibilities of his time. His dealings with Frederick the Great, for instance, in great contrast to what they could and should have been ran their course in the form of a fundamental mutual misunderstanding: Lessing, like so many of his younger contemporaries, honoured and celebrated a fictional, mythical Frederick, not the real one as he lived and had his being at Potsdam;

and thus it was inevitable that in his turn the real Frederick should be completely unable to recognize flesh of his flesh and spirit of his spirit in Lessing. While Lessing was still a young man he had quarrelled with the great Voltaire (we remember Rousseau's relations with the same person) and in later years, in spite of all he undoubtedly owed him as a critic, he became objectively his most bitter opponent. He likewise became the opponent of his compatriot Gottsched, in spite of the fact that the aims they were striving for were related. In theology he came to oppose not only people like Goeze and the orthodox churchmen, but Semler, and those who shared Semler's neological views; further he lent his support to the achievements of Reimarus only because their radicalism interested him from the standpoint of method, and supported them only to reject them eventually dialectically, just as he abandoned the position of the apologists who opposed Reimarus. And even though he did to the last remain the friend of the last great Enlightenment philosopher, Moses Mendelssohn of Berlin, it is nevertheless more than likely that Mendelssohn was fundamentally mistaken in thinking he could command Lessing's services in support of his own harmlessly theistic interpretation of Spinoza against Heinrich Friedrich Jacobi. With or without Spinoza, Lessing had certainly long been on the road which led to Goethe, to interpreting God, in an at any rate quite untheistic way as the immanent principle of the human microcosm and macrocosm. Lessing in fact, although he was everywhere aligned with the front rank of his contemporaries, and functioned as their most eloquent and respected spokesman, had likewise broken away at every point from the positions they characteristically occupied. We must also understand him in relation to the play of the dialectic of tendencies to which this fact gives rise.

In recent years more than one commentator has appraised Gotthold Ephraim Lessing (1729-81) as a specifically masculine genius. There is certainly something illuminating about this remark, especially when we read Lessing after Rousseau. The two have in common the discovery of the second dimension we were talking about, the discovery of human existence as such, as distinct from what man can know and desire. Lessing was more of a scholar than Rousseau. He was, like Rousseau, a moralist. Moreover he had, like Rousseau, the knowledge of something beyond science and morals. He spoke of the heart and of feelings less often and with less emphasis than Rousseau, but he, too, did refer to them, especially at decisive points. The sober Lessing did not advance to that revolution of the heart against science and morals which Rousseau so stormily implemented; therefore he did not come to the self-analytical reveries and constructions, nor, for the same reason, to the educational and political ones, which are so characteristic of Rousseau. Coming from Rousseau to Lessing is like emerging from the twilight into a clear daylight, almost painful in its intensity. But the knowledge of that inner place of existence and of its significance as the source of the whole, the enjoyment of freedom in one's relation to the outside world which springs from this knowledge; these things are also typical of Lessing. For him, too, the ultimate reality is this free, stirring communion of the ego with the object, in which, however, the ego ever retains and regains the mastery. But whereas the use of this freedom which typifies Rousseau consists in a withdrawal from without to within from the object to the ego, Lessing rejoices in this same freedom as the freedom to make contact, the freedom to act. Whereas Rousseau above all always seems to be wanting to draw back from the thing facing him, Lessing rather seemed as if he were constantly wanting to seek it out, without mistaking the tension to which this attitude gives rise, and without relapsing into the naïve individualism of his older contemporaries. Rousseau was the lyric poet, and Lessing the dramatist. This is what might perhaps be meant by the reference to his 'masculinity'. But common to both Rousseau and Lessing was the standpoint of a wider, deeper rationalism, a rationalism deepened in the direction of an independent and permanently independent awareness of one's own existence. It was the same new feeling for life which in the midst of the eighteenth century triumphed both in Rousseau's revulsion, which easily affects us as being childish, and in the maturely tragic quality of Lessing's life.

It is thus not merely by chance that it was the drama and the theory of the drama which outwardly formed the peak of Lessing's life achievement. The drama was for him the highest genre of the poetic art, and therefore of art in general, because, as he intended to show in the continuation of his Laocoön which he never wrote, 'all art should strive to be a direct representation of nature, and poetry, which can depict and represent only indirectly, only by means of words, rises solely in the drama to a true modelling or imitation of life, to developing actions, and to effective speeches, feelings and passions'.[1] What interested Lessing so much about the drama in particular was therefore (as he taught in opposition to the French classical dramatists and together with Sophocles and Shakespeare) that it is to be defined as the poetic representation of an action, whose parts should be formed by their presentation into a unity in such a way that they are bound to appear

[1] Scherer-Walzel, p. 353.

alone and in their relation to one another as a necessary expression of the nature of the human characters taking part; in such a manner, therefore, that what is actually presented is the inner life of these characters, the sight of which must evoke in the spectator feelings of sympathy and of compassion, and compel him to the admission that in the same situation, and at the same stage of such a passion, he would have been bound to act in exactly the same way. Lessing thought that the drama should not arouse mere wonder at this or that sad or merry event, and that it should not therefore present such events to men at all as events but as revelations, and by this method of presentation evoke feelings of sympathy in others, that is, make these others participate in the action which was being presented. For this reason Lessing gave to his own dramas that proximity of the subject to life, that firmness in the construction and execution of his plots, that pregnant quality in the dialogue, which made his contemporaries sense that there was something quite new about them. This was an art which suddenly dared to take as its real object the nature of man himself, which is subject to so many varied influences, as it is seen in the unfolding of human actions. In this conception of art we have before us at the same time the deepest meaning of Lessing's conception of life: his particular problem and theme was man, but man in action, or to put it the other way, action, but action always as human action.

At this point we can very well transfer our gaze directly to Lessing's contribution to the history of Protestant theology, which is of especial interest to us. The son of a pastor in Saxony, he played a part in theology both in his youth and when he was older. It was not only an incidental one but fraught with such passion and with such an extensive knowledge of the subject that it is very much open to question whether it was not here, rather than in the field of art and the theory of art that his true central interest lay. In the last ten years of his life at any rate theological matters claimed his attention, outwardly as well, as nothing else did. We have in our possession a whole series of very characteristic essays and fragments on church history and the philosophy of religion which he wrote when he was still quite young. The decisive step—it has perhaps rather exaggeratedly been called 'one of the most important events in the history of the Protestant church and theology'[1]—came in the years 1774-8. Lessing published a series of fragments which he alleged he had found among the shelves of the Wolfenbüttel library, of which he was in charge, from the *Apologie oder Schutzschrift für die vernünftigen Verehrer Gottes* (Apology or defence for the reasonable worshippers of

[1] Scherer-W., p. 357.

God), written in 1767 by Hermann Samuel Reimarus, Professor of Oriental Languages in Hamburg, who was born in 1694 and died in 1768. He was probably given this manuscript, which its author did not intend to have published, by the dead man's sister, Elise Reimarus, a gifted woman who also numbered Mendelssohn and Jacobi among her friends. The fragments published by Lessing developed in an intensity which until then, in Germany at least, had been absent from public discussion of the matter, a fundamental denial of the necessity and possibility of all revelation and especially of the biblical Christian revelation when seen against the background of the implemented conception of a purely natural religion, a religion, that is, representing a universal, timelessly valid human possibility, such as forms the basis of every historical, positive and allegedly revealed religion and which is more or less decayed in all of them and to which, therefore, a reasonable worship of God must now go back whatever its present position may be. It was essentially the same reduction which we know from Rousseau's confession of the Vicar of Savoy, written a short time before.

Lessing provided this publication with a continuous commentary in which, as its title, *Contrasts*, states, he expressed his material denial of much that Reimarus presented, but also his partial agreement with it, and above all his belief that the problem which Reimarus had raised was highly important from a fundamental and methodological point of view. The violent polemical repercussions which the publication immediately called forth provided him with a favourable opportunity, in the famous series of polemics in which he gave his further views on the subject, *Über den Beweis des Geistes und der Kraft* (Concerning the proof of the spirit and the power), *Das Testament Johannis* (St John's Gospel), *Eine Duplik* (A Rejoinder), *Eine Parabel* (A Parable), *Axiomata*, *Anti-Goeze*, etc., of engaging less in a defence of Reimarus than in an attack upon and exposure of Reimarus' opponents. It was the censor's office at Brunswick which put a stop to the continuation of the fragments and to the further development of the dispute in 1778. This could not, however, prevent Lessing in 1779 from giving classic expression, in *Nathan der Weise* (Nathan the Wise), his most mature dramatic work, to his notions concerning the relationship between natural and positive religion which had matured in the course of the struggle he had been engaged in. The series of theses, *Die Erziehung des Menschengeschlechts* (The Education of the Human Race), published in 1780, which belong with *Nathan*, are a last systematic exposition of the same ideas. Their genuineness as Lessing's work is in dispute. Their content, however, coincides so exactly with the views

Lessing expressed elsewhere that the question as to whether and to what extent he perhaps allowed someone else to speak as a witness, as he in fact loved to do, is for all practical purposes an idle one. (It is considered that his collaborator was most likely the young farmer Albrecht Thaer.)

If we wish to understand Lessing's aims as a theologian we must proceed from the fact that every one of the positions of the theological neologians of that time, up to and including the thoroughgoing neologism of a man like Reimarus, which tended to turn into rationalism, were also contained and preserved in Lessing's own position. His early theological works testify that here he had his origins. But *Nathan* and the *Education* still show this very plainly. It would be possible to put a construction upon Lessing's theology which would show him to have been simply a particularly bold and advanced but ultimately typical neologian. Lessing was one when already in his younger days he was of the opinion that the Christian religion was not something 'that should be taken on trust and belief from one's parents'.[1]

> A man like you does not
> Stay in the station birth by chance
> Accords him: or if he stays, he stays
> From choice, by reason of his insight[2]

is still the view expressed by Saladin to Nathan (Act III, Scene 5). Just as Lessing in 1751 already thought it a great thing 'to think for oneself and challenge accepted prejudice', 'to convince oneself of one's belief', and indeed by the method of a comparative testing of the various religions in the form of a religious discussion, the form in which, twenty-five years later, he actually presented it in *Nathan*[2]—so in 1760 he exhorted himself with the words: 'I say to myself, submit to this investigation like an honest man! Look everywhere with your own eyes! Distort nothing! Embellish nothing! Let your conclusions flow as they will! Do not impede, do not attempt to guide their course!'[3] and so in 1778 still he declares it his duty 'to test with his own eyes, *quid liquidum sit in causa Christianorum.*[4]

We hear the typical moralistic refrain of the entire theology of the eighteenth century in the young Lessing's angry growl at the supposed believer, 'who has memorized and who utters, often without understanding them, the principles of Christian doctrine, who goes to church

[2] *Theologische Schriften*, I, 25-33 (Theological Writings).
[3] Ibid., I, 222.
[4] Ibid., IV, 166.

and takes part in every ceremony because it is customary', at that 'majority of people' who show by their 'comportment' 'what proper Christians they are'.[1] And we hear this refrain again when Nathan (Act I, 2) breaks into the famous words:

> But do you comprehend
> That it's far easier to be in ecstasies
> Than to act well? How willingly the feeblest
> Welcome ecstasy, but to escape—
> And be they of their object unaware—
> The task of being virtuous in life?[2]

We hear the well-known neological rejection and re-interpretation of the dogma of original sin in hearing[2] and its truth consists in the fact that man at the first and lowest stage of his humanity was simply not sufficiently master of his actions to be able to act in accordance with moral laws, or in hearing[3] of original sin that it consists in the 'superior power of our sensual desires, our dark imagination over all knowledge be it ever so clear', a power which 'we have it in us' to weaken and which we can even 'use just as much for the doing of good as for the doing of evil'. The characters in *Nathan* are thus accordingly (with the exception perhaps of the odious patriarch) all splendid, lovable people,[4] well able to take comfort even after their less glorious deeds:

> Why should I be ashamed of a mistake?
> For is it not my firm resolve to right it?[5]

For the same reason the truth of the doctrine of the atonement through the Son of God is therefore held to consist simply in God's giving moral laws to man, in spite of man's original incapacity for them, out of consideration for his Son; but this, according to Lessing, means out of consideration for his own perfection, the perfection which annuls individual man's imperfection, and thus in his not excluding man from the prospect of moral blessedness. For the doctrine of justification by faith Lessing can altogether find only the angrily derisive cry: to faith 'you give the keys of heaven and hell, and sufficient good fortune to make for virtue, so that by the skin of your teeth you can make virtue into some sort of companion to faith! With you the worship of sacred chimeras makes blessed without righteousness, but not righteousness without the worship. What a delusion!'[6]

---

[2] In the *Erziehung des Menschengeschlechts* (Education of the Human Race), para. 74.
[3] In the *Theologische Schriften* (Theological Writings), II, 265f.
[4] Scherer-W., p. 363.   [5] *Nathan*, V, 5.
[6] *Theological Writings*, I, 39f.

The Christology to go with this has as its main tenet the affirmation of a 'Religion of Christ' most clearly and plainly contained in the Gospels: 'The religion of Christ is the religion which Christ himself knew and practised as a man; which every man can have in common with him; which every man must wish more and more to have in common with him, the more sublime and lovable he conceives the character of Christ as a mere human being to have been.' The 'Christian religion', on the other hand, is something quite different, consisting essentially in the acceptance of the belief that Christ was more than a mere human being. It is inconceivable, says Lessing in this fragment, that anyone could hold these two religions simultaneously.[1]

Also most genuinely in the style of the eighteenth century, having become typical since Gottfried Arnold, are the young Lessing's ventures upon all sorts of 'saving' actions, i.e. his defence of certain historical figures which the writers of official Protestant church history were alleged to have treated badly: the Renaissance philosopher Cardanus, Cochleus, the Roman Catholic writer of polemics, the anti-Trinitarian Adam Neuser, who embraced the Islamic faith in the second half of the sixteenth century, and other similar figures. In a piece of 1750, about the Moravian brethren, which he unfortunately only managed to begin, Lessing glowingly compared this community with Socrates, as opposed to his pupils Plato and Aristotle, who had already fallen short of the simplicity of their master; with Descartes, as opposed to Newton and Leibnitz, philosophers who simply filled the head but left the heart empty, with the 'simple, light and lively religion of Adam as opposed to the religion of Judaism, with the Christianity of Christ and of the first century as opposed to that of the Middle Ages, with the beginning of the Reformation as opposed to everything which had followed the dispute about the Eucharist'.[2] And the historical phenomena which traditional church history usually accords a positive value, he treats with sound neological scepticism and malice in just the opposite manner.

> When was I not all ear as often as
> It pleased you to recount the story of
> The heroes of your faith? Have I not ever
> Gladly paid their deeds the constant tribute
> Of my wonder, their sufferings the tribute
> Of my tears? Their faith, I must confess,
> I never found their most heroic part[3]

we hear Nathan's ward Recha, who, as we know, has been brought up in two faiths, saying to Daja, her nurse. And the young Lessing does not

---

[1] *Theological Writings*, IV, 248f.   [2] Ibid., I, 204f.
[3] *Nathan*, III, i. For original, see Appendix, p. 401.

shrink from stating that he has noticed that amongst the much praised
early Christian heroes there had been some who deserved the name of
fools or madmen rather than that of martyrs and he makes no secret
of his belief that a bee in somebody's bonnet can achieve as much as the
truth in all its glory.[1] Concerning the persecutions of the early Christians he remarks that they were never so general or official as they have
often been represented and, moreover, he thinks he is right to ask whether
the Christians were really quite without blame in the matter. Did
they not deserve to be punished for their nocturnal gatherings, which
gave offence and were after all forbidden in Rome? 'Since their religion
did not in the least demand such meetings, why were they always
running to meet each other? Why these night-gatherings of whole
hordes of people of every age and sex? They were bound to be suspect
to any good police force.' And their love-feasts! 'What was the point of
these sacred revels?'[2] And then again, in his *Rettung des Cochleus* (Deliverance of Cochleus) in 1754 Lessing makes it quite apparent that in
his opinion the sixteenth-century Reformation too, for all the infinite
good it may have done, rests historically on a 'monks' quarrel', the
one between the Augustinian and the Dominican orders.[3] Relevant
here is the caricature of the Patriarch in *Nathan*, and also the other
caricature on which it is based, that of his enemy Melchior Goeze,
a figure which in Lessing's polemics belongs as much to fiction as to
truth.

Behind this criticism of dogma and of church history there stands,
however, a criticism of the concept of revelation as such no less definitely than with a man like Reimarus. Lessing holds that man's only duty
that can in any real sense be called a duty, is to practise 'natural
religion', i.e. to recognize God, to form only the noblest conceptions of
him, and to bear these in mind in all his thoughts and deeds. It then
became necessary, purely sociologically, 'conventionally', for people
within this one natural religion to come to some agreement concerning
certain things and concepts, and to attribute to the concepts and things
thus singled out the same force and necessity which the naturally perceived religious truths had of themselves. 'From the religion of nature
a positive religion had to be constructed, just as a positive law had
been made out of the natural one.' 'This positive religion acquired its
sanction by the respect accorded to its founder, who alleged that the
conventional element in this religion came just as certainly from God,
only indirectly through himself, as its essentials came directly through
the reasoning powers in each one of us.' The inner truth of a positive

---

[1] *Theological Writings*, I, 35.   [2] Ibid., I, 231f.   [3] Ibid., I, 82f.

religion as such cannot consist of anything but its practical indispensability. 'All positive and revealed religions are thus equally true and equally false': equally true to the extent that an agreement concerning non-essentials.was everywhere necessary, and equally false as far as every such convention signified a weakening and suppression of the essentials. 'The best positive or revealed religion is the one containing the fewest conventional additions to natural religion and least limits the good effects of natural religion.'[1] His tone in 1760 is much more malicious still, and reminiscent of the Voltairean style in religious criticism: 'This is the real artifice of a founder of a religion. He must not say: "Come, I want to teach you a new religion!" Such a speech evokes dread in his audience. He begins by instilling scruples against the accepted religion, and instilling them in confidence, like a man who has his friend's welfare at heart. This cavilling gives rise to assertions. The assertions give rise to voluntary dissociations, first in trifles and then ultimately embracing the whole. The religious founder's most difficult task is to procure his first dozen followers, really blind, obedient, enthusiastic followers. But once he has them, his work begins to go much better. . . . Who is there, believing himself inspired, who will not gladly in his turn inspire? It is always the most ignorant, the most simple who are most busy at it . . . Especially the women! It is too well known how surpassingly well all the heads of new religions and sects, like the first founder . . . in paradise, have understood how to make use of them.'[2] Corresponding to this historical denigration of revelation there is the factual one Lessing presented in 1754: 'They all refer to higher revelations which have not even been proved possible. They want truths to have been received through these which might be truths perhaps in another possible world, but not in ours. This they recognize themselves, so they call them mysteries, a word which refutes itself. I will not name these mysteries to you, but simply say that they are like the ones which give rise to the most sweeping and material notions of everything that is divine. They are the ones which never allow the common people to think of their Creator in a becoming fashion. They are the ones which tempt the mind away to all sorts of barren reflections and create for it a monster, which you call faith.'[3]

That is why Lessing's judgment of miracles is exactly the same as the one we can find in his edition of Reimarus' works.[4] It is that: 'Only those men need to perform miracles, who wish to convince us of inconceivable things, in order to make inconceivable things conceivable

[1] *Über die Entstehung der geoffenbarten Religion* (Concerning the origin of revealed religion), 1755-60; *Theological Writings*, I, 219f.
[2] Ibid., I, 234f.   [3] Ibid., I, 39.   [4] Cf. ibid., II, 387.

by means of miracles. But those who have nothing to present but teachings, whose touchstone every man carries with him do not need them.[1] And that is why the foolish Christian woman Daja, when she asks what harm there is in attributing an unexpected deliverance to an angel rather than to a man and thereby feeling all the nearer to God, the first inconceivable cause of such an event, receives from the wise Nathan the answer:

> Pride! and nought but pride! The pot
> Of iron would fain be lifted from the fire
> With silver tongs, to think itself more precious.—
> Bah!—And what's the harm, you ask, the harm?
> —What good is it, I might but ask in turn—
> For your 'To feel oneself the nearer yet
> To God' is folly or a blasphemy.—
> It only harms—it's harmful utterly.[2]

It is harmful in fact—and at this we have arrived once again at the beginning of this line of Lessing's thought—because it leads man to ecstasize where he should quite simply do good.

The existence of this line of thought, and the entirely unequivocal and decided way in which Lessing expresses it, must be borne in mind. One must, however, note simply that it was precisely the most pungent of the passages written by the young Lessing and quoted beforehand which was published from the papers found after his death, and the ones, therefore, which strictly speaking, while he thought them and committed them to paper, were never actually uttered by him. And we must above all be clear that here it is a question of only one line of Lessing's theological thought. Anyone wishing to attribute to him only this one line of thought would be misunderstanding him just as much as anyone who overlooked it altogether. Lessing could speak quite differently —and did speak quite differently. Friedrich Nicolai, his Enlightened friend, once wrote of him, as one who knew him well: 'Lessing could not tolerate anything which was all too clear-cut, and was in the habit, in polite or learned discussion, of espousing the weaker cause or the one whose opposite someone was trying to assert' and he adds the lovely illustration: 'Many of Lessing's friends will still recall that during the Seven Years War he always supported Prussia at social gatherings in Leipzig, and in Berlin the cause of Saxony. He was thus an object of heartfelt hatred to the true patriots in both places, who, as is well-known, were a trifle fierce while the war lasted.'[3] Lessing the dramatist was doubtless glad to keep this attitude, not only in society, but also

---

[1] *Theological Writings*, I, 40.   [2] *Nathan*, I, 2. For original, see Appendix, p. 401.
[3] *Theological Writings*, IV, 267.

as a writer, and indeed as a theological writer particularly. The impression which this attitude made must, in his lifetime at least and especially among free thinkers, have been that of a conservative thinker rather than that of a free thinker. No, we hear him declaring just as definitely, although after what has gone before something different might have been expected, that what he means and intends is precisely not the 'reasonable Christianity' of his time. 'What a pity nobody really quite knows where his reason or where his Christianity is'[1] we hear him mocking. No, he has no love at all for the people whose leader we were just thinking we should have to take him to be, the 'new-fangled clergy, who are far too little theologians and not nearly philosophers enough'.[2] But certainly he wished to be a disciple of the Enlightenment, also, and especially, in matters affecting religion, 'I should despise myself if my scribblings were devoted to any end but that of helping to further these great intentions. But do leave me my own way in which I think I can do this.'[3]

What is there then about his own way, in opposition to that of the neologians—now so abruptly dismissed? Why do they please him neither as theologians nor as philosophers? What can he mean when he protests, over against Goeze, that he is no less well-intentioned towards the Lutheran Church than Goeze—when he, too, thinks he can appeal to the 'great misjudged man' Luther? 'The more insistently one man wanted to prove Christianity to me, the more doubtful I became. The more wilfully and triumphantly another sought to trample it completely underfoot the more inclined I felt like upholding it, in my heart at least.'[4] What is the meaning of this defiance of Lessing's towards that standpoint too, and in particular the point where we thought we saw him stand himself, without any qualification whatsoever? The answer sounds enigmatic enough, but is highly typical of Lessing: 'The freemason quietly waits for the sun to begin to shine and lets the lamps burn as long as they are willing and able to burn. But to put out the lamps and take note, when they are put out, that the candle-ends must be relit, or even be replaced by others—this is not the freemason's concern.'[5] 'Take care, more capable individual, you who paw the ground and are aglow on reaching the last page of the first primer (the Jewish-Christian revelation!), take care not to let your weaker school-fellows feel what you are sensing or already beginning to see. Until these weaker school-fellows have caught up with

[1] *Theological Writings*, II, 103.   [2] *Letters to Nicolai*, 1777, II, 11.
[3] *Letters to his brother*, 1774, II, 11.   [4] *Theological Writings*, IV, 169.
[5] *Ernst and Falk*, 5.

you, turn back the pages of this primer again, and find out whether
what you take to be the result of mere expressions of method, make-
shifts of the teaching system, is not perhaps something more.'[1] Or
concretely, about the relation between orthodoxy and neology: 'I
should not wish the impure water, which has long been unusable,
to be kept; it is only that I should not wish it to be poured away before
we know where we can get purer; I simply do not want it poured away
unthinkingly, and the child to be bathed thereafter in manure. And
what else is the new-fashioned theology, as compared with orthodoxy,
but manure as compared with dirty water? . . . I beg of you, dear
brother, enquire just a little more closely into this point, and look
rather less at what our new theologians reject than at what they want
to put in its place! I agree with you that our old system of religion is
false, but cannot agree with you in saying that it is a makeshift contrived by bunglers and pseudo-philosophers. I know of nothing else
in the world where men have shown and practised their judgment more
than in this. It is the new system of religion which is intended to replace
it which is a bunglers' and pseudo-philosophers' makeshift and it has
at the same time far more influence over reason and philosophy than
the old one presumes to exercise. And yet you take it amiss that I defend
the old system? My neighbour's house is on the point of collapsing.
If he wants to pull it down I will willingly help him. But he wants to
prop it up and support it . . . by means entailing the complete ruin of
my house. He must stop this or I shall take care of his collapsing house
as if it were my own.'[2]

These were Lessing's reasons for remaining largely silent, after the
manner of the freemason, about his objections to orthodoxy—'The
wise man cannot speak about the things it is better he should keep
to himself'.[3] They were also his reasons for actually taking up from
time to time the cause of the orthodoxy which was under attack, or
of the old system of dogma, to the horror of his Enlightenment friends.
There can be no doubt: Lessing considered the orthodox position, he
considered the whole Jewish-Christian revelation upon which this
position rests, not to be something that is absolute but something we
can in principle rise above. It is not the rising sun, but a man-made
lamp, burning for the time being, which will later be extinguished;
it is to be likened to impure water, to a house in need of reconstruction.
It is not the final terrible truth that mankind must and indeed shall
know for his salvation, but only a first primer intended to prepare

---

[1] *The Education of the Human Race*, paras. 68-9.   [2] *Theological Writings*, II, 11f.
[3] *Ernst and Falk*, 2.

man for the final truth. Lessing is aware that in this critical insight
he is at one with the neologians. He thinks that he too knows everything
there is to be known in this respect. But that the sun might already
be risen, and clean water at hand, that the tottering house could be
transformed into a new one by the addition of a supporting wall—
these things he denied. In other words he denied that the Jewish-
Christian revelation had in fact already been superseded and relieved
of its task by something better. It is still better and stronger than the
reasonable Christianity of the neologians, provided it is properly
represented. This Christianity of reason, which is no longer Christian
and not yet reasonable, is a hybrid. Thus there is no point in putting
this critical insight already into practice and in wanting already to
dispense with the first primer. There would only be sense in this if
something better had already come, if the sun had already risen, if
pure water were already at hand, if the old house could really be de-
molished. The poverty of what is offered in place of revelation proves
that this is not the case; that revelation is not yet finished with. The
wise man, the freemason, in Lessing's sense, will therefore not join in
the neologians' direct attack on the Church and on dogma, although he
knows all that they know. He hopes. He is quite sure of himself and his
cause: 'The development of revealed truths into truths of reason is
necessary at all costs.'[1] 'Or could it be that the human race is destined
never to arrive at these highest stages of enlightenment and purity?
Never? Never?—Let me not think such blasphemy, all-bountiful
Lord!—Education has its aim, with the race no less than with the
individual. That which is educated is educated for something.'[2] 'The
time will certainly come, the time of a new, eternal gospel, which is
promised to us even in the primers of the New Covenant.'[3] It is however
precisely the wise man, who knows and hopes for this, who can wait.
'Go your imperceptible way, eternal Providence! Just do not let me
despair of you because of this imperceptibility!—Do not let me
despair of you even if it should seem to me that your steps are leading
backwards!—It is not true that the shortest line is always the straight
one. You have so much to carry with you upon your everlasting way, so
many digressions to make from the path!—And what if it were as good
as arranged that the big, slow-turning wheel which is bringing the race
nearer to perfection, could only be set in motion by smaller, faster wheels,
each one of which contributes its own individual effort to this cause?'[4]
     From this it almost necessarily follows that Lessing was bound to
have a positive interest in revelation, for all that he completely saw,

[1] *Ed.*, para. 76.   [2] Ibid., paras. 81-2.   [3] Ibid., para. 86.   [4] Ibid., paras. 91-2.

admitted and stated that the nature of that interest was relative. From this standpoint Lessing quite honestly found himself placed in a position where he not only could tolerate the belief in revelation and accept it as fact, but was able to ponder on it and express himself on how, *rebus sic stantibus*, it might most properly be represented.

This firstly makes plain the concern which prompted Lessing in the dispute of the Fragments. In it he was in his way really well-intentioned towards the Lutheran Church, without, for all that, being less well-intentioned towards the Enlightenment. As a wise disciple of the Enlightenment, who paradoxically but very subtly does not consider the straight line to be the shortest line, who knows of those digressions eternal Providence must make, in order to set in motion for its own part the smaller, faster wheels which move the big, slow one, he can, no, must in fact have the interests of the Lutheran Church at heart. It was Lessing and nobody else who honestly knew himself to be qualified and called to offer it some good advice. This was Lessing's desire in the dispute of the Fragments: he wanted, from the lofty watchtower of the wise man of the Enlightenment, of the true freemason, to give the Church, Christianity and Christian theology some good advice. He thought it could certainly be surpassed and he thought it was certain to be surpassed in the future, but he wanted to advise it on how it should conduct itself as something which was for the moment not surpassed, so that by its behaviour it should prove that it was not yet surpassed.

Lessing was interested in Reimarus' critique of all revelation including the Christian revelation. It interested him as a sign of the times. His dramatic conception of history perhaps contained certain traces of chiliasm, for a certain passage in Cardanus seems to have made a great impression upon him. It said: *Necesse est anno Christi millesimo octingentesimo magnam mutationem futuram esse in Christi lege*, 'that in the year 1800 a great change will come about in the Christian religion'.[1] It is not impossible that in view of this prophecy Lessing held that the coming of the last things was near, as far as the completion he mentions of the education of the human race and the actual surpassing of revelation were concerned. Be that as it may: Lessing was not interested in Reimarus in the way that Reimarus was bound to interest the common run of men of the Enlightenment. He was not interested in him as the implementer of a simple advance along the way to overtaking the belief in revelation—it was precisely the idea that such an advance could come about simply by means of criticism that Lessing denied. But Lessing was certainly interested in Reimarus as the provider of an

[1] *Theological Writings*, IV, 250f.

opportunity in the face of which the belief in revelation, in so far as it was not yet surpassed, must prove itself in its temporary truth and validity; as a chemical test, so to speak, to which the belief in revelation, the Church and theology must react in a certain way, inasmuch as their last hour had not yet struck. It was to this extent that Reimarus really interested Lessing for the Church's sake. It was to this end that he addressed the theologians in the dispute of the Fragments. And what excited and angered him to the astonishing extent to which he *was* angered and excited in the course of this dispute was the fact that he thought that they were not reacting in the only way possible; they were failing to grasp what was being asked of them and what their answer should be, failing to understand themselves and their own cause, neglecting the favourable time, the great opportunity that was offered them to prove themselves. And now he, the man of the Enlightenment, the one who is convinced that all revealed truth will hereafter be transformed and merged into the truth of reason—he has to tell the theologians how they must behave if in actual fact things have not progressed so far! That, in Lessing's eyes, was the problem, the fierce humour and bitter tragedy of the dispute of the Fragments.

What then was essential about the Fragments of Reimarus? For Lessing it was the fact that they represented a historian's historical attack upon the historical reality and possibility of revelation. Does this historian know, Lessing asks, that revelation—assuming that such a thing exists—cannot in any circumstance be denied historically as a historical quantity? But in this matter Lessing has to do not with Reimarus but with the Lutheran theologians. That is why he is immeasurably more concerned with the other question: Do these theologians know that revelation cannot ever be affirmed, justified and defended historically as a historical quantity? Lessing was the man who held that revelation can be surpassed in principle, who knew the objections against its historical reality and possibility as well as Reimarus did, and who was not at a loss, as we have seen, to produce all kinds of natural explanations for the things the Church declared were phenomena of revelation. But he thought he knew enough about the matter to say that revelation should at all events be interpreted as a fact proved in itself, i.e. not as one which can be either proved or attacked historically, but as one which is certain in itself. He thought that in this he was in agreement with the older theology, i.e. the orthodoxy of the sixteenth and seventeenth centuries, which was in the habit of presenting the historical proof only incidentally and without emphasis, and was not of the opinion that it could and should prove revelation as such by these means.

Lessing, however, did not find himself in agreement with the theology of his own time, not even, especially not, with the allegedly orthodox theology.[1] This theology replied to the historical criticism of revelation with a historical defence. This, Lessing maintained, was to the detriment and obviously in misunderstanding of its own cause; Lessing called it a 'theological innovation', and it was the essence of his complaint against Melchior Goeze that the latter made himself guilty of that innovation! It was against this, and ultimately only against this, that Lessing directed his polemic in this fight. 'They should be ashamed, these men who have the promise of their divine Teacher, that his Church shall not be overcome by the gates of hell, and are foolish enough to believe that this cannot otherwise come about than by their overcoming the gates of hell themselves!'[2] 'When will they cease to want to hang nothing less than the whole of eternity on a spider's thread!—No, scholastic dogmatics have never inflicted such grievous wounds upon religion, as that which the historical exposition of the Scriptures is now daily inflicting.'[3] 'Great God, it is to this mire, to this mire, even if there are perhaps some few specks of gold beneath it, that my neighbour in boldness and defiance transfers the completed edifice of his faith! . . . God! my God! what things men can found a faith upon, by which they hope to achieve eternal happiness!'[4]

Lessing likens the theological apologists to the inhabitants of a palace, oddly constructed to be sure but quite habitable, who each possess different plans of the building, which, they claim, derive from the first architect, which they do not understand and which seem to contradict each other. They are continually quarrelling about which is the right one. Some few, laughingly, and to the annoyance of the others, do not take part in this quarrel, but content themselves with rejoicing at the fact that they are actually allowed to live in this palace, whatever its plan may be. 'Once, when the quarrel about the plans was not so much settled as dormant, once upon a time at the midnight hour the voice of the watchmen suddenly rang out: "Fire! Fire in the palace!" And what took place? Everyone started up from his bed, and everyone —as if the fire were not in the palace but in his own home—ran to get what he believed to be his most precious possession—his plan. "If we can only save that!" each one thought; "the palace can burn nowhere more truly than as it stands described here!" So each one ran with his plan into the street, where he first of all wanted to show the others on

[1] *Theological Writings*, III, 107.   [2] Ibid., II, 287.   [3] Ibid., III, 34.   [4] Ibid., III, 89f.

his plan where the palace was supposed to be burning instead of hastening to save the palace. "Look, neighbour! Here's where it's burning! Here's where we can best get at the fire!" "Or here rather, neighbour, here!"—"What are you two talking about? It's burning here!" "What would it matter if it was burning there? But the fire is certainly here!" "You can put it out here if you like, I'm not going to!"—"Nor am I going to put it out there!"—"And nor am I going to put it out there!" And while they were busily arguing the palace, if it had been on fire, might very well have been burned to the ground. But the startled watchmen had mistaken the northern lights for a conflagration.'[1] Let the historical proofs of revelation rest where they will! 'Would it be a great misfortune if they were put back again into the corner of the arsenal they occupied fifty years ago?'[2] Why are they superfluous, even harmful? Why are the reasons with which the theological apologists work like spiders' webs, mire, a paper plan, and ultimately downright dangerous to religion? Because they divert the question of the truth and reality of revelation on to a track which is the very one where it cannot with certainty be answered. Historical proof of revelation means the historical proof of prophecies fulfilled and miracles which actually came to pass. But this proof cannot serve as proof of revelation. For the certainty which would have to be contained in a proof of revelation would necessarily be lacking in such a historical proof. 'Fulfilled prophecies which I myself experience are one thing, and fulfilled prophecies of which I know from history only that others claim to have experienced them, are another. Miracles which I see with my own eyes and have the opportunity to test are one thing, and miracles, of which I know from history only that others claim that they have seen and tested are another.'[3] The most reliable information about the latter does not therefore make my knowledge of it more reliable than it is possible for knowledge based on historical data to be; it is not possible to place more confidence in it than we are generally entitled to place in any truth shown by history. For no historical truth, even when it is supplied with the best evidence, can be demonstrated. But if 'no historical truth can be demonstrated, then neither can it in turn be used to demonstrate anything'.[4] 'To jump over' with this historical truth—assuming and granting that it is such—'into a completely different class of truths, and to demand of me that I should adapt all my metaphysical and moral notions accordingly . . . if that is not a μετάβασις εἰς ἄλλο γένος, then I do not know what else Aristotle can have meant by the term'.[5]

[1] *Theological Writings*, III, 95f.   [2] Ibid., III, 34.   [3] Ibid., III, 9f.
[4] Ibid., III, 11f.   [5] Ibid., III, 13.

'That, that, I say, is the nasty big ditch I cannot get over, often and earnestly as I have tried the jump. If anyone can help me over, let him do so; I beg him, beseech him to do so. By me he can reap a reward in heaven.'[1]

And now for Lessing's positive thesis, the better suggestion he thinks he can make to theology. This lament about the impossibility of passing over from the historical proof to the faith of revelation is in fact not genuine. Lessing could perfectly well do without what he represented in those sentences as being inaccessible to him, and he wished to make it clear to the theologians that it is not only inaccessible but also superfluous for them, and that for the sake of their own cause they should give it up. Is the situation such that 'I should hold a geometrical theorem to be true not because it can be demonstrated, but because it can be found in Euclid?' 'The fact that it is to be found in Euclid can prejudice us in favour of its truth as much as it will. But it is one thing to believe a truth on the strength of a prejudice, and another to believe a truth for its own sake.'[2] The learned theologian may finally be left in a state of embarrassment as a historian by an attack like that of Reimarus. 'But the Christian too? Most certainly not! Only possibly to the theologian might it be a cause for confusion to see the supports with which he wanted to shore up religion shaken, the buttresses cast down with which, God willing, he had so beautifully secured it. But of what concern to the Christian are the hypotheses and accounts and proofs of this man? For the Christian it is simply there, the Christianity he feels to be so true, in which he feels himself so blessed.—When the paralytic is undergoing the beneficent shock of the electric current, what does he care whether Franklin or Nollet is right, or neither of them?'[3] 'If I see these fruits ripening and ripened before me, should I not eat my fill of them, not perhaps because I deny, or doubt the pious old legend that the hand which scattered the seed for this fruit must be washed seven times in snails' blood at every throw; but have merely left it consigned to its proper place?—What do I care, whether the tale is true or not: the fruit is delicious. Supposing there were a great, useful mathematical truth, arrived at by its author by a palpably false conclusion. (If there are no such truths they might well exist.) Would I be denying this truth, would I be refusing to make use of it: would I be an ungrateful blasphemer against the author, if I did not wish to use his acuteness elsewhere, and did not think that his acuteness elsewhere could be used to prove that the false conclusion by which he had stumbled on the truth could not be a false conclusion

[1] *Theological Writings*, III, 13f.   [2] Ibid., III, 127.   [3] Ibid., II, 261.

at all?'[1] One should 'not act as if someone who doubts certain proofs of
a matter doubts the matter itself. Anyone who as much as points his
finger in this direction is as guilty as an assassin.'[2] 'He who has a more
Christian heart than head' is not deterred in the slightest by these
objections, because he *feels* 'what others are content only to think,
because he at all events could dispense with all the Bible. He is the
confident victor who leaves the fortresses alone and captures the land.
The theologian is the anxious soldier who runs his head against the
strongpoints on the border and in so doing sees hardly anything of the
country.'[3]

We must now try to find out more precisely what Lessing means
when he speaks of this 'victor'. We have not yet quoted the best-
known of the various formulations in which Lessing has expressed his
belief in the superiority of Christianity over all historical polemics,
or alternatively in the fact that it cannot be proved by any historical
apologetics. It runs: 'Accidental historical truths can never become
proofs for necessary truths of reason.'[4] This sentence does not say—in
Lessing's context it cannot say—what Fichte later said: 'It is only the
Metaphysical and on no account the Historical, which makes blessed.'
Lessing does not maintain that the 'necessary truths of reason' are
self-evident, certain without regard to time and space, and that history
has no significance in their knowledge. In the dispute of the Fragments
he most definitely took it as his premise that the education of the human
race was not yet complete, and that revelation, a historical way of
knowledge (as distinct from the continual present—without regard to
time and space—of the necessary truths of reason) was therefore still
possible, indeed necessary.

Lessing, it is true, is aware of one proof of Christianity, i.e. a growth
of a knowledge of God through Christ, through present-day man's
encounter with the Christian tradition. But this proof must be 'the
proof of the spirit and the power' as the title of the famous writing of
1777 runs, from which comes the famous sentence just quoted.
'Accidental truths of history', which as such cannot become proofs of
necessary truths of reason, are, in the context of this writing, to be
understood as such particular, concretely unique historical truths,
about which I am merely informed by others, which are merely handed
down to me as true. I have not myself encountered them, I have not
myself experienced them as true. Truths of history can indeed become
proof for me of necessary truths of reason, but only when they are
not merely 'accidental' historical truths, but have become convincing

1 *Theological Writings*, III, 14.   2 Ibid., III, 107.   3 Ibid., III, 122.   4 Ibid., III, 12.

to me as historical truths, have become necessary, and indeed directly necessary to me. The historical truths which are merely handed down and attested have as such not this power of proof, no matter how well they have been handed down and how definitely attested they are. Historical (from ἱστορέω) is, that which I must first make part of my own experience by investigation, and which is therefore in the first place not experienced by me. Historical truth as such, the truth which is in need of such investigation and is not yet part of my own experience, cannot be the legitimate and fully-authorized messenger of the truth of revelation, i.e. the truth which necessarily imposes itself upon my reason, which is ultimately certain. Historical truth, if it were to have this significance for me, would have to come to me by other means, not as 'historical' and not as 'accidental truth', not as requiring my investigation, and thus not at all merely as truth which has been handed down, and further by no means in such a way, that there should be any question at all of the problem of the 'nasty big ditch'. 'It is impossible for a revealed religion which rests upon human testimony, to afford an undoubted assurance in anything.'[1] There is, according to Lessing, another way.

With Lessing we have seen how at the decisive point the concepts 'feeling', 'experience', 'heart', and the image of the 'beneficent shock of the electric current' occur. This is what he would have us understand as the 'proof of the spirit and the power'. It is not as historical truth but through *experience*, that the historical element in Christianity assumes the power of proof for Christianity itself, and that, by way of historical truth, necessary truths of reason are proved. The way of Lessing's victor is the direct way from historical truth to the *heart* of present-day man. The fact that this way exists is the positive side of the negative sentence we quoted. Lessing knows very well about historical truths which can become proof of necessary truths of reason in this manner. From Luther's writings he appealed to the spirit of Luther;[2] likewise from the letter of the Bible to the spirit of the Bible, and from the Bible as such to religion, which was in existence before the Bible,[3] from the facts narrated in the books of the Bible to the principles of the Christian teaching, which do not all rest upon facts,[4] from the miracles worked by Christ and his disciples to 'the miracle of religion itself, which is still continuing in its effects',[5] and finally from the Gospel of St John to St John's testimony: 'Little children, love one another!'[6] and, as we have already seen, from the Christian religion to the

---

[1] *Theological Writings*, IV, 253.   [2] Ibid., III, 140.   [3] Ibid., II, 271f.; III, 113f.
[4] Ibid., III, 118.   [5] Ibid., III, 33f.   [6] Ibid., III, 14.

religion of Christ himself.[1] 'Surely in Hamburg nobody will any longer wish to dispute with me the whole difference between gross and net?'[2] No: 'the historical words are the vehicle of the prophetic words'.[3] 'It must be possible for everything the Evangelists and Apostles have written to be lost again, and for the religion they taught to remain notwithstanding. Religion is not true because the Evangelists and Apostles taught it, but they taught it because it is true. The tradition handed down to us in writing must be explicable by its inner truth, and no written tradition can give it inner truth if it does not contain any.'[4] 'Within the last seventeen hundred years has the first, the only spring never flowed, has it never found its way into other writings? Has it never and nowhere found its way into other writings in its original purity and healing quality? Must every Christian without exception draw from this spring and this spring alone?'[5] Goeze had asked Lessing whether he thought that without the presence and tradition of the books of the New Testament there would be any trace left in the world of what Christ had done and taught. Lessing answers: 'God preserve me from ever holding the teachings of Christ in such little esteem, that I should dare to answer this question quite directly with no! No, I should not say this "no" you want me to say,—even if an angel from heaven were prompting me to do so, let alone when it is only a Lutheran pastor who is trying to put the word in my mouth.'[6] We are not worse, but better off than the Christians of the second generation, in whose time the eye-witnesses were still present. 'We are abundantly compensated for the passing of the eye-witnesses by something which it was impossible for the eye-witnesses to have. They had only the ground before them, upon which, convinced of its firmness, they dared to erect a great edifice. And we, we have before us this great edifice itself, complete.'[7] The inner truth which no written tradition can give to Christianity and which Christianity therefore cannot derive from it[8]—the inner truth, on the one hand, comes from before the written tradition and, on the other hand, has its place behind it, in the 'edifice' of the whole of Christian history, which we see standing before our eyes. This inner truth 'is not a kind of wax nose that every knave can mould as he likes to fit his own face; it is the fact of revelation which speaks directly and with certainty to us ourselves, to our hearts. It is something, that is, which is capable of being felt and experienced. Because there is such a foundation for Christianity before and after the Bible, and because the Christianity resting

---

[1] *Theological Writings*, IV, 248f.   [2] Ibid., III, 108.   [3] Ibid., III, 112.
[4] Ibid., II, 262, III, 120, 125f.   [5] Ibid., III, 128.   [6] Ibid., III, 118.
[7] Ibid., III, 32.   [8] Ibid., III, 129.

on this foundation is the essential, the true one, objections raised against the historical element in religion as for instance indications of contradictory passages in the various Gospels, and doubts cast as to this or that report of a miracle are on principle irrelevant.[1] And for this reason the theologian should not try to impose his learned study of the Bible, with the pros and cons of his conclusions, upon the Christian as something which is of decisive importance for his religion.[2]

With this theological view in mind Lessing among other things also upheld two historical hypotheses which very significantly explain what he wanted. First, he assumed that there must have been an original Gospel, written in Hebrew, older than that of St Matthew, as the earliest of the Synoptic Gospel Writers[3]—the historical truth with the power of proof *before* the Bible! Secondly, he held that the *regula fidei*, the confession of faith (also in itself, incidentally, older than the New Testament) was the rock upon which the Church of Christ was afterwards built and not upon the Scriptures[4]—the historical truth with the power of proof *after* the Bible!

This teaching of the proof of the truth of Christianity, which must be brought as a 'proof of the spirit and the power', Lessing would no doubt also have us recognize as the meaning of the famous fable of the three rings in *Nathan*.[5] Here also it is a matter of the proof of the truth of Christianity, but not now as regards the problems presented by Christian history itself studied for its own sake, as in the polemics against Goeze. Now it is studied in relation to the fact that the history of Christianity, as a relative phenomenon, is a part of the universal history of religion, together with several other religions. Is Christianity, when ranked with the other religions, really the true religion, or, as was to be said later, the absolute religion? And how should the justification for his claim show itself, if and in so far as it is justified? That is the theological question which is discussed in *Nathan*.

The fable of the three rings is as follows: In an ancient family it is the custom for the father to give his favourite son a ring for his inheritance, a ring possessing the miraculous power of making whoever owns it beloved in the sight of God and man. One father, in this family, has three sons whom he loves equally. In order to hurt none of them he has two perfect imitations of the true ring made, which even he cannot detect and gives each of the three sons his blessing, and one of the rings, and dies. What happens then is obvious, of course. Each of the three sons considers that the other two are deceivers.

---

[1] *Theological Writings*, II, 282; III, 24, 132.   [2] Ibid., III, 129.
[3] Ibid., IV, 119f.   [4] Ibid., III, 215.   [5] *Nathan*, III, 7.

> They search, dispute, lament.
> In vain; the proper ring could not
> Be found; 'twas hid as well almost
> As—the true faith from us today.[1]

The three sons hasten to the magistrate:

> And each swore to the judge
> He had the ring directly from his father's hand—
> And this, of course, was true![2]

The judge then has a timely recollection of the miraculous power the true ring is said to have:

>   This must
> Decide! The rings, if false, will surely not
> Possess this gift! Say, two of you, forthwith
> Whom you do love the most. No word? The rings'
> Effect is just within, does not project?
> Each loves himself the most—all three of you
> Are then deceived deceivers! All the rings
> Are false—the real one was doubtless lost.
> Your father had the three rings made
> To hide the loss and make it good.[3]

The judge, however, like Lessing himself, is not disposed to make practical use of this critical opinion, which simply deprives the question of which is the real ring of its object. Apart from this judgment of his (which was, if it had been simply a question of judgment, the only one he could give), or rather instead of it he had a 'piece of advice' to offer:

> My counsel is, you should accept
> The matter simply as it stands. If each
> Received his ring from his father's hand
> Then let him think his own is without doubt
> The real one.[4]

It might also be the case, the judge now reflects—and in so reflecting hits upon the cause of the whole problem, which the fable pre-supposes as true—that the true ring has *not* been lost, but is there, unrecognizable together with two false ones by the father's own will. How then could judgment be passed? The counsel just mentioned can, however, very well be given, and explained in the following manner:

> So be it then!
> Let each one seek the unbought love that's free
> From prejudice, as promised by the ring!

[1] For original, cf. Appendix, p. 401.   [2] For original, cf. Appendix, p. 401.
[3] For original, cf. Appendix., p. 402.   [4] For original, cf. Appendix, p. 402.

> Each strive in contest to reveal the jewel's
> Strength! And aid this force by gentleness,
> A heart-felt tolerance, good works and deep
> Submission to God's will! And should the powers
> Dwelling in the stones then come to light among
> Your childrens' childrens' heirs, I then, when
> Thousand thousand years are past, invite them
> Once again before this judgment-seat.
> A wiser man will then sit here and speak.
> Now go your ways! Thus quoth the modest judge.[1]

According to this second opinion of the judge, be it noted, one of the rings is in fact genuine, and the decision about which is the genuine one will be made at some future time—in a thousand thousand years, to be sure, in a time completely inaccessible to us—by a wiser judge, when in fact the power of this genuine ring has in the meantime 'come to light'. In other words: a true faith does exist, and this faith will bring the proof of the spirit and the power, and it is then that the judgment, upon what is really the truth in religious history which is at present impossible will be passed. At the present time, however, this cannot come about. The contemporary student of religious history must declare, with Saladin in the play:

> . Nathan, cherished Nathan!—
> The thousand thousand years of this your judge
> Are not yet past. His judgment-seat is not
> My own.[2]

For the present it is only possible to advise the devotees of every religion, the Christian religion included, that they should assume the alleged miraculous power of their faith to be real, and act in a way that will foster it. That is, they must be what people who have this miraculous power must be, with 'gentleness, a heart-felt tolerance, good works and deep submission to God's will', without themselves doing injury to the prejudice inherent in their faith, but also without consideration for it. It will not be this contest of virtue which will decide the argument but the miraculous power of true faith, which is not now discoverable as such. But this contest of virtue is the only possibility which can at present be recommended to all participants, for the miraculous power will certainly be revealed as a fostering of virtue which makes men beloved in the sight of God and man.

There are two elements in the thought of the play which seem to be new. The first that strikes us is just this indication of right, that is, virtuous conduct which is in accordance with the miraculous power of the

---

[1] For original, cf. Appendix, p. 402.   [2] For original, cf. Appendix, p. 402-3.

true faith, which encourages, and even aids it. In the dispute of the Fragments, in the passages most relevant to this question, Lessing always spoke of the experience which had to be acquired. Now we are expressly told, that whichever faith presents itself by experience as the true one, this experience will in all circumstances be an experience of a moral kind. The man who is beloved in the sight of God and man, as is promised to the true believer, will in all circumstances be a man who is graced by definite specifiable virtues, who is triumphant in the spheres where they are exercised.

Another striking element is the expressly stated assumption in the parable of the rings that *one* of the positive historical religions, unidentifiable as it now is among them all, will show itself, by means of the proof of the spirit and the power, to be the true one, and can and must ultimately come to be judged as such. The judge's decision, in the fable, was to give his advice, instead of his judgment, which would inevitably have amounted to a *non liquet* and stamped all three of the brothers as 'deceived deceivers'. In giving preference therefore to the second possible view of the matter over the first, which was also possible in principle, he opts—without knowing it, only sensing it, although the author knows—for the true view in opposition to the false one: the true ring was in fact *not* lost. His counsel rests upon this second view which he prefers and is in accordance with the facts. And that is precisely why no proclamation of a universal religion comes about in *Nathan*. It is true we hear Nathan sighing at the beginning:

> Are Jew and Christian Jew and Christian first
> And not first men? Oh! if only from among
> Your kind I'd found one more who is content
> To bear the simple name of man![1]

We hear the same Nathan soliloquizing, however, just before the scene of the rings:

> It does not do to be an arrant Jew,
> But even less to be no Jew at all.[2]

But Saladin too declares later on:

> I have never wished to find
> The same bark growing upon every tree.[3]

And the Templar likewise knows that he who is thought to stand—and declares he stands—above all parties, in fact supports a party too:

> Since this fact is simply so,
> It's rightly so, I trow.[4]

[1] *Nathan*, II, 5; cf. Appendix, p. 403.   [2] Ibid., III, 6; cf. Appendix, p. 403.
[3] Ibid., IV, 4; cf. Appendix, p. 403.   [4] Ibid., IV, 1; cf. Appendix, p. 403.

The meaning of this conservative aspect of the conclusions presented in the play is of course to be found in the assumption that *one* of the positive historical religions—we do not, admittedly, know which—is the true one and will show itself as such. Because this is so, there would be no sense in changing one's own religion to which one belongs after all for one of the others, and even less in changing it for some kind of universal religion.

These two seeming innovations in *Nathan* can, however, be taken only as elucidating Lessing's basic position, which we know already. The really significant thing is that we find Lessing the theologian in *Nathan* too, and in *Nathan* particularly, in the benignly superior *rôle* of the counsellor—poised upon the lofty watch-tower of the man who he is not so completely tied to any one of the positive religions that he is bound to consider it to be the only true one. On the other hand, he is not so completely inimical to any of them that he would think it out of the question for it to be the true religion. He considers the whole formed by the concrete historical plan or succession of these religions to be so meaningful, and reckons so completely with the inner teleology of this whole, that it is for him certain that one of these religions will prove to be the true one and in doing so justify the whole of which it was a part. But the circle is complete—he feels himself bound to maintain in the face of all opposition, that the superiority of this one religion —'the thousand thousand years of this your judge are not yet past'— has not yet emerged in a manner making it ripe for judgment, and it can therefore for the time being not be made valid in practice. He points out, with this proviso, that the experience of the true religion will manifest itself, come what may, in the practice of the quite definite moral virtues he mentions and thus he points to this practice of virtue as the most promising path, *rebus sic stantibus*, which every religion can and should tread.

We must be clear in our minds that this is Lessing's standpoint (it is simply more clearly recognizable in *Nathan*) when giving counsel to the Lutheran Church in the dispute of the Fragments. He who gives counsel here, does not stand on the ground of the Lutheran faith in revelation but adopts this ground for a certain accidental reason and a higher insight. He is given the certain accidental reason for acting in this way by the fact that he happened to be born on the ground of Lutheran Christianity. The higher insight which leads him to take this fact seriously is not by any means the truth of the Lutheran faith in revelation itself. It is his comprehensive knowledge of the great connexion between the parts of the whole of history, which is moving towards a final decision, and within which there happen to be after all stages and stopping places, i.e. such provisional decisions as that for the truth of the Lutheran faith in revelation, within which, since it is so, everyone must make some such kind of preliminary decision, in accordance with the occasion of his birth and education. 'Let each think his own is without doubt the real ring.'

In this sense Lessing 'believes'. Nothing but this provisional decision, and not, for instance, the necessity for the final decision upon the whole of religious history, does bind him to this particular faith of this particular Church. He knows that we cannot know of the true faith, but that we can only simply assume that some one faith is the true one. This, in fact, he does. And, of course, he knows that his choice may not be without good cause; that his ring may perhaps really be the genuine one. It certainly does not seem out of the question to him that the Lutheran Church itself might at some time show itself to be the true Church and religion. It is because this chance exists that he is concerned about the Lutheran Church and thinks it worth the trouble to give it good counsel, to put its theologians to the test. For the same reason he can become quite angry with them when they fail in this test, and do not accept or understand his advice. He does this, be it well understood, because of that chance! He knows for certain that such a chance exists, for he knows for certain of the related meaning which exists between all such preliminary decisions. Because he knows this he knows for certain that history has a purpose and that one of these preliminary decisions will approximate most closely to history's purpose; that it will be directly responsible for the transition to the age of the new, everlasting gospel and thus prove itself in the sight of the other preliminary decisions to be the true one.

Lessing gave the Lutheran Church advice from this watch-tower of the philosophy of history. Does his advice differ in content and in purport from that of the philosopher of history, from that of the wise judge in the parable of the rings? We have seen that this advice consisted in the indication of experience, the lessons of life, the feelings and the heart: it is as something which reaches and touches us directly, as something which immediately enlightens and enters into us, that historical truth becomes revelation and proves that it has the force of the necessary truth of reason. The advice of the judge in the parable of the rings also consisted in the pointing out of the self-proving miraculous power of the genuine ring. One thing is certain: Lessing was here not pointing out to the Lutheran Church that which, at any rate in its origins and confessional writings, it had understood as revelation; he was not pointing to the 'miraculous power' with which God, as the Lord of history, espouses the cause of historical man in a historical encounter which man comes to share directly. This interpretation of Lessing's *Proof of the Spirit and the Power* from the dispute of the Fragments, which in certain passages is not an impossible one (just as with Rousseau), is shown to be completely out of the question when the *Proof* is seen beside *Nathan the Wise* and beside the *Education of the Human Race*. Within history, in which there are the various religions, and in which there is also a Lutheran Church, there are only human pre-decisions, and human affirmation of this or that historical possibility. But there is no encounter with God decisively intervening from outside or above, and demanding faith as man's final decision to obey; no revelation in the sense in which the Lutheran Church had understood it before the eighteenth century. According to Lessing no Church and no religion can or may call revelation in this sense to witness. It is precisely revelation in this sense which, in Lessing's view of history, is utterly precluded. Now this means that the polemics of the dispute of the Fragments, occasionally so instructive and amusing to read, are in their essential passages without doubt arguments against just this conception of revelation. For in their essential principles they are not relevant, as according to the programme they should be, to the historical apologists who desire to prove historically the revealed character of certain historical truths, but they are relevant to the notion that the Holy Scriptures are the authoritative document for the historical truth which to the Church is identical with revelation. This, however, means that the polemics are relevant to the authoritarian character, upheld by this notion, of what the Church calls revelation, its character as historical truth which descends from above, a particular truth stepping in from outside in distinction from all other historical truth; a truth which is, indeed, uniquely qualified. For that is the character which the Protestant doctrine of Scripture concretely ascribes to revelation.

And it is precisely the Protestant doctrine of Scripture that Lessing is trying to juggle away, with all the means at his disposal, in favour of this historical truth with the power of proof which exists before and after the Bible, in favour of the prophetic word which is not bound up with the vehicle of the historical word, in favour of the original gospel and of the *regula fidei*, in favour of the spirit and the inner truth and the 'ever-continuing miracle of religion itself', in favour of the whole 'edifice' of the Christian Church. In short he seeks to achieve this end in unison with Roman Catholicism and the whole of Protestant modernism (and as one of the first quite obvious heralds of the programme of Protestant modernism) in favour of history itself as distinct from and as against the Lord of history, who is indelibly denoted precisely by the Protestant doctrine of the Scriptures.

With Lessing there is no such thing as a Lord of history within history. Indeed he discusses miraculous powers and events experienced or recounted in history, the 'grateful shock of the electric current' and the like, he believes it possible of the positive religions that such things could actually come to pass, in their sphere, and come to pass so genuinely even, that one of them might finally and at last show itself to be the genuine, the true religion, he shows enough trust in Lutheranism in spite of everything to urge its believers to let the empirical nature of the historical fact which gives the Church its foundation be the decisive factor. But in discussing these things he is thinking simply of possibilities within history, which can and may be reckoned with and pointed out, but which are all subject to the proviso that it is ultimately impossible to pass any judgment upon their truth or genuineness. *History is revelation;* this is the principle denied by the Protestant doctrine of Scripture, but upheld by Lessing, the counsellor of the Lutheran Church. The meaning of revelation in Lessing's sense was the successive or simultaneous working-out of the possibilities proper to and inherent in historical humanity. Revelation is the 'education which the human race has undergone and is undergoing still'.[1] Education, however, 'does not give man anything he might not also take from within himself; it is just that it gives him more quickly and easily what he might have from within himself. Revelation too therefore does not give man anything which human reason left to itself would not also discover; it is just that it gave and is giving him the most important of these things sooner'.[2] The concise parallel to these sentences, in themselves already concise, is quite simply the fact that the judge in the fable of the rings knows as a matter of course wherein the quality of being beloved of God and man, promised to the owner of the genuine ring, will at all events consist: it will consist in a moral virtuousness which can be most directly specified. If this is so, what then is the 'proof of the spirit and the power'—whether it is triumphantly brought by the one religion or by the other—but the event, in which humanity in fact arrives at that which is the goal required by its own nature, the realization of its possibilities.

Can a Lord of history exist in these circumstances, even solely as a Lord over history? Lessing speaks of 'God' as the educator of the

---

[1] *Ed.*, para. 2.　　　[2] Ibid., para. 4.

human race. He speaks of the steps of 'eternal Providence' which are accomplished in this education. But he can also (as in the foreword to the *Education*) simply speak of the course visible in the history of the religions, 'which is the one and only thing by which human understanding everywhere can develop itself, and is meant to develop itself, even further'. This is new in Lessing as opposed to the other neologians: the fact that for him such a 'course' of history does exist, and it was in all probability this discovery, the discovery of the dramatic quality active in history, which gave him the courage to utter the old word 'revelation' with a new solemnity as a description of this course. But does it make any difference to his interpretation of this 'course' whether we say 'God' or whether we say 'human understanding' in the significant places, and whether we interpret revelation as being education by an educator or self-education or even more simply development, and thus allow the Lord of history to coincide with history itself, or alternatively with its subject, with the humanity educating, or alternatively, developing itself? It is difficult to say in what respect there is meant to be a distinction, and perhaps it is only a part of Lessing's freemason's wisdom that he did not go so far as to say openly that it really does not make any difference. As Lessing, in *Minna von Barnhelm*, presented the noble Tellheim, the surly Just, the faithful Werner and the thankful 'Lady in mourning', and in *Nathan* the Christian Templar, the Mohammedan Sultan and the Jewish merchant, the highest law to which all these figures are subject, in the one play just as much as in the other, is apparently: 'Act in accordance with your individual perfections!' (as Lessing put it in formulating the categorical imperative in a strange early work of his[1]), and in each of them it is a 'course' which welds these figures into a dramatic unity. Is it actually a God which is necessary in *Minna* and in *Nathan* to set these characters in motion either in isolation or in their relationship one to another? Is not the thought of a God in both of them bound to appear like that of a fifth wheel on a carriage? Is not all that is necessary in both of them a poet and thinker, perhaps, a playwright of genius? To put it differently: is man not, in the one play just as much as in the other, best understood when he is understood as being sufficient unto himself? Did Lessing really even count upon God's final word concerning the dramas and drama of human history, after having in principle cut God off from every word previous to the last word spoken, or to be spoken, within this history? Is it not a fact that Lessing's man is self-sufficient, and has no need of God in any event?

[1] *Th. Wr.*, I, 217.

And now in conclusion let us quote the most famous words which Lessing wrote, without comment, since they of themselves best bring the proof of Lessing's spirit and of his power. They are to be found in the polemic *A Rejoinder*, written in 1778.[1]

'A man's worth does not consist in the truth any one man may happen to have in his possession, or thinks he has in his possession, but in the honest endeavour he has brought to bear in his attempt to discover the truth. For it is not by the possession of truth but by the search for the truth that his powers are enlarged, which alone go to make for his ever-increasing perfection. Possession makes men placid, indolent and proud.

'If God were holding all the truth that exists in his right hand, and in his left just the one ever-active urge to find the truth, even if attached to it were the condition that I should always and forever be going astray, and said to me, "Choose!" I should humbly fall upon his left hand and say: "Father, give! Pure truth is surely only for thee alone!" '

[1] *Th. Wr.*, III, 26.

7

KANT

1. IT was in the year of Lessing's death, 1781, that Kant's *Critique of Pure Reason* appeared. What was the significance of this man and of this work? In connexion with our observations in this book our answer must simply be that it was in this man and in this work that the eighteenth century saw, understood and affirmed itself in its own limitations. Itself—in its limitations! In saying this we are saying that Kant, like Rousseau and Lessing, stands at the turning-point of his age. We must, however, immediately add that he does this because in him just this one simple thing happens. There is no disclosure of a new dimension, no discovery of new provinces and powers, as with Rousseau and Lessing—if that were the point, we might very well find that Kant after Rousseau and Lessing might appear to us to be a reactionary—but just this one simple thing: the century's coming to an understanding of itself—but of itself in its limitations. With Kant only this one simple thing happened and for this reason he stands, in effect, much more basically, much more comprehensively and more radically, and, in historical terms, much more interestingly and more significantly at the turning-point of his age.

The singularity of Kant's position can be seen already by the fact that, comprehensive and typical in both directions as it is, it is a solitary one. Just as on the one hand he lent the eighteenth-century spirit a pregnancy of expression which, for all the connexions he has here, makes of him an incomparable figure, so on the other hand in spite of every connexion, as a surmounter of this spirit he does not align himself with the companion figures of the new age—the line of succession leading from Rousseau by way of Lessing and Herder to Romanticism. He stands by himself—in this respect he can only be compared to Goethe after him—a stumbling-block and rock of offence also in the new age, someone determinedly pursuing his own course, more feared than loved, a prophet whom almost everyone even among those who wanted to go forward with him had first to re-interpret before they could do anything with him.

The singularity of Kant's position can also be seen, particularly in his special position in relation to the theological problem: he and only he was in fact the man, also here, and here in particular, in whom the the century saw 'itself in its own limitations'. Nobody from China to Peru brought into the open the theological viewpoint, thought and intent of the eighteenth century with so much determination, in such concrete and logical terms with so unemotional a clarity (in contrast to Rousseau), and with such an unfreemasonly candour (in contrast to Lessing) as he did. There was moreover nobody at all who saw so clearly that this theological thought and intent were one, given their limits by a theological possibility not only relatively but absolutely different. Kant personally never considered passing these limits for one moment. He did really stand with both feet within them. And yet he saw them, no matter how deprecatingly, how polemically. Rousseau and Lessing and later Herder, Schleiermacher and Hegel did not see them. Of Goethe too we must probably say that he did not see them. It is fundamentally impossible to conduct a conversation with them from the point of view of this altogether different theological possibility, because they simply did not recognize it as a distinct opposite of their own possibility, because it simply did not exist for them as an opposite. Kant, however, recognized this other possibility, even though it was at a distant periphery of his thought. He recognized it as an opposing force which he rejected, but still as an opposing force, as an instance which he dismissed in practice but not in principle, as an instance, that is, which he was not capable of including in his own position. Kant did not, like Rousseau, go to Holy Communion, did not, like Lessing, call Luther to witness. Instead, when the university of Königsberg was proceeding in solemn procession from the Great Hall to the church for the university service on the *dies academicus* Kant used ostentatiously to step away from the procession just as it was entering the church, make his way round the church instead, and go home. We have before us in all his writings the same refreshingly unequivocal attitude. With such a man a conversation from the other point of view, from the point of view of a completely different theology, is possible, because it is precisely when it is seen from there that it has quite definite outlines. The confusion of both worlds, which is more or less likely to lead one astray with everybody else, is almost impossible with Kant. Particularly in our field he points beyond the relative distinction between the old and the new time which concerns us here. And he points beyond what is common to them both.

In a little essay he wrote in the year 1784, Kant gives the following answer in the first few decisive sentences to the question of the title, 'What is Enlightenment?': 'The Enlightenment represents man's emergence from a self-inflicted state of minority. A minor is one who is incapable of making use of his understanding without guidance from someone else. This minority is self-inflicted whenever its cause lies not in lack of understanding, but in a lack of the determination and courage to make use of it without the guidance of another. *Sapere aude!* Have the courage to make use of your own understanding, is therefore the watchword of the Enlightenment.' Nobody saw, knew or said in the way that Kant did what this mature, courageous man who makes use of his own understanding looks like, what his position is and how he conducts himself. Nobody strikes us as so worthy of belief and so honourable as he does when he baldly announces the advent of this kind of man, and when he naïvely expresses the conviction that his own present, as the time of this man, is without doubt the best of all the ages which have gone before.[1] Perhaps the reason for this is simply that nobody really lived the life of the man Kant had in mind as economically and as existentially as it was possible for Kant himself to live it, as he lived it in his study and during the measured walks he took in the town he never left in all his days. It was the life of one who vigorously, indefatigably, and in every respect made use of all his human capacities. But the deeper and more significant reason why he strikes us in this way is the fact that the naïveté with which he praised his time and the man of his time, and the complete and unquestioning way in which he embodied this man in his own person were based upon a most scrupulous and calculated testing of these capacities, upon a most logical carrying to its conclusion of the 'emergence from minority', upon a complete understanding of the problems with which—as well and particularly—the man who makes use of his own understanding is faced.

Kant inspires our awe as a representative of the spirit of the eighteenth century. We cannot help feeling that in him this spirit has not only reached maturity and beyond. In him, we feel, this spirit is not merely at loggerheads with itself in a riotous way; it does not merely strive beyond itself in enthusiastic or poetic fervour and it does not become a prey to Mephistophelean self-mockery. It has quite simply come to terms with itself; it therefore knows where it stands and it has thus acquired humility. With Kant we do not find any narrow-minded, ignorant self-satisfaction within the confines of this spirit,

---

[1] *Die Religion innerhalb der Grenzen der blossen Vernunft* (Religion within the Bounds of Reason Alone), p. 197, quot. from 2nd ed., 1794.

neither do we find any exuberant, lawless unrest in the face of these confines, according to the prescription:—
Any fence we find we'll crash·

> What else are fences for, now?

Any lamps we find we'll smash—

> Our lights are lit, we trow!

In Kant we find this spirit at a point beyond self-satisfaction and rebellion in being what it is, namely, distinct, existing in history as it does, keeping within its confines, being completely itself and completely self-conscious, and in its limits. In its limits, as they are understood by Kant, something of humanity's limits in general, and at this something of wisdom seems to become visible. In Kant's philosophy, as in the music of Mozart, there is something of the calm and majesty of death which seems suddenly to loom up from afar to oppose the eighteenth-century spirit. That is why, in Kant, thrown completely back upon humility, it shines forth once again in its full splendour. That is why it here commands our respect.

In a more important passage than the one previously quoted[1] Kant gave another answer to the question about the meaning of his time or rather he gave the same answer in more fundamental and significant terms: 'Our age is the true age of criticism, to which all things must be subjected.' In the way Kant meant it this was an interpretation or characterization of the age completely new to his contemporaries, and was, strictly speaking, only applicable to one single man of the age, namely to Kant himself. In Kant's sense 'criticism' does not mean a kind of knowledge fundamentally consisting in the total or partial negation of another merely alleged or at any rate disputable piece of knowledge. Criticism in Kant's sense does not consist in casting doubt upon or denying certain propositions, or alternatively certain things contained in these propositions, which are declared to be objects of knowledge. He could not, it is true, embark upon or set forth his own kind of criticism without using the usual kind of criticism as well. But his own criticism is essentially quite different from it: it is criticism of knowledge itself and of knowledge as such. This does not mean that it is a complete or partial denial of the possibility, validity and worth of the human method of forming knowledge. Even if it was David Hume, the 'sceptic', who by Kant's own admission first roused him from his 'dogmatic slumbers', i.e. first shook him in his untested

---

[1] *Critique of Pure Reason*, 1st ed., Preface V.

assumption that human knowledge was possible and valid, this does not mean that Kant intended to pursue the same road as Hume, i.e. that he intended to make the challenging of this assumption his actual goal. Those have truly been guilty of misunderstanding him who have taken him to be a kind of super-sceptic, who have looked upon him as the 'all-annihilating one', as far as the reality of knowledge, the reality of science and morality, art and religion are concerned: and have regarded him as the man who contemplates civilization from outside, and challenges its values, so to speak, in order to provide it, on his own initiative, with a new basis, or in order to refrain resignedly from the possibility of giving it a basis.

Kant himself, although he compared his enterprise with that of Copernicus, or rather precisely because he made this comparison, looked upon it as anything but a venture in criticism in this sense. Kant was not Rousseau, and Rousseau himself cannot be understood only in this sense. In Kant's eyes civilization has its basis. For him civilization, the achievement of his age, the achievement which is also and in particular the achievement of human knowledge in all these fields, is an event beyond question. It is this event that provides him with the ground upon which he stands. His investigation does not seek to answer the question of whether this achievement has any basis, but the question as to what its basis is. It seeks to establish the method of this civilization: it seeks, in so far as this civilization is firstly and lastly that of the Enlightenment, to bring about an enlightenment of the Enlightenment about itself, so that, safe from all misunderstanding of itself, it might thenceforward adopt a certain, sure and tranquil course. Kant intends to see to it that the man who has come of age, whom he believes he can recognize and may praise in Enlightenment man, does not use his understanding wilfully and as he thinks fit, now that he has mustered the courage to use it at all. This does not mean that he should make his understanding the object of a sceptical mistrust. It means that he should understand it and thus, knowing about it, for this reason use it calmly and surely and constantly. And the courage (*Mut*) demanded here from him is not meant to be arrogance (*Hochmut*), let alone faintheartedness (*Schwachmut*), but—lying midway between the two—humility (*Demut*), enabling man to subject himself to a searching criticism of his capacities which will show him the right course and which, precisely because it is searching and showing the right course, will clarify and confirm his ability to subject himself to, and, once he has done this, to be guided by the results of this self-criticism. The critique of reason is reason arriving at an understanding of itself. Its pathos is not by any means that of a denial; it is rather, in the most explicit manner possible, that of an affirmation of reason. Kant is not Jacobi. Kant is not Hamann or Claudius or Lavater. Kant is Kant and his critique of reason has nothing at all to do with a weariness of civilization or a weariness of the Enlightenment. Kant both has and demands an almost unconditional faith in reason. But the only kind of reason he considers worthy of his trust is the reason which has first of all come to be reasonable as regards itself. The meaning of his critique of reason consists in the attempt to bring this kind of reason into prominence.

The essential quality of eighteenth-century man before Kant was a joyful affirmation of the actual capacity of human reason, which stood, so it seemed, as an incontrovertible fact visible to all in the irresistible forward march of natural and technical science, of historical knowledge, and surely also of moral feeling. As a true child of his age Kant is also to be found among the joyfully participating admirers of this process. He conceives and announces his teaching as one who is engaged in furthering this process, as one who is to a great extent himself actively concerned with it. It is well known that with the astronomical theory which shares his name and that of Laplace he intervened significantly in the sphere of natural science, and with his shrewd and lively spectator's eye he was, so to speak, always present whenever there was something to be seen. He never stood apart but always faced, was always in the middle of the real intellectual movement of his age. 'Such a phenomenon in human history will never again be forgotten, because it has revealed a disposition and capacity for betterment in human nature.'[1] This he said of the French Revolution, the outbreak and development of which he followed with the closest attention and with an almost boyish sympathy and expectancy, in this resembling only too closely a contemporary like Lavater, from whom he was in every other respect totally dissimilar. But we must note that only because and in so far as it reveals a disposition and capacity in human nature does Kant affirm the tendency of his time. 'It is already a beginning of the reign of the good principle and a sign "that the kingdom of heaven is at hand", even if only the fundamentals of its constitution come to be commonly known. For something is already present in the world of the understanding, and the roots, from which alone it can spring, have already established themselves everywhere, although the complete development of its appearance in the world of

[1] *Streit der Fakultäten* (Dispute of the Faculties) Vol. 46D of the Phil. Libr., 2nd ed., p. 135.

the senses still lies in the unforeseeable future.'[1] Kant, faced by the actual capacity for human reason as manifested in the trends of science and morality, of art and religion in his time, is not interested in this actual capacity in itself and as such, but in the deeper actuality of this capacity in principle. Faced with what reason has brought into being he is interested only in its *a priori* capacity for achieving these things; faced with the accidental historical aspect of civilization he seeks instead what is essential and necessary about it, the quality which makes it into an unforgettable phenomenon.

And now the question he asks is about the nature of this basic capacity, about the definite order and structure of this necessity, about the laws governing its essential quality, without perception of which the actual capacity could not in the long run remain certain of its objectives and its course. Thus he himself called his great main work a *Treatise on Method*.[2] He might also have said the same of his other three main works and of the lesser works which accompanied them. Man has come of age. But in what does man's majority consist? Only Kant, the perfect man of the eighteenth century, could dare to accept the assumption which underlay this question: the assumption that reason is right in its activity, as an actual capacity, as and in so far as, *a priori*, preceding its activity, it necessarily rests upon itself. But the question which was put on the basis of this assumption, the question about this 'as and in so far as', in bringing the spirit of the age to its culmination, also overcomes it.

The Enlightenment before Kant was the absolute and boundless self-affirmation of reason, which, as such an affirmation, was ultimately bound to be uncertain of itself. Even if we wish to characterize Kant's intellectual quality and that of the time after him as part of the Enlightenment—as in a certain sense we not only can but must—it is now at all events a relative and bounded self-affirmation of reason, critical and now for the first time sure of itself, to the extent that it possesses these qualities. That is what is new in Kant. And it is also a new side of the intellectuality of the nineteenth century, as opposed to that of the eighteenth. The actual capacity of human reason was destined to march onward in this new century, in which Kant himself, grown tired, and the balance of his mind somewhat disturbed, was to live only for a few years. It was destined to assume quite different dimensions from those of which Kant could have any idea; there would be quite different and ever-increasing occasion for the self-consciousness which

[1] *Rel.*, 225.
[2] *Critique of Pure Reason*, 2nd ed., Pref. XXII.

distinguished the old Enlightenment and which was also alive in Kant. But from now onwards, from Kant onwards, all self-affirmation of human reason would be asked, and would continually have to bear with 'being' asked, whether it in fact rests upon a true maturity. And everyone who used this reason would be asked from now on whether his use of it might not perhaps just be sophistry masquerading as reason, an uncritical adventure of the understanding prompted by obscure feelings. With Kant and from Kant onwards the human use of reason has left the broad way and finds itself within the 'strait gate'.[1] This was also, and particularly, true of theology. From now on theology would no longer be able to formulate its tenets, no matter on what foundation it might base them, without having acquired a clear conception of the method of reason, which it also uses in the construction of its tenets. Any theology which had not at least faced this question and presented its credentials was backward, from now on, superseded in its relation to the age, no matter how valuable or worthless it might otherwise be; it would not be the theology of the new century which was just coming into being. Further, it would in any case be typical of the theology of the new century to absorb the idea of the critique of reason, in a vastly different form perhaps from that of Kant himself, but in consideration, nevertheless, of the problem which Kant raised.

It cannot be our concern here to develop even at moderate length Kant's critique of reason in its historical course and philosophical content. We shall content ourselves with establishing what its result was and with establishing its two basic trends, which have an especially important bearing upon theology.

The one has its goal in the insight into the ideal character of all knowledge achieved by pure reason. (From it the way of thought Kant founded and which was developed directly after him acquired the ambiguous title of 'Idealism'; 'Criticism' or 'Rationalism' are terms which would have typified much more clearly and comprehensively all that Kant, at any rate, wanted.) By pure rational knowledge Kant means that necessary knowledge which refers not to what is, but to an object that transcends all experience, to what must be and only in this sense 'is'. This pure rational knowledge which is necessary since it accompanies and directs all empirical knowledge—in substance Kant here simply follows the metaphysics of his time—is the knowledge of the ideas of God, freedom and immortality. It is clearly in the realm of this knowledge of ideas, the realm of metaphysics, that there take place all the reason's misconceptions and deceptions about

[1] *Critique of Practical Reason*, 1st ed., p. 163.

itself. To clarify and lay foundations for this knowledge of ideas, and to provide in this sense a criticism of it, is the task of the *Critique of Pure Reason*. That is why Kant gave its distinctive title to the, as he intended, popular compendium with which he at once followed up the longer work: *Prolegomena to any future metaphysics which can possibly pretend to be a science*. Empirical knowledge is not knowledge of ideas and knowledge of ideas is not empirical knowledge, indissolubly interconnected as they are—that is what, above all, human reason must make clear to itself, in order to understand itself.

Empirical knowledge is constituted by intuition (*Anschauung*—immediate perception) and the Understanding, the two forms of knowledge peculiar to human reason. Their object cannot be the 'thing-in-itself', that is a thing manifest to us in its essential nature; but is the thing as it is given and comprehended by virtue of these two forms of knowledge. Their object is *given* to us under the forms of space and time, so that its existence and characteristics become to us intuitively evident. We *comprehend* however its existence and characteristics by means of the Categories or forms of the *Understanding* which correspond to the forms of intuition (the forms of space and time). By means of the Categories of the Understanding we attempt to think what we have intuited. Genuine empirical knowledge is achieved when there is a concrete unity of intuition and concepts. This is what corresponds to the transcendental act of apperception, that is to what underlies this achievement, the synthetic *a priori* determining principle of our reason. Only empirical knowledge is genuine theoretical, rational knowledge, that is, knowledge of what exists. For only in the *unity* of intuition and concepts is there knowledge of what exists.

As intuition without concepts would be blind, so—and this is the aspect of the matter emphasized by the Kantian teaching—concepts without intuition are empty, that is, they cannot be made to yield any knowledge of what exists. When assertions or denials about what exists are made by means of forming concepts which lack any actual or at least possible intuition, the illusion of genuine theoretical knowledge and not the reality is achieved. For there is wanting any basis in transcendental apperception and thus any test of pure rationality. This illusion will very soon produce difficulties in its train by developing antinomies, necessary self-contradictions in which at once such a desire for ideal knowledge of a merely conceptual kind will be entangled. Examples are the contradiction between the assumption of a First Cause and that of a *regressus in infinitum*; or that between the assumption of human free-will and the assumption that there is no such thing. So far as the objects of intuition and the Understanding, of empirical knowledge, are concerned, God, Freedom and Immortality are not objects of our knowledge. That means: they are not objects of our theoretical knowledge. They are not to be comprehended simply as existent reality. Only sophistry can present them and treat of them as such. Metaphysics—metaphysical cosmology, psychology and theology—is impossible, if one understands by it a theoretical knowledge of objects, the concepts of which must be devoid of corresponding intuitions. They are impossible 'since for determining our ideas of the supersensible we have no material whatever, and we must derive this latter from things in the world of sense, which is absolutely inadequate for such an Object'.[1] All theoretical proofs and disproofs of God's existence, for example, fail equally, since the propositions, 'God exists' and 'God does not exist', can express in their theoretical meaning only the illusion of knowledge and not knowledge. For they apply the Category of being, positively and negatively, to an object which lacks intuition. God is a limiting concept, a regulative idea, a pure thing of thought. We imagine that when we assert or deny God's existence we have said something about God. In fact to speak of existence or non-existence is *per se* not to speak of God.

Be it well understood: the significance of this, the negative aspect, of Kant's endeavour to bring reason to an understanding of itself, does not consist in an attempt to dispute or even only cast doubt upon the metaphysical reality or unreality of God, freedom and immortality. It certainly does consist in criticism of the means by which they are known, in the attempt to demonstrate that this knowledge is that of pure reason, that its nature is strictly ideal; and in the making of the proviso, that it may on no account claim to be theoretical knowledge.

There is, however, a second aspect, a positive aspect to Kant's undertaking. According to Kant knowledge by pure reason is also and in particular true knowledge by reason, however necessary it is to all empirical knowledge. Reason must, however, learn to understand itself as pure reason. It will not have come to an understanding of itself so long as it imagines itself merely to be theoretical reason and not active, practical reason. In Kant's teaching 'practical reason' is not a second kind of reason existing beside the theoretical form; it is rather that the one kind of reason, which is also theoretical, is also and, it must actually be said, primarily, practical reason. Surely the union of intuition and concept, whence empirical knowledge derives its

---

[1] *Critique of Judgment*, 3rd German ed., p. 453; transl. by J. H. Bernard, 2nd ed., p. 403.

reality, is in fact action, practice, having its basis in transcendental apperception. It is in this act as such that man is laid hold of not only by the being of things, i.e. by nature in its reality in time and space, but beyond this and above all by the thing that must be, hidden from us as a 'thing in itself' which is, as a thing, undiscoverable; by the world of freedom which limits time and space and resolves them in itself. I am laid hold of, to use the words of Kant's famous passage,[1] not only by the star-strewn heavens above me, but also, at the same time, and chiefly, by the moral law within me. Abstract man, the man who is held to be a creature of theoretical reason, is not the real man. I am not a real man, a real creature of reason, simply by virtue of this capacity I have for perceiving things in time and space, but this capacity for perceiving things in time and space is itself based upon the true and essential reasoning capacity, namely that by which I perceive necessity and law, in such a way that law and necessity are imposed upon me as a person who acts. God, freedom and immortality—these ideas which in their regulative use are indispensable also in empirical knowledge—cannot be perceived *in abstracto*, i.e. by contemplation in isolation, but they can be perceived *in concreto*, i.e. in actual fact. It is in and with the *fact* that their true contemplation is accomplished; it is in practice that the true thing is accomplished, the theory which accompanies, provides the basis for and contains within itself all empirical knowledge but which now also rises truly and legitimately above it. They have no truth in a theory by itself.

Their truth is contained in the truth of the will for good, beside which 'it is not possible to conceive of anything anywhere in the world, or, indeed, outside it which could be taken as good without restriction'.[2] The will for good is a will not governed by any object, nor significantly guided by any desire or end or authority, but subject by its own decision to the categorical imperative of duty, in its quality as the rule for that which is universally valid, as the quintessence of the law, as the voice from the world of freedom Kant alludes to. Pure reason, reason as the capacity for knowing ideas, is practical reason. Knowledge by pure reason too, the true knowledge of God, freedom and immortality, is knowledge by practical reason, as it is implicitly accomplished in the deed performed in accordance with duty, and knowledge by practical reason is knowledge by pure reason. The act performed in accordance with the will for good, the moral act, is not

---

[1] *Critique of Practical Reason*, V, 161.
[2] *Grundlegung zur Metaphysik der Sitten* (Background for a Metaphysics of Morals), Phil. Libr., vol. 41, p. 10.

possible without, but comprises, not the establishment but certainly the *pre-supposition*—Kant's word for these, not a very happy choice linguistically, was 'postulates'—that all these ideas which transcend every experience and yet for their own part comprise all empirical knowledge are *true*: There are:

1. The pre-supposition of the truth of the idea of *God*, of the truth, that is, of an ultimate unity of nature and freedom, of that which is with that which must be, and thus of duty and desire.

2. The pre-supposition of the truth of the idea of *freedom*, of the idea, that is, that our moral existence is superior in its origins to our natural one.

3. The pre-supposition of the truth of the idea of *immortality*, of the idea, that is, of the infinite convergence of the two lines upon which our existence runs.

The truth of ideas (this, however, means truth in general, in so far as the truth of things is comprised in the truth of ideas) is practical truth, truth, that is, which is perceived in the form of such pre-suppositions (Kant says, in the form of 'postulates') which are accomplished in the moral act. As theoretical knowledge (whose objects can only be objects of experience), knowledge by pure reason is impossible, having its inevitable, true and sure basis in the knowledge of ideas, a knowledge which cannot be affirmed or denied, but which can certainly be believed, and believed, furthermore, as something jointly based with the moral demands on reason, as something, therefore, which is to be believed to be reasonable. It is impossible to bring forward the proof of God as an ontological, cosmological or teleological proof, as ultimately the school of Wolff still wanted to bring it. The proof of God is ever to be adduced as a demonstration of the presupposition that is assumed in deciding to accept the commandment of the inscrutable Law-giver, in subjecting oneself to the judgment of the inscrutable Judge. It must be brought forward as a moral proof of God.

There is, therefore, according to Kant, one knowledge of God, namely that one which lay a practical basis and meaning: 'After the analogy with an understanding I can very well . . . conceive of a super-sensory Being, without however wishing to perceive him thereby theoretically; if, namely, this definition of his causality concerns an effect in the world containing an intention which is morally necessary but which sensory beings are incapable of implementing; since then a knowledge of God and of God's existence (theology) is possible by means of qualities, and definitions of his causality, attributed to him simply by analogy, the which (*sc.* existence) in its practical aspect, but then again only in respect to its practical (i.e. moral) aspect, has all the reality anyone might wish for.'[1] The critique is therefore meant to have brought honour, and not discredit, to knowledge by pure reason in particular: Kant does not think that in clarifying the relationship of knowledge by pure reason to empirical perception he has destroyed metaphysics, but rather that he has first and foremost made it possible as a science: metaphysics as knowledge by means of practical reason.—That then is the true use of pure reason as it at last and finally emerged from the fire of Kant's critique of reason.

As a result of this teaching theology, at least as much as philosophy and every other branch of learning at that time, found itself faced with the problem of determining its future attitude to Kant's critique of reason in the formation of its peculiar and necessary propositions. Kant, however, did not first wait for the theologians to declare their attitude to his philosophy, but immediately advanced to meet them—in accordance with the careful thought and precision he devoted to all his work—by dictating his own terms for peace, i.e. by giving an explicit and exhaustive explanation of the way he thought this attitude should be formed. These terms for peace are contained in his philosophy of religion, set down in his fourth main work, *Religion Within the Limits of Reason Alone* (1793), to which in 1798, with the *Dispute of the Faculties* (which, significantly, concerns only the dispute between the philosophical and theological faculties!), he added a rider which was meant to emphasize and enjoin upon them what he had said in the previous work. It is to these works and to the very categorical proposal made to theology in them that we have now to devote our attention.

It is possible to distinguish in Kant's dictation of peace terms—just as with every such dictated peace, however severe—between what the dictator definitely wants, and what he does not necessarily require, according to his explicit or tacit explanation of his terms—but leaves to the discretion and decision of the second party to the contract, until he has seen how things are going, at any rate. We cannot therefore explore all the possibilities of characterizing Kant's theology and describing its historical significance simply by explaining and assessing the content of his teaching, or alternatively of his terms for peace as they stand. We shall have to pay strict attention also to the passages where the philosopher has not expressed his own opinion, or has not stated any conclusion, but has merely left the question open. It is fitting to set out first in pursuit of what Kant in his works expressly stated and definitely wanted in his discussion of the theological problem. We shall then in

[1] *Critique of Judg.*, 482, cf. 424, footnote, 434, 472.

conclusion examine the other things, those upon which he was strikingly
unwilling to express himself either explicitly or tacitly, and in which,
therefore, he did not wish to act as a dictator towards theology.

What are Kant's aims as a philosopher of religion? The answer we
must give is a double one: he wants on the one hand, as a philosopher,
i.e. as the advocate of human reason in the general sense—which is
seeking to understand itself and is thus self-critical—to remind religion
too and theology as religion's mouth-piece of the significance of the
fact that it too is a matter in which reason plays its part, an additional
part, at all events, just as certainly as it too at least *makes use* of reason
in-the establishment of its propositions. And on the other hand, once
again as a philosopher, he wants to assess religion as a phenomenon
of reason, as a cultural manifestation, in so far at least as it is these
things; he wants to make it intelligible within the frame-work of all the
other phenomena of reason, to construct it by applying the general
principles pertaining to all civilization. The theological propositions are
at all events also, those of reason. And reason for its part has the 'idea
of a religion'[1] as something which is, at all events, also peculiar to it.

In respect to theology philosophy therefore has on the one hand the
task of critically examining in principle theology's 'interpretations', i.e.
the tenets calling revelation to witness.[2] This at all events theology
cannot disallow: 'The theological faculty's proud claim that the
philosophical faculty is its handmaid (which still leaves open the
question as to whether the latter carries her mistresses' torch before her
or her train after her) can be conceded only so long as the maid is not
driven out or gagged.'[3] Kant is bold enough to make the suggestion
that candidates for theology should be compelled upon completion of
their instruction in theology proper, biblical theology, to hear a special
lecture upon purely philosophical religious teaching, as something
necessary to their complete preparation.[4] 'It doesn't matter whether
this makes the theologian agree with the philosopher or makes him
feel that he must defeat his arguments, so long as he only hears
him.' We shall hear what there is to hear for the theologian on this
subject.

On the other hand, however, the philosopher is bound to feel it
important for his own sake 'to form some coherent idea of those things
in the Bible, the text of a religion which is held to have been revealed,
which can also be perceived by reason alone',[5] and 'to seek that meaning in the Scripture which is in harmony with the holiest of reason's

---

[1] First draft of the Foreword to the *Rel.*   [2] Loc. cit.   [3] *Disp. of the Facs.*, 67.
[4] Foreword to the 1st ed. of the *Rel.* XIX.   [5] *Disp. of the Facs.*, 44.

teachings'.[1] The revealed or church faith, the positive religion, contains the inner, smaller circle,[2] Kant says (but he means to say: as the shell contains the kernel). It is this religion of reason as such, or the inner circle of positive religion, where it too is comprehensible as a religion of reason, and only in so far as it is here comprehensible as a religion of reason too, which interests the philosopher. It is in this respect that the philosopher is interested in positive religion as such too. It and it alone (*sc.* the religion of reason) is the object of the philosophy of religion. Only seemingly does the latter trespass upon theology's ground, in for its own part, for instance, basing its arguments upon quotations from the Bible; only seemingly because it does this simply to explain, and at most to affirm its own tenets relevant to this inner circle. It is on principle concerned with Christianity in particular and the documents of Christianity only as an example, in order to reveal by it the sole conditions 'whereby the idea of a religion can be realized',[3] i.e. in order to demonstrate by such examples the universal truth of religion.

Such then, in very general terms, are the two aims expressed in the title 'Religion within the limits of reason alone'. This title does not at all imply that religion exists solely within the limits of reason. It does, however, state that religion at all events is to be contemplated also within the limits of *reason* alone, and secondly that within the limits of reason alone *religion* too is to be contemplated. In this it must be borne in mind that 'reason alone' must in no circumstances be confused with 'pure' reason, the capacity for the knowledge of ideas, but stands in contrast to the reason illuminated by revelation, the reason which believes positively and concretely. Kant's undertaking in the philosophy of religion is not concerned with this last kind of reason as such and in itself. The contemplation of revelation, or alternatively of the reason which believes positively and concretely as such and in itself, has for the philosopher the significance of contemplating the border beyond which he feels, declares and conducts himself as one not competent, as a spectator, as a member of another faculty which is not qualified to judge of the matter, giving way respectfully and a little maliciously to the theologian, not contesting what he says, but not expressing agreement either, interested, but disclaiming all responsibility, waiting to see whether the other, the theologian, will find the desire and the courage really to take up the position which is his due as the proclaimer of revelation, of religion, that is, within and without

---

[1] *Rel.*, 115f.   [2] Foreword to the 2nd ed. *Rel.*, XXIf.
[3] Second draft of the Foreword to the *Rel.*

the limits of reason alone. Such is the strange restriction of the problems dealt with in Kant's philosophy of religion, concerning which we
shall have several things to say later. Let us turn first of all to the details
of the Kantian teaching of religion *within* the limits of reason alone,
within the reason, that is, which in respect of any kind of positive faith
based on revelation is, so to speak, merely a void, but which, precisely
because of this, is the necessary form in all reason too which is filled by
faith based on revelation.

Kant himself described his standpoint in the philosophy of religion
as being that of 'pure rationalism'.[1] In order not to misunderstand him,
being misled by the narrower sense which this word normally has when
we use it, we must once again reflect that with Kant *ratio*, reason, does
not refer to the isolated theoretical, intellectual human capacity but to
that human capacity which is, decisively even, determined by practice.
It is precisely Kant's 'rationalism' which remains untouched by the
arguments it is customary to raise against 'intellectualism'. Taking
Herder or Rousseau as one's guide it is possible to attack Kant's
rationalism for its narrowness, as the Romantics who followed them did
in fact attack it. But it is precisely as intellectualism that it is impossible
to condemn it. Kant is only carrying out an analysis of the problematical
notion of 'religion within the limits of reason alone' when he explains his
'purely rationalistic' standpoint by saying that as far as the latter is
concerned the reality of a divine revelation is indeed 'admitted', left
undecided, that is, as a possible answer to a question which is deliberately not put but which is merely alluded to, but that it must also be
affirmed that it is not necessary to religion (within the limits . . .) that
such a revelation should be known and assumed to be real.[2] Religion
(within . . .) is 'knowledge of all our *duties* as a *divine* commandment'[3] or,
conversely, it is 'that faith which sees man's *morality* as the essential part
of all worship of the *Divine*'.[4] Religion, the religion of reason as we
shall now always call it, using Kant's own abbreviation, is distinguished
from morals as the primary use of reason not in its content but merely
in its form, inasmuch as it represents morals in a certain connexion,
inasmuch, namely, as it gives to the idea of God which is evolved from
morality itself an influence upon the human will for the fulfilment of
every human duty.[5] 'When morality knows in the holiness of its law
an object worthy of the greatest esteem, it (morality) represents the
cause of that law's fulfilment on the level of religion at its highest as
an object of adoration and it appears in its majesty.'[6] This then, the

---

[1] *Rel.*, 231f.   [2] Loc. cit.   [3] *Crit. of Judg.*, 477; *Rel.*, 229.   [4] *Disp. of the Facs.*, 93.
[5] Ibid., 77.   [6] Foreword to the 1st ed. of the *Rel.*, Xf.

fact that morality in religion appears 'in its majesty', is the formal distinction, i.e. the sole possible distinction, between religion and morals as such. 'Morality inevitably leads to religion, and in so doing extends itself into the idea of a moral legislator possessed of power and existing outside man.'[1]

Revelation is not in itself necessary to this extension of morality, to this emergence upon the higher plane. The movement from morality to religion consists in fact in the moral mode of thought of reason itself, namely 'in the belief that those things are true which are inaccessible to theoretical knowledge, in the belief that the ideas, and especially and most decisively the idea of God, are true, the belief which comes about implicitly, which is pre-supposed, in every act performed in accordance with a genuine will for good. And just as it is not an object that can be proved theoretically which we accord this supposition of truth, we are not bound either by any external authority to that supposition, but accomplish it spontaneously, in accordance with the laws of freedom.'[2] Kant expressly declared that while indeed it had a dubious sound it was 'by no means reprehensible to say that every man makes a God for himself, and indeed, according to moral concepts, . . . must make a God for himself, in order to worship in him the One who made him'. He has to be in a position to measure the God who is, perhaps, proclaimed to him or who, perhaps, even reveals himself to him, against an ideal conception of God which he has set up for himself, in order (it is surely only thus that it is possible!) to recognize the former as God.[3] He must therefore have already perceived God directly and in himself before any act of revelation has taken place. Kant finds himself in agreement with Augustine's teaching that the knowledge of God is a recollection of a notion of God which has already dwelt within our reason beforehand, because it has always been within us from the very beginning. And that is why he is not afraid to speak expressly—a thing impossible even on the basis of the teaching of Augustine—of the 'God within ourselves', who must be the authentic interpreter of all revelation, 'because we do not understand anyone but the one who speaks with us through . . . our own reason'.[4]

We shall certainly not find any criterion in the sphere of our experience by means of which a revelation which is thus encountered, as experience, might be distinguished from other experiences, and which might be perceived as revelation as distinct from these. 'For if God really spoke to man, he would never be able to know that it was in

---

[1] Loc. cit., IX.   [2] *Crit. of Judg.*, 462.
[3] *Rel.*, 257.   [4] *Disp. of the Facs.*, 91.

fact God who was speaking to him. It is an utterly impossible demand
that man should grasp the Infinite One by means of his senses, distinguish him from sensory beings, and perceive him thereby.'[1] But
neither is it permissible to characterize such experience, difficult and
impossible as it seems to us to exalt it to the level of empirical knowledge on account of its incomprehensibility, as divine revelation, since
in order to do this we should already have to have some prior knowledge of what revelation is, and of what God is. 'It might at most be
allowed, that man had had some inner experience of a change which
he was at a loss to account for other than by a miracle, an experience,
therefore, of something supernatural. But an experience concerning
which he cannot even be certain whether it was in fact an experience,
because (being supernatural) i̇ cannot be reduced to any rule partaking of the nature of our understanding, and thus substantiated, is an
interpretation of certain sensations we do not know what to make of,
and concerning which we do not know whether, as something belonging to knowledge, they have a real object, or whether they are mere
fantasy. The wish to feel the direct influence of the Deity as such is a
self-contradictory piece of presumption, since the idea of the Deity
has its seat in reason alone.'[2]

If then there is no empirical criterion, and therefore no empirical
knowledge either, of true revelation of the true God, this criterion can
only ever be perceived by its 'correspondence with that which reason
declares to be proper for God',[3] and it should now be clear where in
fact we must look—judging always from the standpoint of the religion
of reason—for the true, original revelation, if we might speak of such a
thing. The true miracle of revelation, or, at least, what is the highest
degree to be wondered at in the founding of the religion of reason is—
reason itself in its own eyes, as moral reason, namely—'There is in fact
something within us which we can never cease from wondering at,
once we have looked well upon it, and this is the thing which at the
same time exalts mankind ideally to a dignity which one would not
expect in man as comprising objects of experience', 'the superiority',
namely, 'of the super-sensory man in us over the sensory', the moral
disposition in us which is inseparable from humanity.[4] 'The incomprehensibility of this disposition which proclaims our divine origin must
affect the mind with the force of an inspiration.'[5] It is the object of our
highest wonder, 'which can only ever increase, the longer one gazes
upon this true (and not invented) ideal; so that those men can well be

[1] *Disp. of the Facs.*, 109f.   [2] Ibid., 102f.   [3] Ibid., 89.
[4] Ibid., 103f.; cf. *Rel.*, 57.   [5] *Rel.*, 58f.

pardoned who, misled by its incomprehensibility, consider this super-
sensory quality in man, because it is practical, to be supernatural,
something, that is, which does not lie in our power at all and belong to
us as our own, but which is rather to be ascribed to the influence of
another and higher spirit; in which belief they are, however, very much
at fault'.[1]

We see, then, upon the one hand the inspiration, whose object
resides within ourselves, in so far as the idea of humanity and therefore
this moral disposition reside within us too; and, upon the other, the
'influence of another, higher spirit'. It is between these two, between
the notions of a 'disposition' proclaiming a divine origin on the one
hand, and 'revelation' on the other, between the 'supersensory' and the
'supernatural', that the exact border between the things which can be
supposed and the things which may not be supposed, runs, in matters
concerning the religion of reason. Anyone who speaks of revelation is
bursting the religion of reason asunder, for he is bursting asunder
'mere' reason, he is speaking of something which cannot be an object
of empirical knowledge. The critical philosophy of religion cannot
therefore speak of revelation. This, then, is Kant's 'pure rationalism'
in this matter.

From the point of view of religion which has its foundation in reason
itself, i.e. the religion which refers to this disposition to be discovered
in ourselves, the following may be said concerning positive, allegedly
revealed, statutory religion, in so far as it, also at any rate, presents
itself as a phenomenon of reason, and is to be judged as such: it rests, as
distinct from the religion of reason, upon 'a teaching which has been
passed on to us'.[2] It is 'based upon facts'.[3] It is a 'historical faith'.[4]
It has need, in so far as it has its basis in books, of the control of historical science.[5] In consequence 'its validity is always only of a particular kind'—it is valid, that is to say, only for those who have been
reached by the history upon which it rests. Its knowledge is not necessary and uniform, but accidental and diverse, it is not *per se* the one,
pure religious faith which should distinguish the one true Church.[6]
Such a historical faith is, however, as such not a living, not a salutary
faith, and is therefore not necessary either. It is 'dead in itself'.[7] The
idea that 'it is our duty and essential to salvation, is superstition'.[8]
Those who represent it are in error in attempting to take 'its statutes
(even if they were divine revelations) to be essential parts of religion,

[1] *Disp. of the Facs.*, 104.   [2] Ibid., 91.   [3] *Rel.*, 145.   [4] Ibid., 161.
[5] Ibid., 194.   [6] Ibid., 167; cf. 154; *Disp. of the Facs.*, 91.
[7] *Rel.*, 161; cf. *Disp. of the Facs.*, 113.   [8] *Disp. of the Facs.*, 112.

thereby foisting rationalism upon empiricism in matters of faith [Kant means foisting the necessary quality of reason itself upon the empirically determined nature of the reason which positively believes], and thus representing that which is merely accidental as something necessary in itself'.[1] For 'in itself, looked upon as a confession, it contains nothing which might have moral value for us'.[2] Historical knowledge, which bears no inner relationship valid for all to the betterment of mankind, 'has its place among the things (*adiaphora*) which may or may not be believed, which each one may treat in the manner he finds most edifying to himself'.[3]

Kant does not, however, wish to say outright that revelation is therefore completely unnecessary and superfluous.[4] He does, admittedly, say quite openly that it is a consequence of a special weakness in human nature, that the religion of reason 'can never be relied upon to the extent it certainly deserves, namely to the extent of the foundation of a Church upon it alone'.[5] But since this is once and for all so, the faith of a Church must be determined, in contrast to this religion *a priori*, as religion *a posteriori* or as religion *in concreto*, as a 'working-out' of the former's demands,[6] as a 'means to its furtherance',[7] as its 'vehicle' as Kant was especially fond of saying.[8] Dogma might, for instance, be honoured as the 'shell' which has served to set the religion of reason publicly in motion.[9] Taking the ideal case it might so be that the revealed and the natural religion were one and the same, in the case, namely, 'when the positive religion is so constituted, that men might and should have been able to discover it for themselves by the sole use of their reason, albeit they would not have discovered it so early or in such large numbers as is expected of them, so that at a certain time and in a certain place a revelation of the same might be wise and very advantageous to the human race; a revelation made, however, in such wise that all men thenceforth, once the religion thus introduced is there, and has been made publicly known, can convince themselves of its truth by their own inner resources and by their own reason. In this case the religion is objectively a natural one, although subjectively it is a revealed religion, for which reason also it is the former name which truly befits it.'[10] Thus pure rationalism prevails in this case too. This supposition that the revealed and the natural

[1] *Disp. of the Facs.*, 93.   [2] *Rel.*, 161.   [3] Ibid., 47; *Disp. of the Facs.*, 82.
[4] *Disp. of the Facs.*, 50.   [5] *Rel.*, 145.   [6] First draft of the Foreword to the *Rel.*
[7] *Rel.*, 148, 250.
[8] Ibid., 152, 153; *Disp. of the Facs.*, 78, 91, 95—'vehicle' means a 'conducting substance', and is a technical term which was used in pharmaceutics at Kant's time.
[9] *Rel.*, 118.   [10] Ibid., 233.

religion might be one and the same, is, in Kant's opinion, true of Christianity. And thus the Christian preaching has also at any rate the task of presenting the biblical teaching of the faith in the form in which we can develop it from within ourselves by means of reason.[1]

What there is to be said, from the point of view of Kant's conception of the problem of a 'religion of reason', concerning the significance of the Bible can now to a certain extent already be foreseen. There is above all this to be said that the Bible too, like religion itself, 'is made up of two unequal parts; the "canon", which contains the pure religious faith, and the "organon" or "vehicle", containing the church faith which allegedly rests upon revelation'.[2] The thing which affirms its truth (judged always from the standpoint of the religion of reason) is not the especial 'learnedness in divinity' of those who wrote it, but the popular effect of its popular content, and it is precisely thereby that it betrays itself as an affirmation 'from the pure spring of the universal religion of reason, which dwells with every common man'.[3] This acknowledged effect which it has of 'giving rise to religion in human hearts' surely has its quite simple explanation as the 'effect of nature and result of progressive moral civilization in the general course of Providence'. And it is precisely because this effect is ultimately the effect of the religion of reason itself that it is independent of all historical and critical investigation of the Bible. May the latter even be 'greatly or little lacking in items of so-called historical proof', the divine nature of its moral content yet justifies the pronouncement, 'that the Bible just as if it were a divine revelation deserves to be preserved, used in moral questions and employed as a manual for religion'.[4]

Since this is the position in respect of the authority of the Bible, its exegesis must consist in a thorough 'interpretation' of the Bible 'into a meaning which concords with the general practical rule of a religion of reason. For the theoretical element in the church faith cannot hold any interest for us from a moral point of view, if its effects do not tend to the fulfilment of every human duty as a divine commandment'. Even if this exegesis then 'often seems forced, and often really is so too', it is nevertheless resolutely to be preferred to a literal but morally insignificant one.[5] The learned man of Scripture is subordinate to the interpreter of Scripture.[6] And the interpreter of the Scripture, should the occasion arise, is quite entitled to 'convey' the true teaching of the religion of reason into the Bible, if by any chance he does not find it

---

[1] *Disp. of the Facs.*, 105.   [2] Ibid., 78.   [3] Ibid., 110.
[4] Ibid., 111.   [5] *Rel.*, 158.   [6] Ibid., 162.

there.[1] 'Passages in the Scripture containing teachings which, while they are theoretical and proclaimed sacred, yet transcend every concept of reason (even the moral one), *may* be interpreted to practical reason's advantage, but those containing tenets which contradict practical reason *must* be thus interpreted.'[2] The words 'He that believeth and is baptized shall be saved' (Mark 16.16), for example, must not be interpreted literally and historically.[3] 'It is therefore only the doctrinal exegesis, which does not seek (empirically) to know what sort of meaning the holy author might have attached to his words, but to know with what sort of teaching reason (*a priori*) can support the Bible, in regard to morals, with a scriptural saying giving occasion for its text, which is the sole evangelical-biblical method of instruction for the people.' And it is precisely this interpretation, Kant thinks, which is in fact the authentic one, i.e. 'it is thus that God would have his will as revealed in the Bible understood'. 'The God who speaks to us through our own reason (reason practical in what concerns morals) is an infallible and universally comprehensible interpreter of this his word.'[4] 'The God who is within us is the interpreter.'[5] Such therefore is the doctrine of the Scriptures and such is the interpretative method (Hermeneutics) of pure rationalism.

What form will the Christology of this teaching take? It is typical of Kant (and indeed typical of him in a way which is also entirely to his credit) that the name Jesus or Christ never, so far as I can see, flowed from his pen in any of his writings, and that he even found a way of avoiding it in the numerous quotations from the Bible which he used in the 'Religion within'. He allows him to appear only as the 'teacher of the Gospel', as the 'founder of the Church', as Son or Ambassador of God, and of course as the preacher too who is legitimized by the content (in accordance with reason) of his preaching, and who is therefore on principle subordinate to it. He grants him that, seen historically, he brought about 'a complete revolution' among the race of men, in respect of religion, at least.[6] But Kant's interest did not stop here. He was also interested in the Christological dogma and tried to derive a meaning, his own meaning, of course, from it. There is even a Kantian doctrine of the Trinity, held together by the idea of love, in so far as one 'can' (!) worship in God: firstly, the loving one, who loves with the love inspired by his being well-pleased morally with mankind (in so far as man lives up to his holy law), as the Father; secondly, representation in the idea of humanity which is begotten

[1] *Disp. of the Facs.*, 116. [2] Ibid., 80. [3] Ibid., 84.
[4] Ibid., 114. [5] Ibid., 91. [6] *Rel.*, 79.

and loved by him himself, as the Son; thirdly, his wisdom, in which he bestows his favour upon those who fulfil this condition, as the Holy Ghost.[1]

The specifically Christological doctrine of Kant takes a form in which the incarnate Son of God is interpreted as 'the idea set before us for our emulation' of moral perfection, an idea which as such cannot be any created thing, but only God's only begotten son.[2] We cannot conceive of the 'ideal of the humanity in whom God is well-pleased' other than as it is contained 'in the idea of a man who is prepared not only himself, to exercise every human duty . . . but also, although . . . tempted, to take upon himself every suffering, even a shameful death for the best good of the world and for the sake, even, of his enemies'.[3] On principle, however, this ideal does not require any historical realization, either, in order to be an example, but it, too, as such resides already in our reason, and even if its historical realization must on principle be possible, its true and original source is still to be found in reason itself. 'Even the Saint of the Gospel must first be compared with our ideal of moral perfection, before he can be perceived as such; he too says of himself: Wherefore do ye call me (whom you see) good? No one is good (is the archetype of goodness) but the one God (whom you do not see). But whence do we derive the notion that God represents the highest good? Solely from the idea, which reason *a priori* traces of moral perfection and inseparably links with the notion of a free will.'[4] This 'archetype residing in our reason' which we use to 'attribute' to the phenomenon Jesus, is 'the true object of the faith which saves',[5] so that we have no reason to suppose in Jesus anything but the example of a life well pleasing to God, i.e., however, 'a man of natural origin'. An exaltation over our frailty, such as would be postulated by a different kind of pronouncement concerning him, would even actually impede the practical application of the idea which he preached.[6]

Thus if, according to Kant, something corresponding to what is called the 'Word' in the prologue to St John's Gospel exists, there is certainly, according to him, no suggestion that this Word might by any chance have become flesh. To the religion of reason the Son of God is not a man, but 'the abstraction of humanity'.[7] Thus the belief in him should not rest upon miracles either, the demand for which is rather to be characterized as 'moral disbelief',[8] which the man guided by reason does not consider as a possible factor in the present at all,

---

[1] *Rel.*, 220   [2] Ibid., 73.   [3] Ibid., 75.   [4] *Basis for a Metaph. of Morals*, 29.
[5] *Rel.*, 175.   [6] Ibid., 79.   [7] *Disp. of the Facs.*, 81.   [8] *Rel.*, 77, 116.

but only at best as something belonging to the distant past[1] and which at all events cannot have any other significance but that of 'effects of nature', and not that, therefore, of objects of belief.[2] The *work* of the Son of God, however, in so far as it exceeds his teaching—his vicarious suffering above all—is, according to the one passage in Kant, to be interpreted as meaning that from a moral point of view *intelligible* man is in God's eyes different from empirical man; that as the latter's vicar he carries empirical man's guilt incurred by sin, meets the demands of the highest justice through suffering and death and is therefore his Saviour, so that empirical man, in so far as he is yet identical with intelligible man, can hope to appear before his Judge as one vindicated by him.[3] According to the other, less profound, passage the vicarious suffering is interpreted as meaning that Jesus by his death 'represented the good principle, mankind, namely, in its moral perfection, as an example to be imitated by everyone' and thus made visible 'the freedom of the children of heaven and the slavery of a mere son of earth in the most striking contrast'.[4] The belief in Christ, the Christian belief, whereby a person becomes well pleasing to God, must therefore, according to Kant, consist in placing in oneself the well-founded confidence that one will, 'while subject to similar temptations and sufferings . . . unwaveringly cling to the archetype of humanity and remain true to his example in faithful imitation'.[5]

It has to do with the primacy Kant bestows upon practical reason that, as compared for instance with Lessing, he takes a quite strikingly systematic interest in the notion of the Church. It is here for the first time that something becomes visible of the borders of the conception of the problem peculiar to him. The reign of the good principle of humanity demands and makes necessary—as he puts in at this point—the setting-up and spreading of a 'society in accordance with the laws of virtue and for the purpose of the same'.[6] This demand, however, presupposes a higher moral being beyond the insufficiency of the individuals, upon which this demand is made[7] a supreme law-giver and universal searcher of hearts, a moral world-ruler.[8] It would be 'against all reason to say that the kingdom of God should be instituted by men. . . . God himself must be the originator of his kingdom'.[9] 'The creation of a moral people of God is therefore a work the execution of which cannot be expected of men, but only of God himself.' Kant hastens to add that this still does not permit man 'to be inactive in the expectation of this work and to allow Providence to reign'. 'He must

---

[1] *Rel.*, 118. [2] Ibid., 124. [3] Ibid., 98f. [4] Ibid., 112f. [5] Ibid., 76.
[6] Ibid., 129. [7] Ibid., 136. [8] Ibid., 138f. [9] Ibid., 227.

rather proceed as if everything depended on him, and it is only upon this condition that he dare hope that a higher wisdom will allow his well-meaning efforts to blossom into fulfilment'.[1] As God, as the founder, is the creator of the constitution of this kingdom, thus men as its members and free citizens are at all events the creators of its organization.[2]

Ideally this kingdom coincides with the Church;[3] empirically, as the visible Church, 'it is diminished at the hands of men into an institution, which, . . . so far as the means for the setting-up of such an entity are concerned, is very restricted, according to the limits imposed upon a sentient human nature'.[4] But from its identity with the invisible Church, there yet result certain demands upon the visible Church, the entire meaning of which is to make the invisible Church as visible as possible in it. These are unmistakably the well-known predicates of the old Christian conception of the Church: *ecclesia una sancta catholica et apostolica;* which Kant has in mind when he says: (1) that only those elements in the Church should be considered essential, which must necessarily lead to a universal union into one single Church;[5] (2) that only morality, but not superstition and enthusiasm, might be the principle of ecclesiastical union;[6] (3) that this Church must distinguish itself from a political entity by its tendency to achieve unanimity in all men, by its tendency to be an ethical entity in which only the pure religious faith, the *catholicismus rationalis*, and not the *catholicismus hierarchicus*, whose aim is to establish one particular church faith as the universal one, may hold the reins of government;[7] and (4) that its constitution must be inalterable, and only its administration alterable, the accidental order which adapts itself in accordance with the demands of time and place.[8] This inalterable constitution of the Church is the work of God and of God alone. But Kant saw clearly enough and he thought practically enough, that 'if there is simply no means of arranging things otherwise' regarding the fact that the pure religious faith has need of a statutory church faith as its vehicle, that there must be, as against this divine constitution, a statute on the human side, which, even if it is not to be considered as divinely statutory, is yet an equivalent raised publicly to the status of a basic law; a humanly inalterable, humanly qualified statute, as it were: the Scripture, beside which, however, no tradition and no symbols must then be set up as equal to it in value.[9]

---

[1] *Rel.*, 141.   [2] Ibid., 227.   [3] Ibid., 142.   [4] Ibid., 141.
[5] Ibid., 143; *Disp. of the Facs.*, 91, 96.   [6] *Rel.*, 143.
[7] Ibid., 143; *Disp. of the Facs.*, 93.   [8] *Rel.*, 143f.   [9] Ibid., 143f., 150, 152.

I say that something of the borders of Kant's conception of the problem become visible here. This it is possible to say, but more cannot be said. Kant, in wishing to show that the conception of the Church is rationally necessary, and in passing swiftly (a thing we are already accustomed to in him) from the proposition that God alone can be the founder of the Church to the other, that man must therefore proceed in the Church as if everything depended upon him alone—suddenly speaks of the Church in its visible form in quite different tones and with a quite different emphasis, surely, from that with which we heard him speak of the parallel notions of positive religion, the Bible and the historical Christ. It is here precisely not the divine constitution alone which is rationally necessary, but, on principle, the human organization of the kingdom of God also, even if Kant does establish here, too, the fact that this kingdom dwindles in the process into an institution and becomes subject to the limitations of sentient human nature. For the first time unequivocally in this philosophy of religion he says that the concretion, the thing which he otherwise treats above all with suspicion or at least as a mere *adiaphoron*, is on principle necessary, and that it is worth the trouble to devote serious thought to it in itself.

The fact that Kant did in fact do this, to a certain extent at least, is evidenced by the qualified significance he yet attributed in particular to the Bible within this concretion. And what are we to think when we hear him declare in respect to the constitution, not of the invisible *civitas Dei*, but of the concrete, visible Church, that it must not, according to its principles, be similar to a political constitution, must not, therefore, be either monarchical (papal) or aristocratic (episcopal), or democratic (after the fashion of the 'sectarian *Illuminati*'), but 'might best be compared with that of a household (family) under a common, albeit invisible moral Father, inasmuch as his holy Son, who knows his will, and at the same time stands in blood-relationship to all its members, represents him by making his father's will more clearly known to them, who therefore honour the Father in him, and thus enter into a voluntary, universal and perpetual union of the heart one with another'.[1] Is this still the Church of the religion of mere reason? If it is, it is certainly at the same time a picture of the Christian conception of the Church showing no lack of careful study. And if the philosopher should answer that it is precisely in this that the occasional happy coincidence of the Christian with the reasonable element comes to light, we could then ask in return whether it was in fact the reasonable element which served as the archetype in this construction, the Christian element

[1] *Rel.*, 144.

serving only as an example or vehicle, or whether perhaps things turned out differently from what Kant planned and intended, whether he might have used the text of a religion other than that of his religion within. . . . And even if all these questions could be controverted, it might still be affirmed that it was precisely at this point, where the gaze of the philosopher turned to the phenomenon of the Church, that this coincidence of the Christian and the reasonable must have met him in a quite particularly pregnant fashion.

The observation that the conception of the problem contained in Kant's philosophy of religion in fact has its frontiers, and the supposition this implies, that he could or would not say more, with this conception of the problem, in his philosophy of religion than it was, quite simply, possible for him to say, once he had chosen it as the instrument for his work—this observation and supposition are confirmed when we turn finally to the decisive part of his teaching of the religion of reason: to his reflections on the complex of questions which directly concern the *reality* of religion in the individual man, and which therefore directly concern the reality of practical reason in the human will for good, the will, that is, which is in accordance with the law, and which thus contains the knowledge of God and the hope in him. Kant did not try to evade this question. He makes its discussion the starting-point for his philosophy of religion, even, and thus it comes about that the reader of the 'Religion within . . .'—his first contemporary readers found it so, too—finds himself at once confronted in the very first pages by the most difficult questions of interpretation. One certainly does not expect, having a knowledge of Kant's ethics from his earlier writings, and looking at the rest of the contents of his teaching of religion after this beginning, to be met here immediately on the doorstep with a detailed doctrine of the problem of evil, and above all with that kind of doctrine. It is in fact the last thing one would expect.

'The lament that the world is wicked is as old as history', Kant begins. He develops the biblical form of this 'lament', without, surprisingly, attempting to criticize or dissociate himself from it in any way, and then goes on to oppose it to the 'heroic' belief—'held, perhaps, only by philosophers and, in our time, especially by educationalists', 'that the world is constantly (albeit almost imperceptibly) advancing from worse to better', and that there is a corresponding disposition in human nature, and therefore a kind of *a priori* necessary superiority of good in us. Kant, however, objects that this belief is certainly not drawn from experience. The history of every age speaks strongly against it and it is 'presumably merely a benevolent pre-supposition of the moralists, from Seneca to Rousseau, made in an effort to encourage the cultivation of the germ of good which perhaps resides within us'.[1] To anyone who knows Kant this is indeed a legitimate cause for surprise. We saw that he held the view that his time was the best there had ever been, and saw his joyful appreciation of the historical advance of the human life of the spirit. Even in the *Dispute of the Faculties* we find in that request still the remark that it is 'no merely well-meaning and for practical purposes expedient proposition, but one which is tenable also, having regard to the strictest theory, in face of all unbelievers, that the human race has always been advancing to a better state and will continue to do so . . . a fact which reveals a prospect into an unforeseeable time; always provided that the first revolutionary epoch of nature, which buried only the animals and plants, is not followed by a second which will also include the human race, so that other creatures may walk upon this stage'.[2] But in this passage too Kant means something quite different from the 'heroic' or even 'well-meaning' conviction held by all moralists from Seneca to Rousseau; he is in fact simply thinking of the actual decrease of merely outward violence, the increase of lawfulness, of beneficence, etc., of the trend in politics, even, towards a 'society of world-citizens', of the victory of democratic principle, and the gradual elimination of war (against which he always expressed himself in the strongest terms);[3] as—optimistically enough, we are now tempted to say—he imagined all these things to be coming.

He is, however, explicitly *not* thinking of a progress 'consisting in an extension of man's moral basis, . . . for which a kind of re-creation (supernatural influence) would be required'.[4] He expects this progress to be achieved 'not by what happens from below to above, but by what happens from above to below'. To bring this progress about by the education of youth, for instance, namely to an intellectual and moral civilization, 'strengthened by the teaching of religion', is a plan which Kant considers 'has very little hope of meeting with the desired success'.[5] Instead he sees this progress—we have met, by the way, with a similar train of ideas in Rousseau—quite dispassionately, as being founded primarily in part upon the love of honour, and in part upon the enlightened self-interest of men and peoples. Such is the foreground. The background, however, has as its basis not an advance in reason, but 'a wisdom descending from above (which, when it is invisible to us, is called Providence)'.[6] This flat denial of an actual moral progress in

---

[1] *Rel.*, 3f.   [2] *Disp. of the Facs.*, 135f.   [3] *Rel.*, 30; *Disp. of the Facs.*, 132, 141
[4] *Disp. of the Facs.*, 139.   [5] Ibid., 140.   [6] Ibid., 141.

history, of a progress 'within the limits of reason alone', a denial made in face of the importance which Kant yet certainly attached to this very idea of progress; this and his act of founding what he recognizes as progress upon eudemonism on the one hand and providence on the other—both of them motives which clearly have no indigenous claim to belong to the teaching of the religion of reason as such—these things present us with the first riddle we have to face here.

It is indeed not at all Kant's wish in this beginning to the 'Religion within . . .' to place himself on the side of the moral pessimists whose views he had first of all presented. His intention is stated rather in the title to the first part of the work, which runs: 'Concerning the inherence of the evil *principle* together with the good.' It is, however, precisely this inherence—let us reflect: the inherence of an evil principle *together with* the good!—which evidently prevents him from affirming the existence of moral progress in its true sense (because he sees, in the very moral foundation itself, whose 'extension' would be in question if such a progress were to come about, an evil principle firmly rooted together with the good)—it is precisely this inherence, which Kant believes he must assert here, which presents us with a second and greater riddle. 'The inherence of the evil principle together with the good' surely means—and it is thus that Kant did in fact mean it—that in the same incomprehensible freedom of reason in which the good, lawful will can be made actual, its great opposite, a will for evil, can be made manifest too.

This was, perhaps, implied in the philosophy of practical reason as Kant had represented it prior to 1793, but not, at all events, expressly stated. How startling were the effects of his statement of it now upon his contemporaries can be seen by Goethe's outburst in a letter to Herder (7th June 1793, from the camp near Mainz) in which he said that Kant, 'had criminally smeared his philosopher's cloak with the shameful stain of radical evil, after it had taken him a long human life to cleanse it from many a dirty prejudice, so that Christians too might yet be enticed to kiss its hem'. It is not the fact *that* the philosopher takes evil into account at all, or the fact that he does this earnestly and emphatically, which was and is astonishing here—what moral philosopher could do otherwise?—but certainly the *manner* in which he takes it into account, i.e. that he speaks of an evil *principle* and therefore of a source of evil within reason, and of a *radical* form of evil in this sense. It might once again well be asked whether Kant has here not, willy-nilly, incurred the guilt of falling in with the scandal and folly of the Christian-dogmatic teaching. Surely, he could have

remained on the broad highway of the usual philosophical interpretation of the notion of evil, which was also largely usual for theology too,
and therefore he could have allowed evil to appear as the opposite of
good just as sensuality appears as the opposite of reason, and folly as
the opposite of wisdom, proceeding then to explain evil in the way of the
Augustinian teaching, from which in other respects, he is not quite
removed, as a *privatio boni*. It may seriously be asked whether it might
not have been more befitting to Kant's whole starting-point, and, at
all events, to the conception of the problem underlying his philosophy
of religion if he had in fact so treated it. Instead of this he now embarks
upon a polemic against the Stoics, of all people, because they had
sought to find the foe in the natural *inclinations*, which after all, considered in themselves and for themselves, were yet good, and by no
means were to be stamped out. They had summoned up wisdom against
folly, instead of calling it to aid against the *malice* of the human heart,
against the much more dangerous, because, as it were, invisible foe,
concealing itself behind reason.[1] In opposition to the Stoics Kant
declares himself in due form for the words of St Paul in Ephesians 6.12:
'For we wrestle not against flesh and blood (the natural inclination),
but against principalities and powers—against spiritual wickedness.'[2]
The essence of wickedness, Kant tells us in interpreting the biblical
story of the Fall, consists firstly in doubting the strictness of the commandment itself, then in giving it the new meaning of a commandment
to self-love, and finally in the subsequent over-emphasis of the sensual
impulses in the maxims, i.e. the fundamental orientation to which
man's conduct, governed by this undue emphasis, is for ever subject.[3]
Kant describes wickedness elsewhere as being primarily the weakness
of the human heart, the frailty of human nature in respect to the
decision to perform the act which is in accordance with the law—he
quotes here Romans 7.18: 'For to will is present with me; but how to
perform that which is good I find not'; then as the self-interest in
which man is able to link moral and amoral motives, and thus deceive
himself, and finally as the malevolence in which he is able to acquiesce
to the amoral motives made tangible in this manner.[4] 'Man is wicked,
i.e. he is aware of the moral law and has yet incorporated the (occasional) deviation from it in his maxims.'[5]

On the basis of this primary frailty or self-interest or malevolence,
which Kant himself describes as the *peccatum originarium* and concerning
which he declares himself in agreement with another saying of St Paul,
Romans 5.12: 'In Adam we have all sinned'[6]—on the basis of this

[1] *Rel.*, 67f.   [2] Ibid., 72.   [3] Ibid., 44f.   [4] Ibid., 21f.   [5] Ibid., 26f.   [6] Ibid., 45.

pre-supposition all man's actions (in so far as the freedom to do good has not snatched some place for itself) are to be described as wicked. For 'the first incurring of guilt remains, even if the second (the wicked deed) be very often avoided'.[1] Yet another quotation from St Paul makes its appearance here—Romans 14.23: 'For whatsoever is not of faith (of the moral law as the sole motive-force) is sin.' Man can and must then, even if he only does good deeds—the accidental coincidence with the law helps him then not at all—nevertheless be wicked.[2] It is a question of a 'bent for wickedness',[3] of a guilt which is inborn because it can be shown to have been in man just as early as the use of freedom in any form was in him,[4] of an 'attitude which is part of his nature' that was not merely acquired with the passage of time,[5] of 'an inscrutable reason for the acceptance of maxims which are counter to the law', which typifies man as such and the human species.[6] That the manifestation, the actualization of this evil principle concerns human freedom just as much as does obedience to the law, that we are accountable and responsible for it, as Kant emphatically points out,[7] and that it must be thought of as something which it is possible to overcome, all this only serves to confirm the original and inscrutable quality of this evil principle, a quality comparable to and vying with that of the freedom to do good. It is called 'radical evil', however, because it is a corruption at the very source, a corruption of the chief subjective basis for all maxims. It cannot actually be rooted out by any human endeavour, since this could only be achieved by means of good maxims, by means of a betterment at source—precisely by means of the good maxims which are threatened and annulled by this principle![8]

To say that this doctrine of radical evil is in the nature of a 'foreign body' in the Kantian teaching is a possibility so obvious in interpreting his work, and one which has been presented so often, that simply for this reason one is unwilling to concur in it. It would perhaps not be a foreign body at all if it were part of a total survey given from the Kantian point of view, a survey which we must say Kant neglected to give, both to his own time and to us, and which, considering his position, he was bound to refrain from giving; a total survey embracing not only the truly wide horizon of the field he in fact chose as presenting his problem, but also the horizon of the neighbouring fields upon its borders, and not merely regarding these as marking its limits. It cannot, however, well be denied—and to this extent we cannot dissociate

---

[1] *Rel.*, 25. [2] Ibid., 24. [3] Ibid., 27. [4] Ibid., 36f.
[5] Ibid., 14. [6] Ibid., 7. [7] Ibid., 46f., 42. [8] Ibid., 35.

ourselves from the general judgment just mentioned—that the closed and rounded quality of the Kantian system as it stands, i.e. the rounded quality of the Kantian conception of reason and of the religion of reason as postulated in his philosophy of religion, is disturbed by the doctrine of radical evil. That this is so is shown in the developments which this teaching brought about in the further course of the Kantian philosophy of religion.

If it should be so that the notion of evil must in all seriousness be accepted as a concept of reason, which, even if it greatly conflicts with the general plan, must yet be considered as necessary; if there is really an *evil* of reason, an *a priori* evil, an evil principle, opposing the *law* of reason; and if, as the title of the second part of Kant's book says, a 'Conflict between the good and the evil principle for the mastery of mankind' must take place, then we are at liberty to ask whether Kant's doctrine of this conflict, of religious reality being the reality of this conflict, and his doctrine of man's *redemption*, might not, at least, and perhaps should, have been cast in a mould entirely different from the one which they did in fact receive. Is it possible with impunity to be so far in agreement with St Paul as Kant after all was in his doctrine of sin? Indeed the fact that he did go so far in this respect, as we have just discovered, also affects his doctrine of salvation. In this conceptions like those of vicarious atonement, justification, forgiveness, re-birth and even predestination, make their appearance here, like strange visitors from another world, upon the horizon of a philosophy of religion, without there being any attempt to disguise the mystery that is implied in them. They are greeted with a mixture of understanding and surprise, of request and a respectful shaking of heads, and they are acknowledged somehow as conceptions which are at any rate possible, as indicative of open questions, at the least.

One is apt to wonder, arriving at this point by way of Kant's doctrine of radical evil, why Kant does not seize upon this subject even more forcefully. But then again we should not really feel any surprise at all —in view of the rest of the general purport of this doctrine of religion and of the philosophical frame within which it is set—that this does not happen, and that these concepts, for all the reverence with which they are treated, are in effect eliminated in so far as Kant finds that their mystery cannot subsequently be resolved in terms of practical reason, or, wherever Kant thinks this possible, they are simply given a new meaning as concepts of reason, in accordance with the method of interpretation (hermeneutics) already referred to. The end-effect of all this is doubtless to show that here, too, the problem-concept which was postulated is victorious at the last; only the difficulty of carrying it through to victory in this field too has been plainly revealed, and its limited nature has once again, and here most palpably, been made visible—the limitation imposed by problems in other fields which Kant avoided, but which *were* only avoided by him, and not refuted.

Let us once again go into detail. Kant felt himself able to repeat also in the later parts of his book the proposition that 'Man as we know him is corrupt and not by any means in himself a fit subject for this holy law'.[1] He goes on to state what may be inferred from this, too: 'How it is possible for a man who is by nature wicked to make himself good is something which passes all our comprehension; for how can a corrupt tree bear good fruit?'[2] Passes all our comprehension! It is with this statement that these conceptions of the biblical and church doctrine of salvation come within the sphere of Kant's observation, commanding, as it were, consideration of themselves. 'That someone, however, . . . should become . . . a morally good man (one well-pleasing to God) . . . is something which cannot be accomplished by gradual reform so long as the basis of man's maxims remains impure, but which must rather be brought about by a revolution in his mind; and a new man can come into being only by means of a kind of rebirth, like that achievable by a new creation (John 3.5; cf. Gen. 1.2) and by a change of heart.'[3] Kant knows that 'it is possible to conceive of guilt-laden humanity being granted absolution by divine justice only provided that humanity undergoes a complete change of heart,[4] and that the revolutionary change in man's way of thinking must not only correspond to the reform of his disposition which is to be demanded of man but must precede it on principle—that man would have 'to put on a new man'.[5] Kant also knows, however, that observation of his previous course of life can never provide man with the conviction that such a change has taken place, and that he could never have an immediate awareness of it either, since 'the depth of the human heart (the subjective first basis for his maxims) is unfathomable to man himself'.[6]

Kant goes on to say that we can only hope at least to arrive on the way which leads there (to righteousness in God's sight, that is) by the employment of our own powers: for only that can be morally good which can be attributed to us as performed by ourselves; we can, however, only *hope* for even such a 'being on the way' since, and in so far as, this way has already been 'pointed out' to us 'by a disposition

---

[1] *Rel.*, 216. [2] Ibid., 49. [3] Ibid., 54.
[4] Ibid., 102. [5] Ibid., 55. [6] Ibid., 61.

that is fundamentally improved'.[1] The quality our deeds have of being well-pleasing to God can 'with us in our earthly life'—but also perhaps in all future ages and in all possible worlds—only ever be something that is coming into being, and we cannot base any claim that we are right upon what we ourselves know of our deeds. From what we know of ourselves the prosecutor in us must rather always demand the sentence of damnation. 'It is therefore always only a sentence of judgment prompted by mercy, albeit one . . . completely in accordance with everlasting righteousness, if we are relieved of all responsibility for the sake of the goodness contained in our faith.'[2] It is solely in the *idea*, known only to God, of the improved disposition, that justice can be done to eternal righteousness. It is this ideal right-eousness which is thus our righteousness, and not the righteous-ness of a disposition which we might actually find present within us! It will therefore 'always remain a righteousness which is not our own'.[3]

Does Kant after all perhaps know what justification is, in the sense of the Reformation? This question at least one cannot possibly escape, after carefully analysing the multifariously involved utterances of this, the work of his old age—and it is inescapable at this point in particular. It is, of course, impossible, in face of the Kantian re-interpretation, of the Christological dogma, to answer this question in the affirmative. But how can it be denied, when it is so plain that it was none the less precisely the Christological dogma by means of which he has here interpreted the text, that text, he alleges, which was the only one which interested him of practical reason? Kant, it is true, very strongly denies the validity of all 'expiations' which seek to replace this 'change of heart' as the true and decisive, but also at the same time non-intuitive human deed, be they of the atoning or of the sacramental kind; he rejects all invocations and promises of adoration, even that of the vicarious ideal of the Son of God, because this ideal must be taken up into our disposition in order to intercede for us in place of the failure to act. In Königsberg, for example, where he lived near the castle, which also served as a prison, Kant was angered by the loud and persistent hymn-singing of the prisoners, which was particularly irk-some to him in the summer, when he liked to philosophize with his window open, and complained to the town-president about the 'sten-torian devotions of those hypocrites in the gaol', the salvation of whose souls would certainly not be imperilled even if 'they listened to them-selves behind shuttered windows and then even without shouting at

[1] *Rel.*, 61. [2] Ibid., 101. [3] Ibid., 83.

the tops of their voices'.[1] 'Everything that man imagines he can do to
win favour in God's sight over and above living the good life is mere
religious illusion and mock-service of God.'

But note how the continuation of this very sentence, for all its sharpness: 'I say: What *man* thinks he can do; for whether there is not
something more, beyond everything *we* can do, something residing in
the mystery of the highest wisdom, which only *God* can do, to make
men well-pleasing in his sight, is not negatived thereby.'[2] For 'one
cannot prove either that this is impossible, since freedom itself, although
it contains no supernatural element as a concept, yet remains just as
incomprehensible to us, in what concerns its possibility, as the supernatural, which one is tempted to embrace as a substitute for the self-
active but defective determination of the same'.[3] In 1789 Kant wrote
the following to Jung-Stilling: 'You also do very well to seek the final
satisfaction for that mind of yours which is striving for a sure basis
for hope and doctrine in the Gospel, that immortal guide of true
wisdom, which is not only met by a reason which has brought its
speculation to a completion, but whence reason also acquires a new
light in respect to that which, even when it has marked out its entire
field, still remains hidden from it, and from which it is still in need of
instruction.'[4]

Kant, it is true, takes as it were a step backwards at this point with
truly remarkable alarm, with alarm, one is tempted to say, which
is worthy of imitation: in the conflict between his duty and his incapacity man finds himself drawn to the belief in a moral world-
ruler's helping or shaping hand, 'and now the *abyss* opens before him
of a secret, the secret of what part God plays in this respect: of whether
anything at all is to be attributed to him, and if so, *what* in particular'.[5]
'This idea is one that knows no bounds, and it is moreover salutary
that we should keep at a reverent distance from it as from a thing
which is sacred.' What cause is there for alarm here? Kant, of course,
feared above all, from an actual vindication of the 'idea' of God's
autonomous action, the result that it might 'make us all incapable of
any use of our reason, or encourage the indolent habit of expecting in
passive ease from above that which we should seek in ourselves'.[6]
But he also further saw and above all did so with great clearness, that
that 'which God alone can do to make us into men well-pleasing in his
sight', must be to *forgive*; it is forgiveness which must be the decisive
justification of man who, as we know him, is corrupt. But it is precisely

---

[1] Vorländer, *Life of Immanuel Kant*, p. 138.   [2] *Rel.*, 261.   [3] Ibid., 297.
[4] *Corres.*, XI, 10.   [5] *Rel.*, 210.   [6] Ibid., 298.

of divine forgiveness that Kant says that 'an immediate divine revelation in the comforting utterance: "thy sins are forgiven thee", would be a super-sensory experience, because it is impossible'.[1] And he saw moreover with an equal clarity that the notion of a historical faith that justifies, i.e. one achieving this unfathomable improvement of mankind fundamentally, just as much as the notion of vicarious atonement as the object of this faith 'ultimately leads to the conception of an absolute divine decree: God "hath mercy on whom he will have mercy, and whom he will he hardeneth"', which, as Kant at one point says, 'represents, if taken literally, the *salto mortale* of reason', whereas elsewhere he says: 'It must at all events refer to a wisdom the rule for which is utterly and completely hidden from us.'[2]

It is at this point that Kant resolutely turns back. 'God has revealed nothing to us concerning these secrets, and cannot reveal anything either, simply because we should not understand it.' We certainly understand the individual words, but not what the words are saying. And even a supernatural prompting could not at all alter the fact that it 'cannot inhere in us at all, since the nature of our understanding is incapable of it'.[3] Grace, miracle, the mysteries of the call to faith, of atonement and of election, and the possibility of means of grace, are '*Parerga* of religion within the limits of reason alone' as the methodically very illuminating expression runs; 'they do not belong within it, but are yet adjacent to it. Reason, in the knowledge of its incapacity to satisfy its moral requirements, extends itself to extravagant ideas, which could supply this need, without, however, appropriating them as its own extended possession. Reason does not dispute the possibility or reality of the objects of these ideas; it is just that it cannot include them in its maxims for thought and action.'[4]

It should be clear from the foregoing that Kant, whenever and wherever he did not tend to characterize these *parerga* simply by remaining silent, was forced to have recourse to the method of re-interpreting them in order to point them out. He adopts two ways of re-interpreting justification. The first is the way which has over and over again been trodden through the ages, by Augustine first and latterly by Holl and his disciples: the indirect equation of divine justification with the event of the good human will, the interpretation of the imperfectly good human deed as a *larva* of the perfectly good reality of the divine grace. 'If by nature (in its practical significance) we understand the capacity to achieve any certain aims by our own strength, then grace

---

[1] *Disp. of the Facs.*, 90.   [2] *Rel.*, 177f., 217; *Disp. of the Facs.*, 83.
[3] *Rel.*, 217.   [4] Ibid., 63.

is nothing else but human nature, in so far as man is determined to actions by his own inner, but super-sensory principle (his conception of his duty), which we imagine to be the impulse to do good imparted to us by the Godhead, the basis for which we have not ourselves laid down in us, and which therefore we imagine to be grace.'[1] ' "A yearning for the kingdom of God"—if only one were assured of the immutability of such a feeling(!)—will be tantamount to knowing that one is already in possession of this kingdom.'[2] 'The Comforter (paraclete), whenever our transgressions trouble us by reason of their persistence', is 'the good and pure disposition (which may be called a good spirit which governs us) of which we are aware'.[3] And rebirth is the 'revolution of the mode of thought', the 'foundation of a character', in which man 'reverses the supreme basis for his maxims, on account of which he was a wicked man, by one single immutable decision', so that 'he puts on a new man', and becomes 'a subject receptive to good'. A 'reform of the disposition' must then correspond to this revolution, a reform, that is, which consists in a gradual but constant advance from worse to better, which is taken by God to have been completed in consideration of the revolution which has supplied the basis for it.[4] We have only to think of Kant's aforementioned explanation, that it is rather the idea of the disposition which shall justify us, and precisely not a disposition of which we are *aware*, precisely not the 'foundation of a character' which is conceivable as something which we can achieve ourselves, in order to see the seam hiding a tear which is palpably ill-mended here. 'If only one were assured of the immutability of such a feeling!' But how then is man to be able to recognize in his empirical goodness any analogy even, and thus any guarantee, for his intelligible goodness, his quality of being well-pleasing to God? What the belief in divine justification should achieve in view of the radical evil, according to Kant's own premises, it manifestly cannot achieve in this interpretation (an interpretation, that is, which is bound to a good disposition that is to be empirically established).

Kant's other re-interpretation of justification is in its groundwork identical with that known to us from the old Catholic Church of the second and third centuries, from the Greek fathers, and especially from the Franciscan scholasticism of the late Middle Ages: each one of us must *do as much as is in his power* (*facere quod in se est*) to become a better man. He may then hope that what lies beyond his capacity will be supplied by a higher power which is aiding him. This can come about, according to Kant, without it being necessary for us to know in

[1] *Disp. of the Facs.*, 85.   [2] *Rel.*, 86f.   [3] Ibid., 91f.   [4] Ibid., 54f., 85.

what this extra help consists and how it takes effect.[1] Whether it consists in a diminution of the obstacles standing in the way of the will for
good, or in positive aid for this will, man must previously make himself
worthy of it and he must also, which is, after all, no mean thing either,
be prepared at all events to accept this aid of his own accord.[2] Of the
two conditions for salvation, the belief in the atonement which inter-
cedes for the transgressions we ourselves cannot make amends for, and
the belief that we can in future become well-pleasing to God by living
the good life, the second must in all circumstances be placed in the forefront and the first, as a reinforcement of our determination to stand on
our own feet, in the background.[3] 'The right course, is not to proceed
from the receiving of grace to virtue, but rather from virtue to the
receiving of grace.'[4]

It is clear that it is this doctrine of grace or the Augustinian one or a
combination of the two (with Kant they frequently merge with one
another), or, in short, the Roman Catholic, the decidedly non-refor-
matory doctrine of grace which emerges as the result of these re-
interpretations, and which also doubtless accords with the true line of
Kant's undertaking, or, to put it more cautiously, with that of Kant's
philosophy of religion. Where else is a doctrine of salvation to end,
which is intended to be anthropology and nothing but anthropology,
even if it does have as its background a metaphysics with an ethical
foundation—where else could it end, but in the twofold possibility
of the Roman Catholic doctrine of salvation? Kant's emergence
into the Augustinian mystic teaching of the dual picture of reality
and into the vulgar Pelagian doctrine of justification by words is no
less necessary after its fashion than the emergence of Lessing's theology
of history into the Roman Catholic principle of tradition. These roads
must all lead to Rome! Those features in Kant's philosophy of religion,
then, and those especially which are relevant to this last point, which
have struck us as being upsetting to the general plan, can certainly
only be adjudged deviations which have their origin in another field
of magnetic force, and not peculiarities of Kant's own system, as
Kant himself wished it to be understood. We must be well on our
guard against the desire to re-interpret Kant, according to the rules
of his own hermeneutics, as if what he said and meant were at bottom
the same as what Luther and Calvin said and meant. It is not, however, a re-interpretation for us to note the presence of these deviations,
which are to be found precisely at the most significant point: there

---

[1] *Rel.*, 62, 262; *Disp. of the Facs.*, 86   [2] *Rel.*, 47f.
[3] Ibid., 168, 173, 284.   [4] Ibid., 314.

are '*parerga* of religion' which, according to Kant's own explanation, *abut* upon the 'religion within the limits of reason alone'. And in this, incidentally, we are certainly at liberty to take this 'abutting' as implying not only adjacency but a clash.

To summarize: Kant's philosophy of religion has the significance of an attempt to interpret religion, too, as a necessary phenomenon of reason, in pursuance of his general undertaking of the critique of reason; an attempt, that is to say, to reduce it to a capacity *a priori* and measure its concretely empirical content against this capacity as if this were its inner law. Kant interprets religion by means of the two most significant results of his general critique of reason: the ideal and practical nature of all knowledge by pure reason. Since it is reason itself which has alone been able to perform the critique of reason and has thus supplied those results of the critique of reason which have now become criteria, it is already taken for granted by the very starting-point of this philosophy of religion, and by the conception of the problem it is supposed to involve, that it is the agent of reason, man, that is, who, just as he is the measure of all things, is here thought of and provided for as the measure of religion, too: of its practical and theoretical possibilities, and also, and in particular, as God's measure. This conception of the problem proves itself faultlessly in execution for precisely as long as it is merely a matter of its own development, of drawing the limits, that is, between it and the notion of a revealed positive religion, between it and the authority of the Bible when this authority is conceived as a merely historical one, and between it and the merely historically conceived instance of a Word of God made flesh confronting man. Kant's programme is unfolded over against these notions in such a way that he shows, or alternatively affirms, in each case that the allegedly revealed knowledge of God which is claimed along these lines bears a relation to the ideally practical knowledge of God by pure reason akin to that of a vehicle to the actual remedial substance; it is to be understood, that is, in comparison with the other, as something only relatively necessary, as something which in case of conflict is always to be understood from the standpoint of and to be measured by the ideally practical knowledge of God by pure reason, and not the other way round.

It first struck us, however, in the discussion of the notion of the Church that Kant himself feels he has occasion to place a positively historical factor, in the form of the notion of the organization of the kingdom of God, or alternatively, of the visibility of the Church, in close proximity anyway to the timelessly reasonable necessity of his conception of religion. It struck us that the necessity of this conception of religion seemed to show, in this context even, at least a strong relationship to the 'statute' of the positively historical, the Christian religion.

We were secondly surprised to find that Kant is unable to speak of the reality of religion in the individual without at once introducing a principle which in the rest of his analysis of what generally appertains to reason is not, at all events explicitly, held up to view, a principle which is against reason, but which yet, surprisingly, precisely as such belongs to the order of reasonable things, the principle of *radical evil*.

And thirdly it struck us in Kant's teaching of atonement, that he, the philosopher, cannot help but acknowledge the presence, at the back at least of the atonement by one's own good deed, which, according to his teaching, is apparently the only possible kind, of certain problems of another order; these problems are concentrated in the notion of *grace*, mysteries which he leaves undiscussed, as *parerga* of the religion of reason, or attempts to make accessible to a degree by re-interpretation; but whatever his treatment, Kant still acknowledges that they 'abut' upon the religion of reason.

With this we return to the introductory sentence, in which we said that the dictation of peace terms with which Kant, commandingly enough, advanced upon theology, does at least contain a certain gap. Seen in relation to the entire Kantian plan this gap doubtless signifies the presence of a certain inconsistency. The inconsistency becomes visible in the execution of the Kantian enterprise: the conception of the problem which Kant takes as his instrument cannot be equally triumphant all along the line. For the Kantian enterprise consists in a great 'if . . . then' sentence: *if* the reality of religion is confined to that which, as religion within the limits of reason alone, is subjected to the self-critique of reason, *then* religion is that which is fitting to the ideally practical nature of pure reason, and that only. It is in the execution of the 'then' part of the sentence that the inconsistency shows itself. I say, shows itself, and the question now is, whether it could show itself if it was not somehow contained in the 'if' part too, in the premise. This once again might have two meanings: it can mean, firstly that the premise Kant made is, in the way in which he fashioned it, perhaps not complete, but in need of improvement. It could, however, also mean that there is an entirely different premise apart from and opposing the one made by Kant, which he has not made at all, and which yet should have been made. According to the place at which the source of the error is sought three possibilities arise, then as now, for the understanding of the theological relevance of Kant's teaching:

First, theology can take the Kantian premise just as it is as its standpoint; the premise that the criteria Kant took from his philosophy are correct, complete, and that they really set the standard, in order then, with this as its basis, to execute the Kantian programme in a way which is somewhat different after all from that of Kant himself, be it in an even more compact way, or in an even freer way, moving in the latter case in the direction of the gaps existing in Kant's own work. We find following this line of development, firstly the so-called rationalistic theologians, at the end of the eighteenth century and in the first half of the nineteenth, whose only completely thorough-going representative of note was in fact Wegscheider of Halle; and then much later and of a quite different stamp, as a result of the great Kant-revival of the second half of the nineteenth century, A. Ritschl, and particularly distinct among his pupils W. Herrmann.

Secondly, theology—now convinced that the Kantian premise should not be accepted just as it is—can, while it indeed affirms it in what concerns method, subject it to an immanent critique. For it can undertake to broaden and enrich the conception of reason which forms the premise by pointing out that there is yet another capacity *a priori* which is part of the necessities of human reason, apart from the theoretical and practical ones: the capacity of feeling, as Schleiermacher put it, or that of 'presentiment', as de Wette preferred to express it, linking up with the philosophers Jacobi and Fries. It is this second possibility, that of correcting Kant's conception of the problem— a correction which was then of course bound to bring about also a change in the execution of the programme—which became characteristic of the stamp of theology in the nineteenth century, and in particular, of the so-called conservative or positive theology, just as much as of the so-called liberal theology of this century. Both these first possibilities have it in common that theology desires in principle to keep to the Kantian terms for peace, and to enter into negotiations, merely, with their dictator, whether it be upon the conditions he has laid down for their execution, or upon the actual terms for peace themselves. It is in pursuing these two lines of development that nineteenth-century theology is destined to be the direct continuation of the theology of the Enlightenment.

The third possibility, which also clearly exists, was not taken seriously into account throughout the whole of the nineteenth century, the possibility, namely, of at least questioning not only the application of the Kantian conception of the problem, but that conception itself, and therefore the autocracy and its competence to judge human reason in relation to the religious problem. It might perhaps well be possible to concur with an untroubled mind in the premise of Kant's undertaking, be it in the form set down by Kant, or in its corrected form, but at the same time have it emphatically understood that this premise is not the only one to be made in an objective treatment of the religious problem. It might be possible to object that with the problem conceived as 'religion within the limits of reason alone' only the one side of the problem, namely religion as a human function, is seen, and not the other side, the significant point to which this function is related and whence it springs, the dealings, namely, of a God who is not identical with the quintessence of human reason, with the 'God in ourselves' —thus restricting the validity of the enquiry in a manner which must also of necessity adversely affect the presentation of the first side, the interpretation of this human function. This third possibility would, in a word, consist in theology resigning itself to stand on its own feet in relation to philosophy, in theology recognizing the point of departure for its method in revelation, just as decidedly as philosophy sees its point of departure in reason, and in theology conducting, therefore, a dialogue with philosophy, and not, wrapping itself up in the mantle of philosophy, a quasi-philosophical monologue. It can only be said of this third possibility, which becomes visible on the borders of the Kantian philosophy of religion, that it is at all events observed by Hegel and by several of his pupils in theology—I am thinking of Marheineke in the first half of the nineteenth century and of I. A. Dorner in the second—further that it was tackled by certain outsiders (often, unfortunately, without taking sufficiently into account the problems as raised by the Kantian enquiry), again, that it was more or less clearly aimed at by the conservative schools (which for the rest were under the influence of Schleiermacher) as part of their teaching, but that right up to our own time it could not get the better of the actual trend of the time, which at first took its course from Schleiermacher (with the detour via Ritschl) to Troeltsch.

There remains for us, in our study of Kant, the task of ascertaining whether, and if so, in what respect the prospect of this third possibility might really present itself even from Kant's own standpoint. We shall now make no further reference to the inconsistencies we have been discussing in his philosophy of religion. They speak for themselves in this respect, in their unmistakable equivocality, at least. It would also be better for us to renounce the bold attempt to try to understand

Kant better than he understood himself, to renounce the wish, that is, to deduce and construct a philosophy of religion from the philosophy of Kant, other than that with which he himself thought he should and could crown his work in the field of theology. The question as to whether this might not be possible is a permissible one, but even assuming that the question of the theological significance of such an improved philosophy of religion based on Kant were clarified, the task of developing it would at all events be one of a purely philosophical kind. Philosophy, however, is in itself a strict study covering a vast field, and it is not for the theologian to conduct himself as if he were in a position to propound a philosophy, as if this were some subsidiary part of his office, and to pull a philosopher's work to pieces, especially if that philosopher happens to be Kant. We shall remain, therefore, within the framework of an immanent interpretation of Kant, of the Kant who, upon the border between philosophy and theology and in that he was not able to avoid taking half a step over this border, did in effect intrude upon theological matters as a philosopher. In remaining true to this Kant, and in taking him as he presented himself, we are enabled to establish the fact that he yet said several things upon this border which might at least have led theology to take this third way into consideration too, together with that leading from Wegscheider to Ritschl and Herrmann and that leading from Schleiermacher to Troeltsch.

Kant, as we have seen, with the notion of the Church as his starting-point, pondered the possibility of the Bible having a position and significance, which, even if it were not 'divinely statutory' would yet be extraordinary and qualified, and he went on from this to ponder also the possibility of a theology which would be *different* from the philosophical theology he himself was propounding. He explicitly calls this other theology, which limits philosophical theology, '*biblical* theology', and it is his wish that the affairs of this biblical theology should not 'be allowed to mingle' with those of philosophy. He wants rather to form for it a definite distinct idea as befits its own peculiar nature.[1] For Kant the possibility for such a discipline or faculty, which is theological in the narrower and specific sense, is given, first of all formally, simply with the existence of the Church which has its foundation in the Bible. Philosophy would be exceeding its rights if it were by any chance to proceed to the formation of a Church, to a special philosophical preaching, on the basis of its own understanding of religion.[2] Philosophy does not offer itself as a rival to theology, but as a

---

[1] *Disp. of the Facs.*, 63.   [2] First draft of the Foreword to the *Rel.*

'friend and companion'.[1] 'A minister of a Church is bound to convey
his message, to those he is teaching the catechism, and to his congregation, according to the symbol of the Church he is serving.' Kant disputes the idea that a minister's task as an office-holder is dependent
upon any historical-philosophical convictions he might hold as one
learned in the subject. A preacher would be bound to abandon his
office for this reason, only if he should find something flatly in contradiction of the 'inner religion', as he must understand it as a philosopher, in the teachings of his Church, but not if these teachings do
not happen to correspond exactly with his historical-philosophical
convictions. Even if such a conflict between the office-holder and the
scholar in him should take place, the scholar can always explain that
it is not completely impossible for 'truth to lie hidden' in the things he
has to represent in the Church as one holding office.[2]

And with this we have arrived already at what, according to Kant,
constitutes the material possibility of a biblical theology. Kant guards
against the reproach that it seems as if his critical religious teaching is
presuming to dispute revelation. This is not his intention, 'since it
might be after all, that the teachings of revelation stem from men
supernaturally inspired'.[3] He does not wish to assert that in matters
of religion reason is sufficient unto itself, but acknowledges (let us
think once again at this point of that letter to Jung-Stilling) that
reason, after it has established in religion those things which it is fitted
to establish as such, 'must await the arrival of everything else, which
must be added beyond its capacity, without reason being permitted
to know in what it consists, from the supernatural helping hand of
heaven'.[4] 'Even at that point where philosophical theology seems to
accept principles in opposition to those of biblical theology, e.g. in
respect of the teaching concerning miracles, it confesses and proves that
it does not assert them as objective principles, but only as subjective ones;
they must, that is, be understood as maxims, *when* we merely wish to
make use of our own (human) reason in judging of theological matters;
and in so doing we do not dispute the miracles themselves, but merely
leave them without restraint to the biblical theologian, in so far as he
wishes to judge solely as a biblical theologian and scorns any alliance
with philosophy.'[5] What Kant does dispute is the idea that the reality
and possibility of revelation, its availability as data for human reason
and its perception by human reason, are things which can be accounted

[1] Second draft. [2] *Was ist Aufklärung?* (What is Enlightenment?), 9.
[3] *Disp. of the Facs.*, 44; cf. *Rel.*, 87. [4] *Letters*, II, No. 542.
[5] *Draft of Writings to a Theol. Faculty*, 1793.

for by philosophical means, the idea that over and beyond the philosophy of religion there is a philosophy of revelation and of faith, and
that by its theology might be represented, or make its position secure.
At the same time, however, he disputes the philosopher's right to deny
revelation because it cannot be accounted for by philosophical means.
He therefore advises both the theologian and the philosopher 'not to
indulge his curiosity in those things which do not pertain to his office
and of which in general he understands nothing'. For him theology is a
'privileged body', which he quite plainly instructs to do precisely those
things in matters of religion which philosophy dare not do, and to refrain from doing precisely those things which philosophy is bound to do.

What may theology *not* do? It may not 'interfere in the free profession of philosophy and attempt to prove or refute its principles of
belief least of all, by philosophy', just as philosophy for its own part
has to resign itself that it cannot pass any definitive judgment upon the
authority and exposition of the Scriptures.[1] Theology 'does not speak
according to the laws of the pure and *a priori* knowable religion of
reason, for in so doing it would debase itself and set itself down upon
the bench of philosophy'.[2] It may not, 'in what concerns the fulfilment
of the divine commandments in our will . . . by any means count upon
nature, upon man's own moral capacity (virtue), that is'. The interpretive method of 'giving another meaning to something' is forbidden
for theology: theology cannot be entitled 'to give the sayings of the
Scripture a meaning which does not exactly suit what is expressed in
them; with a moral meaning, for instance', 'and since there is no human
expounder of the Scripture authorized by God, the biblical theologian
must rely upon a supernatural enlightenment of the understanding by a
Spirit which guides into all the truth, rather than concede that reason
intervenes'. 'The biblical theologian as such cannot and may not
prove that God himself spoke through the Bible, since this is a matter
of historical fact, and thus belongs to the philosophical faculty.'[3] He
must, as Kant at one point says, certainly not without malice, as a pure
(*purus, putus*) biblical theologian, be 'still uninfected with the accursed
free spirit of reason and philosophy'.[4] What, on the other hand, should
theology do? The answer: 'The biblical theologian is really the scribe
of the Church faith, which rests upon statutes; laws, that is to say, which
stem from the arbitrary choice of another authority.'[5] Theology
'speaks according to statutory prescriptions for belief which are contained in a book, preferably called the Bible; contained, that is, in a

---

[1] First draft of the Foreword to the *Rel.*   [2] *Disp. of the Facs.*, 106.
[3] Ibid., 62.   [4] Ibid., 63.   [5] Ibid., 77.

codex of the revelation of an Old and New Covenant of men with God, which was joined many hundreds of years ago, and whose authentication as a historical faith (and not, particularly not, as a moral faith, for that might also be drawn from philosophy) should surely be expected from the effects of the reading of the Bible upon the human heart rather than from . . . proofs'.[1] 'The biblical theologian proves that God exists by means of the fact that he has spoken in the Bible.' He may, in the question of the realization of the will for good, count only upon grace, 'which, however, man cannot hope to partake of in any other way than by virtue of a faith which fervently transforms his heart; which faith itself he can, however, in his turn expect of grace'.[2] Theology, with these premises it has: the Church, the Bible, historical revelation, and grace, should allow itself to be ranked together with other branches of learning and content itself with the influence it can acquire as such by its own dignity.[3]

Such was the advice Kant had to give to the theologian. What comment should we make upon it? We should certainly not forget that it was to some extent conditioned by the historical events of Kant's time, and that it must be understood accordingly. His philosophy of religion was written subject to the pressure, or in the shadow, at least, of Wöllner's edict of religion. We must therefore certainly bear in mind the fact that he was prevented from developing a decidedly anti-theological absolutism by restraints imposed from without, too. But he cannot be understood solely from this point of view either, unless we intend to question his character in a way for which we have no reason. Once again we must not fail to appreciate that kind of philosophical irony with which Kant carried out this deeply serious segregation of the matters in which the two faculties were to be considered competent, on the basis of which he finds himself after all, unexpectedly in a position to allocate to a biblical theology its place beside philosophy. But what is the ultimate significance of this irony? Perhaps the placing of philosophy and theology side by side is after all a matter which cannot be spoken of without irony—and from the theological side too! It is only to be regretted that there was apparently no one among Kant's theological contemporaries who had the insight, the courage and the humour expressly to draw the great man's attention, in all respect, to the mutual quality of this relationship.

Be this, however, as it may: looking at the matter purely objectively there is just the one question as to whether, behind Kant's segregation

[1] *Disp. of the Facs.*, 107.   [2] Ibid., 62.
[3] Second draft of the Foreword to the *Rel.*

of the philosophical and theological function, with or without irony, an *insight* lies hidden, which had, and still has, a right to be heard, an insight which, it is true, was of no direct usefulness within the framework of Kant's undertaking, but one in which that determination of the place of theology might well have its deep and justified reason. We do not overlook the fact that with more than one of the passages just quoted Kant may have laughed up his sleeve as he wrote them, happy not to be in the shoes of such a 'biblical theologian', and that for his part he need not take up his uninvitingly portrayed position. But it cannot be maintained that the old gentleman's smile by any chance detracts from the weight of the train of thought which was becoming visible as he wrote, whether he would have it so or not. We cannot see, however, why the smile of the old man should impair the importance of his train of thought, which willy-nilly becomes visible. Again we cannot see why his determination of theology's place should not be right simply because the place he indicates for the theologian is in fact such that in it the theologian—seen from the point of view of a philosophy attentive to the concerns of 'mere reason'—must right at the outset feel himself threatened and also probably an object of ridicule. It is only necessary to take quite seriously what Kant said half in mockery, in order to hear something very significant, even though we reserve in every respect our right to object to his formulations. Or is it not the case that the philosopher of pure reason has said something very significant to the theologian in telling him in all succinctness that '*The biblical theologian proves that God exists by means of the fact that he has spoken in the Bible*'?

8

HERDER

I. BEFORE and during the time when Kant was painstakingly engaged in writing the *Critique of Reason* other, completely different men had long been at work, who in a more daring and sweeping way than it was given to Kant were bringing the spirit and cast of thought of the eighteenth century to its culmination, and ultimately overcoming it. They were so different from Kant that turning to them after studying him is like suddenly finding oneself in another world, even though they were his contemporaries, and their assumptions and aims were ultimately the same as his. Kant's way of pursuing the path of the Enlightenment to its end, his striving for basing everything on principle, his severity and asceticism, the very method which led to a glimpse of new horizons beyond the Enlightenment and beyond the eighteenth century generally, were bound to have a limited appeal. It needed too much patient study and too little prejudice to discover that his work not only signified the fulfilment of the old era, but paved the way into a new one. Kant's works are so demanding that the majority even of his present-day readers remain unaware of the fact that his cold deliberateness was capable of hiding more enthusiasm than is to be found in any number of frankly enthusiastic proclamations. The air at the goal to which Kant's path finally led seemed too rarefied and chill; the gateway to the knowledge of the last things formed solely by the twin pillars of pure and practical reason, to which he pointed in conclusion, too narrow; the demand that we should actually persevere beneath this narrow portal to metaphysics, too inhuman. Further, even if Kant was well-acquainted with the message of the Christian Church, or at any rate acutely conscious of its significance, we cannot deny that it figured too imprecisely and too insignificantly in his scheme of things for his philosophical system to appear as necessary, meaningful and promising from the Christian point of view as it might otherwise well have done.

Thus it happened that Kant's work as a whole did not satisfy his contemporaries, however impossible they found it to escape its influence in detail. Kant was respected, admired and praised by all. Herder himself in his formative years experienced the exalting effects of Kant's personality as a thinker and a teacher, an influence which continued to affect his work even when he was devoting it to attacks, both direct and indirect, upon his former master. But even in those days it was probably only relatively few people who read Kant's work in detail and in its entirety, let alone truly accompanied him to his goal: and Herder was most definitely not one of them. In the very act of praising Kant his fellows began to chafe and argue against his conclusions, without always having used his guidance to think them out for themselves. They tried to circumvent him, imagining that they could turn his findings, and especially the negative ones, to a far richer and more fruitful purpose, and that they were already in a position to advance beyond him and put him behind them. The most that Kant could promise for the possibility of uncovering the secret of the existence of man and of the universe—an activity to be performed by man himself—had been his indication that only an ideal knowledge by pure reason understanding itself solely in the form of practical reason was possible. This was not enough to satisfy the yearning of the eighteenth century. No one, it is true, was capable of refuting the deductions of Kant's logic, and still less those of his ethics, which had shaped the final expression of his logic and determined its limits. But the yearnings mounted like a flood against the barrier of Kant's conclusion that the knowledge of the last things possible to man should now actually consist in thinking the *action*, in *thinking* the action, and that rational knowledge should be confined within such narrow limits.

Was it not the case that Kant himself in reaching this conclusion, and reason as he had defined it, had once again, and more than ever, encountered the secret, the unfathomable and yet undeniable secret, of man as he really is and of the real world? Had he not himself proved by this that reason knows and pursues also a way different from the one he had described as the only one? Do we live only in the interlacing of idea and action which seems to be Kant's single preoccupation, or do we not begin to live *until* we reach that stage? Does not man again and again push forward to the utmost limits of the possible, to the source of things, to the 'mothers', and to truth, and in doing so discover himself and the self's absolute power?—Does he not do this also in ways entirely different from the one described by Kant as the only one? Must thought and speech allow themselves, dare they allow themselves, to be restricted to the sphere of learning and morality, and to the postulates and hopes possible and necessary within the limitations of those two spheres? Was this not wrongly allowing a fount of reason itself to become choked, allowing a justification for human speech to be wrongly suppressed? Could it really be that we dare not recognize and may not speak of the very thing which is our true and ultimate source of life, beyond this interlacing of idea and action? Did this not mean that Kant had overlooked the most decisive, the deepest and most comprehensive possibility open to mankind, and that his philosophy, signifying a calamitous impoverishment, was therefore in need of the speediest re-orientation, a process which would, however, by no means injure its truth and greatness within its own particular field? Was there no other, better fulfilment of the Enlightenment in prospect, apart from and beyond that offered by Kant, and with it a different, better and new self-understanding of the eighteenth-century spirit? Was not the *sapere aude* capable of being interpreted far more deeply than Kant had interpreted it?

It was in discussing Lessing, in connexion with his reflections upon the significance of the historical element in Christianity, that we came across the concepts 'experience' and 'feeling', and the image of the decisive 'grateful shock of the electric current'. Lessing was sufficiently a representative of the Enlightenment, sufficiently a Kantian in advance of Kant, one is tempted to say, to refrain from pursuing this line of enquiry, from interpreting experience and feeling as means to an end, and reaching out after all to grasp the plain truth beyond the limits of human reason. It was Lessing's desire to leave pure truth to God, experience and feeling notwithstanding, and to be himself content with striving after it. We have already heard what Kant thought of the idea of introducing the concepts of experience and feeling into the teachings of religion: who is to convince us that an experience is even really an experience, if, as is the case with religious experience, we are unable to derive it from any principle of our understanding? 'The wish to feel the direct influence of the Godhead as such is a self-contradictory piece of presumption.'[1] 'Feeling is something entirely personal, and no one can assume its presence in others, which means that it cannot be taken as a touchstone for the truth of revelation. It does not teach us anything at all, consisting as it does merely in the effect of pain or pleasure upon one particular person, and cannot possibly form the basis for any knowledge at all.'[2]

It was the successful ignoring of this objection which formed the starting-point for the circumvention of Kant. That circumvention would be embarked upon with a low obeisance to his genius. It could

[1] *Disp. of the Facs.*, 103.   [2] *Rel.*, 165f.

be perfectly reconciled with his methodological starting-point, his enquiry concerning the 'capacity' of the human mind, and also with the answer he discovered, the interlacing of idea and action. It was possible for those carrying out the outflanking movement to declare that they merely wished thought and action to be looked upon as relative things, considered in relation to experience, within the totality of phenomenon, of human reason that has to be taken into account; that they were only proclaiming that which we sense immediately as a source of knowledge of a higher order. They could let the Kantian concepts of science and moral philosophy stand, grant their validity, as they were, in their rigour and more or less understood, and content themselves with saying that Kant had merely overrated their significance, depriving them of their force by making evident the possibility of a quite different kind of intellectual activity and communication, a far more fruitful and much more promising one, that, namely, which is founded upon experience and feeling, upon the lessons of life. In actual fact this reducing of thought and action to a position of merely relative importance, and the award of pride of place to experience, had appeared upon the European scene long since, in the person and writings of Jean-Jacques Rousseau. It was when German philosophy, with typical German thoroughness, took its stand as a matter of principle in the position Rousseau had discovered that the success of the circumvention of Kant became inevitable.

The master in the art of circumventing Kant was Johann Gottfried Herder. He has been called the 'theologian among the classical writers'. He was also truly a classical theologian, because he was the first to discover in convincing manner a way of making a theology possible which was able to bypass Kant. The possibility which Lessing was too cautious to exploit, and which, according to Kant, was forbidden, is to Herder a joyous event, in the course of which, as I. A. Dorner has well expressed it,[1] his mind stands like a help-meet beside the masculine mind of Lessing. Herder's significance for those theologians who came after him can scarcely be rated highly enough. Without him the work of Schleiermacher and de Wette would have been impossible, and also the peculiar pathos of the course of theology in the nineteenth century. Without Herder there would have been no Erlangen group and no school of religious history. But for Herder there would have been no Troeltsch. There are three different ways of characterizing Herder's significance for theology and the emergence of his philosophy of religion to take its place beside Kant's. I make the

[1] *Geschichte der protestantischen Theologie* (History of Protestant Theology), p. 737.

distinction without discussing the relative merits of each, but simply to help make the situation clear:

1. If Kant's philosophy of religion, because of the supreme place consistently accorded in it to the autonomy of reason, was a work of the *hubris* of the Enlightenment turning a somersault, then the reaction instigated by Herder brought about its nemesis with incredible rapidity and force.

2. If Kant's philosophy of religion, by the way it juggled away every revelation presenting itself to mankind, constituted a danger, temptation and difficulty for Christian theology, then it was Herder's incredibly sudden and forceful arrival as its saviour which rescued it, temporarily at least, from all its troubles.

3. If Kant's philosophy of religion, because of the clarity with which it at all events recognized and established the limits of humanity, represented a unique opportunity for theology to call itself to order and to recollect certain fundamental theological premises, then it was Herder, by his sudden and powerful influence, who took care that such an act of recollection did not at once take place.

Be that as it may: it was Herder who restored forthwith to theology the scope of its activities which Kant had apparently reduced to a painfully small space. It was thanks to Herder that the overcoming of the Enlightenment did not merely signify, as it did with Lessing, the overcoming of a system of polemic and apology without objects, by a reminder of the autonomy of ultimate knowledge; nor, as it did with Kant, the subjection of a freely proliferating speculation by arguments to prove that this ultimate knowledge was limited both ideally and practically. With Herder the vanquishing of the Enlightenment influence means the vanquishing of the supremacy of logic and ethics in general, of the categories of the understanding and of the categorical imperative as well, by means of the discovery of feeling and experience, the discovery that there is a form of knowledge and speech which arises directly from the events of life. This not only saved the discovery of man as the measure of all things which was common to Rousseau, Lessing and Kant, and to the eighteenth century as a whole, and ensured its passage into the new era, but meant that it was in turn immensely enriched and strengthened by the discovery of another potentiality inherent in man himself. Let us suppose religion should prove to be a matter of immediate feeling and immediate experience, perhaps in direct contrast to science and morality, and more deeply rooted than these; again, let us suppose religion should prove to contain the deepest meaning of the faculty for recording and applying the teachings of life, and thereby also the deepest meaning of the processes of thinking and willing. In this case does not the man who proclaims this truth, by virtue of an equal, nay a superior consciousness of self, take his place beside the man of the Enlightenment, beside the proclaimer of science and moral philosophy, and even beside the philosopher of self-criticizing reason? If this should be so then it erases the memory of Kant's smile as he presented theology with a task which he held to be impossible. Then it is possible once again to be a theologian, on the heights, and above and beyond the Enlightenment!

'I see no reason why theologians should not be just as open-minded and cheerful in their subject as students of the other branches of learning. Theology is in a certain way the most liberal of all the arts, a free gift of God to mankind, and one which has aided him in the acquisition of all the liberal benefits of reason, high-minded virtue and enlightenment. It was the theologians who were the fathers of human reason, and of the human mind and heart. It was from the sacred grove of theology that the first sages, law-givers and poets went forth, and it was only much later that the most diverse and lucid studies emerged from the old form of theology like flowers from the bud. . . . The divine revelation is the red sky of morning, the spring sun-rise for the human race, full of the spring's promise of light, warmth and abundance of life. What has this to do with the theologian's depressed and morose expression; as if this expression were in some way inseparable from the Bible and theology, as the beggar is from his sack?'[1] What tones are these, and what a language! And Herder wrote this seven years before the appearance of Kant's critique of religion. There can be no mistaking the fact that this was a new wind, swelling the sail from another quarter. He who speaks in this manner, remember, was one of the most celebrated thinkers and poets writing in the German language, whose influence gave an unprecedented stimulus not only to theology, but to history, the history of literature, and to natural science, even, as well; the General Superintendent (1776-1803) of Weimar, of all places, he occupied the pulpit beneath which Goethe ought to have sat at least from time to time.

But there was really no need for all these reminders to make us properly aware of what seems to have been here at stake. Herder's thinking underwent a long series of changes in the course of its development: from Kant to Hamann, Hamann to Leibnitz, Leibnitz to Spinoza, and when he was old (a sure sign that he might have pursued

---

[1] *Briefe d. Stud. Theol. betr.* (Letters concerning the Study of Theology), Herder's complete works, ed. B. Suphan, Berlin, 1877ff., vol. 10, 277f.

his previous path a little too hastily at times) there was a kind of weary return which brought him back close to the Enlightenment. We shall not stop to discuss this development here, but we shall try rather to get a rough idea, first of the general compass of Herder's thought, and then of the way he applied it to theology.

II.   I am not here to think!—To be! To feel!
To live! And to rejoice![1]

Thus Herder in the poem *St Johanns Nachtstraum* (St John's Night's Dream), written while he was at Bückeburg during the years 1771-6,[1] which has as its theme the idea that man is entirely alone, and yet not alone, in Mother Nature's great enchanted arbour. The middle and fixed thing between the two poles of this paradox, of this mysterious being alone and not alone, is nothing other than man's being, which is feeling, life and joy and all these things at once—and not thought, or at least not primarily thought! And even if it should happen to be thought, then it is the thought of one particular being, the language of the soul, being that of some person or other at a particular time and place, at a single point of the great process willed and created by God: the soul which is formed by its place as a link in the chain of this process, and which is yet, like the fire-fly, the original and unique 'glowing spark of God'. 'Syllogisms can teach me nothing where it is a question of the first entry of truth into the mind, which syllogisms merely develop once it has been received . . . the great spirit which breathes upon me and shows me the mark of one hand in great and small, and uniform laws in the visible and the invisible, is my seal of truth.'[2] That is one aspect of my being, my being alone, recognized by me by virtue of the inspiration of this great spirit. 'All God's works have this in common, that although they are parts of a whole too great for us to comprehend, they nevertheless all singly are a whole in themselves and bear the stamp of the divine character of their destiny.' God the all-wise 'does not compose any abstract world of shadows—in each one of his children he loves and feels himself with a father's feeling, as if each were the only one in his world'.[3] 'The most fundamental basis for our existence is individual, in our feelings just as much as in our thoughts.'[4]

---

[1] Stephan, *Herder's Philosophy*, Phil. Libr., Vol. 112, p. 249.
[2] *Vom Erkennen und Empfinden der menschlichen Seele* (Concerning the Knowing and Feeling of the Human Soul), 1778, p. 51.
[3] *Ideen zur Philosophie der Geschichte der Menschheit* (Ideas for a Philosophy of the History of Mankind), p. 139.
[4] *The Soul*, 75.

> Forget your ego, but yet never lose
> Yourself. It is the greatest gift
> A bounteous heaven can bestow.[1]

Such is being alone. The other side, however, is the quality of not being alone:

> To live alone?
> The fire-fly is not alone,
> And becoming what it will be
> Will ne'er be so!
> And I, rejoice?—Alone?
> Great Mother Nature!—none to tell
> How beautiful you are
> In the love-heat of summer!
> Having none to share with me
> The music of creation, none to hear
> The wheels' soft hum nor see the angel fly,
> With me imagine immortality!—
> Dream it together and together taste
> This earthly life! In friendliness embrace!
> Thy noblest spark, O wondrous Mother Nature![2]

Continuing in this vein, Herder finds himself able roundly to declare:

> If peace your aim then fly, O friend, that worst
> Of enemies, the personality!
>
> .   .   .   .   .
>
> Rouse up! But no, your soul is not your own,
> You're integrated in the great, good All!
>
> .   .   .   .   .
>
> What were you otherwise? Not self; for each
> And every drop of blood, each cell and every
> Thought and impulse of your heart and mind,
>
> .   .   .   .   .
>
> Each word that issues from your lips, your very
> Countenance are not your own, but yours
> On loan, for passing use. It's thus man goes
> By stealth; inconstant, ever-altered, bears
> A wealth of alien source throughout his years.
>
> .   .   .   .   .
>
> 'Tis only when the mind, which seeks to live
> In all men's souls, o'erlooks the narrow bounds
> Of self, when heart beats with a thousand more

---

[1] *Self*, 256; cf. Appendix, p. 403.
[2] *St John's Night's Dream*, pp. 249f.; cf. Appendix, p. 403.

That you are made immortal, powerful,
Like God invisible, the Nameless One.

· · · · ·

So let us quell the spirit and effects
Of 'I', and let the better
Thou and He and We to banish it
In gentleness, and slowly free from I's
Harsh call; and may the first of all our work
Be self-forgetfulness! It's only thus
Our deeds will prosper, and each act be sweet.[1]

But the two aspects of our being, the quality of being alone and of not being alone, and everything they imply, belong together. They always become one again, and are one in experience. Herder has the same view of the whole of sensate nature, man and the animals and all the lower orders, as he has of the universe: both are moved and quickened by an influence like that of an advancing and receding tide. 'Man is made to receive and to give, to strive and rejoice, to do and suffer. In the well-being of his body he assimilates and gives forth again, conceives easily and achieves an ease in re-imparting what he has absorbed. He does gentle violence to nature, and she in her turn to him. It is this attraction and diffusion, activity and rest, which are the source of health and happiness.'[2] It is really the unity of all these things, their combination and combined effect and mutual dependence, preserved throughout every seeming contradiction, which is the secret of man's experience of himself which forms the hard core of Herder's thought. Our senses reach their object and the objects our senses through the medium of the questing spirit which seethes in us. The incomprehensible heavenly being which brings me all things and unites all things in me might also well be called flame or ether—it is this being in whom we must place our trust, in whom we must believe in the act of knowing, for 'unity, if God's hand be not at work here, where could it be?'[3] If we pay heed to know his works it is impossible for us not to sense on the one hand everywhere a similarity with ourselves in the great spectacle of nature as a living force; not to imbue everything with our own feelings, 'whether the truth of this analogy is a merely human one or not ("so long as I am on this earth I have no knowledge of any truth higher than the human one"), and on the other hand not to seek, implement and work out the analogy of our own nature with the Creator's, our likeness in his image'.[4]

Herder thought of this working out of the image of God in ourselves,

---

[1] *Das Ich* (The Ego); cf. Appendix, p. 404.   [2] *The Soul*, 54.
[3] Ibid., 62, 64, 65.   [4] Ibid., 50f.

so to speak, as a passing through a gateway: if we keep our minds and
spirits open to the influences of the world, which is God's world, then
we come to resemble God, as it were, of our own accord. 'The law of
nature will not change solely on your account: but the more you
recognize nature's perfection, goodness and beauty, the more her living
frame will mould you after the model of the Godhead in your earthly
life.'[1] It was for this reason that Herder was a great believer in the
potentialities of modern science. 'The more the true study of physics
increases, the further we shall emerge from the regions of blind force
and lawlessness into those where a goodness and beauty which are
stable in themselves rule with a most wise necessity.'[2] Necessity, according to Herder, is transformed in man's cognition of it into perfection,
goodness and beauty. In human life also, and indeed in human life
in particular, it is a question of accepting, discovering and truly
implementing what is absolutely necessary. Herder's attitude of
'fervent delight' in feeling the 'balm contained in the laws of human
nature, and watching it spread among men against their will'[3] is far,
far removed from Kant's. Far removed from Kant he declares:
'Stimulation is the mainspring of our existence, and must remain so
even in the case of the cognition of the highest things. What inclination
or passion is there which is not susceptible of being enriched by the
knowledge and love of God and our neighbour, so as to produce effects
all the more noble, sure and strong? The dross is consumed, but the
true gold shall remain. Every force and capacity for stimulation lying
dormant within me shall awake and work solely in the spirit of him
who created me.'[4] Therefore: 'Let no one despair concerning the
purpose and effect of his existence; the more order it contains, the more
it will act in accordance with the laws of nature, the surer will be its
effects. Like God, it works in an almighty way, and cannot help but
reduce to order a state of chaos surrounding it, and dispel darkness
that there be light: it causes everything with which it comes into contact, and even, to a greater or lesser degree, everything hostile which it
encounters to assume the beauty of its own form.'[5] The soul, 'the queen,
whose thoughts and wishes are enthroned within us'[6] 'is the image of
the Godhead and seeks to stamp everything about her with this image:
she creates unity out of diversity, brings forth truth out of untruth,
serene activity and achievement out of restless ease, and all the
time it is as if she turned her gaze inward and with the joyous feeling, "I am the daughter of God, and his image" said to herself:

[1] *Ideas*, 124.   [2] *God*, 206.   [3] *Ideas*, 163.   [4] *The Soul*, 72.
              [5] *God*, 242.   [6] *Soul*, 66.

"Let us!", and holding sway, were engaged in asserting her will.'[1]

It is fitting, particularly at this point where we are trying to determine the concept which underlay all Herder's thought, that we should
allow him to speak for himself at somewhat greater length. The fact
that the piece is a poem is essential to his view of the matter. He wrote
the following, entitled *Die Schöpfung* (The Creation) also during the time
he was at Bückeburg (250f.).

> God's creation, now complete,
> Pauses, silent yet awhile,
> Looks within and fails to find
> What is creator, what created;
> Seeketh one whose mind delights.
> Source of joy unto himself,
> Seeketh one who God-like gazing
> Shineth all creation back!
> Inward, outward. And himself
> Radiates fatherly, reigns supreme
> Is a maker like his God!
> See, this is what God's creation
> Seeketh, having reached its goal,
> Transmits sense to what it misses
> And behold, man-God-exists!
> New-formed creature, how to call you?
> Teach me, Lord, God of creation!—
> But it's I, it is myself
> Who became God's image here!
>   I, like God! Creation's scheme
> Fills me and expands, finds focus,
> Gathers force—the end is joy,
> Great rejoicing and fulfilment.
>   I, like God! At this my soul
> Self-exploring, finds, conceives me!
> Re-creates itself and acts
> Freely, feels how free its God.
>   I, like God! In kingly pride
> Beats my heart, and brotherhood.
> All life here is one, and man
> Feels himself the friend of all.
>   Feels himself full of compassion,
> Reaches even to the flower,
> To the goal of man's God-seeming,
> Far and wide welds all in love,
>   Reaches ever deeper, higher,
> I, the focal point of all,
> Flow through all things and it's I
> Who filleth all things in himself!

[1] *The Soul*, 68.

To the meanest of God's creatures
My sense extends and feels and tastes!
The harmony of every creature
Is one with me, yes, I am they!
Sound of earth's ecstatic choir
Flew on high through me and came
To the ear of God, took shape,
Grew to thought and deed—and man.
    Godly counsel, man, is in thee!
Feel thyself and thou wilt make
That creation feels itself!—
    Feel thyself and thou wilt feel
God is in thee and God feels
That in thee alone he is
As no sun or animal can feel him
Thus fulfilling himself in self! . . .[1]

This makes it quite clear to us that the most significant concept—perhaps with this despiser of the syllogism we should rather say, the most significant word, or sound, even—of Herder's thought, can be nothing but *humanity*. 'Just as our way of knowing is only human, and must be so if it is to be right, so our will can only be human too; something which arises from and is full of human feeling. It is humanity which is the noble standard by which we know and act.'[1] Man has no more noble word to describe him than man itself, in which the image of the Creator of our earth, as it was possible for him to become visible here, lives reproduced. We have simply to outline his form to arrive at an idea of his noblest duties.'[2] In doing this, however, we must once again bear in mind the aforementioned rhythm of attraction and diffusion and not by any chance confuse individual man as such with this human standard. 'Look upon the whole of nature, behold the great analogy of the creation! Everything senses itself and its kind: life intermingles with life. Every string vibrates to its own note, each fibre intertwines with its neighbour, animal feels in harmony with animal; why should not man feel in harmony with man? Our feeling for ourselves should only be the *conditio sine qua non*, the ballast which gives us stability, not an end, but a means to an end—but a necessary means, for it is and must ever be true that we love our neighbour only as we love ourselves. How can we be true to others if we are not true to ourselves? The degree of our sense of self is at the same time the measure of our feeling for others: for it is only ourself that we can as it were project into the feelings of others.'[3] 'It is in absorbing the love of the Creator and imparting love to others by means of the self, and in

---

[1] *The Soul*, 72.   [2] *Ideas*, 116.   [3] *The Soul*, 72f.

continuing in this assured course, that the true definition of the moral sense, of conscience, consists.'[1] It is the sphere of humanity, 'the realm of these propensities and their development, which is the true kingdom of God on earth, the state which has all men as its citizens. . . . Happy he who can help to extend it, for it signifies the human creation in its true, inward sense.'[2]

But the extension of this kingdom is the history of the human race. That is why it is at this point that history becomes the chief of Herder's interests. That is why he proceeded to enquire into the origin of language, into the spirit of Hebrew poetry, and of Oriental verse in general, and why he was one of the first to study the old German folk-song. That is why he laments and condemns the Enlightenment's complete absence of understanding for history, and why he twice attempted to write a philosophy of history, in those days an unprecedentedly novel undertaking (the first, in 1774, according to a more original method, but one less comprehensive than that of the *Ideas* of 1784-91 which have become famous). That is why, by dint of considerable devoted study and receptivity, he was also one of the first to appreciate the achievements of the European Middle Ages, an era the Enlightenment dismissed as one shrouded in darkness and barbarity,[3] and why it was given him to discover that the Reformation, and Luther in particular, represented an event of considerable importance, a view which, strange as this may seem to us, had likewise been completely lost sight of in the eighteenth century.[4] It was just those aspects of history which had made it particularly suspect, and an object of hatred even, to the Enlightenment, precisely those which the eighteenth century, in its tendency to absolutism, looked upon as the most irreconcilable with its tenets, that Herder illuminated and emphasized with love and care, counselling his contemporaries to esteem and respect them as the very ones which were absolutely essential to the concept of history. The ideas he put forward were:

1. That the significance of history is the principle of individualization: it is 'a pure natural history of human energies, deeds and impulses, according to time and place'.[5] 'Set down upon the earth living human forces together with certain local and temporal circumstances, and all the changes of human history take place.'[6]

2. History is composed of facts: in it humanity is not just an idea, a teaching or a kind of poetry, but in one way or another that which happens, no matter how simple or obscure a form the event may take. It

---

[1] *The Soul*, 72.　　[2] *Ideas*, 147.　　[3] *Auch eine Philosophie* (Also a Philosophy), 93f.
[4] Ibid., 100f.　　[5] *Ideas*, 145.　　[6] Ibid., 148.

is precisely this factual quality of history which, it seems, suggests to Herder the 'depth of obscure feelings, forces and urges' to which he wished to draw his contemporaries' attention as important sources of creative power.[1]

3. The wondrous nature of historical reality in its varying content, at the intersection of the co-ordinates of time and space, which is changing and fortuitous, and yet not fortuitous, but necessary in its fortuity: its wondrousness, in which at every point a miracle too lies hidden, the madness or half-madness which produces the greatest changes in the world and which must be given scope and allowed to have its way from time to time, without being either incensed or provoked.[2]

4. Most important: history means tradition. As historical beings we are not monads, but links in a chain, drops of water in a stream, the living cells of a growing organism; not the autonomous subject exercising thought and will, but the mother suckling the infant and encouraging its first attempts at speech, the father of the child, who has fought and suffered to safeguard its inheritance, and the child itself, whose most intimate possession in its totality is at once only what it receives from the father and mother—it is these who become of interest to the thinker in historical terms. 'Why should I become a mind of pure reason when my sole wish is to be human, and when in knowledge and belief I am just what I am in my being, drifting like a wave in the sea of history?'[3]

There can be no disputing the significance of these discoveries, made by Herder as they were in complete defiance of the extreme opposite views prevailing in the time before him. And how often have they been discovered again since Herder's time and proclaimed anew as the principles most precious and most fundamental to theology in particular! Talk in any way you please, just a little unguardedly, but it may be, perfectly logically in the 'rationalistic' Kantian tradition, and you will suddenly and inevitably find that you are consciously or unconsciously getting an answer which is entirely indebted to Herder's way of thinking, conjuring up his conception of history. It is as if his genius had been given the task of continually appearing behind Kant's like a shadow; sometimes as a necessary corrective, but sometimes like a rather excitable schoolmaster, which, of course, was just what Kant, when properly understood, did not require. Herder's genius (whether for good or bad it is no part of our task to decide), the new and

[1] *The Soul*, 59.
[2] *Briefe zur Beförderung der Humanität* (Letters for the Furtherance of Humanity), Suphan, 17, 231f.
[3] *Br. Theol.* (Letters concerning the Study of Theology), Suphan, 10, 290.

epoch-making quality of his mind, is precisely his complete, loving and devoted understanding of the concrete reality of history. It was none other than Goethe who, long after Herder's death, wrote the most affectionate and understanding description we have of him, in the *Maskenzüge* (Masked Processions) of 1818.[1]

> A man sublime, intent upon discerning
> The diverse emanations of the mind,
> Attentive to each sound, each word returning
> From each of sources countless in their kind,
> Both old and new exploring in his quest,
> He studies all things; spirit slow to rest.
>
> And thus he hears the music of the nations,
> The things that move them in their native air,
> And hears recounted all the good traditions,
> The generations' gift that all hold dear.
> And all he heard held both delight and lesson;
> And mood and action harmonized in one.
>
> Events that oft bring ease and often pain,
> A sudden discord or unhoped-for rest,
> Have ever found a similar expression
> In every tongue that ever man possessed.
> Thus sings the bard, thus myth and saga say—
> And move us now as much as in their day.
>
> When crags are veiled in gloom, and heavily
> Is born the dread lament of phantom shapes;
> Or when with sun-beams on the open sea
> The song sublime of ecstasy escapes—
> Their heart is pure—'twas only what we ought
> Each one of us to seek, the human things, they sought.
>
> Wherever it was hid he could reveal it,
> In solemn garb or lightly clad in play—
> With highest sense of time to come he'd seal it:
> Humanity be our eternal lay.
> Alas that he's no longer here to see
> The sorest evils healed by its decree!

In what concerns history, too, Herder shouted what Lessing had whispered. History, for him, is nothing else but living experience understood in the macrocosmic and universal sense, instead of, as previously, in the microcosmic and individual one. That is why, if I may make use of a phrase adapted by a present-day theologian from Luther, God and history are for him part and parcel of the same thing. That is why the acquisition of a feeling for history constitutes *the* task and *the* hope to

[1] Jubilee ed., vol. 9, 350; for original, cf. Appendix, p. 406.

which he directs mankind: 'Our body decays in the grave, and that which bears our name is soon a shadow on earth; only when merged in the voice of God, in the tradition, that is, which shapes the future, can we actively live on, as an unconscious influence, even, in the souls of our fellow-beings', in the golden thread of man's store of knowledge, in which 'the human figure vanishes, it is true, but the human spirit survives, as a constant and undying force'.[1] And civilization, which is the task and source of hope for mankind as a whole, is 'the tradition of an education'.[2]

It is because he finds God in living experience, and this is based upon self-experience, which is itself embedded in the communal experience of history, that Herder is implicitly and unequivocally optimistic in his general view of history, and of its course and development—but in a very different way from Kant, who on principle gave these same ideas a very fragmentary treatment. Kant's doctrine of radical evil did not appeal to Herder any more than it did to Goethe. He fairly shouts the view that all evil is merely negative: 'In God's kingdom nothing evil exists that could be described as real. Everything evil is as if it were nothing. We, however, call hindrances or contradictions or transitions evil, whereas none of them deserve the name. . . . Viewed properly even our mistakes have a good purpose; for they soon reveal themselves as such, and by pointing the contrast, help those who commit them to find the way to more light, and purer goodness and truth, and they do not do this haphazardly, but according to the eternal laws of reason, order and goodness.'[3] 'No force can be lost, for what meaning could there be in the words, a force is lost?'[4] 'Death brings life; individual decease furthers a higher order, and in physical nature nothing is really lost. Can it be otherwise in moral nature, the true nature, where all the main-springs and sources of power are housed?'[5]

Because this is so Herder finds in history 'progress, progressive development, even if no single thing should profit therefrom. Great things are in store! . . . the scene of a guiding intention on earth! . . . even if it is not given us to see the final intention, scene of the Godhead, even if visible only through gaps in the isolated parts of the action, and amid their ruins'.[6] 'The course of history shows that with the growth of true humanity the destroying daemons of the human race have actually decreased.'[7] Herder was for instance of the optimistic but strangely naïve opinion (Schleiermacher later thought so too) that

[1] *Ideas*, 141f.   [2] Ibid., 138.   [3] *God*, 246f.   [4] *Ideas*, 128.
[5] *Letters concerning the Study of Theology*, Suphan, 10, 346; cf. *God*, 246.
[6] *Also a Phil.*, 194.   [7] *Ideas*, 161.

even war was in the process of becoming humanized, 'the more it becomes a studied art, and especially the more technical inventions contribute to it'.[1] It cannot be said that this optimism of Herder's was based entirely in this world. Its prolongation into a kind of beyond, however, is brought about by the cry to the man standing terrified before death, the frontier of his existence: 'What the Giver of all life calls into being, lives—that which is a force is a force everlastingly, in its eternal harmony with everything else.'[2] 'If we look back and see how behind us everything seems to have ripened and developed towards the coming of man,' and how, with his coming, the first promise and propensity of that which he is meant to be, and of the image upon which he was carefully modelled, are present within him, then we are bound to conclude that man also must pass onward if all nature's perfect order and all the evidence that she has a goal and intention are not to be dismissed as an empty illusion.'[3] There *is* therefore a passing onward in store for us; even our earthly blessedness and virtue are merely an education, a journey and an instrument—provided the order of nature and the postulate based upon it are not in fact an illusion.[4] 'All man's doubt and despair concerning the confounding of goodness in history, and its scarcely perceptible advance, have their origin in the fact that the unhappy wanderer is only able to see a very short part of the way before him.'[5] The fact that this very short part of the way happens to coincide exactly with the unhappy wanderer's one brief life on earth, and that in view of this fact Herder's optimistic idea of a cosmic embodiment, 'with great things in store', of the various causes of unhappiness was likely to be a poor consolation for those in need of comfort, seems to have worried him and most of his contemporaries very little, so far, at least, as can be judged from his writings. In his own life Herder found no justification for his optimism, and one is almost tempted to describe it as a consoling fact that he should have ended his life deeply disillusioned, not to say embittered, in a state of mind completely belying the trend of the ideas just described.

It should be clear that on the basis of those presuppositions Herder, as was said as an introduction, brought theology relief when it was hard pressed, gave it a chance, even, to survive and continue to remain active, and provided it with convenient and practical handholds. This will be the subject of our further discussion.

III. What is religion? 'Religion is man's humanity in its highest form.' This weighty sentence[6] says in a nutshell all there is to be said.

[1] *Ideas*, 164f.   [2] Ibid., 129.   [3] Ibid., 133.
[4] Cf. *Letters concerning the Study of Theology*, Suphan, 10, 397.   [5] *Ideas*, 166.   [6] Ibid., 122.

Kant too might have written this sentence; but how sublime, or how meagre, but, to be just, how unmistakably clear also, is the meaning Kant would have attached to it, as compared with the deeply generous but also of course generously ambiguous significance lent it by Herder! Let us at once hear a somewhat more detailed definition, in order to convince ourselves that we are here in fact in another world: 'Religion, even when looked upon solely as an exercise of the understanding, is the highest humanity, the most sublime flowering of the human soul. It is an exercise of the human heart and the purest direction of its capabilities and energies.'[1] Herder, to begin with, has the following idea of the genesis of this sublime flower: 'As soon as man learned to use his understanding when being stimulated ever so slightly, as soon, that is, as his vision of the world became different from that of the animals, he was bound to surmise the existence of invisible, mighty beings which helped or harmed him. These he sought to make his friends, or to keep as his friends, and thus religion, whether true or false, right or wrong, became the teacher of mankind, the comfort and counsel of a life so full of darkness, danger and perplexity.'[2] True religion, however, 'is a childlike service of God, an imitation of the highest and most beautiful qualities in the human image, and hence that which affords the deepest satisfaction, the most effective goodness and human love'.[3]

To Herder there is nothing easier than to pass on from this point to the concept of revelation. The notion of man free of revelation, as Kant ultimately tried to conceive him, is impossible from the very outset within the framework of Herder's thought. Man's distinguishing quality is the fact that he stands within history. And religious man's chief distinguishing quality too is the fact that he stands within history. 'Facts form the basis for every divine element in religion, and religion can only be represented in history, indeed it must itself continually become living history.'[4] We do not know what we were, and there are no physical data available to us to tell us what we shall be. Analogy forsakes us upon both sides. Thus history must truly take the place of arguments, and this history provides the record and commentary of revelation. Standing within history also means on principle standing in the stream of revelation. 'Here also tradition is the transmitting mother, of its religion and sacred rites as of its language and civilization.'[5]

[1] Cf. Dorner, *Geschichte der Protestantischen Theologie* (History of Protestant Theology), 739.
[2] *Ideas*, 123.
[3] Ibid., 124.
[4] *Letters concerning the Study of Theology*, Suphan, X, 257.   [5] *Ideas*, 143.

The fact, however, that we stand within tradition forms part of the notion of our existence. How often after Herder and up to our own times theology has thought further along these lines, without, it must be said, always carefully considering whether the path it was treading might perhaps end in a *cul-de-sac*! Herder's meaning was this: 'If we are now bent upon taking experience as our guide, then we observe that the soul does not contrive, know or perceive anything of itself but what its world contributes from within and without, and what the finger of God assigns it. Nothing returns to it from the Platonic realm of a previous world; it has not chosen to appear in the position it occupies, and does not itself know how it arrived there. One thing, however, it does know, or should know, which is that it perceives only those things which this position reveals to it, and that there is nothing in the idea of the soul as the self-sufficient mirror of the universe, or of the endless upward flight of its positive power in omnipotent selfhood. It is in a school of the Godhead which it has not itself prescribed; it must make use of the impulses, senses, powers and opportunities it has received by a happy and unmerited inheritance, or else it withdraws into a desert where its divine strength falters and falls. It seems to me, therefore, that abstract egotism, even if this be but an academic phrase, runs counter to truth and the apparent course of nature.'[1] In how many studies, where sat theologians who would willingly have believed at that time but were chagrined to find themselves at a loss to answer what Kant had pointed out, must such words have been joyful tidings and like a breath of morning air! Man's existence, according to Herder, with its historical quality, comprises his participation in God's revelation in a manner which is without doubt the most direct possible. With Herder nature in its historical development is the action and speech of the Godhead. 'Is there on this account no Godhead, or is it not precisely the Godhead which is at play so exhaustively, uniformly and invisibly in all its works?'[2]

We may not in these circumstances expect from Herder any precise answer about a criterion of the true religion and revelation. How, in face of the exhaustive, uniform and invisible deity, could there be any criteria? The dispute between reason and revelation, in the form in which it so greatly occupied Lessing and Kant, has its place on the borders of Herder's field of vision. He prefers to speak of it metaphorically as, for instance, that both are surely gifts from God and as such could not be opposed to one another, since two presents are better than one! Revelation is the mother, and reason the daughter she has

---

[1] *The Soul*, 67f.   [2] *Also a phil.*, 92.

educated: 'The mother cannot be against the daughter, and the daughter, if she is the right sort, should have no wish to be against the mother.'[1] Humanity is to be compared with the outline of a statue, hidden in the deep, dark marble. The marble cannot hew and shape itself. 'Tradition and teaching, reason and experience should do this.'[2] Or: 'the book of sacred nature and of conscience was slowly unfolded, ordered and explained by the commentary of tradition.'[3] In the last quotation it is not even entirely clear whether it is reason which is looked upon as the book which provides the foundations, and revelation as the elucidating commentary, or vice-versa.

In his later years Herder came close again, strangely enough, to Kant's and Lessing's view, the Enlightenment view of the primacy of reason. And there can be no doubt that in his evaluation of Christianity as the religion embodying the highest humanity, this quality giving it its truth, he measured it, fundamentally, in sound Enlightenment fashion, by the ideal of humanity already postulated and known, and then he found Christianity, in inspired fashion, but from the well-known lofty watch-tower, to be in accordance with this ideal. The view most characteristic of Herder at the summit of his course is, I think, that in which reason and revelation preserve a mutual balance like the two arms of a see-saw, in a harmony resulting from equal tension, a relationship which cannot be explained intellectually, only experienced, and one therefore which leaves the question open, or disperses it in the gusty whirling of the spirit. We must get used to the idea that with Herder and with the whole line of theological development which began with him there is not that burning interest in the question of truth which we might at first expect where the establishment of a working basis for a theology is at stake which had to come to terms with Kant of all people. Herder's theology finds the reality of revelation so conclusively in living experience or history, in feeling or practical knowledge, that it thought it could dispense with.the enquiry into its legitimacy. 'It is an inner token of the truth of religion that it is utterly and completely human, that it neither senses nor broods, but thinks and acts, and bestows the power and the means for thought and action. Its knowledge is alive, the sum of all its knowledge and sensations is eternal life. If there is a universal human reason and sensation, then it is in religion and it is precisely this which forms the most neglected aspect of religion.'[4]

This position *could* mean that theology was preparing to reflect upon

---

[1] *Letters concerning the Study of Theology*, Suphan, 10, 285f.   [2] *Ideas*, 147.
[3] *Letters concerning the Study of Theology*, Suphan, 10, 295.   [4] *The Soul*, 86.

its own basis for knowledge, upon the independence, in authority and in faith, of revelation. We may ask whether that may not be the ultimate significance of Herder's obscure utterances upon this point. For from time to time we find nuances in his writings which lead us to conclude that the thought was not quite foreign to him that revelation might not only signify the revelation of humanity, but also at least the revelation of a majestic claim to Lordship made upon mankind. I am thinking of the way he rejected the juggling away of the miracles in the Bible, stating as his reason that 'these miraculous *facta* cannot be reasoned away by any conclusion of our practical knowledge, nor can the analogy they themselves contain be defeated by any analogy drawn from our lives'.[1] I am thinking further of how he gave the Christian Church the task of 'preaching *God's* will, not our own, presenting his theme, and not our theme', and of the great energy with which he therefore maintained that the homily was the only form of sermon suited to the subject, and brought good reasons in support of this view.[2] To Herder the sovereignty of a revealed religion over all forms of apologetics and polemic was also apparent: 'Facts can only be documented and preserved by facts; the best proof of Christianity is thus Christianity itself, its foundation and preservation, and most of all its representation in innocence, active hope and in the life such as Christ lived.'[3] 'Shun disputes about religion like the plague: for there can be no disputing about that which is truly religion. It cannot be either proved or disproved by argument any more than we can hear light or depict spirit. The spirit of Christianity flees dispute and strife.'[4]

But we must ask, in face of such statements which perhaps may be understood as being full of promise, whether it is not obvious that reflection of theology upon the presuppositions peculiar to it, has become bogged down in its first stage, in the hasty equation, that is, of revelation and history, of revelation and experience. We must ask whether the enquiry of pure rationalism concerning the independence in authority and in faith of revelation thus affirmed could in the long run fail to come, or be suppressed and whether Herder's own emergence in the neighbourhood of the Enlightenment position does not, clearly, at least show one thing: that in principle he no more succeeded in overcoming the Enlightenment than Kant did in his philosophy of religion. In other words, is the extent to which Herder actually overcame the Enlightenment any greater than that we have encountered in Kant and Lessing, in spite of the fact that his was a different approach? We

[1] *Letters concerning the Study of Theology*, Suphan, 10, 164.
[2] Ibid., 11, 17f.   [3] Ibid., 10, 172f.   [4] Ibid., 10, 260.

can even wonder whether we could not say that Kant and Lessing overcame the Enlightenment more fundamentally than Herder, in so far as they, especially Kant, after all at least saw and acknowledged, in a much more basic fashion, the problem of a realm beyond the human one, containing a truth incomprehensible to us. In the theology of Herder, the saviour of theology and prophet of the religion of God, on the other hand, with its impetuous equation of human experience, religion and revelation, of the quality of being in the image of God and the quality of the Divine, that problem of a realm beyond the human, continually threatens, in spite of several starts in another direction, to founder completely inside this human world. It is enough that Herder decided upon Christianity as the true religion, 'the genuine religion of God, which honours the father as his child and loves him in his children'.[1]

It is clear that Herder's general assumptions were first and foremost bound to give him an entirely new key to the Bible. Whatever we may hold of Herder's conception of the Bible, it must be conceded—and this was something new in the world of learning of those days—that at all events he read the Bible lovingly and with delight, and that he certainly showed many people how to read it as he did. His approach was this—and how could it be otherwise?—the more human (in the best sense of the word) the way in which we read the Word of God, the closer do we approach to the goal of the divine Author, who made men in his image and acts humanly for us in all the works and acts of beneficence in which he reveals himself to us as God. In supposing that this book was written in heaven and not on earth, by angels and not by men, we do not do him honour, but outrage and harm.[2] It should be read, just so that we may be convinced of its divine quality, with eyes and ears as human as those we devote to the study of Horace, Homer, Sophocles or Plato. Nothing unnatural is of God, the things most supernaturally divine become the most natural, for God adapts himself to the creature with whom he speaks: On the other hand we should quite simply desist from all reflections about the inspiration of the Bible. I am 'far more inclined to acknowledge, sense and apply in living fashion the divine element in these writings, than to dispute and ponder its actual form and nature in the souls of those who wrote it, or on their tongues, or in their pens or pencils. Flee, my friend, the scholastic whims and subtle speculations upon this subject, the sweepings of old barbaric schools, which will often destroy for you the best natural impression of the spirit of these writings. From the moment when you

---

[1] *Letters concerning the Study of Theology*, Suphan, 10, 246.   [2] Ibid., 10, 7f.

bar yourself up at the bottom of a precipice and help to weave a spider's web of philosophical questions and distinctions, instead of enjoying and applying a healthy view and the living divine effects, the spirit of these writings will depart from you. It is a natural, free, happy and childlike spirit, and it does not love such caverns and servile examinations. If you do not hear the sound of its footsteps as heralding the arrival of a friend or loved one but slavishly seek to measure and grope out its stride, then you will not hear it coming.'[1]

It is plain that behind these sentences—and they too have been enthusiastically repeated, in countless variations, for more than a hundred years—there is Herder's axiom that in the entire analogy of nature the deity has never acted other than through nature.[2] It cannot be said out of hand that it was essentially Herder's object here to arrive at an aesthetic appraisal of the Bible, in so far at least as 'aesthetic', in accordance with normal usage, would be taken to mean the same as 'artistic'. Even if he did without doubt read the Bible also from this point of view, and wanted to have it read thus, this was nevertheless only a means to his end. He was capable of calling the discovery of the poetical element in the Bible in which he himself played a part, 'tinsel', in tones of contempt, 'and whoever turns a Gospel of Christ into a novel has done injury to my heart, even if he has done so with the most beautiful novel in the world'.[3] He expressly declares: 'I would very much deplore you, my friend, if, being unconvinced of the historical truth of the earliest Christian history, you were to remain a student of theology.'[4] Herder's aim, in the Bible as everywhere, was to discover the 'course of history', the 'spirit of God', which with him means that which was so peculiar, actual and miraculous that it could not have been invented, as it was received and handed down as tradition by this people Israel, and later by the apostles;[5] 'God's course over the nations.'[6]

In this connexion Herder already felt the importance, as the true focal point of revelation, of that feature which, much later, was called the religious 'personality', and proclaimed with particular emphasis by Carlyle, in a completely different sense from that in which Herder conceived of it. 'God works upon earth in no other way than through great and chosen men.'[7] 'Religion is dead in a group where it has no living examples; the dead profession of faith, dead customs, pedantic

---

[1] *Letters concerning the Study of Theology*, Suphan, 10, 145f.   [2] *Also a phil.*, 92.
[3] Ibid., 10, 218.   [4] Ibid., 10, 169.   [5] Ibid., 10, 139f., 143 and 11, 167.
[6] *Also a phil.*, 104.   [7] *Ideas*, 141.

learning and the splitting of hairs, even if it were to perform its work in the original language and upon the lips of the founders, can neither represent nor replace this daughter of heaven, who must be alive in men, or she is no more.'[1]

Already Herder recommends further that we should distinguish in the Bible between the letter and the spirit, between teaching and life. 'What is written is after all only a copy of what is spoken.' It is necessary to bear in mind that behind the test of the Bible there was the living speech and listening, and that the oldest books of the Scriptures are young compared with the beginnings of the human race.[2] 'Never let yourself be diverted from the one truth in the Bible by the way in which its teachings are dressed from the one truth which lives in all its teachings as their soul. . . . In every case the dress is only a means to the teaching; the truth itself is the end, and only weaklings forget the end for the dress.'[3] This is the sense in which it is true that history is the basis of the Bible, 'the roots and trunk of the tree out of which the teachings spread like branches, upon which the duties grow like the flowers and fruit'.[4] This is the sense in which 'the basis for the whole of Christianity is historical event and the pure comprehension of the same plain simple faith actively expressed'.[5] The apostles' 'joyousness both in life and death came solely from the fact that they had, from sheer necessity, at the command of God, to preach a true history they had themselves seen, especially that of the resurrection. It was the very simplicity of this teaching as a certain fact which they had experienced themselves which contributed most to the revolution Christianity brought about.'[6]

And now we can already anticipate what Herder will have to say to us about Christ. 'As a spiritual saviour of his race he sought to form men of God who, whatever the laws to which they were subject, because of their pure principles, would further the good of others and, even suffering, would reign like kings in the realm of truth and goodness.'[7] That he is this saviour is perceived by the fact that the human quality in him speaks to the human quality in all of us. In no other way! Herder had a strong aversion to the Christology of the Early Church, which sought to determine in monastic terms what no human reason will ever be able to determine and thus obscured the 'healthy view' of the life of Jesus as it was presented by the Evangelists, without any such definition of terms. A hundred years before Harnack Herder already declares: 'Our Protestant Church has nothing to do with this Greek,

---

[1] *The Soul*, 79. [2] *Letters concerning the Study of Theology*, Su., 10, 285f. [3] Ibid., 11, 9.
[4] Ibid., 10, 258. [5] Ibid., 10, 171. [6] Ibid., 10, 169f. [7] *Ideas*, 172.

monkish illusion.' In opposition to it he already recommends concentration upon the figure which was later called the 'historical Jesus': 'A divine phantom walking upon earth is something I dare not imitate in thought or deed . . . thus for every Christian and for every Christian theologian the human Christ is not some image in the clouds to be gazed at in wonder, but a perfect example upon earth for our imitation and instruction. Every written work which develops historically and represents morally this perfect example, the figure of the purest man on earth, is an evangelical book. On the other hand, all scholastic sophistry which contrives to turn it into something calculated to dazzle, something devoid of humanity, is diametrically opposed to the spirit of the writings of the New Testament and harmful to it.'[1] But how does it come about that here, and particularly here, humanity as the messenger of divine truth speaks to humanity? Here too Herder's general canon of the theory of knowledge must be applied, and this means, on the one hand, that 'it must be believed, that is to say, it must be experienced and sensed and shuns every form of linguistic generalization and abstract divination. If an object of which we have not dreamed, from which we have hoped for nothing, suddenly reveals itself in such close proximity to ourselves that the most secret impulses of our heart willingly obey it, as the tops of the grasses are moved by the wind, and the iron filings by the magnet, what is there here that we should ponder upon, or debate with argument.'[2] And, on the other hand, it means that the appeal takes root in the universal and pre-known ideal by which Jesus is measured, and which he was found to fit. Herder did this especially over against the person of Jesus. It is self-evident that an intention—of this kind (such as is manifested in the intention of Jesus in his earthly life) must be the sole aim of Providence towards our race, an aim to which all wise and good people on earth must and will contribute the more nobly they think and strive; for what other ideal of his perfection and blessedness on earth could man have except this pure humanity with its universal effect?[3]

It is of course the first of these two arguments which is typical of Herder, whereas the second, which yet again employs the idea of the Platonic recollection, of humanity as something abstractly divined, is to be construed as an unavoidable re-insurance in the style of the Enlightenment.

But it is precisely in the form of this unavoidable link with a secret *a priori* mode of thought that the theory of experience is characteristic

[1] *Letters concerning the Study of Theology*, Su., 10, 238f.   [2] *The Soul*, 60.   [3] *Ideas*, 172.

of Herder, and not only of Herder. Obviously it means something
different from what it is in fact speaking of, something other than mere
experience. It seems somehow as if what is meant is the autonomy and
independence in faith which belief derives from its object, and only
from its object. With Herder, as I said, one is always tempted to construe such pronouncements as evidence of an insight which truly and
finally explodes the Enlightenment conception of religion. It is instructive to find that Herder, on his quite different course, was just as
unable as Kant had been to avoid talking sometimes in such a way that
a conception of things that could and must have directed nineteenth-
century theology along quite different lines, seems to have been staring
them in the face, just waiting to be taken hold of. But with Herder, as
with Kant, we should be mistaken in assuming that such a decisively
different conception had actually come home to him. For Herder's
theory does not in fact extend beyond experience as such. He is far
from basing theological knowledge upon the object of experience but
bases it quite definitely upon experience as such. For the historical
objectivity to which he appeals is quite definitely different from the
objectivity which would, for instance, have to be taken into account in
a theology of faith. The thing which interests him about faith is its
assumedly intuitive *form* in sensation; and what interests him concerning the object of faith is its assumedly tangible and demonstrable
effect in the state of mind already prevailing in the believing subject.
'Rebirth and faith are the principle, the true energizing force, the vital
spark of a new creature for a new heavenly existence.'[1] And thus dogmatics are for him 'a system of the most sublime truths for the human
race, relating to its spiritual and eternal blessedness . . . the most
beautiful, significant and true philosophy'.[2]

Once this point has been reached, however, then the referring back
to reason, the anamnesis, the appeal to the pre-known or to philosophy,
has in actual fact become inevitable. At this point theology yet again
expressly appears in the garb of a philosophy, at which its claim that it
is the most beautiful, significant and true philosophy is clearly at the
outset one very debatable assertion among others. On such a footing
theology will not be able on principle to reject and deplore criticism
from a philosophy which has itself become critical. The dispute of the
faculties cannot by any means be decided by mere assertions. And so
theology abandons, together with its peculiar duty towards its special
object, a duty which could perhaps be the secret of a legitimate constituting of this discipline, also the peculiar dignity which might

[1] *Letters concerning the Study of Theology*, Su., 10, 355.   [2] Ibid., 10, 279.

perhaps accrue to it if it honestly sought to be a science of this object.

Thus the honour Herder won for theology seems from the outset to be at best an ambiguous one, and beset by perils. His theological point of departure is in itself, as a counter-blast to Kant's pure rationalism and the rationalism of the eighteenth century in general, understandable, and historically necessary. To be sure, Kant too had not been able to offer a true solution. But the counter-blast was set afoot in a dimension in which it was bound to be exposed to a possibly lethal counter-blast from the other side, in a sphere where pure rationalism was simply master and would in all probability again and again achieve the mastery. Whoever speaks of humanity, experience, history—and ultimately Herder and the scores of theologians after him who were supposed to be vanquishing Kant did not speak of anything else— does not, it is true, only speak of 'understanding'. But he too speaks of 'reason', and he who says reason must be prepared to give an account of himself before self-criticizing reason. Ultimately and at the deepest level, therefore, will anything remain for him but a retreat to the religion of reason, which Kant had worked out neatly enough in all conscience? A retreat upon which he would after all not be able to escape the temptations and dangers which outcast understanding will set in his path!

And then we must still ask whether it is not more clearly apparent from the standpoint of this self-critical reason (as the authoritative position in all circumstances primary to experience and history) in what a true counter-blast to pure rationalism, one that would destroy the sphere in which it held undisputed sway, would consist. The question arises whether Kant did not understand better than Herder what theology, in pure contrast to pure rationalism at all events, might be. I have said that Kant understood what the idea of a Church was, a knowledge which enabled him to understand what theology might be in certain circumstances in which he himself, admittedly, had no desire to be placed. And I further dare to say that Kant understood what grace was, in the sense of the Church of the Reformation. Without making use of this understanding! He was purely a philosopher and his philosophy is not in the least dressed in the garb of theology. But all the same, Kant would not at all events have let pass the attempt to dismiss the Christology of the Early Church as a Greek monks' illusion. How different things would be if it could be said of Herder, the inaugurator of typical nineteenth-century theology before its inauguration by Schleiermacher, that he too understood what Church and grace were! But this can be said of Herder only with the greatest of reservations, in spite of every recognition of the great significance of what he set out to do. And if in theology it should perhaps be above all a matter of this understanding—it is not for us to decide upon this here—then the fiery dawn of a new age which it was many people's desire to see in Herder may after all have been perhaps only the transient glow of a Bengal light.

9

NOVALIS

I. ROMANTICISM was not the most profound, the most radical or the most mature form of the great intellectual movement which fulfilled and surpassed the Enlightenment and the eighteenth century generally, and established the typical way of thinking of the nineteenth century. Not the most profound: this was in all likelihood the philosophy of Kant. Not the most radical, which we shall come to discover in Hegel. Not the most mature, which we should have to recognize in the wisdom of life of the one and only Goethe. But of all these forms of that great intellectual movement Romanticism probably expressed this movement in its most characteristic and representative form; that in which the general trend was most clearly apparent. Nowhere, probably, were the final aims of the Enlightenment expressed in a form so plastic as to tend almost to caricature, as in this most angry and most thoroughgoing of all the protests against it. And nowhere was the secret of the man of the dawning nineteenth century, of his strength and weakness, of his greatness and of his faults expressed in so plastic a form as to be almost a caricature, as in this very part-manifestation of the great eruption which was establishing the new basis, this manifestion which, after flaring up briefly, was itself in its turn dispatched and extinguished. It was dispatched and extinguished with even greater fury and derision than that with which Romanticism itself had once imagined it could dispatch and extinguish the Enlightenment.

There is a French *bon mot*, which says, scratch the Russian, and you rouse the Tartar. It could equally be said of 'modern man' that you have only to scratch him to discover the Romantic. 'Modern man', and not present-day man! What manner of men are *we*? The question is one which, for the present, cannot be answered historically. I refer to the 'modern man' who once, in a manner typical of the apogee of the nineteenth century, thus consciously and euphorically described himself, who was at his height approximately between the years 1870 and 1914, and who served in theology as a point of orientation already for Ritschl and still for Troeltsch. He was something of a positivist

philosopher, this modern man, a coldly calculating technician, a
Manchester capitalist and Marxist socialist, an exact natural scientist,
relativist historian and impressionist artist—and in all these things he
was apparently worlds removed from the world of Romanticism.
But we must not allow ourselves to be led astray by the changed *décor*.
The melancholy sound of the post-horn and the ruined castle by moon-
light, the fairy princess, the blue flower and the fountains dreamily
playing in the splendour of the summer night—these are the things
which—not without cause—first spring to our minds at mention of the
word Romanticism. They are however nothing more than the stage-
properties of Romanticism as it first was, which to comprehend does
not mean that we have understood the true game that was played here,
for all that they are certainly part of the game in their way. It was
possible to go on playing it with a completely different set of properties
and that is what happened. To illustrate what I mean I shall just
mention the names of five men who lived at the height of the age of this
modern man: Richard Wagner, Friedrich Nietzsche, Ernst Haeckel,
Leo Tolstoy, Friedrich Naumann—all five of them certainly modern
men to the core, and representative of their time. But at the same time
each of them was in his way a solitary, a modern man in a somehow
original way, and just because of this all the more representative of the
hidden striving of his age, which was apparently so far removed from
Romanticism. None of the five of them can truly be understood in
terms of Kant, or Hegel, or Goethe; but, if they are to be understood
at all as stemming from this turning-point in time, then only in terms
of Romanticism. And the golden base of Romanticism, which with
them shines forth from beneath various washes of another colour,
is not only their secret. There can surely be little doubt that ultimately
and finally, when its spirit matured, the unromantic century was after
all bound to have its Eugen Diederich Publishing House and its youth
movement, and that the last German emperor, if all our understanding
of him is not an illusion, was bound, like his great-uncle Frederick
William IV, to be 'a Romantic upon the throne of the Caesars'.
It is precisely for this reason that we cannot pass over Romanticism in
our attempt to discover the elements of the general intellectual structure
of the century.

What has just been said applies however to nineteenth-century
theology as well. It left Romanticism behind, but could not escape it.
Somehow in the last resort it is also Romantic theology. In so far as
it was ruled and determined by Schleiermacher there is no need to
prove this preliminary point. And it is not for nothing that the entire

era ends where it had begun: with a renaissance of Schleiermacher. I spoke just now of the modern man of the turn of the century, as he provided a point of orientation already for Ritschl and still for Troeltsch. It should, however, be said that Troeltsch understood this modern man considerably better than Ritschl. Ritschl took him far too seriously as a positivist, etc. This was rather like making the blue flower and the post-horn wholly characteristic of the man living around 1800. This was one of the reasons that the school of Ritschl was unable to survive any longer than it did. It is well worth noting how Ritschl's most reliable pupil, W. Herrmann, was already unable to get on without leaning heavily upon none other than the young, Romantic Schleiermacher. The victorious element in the teaching of Troeltsch, however, certainly rested last and not least upon the fact that he took up Schleiermacher's programme once again and placed a conception in the centre of his philosophy of religion, which was basically the Romantic one. The decisive main stream of nineteenth-century theology cannot therefore be explained in terms of Herder alone.

What does stem from Herder in the newer theology is all that which can be brought under the heading of psychologism and historicism, its methodical point of departure in the correlation 'experience—history'. G. Wobbermin, for instance, the inventor of the religious-psychological circle, might easily be described as a very schoolmasterly and extremely dull Herder. But if with Herder himself the departure from this correlation was in the nature of a reaction, a counter-blow at Kant's pure rationalism, in the theology following him, but not only *him*, it rests upon the attempt at a more essential, profound and superior understanding of this rationalism; it overcame it, or thought to have overcome it, in passing through it. It sets out from the correlation 'experience—history', after previously setting out with Kant (but in a way which was assumed to be, or actually was, more profound than Kant's) from a synthesis which (assumedly or actually) surpassed, transcended this correlation. It was probably this synthesis too which Herder meant, when he spoke, as, for instance, in his work on the soul, of the spirit. It was possibly also what he was getting at as the true meaning of such outpourings as the *Hymn to the Creation*, for instance. But Herder was too involved in the mere reaction to Kant to be able to gain a clear sight of this Above and Beyond of experience and history. He was too involved in it to be able to prevent himself, whenever he was speaking of the spirit or the soul and its likeness in God's image, or of humanity, from sliding off into the psychological and historical, or from falling back into the very *a priori* methods he was trying to combat. It was this which was bound to put him straightaway at a disadvantage not only with Kant; but also with those who, like Herder himself, were seeking to rise above the Kantian position. The deeper source of the newer theology which in its method is linked with Herder is, however, Romanticism. Thus regarding theology itself we have occasion to concern ourselves with Romanticism. We shall do so before approaching Schleiermacher, who was by no means only a Romantic, and whose Romanticism we must measure against Romanticism in its pure form in order to understand it.

I have taken Novalis (whose real name was Friedrich von Hardenberg) as my particular example just because he represents in a uniquely pure way the intentions and achievement of this entire group—and not because the theological aspect is particularly clear in his work. He did not, like Rousseau, write a *Vicar of Savoy*, nor, like Lessing, theological polemics or a *Nathan*; nor, like Kant, did he write a philosophy of religion. And he did not, like Herder, engage in biblical studies. His direct utterances concerning the problem of religion are few, and, outwardly at least, they carry no particular weight beside his much more emphatic and detailed remarks relating to every other conceivable 'province' of human intellectual life, as the favourite expression then was. Even his famous *Sacred Songs* would not in themselves be sufficient to secure him a place in a history of theology. But he does belong there because he, and really he alone, of all his fellows, succeeded in exposing the meaning of Romanticism with a certain unequivocality and finality, and with a clarity that demands judgment. It is possible to master Friedrich Schlegel, Tieck, Brentano and Eichendorff, but with Novalis it is not so easy. He proclaimed the concern of Romanticism in a form in which it must at least be heard. We cannot dispose of Romanticism without disposing of Novalis.

But that is precisely what has not happened up to now. It has been rightly said of him, that he alone of all the Romantics has assured for himself, through all the numerous changes of outlook of the nineteenth century, 'a singularly certain *succès d'estime*'.[1] We might well add that leaving Schleiermacher out for the moment, Novalis is the only Romantic whose work goes on seeming relevant and new. He is the poet whom we cannot silence by any historical relativizing, any more than we can silence Kant—who was so different—in that way. And it must further be said that we shall perhaps only be able to speak of a true Neo-romanticism for all time when Romanticism is once again

[1] Bölsche, *Novalis' Ausgew. Werke* (Novalis' Selected Works) Leipzig, 1903, p. viii.

seriously taken up in the sense that Novalis understood it and in his spirit.

The peculiar significance of Novalis is closely bound up with the fact that he can scarcely be said to have given the world a true life-work. Those of his works we do possess are a little book of poems, *The Apprentices of Sais*, a story of natural philosophy, a sketch in the philosophy of history entitled *Christendom or Europe*, the unrevised first part of a biographical novel, *Heinrich von Ofterdingen*, planned on a grand scale in the style of Wilhelm Meister, some attempts at a continuation of this work and finally a chaotic collection of 'Fragments',[1] i.e. isolated thoughts set down at varying length for later use.

Fundamentally all these works are fragments. Novalis died of consumption in 1801 at the age of twenty-nine. The lament for the work which by his premature death he was forced to owe his time and all time is understandable. But it is at least open to question whether he has not precisely thereby, in this beginning, which remained a beginning—like Wackenroder, his older contemporary and sharer of the same fate—said everything he had to say in a way truer and more essential than that in which he would have said it in a long life, which would have brought him beyond this beginning. Another reason why he is the pure type of the Romantic is that the Romantic principle hardly achieved in him any length or breadth but remained almost a mathematical point. Perhaps Romanticism is something which should not achieve length and breadth, but which should flare up in this meteoric way if it is to bring forth its concern in a manner impressive and worthy of credence. Would it be possible for a Romanticism which acquired length and breadth to end anywhere but in the psychologism and historicism of Herder, or back again in the pure rationalism of Kant?

Thus it might be that the old saying that those whom the gods love die young has in more than one sense been vindicated here. I am reminded of a scarcely more recent parallel in the history of theology; that provided by the Württemberg revivalist preacher, Ludwig Hofacker, who also, at thirty, at the most fruitful moment of his life, and when he had but given promise of his best, was snatched away as by the scythe. Is it chance that his sermons are still read today—a thing we can very rarely say of sermons, and particularly of those of the past—and that for the most part their effect is topical and relevant! The revivalism too—which incidentally was certainly not unconnected with Romanticism—was ill-suited to the Consistorial Councillor-type

[1] Classified Collection edited by Ernst Kamnitzer, Dresden, 1929.

length and breadth it acquired in the figures of Hofacker's longer-lived colleagues in the middle years of the century. How completely different Schleiermacher's *Addresses on Religion* would seem to us if their author had not the good fortune to be able to carry out, in his further thirty-five years of life, the programme he announced in them—or should we say if he had not had the misfortune to have to carry it out! No wonder Schleiermacher's contemporaries and followers—among the contemporaries, Klaus Harms, and among the followers, W. Herrmann, for instance—again and again tend, so to speak, to shut their eyes to the later, more mature Schleiermacher, and to cling in nostalgic delight to the younger figure in its Romantic purity, which Schleiermacher himself, continuing in his life and influence, simply could not preserve. Perhaps this message was such that it could only sound strong and worthy of belief if it was proclaimed for a short time and abruptly terminated.

The second feature about Novalis, which he reveals in a manner both relevant to the moment and decisive for an understanding of the time which came after him, is the uniquely exact way in which he stands between the ages and between the great problems of the two ages. W. Bölsche wrote of him: 'Of all the figures of the great epoch of Goethe, he is the one who most plainly stands upon the border between the eighteenth and the nineteenth centuries. He is bathed simultaneously in the light of the setting and of the rising sun. He stands in this magic dual splendour as if steeped in an artificial glow. . . . He is an immeasurably concentrated figure, crowned and sometimes also a little bowed by the richness of the hour.'[1] But not only the eighteenth and nineteenth centuries are finely divided in him. Again and again we find ourselves compelled to ask, within the problem-complex of the old and the new age which moves him: Is it philosophy or is it art which is really his true sphere? And if it is both, if his particular problem is in fact the merging of the one with the other, is this philosophical art or artistic philosophy really directed towards nature or towards history? And if once again the answer should be that he is concerned with an attempt at a synthesis, is the personal expression of this synthesis love in the sense of the Platonic *eros*, or *agape* in the sense of the Christianity of Augustine and Roman Catholicism, the direct love for the distant object or the love emanating from this distant object being answered by love and loved again and therefore religion? And if yet again it should be a question of a synthesis, then will the word 'poesy', with which Novalis is in the habit of

[1] Bölsche, V.

defining the creative centre and unity of all these antitheses, remain comprehensively and decisively valid here also? Will it be Mary or will it be Christ—Novalis sang the praise of both of them—who will keep the central position? It is possible to decide all these questions either way with equal degrees of probability. It is just the way these questions remain open which is typical of Novalis, and of him alone in this fashion, and which makes him in particular into the pure type of the Romantic. Pure Romanticism is truly the border: between the eighteenth and nineteenth centuries as it is the border between philosophy and art, between nature and history, and between love and religion. Their border? Romanticism imagines it to be their unity. But strangely enough it is only in actually revealing their borders that it can actually make it plain that it is their unity which it has in mind. It is pure Romanticism only in so far as it draws up its programme, and not by carrying it out. It is surely no mere chance that the life-work of the last great Romantic in theology, Ernst Troeltsch, consisted chiefly in the proclamation and ever-renewed proclamation of programmes. Pure Romanticism must not wish to extend itself in such a way as to become a science or action, or—the science and action of which it is capable will signify its disloyalty to itself. Romanticism is pure as yearning, and only as yearning. That is why Novalis is a pure Romantic. That is why we can scarcely refute and dispose of him. And that is why he is scarcely to be imitated. That is why through him Romanticism became something which was perhaps unassailable, but which is perhaps also never to be recalled. Just in this way it became a word which continues to speak to us in an incomprehensibly real and relevant way. It has spoken also, and spoken in particular, to the theology of the new age. How could it have been otherwise? Possibilities seemed to offer themselves here to theology particularly, which held promise of making fruitful for the first time Herder's somewhat tumultuously inaugurated attempt to come to terms with Kant. Here there was something more than Herder. From this point it was for the first time possible to free Herder from the *cul-de-sac* in which he had landed himself. Only this was Schleiermacher's point of departure.

II. We shall in the first place consider the world of Novalis's thought, irrespective of its theological content. The form in which we find it in his literary remains and which in its incompleteness is its final and perhaps its most perfect form, is like a field of early corn in the spring: open to the view and yet with much that remains hidden from sight. This is also true because in its rather unfixed state of early development it delights, but can also confuse those who would know it at every step in its naturalness, in the apparent secret of a creative life which is reflected and represented there. And the way in which it does this is rare in what usually confronts us as mere literary reality, and unique even within the writings of the Romantics, of which we could generally say this. For the desire to proclaim the miracle of creative life, not without expressing openly the underlying thought that this is identical with the secret of the Creator, is something essential to all the Romantic movement. This intention also leaves its mark upon the language of Romanticism and its mode of presentation. The course of Schleiermacher's thought and his systematic method also has something of the life of a great organism, of a gigantic tropical climbing-plant, for instance, and this is not the least of the qualities which make for its recurring beauty and power of attraction. The novels of Eichendorff, too, seem to breathe—the fairy tales which the Romantics loved so much seem to bud and blossom before our eyes. What is uniquely moving in Novalis is the state of early development, of first germination, in which all his thoughts are to be found and in which they speak all the more eloquently of the creative power which is indeed their true object. We find here no world-tree, with its roots, trunk and spreading branches; here there is truly only a blue flower—which, to be true, is in the process (but only in the process!) of developing into a world-tree,[1] a pretentious lack of pretentiousness, against which we can say everything and nothing, which we should perhaps only look upon, and which perhaps, for all our doubts, we must simply like in order to understand it. I venture to speak in these unusual terms because we may be concerned here with the very heart of nineteenth-century theology, because it is perhaps just in Novalis that the question of the understanding of the entire age, and of the entire age of the Church, with which we are here concerned, is posed with an urgency which compels us to final decisions.

It is, I think, impossible to give an account of the world of Novalis's thought; only Novalis himself could do it if he returned among us. We can only make an attempt at a general survey, without claiming to present everything there is to be seen, much less interpret it all. We shall do this by attempting to see some of the systems of co-ordinates which, all at different levels, seem to weave a criss-cross pattern in Novalis's thought. I have already mentioned the antithetic unities which seem to me to be the most significant in that respect: art and philosophy, nature and history, love and religion. We shall finally

[1] Bölsche, IV.

come to speak of a last antithesis, which raises the problem as to whether it is likewise to be understood as an antithetic unity, or as a disjunctive antithesis, as an either—or: I should like to describe this last one as the Mary-Christ antithesis.

The first three antitheses are antithetic unities because each of them has an exact and therefore neutral and therefore superior centre. This neutral centre is common to all of them: the three systems of co-ordinates intersect, therefore, in such a manner that their points of intersection coincide. Or if instead of conceiving each of them as consisting of two straight lines intersecting at right-angles, we imagine each of them as the two end-points of a straight line, then in this case these straight lines are to be understood as diameters of a circle, which as such can only intersect at one point.

We would be completely mistaken if we thought that this mathematical description of the teaching of the blue flower is one ill-suited to it and contrary to its character. No description could in fact suit it better. It is precisely in its affinity with the spirit of mathematics that the spirit of the blue flower is no stranger on the threshold of the century of the exact sciences. Pure Romanticism regards itself as something of the strictest objectivity: 'The Romantic studies life as the painter, the musician and the engineer study colour, sound and power. It is a careful study of life which is the making of the Romantic.'[1] And it is precisely mathematics which is completely in keeping with this objectivity and care: 'A necessary postulate to the conception of mathematics is its complete applicability . . . its basis is the intimate connexion, the sympathy of the universe . . . its relationships are world relationships . . . true mathematics is the true element of the magician . . . in music it appears formally as revelation, as creative idealism . . . all enjoyment is musical and therefore mathematical . . . the true mathematician is an enthusiast *per se*; without enthusiasm there is no mathematics. The life of the gods is mathematics. All ambassadors of the gods must be mathematicians. Pure mathematics is religion. Mathematics can be arrived at only through a theophany. Mathematicians are the only happy people . . . anyone who does not pick up a book of mathematics with reverence and read it as if it were a divine book will not understand it.'[2] 'Every true system must be similar in form to the numerical system—the qualitative system or the denominator system too.'[3]

Let us return to the subject in hand. It should be clear that the fact that this neutral superior centre of these antitheses is a common one

[1] *Fragments*, Kamnitzer, 1,942.   [2] Ibid., 940.   [3] Ibid., 107.

will give rise to an abundance of mutual relationships, and indeed of new antithetic unities between the antitheses themselves too, so that, strictly speaking, with each single antithesis it is not only its two poles and its centre which we have to reckon, but because this centre is also the centre of all the others, we have at once indirectly to take all the others into account.

1. *Poesy.* Novalis sometimes, in accord with Fichte, defined this centre as the ego, which is confronted by the non-ego, the universe, consisting in the unity of every object of sense, but in such a manner that the positing of the ego is to be understood as a positing of the universe, and the positing of the universe as a positing of the ego.[1] 'It makes no difference whether I posit the universe in myself or myself in the universe.'[2] 'It is all one whether we suit ourselves to things or suit things to ourselves.'[3] That is why Novalis can say: 'One succeeded—he lifted the veil of the goddess at Sais—But what did he see? He saw—wonder of wonders—himself',[4] as well as, in the fairy tale of Hyacinth and Rosebud in the *Apprentices of Sais* having the youth who is seeking the same 'mother of things', find not himself this time but his Rosebud, abandoned and yet loving and beloved.[5] Novalis, therefore, advancing beyond Fichte, defined this centre better and more peculiarly as the life which consists precisely in its defiance of the attempt to comprehend it, because it has its being beyond the ego and non-ego, being and non-being, composed of synthesis, thesis and antithesis and yet nothing of all three.[6] Life is 'the stuff that truly and absolutely binds everything together'.[7]

At the point where he defines the centre as poesy Novalis speaks in terms which are completely characteristic of him and quite original. 'Poesy is that which is truly and absolutely actual. That is the core of my philosophy. The more poetic a thing is the truer it is.'[8] Novalis understood the concept of poesy primarily in its original sense of ποίησις.' work, creation. 'The poetic philosopher is *en état de créateur absoiu.*'[9] He posits subject, predicate and copula simultaneously.[10] 'Transcendental poetics treats of the spirit before it becomes spirit.'[11] 'The poet is *a priori* the inventor of symptoms.'[12] 'The true poet is omniscient, he is a real world in miniature.'[13] It is precisely for this reason that poetry is admittedly ultimately 'something completely personal and therefore indescribable and indefinable. Anyone who does not immediately know and feel what poesy is can never have any

---

[1] *Frag.*, 157.   [2] Ibid., 429.   [3] Ibid., 439.   [4] Bölsche, III, 95.
[5] Ibid., I, 148f.   [6] *Frag.*, 649.   [7] Ibid., 506.   [8] Ibid., 1,871.
[9] Ibid., 53.   [10] Ibid., 54.   [11] Ibid., 1,890.   [12] Ibid., 1,908.   [13] Ibid., 1,909.

conception of it instilled into him.'[1] The poet, the true poet, he of genius, and no other, is the true man: 'It is the poets, those rare nomadic men, who pass from time to time through our dwelling-places and everywhere renew the old and venerable service of man-kind and of its first gods, of the stars, spring, love, happiness, fertility, health and gladness; they who are in this life already the possessors of a heavenly peace and not driven hither and thither by any foolish desires, only breathe in the scent of earthly fruits without consuming them and thus becoming bound irrevocably to the underworld. They are free visitors, whose golden foot steps gently and whose presence causes all men to spread involuntary wings. A poet, like a good king, is to be discerned by the joy and clarity of his countenance, and he alone it is who rightly bears the name of a sage.'[2]

Thus poetry by no means coincides with art and for this reason it would not be fitting in discussing Novalis to speak of 'aestheticism' in the customary meaning of the word. Poetry, according to Novalis, is certainly also art, but is at the same time distinct in principle from all other art, as the art of expression by means of the word. It distinguishes itself from painting on its right and music on its left by the fact that what it does is in no way produced with tools and hands. 'The eye and the ear perceive nothing of it . . . it is all achieved inwardly . . . through words the poet presents us with an unknown splendid world for our perception. Past and future times, countless human figures, wonderful regions and the strangest occasions rise up in us as if from deep caverns and tear us away from the known present. We hear unfamiliar words and are yet aware of what they should mean. The utterances of the poet exercise a magic power; the familiar words, too, appear in delightful assonance and bemuse the enchanted hearer.'[3] This, according to Novalis, is in fact, the essence of Romantic poetry: its way of 'pleasantly surprising art, of making an object strange, and yet familiar and attractive . . .'.[4] But this is something only poetry can do of all the arts, or which all other arts can do only in so far as they, too, are poetic. Making the strange familiar by means of making the familiar strange: this is nothing else but the rhythm of ego and non-ego, the rhythm of life itself, in which Novalis imagines he has discovered the essential nature of poesy, and of the creative process in general.

That is why poetry is the secret not only of this or that person, but the secret of man in general. 'It is a very bad thing, Klingsohr said, that poesy has a particular name and that poets form their own

[1] *Frag.*, 1,887.   [2] *Heinrich v. Ofterdingen*, Bölsche, II, 79.
[3] Ibid., Bölsche, II, 24f.   [4] *Frag.*, 1,941.

profession. There is nothing at all special about it. It is the way of acting peculiar to the human mind. Does not every man give birth to poetry and aspiration at every instant?'[1] Transcendental poesy comprises 'all transcendental functions and in fact contains the transcendental altogether. The transcendental poet is transcendental man altogether.'[2]

To summarize, the concept of the ego or of life or, significantly, poesy, and, therefore, the concept of the neutral superior centre is, with Novalis, to be defined as the endless becoming outward of endless inwardness, or also as the endless becoming inward of endless outwardness, in the way that these processes both can and should and do in fact take place in the human act of living. It is a principle which is not only systematic, which does not only organize, but which is a creative principle that we have thereby come to know. All other principles are applications of this one creative principle, and are identical with it in substance. That is why it and it alone can stand neutral and superior as the centre of all of them. Novalis stated his notion of this principle in a manner entirely and uncannily characteristic of him, in describing it finally also as a magic principle, and the poet, and thus man in general, as a magician.[3] We shall have to return to the question this raises in our third section.

2. *Art.* There can be no mistaking the particular affinity of this poetic or magic principle with art. We have already heard that the two do not simply coincide. But the poet in whom Novalis perceives the true man is yet, primarily at any rate, also the poet in the narrower sense of the word, one identifying him also as one of various kinds of artist. 'Art is the development of our effectiveness.'[4] 'The artist stands upon the man as the statue upon its pedestal.'[5] And on the other hand: 'The poet uses things and words like the keys of a musical instrument.'[6] 'The beautiful is the visible $\kappa\alpha\tau'$ $\dot{\epsilon}\xi o\chi\acute{\eta}\nu$.'[7] 'Beauty is objective goodness.'[8] 'In every genuine art a spirit is realized—produced from within —the world of the spirits.'[9] And for this reason there also exists an artistic realism. In his doctrine of art especially, Novalis is very far from wishing to throw open the flood-gates of an unrestrained immediacy. The poet cannot be cool and composed enough. 'A confused babble results if a tearing storm rages in the breast and the attention is dissolved in a quivering abandonment of thought . . . the true state of mind is like the light, just as calm and sensitive, just as elastic and penetrable, just as powerful and imperceptibly effective as this precious element, which distributes itself upon every object in fine gradations

---

[1] *Heinrich v. Ofterdingen*, Bölsche, II, 97. [2] *Frag.*, 1,875. [3] Ibid., 669. [4] Ibid., 1,771.
[5] Ibid., 1,778. [6] Ibid., 1,904. [7] Ibid., 1,788. [8] Ibid., 1,792. [9] Ibid., 1,793.

of intensity and allows them to appear each one in delightful diversity. The poet is pure steel, just as sensitive as a fragile thread of glass and hard as the unpliant 'pebble'. . . . 'Poesy requires above all to be practised . . . as a strict art. As mere enjoyment it ceases to be poesy. A poet must not idly wander about all day and go hunting after images and states of feeling. That is the wrong way entirely. A pure and open state of mind, skill in reflection and observation, and an adroitness in transforming all his abilities into an activity which in its turn enlivens the mind, and keeping them there; such are the demands of our art.'[1] It is only upon this condition that the identification of life with art, art with poesy, is valid. With this we have already cast a glance from art at the thing which makes it possible and orders it, the power of thought: without philosophy there can be no perfect poetry.

3. *Philosophy.* 'The division between the poet and the thinker is only an apparent one and is harmful to both. It is a sign of disease and a diseased constitution.'[2] Philosophy is only feeling when it is dreaming.[3] This statement is not meant in any derogatory sense. Dreaming, for the pure Romantic, is something to be treated in all earnestness. Philosophy is in its original form feeling. It treats of an object which cannot be learned, of no object, that is to say. That sets it apart from all the other sciences, which have as their objects things which can be learned. Philosophy is the reflected feeling, based on the self-consciousness of the ego, or,[4] seen objectively, it is the proving of things by relating them with the self-consciousness of the ego, in which man perceives the absolute basis for his own existence.[5] All philosophy begins at the point where the philosopher philosophizes himself, i.e. at once consumes and renews himself.[6] In this we further perceive the connexion between philosophy and poesy. 'In its truest sense philosophy is a caress, an attestation of the most fervent love of reflection, of the absolute joy in wisdom.'[7] 'Philosophy is actually nostalgia, an urge to be at home everywhere.'[8] It coincides, in the 'act of overleaping itself', with the original point, with the genesis of life.[9] 'It also, like the activity of genius in general, is not susceptible of description.'[10] And: 'There is no philosophy *in concreto*, because philosophy is intelligence itself.'[11] And it is precisely because philosophy in its perfect form is nothing else but poesy that it must now come together with art in the narrower sense, must conceive of itself as art, the art of 'producing all our ideas in accordance with an absolute artistic idea and of evolving

---

[1] *Heinrich v. Ofterdingen*, Bölsche, II, 92f.   [2] *Frag.*, 1,907.
[3] *Appr. of Sais*, Bölsche, I, 152.   [4] *Frag.*, 64.   [5] Ibid., 65.
[6] Ibid., 95.   [7] Ibid., 69.   [8] Ibid., 70.   [9] Ibid., 95.
[10] Ibid., 73.   [11] Ibid., 77.

by way of thinking a world-system *a priori* from the depths of our spirit, of using the organ of thought actively for the representation of a world to be comprehended only in thought'.[1] 'The poet closes the procession just as he opened it. If the task of the philosopher is only to order everything and put it in its place, the poet loosens every bond. . . . Poesy is the key to philosophy.'[2] Thus we are directed back from the second pole of this antithesis to the first one again.

4. *Nature.* Corresponding to the antithesis of art and philosophy on the ontological there is the antithesis of nature and history on the ontic plane. Nature is 'the quintessence of that which moves us'. It is 'that wonderful community into which our body introduces us and which we come to know according to the body's facilities and capacities'.[3] It is 'an Aeolian harp, it is a musical instrument whose sounds moreover are the keys to higher strings in ourselves'.[4] ' "Where is the man," cried the youth with sparkling eyes, "whose heart does not leap with delight when the inmost life of nature enters his mind in all its abundance, and when, at this, that mighty feeling, for which language has no other name but love and desire, expands within him, like a strong, all-releasing vapour, and he sinks trembling with sweet anguish into the dark, alluring womb of nature, his poor personality being consumed in the breaking waves of delight, and nothing remaining but a focal point in the immeasurable procreative power, a sucking whirlpool in the vast ocean." '[5] With Novalis, as his *Fragments* in particular show, such dithyrambs have as their background a true abundance of observations in natural science, drawn especially from the fields of biology, physics and chemistry, psychology and medicine. 'The essential qualities required of a true naturalist are a long and unrelenting association with the object of his study, free and ingenious observation, an attention to the slightest indications and tendencies, an inner poetic life, practised senses, and a simple and God-fearing mind.'[6] The most significant of these requirements is, however, once again, the 'inner poetic life'. 'The spirit of nature has appeared at its purest in poems. Upon reading or hearing true poems one feels an inner understanding of nature moving there, and hovers like nature's heavenly body, at once in it and over it. The naturalist and the poet, in that they speak a common language, have ever revealed themselves to be as one race and people.'[7]

It is precisely at this point, however, that one is tempted to see the

---

[1] *Frag.*, 1,793. [2] Ibid., 1,875. [3] *Appr. of Sais*, Bölsche, I, 154.
[4] *Frag.*, 498. [5] *Appr. of Sais*, Bölsche, I, 160. [6] Ibid., Bölsche, I, 144.
[7] Ibid., Bölsche, I, 141.

objectivity of that which is observed threatened, in spite of the realism
which Novalis recommends here, too, by the stormy *eros* of the observing
subject. And if this be in doubt then the balance of the rhythm of this
entire system of thought is threatened also! There is a disturbing note
in Novalis's proclamation: 'The secret path leads inwards. Eternity
with its worlds, the past and the future, is within us, or nowhere.'[1]
'What need have we of laboriously journeying through the muddy
world of visible things? For the purer world lies within us within this
fountain-head. It is here that the real meaning of the great, variegated,
confused spectacle is revealed; and if, full of these sights, we step into
the realm of nature, everything there is familiar to us, and we have a
sure knowledge of every form. We have no need of any long research;
a light comparison, a few lines traced in the sand, are enough to ensure
our understanding. Thus all things are like a great book to us, for
which we have the key, and nothing takes us by surprise, because we
know in advance the way the great clock-work runs.'[2] The study of
nature seems to be dispensed with also, the instant it is laid down, when
the following figure appears among the apprentices at Sais, who we
are at first tempted to think are in an academy of the natural sciences:
'One of them was a child still, and no sooner was he there than he
wanted him to take over the lessons. The child had big dark eyes with
sky-blue depths, his skin glowed like a lily, and his curly hair was like
wisps of cloud at the coming of evening. His voice pierced all our
hearts. We would fain have given him our flowers, stones and feathers,
everything. There was an infinite gravity in his smile and when he was
there our spirits were strangely exalted. "One day he will come back
again," said the teacher, "and dwell among us, and then there will be no
more lessons." '[3]

We do not know whether Novalis would have continued further
along this course, which was not without its dangers, or whether he
might have more nearly approached the great maturity of Goethe's
outlook upon nature. What is certainly intended, even in such striking
passages, is, however, the proclamation of the referring back of the
perception which is directed outwards to the principle of the centre.
This is achieved by the proclamation of the necessary counter-pole to
this world of nature, which presses in upon man in an overwhelming
way. This counter-pole of nature coincides, however, in Novalis, with
history. For it is not enough to be able to improvise upon nature, as
upon a great musical instrument. It is only the man who understands
the history of nature, its dimension of depth in time, who understands

[1] *Frag.*, 593.   [2] *Appr. of Sais*, Bölsche, I, 146.   [3] Ibid., Bölsche, I, 138.

nature. History, however, means mind, as it is opposed to nature in the 'counter-image of humanity'. Nature would not be divine if it did not also have a history, did not also have a spirit. 'In order to comprehend nature one must allow nature to grow inwardly in its entire sequence . . . it is comprehensible only as the instrument and medium of the acquiescence of reasonable beings.'[1] Novalis seems after all to have had nothing else in mind but what Goethe said about the relationship between the inner and outer world in the contemplation of nature, however unguardedly and tempestuously he may have spoken of it.

5. *History.* It is now clear to us why Heinrich von Ofterdingen, when journeying to fetch his bride, should have to meet nature and history one after the other in the shapes of a miner and a hermit. Nature and history are in very fact opposed to one another in an antithetic unity. In history, too, according to Novalis, in so far as it is now to be taken especially into account, man seeks and finds the ego in the non-ego, the familiar in the strange. It is characteristic of Novalis that with nature it is primarily a question of finding, and with history, of seeking the great $\times$, the $\times$ which is his subject the whole time. Once again there can be no mistaking the fact that the concept of a historical realism, which now truly seeks the familiar in the strange, is not unknown to Novalis. But far more important to him than an assessment of the significance of exact research into the details of history is here once again the polemic against its degeneration, against every study of history which is merely analytic, unphilosophic, unpoetic, and the canon that 'a student of history must also of necessity be a poet', and the assertion that there is more truth in the fanciful tales of the poets than in the learned chronicles.[2] A few verses from the *Hymns to the Night* might best show the pure Romantic's approach to history:

What seek we in this world below
With all our love and duty?
The old is worthless, let it go!
How shall the new bring beauty?
O sad, forlorn and out of time
Who warmly love the golden Prime.

The golden Prime, when senses light
In upward flames were glowing;
When men the Father's hand and sight
Felt, his own presence knowing;
When high and simple thought was rife,
And time showed forth the perfect life.

[1] *Appr. of Sais*, Bölsche, I, 157f.　　[2] *Heinrich v. Ofterdingen*, Bölsche, II, 71.

The golden Prime, when blossomed full
The primal races flourished;
And children tried in death's pained school
The heavenly vision cherished,
And though life joyous accents spake
Yet many a heart for love would break.

The golden Prime, when glowing young
God came himself revealing,
In sweet love-life went men among
And died young for their healing;
Nor drove he pain and grief away
That he might dearer with us stay.

Restless the golden Prime we see
In night's dark shade enveloped;
Nor stilled our burning thirst will be
By all in time developed,
But we to home must also go
To see that holy season's flow.

What still keeps back our late return?
The dear ones long are waiting;
Their graves shut in life's utmost bourne,
And all is sad and sating;
Nought's left for us to seek again,
The heart is worn, the world is vain.[1]

It becomes clear, in the last verse especially, how greatly, and once again how menacingly, for the equilibrium which seems to have been intended throughout this system of thought, poesy becomes master of this object, too: master to such a degree that the creative, all-too creative man finds himself driven more and more to the edge of an abyss of appalling loneliness. Novalis was capable of saying in the major key also what was said, in the verses just quoted, in the minor:

When signs and figures cease to be
For all created things the key;
When they who do but kiss and sing
Know more than sages' reckoning;
When life to freedom shall attain
And freedom in creation reign;
When light and shade, no longer single,
In genuine splendour intermingle,
And man in tales and poems sees
The world's eternal histories,
Then this corrupted state will flee
Before a secret word's decree.[2]

[1] *Hymns to the Night*, Bölsche, I, 30; for original, cf. Appendix, p. 407
[2] Ibid., Bölsche, II, 143; for original, cf. Appendix, p. 408.

The same impression of an uncanny threat to creative man who is capable of achieving such a break-through, is conveyed also in the sole example of historical art Novalis has left to us, the essay *Christendom or Europe*, written in 1799. In it he draws a mighty circle from the boldly idealized, or perhaps imagined, picture of the peaceable and friendly single Church of the Middle Ages, through the Reformation, which declared a revolutionary government permanent, profanely identified the boundaries of the Church with those of the state, and introduced the highly alien secular science of philology into affairs of religion, on to the farthest point of the orbit, which in so far as it is the farthest point already heralds the return, the Enlightenment, with its hatred of the Church, the Bible, faith, enthusiasm and poesy, and finally back to the time just then coming, that of the resurrection, the conception of a new Messiah, in which one Brother in particular is described and lauded as the 'heart-beat of a new age', who has made for the Holy one, i.e. religion, 'a new veil', which 'clingingly betrays the divine mould of her limbs and yet veils her more chastely than any other'. Novalis awaits the revelation of this new age and with it the coming to life of Christianity, the bringing of awakenment and peace to Europe in every field, from the convocation of a 'venerable European council'. 'When?—and when most likely? That is not the question. Just be patient, the time will come, must come, the holy time of lasting peace, when the new Jerusalem shall be the capital city of the world; and until this day, be cheerful and courageous amid the dangers of the time, sharers of my faith; proclaim with word and deed the holy Gospel, and remain faithful unto death to the true eternal faith.'[1] Once again we see the pure Romantic standing in affecting isolation, and ask ourselves whether it might not be that his need is sprung from a tragic guilt; whether a view which has so largely renounced the ability to see could in fact end anywhere but in this convulsive hope which simply does not speak in tones worthy of credence. And we ask ourselves once again whether, if he had lived longer, Novalis would have proceeded further along these lines, or whether from this point he would have found his way forward or back to an ultimate historical wisdom. Suffice it to say that here the problem of history is at all events passionately felt to be a problem, and poesy, man's creative inward world, has shown itself to be the key to this book of mysteries as well.

6. *Love*. What art and philosophy are on the ontological plane, and nature and history on the ontic one, love and religion are on the personal or ethical plane. It becomes even more difficult than before to

[1] Bölsche, I, 135.

distinguish the antitheses to some extent, both among themselves, and from the creative centre.

It is part of the quality of Novalis as a phenomenon that his utterances concerning love in the most obvious sense have not the breadth which one might perhaps expect. Novalis was of little experience in the sphere of sexual love. His engagement to Sophie von Kühn only really acquired significance for his work by her early death. And his second engagement to Julie von Charpentier never became greatly significant either in his life or in his writings. But the intensity of the few things he said upon this cardinal theme of all poetry speaks all the more plainly for that. According to Novalis sexual love is the decisive event in human life because it is the revealed secret of reciprocal effect. Love is 'a mysterious flowing together of our most secret and most peculiar being'.[1] It is a question in life, in all art and philosophy, in nature and history, of ego and non-ego. Novalis, however, advancing beyond Fichte, wished to have the non-ego understood as Thou. It is, he finds, precisely love which is lacking in Fichte. Love understands the non-ego as Thou in understanding it as beloved and loving Thou and consequently as the 'centre-point of a paradise',[2] as the 'object of all objects';[3] consequently the propositions are valid that 'love is the most highly actual thing, the primal basis',[4] 'the final goal of world history, the Amen of the universe'.[5] 'I do not know what love is, but one thing I can tell you; I feel as if I were only now beginning to live.—My Matilda, for the first time I sense what it means to be immortal.—How deeply you shame me! For it is only through you that I am what I am. Without you I should be nothing. What is a spirit without a heaven, and you are the heaven which contains me and bears me up.—I can conceive nothing of eternity, but should think that must be eternity which I feel when I think of you.—Yes Matilda, we are immortal because we love each other.' Thus we hear the lovers speaking in *Heinrich von Ofterdingen*.[6] But what is decisive in this representation of love is not, after all, the way the lovers find each other for themselves, but the way in which, simultaneously looking at and beyond each other, they each discover in the object of their gaze the new secret world of poesy.

> A darkling pathway love did tread,
> Seen by the moon alone,
> The shadows realm, unfolded wide,
> Fantastically shone.

---

[1] *Heinrich v. Ofterdingen*, Bölsche, II, 100.   [2] *Frag.*, 1,257.   [3] Ibid., 1,260.
[4] Ibid., 1,677.   [5] Ibid., 1,745.   [6] Bölsche, II, 98.

An azure mist with golden edge
Around her hung in play
And eager Fancy bore her fast
Oe'r stream and land away.

Her full and teeming breast rose up
In wondrous spirit-flow;
A presagement of future bliss
Bespoke the ardent glow.[1]

The *eros* which is the subject of this poem has become the divine *Eros*, or is at any rate no longer merely that *eros* which unites two human beings. For when this *eros* reaches its goal the human couple, the man and the woman, have vanished in the eternally-human, that the one has found in the other, the romance is lost in the purely Romantic quality, for whose sake alone the romance shall and may exist, and the truth then, is that

Love's kingdom now is opened full
And Fable 'gins to ply her wheel;
To primal play each nature turns,
To speak with tongues each spirit burns.
And thus the world's great feeling looms,
Moves everywhere, forever blooms.
For each thing to all else must strive,
One through the other grow and thrive;
Each one is shadowed forth in all
While it itself with them is blending,
Eager to their deeps doth fall,
Its own peculiar being mending,
And myriad thoughts to life doth call.—
The world's a dream, and dream the world.[2]

And therefore by virtue of this passage through the creative centre the counter-pole must always shine forth in love, too, in magical identity with love itself. That is why the lovers' conversation goes on as follows: 'O beloved, heaven has given you to me to worship. I pray to you, you are the saint who carries my wishes to the ear of God, through whom he reveals himself to me, through whom he declares to me the abundance of his love. What is religion but an unlimited understanding, an eternal union of loving hearts? Where two are gathered together he is there. It is through you that I have to draw breath forever; my breast will never cease to draw you in. You are the divine splendour, eternal life in most alluring guise . . . I swear to be yours eternally, Matilda, as truly as love, God's presence, is with us.'[3] That is

---

[1] *Heinrich v. Ofterdingen*, Bölsche, II, 107; for original, cf. Appendix, p. 408.
[2] Ibid., Bölsche, II, 126; for original, cf. Appendix, pp. 408-9.　　[3] Ibid., II, 98f.

why Novalis himself was able to write in his diary: 'I feel religion for Sophie—not love. Absolute love, independent of the heart, based upon faith; such is religion.'[1]

7. *Religion.* 'Through absolute will love can be transformed into religion.'[2] We were already prepared for that sentence. Like art and philosophy, like the study of nature and history, and like love, religion for Novalis is without doubt in the first place a work of man, something to do with Romantic civilization. 'There is as yet no religion. First of all a lodge for training in true religion must be founded. Do you believe that religion exists? Religion must be made and put forward by the union of a number of people.'[3] The concept of God is achieved 'from the union of every capacity for feeling' . . . 'by means of a moral revelation, a moral miracle of centralization'.[4] For the finding of God an intermediate link is of course necessary. But this intermediate link must be chosen by ourselves, and this choice must be free. Regarding the intermediary as God himself is idolatry. The intermediary is the organ of the Godhead, its sensory manifestation, and Novalis declares himself a believer in Pantheism in the sense that he wishes to understand by it the idea that everything can be the organ of the Godhead, the intermediary, if I exalt it to that position. He rejects monotheism, which seeks to acknowledge only one such organ, but believes it possible to unite pantheism and monotheism by making the monotheist intermediary the intermediary of the intermediate world of pantheism, through it centring this world, as it were.[5] I believe that it is these very sentences which justify my tracing of the line, in the introduction, from Novalis via Schleiermacher to Troeltsch. That is why we now find that Novalis furthermore thinks that the Bible is still in process of growing.[6] 'The history of every man is intended to be a Bible; will be a Bible. . . . A Bible is the highest task of authorship.'[7] 'There is no religion that would not be Christianity.'[8] 'Our whole life is service of God.'[9] No wonder Novalis speaks of 'the infinite sadness of religion': 'If we are to love God he must be in need of succour.'[10] No wonder he has given us, one might well say, an absurd philosophy of the Lord's Supper, the existence of which could not be well enough noted by the present-day adherents of symbolism. Its climax is contained in the sentence: 'Thus daily we enjoy the genius of nature, and thus each meal becomes a commemorative one, a meal which changes our soul just as it sustains our body, a mysterious means of transfiguration and deification on

---

[1] *Frag.*, 47.   [2] Ibid., 1,746.   [3] Ibid., 1,676.   [4] Ibid., 1,679.
[5] Ibid., 1,688.   [6] Ibid., 1,707.   [7] Ibid., III, 202.   [8] Ibid., 1,714.
                     [9] Ibid., 1,733.   [10] Ibid., 1,747.

earth, of a quickening intercourse with that which lives absolutely.'[1]
Let us hear this philosophy in its entirety in the following hymn, taken
from the *Sacred Songs*:

Few men know
The mystery of love,
Feeling contentless
Appetite and thirst.
The Holy Communion's
Divine significance
Is a riddle to our earthly senses;
But he who once
Drew breath of life
From warm beloved lips,
Whose heart in trembling
Waves was melted
By the sacred glow;
Whose eye was opened
To survey the endless
Ground of heaven
Shall eat of his body
And drink of his blood
Eternally.
Who has guessed the high
Purpose of earthly flesh?
Who can say he
Understands the blood?
All will be body once,
One flesh,
The blessed pair
In holy blood imbued.—
    O that the world-sea
Might now redden,
The rock break forth
In fragrant flesh!
The sweet repast is never ended,
Love never will be satisfied,
Never enough his own
Can it possess
The loved one.
Constantly more tender lips
Transform the joy to something
Even deeper, closer.
A more intense desire
Besets the soul,
Hungrier, more thirsty
Grows the heart:

[1] *Frag.*, 1,766.

And thus the joy of love endures
From eternity to eternity.
If they of sober mind
Did taste it, though but once,
They would forsake their all
And join us at the table set
For those who yearn,
The never-empty table.
They would see the endless
Fulness of love
And praise the fare
Of body and blood.[1]

If we are justified in speaking of a *hubris* of the Enlightenment, then it is here, in the magic religious teaching of pure Romanticism, that it broke out, and if perchance it was precisely the religious teaching of pure Romanticism which was to become the esoteric secret of nine-teenth-century religious teaching, then it is just in this event that the uninterrupted connexion with eighteenth-century absolutism would stand revealed. It is surely clear, indeed Novalis says it himself, that his teaching of religion is the teaching of love, of heavenly love indeed, but of love nevertheless. For all this, however, we should not perhaps bear him ill-will, in the last assessment, not even in a survey such as this. For precisely at this point a final problem obtrudes, a heterogene-ous line of thinking providing a point of vantage from which we can see how his teaching on religion, if it does not annul—that indeed we cannot say—at all events calls into question in significant fashion his entire teaching, and, further, poesy as the last word of this teaching, as it celebrates its ultimate triumph in this religious teaching particularly.

III. Somewhere among Novalis's mathematical fragments there is enclosed in brackets the little sentence, fraught with meaning: 'God is sometimes $1 \times \infty$, sometimes $\frac{1}{\infty}$, sometimes 0.'[2] In the 'some-times $1 \times \infty$, sometimes $\frac{1}{\infty}$' is contained the whole ideology of pure Romanticism, while the added 'sometimes 0' contains its whole problem.

1 of course represents the given quality of the ego or of life, or the reality of poesy, in which the individual affirms, engages, possesses and enjoys himself. And the multiplying and dividing of this 1 by ∞ signifies the rhythm of transforming things inwards and outwards, of gathering and deployment, of things becoming familiar and strange, in which poesy, and with it the individual, and with him the ultimately real,

---

[1] Bölsche I, 73f.; for original, cf. Appendix, pp. 409-10.   [2] *Frag.*, 909.

and with it God, is actual. Seen from the opposite pole, seen, that is, through the constant 1, which is to be thought of as transparent, art and philosophy, nature and history, love and religion can just as well signify $1 \times \infty$ as $\frac{1}{\infty}$; the creative subject can just as well give his life, himself, the highest, as the least value, without, however—for even infinity cannot arrive higher than the highest once the basis 1 is postulated—abandoning or even only endangering his substance and therefore himself, in scaling the value either up or down. The extreme is reached now on the one side and now on the other—philosophy seems to be merged and to disappear in art, art in philosophy, love in religion and religion in love. But it always only reaches the extreme, and care is taken that there is always a safe return from whichever extreme it may be. The creative subject plays and dances, on a high wire in peril of its life, to be true, but it dances well, and will for this reason not fall in spite of everything. It achieves infinite rejoicing and infinite sadness. But that is all it does achieve. And why should not this $\times$, which can sometimes be $1 \times \infty$ and sometimes $\frac{1}{\infty}$ be God? Its beauty surely cannot be in dispute. It is surely a God at least, this dancer, this *perpetuum mobile*, a God whom to serve as God might make a human life truly rich enough, and in view of whom it might seem folly to begin to look out for another. Who needs yet more if he has that, having himself as a premise of the whole?

What could Novalis have been thinking of when he added that God could also be 0? The sentence could of course be intended to convey the negation: 'and there is no other God'—beside this dancer, that is, whom we have in having ourselves. Does not Romanticism truly seem to wish to raise itself to a denial of this other God? And if this is not its wish, is not this denial necessarily contained in the natural sequence of Romanticism? But even if the sentence 'God is 0' were intended to mean that, would it not after all, in saying it, have set up the notion of this other God, even if merely as a notion which is denied, and have placed it beside the true notion of God, the notion of God the dancer? And it now seems after all that it is not this negation which the sentence is meant to signify. Novalis placed that third 'sometimes' beside the first two in too disinterested and unpolemic a fashion for that. He seems to have intended it in the same positive sense: God can also be 0, just as he is sometimes $1 \times \infty$, sometimes $\frac{1}{\infty}$.

Do we not look upon Novalis in this as we would look upon someone who, for the sake of perfection or caution or beauty, or for some other reason, has walled up a bomb in the cellar of his house, with a fuse running up to his writing desk? Let us hope there is no accident! The concept o is a dangerous thing to play about with. For o is certainly not merely a harmless little point which is passed through between $+ 1$ and $- 1$, between $+ \infty$ or $- \infty$, or between $1 \times \infty$ and $\frac{1}{\infty}$. Novalis himself defined o as the 'positive non-determinate'.[1] o stands at least as an emphatic question, not beside but above and below the 1, cutting through the whole series of numbers perpendicularly from above; above and below the 1 as it is above and below the million and the billion, and above infinity even. What would it avail the 1 if it were to gain the whole world, of what avail to it would be infinity, of what avail any addition, multiplication and scaling-up, and (assuming that it might be even more beautiful the other way round) any subtraction, dividing and scaling down, if it were not the 1 but the o which is the ultimate reality? And together with the million and the billion, and with infinity, the 1 stands in the light or shade of the o. o is the end or the beginning, not the 1 and not infinity either, whether it be infinity scaled up or down. o, if we have interpreted the $1 \times \infty$ and $\frac{1}{\infty}$ correctly as a mathematical formulation of the Romantic dialectic, is the equally exact mathematical formulation of the question which opposes the premise of the Romantic dialectic, this idea that we have ourselves. And now this o is to be thought equivalent to God, or at all events a possible equivalent to God. What weight the o which confronts the 1 acquires in face of this possibility!

What does the sentence 'God is sometimes $1 \times \infty$, sometimes $\frac{1}{\infty}$, sometimes o' mean? The third part evidently means a μετάβασις εἰς ἄλλο γένος, conceived in a manner which could not be more energetic or more dangerous. It signifies the most radical splitting-up of the notion 'God', who is the subject of the whole sentence. God is then on the one hand the x that can be everything between the extreme values $1 \times \infty$ and $\frac{1}{\infty}$, on the basis, be it well understood, that would be God the dancer. And God is then, on the other hand, the y which opposes this very basis 1 as an irremovable question and exclamation mark: it stands in opposition and does not dance at all (as x can dance between art and philosophy, between nature and history, between love and religion), the y which stands there like the visitor of stone in *Don Giovanni* or like the Christmas angel among the shepherds, as the *dies irae* or as the day of resurrection, in short, as the end of time whatever its equal may be. In standing there God either makes the whole dance completely impossible: 'Thou hidest thy face, and they are troubled: thou takest away their breath, they die, and return to their dust'—or he makes it possible: 'Thou sendest forth thy spirit, they are created:

[1] *Frag.*, 910.

and thou renewest the face of the earth.' What is to become of x, if there is also a y? x and y cannot be God in the same sense, and if they are God at all then they are God as differently as heaven and earth are different, as something and nothing, as creator and creature are different. Only one of the two can be the true God, God in the ultimate, true sense. A decision must be made between these two, or perhaps as the secret of this decision a revelation, as upon Mount Carmel: 'and the God that answereth by fire, let him be God.' We are not in any position, either as regards Novalis or any other person, to be able to know or say whether this decision or revelation has or has not taken place in his life, will and thought. But there can be no mistaking that the question of the o and the question of the God y underlying it played a definite part in his life, will and thought. And there are more eloquent indications that this was so than this 'sometimes o', which he wrote down so smoothly and without perhaps giving the matter overmuch thought.

There was in fact a very universally human factor which played a very special part in the life of Novalis, and one which stands in close relationship to this 'sometimes o': namely, death. It was of special significance for him first because his own early demise was brought about by an incurable disease, so that for him death cast its shadow a long way before. Its second and chief significance for him was, however, the fact that in the spring of 1797—a remarkable repetition of Dante's experience with Beatrice—he lost his intended wife, Sophie von Kühn, whom he had met three years before, when she was thirteen years old, and fallen in love with immediately. We have already seen how, as was indeed inevitable in the light of all Novalis's set theories, his erotic relationship with this girl was irresistibly sublimated and transfigured, even while she was still alive, into a religious one. At her death, however, it became characteristic of this love, that being that of someone himself doomed, it should become a love for a dead person. It is safe to say that the poet's second engagement, biographically so curious, which took place scarcely a year afterwards, is the best proof of the incomparable way in which this first relationship was set apart in his mind—set apart in such a manner that a second relationship of a quite different order was possible and perhaps even necessary beside it. Let it be noted that every more or less completed work which we have from Novalis: the *Apprentices at Sais*, *Christendom or Europe*, the beginning of *Heinrich von Ofterdingen*, the *Hymns to the Night* and the *Sacred Songs*, was written in the years 1798-1801, and therefore stands already in the shadow or light of this experience, or of the insight which the poet owed to this experience. It cannot, therefore, he said that this insight, falling like a frost in a spring night, beat or destroyed another tendency; instead, just as it precedes in time all Novalis's work which has some pretence to a finished form, so it was the beginning of this work, in principle and in content. Upon it stands everything, the entire teaching of poesy, which, anticipating, we have studied on its own. It is the high wire upon which, with Novalis, the dance of the Romantic dialectic takes place. It was the thing that made Novalis what he was.

What is the nature of this insight? It can be described by a linking up with the previously quoted definition of the concept o: it is a question of the insight into the 'positive non-determinate' of the ego, of life, of poesy. The Romantic doctrine of poesy proceeds, to begin with, from the point of determination 1: in poesy man posits himself as the ultimate reality. It is upon this basis that he dares to establish the Romantic doctrine of poesy, upon this basis that he makes $1 \times \infty$ and $\frac{1}{\infty} = $ God. But the secret wisdom which Novalis acquired in 1797 says that beyond this point of determination 1 there takes place the positive non-determinate! Let it be noted: *positive* non-determinate; this border, this Beyond of the Romantic synthesis requires therefore to be construed not merely negatively, but positively. It seems as if a new field of at least equally serious problems were unfolding itself, above this synthesis and its problems. It seems! For it is precisely this which we do not know, and we must take good care not to feel tempted to decide positively (just as little as we can decide negatively) whether this new field of problems really disclosed itself to Novalis's thought; whether a shaking of the somnambulist feeling of security with which we see the pure Romantic going his purely Romantic way, took place, therefore, or not. It may also be that as a result of this insight he felt himself yet again, all the more confirmed and strengthened in this security. It is also possible that he succeeded in relating the antithesis of life and death which revealed itself to him beyond the antithesis of love and religion, to the Romantic synthesis. He may have succeeded in dissolving death 'in a play of harmonies', in 'pointing to it as an arabesque in the poetry of each individual life', as Bölsche has approvingly remarked.[1] It may also be that the figure before whom he apparently desires to clasp his hands, having come up against this positive frontier, was after all only that of Mary and not of Christ. We must content ourselves with establishing the fact that it could, none the less, have been otherwise: it might also be (and judging by the nature of

[1] Op. cit., p. xxxviii.

the matter there are no strong indications against this) that a perception
of a radically different kind had announced itself, that the Romantic
synthesis in the entire splendour of its self-given sense of security
yet ultimately bore within it a great, fundamental and inescapable
flaw, capable of shaking, challenging, and even of destroying it, and
that, therefore, it was after all Christ and not Mary whom Novalis
encountered at this frontier.

The facts of the matter are these: In the *Hymns to the Night* Novalis
speaks of his discovery that in the conflict between the Daylight, the
most beloved of all the miraculous manifestations of space by those
living and endowed with sense—and the Night, the sacred, ineffable,
mysterious Night, it is the latter which should be accorded pride of
place and greater honour.

> Have you too
> A human heart,
> Dark Night?
> What do you keep
> Beneath your cloak
> That moves my soul
> With unseen power?
> You do appear but fearful—
> The poppies in your
> Hand dispense
> A precious balm.
> In sweet delirium
> You spread the heavy magic of your wings.
> And give us dark
> Ineffable delight,
> Secret as yourself.
> Joys which give us
> Sense of heaven.
> How poor and childish
> Is the light
> With its gaudy things,
> How blessed a relief
> The day's departure.
> For this alone, then,
> Since the Night steals from you
> These your servants,
> Did you sow,
> Among the widths of space,
> The gleaming globes
> Proclaiming your omnipotence,
> Your return
> In the time when you are far.
> I think the endless eyes

More heavenly
That Night unveils within us
Than these resplendent stars,
In that vastness.[1]

How did he come to make this discovery? The following hymn in prose gives us the answer:

'Once, when I was shedding bitter tears, hope melted in grief and drained away, and I stood lonely by a barren mound that concealed in a small, dark space her who was my life, lonely as no one else had ever been, driven by unspeakable fear, without strength, remaining nothing but a thought of wretchedness, as I looked about me for help, powerless to move either forward or back, and clung to the fleeting, extinct life with infinite longing, there came from the distant blue, from the heights of my former happiness, a twilight tremor, and all at once the birth-bond, the fetters of light, were broken, earthly splendour fled away, and with it my mourning. My sadness was gathered into a new, unfathomable world. You, excitement of the night, slumber of heaven, did fall upon me. My surroundings rose softly upwards, above them hovered my liberated, new-born spirit. The mound became a cloud of dust, and through it I beheld the transfigured features of my adored one. Eternity lay in her eyes. I seized her hands and the tears became a sparkling, unbreakable band. Millennia vanished into the distance like blown storm clouds. Upon her neck I wept enrapturing tears in tribute to this new life—that was the first dream in you. It passed, but left its reflected glow, the eternal, unshakable belief in the night-sky and its sun, the beloved.'[2]

Novalis did not then renounce the world of light as a result of this discovery and change of attitude. On the contrary: it is Platonic, doubly reflected negation which is in question here.

Gladly will I move
With busy hands,
And ever look to see
Where you need me,
Praise the utter glory
Of your splendour,
Tirelessly pursue
The wonderful contrivance
Of your work.
Gladly I observe
The meaning course

[1] *Hymns to the Night*, Bölsche, I, 14; for original, cf. Appendix, pp. 410-11.
[2] Ibid., Bölsche, I, 17.

Of your great glowing
Measurer of time,
Plumb the regularity
Of forces
And the rules
Of the fantastic play
Of spaces numberless
And all their periods.
But my most inward heart
Remains the thrall of night
And of her daughter,
Creative love.[1]

For night is at once the secret, the true principle of the world of light.
Why are they who do not know it fools? Because they do not know its
creative significance for the world of light especially:

They do not feel you
In the grape's gold flood,
In the magic oil,
Of the almond tree
And in the brown juice of the poppy.
They do not know
That it is you
Who hovers round
The gentle maiden's bosom,
And makes a heaven of her womb—
Do not divine
That you come towards them from ancient tales
Revealing heaven,
Bear the key
To the dwellings of the blessed,
The silent messenger
Of never-ending mysteries.[2]

Novalis sings the praises of Night as the high proclaimer of a holy world,
as the nurturer of blissful love:

You come, beloved—
It is night—
My soul is entranced—
The earthly path is ended
And you are mine again.
I look into your deep, dark eyes,
Revealing nought but love and blessedness.
We sink upon the altar of the Night
Upon the gentle couch—

[1] *Hymns to the Night*, Bölsche, I, 18; for original, cf. Appendix, pp. 411-12.
[2] Ibid., Bölsche, I, 16; for original, cf. Appendix, p. 412.

The veil falls,
And fired by the warm embrace
The limpid glow transpires
Of the sweet sacrifice.[1]

But that, of course, is the earthly love which has already been purified by heavenly love, which has passed through the catharsis of death; it is only from the night that the world of light and its love acquires its possibility and truth; and even then it is possible and true only in a very preliminary sense and in the light of this its own transcendence:

'A heavenly weariness now never more forsakes me. The way to the holy sepulchre was long and toilsome and the cross was heavy. He whose lips have once been moistened by the limpid wave which flows in the hill's dark womb invisible to common earthly sense, the hill at whose foot the earth's sea breaks; he who has stood aloft upon this border mountain of the world and gazed across at the new country, the dwelling-place of Night; truly he does not return to the turmoil of the world, to the country where light reigns and constant unrest has its abode. He builds humble lodgings, huts of peace, up there, yearns and loves, gazes across, until the most welcome hour draws him down— into the spring's source. The earthly element rises to the surface and is washed down from the height, but that which was made holy by the touch of love flows liberated in hidden channels to the land on the other side, where, like clouds, it intermingles with departed loves.'[2]

That the Night which the poet thus extols is the night of death, as we just found suggested, is something which finds direct expression in that very artistic part of Novalis's poetry written in the form of a mythical history. Life was once:

An endless feast
Of gods and men.
In childlike awe
Each race revered
The tender, precious flame
As the highest thing in the world.[3]

But there is one thing which mars and irrestistibly, irreparably interrupts this feast:

One thought alone was there,
Which, its dread form amid gay revels showing,
Did sudden fill their heart with horror wild;
Nor means had all the gods within their knowing

---

[1] *Hymns to the Night*, Bölsche, I, 15f.; for original, cf. Appendix, p. 412.
[2] Ibid., Bölsche I, 17f.
[3] Ibid., Bölsche, I, 22; for original, cf. Appendix, p. 413.

To still men's troubled mind with comfort mild;
Mysterious ill the spectre e'er went sowing;
Nor prayer subdued his rage, nor gift beguiled;
For Death it was who all their merry cheer
Suppressed, with pain and anguish and with tears.

> .   .   .

With daring spirit and impassioned breast
Man sought to beautify the mask of dying,
A pallid youth puts out the light and rests,
The end as gentle as a harp's low sighing—
And memory melts mid shadow-waves' cool crests,
The poet sang, to this sad need replying.
But still unfathomed was the endless Night,
The awful symbol of a far-off might.[1]

Until the great reversal of death actually came about:

> The night became
> The fruitful womb
> Of revelations
>
> .   .   .
>
> The deep divining
> Fertile wisdom
> Of the East
> Did first perceive
> The new millennium's dawn.[2]

Christ was born and lived, an event which Novalis describes as follows:

> The heavenly heart
> A lonely flower unfolding,
> Turned towards
> The glowing source of love,
> The Father's countenance sublime—
> Resting on the loving-earnest mother's
> Breast, which dreamed of blessedness.
> The growing child's prophetic gaze,
> With fervour to ensure divinity,
> Was turned towards the future,
> To his loved ones, future
> Bearers of his name,
> Not caring for the earthly
> Fate in store.
> Around him soon,
> Miraculously drawn by
> Love all-powerful
> The child-like hearts assembled.
> A new and unknown life

---

[1] *Hymns to the Night*, Bölsche, I, 22f.; for original, cf. Appendix, p. 413.
[2] Ibid., Bölsche, I, 24; for original, cf. Appendix, p. 413.

Grew up like flowers
Where he was—
From his loving lips
Undying words
And tidings most rejoicing
Fell like sparks
Of a divine spirit.[1]

And then Novalis causes this wondrous child to be addressed by a
minstrel hailing from a far-off shore, and who then joyfully journeys
onward to Hindustan, as follows:

The youth art thou who all these years hast stood
In thought inclined o'er graves of mortal beings;
A sign of comfort in dark solitude,
And of a higher manhood's glad beginning;
That which hath made our soul so long to pine
Now draws us hence, sweet aspirations winning.
In death eternal life hath been revealed,
And thou art Death, by thee we first are healed.[2]

For while Christ is dying, while his holy mouth, drawn in dreadful
anguish, is draining the dark cup of suffering, the birth hour of the new
world is drawing near him.

Awakened to new glory,
He ascended to the height
Of this new world made young again;
The old world that had died with him
With his own hand he buried
In the empty tomb;
And set upon it with almighty strength
The stone which no force can remove.[3]

Long ages since
Have passed:
Thy new creation grew
In ever-greater glory.
From out of misery and pain
A multitude has followed thee
In faith and longing
And in loyalty.
They reign with thee
And with the holy virgin
In the realm of love,
And serve within the temple
Of Death that is in heaven.[4]

[1] *Hymns to the Night*, Bölsche, I, 28; for original, cf. Appendix, pp. 413-14.
[2] Ibid., Bölsche, I, 25; for original, cf. Appendix, p. 414.
[3] Ibid., Bölsche, I, 25f.; for original, cf. Appendix, pp. 414-15.
[4] Ibid., Bölsche, I, 27; for original, cf. Appendix, p. 415.

I

Death sounds his bridal call;
The lamps are brightly flaring;
The virgins stand preparing
With oil in full for all;
If on the ear came falling
The far sound of thy train,
And all the stars were calling
With human tongue and tone!

To thee, Oh Mary, hallowed,
A thousand hearts are sent,
In this dark world and shadowed
On thee their thoughts are bent.
They hope for gracious healing
With joy more fully guessed,
By thee pressed, holy Mary,
Upon thy faithful breast.

.   .

By no cold grave now weepeth
A faithful love, forlorn;
Each still love's sweet rites keepeth,
From none will they be torn.
From heaven cherubs thronging
Hold watch upon our heart;
To soften our sad longing
Her fires doth Night impart.

Content, our life is hasting
To endless life above,
Now greater longings tasting
With sense transformed in love.
The starry host shall sink then
To bright and living wine,
The golden draught we drink then,
And stars ourselves shall shine.

Love released lives woundless,
No separation more;
While life swells free and boundless
As a sea without a shore.
One night of glad elation,
One hymn that cannot die,
The sun of all creation
Is the face of the Most High.[1]

And now in conclusion there follows that song of triumph in a minor
key from which we have already quoted those verses of painful nostalgia
for the wonderful 'golden Prime':

[1] *Hymns to the Night*, Bölsche, I, 28-9; for original, cf. Appendix, pp. 415-16.

Down into earth's dark bosom, down!
From realms of light departing;
The sting of pain, wild tortured frown,
Are signs of happy starting;
The slender bark will bear us o'er
Like lightning, to the heavenly shore.

Eternal Night! Then praised be thou!
Be praised eternal slumber;
The day has made us warm; pale now
Press cares we cannot number;
No more 'tis joy abroad to roam,
We rise to seek the Father's home.

.　　.　　.

Down to the soul's own sweetest Bride,
To Jesus, the Beloved!
Rejoice! the evening glimmers wide,
To hearts by sorrow proved;
A dream breaks all our bonds apart,
And sinks us in the Father's heart![1]

And now once again in truly triumphant tones the 'Song of the Dead'
in *Heinrich von Ofterdingen* can ring out:

First with us grew life from love;
Closely like the elements
Do we mingle Being's waves,
Pounding heart with heart.
Longingly the waves divide
For the strife of elements
Is the highest life of love,
And the very heart of hearts.

Whispered talk of gentle wishes
Hear we only, we are gazing
Ever into eyes transfigured
Tasting nought but mouth and kiss.
All that we are only touching
Change to balmy fruits and glowing,
Change to soft and tender bosoms,
Sacrifice to bold desire.

The desire is ever springing,
On the lover to be clinging,
Round him all our spirit flinging,
One with him to be—
Ardent impulse ever heeding
To consume in turn each other,
Only nourished, only feeding
On each other's ecstasy.

.　　.　　.

[1] *Hymns to the Night*, Bölsche, I, 29-31; for original, cf. Appendix, pp. 416-17.

And in flood we forth are gushing,
In a secret manner flowing
To the ocean of all living
In the One profound;
And from out his heart while rushing,
To our circle backward going,
Spirit of the highest striving
Dips within our eddying round.

O could men, our future partners,
Know that we in all their joyance,
Are about them and do share
All the bliss which they do taste,
They would burn with glad upbuoyance
To desert the life so hollow—
O, the hours away are streaming;
Come, beloved, hither haste.

Help to fetter the earth-spirit,
Learn to understand death's meaning
And the word of life discover:
Turn around but once.
Soon will all thy power be over,
Borrowed light away be flying,
Soon art fettered, O earth-spirit,
And thy time of empire past.[1]

The *Hymns to the Night* and this *Song of the Dead* are balanced by the two songs to the Virgin Mary and the thirteen Sacred Songs. Their thought-content is apparently the same as that of the first two works, the only difference being that now, instead of the ideas, night and death, it is the ideas, Mary and Christ, which occurred in the mythical-historical turn of the first train of thought, which acquire central importance, so that, accordingly, the positive, affirmatory significance of the entire new insight is stressed even more strongly and one-sidedly, being indeed the sole subject of emphasis. It is, however, precisely at this particular point inevitable, in face of this specifically religious, and indeed Christian writing by Novalis, that this entire final problem which he raises should once again itself become highly problematical, in so far as the *Song of the Dead* has not already made it so: problematical in its ultimate seriousness as regards the genuineness of the transcendence which, seemingly, makes itself noticeable here, and as regards the solidity of the ground upon which all the rest of his work, as a thinker and poet, is here seen to be standing. Has the 'awful symbol of a far-off might' in death become visible with such complete clarity here

---

[1] *Heinrich v. Ofterdingen*, Bölsche, II, 144-6; for original, cf. Appendix, pp. 417-18.

that the thought of the overcoming of death does not have the significance of a renewed attempt to beautify the gruesome mask of dying, with
daring spirit and impassioned breast? Be that as it may—it is now the
faith in the love for Christ which overcomes death, which is declared
loudly, and with spirit and persistence.

> O what would I have been without thee?
> What would I not be without thee?
> Dark fear and anguish were about me,
> In all the world alone I'd be.
> No certain love had I been proving;
> The future, an abyss concealed;
> When sorrows deep my heart were moving
> To whom had I my care revealed?
>
> . . . .
>
> But if now Christ, himself revealing,
> Has shown to me the truth, the way;
> The light of life, past all concealing,
> Drives anxious darkness fast away:
> With him is manhood crowned by duty,
> And fate through him doth glorious show;
> Ev'n in the north all India's beauty
> Must round this loved one joyous blow.[1]
>
> Of the thousand hours of gladness
> Which I found amid life's sadness
> One doth still supreme abide;
> One 'mid thousand sorrows growing
> Taught my heart its highest knowing:
> Who for me hath lived and died.[2]
>
> If I do but have him,
> If he is but mine,
> If even to the grave's dark rim
> His trust I ne'er resign,
> Naught I'll know of sadness,
> Only worship, love and gladness.[3]

It must be said that in all this things seem remarkably easy for the
lover; here at all events it is remarkably easy to forget the passage from
the abyss which he claims he has made in saying such things. For him
there is no problem as to whether Christ is there for him to have; he
takes it completely for granted that he can take hold of him.

> He died, yet with each day's appearing
> He and his love are heard anew,

[1] *Heinrich v. Ofterdingen*, Bölsche, I, 61; for original, cf. Appendix, p. 418.
[2] Ibid., Bölsche, I, 65; for original, cf. Appendix, pp. 418-19.
[3] Ibid., Bölsche, I, 66; for original, cf. Appendix, p. 419.

We can approach whate'er the place,
And fold him in a fond embrace.[1]

Boldly seize those hands appealing,
By his radiant face be won;
Turn to him with all thy feeling
As a flower to the sun—
If thou but turn to him, thy whole heart showing,
He'll prove thy faithful bride, his heart bestowing.[2]

That he is there for Christ, too, is something which seems to him to contain no problem either:

Then conquered sin did lose its terror,
And joyous every step was now;
And this pure faith to guard from error,
We wreathed about the children's brow.
And by it life new-consecrated
Flowed onward like a blessed dream;
And by eternal love elated,
The glad farewell no death did seem.[3]

We have already heard that 'the virgins stand preparing, with oil in full for all'.

If I do but have him,
The world as well I gain.
Happy as the heavenly boy
That holds the Virgin's train.
Rapt in contemplation
I'm safe from earthly consternation.[4]

It is only in respect to other people that some doubt or question can arise:

If all were faithless proving,
Yet faithful I'd remain,
That gratitude unmoving
Ne'er die on earth again.

.   .   .

Oft I go bitter weeping,
That thou in pain hast died,
While those thou lov'st forgetting,
Have not thy love descried;
Thy love alone constraining
Thy great work thou hast done;
No fame wert thou here gaining
And no-one thinks thereon.

But I:

[1] *Heinrich v. Ofterdingen*, Bölsche, I, 65; for original, cf. Appendix, p. 419.
[2] Ibid., Bölsche, I, 64; cf. Appendix, p. 419.
[3] Ibid., Bölsche, I, 63; for original, cf. Appendix, p. 419.
[4] Ibid., Bölsche, I, 66; for original, cf. Appendix, pp. 419-20.

> I have felt thy goodness,
> O leave me not again;
> Let all the love that binds me
> To thee for aye remain.
> And yet may all high thinking
> Look heavenward for its rest;
> Men, brothers, in love sinking
> And falling on thy breast.[1]

And thus after the fashion of the others this question also is resolved in the most direct manner imaginable:

> O go ye out o'er all the highways,
> And bring the wanderers gently in,
> And even in the darkest by-ways
> Let love's glad call the faithful win;
> For heaven is now on earth appearing,
> In faith we can behold it plain;
> To all it opens who are loving
> With us the truth that shall remain.[2]

For he really seems to be present everywhere and to offer himself to man always in a manner which will never admit of the smallest doubt that he is in fact there to be taken:

> I see thee in a thousand pictures,
> Oh Mary, lovably expressed,
> But none of them can equal that
> I find upon my soul impressed.
> I only know that since I saw thee
> My heart has banished earthly strife;
> A heaven of undreamed-of sweetness
> Holds my mind eternally.[3]

> Our eyes behold the Saviour true,
> The Saviour lights those eyes anew;
> His head the fairest flowers adorn,
> From which he shines like smiling morn.

> He is the star, he is the sun;
> The fount whence streams eternal run;
> From herb and stone and sea and light
> Shines forth his radiant vision bright.

> His child-like heart, supreme affection,
> Are universal in their action.
> He hugs himself, unconscious, blest,
> With endless power to every breast.[4]

---

[1] *Heinrich v. Ofterdingen*, Bölsche, I, 67; for original, cf. Appendix, p. 420.
[2] Ibid., Bölsche, I, 62; for original, cf. Appendix, p. 420.
[3] Ibid., Bölsche, I, 61; for original, cf. Appendix, pp. 420-1.
[4] Ibid., Bölsche, I, 72f.; for original, cf. Appendix, p. 421.

And we might well at this point call to mind again the hymn of the Lord's Supper, with its interpretation of the communion with Christ into the communion with the non-ego in general.

In short: Novalis has suddenly become remarkably ripe for the hymn-book. This is not without its more doubtful aspects. For it is certainly the modern hymn-book he has become ripe for. The Christian song we hear him singing is certainly not the first person plural song of the Reformation, praising the great deeds of the Lord, but a species, and perhaps the most pronounced species, of the first person singular song which has advanced mightily since 1600, in which the congregation thinks to find edification by letting each individual say and sing that he has felt the hand of God in such and such a way, and how his works have been of benefit to him, to him, to him.

We wonder where death is now, a figure full of menace, warning and promise, who after all confronts too this entire Christian heaven, in so far as it is part of earthly experience. Can it perhaps be that the poet does not intend to express this opposition as something so dangerous, so critical, so full of promise, as he seems to portray it in several passages? Has not death, after all, been resolved in a play of harmonies? And can it be thus resolved? Can the 'positive non-determinate' be included in such a manner; can it, after all, carried away by a powerful 'enthusiasm for Night', be included in the point of determination 1? Was the poet's whole meaning no more serious than in this way when he spoke of the visitor, 'its dread form amid gay revels showing'? Can one dispose of him by simply, in the twinkling of an eye, giving him the name of Christ? And what has Christ become, if he is deemed just good enough to appear as a mythical symbol—or is the poet's meaning different?—at this point, where it is a question of replacing the negative by the positive sign? If it is possible to mention 'Jesus' and 'the sweet bride' in the same breath and sense? If the name Mary can simply be set down with equal meaning for the name Jesus? If he is omnipresent in this way and only seems to have been waiting for the inclination of our hearts, to become our own? Has the poet really seen the majestic distance between the $1 \times \infty$ and $\frac{1}{\infty}$ on the one hand, and o on the other, between the god x and the god y, or has it for a long time, or even from the outset, been submerged in the unity of the one true God x? Is there a knowledge here of the decision between Baal and Jehovah, or has not Baal been chosen unconsciously a long time previously—an act suppressing from the outset, perhaps, the question which flashed into the mind like lightning? Was Novalis in the *Hymns to the Night* and in the *Sacred Songs* singing another melody or was he not rather singing the same one as he usually sang an octave deeper: the song of the magic identity between the ego and the non-ego, with Night now additionally included, with death now additionally included, with Christ himself now additionally included? These things we can only ask. And we are not entitled to ask them as if perhaps we knew the answer. We do not know it. But in order to understand Novalis we must ask, sharply, remorselessly.

The question is concentrated with much symbolic force in the question concerning the meaning of the opposing of Christ and Mary. If the *Sacred Songs*, in spite of all the talk of Christ, are, in the final and decisive assessment, songs to the Virgin Mary, then that would mean that Novalis has in fact succeeded in understanding death too, and death in particular, as a 'romanticizing principle', as he once said,[1] as the ultimate principle of this great process of things growing more strange and more familiar, in making it part of the reality of this dancing god, and in including Christ too in the train of Dionysus. For if Mary is the final word—Mary in the sense of Roman Catholic Church doctrine, to which, upon this point, Novalis was receptive enough—then that means that the final word is the creature open to what is above, open to God, capable of participating in God. The creature thus described can at most be regarded with fervour, at most also with infinite sadness but by no means worshipped. In what concerns Mariology the Roman Catholic Church doctrine too in fact— whatever else may be said of it—is still confined within the frame of the ancient and ever new religion of immanence, which one hundred years ago was called Romanticism. The meaning of 'Star of the sea, I greet thee' may well be one of wondrous beauty, but is not sufficient to make plain the decision or the revelation.

Everything would be different if the *Sacred Songs* could really be referred to by the title they lay claim to, that, namely, of songs of Christ. As we have seen, however, there is a great deal which argues against this. But once again we do not have the final right not to recognize them as what they claim to be. Behind them lies a life that might well have known, and seems to have known, enough of the 'dreadful anguish' to compel us at all events to respect its confession of faith, for all the doubts it might awaken in us. Thousands and thousands of people over the last hundred years have believed that in these poems they have heard a most genuine testimony. Who would argue that they have not really heard it? The fact that *our* confession and testimony, for serious reasons, perhaps, cannot be this one is another question. At all

[1] *Frag.*, 660.

events the simple fact that Novalis wrote these *Sacred Songs* (and in such quantity, too, in relation to the sum-total of his output) is evidence that his gaze was in some way fixed upon the point which forms their subject, and fixed so strongly that it cannot be explained as the conduct of the pure Romantic, for whom things Christian also became a symbol, as has often been said. Certainly that aspect is also part of the matter. But the emphasis with which here just things Christian become a symbol, and the proximity in which things Christian find themselves to the critical concept of death, would still remain striking and singular, even if our final judgment must be that in the last resort the riddle of death has been juggled away once more and that Christianity has yet again been interpreted in humanistic terms. In that event we should be compelled to say that pure Romanticism, in order to mark out the field containing its particular problem, had inevitably to approach extremely close to this other quite different field of problems.

And now let us once again consider that Novalis's confession of faith and testimony is known to us only in the incomplete form in which the twenty-nine-year-old poet left it at his death. Truly it is much more question than answer! Novalis relates of the hero of *Heinrich von Ofterdingen* that, in the cave of the hermit, who personifies history, he came upon an old book containing pictures, and written in a foreign language. To his astonishment he suddenly found amongst its diverse pictures a picture of himself: he saw his likeness, in fact, in different situations. 'Towards the end it seemed to him that he looked bigger and nobler. The guitar lay in his arms and the countess handed him a garland. He saw himself at the imperial court, on shipboard, now in close embrace with a slender and beautiful maiden, now fighting with fierce-looking men, and again engaged in friendly conversation with Saracens and Moors. Frequently he was accompanied by a man of grave aspect. He felt a deep reverence for this august form, and was glad to see himself arm in arm with him. The last pictures were dark and incomprehensible; yet some of the shapes of his dream surprised him with the most intense rapture. The conclusion of the book, it seemed, was missing. This upset Heinrich considerably, and he wished for nothing more earnestly than to have and be able to read the whole book. He looked over the pictures repeatedly and was startled when he heard the company return. He was beset by a strange feeling of shame. He did not dare make known his discovery, closed the book, and merely asked the hermit generally about its title and language. He learned that it was in the tongue of Provence. It is long since I have read it, said the hermit; I do not now remember its contents very distinctly.

As far as I can recollect, it is a romance relating the wonderful fortune of a poet's life, wherein the art of poesy is represented and extolled in all its various relations. The conclusion is missing to the manuscript, which I brought with me from Jerusalem. . . .'[1]

The conclusion to this manuscript is missing. It is missing in every respect. And in so far as we all, as children of the age which began with Novalis, have something of the Romantic, or at least, it is to be hoped, the pure Romantic, in our blood, the same might well be said of us too. This manuscript cannot have a conclusion, and that, perhaps, is the best that can be said of it.

[1] *H. v. Ofterdingen*, Bölsche, II, 77.

IO

HEGEL

IT is well known that Hegel was of the opinion that his philosophy, unlike that of his predecessors from Descartes to Fichte, should be understood not as a stage, a particular period in the development of the course of the history of philosophy in general, leading to heaven knows where, but as the final culmination of this history, uniting and doing away with all previous knowledge within itself. The ridicule, open or subdued, regretful or malicious with which historians of philosophy generally describe this view of Hegel's, the astonishment greeting such an almost mythical or pathological sense of self-importance in a man who in everything else seems to have shown that he had some intelligence, the gratification at the thought that after Hegel's lack of success in thus assessing his own work nobody else would dare to say such a thing again—all these attitudes are fundamentally both petty and irrelevant.

For fundamentally the astonishing thing is not that Hegel believed his philosophy to be an unsurpassable climax and culmination. It is that he was not right in thinking that after him the development was possible of a school of positivism, of pessimism and even of materialism, of Neo-Kantianism and whatever else the other modern philosophies may be called. The astonishing thing is that nineteenth-century man did not acknowledge that his concern in the realm of thought, his basic intellectual concern, had truly achieved ultimate recognition in Hegel's philosophy. It was astonishing that he broke out and made off in all directions as if nothing had happened, and that he was not content with pondering Hegel's wisdom, at most constantly re-formulating it, perhaps cautiously correcting certain weaker parts, and for the rest thankfully applying it in everything. Why did Hegel not become for the Protestant world something similar to what Thomas Aquinas was for Roman Catholicism? How could it come to pass that, very soon after Hegel's death and ever more plainly from the middle of the century onwards, it was exactly his achievement which began to be looked upon, with a pitying smile, as representing something which was in the main already superseded? This happened, though the same people who pitied his achievement were still secretly drawing intellectual sustenance from certain isolated elements of his thought. How did it come about that as early as the eighteen-sixties those who professed Hegelianism openly found it necessary to be defiant, not to say embittered in tone—as for instance in the foreword of Biedermann's *Dogmatics*? How did it come to pass that pure Hegelians, Michelet, for instance (from 1829 to 1893 a lecturer at Berlin), became a species as rare as the ibex and were close to being figures of fun? And how is it that the Hegel renaissance in our day too is but one of many other renaissances and is far from being generally recognized, even in a limited way, as the one true and necessary renaissance as according to Georg Lasson, for instance, one of the faithful few, it should inevitably be? That is what is astonishing. That Hegel, at all events outwardly, should temporarily at least appear to have been put so much in the wrong by the events of history; that is the amazing fact. If the eighteenth and nineteenth centuries formed a unity in such a way that the nineteenth century was the fulfilment of the eighteenth, then it was Hegel who represented this unity in his philosophy as no other man did. Is it not in Hegel that the man who is free from all the ties of tradition and from all conflict with tradition, who rejoices equally in reason and in history, as Lessing, still groping and uncertain, had set him upon the stage—is it not in Hegel that this man has for the first time achieved complete, clear and certain self-awareness? Is it not Hegel who exploited and made fruitful to the last detail Kant's great discovery of the transcendent nature of the human capacity for reason? Is it not he in whom the extremely vulnerable attempt to form an opposition to Kant's real or supposed one-sidedness, as it had been undertaken by Herder and others like him, came most legitimately into its own? Is it not he who is above all the great systematizer and apologist of the concern of Romanticism, of the discovery of Romanticism, of the immediacy of the creative individuality, and of the dialectic of the way his life moves? Was not Hegel he who should come as the fulfiller of every promise, and was it worth waiting for another after he had come?

Such was the view of the new age itself, in the early days at least, in the years between 1820 and 1830, which were so remarkable in every respect. It was at such a time that the Prussian state, just struggling to power, and preparing to take the lead in things German and perhaps European, called Hegel to its first chair of philosophy at Berlin, and that the liveliest students from all Germany, and with them the educated of all ages, flocked to hear him with an enthusiasm of which we can scarcely form any idea today. Again, it was at such a time that learned literature in every sphere spoke something of his language, and that philosophy, and thus fundamentally concentrated knowledge in general, was actually thought to be synonymous with Hegel's philosophy, with a naïveté that almost succeeds in becoming credible again. Was Hegelianism really just another 'ism' among and before and after many others? Was it something comparable to a new fashion in dress? That is how it was regarded afterwards. But if all things do not deceive us it was precisely when it was utterly and completely ruled by Hegel that the new age best understood itself, and it was then at all events that it best knew what it wanted.

It was the first sign that the new time was growing old, the first harbinger, we might perhaps say, of the catastrophe of 1914, the first hint that men were themselves beginning to doubt their own desires, when they became unfaithful to Hegel, who had only just been glorified. It should not have happened. In making Hegelianism the subject of irony they were making themselves the subject of irony. In rejecting this Messiah they were rejecting the whole promise, the very thing they themselves had thought to have received as a promise. In doing so they declared their belief that the first culmination and overcoming of the Enlightenment, as it reached its peak in Hegel, had not succeeded, that a new start had to be made, a return behind Idealism and Romanticism. They declared their belief that the inheritance of the Enlightenment must be entered into once again, with the claim that they were as competent and capable of entering into it as the generation of 1770-1800, and with the risk that this time they might perhaps not attain either to the overcoming of the Enlightenment, which they sought, or to a true culmination of it.

And did this second attempt succeed half as well as the first which had been given up? The first half of the century was still chiefly under the sign of the first approach culminating in Hegel. In the second half of the century the desire was to go behind Idealism and Romanticism to link up with the Enlightenment again and make a better job of things. Today we are already, to a certain extent at least, in a position to survey the scene as a whole: can there be any question that the intellectual atmosphere of the first half of the century was distinguished from the second not only by a far greater sense of self-importance but also by a far higher standard, intrinsic value and dignity? We need only compare the representative figures of the two eras in our own field, the field of theology, the two church fathers,

Schleiermacher and Ritschl, to be shocked at once at the era of meaner things, of smaller stature, which has manifestly arrived. The resurgence of the exact sciences, both natural and historical, to which this new age, the supposedly adult period of the nineteenth century, can lay claim as its title of particular honour, was after all a modest substitute for the clarity and confidence in matters of principle with which the basis was laid between 1820 and 1830, a basis which was later to be abandoned, and with which, even into the forties, people worked at the German universities. It was a meagre consolation for the deep resignation with which as early as 1870 the more far-sighted representatives of this second era, like Frank Overbeck, for instance, did their work, aware that the new time had completely lost the ground beneath its feet. In the eighties and nineties this resignation began to lay itself like a paralysing spell upon all intellectual life, in spite of the thinly chirping pathos to which this age, too, on occasion was once more capable of rising.

At all events, and despite the outward splendour of the era of Kaiser Wilhelm which was just beginning, there can be no suggestion that a second spiritual peak was reached like that around 1830. Hegel's professorial chair was now occupied by Friedrich Paulsen; Schleiermacher's by Julius Kaftan, and in F. C. Baur's place Adolf von Harnack now determined how things stood with the 'essence of Christianity'. And with all due respect for such figures, that is a different matter, if we think of their specific weight. The century had become tired and somehow sad for all its enforced jollity. The age of Hegel and the age of the superseding of Hegel are related as is the battle of Sedan to the battle of the Marne. This time, too, there was an abundance of victorious bulletins, but something had gone wrong at the top, and there was a premonition that things would turn out badly. The century had denied its truest and most genuine son and since then it no longer had a good conscience or any true joyousness or any impetus. It would have liked very much to achieve these things, but it could not. Looking back became its typical attitude of mind, a somewhat aimless and unrelated looking back to various periods of the remote past, a historical stocktaking. It drew its sustenance from memories drawn from earlier centuries, but without taking the opportunity to make them material for a new basis; it did so impelled more by curiosity than by an inner affinity with the concerns of these earlier ages. The century reproached its own youth for having been neglectful particularly of this, for having been far too unhistorically-minded— completely overlooking the fact that in its youthful days it was not only young, but dared to take itself seriously, dared to live from its own resources, and could therefore afford the enthusiasm, the poesy, and the sense of self-importance, too, which it now looked back upon with a senile smile. It did not reflect that in those early days, even though it had less curiosity about history, the century perhaps thought and lived truly historically in a better sense, because it was claimed by history, because it was engaged in conversation with history. But however we may judge all that in its details, a synthesis, and with it a definite feeling for the needs of the age, such as was peculiar to the age of Hegel, was not achieved again once people thought they had left the age of Hegel behind them. In turning away from Hegel the age acknowledged that, having reached the summit of its desires and achievements, it was dissatisfied with itself, that this was after all not what it had intended. It set Hegel aside and tried again, but did not even reach such a peak a second time, and thus manifestly it was bound to be even less satisfied than it was before, although it pretended to be.

Where does the fault lie? In Hegel? Those who study him will not receive this impression. If it is a question of doing what the entire nineteenth century evidently wanted to do, then Hegel apparently did it as well as it could possibly be done. Or is the reason that afterwards the age of the great men was past, that there was no genius present in the second half of the century to carry out the better things which the century it seems had in mind in turning away from Hegel? But it is always a bad sign when people can find nothing to say but that unfortunately the right people were lacking. This should be said either always or never. Every age, perhaps, has the great men it deserves, and does not have those it does not deserve. The question only remains, whether it was a hidden flaw in the will of the age itself, perfect as the expression was that it had found in Hegel, which was the reason why it could not find any satisfaction in Hegel and therefore not in itself, and yet could not find any way of improving upon and surpassing Hegel, and therefore itself.

It might of course be possible that Hegelianism indeed represented in classic form the concern of the nineteenth century, but precisely as such came to reveal the limited nature of this concern, and the fact that it was impossible to proceed from it to the settlement of every other question of truth. And that for that reason it was, curiously, condemned. The rejection of Hegel might have been the fig-leaf with which man at this time sought to hide what he himself was aware of as his pudendum from his own sight, from the sight of others and from the sight of

God. It might of course be that Hegel was in fact the Messiah, the fulfilment of the age, as he himself thought, and was held to be in the eighteen-twenties, but this fulfilment would have been after all only the fulfilment of the promises which had been received, and as they had been received, whereas better or at any rate different promises, which we thought we could see round the edges of the pictures of Lessing, Kant, Herder and Novalis, and which could be much more clearly indicated in many other manifestations of the time, did not exist either for Hegel or for his contemporaries (in the narrower sense of the word). These latter promises did not receive their fulfilment in Hegel either, but were at best only reaffirmed as promises. It is possible that different needs made necessary new promises, different from those which figure centrally in the pictures we have so far studied, and which now in fact seem to be fulfilled in Hegel. It is possible, moreover, that these different promises are in fact present, even if at the edge, indistinct, and in the form of open questions, presented by Kant and Novalis as glimpses beyond the border: problems which were suppressed, which did not get their fair share of attention, and which were calling for treatment. Hegel, fulfilling what he could, did certainly not provide an answer to these problems, except for the fact that with him they are perhaps suppressed and did not get their fair share of attention in a particularly obvious way. If all this was the case, then both the triumph and the tragedy of Hegelianism were meaningful, seen in relation to history.

There would then have to be a break with the idea of a historical progress moving in a straight line, which was so important to Hegel particularly; and it would then have to be acknowledged that a time like the nineteenth century can also take some guilt upon itself for the way it worked out its own peculiar concern: the guilt incurred by the neglect, the overlooking, the covering up and denying of other concerns by the existence of which it was bound to feel itself hindered, limited and channelled in asserting its own concern; again, the guilt for a crime against the truth in not allowing such hindering, limiting and channelling to take place, but rather all too constantly affirming and asserting itself; a guilt all the more manifest the more classically the will of an age is expressed in its leaders and heroes. It is a guilt which must sooner or later be paid for, and which, naturally, will be paid for above all by its leaders and heroes, by those in whom the age itself was great. It will be paid for first in such a way that the age itself will, by degrees, or all at once, find the greatness of these leaders and heroes (and hidden in it its own greatness) unworthy of trust, repugnant, and rotten. This of course need not mean at all (and in the case of Hegel and the nineteenth century it did not mean at all) that the age itself has done penance and is about to perform a *volte-face*. What it does signify, objectively, is that judgment is about to be passed, that the inner impossibility of the crime committed is about to come to light, and that the way will then be free for remembering forgotten things, resuming neglected things, facing the problems which have been suppressed, and in so doing honouring the truth. The fact that this in its turn cannot be achieved without guilt is something that will perhaps be granted by this new age more willingly than Hegel himself granted it in relation to the age preceding him. Perhaps in fact the new age would prefer to dispense from the outset with the idea of historical progress. But precisely in this way will it then be possible really to become aware of the concern of the preceding age, in our case that of the age of Hegel, without failing to realize that that time is truly past.

Everything we have said so far must admittedly be put in parenthesis, for we do not know whether the age of Hegel is in fact entirely past, even if we should, in all seriousness, consider it to be so as far as we ourselves are concerned. It was only in the course of centuries that Thomas Aquinas acquired the position at present accorded him in the Roman Catholic world. It may be that the dawn of the true age of Hegel is still something that will take place in the future. But that would mean that we are in fact standing only at the beginning of the era of the man whom we here provisionally described as the man of the nineteenth century. The fact that people were weary of Hegel in the second half of the nineteenth century would then have to be judged a resting-period, brought about by a state of weakness in modern man, because he had not quite comprehended his salvation at that juncture. And the denial of Hegel, which to us today perhaps seems necessary in a more comprehensive sense than it did to man in the second half of the nineteenth century, would then have to be understood as a reactionary current approaching the point where it will be annihilated or at least rendered harmless, a current which might then only hope for its concern to reach fulfilment at a much later time. The day of judgment and of freedom, which somewhat boldly perhaps we previously set in the past, would then lie in a possibly distant future. Anyone who is aware of serious considerations which cannot receive justice at Hegel's hands, and which in fact Hegel suppresses, will not hesitate, while simultaneously paying his due respects to Hegel as a spirit of undoubted greatness and as the spirit of our time too, to associate himself already now with the necessary protest against him and against this time of ours, even if it is as the supporter of what is already a lost cause. Whether the age of Hegel is already past or whether it is still to come and to come even more than ever before, cannot perhaps be decided, and it is not necessary for us to know for certain.

I. Hegel's philosophy is the philosophy of *self-confidence*. It was because it at once postulated and affirmed this principle, which this age in particular found to the highest degree comprehensible, that it seemed so suited to its time, that it was so much a fulfilment in relation to what the whole century felt as a promise within itself. It was because this principle, for all the artistry with which it was developed and applied, was so startlingly simple that this philosophy seemed so grand and fruitful. And the reason why Hegel's philosophy seemed so convincing was that Hegel dared in all earnestness to pursue this simple principle, which every true contemporary in some way agreed with, to its ultimate conclusion and with all imaginable faithfulness. Anyone who has once understood that here we have a man who absolutely and undeviatingly believes in himself, who can doubt everything because he does not for a moment doubt himself, and who knows everything for the simple reason that he has complete trust in his own self-knowledge—anyone who has once understood *that*, has at least the key to this labyrinth, even if he cannot avoid the trouble of finding his own way about it. It is a question of philosophy and thus of the self-confidence of thinking man. Hegel puts his confidence in the idea that his thinking and the things which are thought by him are equivalent, i.e., that his thinking is completely present in the things thought by him, and that the things thought by him are completely present in his thinking.

He trusts that these two things are equivalent because he trusts—and this is the secret of his secret—in their *identity* which comes about in the performance of the act of thinking. The identity which exists between our thinking and what is thought, in so far as it is achieved in the act of thinking, is, with Hegel, called mind. So Hegel's brand of self-confidence is also confidence in mind which for its own part is one with God and the same with God. The characteristic thing about this, however, is that the confidence in mind or in God must also to the fullest extent and in ultimate seriousness be self-confidence, because there is likewise and in the same sense a final identity between Self and mind, as there is in general between thinking and the thing thought. It is the purpose of Hegel's philosophy to proclaim this confidence, and to summon people to it. He does these things because he does not conceive of it as a personal distinction to have occasion for such confidence, since there is no kind of inspiration or individual enlightenment behind it, because it is meant to be understood utterly and completely as confidence in universal human *reason*, the reason known and available to everyone.

Here Hegel takes up the inheritance of the Enlightenment: in fulfilment of the concern of the whole movement between himself and the Enlightenment, but also criticizing and correcting the courses it had taken acting in an independent direct relationship to the Enlightenment. In affirming this equivalence and final identity of things within and things without, of ego and non-ego, of the familiar and unfamiliar, Hegel affirms the insight of Romanticism. Of the minds we have studied here he is unquestionably most akin to Novalis. For just three years (Jena, 1801-3) he was closely associated with Schelling, the true philosopher of Romanticism, and even though he turned away from Schelling later this did not mean that he had rejected the things Romanticism wanted, but that he was attempting to provide for it a better system and apologetics than that of Schelling. He found the Romantic synthesis and identity to be lacking in a firm and universally valid basis. It seemed to him that the truth and force of this synthesis was imperilled by the mere appeal to poetry, to creative experience, to the individual genius. That was why he was also Schleiermacher's determined opponent and opposed his metaphysics of feeling, and the doctrine of faith which called this instance to witness. For him it is a question of understanding the synthesis which he also affirmed as Novalis, as Schelling, and as Schleiermacher wanted it to be, as solid knowledge, as a free, conscious and responsible act of the capacity for reason, which is in principle always and everywhere present in man and can be appealed to.

Hegel of course also affirms Herder's ideal of humanity and his experience of totality. He it was who put into effect the testament of Herder, and further, of Lessing, by his very thorough inclusion of history in the concept of reason. It has been regarded as Hegel's greatest achievement that in his concept of reason, which also embraced historical reality, he finally and justifiably overcame the dualism of transcendental and historical-empirical thought, the dualism of the eternal truth of reason and the accidental truths of history, of destiny and the idea, which had already been disputed by Herder. This was, however, the case because he actually achieved it within his concept of reason, and not by referring to some intuitive and emotional Beyond, which could not be apprehended, but only experienced! It is in fact

Hegel's criticism of Romanticism, solely and entirely, which distinguishes him from Herder. Hegel believed in the possibility, legitimacy and sovereignty of pure thought. He was never so fiercely aggressive as when, rightly or wrongly, he thought he could detect, behind the appeal to such supposedly given and yet inapprehensible instances, an example of lazy thinking, or fear of thinking, or mistrust of the power of thought. He would have had only the greatest contempt for a collective concept, like that, for instance, of the irrational, as it was evolved by a later age. It was not in a capitulation of the reasonable to the real, as to something which was unreasonable, or against reason, that he sought and found a way of overcoming the dichotomy which Herder had all too tumultuously disputed, but in the knowledge that the reasonable is just as real as the real is reasonable.

And Hegel of course also affirmed Kant's transcendentalism. He did so in the same sense that Fichte did; following in his footsteps, but excluding, admittedly, the specifically ethical turn Fichte had given to his affirmation. Reason critically understanding itself is reason which is self-established and liberated, which is now as a matter of principle the master of all things. But just for this reason Kant's critique of knowledge seems to Hegel to have after all rather the character of a carter's job, that had to be done sometime but could not have any lasting significance. It was in him to ridicule the demand for a theory of knowledge by saying there was as much sense in it as the demand of the Gascon who did not want to go into the water before he could swim. The interests of the theory of knowledge, he said, were best served in the act of a truly rational knowledge. 'If we are not to go to philosophy, to rational thought, before we have rationally known reason, then we can do nothing at all, for it is only in knowing that we rationally apprehend. Rational activity cannot be investigated before we are rationally active. In philosophy reason is for reason.'[1] In this act of rational knowledge the Kantian distinctions between the knowledge of ideas and empirical knowledge on the one hand, and between theoretical and practical knowledge on the other, also fall away, as necessary but secondary preliminary stages of mere reflection. All knowledge comprehending and surpassing these distinctions, is knowledge of God. True logic, including from the outset physics, is as such also the true metaphysics, the metaphysics of the mind which unites within itself thinking and the thing thought—the true metaphysics in mind. It is unnecessary to point out that Hegel's reaction to

---

[1] *Vorlesungen über die Philosophie der Religion* (Lectures on the Philosophy of Religion), ed. Lasson, Philosophische Bibliothek, Vols. 59-63, I, 57f.

certain elements of Kant's teaching, like his theory of postulates, for instance, or his theory of the theoretical unactuality of all knowledge of ultimate things, or his distinction between the religion of reason and historical religion, could only be one of sovereign displeasure. From Hegel's standpoint the good Kant is looked back upon as a manikin loyally improvising his resources, however sadly limited by the cave in which he plies his handiwork. Kant receives an honourable mention, and Fichte, as the man who with his teaching of the ego was the first to understand Kant better than he understood himself, receives a crown of oak: but we should on no account allow either of them to detain us. The distinction between knowledge and the thing in itself, between ego and non-ego is a provisional matter. Upon this point Hegel proceeds with Herder and Romanticism.

Hegel's direct, independent linking-up with the Enlightenment was done in this way: the confidence of the Enlightenment in the right and the power of rational thought was naïve, untested and therefore unsecured, stuck fast in half-truths and open to all kinds of counter-blows. Hegel called this confidence in the right and power of rational thought to self-awareness, worked out and defended its deepest truth *vis-à-vis* its own weaknesses as *vis-à-vis* its attackers, and in so doing exalted it from the level of a one-sided view of the world to a comprehensive world principle. We cannot of course name Hegel in the same breath as Christian Wolff, but we can liken him to Leibnitz, corrected and supplemented by Spinoza, the secret patron saint of all enlightened opponents of the Enlightenment. Hegel is the Enlightenment philosopher with an entirely good conscience, with a completely protected rear. These things the earlier philosophy of the Enlightenment did not have. Somehow it was still not at peace, it was still at loggerheads with the object as the object confronted it, in history particularly, with an irksome refusal to be dismissed. The reality of destiny, to which it shut its eyes, stood like a shadow behind it. That is why the fight against the Enlightenment was bound to emerge from the Enlightenment itself, as we saw it break out in Lessing's discovery of historical experience, in Kant's teaching of radical evil and of the primacy of practical reason, in Herder's protest against pure rationalism and in his enraptured hearkening to the voices of the peoples, and in the Romantic discovery of the immediacy of the individual. The Enlightenment had no safeguard against this assault upon it by opponents who were themselves enlightened, and it was therefore also ultimately unsecured against the never entirely suppressed opposition of such of its opponents as, in a manner which was not in tune with the age, did not even meet it upon its own ground. It was unsecured because the watchword 'Have the courage to use your own understanding' could only ring true when the idea of one's 'own understanding' was so deepened that the conflict with the object, the ignoring of history, and shutting one's eyes to the reality of destiny was superfluous, because all these things, the object, history and destiny, were included in it. God must not any longer be an offence or foolishness to one's 'own understanding'. The individual understanding had to learn to recognize that it must not be so diffident and defiant in understanding itself merely as *individual* understanding or merely as individual *understanding*, but that it must understand itself as *the one and only reason* which is already prevented from quarrelling with God, and which cannot be either openly or secretly atheistic, because as the one true reason of man it is *eo ipso* also the reason of God, a generic object which when thought out to its conclusion must necessarily be transformed into the generic subject, and in fact finally thus transformed. Because to Hegel the rational was historical and the historical rational, he completely and finally disposed of the God who had somehow stood in opposition to reason, who was in some way an offence and a foolishness to reason, and who could perhaps be denied through reason. He did not do this by denying him, and not even by denying that he stood in opposition, but by making the offence and foolishness of this opposition relative, by seeing that this relationship with God was something which was necessary but which was also provisional, by seeing that it could finally be resolved in the peace of reason, which is at once and as such the peace that is higher than all reason. That is what is fundamentally new about Hegel in relation to the Enlightenment, and in it Hegel brought the Enlightenment in its old form to honour in a way of which it would never have dared to dream.

And this makes for the peculiar momentum of Hegel's philosophy of self-confidence; it does not allow itself to be surpassed in cold-blooded rationalizing by any worldling, nor in depth of feeling by the most pious. It is Titanism to the highest degree and at the same time to the highest degree humility. The *self*-confidence it proclaims and to which it summons is at once and as such confidence in *God*, a qualified confidence, a most true and most actual confidence, imbued with the entire mystery and majesty of true confidence in God. Its intention is to give the honour as expressly as possible to *God* and not to man; and this it expresses quite directly and consistently not *only* in the form of a most naïve human *self*-confidence, but *also* in this form, as explicitly as possible. Every formal peculiarity of Hegel's philosophy can be understood when seen in this light. The method of thinking which is based upon the identity of confidence in God and self-confidence must become one that never fails, which is inexhaustible. As the result of the thought which is based upon this identity a *system* must emerge, a complete settling of the account with knowledge and the striking of a balance with truth. Based upon this identity questions which remain *open*, which play so large a part in Kant's philosophy of religion, for instance, simply cannot arise. Here problems are simply there in order that they may be raised and *settled* with all certainty. With this identity as the basis for his thought Hegel is able and indeed bound to be present himself as the man who has an implicit knowledge of *everything*, and is empowered to hale *everyone* before his judgment-seat. Based upon this identity there must be here a fierceness of controversy which is only possible otherwise in the form of a *rabies theologorum*. Wondrous to relate, it is accompanied by a fundamentally conciliatory spirit, and an open-mindedness towards all things. Of this spirit one is at first tempted to believe that it is thinkable only on assumptions which are to some extent theological. If all theology seems at first to pale beside this philosophy, then the reason is not that it confounds and disperses theology in a particularly dangerous and victorious way. Hegel had no thought of undertaking any such unfriendly task, and at bottom he remained throughout his life a loyal son of the Tübingen seminary. It is rather that everything that seems to give theology its particular splendour and special dignity appears to be looked after and honoured by this philosophy in a way incomparably better than that achieved by the theologians themselves (with the possible exception of Thomas Aquinas). Theology, taken care of once and for all, is here not surpassed in the act of this philosophy, but in fact surpasses itself.

Only someone who does not understand Hegel's philosophy can miss its peculiar greatness. Again and again we find we must think three times before contradicting it, because we might find that everything we are tempted to say in contradiction of it has already been said within it, and provided with the best possible answer. It is great in two ways: first, looked at in itself, because it has seized upon and implemented an idea that is at once simple and all-embracing, the at least relative truth of which is self-evident. It has done this so energetically, that whatever attitude we adopt towards it we cannot help hearing it and coming to terms with it. It is possible to bypass Fichte and Schelling, but it is as impossible to pass by Hegel as it is to pass by Kant. And the promissory nature of the truth Hegel enunciated and the ease with which it lends itself to equalization will perhaps be even greater than in the case of Kant for someone who, as a theologian, must finally say 'No' to Hegel.

The other great quality in Hegel's philosophy is the very fact that it is not at all the accidental discovery of one particular, gifted individual —this is what Hegel, in contrast to Schelling, did not wish to be—but the mighty and impressive voice of an entire era, the voice of modern man, or of the man who, from 1700 to 1914, was called modern man. 'Philosophy does not stand above its age in such a way that it is something completely different in kind from the things which generally condition the age; one spirit, rather, moves through the realm both of reality and of philosophical thought; it is only that the latter is the true self-understanding of the real. Or it is one movement which bears along the age and its philosophy. The only difference is that the things which condition the age still appear as accidental, are not yet justified and thus can still stand in unreconciled, inimical contrast to the truly essential content of the age, whereas philosophy, as the justification of the principle, is also the general tranquillizer and reconciler.'[1]

Quite apart from the intrinsic weight of the thought Hegel represents, it is impossible to pass him by, simply because we cannot pass by that modern man. We must not be led astray by the fact that modern man became unfaithful to Hegel. He meant and means what Hegel meant, even if he did, ungratefully enough, blushing, ashamed, and with a smile of embarrassment, turn away from Hegel; after Hegel, to his applause at first, had said that which he himself wished to say in a thousand tongues, but which he simply could not say nearly so well. Self-confidence, qualified as confidence in God, confidence in God given concrete form as self-confidence—where is the man who, with the blood of this modern man in his veins, would not listen to this and hear the finest and deepest echo of his own voice? If we wish to take this modern man seriously, to hear him and put his desires on record— if we wish to take ourselves seriously κατὰ σάρκα, but in the best and deepest sense of what must ultimately come under the notion of σάρξ, then Hegel also must be taken seriously. That is why it is fitting that he should have a place of honour in our investigation of the foundations of nineteenth-century theology. We ourselves are involuntarily thinking along Hegelian lines when we state that his greatness as a thinker consists in the objective and historical significance, the reasonableness and reality of his teaching, which are all present in equal measure, and which form a unity of mysterious clarity.

[1] *Phil. of Rel.*, Lasson, I, 53.

II. We have said that Hegel's philosophy is the philosophy of self-confidence. It is, first of all, the philosophy of the confidence of thinking man in the dignity, strength and value of his thought. And man, according to Hegel, cannot understand himself more deeply, more exactly, more definitely, than simply as thinking man. It is in thinking and in thinking alone that he is different from the animals, that he is, as man, himself. Thus in trusting in the dignity, strength and value of his thought he is in the most fundamental sense putting his trust in humanity, in his own dignity, strength and value. These qualities in his thought are based upon the fact that the act of his thinking, provided it is truly both an *act* of thinking, and an act of *thinking*, is identical with the event of reason, or of the concept or the idea or the mind. With Hegel all those things are synonymous, and indeed they are all synonyms for the reality of all reality, which is one and the same as God.

Reason understood in this sense is *absolute* reason, the concept in this sense the *absolute* concept, truth the *absolute* truth, the idea the *absolute* idea, mind the *absolute* mind. By absolute is meant set free from all, definitely all limitations, such as apply to history in relative contrast to reason, but also to reason in relative contrast to history, to Being in relative contrast to the concept, but also to the concept in relative contrast to Being, to reality in relative contrast to truth, but also to truth in relative contrast to reality, to experience in relative contrast to the idea, but also to the idea in relative contrast to experience, to finite nature in contrast to infinite mind, but also to infinite mind in relative contrast to finite nature. The qualities of absolute reason and its synonyms are absolute dignity, strength and value. That is to say, they are dignity, strength and value, which are not limited by any contrast, which cannot be called into question by any contrast, since they unite all contrasts within themselves, since they are in themselves in motion and at rest, since they stand in and of themselves, or rather set themselves up.

It is by virtue of the fact that the act of human thinking—provided only that it is truly both an *act* of thinking, and an act of *thinking*—is identical with the event of reason, that it merits this confidence, in its dignity, strength and value, a confidence which is therefore absolute, and not to be led astray by any quality of contrast, for this reason it is the occasion for the absolute self-confidence which is the secret of Hegel's philosophy. Identical with the *event* of reason, we say. And that really is the key to everything; that reason, truth, concept, idea, mind, God himself are understood as an *event*, and, moreover, only as an event. They cease to be what they are as soon as the event, in which they are what they are, is thought of as interrupted, as soon as a state is thought of in its place. Essentially reason and all its synonyms are life, movement, process. God is God only in his divine action, revelation, creation, reconciliation, redemption; as an absolute act, as *actus purus*. He is a graven image as soon as he becomes identified with one single moment, made absolute, of this activity. And reason, likewise, is unreason as soon as the process in which it is reason is thought of at any stage as something stationary, when any of the moments of its motion is identified with reason itself. Just because of this it is only the act of human knowing as such which deserves the confidence Hegel speaks of, because it alone is identical with the act of reason itself, and thus partakes of the absolute qualities of dignity, strength and value. Hence as soon as we seek to understand by reason something other than the act in which it is itself, the act in which the idea is idea, the mind mind, etc., we shall inevitably be guilty of treating Hegel with the grossest misunderstanding. The picture he had before his mind's eye in his great apotheosis of thinking, the picture of speculative philosophy in his sense, is not one that could be reproduced by means of a drawing in points, lines and outlines, however much the hints of this picture which Hegel himself gives over and over again seem to invite such treatment. Even in speaking of the Hegelian system we must not think of a rigid, stable construction. Relevant here is the fact that Hegel's terminology is in fact not so unambiguous as one might expect, especially from one who worshipped logic as he did, and it is certainly not as clear as the reader might wish. Anyone who has studied the textbooks of the history of philosophy and then begins to read Hegel, finds himself continually nonplussed and bewildered by the—so unlike the textbooks—overlapping in the application of the individual terms the master allowed himself, for all the consistency of what he wanted to say and did in fact say. And yet somehow it seems fitting, this freedom which brings with it the notorious obscurity of Hegel's writing and which does in fact cause considerable suffering in the reader. From page to page Hegel does in fact wrest from us the possibility to compromise for ourselves a tranquil picture of his views. With him we are only to look, and look again and again, and anyone who thinks he sees stable points and lines, quantities and relationships, is not in fact seeing what Hegel is seeking to show us.

Hegel sees life, the life of reason, of the mind, of truth, admittedly, but nevertheless life, in the full movement of life. Only a kaleidoscope or the moving film of the cinematograph could offer the visual quality that would be required. What is here called a system is the exact recollection of the observed fulness of life. It is only in the form of this recollection that it has permanency and validity, and only when the recollection is itself event, a continual re-creation of the picture itself. And what makes this system a system, that gives the order and regularity running through the whole of this recollection, is nothing but the rhythm of life itself, recognized as running through the fulness of history. This rhythm, considered in itself, is the regularity inherent in the system, its heart-beat, as it were. It is the famous dialectical *method* of thesis, antithesis and synthesis, in pursuit of which Hegel described, or rather reconstructed, in constantly new and changing aspects and insights the event of reason as the sole object of knowledge and learning. That this object is in fact an event, the event pure and simple, is as much as to say that the method here must be the one and all (*Eins und Alles*). Anyone unwilling to allow himself to be seized by the rhythm of the method, anyone seeking to acquire wisdom while standing instead of moving, would remain in ignorance, would not achieve the slightest glimpse of this object.

Nothing is more characteristic of the Hegelian system of knowledge than the fact that upon its highest pinnacle, where it becomes knowledge of knowledge, i.e. knowledge knowing of itself, it is impossible for it to have any other content but simply the history of philosophy, the account of its continuing self-exposition, in which all individual developments, coming full circle, can only be stages along the road to the absolute philosophy reached in Hegel himself. But that which knowledge is explicitly upon this topmost pinnacle as the history of philosophy, the philosophy completed in Hegel, it is implicitly all along the line: the knowledge of history and the history of knowledge, the history of truth, the history of God, as Hegel was able to say: the philosophy of history. History here has entered so thoroughly into reason, philosophy has so basically become the philosophy of history, that reason, the object of philosophy itself, has become history utterly and completely, that reason cannot understand itself other than as its own history, and that, from the opposite point of view, it is in a position to recognize itself at once in all history in some stage of its life-process, and also in its entirety, so far as the study permits us to divine the whole. It is a matter of the production of self-movement of the thought-content in the consciousness of the thinking subject. It is not a matter of reproduction! The Hegelian way of looking is the looking of a spectator only in so far as it is in fact in principle and exclusively theory, thinking consciousness. Granting this premise, and setting aside Kierkegaard's objection that with it the spectator might by chance have forgotten himself, that is, the practical reality of his existence, then for Hegel it is also in order (only too much in order!) that the human subject, whilst looking in this manner, stands by no means apart as if it were not concerned. It is in his looking and only in his looking that there is something seen. It is in his looking and only in his looking that the something seen is produced. And the thing seen actually has its reality in the fact that it is produced as the thing seen in the looking of the human subject. Man cannot participate more energetically (within the frame-work of theoretical possibility), he cannot be more forcefully transferred from the floor of the theatre on to the stage than in this theory.

But what is the meaning of this self-movement of the thought-content which is identical with the self-movement of the thinking subject? In this we must most particularly bear in mind Hegel's dialectical method. Reason is concept, i.e. reason conceives, reaches within itself, and, in completely penetrating, embraces reality within itself, embraces it so much that reality is reality only within reason, only as conceived reality. That, however, is not simply so; it comes about. The concept, to be exact, the absolute concept, is event. Its absoluteness is not a result to be discovered somehow and somewhere but is the absoluteness, the unlimited necessity of its execution. And the self-execution in which the concept is an absolute concept, brings itself about according to Hegel, in an endless circling, in a triple beat in which we are meant to perceive the very rhythm or heart-beat of the Hegelian system. Here we have to deal with Hegel's boldest and most weighty innovation. This movement comes about because of the fact that the concept does not so much exclude the concept that contradicts it, as the fundamental axiom of the whole of western logic had previously held, but includes it. It comes about because the contradiction of the concept, far from neutralizing it, is on the contrary a necessary moment of the concept itself. As an absolute concept the concept not only can but must 'swing over' to its opposite, 'release' its opposite, as Hegel puts it. It must do this not, it is true, in order to allow this opposite as such to stand and be valid, but in order to have it swing over forthwith into a second opposite, and finally and thirdly, that it might adjust and reconcile both in itself, call both back into itself again, and dispose of them within itself. 'Dispose' here does not have the meaning of *tollere*, but of *conservare*, so that the 'play'—Hegel's own name for the process—that is now finished can and must begin again immediately. It must begin again because it is only in its eternal self-execution that the concept is the absolute concept, the concept which is unlimited and unsurpassable in dignity, strength and value, which is absolute reason, the mind, the

idea, God himself. The concept is therefore absolute, it is God, in such
a way that in being and remaining the *dictum* it is also always the
contra-dictum, and always the contradiction of the contradiction and
always the reconciliation and the higher unity of both: thesis, antithesis,
synthesis—subjective-finite, objective-infinite, absolute-eternal—being
in itself and of itself, existing in and of itself, and however else the three
dialectical stages in Hegel are generally described.

Speculative thinking is defined as: 'dissolving something real and
setting it in opposition to itself in such a way that the differences as
determined by one's thinking are set in opposition and the object is
conceived as a unity of both'.[1] All truth is to be found in the ceaseless
completion of this circle, all error is contained in stopping and staying
at one of the moments of the concept, which are necessary as stages,
but are thought of not as points to be stopped at but as points to be
passed through. Error, lying and sin, with Hegel, can only signify
obstinate one-sidedness, a blind lingering and stopping which represents a departure from obedience to the self-movement of the concept.

There is no limitation or exaggeration, no folly or wickedness in the
whole range of real human thinking, from that of the most distant
times and places, right up to what is taking place here and now in the
philosopher's study, which would not be in principle included in the
rational quality of the concept which conceives all reality within itself.
Even that which is most questionable in itself can appear in this
context as the exponent of the mind. It was in this sense that Hegel
wrote in 1806, after the battle of Jena: 'I saw the Emperor, this world-
soul, riding out through the town to go on reconnaissance; it is indeed
a wonderful feeling to see such a person who, concentrated here upon
one spot, sitting on a horse, reaches out over the world and rules it.'[2]
In this sense Hegel could even speak of the Devil in tones of unfeigned
admiration. But precisely in being made relative in this way that one-
sidedness is shown its limits, and the means of rising above it is displayed. *Tout comprendre c'est tout pardonner!* From the height occupied
by the concept a soft and reconciling light can be shed upon everything
and everyone, and even more than that, *tout comprendre c'est tout admirer*,
might well be added to the saying to embrace Hegel's meaning. But
it must be said at the same time that one-sidedness must submit to
being seen and described as such, to being shown up in its merely
relative necessity and in the badness of its habit of stopping and staying.
It must be content to be summoned and aroused to go on by the magic

[1] *Phil. of Rel.*, Lasson, I, 33.
[2] Überweg, *Geschichte der Philosophie* (History of Philosophy), IV, 85.

wand of self-knowledge, which is as such knowledge of God. Theodicy and categorical imperative, the discovery of the meaning of all history, and one's own continuation of meaningful history, to put it in terms of Christian dogma, justification and sanctification, coincide perfectly within the act of this knowledge, at whatever stage it is completed, and whatever point the individual takes as his point of departure—if only this departure from the realm of one-sidedness comes about. And forthwith, as soon as this departure is made, an outlook in principle presents itself, is made possible and real upon the entire inner life of the concept or of the idea or of the mind. The Hegelian universal wisdom is there, like Pallas Athene sprung from the head of Jupiter, the moment this departure from one-sidedness, and with it the entry into the self-movement of the concept, has come about. Accordingly science, the one and only science, must be:

1. Proceeding from immediacy to objectivity: natural philosophy.

2. Passing into the non-immediacy of reflection, of imagination: logic.

3. Turning back into itself, as pure knowledge taken up once again into the higher unity of these opposites: the philosophy of mind.

In accordance with the same principle of motion logic forms itself into the teaching of Being at the first stage, into that of Essence at the second, and at the third and highest stage into that of the concept— natural philosophy forms itself into mechanics, physics and organic sciences—the philosophy of mind forms itself into the teaching of subjective, objective and absolute mind.

Leaving logic and natural philosophy, which are always divided and sub-divided according to the same principle, let us further note from the ordering of the philosophy of mind, which represents the third and decisive moment of the whole course, that Hegel understands by the teaching of the subjective mind psychology in its most comprehensive sense; by the teaching of objective mind, once again in the most comprehensive sense, ethics, which in its highest stage unfolds into the teaching of the family, the society and—characteristic of Hegel—at the highest level, the State. Finally the teaching of absolute mind moves from aesthetics via the philosophy of religion to this philosophy κατ'ἐξοχήν, the history of philosophy, in which Hegel's own teaching is understood as the crown and conclusion of a development which had taken place over three thousand years.

That, presented in the roughest outline, is what may be called the

Hegelian system of knowledge. Involuntarily we ask ourselves at what place in the wide ramifications of this structure we could look for the central point, the decisive concern of Hegel's thought. It might be reckoned as logic, in so far as logic has its peak in the doctrine of the concept, which plays a decisive part throughout. But we learn just as well, or better, of the most significant qualities of the concept of the concept, which is, admittedly, central to the entire teaching, and of its life and activity, in different places, where it lives its life, as distinct from the place where its life as such forms the centre of the discussion. Hegel's logic seems to be one of the less significant parts of his system, or at all events one which is less heeded and effective than many others. Natural philosophy has no clear claim for consideration either: it must be the result of personality that the strength of Schelling and Goethe, a receptiveness for nature, did not constitute Hegel's strength to the same extent. Someone whose view of the history of mind is predominantly political will be inclined and also justified in his way, whether stressing it positively or negatively, to see the Hegelian teaching of the State, with its singular conservative streak, as the master's most significant achievement. But this doctrine of the State, as a possible and necessary consequence, is probably more characteristic of than enlightening about Hegel's actual intentions. It is usual, then, to lay claim to his philosophy of history, which in the system follows upon the teaching of the State, as constituting Hegel's most significant thought. It is true, and was revealed already in his youth (Berne), that his interest in historical matters was incomparably greater than that which he showed, for instance, in research in the natural sciences. But the fact that his philosophy as a whole is the philosophy of history, philosophy of the history of God, is more important, in principle at any rate, than the expositions, given under this particular title, of reason in history, of world-history as the judgment of the world, and of this historical reason as having had its childhood in the oriental world, its time of adolescence and adulthood in the world of Greece and Rome, and its mature old age now in the Germanic world, however stimulating and important these ideas may be in themselves. Hegel's scheme of aesthetics is also certainly highly typical. In it, in opposition to the symbolical art of the East, whose characteristic form is architecture, and to the classic art of Greece, whose characteristic form is sculpture, there appears the 'romantic' art of Christendom as the higher unity, in so far as in it for the first time the spiritual element, infinite subjectivity, is said to predominate, and a reaching of art beyond itself is said to take place, whose characteristic forms are painting, music and poetry, of which, once again, the last takes up the totality of all forms within itself. At this point Hegel's connexion with Romanticism becomes palpably clear, but clear also is his going beyond Romanticism. This is shown in the view he held that the appearance of Goethe meant the beginning of a complete revolution, in terms of what had gone before, in the sphere of art. All the same, once again it cannot be said that Hegel's thought was actually centred in his teaching of art more than anywhere else. Likewise the history of philosophy, which forms the summit of the whole, should probably be looked upon more as the characteristic exponent than as the organizing centre of the whole. Finally, if anyone has wanted to find this whole in Hegel's philosophy of religion, it must indeed be said that here, where it is expressly a question of the things which clearly claim to be the last things, the nerve of all that Hegel wanted is laid bare as nowhere else. Once again, however, it cannot be said that Hegel attached particular importance to this philosophy of religion. It is for him one concern among many others, antithesis to the thesis of aesthetics, subordinate to the synthesis of philosophy; no more and no less. The fact that the philosophy of religion, too, is a motive force and this particular motive force in the self-movement of the mind, makes it relatively important, but it is definitely not important as a motive force in this movement which in some way embraces the others.

We shall ultimately understand Hegel best by believing him that, even if he does not speak with the same weight everywhere, he does after all wish to speak quite weightily absolutely everywhere, and not merely at certain points. Fundamentally there can be no centre here at the expense of a periphery. Or rather: the centre moves with the thinker himself; it is always at the point where the self-movement of the mind in the consciousness of the thinking subject is taking place. There is no outer thing that drawn into this movement could not forthwith become the most inward; there is no second to the last or third to the last thing that could not here forthwith acquire the tone and central significance of the last. Where the triple beat of thesis, antithesis and synthesis rings out, and it rings out everywhere, the Hegelian universal wisdom resembles one of those old villages of weavers or lace-workers where once, day after day, the sound of the same machines could be heard from every house: where this rhythm sounds there is the whole and the centre of this philosophy, possessed of the greatest strength within the smallest space. It is not this or that discipline, not a particular aspect of life or of learning, not that of the State either, or of history, or of religion, which is here in itself the

organizing centre. The only centre is the *method* which is to be applied
and proves true in every discipline and in every field of life
and learning.

One could perhaps go a step further and say that the really vital
interest, the true life-force of the Hegelian method of thinking, does
not lie even in the peculiar nature of this method as such, that it is
this particular method of the triple beat which is given by the division
and re-union of the concept. It is of course significant, and will concern
us further, that what Hegel wanted and was capable of found and was
bound to find expression in this particular method. But Hegel's will
and achievement itself does not consist in the invention of the dialectical
method as such, but in the invention of a universal method altogether.
That is what makes for Hegel's genius, what makes him typically
modern, and suited to his time: the fact that he dared to want to invent
such a method, a key to open every lock, a lever to set every wheel working at once, an observation tower from which not only all the lands of
the earth, but the third and seventh heavens, too, can be surveyed at a
glance. That was the characteristic and specific desire and achievement of Hegel: the invention of a rule for thinking whereby one can
arrive at the thought and its rule itself just as much as at the things in
themselves as the object of thought, at the problems of natural reality
just as much as at the incomparably harder concreteness of history, at
the secret of art just as much as at the texts of the Bible, which was
completely affirmed as revelation, at the most primitive paths of the
human psyche just as much as at the decisions of the Lord himself. This
was a rule of thinking which meant that riddles exist only to be seen
through at once from above and solved. Hegel's method makes it
possible for him to have to overlook, suppress or forget nothing,
seemingly nothing at all. It enabled him to be open, free and just in all
directions. By virtue of it he could meet every request and complaint,
no matter how alien it was to him, with the answer that it had already
been taken into consideration in its place, or at any rate could be considered. It enabled him to understand everything great, true, beautiful
and good as singly connected—nay more than that, as one. By it he
could somehow comprehend and welcome all imperfect things too,
the defiant resistance of the Devil not excepted, in the positive quality
of this unity, and would take them up and affirm them on the condition
that they allowed their place to be pointed out to them in the process
of life and therefore in the system of knowledge.

Is not a principle which promises and offers such things, which
emits such force and splendour, really the quintessence of dignity,

strength and value? Does thinking not merit confidence, if its principle is shown to be identical with this principle? Is self-confidence, the highest possible self-confidence, not possible and necessary if we ourselves are capable of thinking thus, and of thinking this? Once again we are confronted by the mystery: why did not modern man once and for all stretch out his hand and take this key to every lock which Hegel's method offered him? Even if Hegel's method was disputable, and the system unfolded by it—what did that matter? How could modern man, how dared he let it drop before another had been invented which, even if in a better way, perhaps, promised and offered at least the same and was just as universal, just as superior and fertile, just as possible to apply as Hegel's? It is of course true that the philosophers both before and after Hegel believed they, too, could make keys to fit every lock. But how one-sided, how abstract or material were the offerings which were made before Hegel, how many questions of truth, even those held by someone like Kant, seemed to be simply brushed aside! And why was it not noticed that the attempts made after Hegel, although they sought to achieve the same, once more fell short of Hegel's achievement, that they all have the significance of being mere relapses into the one-sided modes of thinking which Hegel had overcome? Again: how, after Hegel, could materialism, positivism, pessimism, neo-Kantianism become possible? Could Hegel's picture, once it had really existed, be forgotten again? Could the prodigal son, once he had returned to his father's house, and had eaten of the fatted calf, really depart again and fill his belly abroad with husks?

Or was it in fact not his father's house to which he then had returned? Had he become the victim of a second great illusion when this picture, Hegel's picture, which seemed perfectly to correspond with and to gratify his own desire, became real? Did the self-confidence which was presented to him by this picture prove finally to be without strength or foundation? If so, then it was certainly not because of the failings which might be part of the Hegelian system as a historical quantity, as they are part of every other, nor because of the questionable things by which the Hegelian method, in the peculiarity of its nature, might be surrounded. Failings and doubtful points of detail can be no reason for rejecting a scheme such as this.

In the depths of the consciousness of the time a violent shock must have befallen the will common both to Hegel and to it, the attempt to make a key to every lock must itself have come under suspicion, a deep resignation must have been born not only as far as the How of the Hegelian method was concerned, but also as regards its That, as regards the possibility of such a universal method at all. There is no other way of explaining the retreats which now began in every sector of the front. The natural scientists withdrew into their laboratories. The historians retired to a consideration of the none-too-subtle question: how was it in those days? The philosophers fell back upon psychology and the theory of knowledge, the theologians upon the historical Jesus and upon the history of religion in general.

There is no other way of accounting for the complete bursting asunder of the *Universitas litterarum* which Hegel had once again saved. It was not only that people had happened to tire of Hegel, but that they had become fundamentally weary of the path which leads to a universal knowledge in general. They were frightened by the ideal that had been achieved, and it seems that they could not think of anything else to do but to drop it. They contented themselves once again with knowing this or that, rejoiced to think that their knowledge was at all events much greater than that of the eighteenth century, and they gave up the idea of knowing one thing, the whole, with those who wanted to surpass the eighteenth century. From this time on their habit of speaking of a scientific method as if it were a unity was but a fond illusion. Fundamentally from this time on not only theology and the other sciences but philosophy and the other sciences, even the science of history and the natural sciences among themselves, stood again helplessly confronting one another. The time was now beginning when the more people talked of method the less they could be content with any method at all, however well founded and worked out it might be; and the more the method, the one method that alone would allow them to speak of a single science, a single culture, was conspicuous by its absence. The self-confidence of modern man which still wanted to assert itself and seems to assert itself even in these changed circumstances, could only be a broken self-confidence. Anyone seeking to look at the intellectual situation of the age after Hegel as an advance upon the age of Hegel himself—and the possibility of interpreting it thus is not precluded—will not be able to seek this advance in the line in which the Enlightenment and the surpassing of the Enlightenment took its course up to and including Hegel. Measured by this line, in the light of the question of whether we have advanced along this line, the intellectual development which has taken place since Hegel can only be regarded as a decline and a retrogression.

The two questions with which we began will now perhaps have become clearer: Why did Hegel meet with no belief? Why did not his philosophy of self-confidence, a self-confidence which was unbroken because it was founded in itself, in a homogenous method, assert itself and win through? Was not his offer, even if he had been in fundamental error, still better, incomparably better as a fulfilment of the promise in which modern man still claimed he believed, than everything that came after? Or should the time of its effectiveness which we can survey perhaps be still too short? Is the time only coming, in which Hegel will meet with belief, in which his offer will be accepted?

III. Hegel is also the great perfecter and surpasser of the Enlightenment because he brought the great conflict between reason and revelation, between a purely worldly awareness of civilization and Christianity, between the God in us and the God in Christ, to a highly satisfactory conclusion. Is it any wonder that Hegel found a following above all among theologians? It seemed that after a long winter a theological spring had come such as had never been known. What had now become of all the arguments against theology which it had had openly or secretly to face since the time of Descartes, indeed for even longer, since the men of the Middle Ages who had disputed revelation? All criticism of revelation was evidence of a lamentable one-sidedness, and the wretched limits within which Kant and Lessing were still prepared to grant it validity were also evidence of one-sidedness; these were all murderous attempts upon the wealth and depth of the truth. Hegel put down each and every one of them. In a most thorough fashion Hegel himself showed the disturbers of the peace, and not least the theologians who were capitulating to them, who was master. He produced a philosophy, as we have seen, in which theology seemed to be taken better care of than in theology itself. 'Because of such a finite perception of the Divine, of that which is in and of itself—because of this finite conception of the absolute content it has come to pass that the basic teachings of Christianity have for the most part vanished from dogmatics. It is now philosophy, not alone, but chiefly, which is essentially orthodox; it is philosophy which maintains and safeguards the tenets which have ever been valid, the basic truths of Christianity.'[1] 'Much more of dogmatics has been preserved in philosophy than in dogmatics in theology itself.'[2] For it is a fact 'that the content of philosophy, its requirement and interest, is also completely that of religion; its object is eternal truth, nothing else but God and the explanation of God. Philosophy, in explaining religion, is only explaining itself, and in explaining itself it explains religion . . . Thus religion and philosophy coincide . . . philosophy is itself in fact an act of divine worship'.[3]

[1] *Phil. of Rel.*, Lasson, III, 26.   [2] Ibid., I, 40.   [3] Ibid., I, 29.

Could theology demand more than such a declaration of solidarity, indeed of a complete identity of interests from its ancient foe?

And the fascination of the form of this declaration lay in the fact that at last, at last it did not mean what the philosophizing of theology had meant during the Enlightenment, and what it had still meant with Kant. There was no de-historicizing, no forsaking of what had once actually happened in history in favour of the timelessly rational. It meant that at long last the historical element in Christianity was not only brought into a tolerable relationship with the rational one, a relationship to some extent in accordance with its dignity, but that it was actually exalted to the position of the most significant factor, that the universal quality, reason itself, was understood entirely historically. The concern which Herder particularly had expressed was given the most thorough consideration here. Anyone who thinks that he can help theology by establishing an organic relationship between revelation, faith and history, should be quite clear in his mind that it has long ago received this help from Hegel. And with history it was dogma, mystery, and primarily those teachings of Christianity which were most profound and most inaccessible to rationalism, which were splendidly rehabilitated by Hegel's philosophy of religion and which were honoured and received protection against the assaults of philosophy and of the faint-hearted among the theologians themselves.

The offer here made was, however, not only that to help save Christianity, or theology. The Middle Ages had possessed a uniform culture, which even the Reformation had not destroyed. What did destroy it was the relentless progress of the intellectual movement of the Renaissance, of the seventeenth and eighteenth centuries. The emancipation of culture from the Church which compelled the Church's emancipation from culture seemed an accomplished fact. The entire intellectual surge of the Enlightenment, but the struggle against the Enlightenment, too, had had the effect of widening this rift. It meant a threat not only to the Church, but also, truly, to culture. In spite of Kant and in spite of Goethe there could be no really quietened cultural conscience, no assured self-confidence for modern man, so long as religion was behind him in the *rôle* of an insulted enemy. A mere 'treaty' such as Schleiermacher wanted to propose to the opposing parties, along 'let us depart in peace' lines, and suggesting that faith must not hinder scientific research and that scientific research must not exclude belief—such a treaty could truly not suffice here. It did not restore what had been lost since the Middle Ages, the unity of the human and the Divine. It still caused man to appear as a spirit divided within himself, and still set up in opposition to free thinking a threateningly independent authority. At the back of Schleiermacher's proposed treaty was admittedly something quite similar to the Hegelian declaration of solidarity, and indeed of an identity of interests, as we shall see. But Schleiermacher, with his teaching of the feelings as the seat and basis of religion, remained too deeply rooted in Romanticism to be able to make clear the unity he too had in mind. This decisive achievement was something of which the speculative idealism of Hegel could alone be capable, and it did not fail in bringing it about. How indeed could it have been otherwise, after all we have seen of it? Hegel wanted to do justice to both sides, with an equity and a circumspection such as none had summoned before him. He wanted to be a modern man, without forsaking or conceding anything, and we must also credit his other desire, his wish to be a Christian, and indeed a Lutheran Christian, without forsaking or conceding anything. He acted as a true attorney, or judge, rather, between the two parties.

He had therefore to make demands of both parties. In his eyes these demands required no sacrifice, nor any compromise or concession. They rather required, upon both sides, a deeper, more radical understanding of its own case by each party, an achievement of greater self-awareness, and upon this basis the arrival at mutual understanding, at a new mutual recognition. It was perhaps the strongest expression of Hegel's self-confidence that he felt able to point out this basis and make the demands upon both sides which rested upon it. These demands were finally rejected by both sides. Modern man, without knowing of a better unity than that proposed by Hegel, yet split himself once again, as oil and water separate, into the Christian and the man. The grip whereby Hegel sought to unite him in himself turned out to be premature, too strong, or too weak, even, to prevent the centripetal forces of both sides from once again shattering the unity. That was probably the deepest, and perhaps the tragic meaning of the catastrophe of Hegelianism.

Let us begin with the demand which Hegel's philosophy of religion made upon modern cultural awareness. Hegel certainly made this demand to its own best advantage, as its own advocate, but also as its judge, in so far as, in the depths of which it had no knowledge, he sought to understand it at the same time as Christian self-awareness. Hegel interpreted modern cultural awareness to itself in an unprecedented fashion by saying that at the deepest and ultimate level it was concerned with the claim of truth. This claim takes a form possible only if the truth is God, and God is the Master of men. This is the meaning of the Hegelian apotheosis of thinking, thinking as distinct from mere feeling; this is the meaning of Hegel's intellectualism, which has so often been condemned: man lives from the truth, and only from the truth. Truth is his God, whom he dares not forsake if he is to remain human. Truth is necessary to him, and, indeed, necessary to him in its unity, in its entirety, in the divine rigour inherent in it. Such was the claim which Hegel hurled at modern man more forcibly than any theologian, at any rate, had done for centuries, although it was without doubt fundamentally a theological claim. 'Our subject', the *Philosophy of Religion* begins, 'is that which is utterly truthful, that which is truth itself, the region, where every mystery in the world, every contradiction confronting deeper thought, every emotional pain, is resolved, the region of eternal truth and eternal peace, absolute truth itself.'[1] The Enlightenment, and thinking since the Enlightenment, had admittedly also been concerned with truth, but where was it concerned in this manner with the imperious and indeed imperialistic claim of truth, with the premise that it, and ultimately it alone, formed the agenda? Where was it concerned with this unity, entirety, rigour, and divinity of truth? 'Knowledge is not only knowing that an object is, but knowing also what it is, and not only knowing in general what it is, and having a certain knowledge and certainty of it, but knowing of that which determines it, of its content, in which the necessity of the relations between these things determining it is known.'[2] The simple principle of philosophical knowledge itself should now be 'that our consciousness knows immediately of God, that knowing of the existence of God is a matter of utter human certainty . . . that reason is the place of the spirit where God reveals himself to man'.[3] 'God is not *a* concept, but *the* concept.'[4] Will modern man recognize his joy in truth, his quest for truth, his fanaticism for truth (we are reminded of Lessing) in this looking-glass? Will he put up with being taken so seriously, with being thus seized upon in his penchant for truth? Will he affirm that it was just this, something of such deadly seriousness, which was the object of his intention and desire? Or will he shrink back before the last things, which are pointed out to him as his own; before the discovery of the revelatory nature of absolute truth and all real knowledge, and still, now as ever, seek to fall humbly into the left hand of God, instead of exalting his thinking to a divine service, as is here demanded of him?

Hegel's demand consists secondly in his insistence on having truth and with it knowledge most strictly understood as a movement, as a

---

[1] *Phil. of Rel.*, Lasson, I, 1.   [2] Ibid., I, 50.   [3] Ibid., I, 49.   [4] Ibid., III, 42.

history. Science to Hegel means knowing and he enforces this definition with an adamant consistency and exclusiveness. Science is present only in the deed, in the event. The concept, the idea, the mind, God himself is this event—not anything outside this event. Science is applied method, and that means the applied method of truth itself, the method of God which lays claim to man in the ultimate sense. This science cannot have assured results, cannot pause for rest after achieving its discoveries. It cannot proceed from axioms unsurpassable in their certainty, from established presuppositions which lie behind it. It is nothing less than everything which is in question, and everything must continually be in question, the ultimate included, for the ultimate too, in the self-movement of truth, must ever and again become the first. This understanding, too, of truth towards all truths apparently rests upon a theological premise. The truth can only be so menacing, so disquieting, all truths can only be so unstable, all science can only be so relativized, if truth, as Hegel constantly assumes, is identical with God himself. Will modern man suffer this threat, permanent in its nature, to all certain science, this dissolution of all science into the act of knowing, into method? Will he acknowledge that Hegel has told him nothing new, but has only described the actual situation of modern man in all his research into truth? Or will he hide his eyes and not be willing to admit this after all? Will he turn away in disgust at having the background to his actions thus disclosed, and devote himself anew to his positive, exact, detailed work in history and the natural sciences, convinced that one can have a wonderful trip on Lake Constance when it is frozen, without having to think every instant where one is going?

And Hegel's demand consists thirdly in the fact that he asserts the contradiction as the law of truth understood as history. It consists in the fact that he thought he could show that the dialectical method was the one which alone exhausted and comprised the truth. The truth is God, God, however, is God only *in actu*. This means for Hegel, only as the God who is Three in One, the eternal process which consists in something distinguishing its parts, separating them, and absorbing them into itself again. Life itself is not a unity resting in itself, but a perpetual $a = non\text{-}a$, in despite of the whole of western logic. It is, quite simply, the task of logic—and of science with it—to order itself according to life, and not the task of life to adapt itself to logic. The unity of truth—and no one fought for it more vigorously than Hegel— is the unity of contradictions, more, the reconciliation which is effected between them. It is their reconciliation, but also the establishment of their basis, their necessity, and their adjustment and dissolving. It is not in the setting aside of contradictions, but in the act of making them relative that the absoluteness of mind consists. This means that it exists in the mutual relationship between the contradictions of being and thinking, object and idea, nature and spirit, object and subject, etc., the relationship they have both among themselves and with their higher unity, the unity which must, however, forthwith emit them again, and in fact itself set them up.

Looked at from this point of view, too, Hegel's demand can be understood only as a theological one. His doctrine of the Trinity, unsatisfactory as it may be from the theological point of view, is anything but a retrospective adaptation of his philosophy to comply with the wishes of the theologians. The leading theologians of Hegel's time had absolutely no desire for a renewal of the doctrine of the Trinity, and least of all for such a one as Hegel's, which threatened to place them yet again and now more than ever in conflict with all single-line logic. In propounding it Hegel was theologizing in his own way, alone and acknowledging no master, against the philosophers and against the theologians. The meaning of his dialectic method is apparent, much clearer than Schleiermacher's meaning, for instance, since Hegel in contrast to Schleiermacher presented his method under the sign of a necessary and certain knowledge of truth: the knowledge of the Creator of heaven and earth, of the Lord over light and darkness, over life and death. Knowledge of God could be the knowledge of irreconcilable contradictions and their eternal vanquishing in the mind. Knowledge of God could mean the passage through the contradictions of reason to the peace that is higher than all reason, and the emergence into these contradictions in comforted despair. Knowledge of God could make this method possible and necessary. It is a question of whether the definitions with which Hegel surrounded his method allow us to recognize that which he intended and achieved, as knowledge of God. There can be no denying that knowledge of God was what he meant, and that he was speaking from very close to the heart of the matter. But once again: will modern man tolerate such a theological invasion, and one of such a particularly menacing aspect? Will he recognize himself in this looking-glass? Was it really this which he had wanted and intended? Or had not Hegel already understood him in far too deep and far too Christian a way, by demanding of him that he should thus found his philosophy upon theology, and eventually allow his philosophy to be transformed into theology?

This partner, modern cultural awareness, did in fact let Hegel down. It neither sought to understand itself thus in its own depth, nor did it want to be reconciled in this depth with Christian awareness in such a way as Hegel thought it should be. Why not? Because the demand was too great, its conditions too theological? That in fact is how it was felt and how it is usually represented. It could also have been for the other reason, that the demand was still not radical enough, that there was not too much, but too little theology in it, for it to seem worthy of belief.

This leads us to the other demand, the demand which Hegel's philosophy of religion presented to theology. We must first of all establish that with what we have come to know as his Christian opposite to modern consciousness, Hegel had something of decisive and lasting importance to say, or to recall, to theology, and not only to the theology of his age. A theology which is jostled by philosophy—and what theology is not—is just the one which has often forgotten and still forgets that truth should not concern it less than philosophy but, on the contrary, much more. It should not be concerned with manifestations of life in general, with some kind of expressions, declarations, avowals, assertions and symbols attempting to express the inexpressible in some form or another, nor with a kind of verbal music-making, nor with a description of conditions and circumstances, nor even with a view of essentials, however deep, but with truth, with a kind of knowledge which does not have its foundation in some kind of given thing, as such, but in the link of this given thing with the final origin of everything given. If theology does not speak the truth in this sense, then in what sense can it assert that it is speaking of God? Can it perhaps absolve itself from the earnestness with which Hegel equated the knowledge of truth and the knowledge of God? Dare it fall short of Hegel in this respect, if it is not to stand—for all the supposed independence of its source of knowledge—in the shadow of philosophy, philosophy being regarded as something much more important. A theology whose basis was merely historical, merely psychological, merely phenomenological, could in fact stand in this questionable shadow. And did not nineteenth-century theology to a large extent stand indeed in this shadow when and after it passed by Hegel's doctrine?

Secondly, theology too and theology in particular was and is reminded by Hegel of the possibility that the truth might be history, event; that it might always be recognized and discovered in actuality and not otherwise. Theology might and should have known, not less well but better than Hegel, that its knowledge, its knowledge in particular, was only possible in the form of a strict obedience to the self-movement of truth, and therefore as a knowledge which was itself

moved. It could let itself be reminded by Hegel that the source of
knowledge of Reformation theology, at all events, had been the Word,
the Word of God, the word of truth. But this also means, the event of
God, the event of truth. An event that comes and goes, like a passing
thunder-shower (Luther), like the angel at the pool of Bethesda, an
event at which the man for whom it is to be an event must be present;
an event, which by repetition, and by man's renewal of his presence,
must ever become event anew. Should not theology have let itself be
reminded, by what Hegel had said to it and beyond what he said to it,
of the biblical concept of revelation, of the God who presents himself
to our knowledge, and can be known, only as the Living God? Did
not theology fall short of Hegel in this respect as well, instead of
surpassing him? Did it not, together with his strict concept of truth,
also lose sight of the concept of real history? Could this loss be made
good by the fact that, in the time which followed, theology was capable
of surpassing Hegel by means of an understanding of the historical as
such that was in fact more extensive than his? Of what use to theology
was all knowledge of reported history, that of the Bible too, and of the
Bible in particular, if at the same time it was incapable of recognizing
real history, of recognizing the Living God?

Thirdly and finally, theology was reminded by Hegel of the contradictory nature of its own particular knowledge. How on earth was
it possible for theology after Hegel to allow itself to become involved
once again in the discussion on the rational and historical qualities of
Christianity? More than that: how could it allow itself to be pushed
into the problem of the natural world and the world of the spirit?
How was it possible for it to enter into the fight against materialism,
just as if it stood and fell with the spirituality materialism was attacking? How was it possible for all its hopes and plans to be directed
towards finding a humble refuge beneath the sheltering wings of the
so-called science of the spirit? How was it possible for theology to be
exactly at the same point again around 1900, at which Kant had
arrived a hundred years before, at an *a priori* way of thinking, within
which it imagined it was well housed and secured in producing a
special, religious *a priori* method? Could it not have understood Hegel
better than he perhaps understood himself? Could it not have understood, namely, that Hegel with his concept of mind, must wittingly, or
unwittingly have been thinking of the Creator of heaven and earth,
the Lord over nature and spirit, precisely by virtue of the unity and
opposition of *dictum* and *contra-dictum*, in which Hegel had the spirit
conceiving itself and being real? Did the theologians, if they knew

about God, need to be so superstitiously respectful of natural science, and so eager to present themselves as scientists of the spirit, as they were—so typically for the theology of that period—in the second half of the nineteenth century? And if they knew about God ought they to have allowed the other Hegelian synthesis, that of reason and history in Christianity itself, to be wrested from them again? Was it really impossible to take up and make fruitful the entire Hegelian concept of the synthesis, so soon as it was taken seriously, more seriously perhaps than Hegel himself took it, with the realization that it could be a question only of the incomprehensible synthesis of God?

Doubtless, theology could and can learn something from Hegel as well. It looks as if theology had neglected something here, and certainly it has no occasion to assume an attitude of alarm and hostility to any renaissance of Hegel which might come about. It might then perhaps open its eyes more than the first time to the most highly positive element in this philosophy, to what is theologically at least indirectly significant in it. It might perhaps for that very reason be more capable than the first time of avoiding its undeniable pit-falls and temptations.

With this we come to the other thing we must say here. It may in fact be that the Hegelian demand is unacceptable to theology for good reasons, or rather that it can only become acceptable and salutary to theology if it is very vigorously translated and transformed. In order to keep sight of the complete picture we shall once again take as our guide the three landmarks of Hegelian thinking which we have already singled out: truth, the moving cognition of truth, and the dialectical character of this movement.

The first question which arises is whether the Hegelian concept of truth can do justice to theology. Hegel thinks of truth as the thinking which is conceived as the pinnacle and centre of humanity. But has humanity *this* centre? *Has* it any such centre at all? Does not man always exist at the invisible intersection of his thinking and willing? Did not Kant's doctrine of the primacy of practical reason at least put forward a reminder of this unity in man? Was it not this with which Schleiermacher's teaching of the central significance of feeling was truly concerned? It was a reminder—Hegel was right in this—which should of course not be allowed, by discrediting thinking, to lead to a vitiation of the notion of truth, but one which must protect the notion of truth from one-sided theorizing. Is a theory of truth which builds itself up upon the inner logic of a thought which is divorced from practice still the theory of man as he really is, the theory of his truth? Can the theory of truth be any other theory but the theory of human practice? From the point of view of theology perhaps it really cannot. But then doubt arises about the uninhibited way in which Hegel, at two decisive turning-points, used to think further, unperturbed—at points where a theory of practice would be bound to stop, and precisely in doing so prove itself as a theory of truth. Hegel in his paraphrase of the relation of man to God did not call a halt before the concept of sin. He included it in the unity and necessity of mind. He sought it in the finite nature of man as such, and in the freedom of mind. He thought he could see one point whence it could be understood at once as fate and as guilt, and at one and the same time the poison-cup of death and the fountain-head of reconciliation.[1] He thought he could understand sin as a 'point to be passed through in a moment or longer'.[2] He accordingly understood reconciliation not as an incomprehensibly new beginning, but simply as a continuation of the one eventual course of truth, which is identical with the existence of God himself. 'The idea of mind is this: to be the unity of divine and human nature. . . . The divine nature itself is but this: to be the Absolute Mind, that is to say, to be the unity of the divine and human nature.'[3] The consciousness of reconciliation 'completes religion as the knowledge of God as mind; for he is mind in the differentiation and return which we have seen in the idea, which implies that the unity of divine and human nature is not only significant in determining human nature, but equally so in determining divine nature'.[4] If the basis of theology for knowledge should be revelation; and if revelation should be the revelation of God to man who is lost in sin, and the revelation of God's incomprehensible reconciling, then here, where we seem to be permitted to think beyond the mystery of evil and salvation, and where it seems to be permitted and possible to solve in this way this dual mystery, we have before us another basis for knowledge, a concept of truth which cannot be acceptable to theology.

That leads us to something further. The Hegelian self-movement of truth is identical with the self-movement of the thinking of the human subject, and in so far as the human subject is to be considered entirely himself while he is thinking, it is identical with the self-movement of this subject altogether. The Hegelian doctrine of the Trinity coincides with the basic principles of Hegelian logic, which is at the same time quite explicitly the basic principle of Hegelian anthropology and the Hegelian teaching of life. 'God is this: to distinguish oneself from oneself, to be object to oneself, but to be completely identical with oneself in this distinction.'[5] Certainly, but Hegel might just as well have

[1] *Philosophy of Religion*, III, 110.   [2] Ibid., III, 105.   [3] Ibid., III, 38.
[4] Ibid., III, 131.   [5] Ibid., III, 6.

said that knowledge is this and man is this. Hegel did not dispute the positive and historical nature of revelation, the uniqueness of Christ; rather he emphatically affirmed it. But with Hegel God and man can never confront one another in a relationship which is actual and indissoluble, a word, a new word revelatory in the strict sense, cannot pass between them; it cannot be uttered and cannot be heeded. It is only in so far as 'everything which exists for consciousness is objective to it that there is an objectivity of revelation. Everything must come to us in an outward way.'[1] Revelation, therefore, like all knowledge of whatever kind, also passes through objectivity, inasmuch as knowledge also comprises the moment of perception. And this objectivity, and similarly and to the same degree the objectivity of revelation, is anything but indissoluble. It is distinguished as a stage of revelation upon the level of the mere 'imagination', which it is the task of philosophy, as being the delegated authority of mind, to raise to the form of thought as the form suited to the reality of mind. This also means, however, that philosophy has to reduce it to its purely logical content,[2] even if, now as before, those who are still immature are still allowed to perceive pure thought in the form of the imagination. Reason, whose ordained task it is to perform this operation, and which must set about performing it without being able to stop, is just as much divine revelation as is the imagination.[3] When God manifests himself the philosopher of religion has already understood him in the preliminaries of this act, and he already has the lever in his hand which he has only to depress to advance from God's act of revealing to the higher level of God being manifest, in which every given thing, all duality, is annulled, all speaking and listening has lost its object and been transformed again into pure knowing, the knowing of the human subject, as it originally proceeded from him. Hegel's living God—he saw God's aliveness well, and saw it better than many theologians—is actually the living man. In so far as this living man is only after all thinking man, and this abstractly thinking man might be a man who is merely thought, and not a real man at all, it is possible that this living God, too, Hegel's God, is a merely thinking and merely thought God, before whom real man would stand as before an idol, or as before a nothing. At all events he would stand in boundless loneliness, 'without a God in the world'. The self-movement of truth would have to be detached from the self-movement of man—and here it is equated with it with the utmost explicitness and rigour of logic—to be justly regarded as the self-movement of God.

[1] *Philosophy of Religion*, III, 19.   [2] Ibid., I, 67.   [3] Ibid., I, 54.

And the third thing there is to be said is that the identification of God
with the dialectical method, even if it did not signify that he was
identified with man's act of life, implies a scarcely acceptable limitation,
even abolition of God's sovereignty, which makes even more questionable the designation of that which Hegel calls mind, idea, reason, etc.,
as God. This God, the God of Hegel, is at the least his own prisoner.
Comprehending all things, he finally and at the highest level compre-
hends himself too, and by virtue of the fact that he does this in the
consciousness of man, everything God is and does will be and is understood from the point of view of man, as God's own necessity. Revelation
can now no longer be a free act of God; God, rather, *must* function as
we see him function in revelation. It is necessary to him to reveal himself. 'A mind which is not manifest is not a mind.'[1] 'God is utterly
manifest.'[2] The finite consciousness, which partakes of revelation, thus
shows itself as a motive power in the concept, in the process of God
himself. Creation is necessary, and reconciliation too is necessary. The
Church is necessary to God himself, for in it he can be the mind of the
Church; and it is this alone which first makes it possible for him to be
mind and God. If he were not the mind of the Church he would not be
God. And he is God only in so far as he is the mind of the Church. I
am necessary to God. That is the basis of Hegel's confidence in God,
and the reason why this confidence can immediately and without
further ado be understood as self-confidence as well, and why it did thus
understand itself. Hegel, in making the dialectical method of logic the
essential nature of God, made impossible the knowledge of the actual
dialectic of grace, which has its foundation in the freedom of God.
Upon the basis of this dialectic the attempt to speak of a necessity to
which God himself is supposed to be subject would be radically impossible. But at all events the dialectic in which we ourselves exist, a
method which we are ourselves at all times capable of using—this is
not the actual dialectic of grace. Hegel did not open the gate-way of
this knowledge to theology, and it seems that it remained closed to his
own perception too. That is probably the weightiest and most significant of the doubts about him which might be raised from the theological point of view. The two points previously mentioned, the single-
track nature of his concept of truth and the confusion of human with
divine self-movement also have their origin in this: in the failure to
recognize that God is free—one might perhaps say in all succinctness:
in the failure to recognize double predestination. They have their
origin in the fact that Hegel's dialectic cannot, by theology at all

1 *Philosophy of Religion*, III, 35.   2 Ibid., III, 6.

events, be acknowledged as a dialectic which could be accepted in all seriousness.

Theology was just as incapable of accepting Hegel's philosophy as was modern cultural awareness. Of course it cannot be said that it rejected him at that time because it knew better and because it clearly recognized the things which were unacceptable to it in his teaching. It would only have been able to do that if it had previously allowed itself to be taught by him much more thoroughly. Ultimately theology rejected him merely for the same reasons which also made him unacceptable to modern cultural awareness. Who knows whether it was not in fact the *genuinely* theological element in Hegel which made it shrink back? Conversely, openly or secretly, it adopted at any rate enough of the very things that were questionable about him, without being able to overcome their effects by means of his genuine insights. Theology had, and still has, no occasion to throw stones at Hegel, as if it had not trodden the same path as he, only not in so firm or so logical a manner as he did. When we come to consider Schleiermacher we shall have to ask very seriously whether his secret is a different one from that of Hegel, only that with Hegel it might be a secret which was to a great extent more respectable and at all events more instructive than that of Schleiermacher. And we shall also find strong traces of Hegel elsewhere and not only among Hegelians, but in places where people considered themselves to be far above Hegelianism. All too much had he, the misunderstood one, taught those things which his whole century, and the theologians of his century as well had at heart. Would modern man and the modern theologian have understood him better and accorded him a better reception, if there had not been these known theological objections to be raised against him, if he had at once gone one step further all along the line, and if he had at once been a little more in earnest from the theological point of view? Many and great things would then have assumed a different aspect in the intellectual life of the nineteenth and twentieth centuries, and perhaps in their political and economic life too. But in that case Hegel would not have been Hegel, and we must therefore be content to understand him as the man he was: as a great problem and a great disappointment, but perhaps also a great promise.

PART TWO

HISTORY

II

SCHLEIERMACHER

THE older Gass, impressed by a reading of Schleiermacher's *Doctrine of Faith*,[1] once wrote to its author saying: 'There is no one who can make me waver in my belief that your dogmatics herald a new era, not only in this one discipline, but in the whole study of theology in general.'[2] And A. Neander went even further, saying to his students on the day after Schleiermacher's death: 'From him a new period in the history of the Church will one day take its origin.'

These prophecies have been fulfilled. The first place in a history of the theology of the most recent times belongs and will always belong to Schleiermacher, and he has no rival. It has often been pointed out that Schleiermacher did not found any school. This assertion can be robbed of some of its force by mention of the names of his successors in Berlin, August Twesten, Karl Immanuel Nitzsch of Bremen, and Alexander Schweizer of Zürich. But they are correct in so far as Schleiermacher's significance lies beyond these beginnings of a school in his name. What he said of Frederick the Great in his Academy address entitled 'What goes to make a great man' applies also to himself: 'He did not found a school, but an era.'[3] The man who published an essay in 1907 called *Schleiermacher der Kirchenvater des 19. Jahrhunderts* (Schleiermacher, the Church-father of the Nineteenth Century), was speaking the historical truth. The nineteenth century brought with it many deviations from Schleiermacher, and many protests against him; often his ideas were distorted to the point of unrecognizability, and he was often overlooked and forgotten. But in the theological field it was nevertheless his century. After describing all sorts of curves, both great and small, it none the less always returned to him. His influence did not decrease, it increased as time went on, and his views established themselves more and more. He was studied,

[1] *Der christliche Glaube, nach den Grundsätzen der Evangelischen Kirche im Zusammenhang dargestellt* (The Christian Faith, systematically set forth according to the principles of the Evangelical Church). References in this chapter to the *Doctrine of Faith (Glaubenslehre)* are to this work, known in England as *The Christian Faith*.
[2] *Briefwechsel* (Correspondence), ed. W. Gass, Berlin 1852, p. 195.
[3] *Philosophische Werke* (Philosophical Works), Berlin 1835, III, 83.

honoured and made fruitful much more in 1910 than in 1830, when
people outside the closest circle of his acquaintances had no hesitation
in naming him in the same breath with theologians like Daub,
Marheineke, Bretschneider and others like them. Even if at this time,
when he was producing his greatest work, he doubtless stood in the
shadow of Hegel (when the young D. F. Strauss, just arrived in Berlin
on the journey customary for Tübingen seminarists, heard in Schleiermacher's study of Hegel's sudden death he wounded him with the
unreflecting painful words: 'But it was on his account that I came
here') his star rose all the brighter after the fairly rapid passing of the
age of Hegelianism. From that time on, after the stimulation of Hegel
had, partly rightly and partly wrongly, been withdrawn, only Schleiermacher could be the saviour. The great exception, the original school
of Ritschl, was also but a proof of this fact. And it is truly a sign of the
extraordinary extent of his influence that E. Brunner, in 1924, was the
first man writing against Schleiermacher whose premises were really
different, really free of him (even if they were perhaps only relatively
free of him!). Until then every attack had shown such a close similarity
of content with his own writings that an effective antithesis had been
impossible. Nobody can say today whether we have really overcome
his influence, or whether we are still at heart children of his age, for all
the protest against him, which now, admittedly, has increased in
volume and is carried out according to basic principles.

If we ask ourselves how it was that Schleiermacher could become so
much our—and perhaps really still *our*—man of destiny, we are once
again faced by the mystery of the great man, which possibly consists in
the indissoluble unity of his timeless individual power on the one hand,
and on the other of the temporal, historical conditions into which he
was placed.—We have no occasion to adopt the style of that man
Lülmann, who in his work on 'Schleiermacher the church-father of the
nineteenth century' referred to Schleiermacher as a 'gigantic personality', and then, as if this were not enough, as a 'priest and prophet in
one person and a king in the realm of the mind' (p. 12). But it is
impossible to consider Schleiermacher thoroughly without being very
strongly impressed. Indeed one is more strongly impressed every time
one does consider him—by the wealth and magnitude of the tasks he
set himself, by the moral and intellectual equipment with which he
approached them, by the manly steadfastness with which he trod the path
he had once embarked upon right to the end as he had entered upon it,
unheedful of the favour or disfavour of each passing decade—and by
the artistry which he displayed, playfully, and endowing it by this very

playfulness with the ultimate gravity of all true art—an artistry he
showed in all he did, almost down to his last Sunday sermon. We have
to do with a hero, the like of which is but seldom bestowed upon
theology. Anyone who has never noticed anything of the splendour this
figure radiated and still does—I am almost tempted to say, who has
never succumbed to it—may honourably pass on to other and possibly
better ways, but let him never raise so much as a finger against Schleiermacher. Anyone who has never loved here, and is not in a position to
love again and again, may not hate here either. H. Scholz wrote with
perfect truth of the *Doctrine of Faith*: 'Schleiermacher did not succeed
in everything; but his achievement as a whole is so great, that the
only threat to it would be a corresponding counter-achievement, not a
cavilling criticism of detail.'[1] This counter-achievement, and indeed
the man who could not only criticize Schleiermacher but measure
himself against him, have not yet appeared. Let it be said in warning
that with every step which exceeds careful listening and the careful
asking of questions one may, not inevitably but very easily, make
oneself look ridiculous. That is the first thing there is to be said about
the secret of Schleiermacher's peculiar position: the drawing of attention to Schleiermacher himself, who indeed won for theology a little
more honour in the circle of the classic writers than the good Herder
had done before him.

The other thing we have to do in trying to assess Schleiermacher's
merits is to remember his time, with some outlines of which we have
become acquainted in the first part of this book. We may bear in mind
Lessing's advances in the direction of the concepts 'history' and
'experience', or the straits into which theology had been driven by
Kant's philosophy of religion, or the concern which Herder, stammering rather than saying anything of real importance, produced in
opposition to Kant. We may remember the discoveries in the mysterious wealth of the centre, on the basis of which Novalis, rather suddenly
as we saw, attempted to proclaim Christianity with a new voice,
together with much mathematics and love and poetry, or the greatness
and downfall of Hegel's philosophy. Positively or negatively we can
draw lines from everywhere leading to Schleiermacher; from every
point we can come to understand that for his century he was not one
among many others, with his theology and philosophy of religion, but
that it was possible for him to have the significance of the fulness of
time. I do not say it was inevitable that he should have this significance,

[1] *Christentum und Wissenschaft in Schleiermachers Glaubenslehre* (Christianity and Learning in Schleiermacher's Doctrine of Faith), 1911, p. 201.

but possible. Whether the century understood itself rightly in thinking it heard the liberating word from Schleiermacher, whether it might not have been possible to gain further insights of an entirely different kind from all the points which Schleiermacher had touched upon—that is a different question. With all the figures we have so far considered we have tried not only to look from them to Schleiermacher, but wherever possible to look from them to points beyond Schleiermacher, to look out for the possible answers to the questions raised there which Schleiermacher just did not provide. But one thing is certain, that this century could and did hear from Schleiermacher a liberating word, in some way an answering word. If it is not in itself certain that 'the man who has done justice to the best men of his age has lived for all time', it is beyond doubt that Schleiermacher, in the theological sphere, really did do justice to the best men of his age. And for that reason he did really live, for that age at all events, and still lives, in so far as we might perhaps still find ourselves within this age. He will in fact live for every age, if we construe his age, too, as an age of the Church. That is the other thing that must be said here.

We shall now attempt to look at some of the most important motifs, as regards content, which played their part throughout while Schleiermacher's life work came into being, and which must be borne in mind throughout the appraisal of it. We shall attempt both to see them and to see them in relation to each other.

I. The factor which is decisive in making a theology theology does not belong to the motifs whose presence can be asserted or denied in anyone's work. Even of Luther or Calvin it cannot simply be said that they represented and proclaimed the Christian faith, the Gospel. The Gospel in the full sense of the word, according to the *Confessio Augustana*, Article V, is represented and proclaimed *ubi et quando visum est Deo*, not at the point where, applying this or that yardstick, we feel we can affirm the Christian quality of a theology or philosophy—however superficially or thoroughly we are observing. The Christian quality of a theology does not belong to the motifs of a theology which can be vouched for, just because it is always the motif, with Calvin and Luther too, which is to be questioned. It is not on the same plane with the motifs of a theology that can truly be vouched for. I say all this in opposition to Brunner. He plays off 'the Christian faith' as a solid quantity against the other effective motifs in Schleiermacher's work in a way which, carried to its logical conclusion, would mean that the Christian quality would inevitably have to be denied to the theology of Luther and Calvin as well. Upon this point, which is admittedly a decisive one, one can only speak of indications. This also applies to Schleiermacher, with whom we are possibly more tempted to ask questions than with Luther and Calvin, and one must then, in order to be fair, not only treat the positive indications as seriously as the negative ones, but even more seriously, provided one wishes to treat with Schleiermacher also within the sphere of the Church and not elsewhere. However weighty the questions we wish to put we must reckon without reserve with the fact that Schleiermacher was a Christian theologian at all events as well. We must remain true to the indications which support this fact. I do not mean to say that we should consider that these indications go to prove it. Led by these indications we should, however, believe it of him, just as we are led by indications which are perhaps stronger, to believe it of Luther and Calvin. I should like to point out four things which should be considered here:

(a) Schleiermacher, who proved by distinguished achievements in the field of philosophy, and above all of philology, that he had a mind which offered him other great possibilities, chose theology in his youth as his life's profession. He allowed himself to be led still deeper into it, into Enlightenment theology at first, as a result of the dénouement of his relationship to his father and the Moravian brethren. He did not allow himself to be led out of it again either by all the intensive investigation he then began of the intellecual life of the time, which was indeed unfavourable to theology, or by an intensive study of the history of philosophy, of Plato especially. And we cannot overlook the fact that he felt himself responsible for the interest of the Christian Church in this very field of learning, in answering the question of truth which was directed also at Christian preaching. We must remember that he dedicated to this interest what was after all a considerable part, and quantitatively at all events the greatest part, of the strength and work and time he had it in his power to dedicate. We must not overlook these things even if we feel that he was not the best man to protect this interest.

(b) We cannot be mindful enough of the fact that Schleiermacher was not one of those theologians who are in the habit, under some pretext or other, of dissociating themselves from the most difficult and decisive theological situation, that in which the theologian, without security of any kind, must prove himself solely as a theologian. I refer to the situation of the man in the pulpit. Schleiermacher did not only not avoid this most exposed position, but actually sought it, throughout

his life, as the place for his 'own office'.[1] He sought it 'with enthusiasm',
as one of his friends avowed in 1804, almost with astonishment.[2] More
than one of the pupils of his who understood him best have testified,
and Dilthey, his biographer, has added his historical testimony to their
contemporary one, that it was precisely in his sermons that Schleiermacher's characteristic desires and achievements were made evident
at any rate in their liveliest and most impressive form. To be true, it
sounds terrible to us to hear Schleiermacher's pupil Sydow praise his
sermons because they presented 'the outlook of a highly-gifted and
thoroughly educated personality in the moments of its most noble
expression of life'.[3] But we must not be prevented by that and the even
more enraptured effusions of the dreadful Bettina von Arnim from
seeing what there is to see here. Whatever may be said of and against
the content of these famous sermons, one thing is certain. It is that in
accordance with the sound Reformed tradition from which he sprang,
Schleiermacher saw the *Kirchen-regiment* (Church polity), for which
theology provides the premise, as consisting essentially in the office of
the preacher, and that he did not only declare himself consistently for
this belief theoretically, but—equalling Luther and Calvin—in uninterrupted practice—without, be it said, achieving extraordinary
outward success. Those who know what preaching and academic work
involve should be truly impressed by the fact that together with all the
other things that claimed his attention, Schleiermacher managed to
perform this office year in and year out, almost every Sunday. Nobody
does that who does not feel impelled to do it, which at any rate is
remarkable. All the questionable things we learn from the *Addresses on
Religion* and *The Doctrine of Faith* about Schleiermacher's fundamental
idea of this office: namely that the decisive factor is a 'self-imparting'
of the preacher—cannot alter the fact that Schleiermacher performed
this office with a noteworthy loyalty, whether or not his idea of it was
correct.

(*c*) In academic theology, too, Schleiermacher did not make things
easy for himself. In the history of Protestant theology the nineteenth century brought with it the none too dignified sight of a general flight, of
those heads that were wisest, into the study of history. From the safe,
distant regions of the history of religion, the Church, dogma and the
mind the practice of theology is a gentle exercise, if one has the necessary equipment. Schleiermacher set a different example in this, at all

---

[1] *Schleiermacher's Leben in Briefen* (Schleiermacher's Life in Letters), Berlin, 1859-63,
II, 16.

[2] *Letters*, III, 376.   [3] *Predigten* (Sermons), VII, p. viii.

events. What decides whether theology is possible as a science is not whether theologians read sources, observe historical facts as such, and uncover the nature of historical relationships, but whether they can think dogmatically. Schleiermacher attempted to show that theology was possible as a science by writing his dogmatics—it was really his only large work, apart from his lectures. Questionably enough, he called it a *Doctrine of Faith* and conceived of it as a historical discipline. At bottom it is perhaps more apologetics than what, by pointing to its better part, could be understood as comprising a doctrine of faith. It raises a most urgent question whether with these very dogmatics theology was not consigned to a branch of the general science of the mind, so that the historicizing of theology was most thoroughly prepared for. But all this does not alter the fact that Schleiermacher at least attacked the problem of theology at the point where it must be attacked if it is to be attacked at all: with a basic consideration on what the Church may, can and should teach in its prevailing present, in connexion with the biblical norm upon the one side and with the Church's past upon the other. We must compare Schleiermacher's attitude with the thorough distraction with which Troeltsch was a theologian a hundred years later. We must set the doctrine of faith of the one beside that of the other, in order to discover which of them had his work completely at heart, and which of them had it definitely less at heart. Then we can grant Schleiermacher what even the most negative judgment upon the theological content of his work must grant: that he was deeply in earnest, not only concerning theology in general, but in the trouble he took to safeguard the specifically theological quality of theology.

(*d*) One thing at all events must be said of the content of Schleiermacher's theology: he did at least see the danger of a theology which is essentially apologetic in its approach—its impending metamorphosis into a philosophy; and if there was one thing he fought almost desperately against as an academic theologian, it was this danger. He saw also what the offence was wherewith he had to present philosophy, or at least the philosophy of his own time, if he wanted to be a theologian, and he did in fact dare to offend it in this way. It is the problem of Christology which is here at stake. It can be asked whether what he wanted to say about the relation of God and man could possibly be said also in the form of Christology. And it can, moreover, be asked whether Christology can possibly serve as the form for what Schleiermacher wanted to say. The Christology is the great disturbing element in Schleiermacher's doctrine of faith, not a very effective disturbance, perhaps, but a disturbance all the same. What he wanted to say might perhaps have been said better, more lucidly and more concisely, if he had been able to say it in the form of a circle with one centre, instead of as an ellipse with two foci. But Schleiermacher could not avoid this element of disturbance. He could not present his views in any other way; he had to present them as he did. Jesus of Nazareth fits desperately badly into this theology of the historical 'composite life' of humanity, a 'composite life' which is really after all fundamentally self-sufficient; in Schleiermacher's sermons, too, Jesus only plays the striking *rôle* he does because, one is tempted to think, he is simply there. He obviously gives Schleiermacher, the professor and preacher, a great deal of trouble! But nevertheless he is in fact there. And the professor and preacher goes to this trouble, swims ceaselessly against his own current, and wishes under all circumstances, and be it at the cost of certain artifices and sophistries, to be a Christocentric theologian. Whether he really is, who can say? Perhaps in fleeing from one kind of philosophic speculation he became all the more deeply embroiled in another. Perhaps after all he avoided the offence of a real Christology.

Perhaps after all he transformed *pistis* into *gnosis*. There is much to support this view. Schleiermacher, as we know, on his death-bed celebrated Holy Communion with his family: with water instead of wine, which the doctor had forbidden him to drink, and recalling that Christ, in blessing wine, had also blessed water. It can be asked whether the water in the wine was blessed in order that in the last resort it could take the place of wine, or whether it all ceases to be the Lord's Supper when the one is exchanged for the other in this way. But there can be no doubt of the fact that Schleiermacher wanted to celebrate the Holy Communion. He wanted in his Christology, whose content might perhaps be compared with the water, to proclaim Christ. And the fervour with which he did it, as a dogmatician and preacher, is also beyond all doubt in the minds of all who know him. If anyone was most deeply in earnest in this matter then it was Schleiermacher. That cannot of course be regarded as a last word upon the subject; the theological question of truth must remain open here as everywhere, even in the face of the greatest personal sincerity. But we must bear in mind the phenomenon of this personal sincerity, which cannot be overlooked, just as we must bear in mind the other indications. Ultimately we can only believe that Schleiermacher, too, was a Christian theologian; that, I repeat, is something he has in common with Luther and Calvin and (lest it be forgotten!), upon the lower plane, with all of us.

II. The quality of being a Christian is the motif in Schleiermacher's
theology for which there are indeed indications that it is present, but
which we cannot vouch for and the presence of which, therefore, with
him as with all other theologians, we can and must ultimately take upon
trust.

But the second motif which we shall now discuss is one that can
without doubt be vouched for. At the same time as he sought to be a
Christian theologian Schleiermacher also felt responsible—I should
like to understand and weigh this as earnestly as possible—for the
intellectual and moral foundations of the cultural world into which a
man was born at the end of the eighteenth century. He wanted in all
circumstances to be a modern man as well as a Christian theologian—
we must not seek to decide whether he was striving for the former aim
with the same or perhaps with even greater earnestness than that with
which he sought to be a Christian theologian, at any rate he did so
with similar earnestness. The fact that in his famous first work he
addressed himself to the educated among the despisers of religion is
something which would have been characteristic of his own position,
even if he had not at once, in the first lines of the book, emphasized
that 'one of those who have raised themselves above the common level
and are steeped in the wisdom of the century' here demanded their
attention. With him his participation in the cultural awareness of his
time, and indeed his participation in its deepest possible content, in
its strictest possible form and liveliest expression, was a deeply serious
concern which was not suspended for an instant. But it was not only
his passive participation as an educated person, but also his participation as one who himself educated, as one who helped sustain this
cultural awareness which is here in question. He affirmed its presence
in feeling that he had received a call to struggle, together with his best
contemporaries, for an ever-increasing depth in its content, for an
ever-greater strictness of its form, for an ever-greater liveliness of its
expression. He took part in the philosophy, science, politics, social life
and art of his time as if they were his own concern, as the man who
was responsible in all these fields, the man who was called to achieve
and to lead in the general achievement. He wants to be and is entirely
this man, the man moved by this concern. And he wants to be and is
this man also as a theologian—and indeed in the pulpit just as much,
and perhaps even more so, than in the professorial chair. It was
only in his time, the time which fulfilled and overcame, overcame
and fulfilled the Enlightenment, that this personal union became
possible: beyond Rousseau's outbreaks, beyond Lessing's struggles,

beyond Kant's critique, in the time which found it possible to take
Hegel's synthetic philosophy as its sign. Schleiermacher so wonderfully
fulfilled that time of his, in realizing the possibility of the theologian's
being at the same time entirely a modern man, with a good, and not
with a divided conscience. How, as a modern man, he was at once a
theologian with a good conscience, is something that will be discussed
later, under Point 3.

For the time being we shall continue to discuss the first thing: the
fact that Schleiermacher was a theologian did not hinder him in the
slightest from also wanting, seeking and effecting, all the things that,
wisely understood, were best in what the non-theological world of his
time was wanting, seeking and effecting. He did not do this retrospect-
ively, trotting behind the times, as theologians so often do, but in
advance of the time, as a born man of the age, and, further, as 'one
dedicated to the achievement of a better future'. To say that it 'did not
hinder him in the slightest' is to put it much too mildly. Precisely
because he was a theologian, and precisely upon the basis of his interpretation of Christianity he felt himself compelled to be a modern
man with all his heart, with all his feelings, and with all his strength.
He did not achieve any synthesis; he lived from a unity which had been
completed for him, he loved this modern man in himself and in the
others with all the strength of a love which is just as sincere as it is a
matter of course. And thus we find him at the turn of the century among
the Romantics, the Berlin hospital chaplain, who yet found it possible
also to come and go in the intellectually advanced circles of the capital
without acquiring that rather unfortunate flavour of the clever eighteenth-century abbé—as one who, honestly and as a matter of course,
belonged there. And thus we find him at Halle, devoting at least as
much attention to his translation of Plato and researches into this
philosopher, as to his studies of St Paul and the beginnings of his dogmatics, inspired to the writing of his *Weihnachtsfeier* (Celebration of
Christmas), as he himself attests, by having heard a flute concerto, of all
things. And so we find him at the height of his career, in the years
1809-34, in Berlin once again, at least as much at home in the Academy
of the Sciences as in his pulpit in the Church of the Holy Trinity.
Schleiermacher, so to speak, had no distance to go from the one concern to the other, from the one activity to the other. By birth and upbringing in its innermost sanctuary his theology is cultural theology:
in religion itself which is the true object of his theology, it is the exaltation of life in the most comprehensive sense, the exaltation, unfolding,
transfiguration, ennobling of the individual and social human life

which is at stake. Civilization as the triumph of the spirit over nature is the most peculiar work of Christianity, just as the quality of being a Christian is for its own part the crown of a thoroughly civilized consciousness. The kingdom of God, according to Schleiermacher, is utterly and unequivocally identical with the advance of civilization. The way in which Schleiermacher himself realized in his own person this idea of religion and Christianity, as researcher, teacher, author and preacher, and what he was as an intellectually and morally thoroughly educated person, what an *opus ingens* the *Doctrine of Faith* was, for instance, which was in its way of intellectual achievement possibly completely unique: all these things are in fact so far above the average that to anyone who does not know them one can only say that he should go and learn here what civilization might be. It is very necessary for theologians that they should have ever before them a clear and lively notion of it, in order to make sure that they do not talk nonsense if, unlike Schleiermacher, they seek to find the secret of Christianity at some point beyond all culture.

But what interests us here is the principle Schleiermacher proclaimed along these lines to others, to the Church, and to society. Above all, it is clear that as a theologian Schleiermacher is relentlessly in earnest down to the last line, in the material sense, too, about thinking and speaking in terms of the premises achieved by the philosophy and history and natural science of his day, and on no account in any others. In the case of the conflict between the Christian and the modern quality of his thoughts this can lead to concealments and ambiguities in his writings. There is in fact no lack of them in his *Doctrine of Faith* and in his sermons. But we can be assured that within this certain element of obscurity—whatever becomes of the Christian quality— the feeling of responsibility for modernity was at all events consistently maintained, either openly or secretly. Schleiermacher did not permit himself any real concessions from this sense of responsibility to any other claim. This participation of his in modern cultural awareness was not only an actual one and not only a defensive one. He did not only advocate modern civilization, but proclaimed and demanded it. In order to become acquainted with Schleiermacher we must not neglect to take as our guide the *Philosophical Ethics* and the *Christian Morality*, and above all the sermons as well as the well-known *Address* and the *Doctrine of Faith*. We must do this if only because in these better-known works it is not nearly so clear as in the former writings that Schleiermacher as a theologian wanted something quite definite from his hearers and readers, something in relation to which everything

else he propounded was only in the nature of a means to an end, as
the lever is to the load to be moved.

What did he want? He wanted to draw men into the movement of
education, the exaltation of life, which at bottom is the religious, the
Christian movement. I venture to assert that Schleiermacher's entire
philosophy of religion, and therefore his entire teaching of the nature
of religion and Christianity, the things we first think of when his name
is mentioned, was something secondary, auxiliary to the consolidation
of this true concern of his, the ethical one. The fact that, in academic
theory, he ranked theology below ethics, is but an expression of this
state of affairs. With Schleiermacher it is not a matter of doctrine, nor
of his particular doctrine, or a matter of his particular doctrine only
for the sake of the end to be achieved; with him it is a matter of life.
The life he means is not, as a superficial observer might suppose, a life
playing itself out in the inwardness of the soul, a life which takes
pleasure in itself, and is essentially passive, a mystical introspection.

This might well be the impression given by the famous introduction
to the *Doctrine of Faith*, and perhaps also by the *Addresses on Religion*.
But it must not be forgotten that in the *Addresses* and in the introduction
to the *Doctrine of Faith* it is a question of Schleiermacher's apologetic
representation of religion, and not actually of his objective one. And
we must not overlook the remarkable Paragraph 9 in the introduction
to the *Doctrine of Faith* where Christianity is suddenly described—
contrary to all the expectations the reader acquires from the previous
paragraphs—as a theological religion, one, that is, which is determined in the direction of activity, in which the consciousness of God is
entirely related to the sum-total of the states of activity in the idea of a
kingdom of God. After the apologetic beginning of the introduction
such a description of Christianity as the highest religion should have
been impossible: the feeling of complete dependence, which had been
the definition of religion in this beginning, could only have found its
fulfilment in the aesthetic, i.e. passive type of religion. It is by deviating
in this way that Schleiermacher returns to the understanding of Christianity he presented when he was concerned with it objectively, and not
apologetically.

We must therefore take the greatest exception to Brunner for completely failing, as the very title of his book *Die Mystik und das Wort*
(Mysticism and the Word) shows, to look in the place where Schleiermacher was truly at home, the place whence he exercised his decisive
influence. For just as Schleiermacher did not seek to identify Christianity with mysticism (although this was in fact what he did achieve as

an apologist) but with the movement of civilization, so the theology of the nineteenth century which took over from him is least characterized by its affinity to mysticism, and most definitely by its unqualified and direct affirmation of modern cultural consciousness. Schleiermacher's entire intellectual attitude, as we have it in his writings, and as it must personally have influenced his contemporaries, is, after all, so completely unlike that of a mystic. This can best be observed in Schleiermacher's doctrine of prayer, which no pious person with a true bent for mysticism could accept. For the moment of withdrawal into self, the gathering of internal forces, the severing of connexion with the outside world, the achievement of a pure stillness, which he describes as the one aspect in the process of prayer, and describes, be it said, with great power, is only the beginning of transition to a quite different activity. In seeking and finding God in prayer man reaches, as it were, the watershed between receptivity and self-activity. In reaching it he has already passed beyond it, and he also once again finds himself, now more than ever, upon the ground of his own free, creative activity. In prayer there takes place, as it were, a crystallization of religious life into a particular act of life, which is forthwith dispersed and dissolved again, at the climax of this process, in the communion with God, in which the general act of life can and should take place, and will take place again after this concentration. It is only for the sake of this second state that Schleiermacher describes the first one. He prays because he wants to work; he is a mystic because without mysticism there could not be any civilization. Thus, Schleiermacher does not seek this particular act of life as such, but its dispersal and dissolution for the benefit of the general act of life taking place in the communion with God. The prayer of this moment is the anticipation of the enhanced will for civilization of the next. It is the *homo religiosus* himself who is in the deepest sense involved in the process of education. He must pass through the mystical sanctuary—but he must really only pass through it, and quickly and without delay—just at the point where the true mystic likes to stop and likes best of all to stop finally, in the pure confrontation and oneness of God and the soul; it is here that Schleiermacher unmistakably urges us speedily onwards, from the act of introversion to the act of forming, from contemplation to construction.

If Schleiermacher considers the first step to be important, then he undeniably sees the second as being even more important and the first is important only for the sake of the second. It is here, in this tendency towards an ethical interpretation, that I am moreover tempted to see the true cause of the undogmatic character, using the word in its usual

sense, and indeed the anti-dogmatic, anti-intellectualizing, anti-
doctrinal character of Schleiermacher's theology. What strikes us in a
study of Schleiermacher's sermons is the fact that whenever he engages
in true polemics these are always directed against the same three
things: against all over-assessment of the importance of religious
doctrine and of the religious word altogether, against every kind of
particular religious excitement, and against the tendency associated
with this, to religious sectarianism of individuals or whole groups.
This must not only and not ultimately be understood as arising out of
Schleiermacher's concept of religion, which does, it is true, coincide
with that of mystical theology, but definitely as the result of the
teleological, activistic intention of his theology, which affirms civilization. Schleiermacher's favourite interpretation of biblical miracle was
that it was the prophecy of the astonishing victory of spirit over the
natural world, which was being fulfilled more and more in human
history, and especially in the present, and was thus, far from being
important in itself or in need of repetition, the incitement for us to
devote our energies to the achievement of this victory.

In this connexion Schleiermacher first and above all celebrated the
state as the guardian of order and of peace. Although throughout his
life he supported the idea that the Church should be independent of
the state this did not mean at all that he thought that the Church
particularly, as the free community of those moved by religious feeling,
should not affirm, tackle and further in the most ideal sense those
desires which had already found their powerful embodiment in the
modern state. Schleiermacher no less than Hegel admired and loved
the modern Prussianism, and cherished and proclaimed the myth of
Sans Souci. But his whole frame of mind in his relation to the state, was
incomparably more liberal than Hegel's, and the idea of progress he
proclaimed, in this as in everything, was much more in the nature of
an ethical demand than it was with Hegel, although with Schleiermacher too it was at the same time borne up by the glorification of a
victorious historical destiny. Together with Fichte, Arndt, Scharnhorst
and others Schleiermacher, in the years 1806-13, as is well known,
became through his sermons—in a way quite different from that of
Goethe and Hegel—one of the educators of the generation which
sustained the wars of freedom, and some of the unpleasantness this
generation had to face in the time of the Students' Association movement affected him also.

The second ethical point that Schleiermacher constantly stressed in
his sermons concerned the civil *profession* in the exercise of which the

Christian is called to prove himself as such. Here Schleiermacher, after his own fashion, was taking up a motif of the Lutheran Reformation. Of this motif it has often been said quite wrongly that it was first given renewed prominence by Albrecht Ritschl. And it did not matter to Schleiermacher to turn the clearest New Testament texts into their opposites when he wanted to state this motif once more.

Schleiermacher's third sphere of interest embraces the problems of marriage and family life, to which, even as early as in his Romantic period, he devoted a penetrating attention, and to which in 1818 he dedicated his famous Household Sermons, which we may, I think, be justified in taking as a perfect example of what Schleiermacher meant by the exalting, ennobling and transfiguring of human life.

Fourthly, there is the social problem, mentioned here with special emphasis because there is scarcely any mention of it in the literature on Schleiermacher. This must have been an object of his strong concern, expecially in his last years, in connexion with the events of the July revolution. Within the frame of an outlook which today would probably be described as that of Social Liberalism he appealed very definitely and courageously to the sense of responsibility of the upper classes towards those placed at a material disadvantage by the advance of civilization. He expressed his belief in economic equality, in social insurance, and in social services (as a right, and not as a benefit!). He demanded a shortening of the hours of work for the lower classes. He gave numerous warnings of the possible dangerous consequences of a further uncorrected social development.

These are things which the great revivalist preachers of his time did not say, and did not even see. We need not mention the complacency with which the Church in general confronted the development which had its origin in these things! Whether his social ideas would have been adequate for the then incipient great conflict between the giants Capital and Labour is another question. But it is in order for us to ask whether one or two things might not perhaps have turned out differently if the educated German public, and if, for example, Schleiermacher's candidate for confirmation, Otto von Bismarck, had really heard and taken to heart what Schleiermacher evidently wished to say upon this subject.

So much, then, about Schleiermacher's positive concerns, the things that can definitely be verified, and which at all events we must see to understand his theology.

III. Apologetics is an attempt to show by means of thought and speech that the determining principles of philosophy and of historical

and natural research at some given point in time certainly do not preclude, even if they do not directly require, the tenets of theology,
which are founded upon revelation and upon faith respectively. A bold
apologetics proves to a particular generation the intellectual necessity
of the theological principles taken from the Bible or from church dogma
or from both; a more cautious apologetics proves at least their intellectual possibility. About the extent and content of these principles
opinions may of course vary among the apologists themselves, and
within the same period of time.

We found that Schleiermacher wanted to be a Christian theologian,
and we found that he wanted, come what may, to be a thinking man
of his time. These two facts inevitably led to his third concern for
apologetics. He formulated the apologetic question, in a famous passage
in his open letter to Lücke,[1] as follows: 'Shall the knot of history be
thus loosed: Christianity with barbarism and learning with unbelief?'
It is clear that his only answer to this question can be, No. His interest
in both Christianity and learning was so great that he even considered
the appeal to the origins of the Protestant Church suitable material to
help underline this No, and thus continues, several pages later: 'If the
Reformation, from whose first beginnings our Church took its life, has
not the aim of establishing an eternal covenant between the living faith
and scientific research, which is free to explore upon all sides and works
for itself independently, so that faith does not hinder research, and
research does not preclude faith: if it has not this aim then it is not
adequate for the needs of our age and we require another Reformation,
no matter how, and as a result of what struggles it may develop. I am,
however, firmly convinced that the basis for this covenant was already
laid in those days, and that all that is needed is to bring about a more
definite awareness on our part of that task in order to be able to
achieve it.'[2]

The intention of achieving this task, and thus fulfilling the contract
in question, is certainly the first clear motif meeting the reader who
traditionally begins with the *Addresses on Religion*, and perhaps also
attempts to work his way into the *Doctrine of Faith* by way of studying
its great introduction. I think I have shown that this intention must
not be understood as a primary motif; and even less primary are the
objective views about the understanding of Christianity which we shall
come to speak of later, which have of necessity emerged from this
secondary theological intention of Schleiermacher's. But let us not be
mistaken: anyone convinced, as Schleiermacher was, that he must, as a

---

[1] Ed. Mulert, 1908, p. 37.   [2] Mul., 40.

Christian theologian, affirm and proclaim the insights and ethos of modern man, must similarly have been convinced that he could and should, as a modern man, be a Christian theologian. It was doubtless only in his maturity, in the two works on ethics and in the sermons, particularly those of his old age, that what he primarily and truly wanted achieved clear predominance. It is none the less understandable, however, that not only in the theological work of his youth, in which he first had to prepare the way for what he really wanted, but also in the most significant part of his *summa theologica*—and such, in fact, is the introduction—he was bound to be concerned with stating this second conviction, that is, with performing the apologetic task.

If we first enquire quite generally into the standpoint which Schleiermacher as an apologist of religion and Christianity sought to take up and did take up, then the first thing we find is certainly that the approach to this task meant for him a certain relaxation of, and indeed detachment from, the essential theological task of interpreting and proclaiming Christianity—however, in general, he might conceive of and execute this task. He declared quite plainly already in the first section of the first paragraph of the *Doctrine of Faith* 'that all the propositions which will occur here cannot be in themselves also dogmatic ones'. The standpoint of the Schleiermacher who later, from Paragraph 32 onwards, was to present the Christian doctrine of faith, and himself represent the Christian faith, is different from that of the Schleiermacher who in Paragraphs 1-31 is explaining what the Christian faith and the teaching of the Christian faith can and should be about.

Paragraphs 1-31 of the *Doctrine of Faith* are written in precisely the same sense as the theological work of his youth, the *Address on Religion*. But what does '*on* religion' mean? It need not mean at all that they are not also talks *out of* religion, but this in fact, according to their actual basic intention, is precisely what they are not. While still a young man, Schleiermacher wanted to show the educated among the despisers of religion that by virtue of their education they are enabled and summoned to understand the nature of religion better than it has been understood previously; and further that it is worthwhile taking note of the nature of religion. Further, that with religion it is a question of the realization of an original, universal and necessary disposition of mankind as such. Further, that of the forms of religion the Christian religion is relatively the highest, the most dignified and the purest. Further, that the intellectual situation of the time, particularly in Germany, is especially favourable to the recognition of these statements and thus to a rebirth of religion among them, the educated. In brief, the speaker

on religion seeks an admission from the educated people to whom he is
speaking that religion in general and the Christian religion in particular is the highest value in life, something which is not only possible,
but real and necessary beside science, art, the Fatherland, etc., something which is already existing in latent form, and only requiring their
correct recognition; and that civilization without religion, without
the Christian religion, is not a complete civilization.

The standpoint from which Schleiermacher could speak in these
terms, and could speak of the nature and value of religion, is evidently
the following. Schleiermacher was not now concerned, directly at
least, with the thing itself, but with the phenomenon of religion as seen
from the outside, and as something which is to be interpreted, understood, perhaps misunderstood, and perhaps better understood from the
outside. Just as he was about to proclaim Christianity he realized to his
sorrow that his fellow men of the day were not listening at all, or at
best shaking their heads over what he had to say. So he left the text he
has already turned to in the Bible to take care of itself for a moment,
and came down from the pulpit again to debate first of all with his
congregation which for this particular moment transformed itself into
an audience. He did this in order to make plausible in advance, apart
from what he was going to say later, the possibility and necessity of
saying it; in order to convince them that religion, Christianity and the
Church were not at all the insignificant or absurd things they considered them to be, and that they should, if they did but understand
themselves aright, give this phenomenon a joyous welcome.

The possibility of taking up this second standpoint, different from
that of the proclaimer of Christianity, evidently had a certain prerequisite. Anyone who seeks to negotiate between faith and a cultural
awareness which at first is assumed to be unbelieving, and then bring
about a lasting covenant between them must, at all events while he is
doing this, take up a position which is in principle beyond that of
both parties, a superior position, from which he can understand both
parties and be the just advocate of both. He must, even if he himself belongs to one side, at least carry a white flag in his hand when
approaching the other for a parley; he cannot at that moment be
engaged as a combatant. To put it unmetaphorically: as long as he is
an apologist the theologian must renounce his theological function.
In so far as the apologist approaches the educated among the despisers
of religion from the standpoint of theology he must not desire to speak
only from faith and with only the faith of his hearers in view. He must
present himself to them in a part which is provided for in their

categories, which really occurs or can occur there.—To judge from Schleiermacher's early work, the part which the apologist, the speaker on religion, must play is that of the virtuoso in religion. Faced by the Romantics, Fichte, Schelling and the others, Schleiermacher would have felt incapable of negotiating simply as a theologian, as a preacher. But why should the *religious virtuoso* not be possible within their field of vision as well, together with the virtuosi of philosophy, of art, of morality? Why should he not exist within the general frame of virtuosity in life? Can he base his claim upon the Church, his ecclesiastical office, his ministry, the Bible, dogma? No. But can he refer to a special kind of virtuosity which had previously not been well known or recognized as such, can he refer to 'the inner irresistible necessity of my nature'? Can he base his claim upon the notion of a 'mediator', indispensable at first, in matters affecting a particular newly-interpreted universal concern of mankind, upon the possibility of an ideally understood priesthood, a religious heroism? Why not? From this position the educated man could and had to and did allow himself to be spoken to.

In his later works Schleiermacher made legitimate the apologist as the confidant also of the opposite side, in an objective way—not so much replacing his former merely personal legitimization as supporting and establishing it. It is true that he did not show the reality of theology, but he did show its possibility and necessity: the space for theology in a comprehensive system of learning. He supported true theology by a philosophical theology, which was meant to demonstrate that the existence of Churches—not the Christian Church in particular, nor any particular Church—was 'an element necessary to the development of the human mind', and not by any means an 'aberration'.[1] And he saw this philosophical theology as founded for its own part in a philosophy of religion which in its turn can be shown to be an integrant feature of ethics—ethics as the science of the principles of history as opposed to those of nature. That is why the introduction to the *Doctrine of Faith*, as Schleiermacher expressly states, proceeded by means of arguments taken first from ethics, secondly from the philosophy of religion and thirdly from apologetics as a branch of what Schleiermacher called philosophical theology. Set in this relationship concretely Christian theology becomes possible as the positive science of this particular Church and its faith. This entire construction, however, evidently implies no more than that which Schleiermacher had already

---

[1] *Kurze Darstellung des theol. Studiums* (Short Account of the Study of Theology), para. 22.

said in the *Addresses on Religion* about the legitimation of the theologian and his playing the part of the apologist respectively: that together with other virtuosi there are also religious virtuosi who may, like the others, in principle justly allow themselves to be seen and heard, according to the judgment also of people who do not profess this virtuosity. The preaching of the Church is no more an aberration— one might also say, an offence—than any other human possibility which can be accounted for in its nature and value from the point of view of ethics as the science of the principles of history.

This white flag, which the theologian must carry as an apologist, means of course for the theologian himself that in so far as he is an apologist he must, as Schleiermacher once more expressly states, take his point of departure (standpoint) above Christianity (in the logical sense of the word) in the general concept of the community of pious people or believers.[1] As an apologist he is not a Christian theologian but a moral philosopher and philosopher of religion. He suspends to that extent his attitude to Christianity, and his judgment of the truth or even absoluteness of the Christian revelation. Together with the other educated people he looks upon Christianity as being on the same level as the other 'pious communities', as being subject to the points of view from which 'pious communities' are to be regarded here. He therefore regards the Christian Church too as 'a community which arises only as a result of free human actions, and can only continue to exist by the same means'.[2] The time will come for him to return completely to his subject and speak as a Christian theologian. Then he will no longer speak *on* religion, but *ex officio out of* religion. Then the nature and value of religion and Christianity in its own inner logic and necessity will no longer interest him. That will be the time for all the things there are still to be said about the concept of the Church and which have to be said also in a completely different way. As an apologist he must say the other things, he must regard the Church as a pious community which has arisen and lives from human freedom, and has to demonstrate its possibility and necessity as such a community.

But what now, according to Schleiermacher, is the meaning of the apologetic act that is to be carried out from this place? What kind of lasting contract is to be concluded from it? At the beginning we distinguished a bolder and a more cautious approach to the apologetic task. The question about which of these two types Schleiermacher's apologetics belongs to cannot be definitely answered.

---

[1] *Short Account*, para. 33; *Doctrine of Faith*, 1st ed., para. 6.
[2] *Doctrine of Faith*, 2nd ed., para. 2. 2.

At first it might seem as if with Schleiermacher it could only be a question of the second, the more cautious kind of apologetics, which seeks to show only the intellectual possibility of the principles of Christianity. In the *Open Letter* to Lücke[1] Schleiermacher says that his aim in writing the *Doctrine of Faith* was to show 'that every dogma truly representing an element of our Christian awareness can also be formulated in such a way that it leaves us uninvolved with science'. In fact Schleiermacher's labours in apologetics can largely be understood along the following lines. He is as a modern man and therefore as a thinker and therefore as a moral philosopher and therefore as a philosopher of religion and therefore as a philosophical theologian and therefore as an apologist and therefore finally as a dogmatist determined on no account to interpret Christianity in such a way that his interpreted statements can come into conflict with the methods and principles of the philosophy and the historical and scientific research of his time.

Schleiermacher's activity as a 'cautious' apologist, and the proof that he was such an apologist consists chiefly in the fact that he himself wrote his dogmatics in such a way that even to someone not so well acquainted with the subject it must be self-evident as something at all events thinkable. The peculiar aesthetic language of the *Addresses* should already be understood as apologetics in this sense. With this language, more musical than argumentative as Schleiermacher himself once said, he adapted himself to the language which the people he was addressing, chiefly the Romantics, happened to love and which they spoke themselves. The very form of the *Doctrine of Faith*, which cannot be sufficiently admired, is also apologetic in this sense. Its strict, artistically ingenious system and the rigid discipline and high intellectual quality of this work are doubtless in themselves meant to form an argument, to justify and defend the content of the work, to speak and testify for it. The feature which is, however, above all distinctly apologetic in this sense is the objective form in which the content of religion and later of the Christian faith is presented, both here and in the *Addresses*. Here the theologian is not only concerned with his subject-matter but as a mediator also with his readers. Indeed he is concerned with readers of a certain intellectual make-up and tendency which is accepted from the beginning by the theologian *qua* apologist. This is revealed at every turn by the fact that this representation of Christianity systematically removes, or is at all events intended to remove (of course he cannot judge in advance the effect of this) each and every stumbling-block which their own intellectual make-up and tendency might

[1] Mul., 40.

prepare for them in such a representation. Christianity is interpreted in such a way that it acquires room by this way of interpretation, that it acquires room in the kind of thinking which is assumed to be authoritative by Schleiermacher's contemporaries, without causing any friction. Whether his readers move into this cleared space, whether they are able and willing to consider and accept this unexceptionable representation of Christianity as part of their own thought; that is of course a question that cannot be answered. But Christianity is prepared for them in such a way that in the author's eyes there no longer exists any obstacle in principle, against the occupation of this space. There must now be other reasons, reasons which are not essential from the standpoint of the cultural awareness as such, which guide them, if they fail to do this.

And now the significance of the fact that the apologist as apologist has to take as his point of departure a point above Christianity becomes clear. It certainly does not mean in itself that for once in a way the apologist has to think like a heathen or atheist in order to convince heathens or atheists of the excellence of Christianity. *De facto*, of course, it can mean this. It should, however, only mean—but this, of course, is in fact meaning quite a lot—that the apologist is a complete master of Christianity, in a position, as it were, to look into it from above just as much as modern cultural awareness is; able to elicit its nature and assess its value. Without having to worry about prejudicing the content of Christianity itself he is in a position to take a pencil to the stock of doctrine he has inherited and boldly 'erase and alter what might in untimely fashion (!) oppress the apparatus of dogma and hamper the living faith in its attempt to walk hand in hand with onward-marching science'.[1] 'Schleiermacher attacked the task of apologetics in the confidence that he knew what Christianity was, and could not be brought to depart from this basic feeling by any church doctrine, no matter how well established the latter was.'[2] It is not right to accuse Schleiermacher of consciously betraying Christianity to science, to the cultural outlook of his time, by always saying when there was a conflict between the two, that civilization was right and traditional Christianity wrong. The only alternative, however, if this accusation is to be avoided—and we must avoid it—is to say that as an apologist of Christianity Schleiermacher really played upon it as a virtuoso plays upon his fiddle: he played the notes and airs which, if they did not cause his hearers to rejoice, could at least be acceptable to them. Schleiermacher did not speak as a responsible servant of Christianity but, like a true virtuoso, as a free master of it.

[1] Scholz, p. 122.   [2] Ibid., p. 121.

Thus the great possibility which has arisen in classic form in Schleiermacher the apologist is that the anxious care to conserve, the advocacy of Christianity at all costs, which had still characterized the apologetics even of the Enlightenment period, can be abandoned. Christianity can be mastered at least in so far as, using the insight we have into its nature and value, we can treat, control and rule the Bible and dogma with unrestricted freedom. It is possible to be a Christian and theologian as one is a philosopher or artist: that is, one can also approach the material of theology in a creative and systematic way, illuminating it in principle, penetrating and forming it out of one's very own power. Like the other secrets of life this secret too can be interpreted. The interpreter need not take into account the fact that it might perhaps be seeking to interpret itself and that the Bible and dogma might perhaps be binding pointers for the understanding of this self-interpretation. And so, creatively forming and interpreting in this manner, and therefore knowing in advance just as much about Christianity as Christianity itself, it is indeed possible to be a Christian and a theologian also as a modern man.

This apologetics is, so to speak, immanent and negative, and in practice essentially turns its point against the Christian tradition itself, and would in fact be of the type of cautious apologetics. But after all it represents only one side of the picture which we can see here. The other appears already in the *Addresses* and is still present in the *Doctrine of Faith*. It is represented by an admittedly strictly limited approach towards a positive proof, an approach towards showing the intellectual necessity of the principles of Christianity. An approach in that direction, I say, and more it is not permissible to say without saying something quite wrong and completely out of keeping with Schleiermacher.

Schleiermacher did not give theology or the principles of Christianity a speculative basis. He did not, that is, conceive of them and treat them as principles to be derived necessarily from the idea of human knowledge. This, as expressed in a much-admired review which he wrote as early as 1803, was what separated him most decisively from Schelling, not to mention Hegel. Schleiermacher, it is true, also had his system of pure knowledge (as presented in his philosophical ethics and in his dialectics), but in this system knowledge and being are set in opposition in such a way that they are held together objectively only by the idea of God, and subjectively only by the feeling correlative to this idea, accompanying all knowledge and action; or, rather, by the dialectician's knowledge of this correlation. In so far as this synthesis of God and feeling as a bracket beyond the antithesis of knowledge and being exists for Schleiermacher, he too is a philosopher of identity, approximating to Schelling's doctrine of the point of identity as the point at which the ideal and the real are seen to be as one, and approximating also to Hegel's philosophy of the mind as the synthesis of logic and natural philosophy. But Schleiermacher did not, like Schelling, consider possible as a proof of Christianity a speculative theology as the science of the point of identity, nor did he, like Hegel, consider a philosophy of religion, replacing theology, as the penultimate stage at least in the dialectic of absolute mind, possible as such a proof. 'I shall never be able to accept the idea that my belief in Christ stems from knowledge or philosophy, whichever philosophy it might be.'[1]

We ascertained while discussing Hegel that this rejection of speculation on Schleiermacher's part also has something to do with the fact that he was not very interested in the truth of theological tenets as such. For he was in the first place interested in the active life of religion, and then in feeling as the true seat of this life, and only thirdly in the tenets by means of which this life—always in fundamentally imperfect form—expresses itself. Schleiermacher quenched his intellectual thirst for truth as a philosopher in fields remote from his theological statements. But this alone is not enough to explain his lack of interest in speculative theology. There is something in him which protests in favour of the peculiar and underivable nature of these very tenets, against the omnipotence of deduction in the thinking of his contemporaries just mentioned, against the elimination of 'high arbitrariness', which might possibly, from one side, at any rate, be the key to Christianity, as he expressed it in his argument against Schelling.[2] And he fears that a theology which is capable of being understood and based upon philosophical terms would lead to the introduction of the un-Christian opposition of an esoteric and an exoteric teaching, of a *gnosis* ranked higher than *pistis*, a 'hierarchy of speculation'.[3] He wished the assertions of the *Doctrine of Faith*—not of the introduction, of course, but of the part which contained the proper representation— to be understood as 'quite simply and honestly solely empirical' (p. 21). The representation itself was meant simultaneously to be the vindication of the *Doctrine of Faith*, 'for everything in it can only be vindicated by being represented as a correct statement of Christian self-awareness' (p. 56). But all the same, this empiricism is that of a science, not rough and unscientific. If it were otherwise, Schleiermacher explains, he would personally, if faced with the choice, decide for a speculative

---

[1] *Open letter to Lücke*, Mul., 38f.   [2] *Letters*, IV, 586.
[3] *Open Letter to Lücke*, Mul., 39f.

vindication of religion, although with the gravest misgivings (p. 39). But Schleiermacher is not faced by this choice. His representation of the Christian faith to be true, does not rest upon the basis of a highest knowledge of God, whose more or less adequate expression it claimed to be. To this extent his apologetics are not of the bolder type, seeking to give positive proof.

Schleiermacher's representation of faith certainly rests, however, upon the basis of a highest knowledge of human feeling or immediate self-awareness in its correlation to God, upon the basis of a highest knowledge of the nature and value of faith and the diversity of ways of believing altogether. It is not the Christian religion, but certainly the type to which this phenomenon belongs, religion as a necessary manifestation of human intellectual life, which is for Schleiermacher an object of speculative knowledge of an *a priori* kind. And this knowledge does not only provide him with a frame within which to establish the nature of the Christian religion as empirically understood, but also with a yardstick by which its value can be measured. To that extent he is in a position to discover and present—and he did this in the *Addresses* just as much as in the Introduction to the *Doctrine of Faith*—not only the necessity of religion, in terms of the science of mind, as completely determined human self-awareness, but also the superiority, relatively at least, of Christianity, as regards its nature and value, when compared with the other religions. Without that highest unity of intuition and feeling, as Schleiermacher said in the *Addresses*, or without the feeling of utter dependence, as he puts it in the *Doctrine of Faith*, cultural awareness would be incomplete, a headless torso. Of the various historical forms this feeling has taken it is the Christian one, the Christian faith, which is the highest and most perfect. It is not the absolute form, the one which is alone true, but it is indeed the highest and most perfect among many which are relatively true as well. In so far as Schleiermacher considers he can show this without fear of objection, to the extent that, as was previously shown, he thinks he can base his dogmatics upon philosophical theology, philosophical theology upon a philosophy of religion, and the philosophy of religion upon ethics as the universal science of mind, he also not directly, but certainly in an indirect way proves the intellectual necessity of the tenets of Christianity. It is a question of the intellectual necessity which is possible within the framework of his system, which is essentially more restrained than those of Schelling and Hegel. It is a question of a relative determined, indirect intellectual necessity of thought to accord with his more cautious conception of speculative identity. The

latter, however, is quite definitely in question and to this extent
Schleiermacher in fact has as his chief support cautious and negative
apologetics but also, without entrusting too much of his weight to them,
toys with the bolder, positive kind. And it is not impossible to see this
relationship as reversed, with positive apologetics as the main prop. For
it must certainly be said that it is only by having as his background the
positive vindication of the doctrine of faith by means of the science of
mind that Schleiermacher is able to form this doctrine of faith into an
apologetics in the way we have previously described: by means of this
bold virtuoso playing on the instrument of Christianity, by this complete freedom in the handling of the store of Christian tradition, and
by the brilliance of the system he applied to it. If Schleiermacher did
not descend from this height 'above Christianity', how should he be
able to appear as a virtuoso and master of Christianity? Thus the
best way of understanding the significance of this third, this apologetic,
motif in his theology, is to imagine him pacing—to continue with the
image of the two props—alternately supported by one of them and
using the other in order to take a step forward. And nobody can deny
that this particular traveller did in fact advance most vigorously
upon his way, after his fashion.

IV. Before proceeding to consider the two motifs in the content of
Schleiermacher's theology which were almost bound to arise from the
attitude he takes in his apologetics, I should like to call attention once
again to yet another of its formal features, which will illuminate the
necessity of the two motifs of the content from yet another angle. The
two motifs of the content, which we shall assess in conclusion, are
experience and history. It is between these two poles that Schleiermacher's interpretation of Christianity takes its course, because these
two poles are also the secret of his general concept of religion; because,
as an apologetic interpretation of Christianity, it cannot take any other
course but one lying between two poles. But why must the secret of his
general concept of religion be that of these two poles in particular?
Why must his philosophy of religion and ethics present him with this
particular polarity, and why must there be this polarity at all?

Here we must reflect that Schleiermacher, the Christian apologist,
was not only one educated and educating in his time, but that his
origins in this respect lay first with the Moravian brethren and secondly
with the Romantic school. Both these facts mean that for Schleiermacher being educated and educating must definitely mean *mediation*
—mediation, uniting vision, synthesis, and peace not only between this

and that opposite, but ultimately between all, even between the most pronounced opposites. Schleiermacher sprang from the Moravian brethren, and was certainly correct in once saying of himself that all his life he had been a 'Moravian of a higher order', to the extent that he had become familiar there with a Christian standpoint which was in principle synthetic, with a Christianity beyond the historical differentiations of Christianity, with the bold idea of a union before union comprising the various confessions merely as various choirs or divisions of the one Church of Christ—and at the same time with the bold idea of a Christianity in which the Saviour and the individual soul as well as the Saviour and the Christian communion were brought, in a correlation quite definitely compared to a form of play, into a synoptic, mediated, polar relationship. And Schleiermacher, passing briefly through the Enlightenment, went from the Moravian brethren to Romanticism. We have already seen what a part the principle of the centre, which was announced already in Herder, played with Novalis. It was the moving principle, in method, with Hölderlin too, and with Schelling and Hegel. Without this principle there would have been no speculative idealism, and no philosophy of identity. Schleiermacher applied it not in Hegel's way, but in his own way, to theology. In doing so he could call to witness the procedure of the Moravian brethren. What he made of it, however, subject as he was to the powerful stimulus of Romantic philosophy, was not a Moravianism merely of a higher, but of the highest order.

It is probably no mere coincidence that precisely in the last years of his life, when he was preparing to publish his *Dialectics*, there was one notion and concern which dominated every other in Schleiermacher's sermons. It can be characterized by the word 'peace'. If he is zealous as a preacher—we have already considered this from another angle— then he is zealous in attacking everything which can divide the Church, or can set the individual hearer at loggerheads with himself, because it calls to mind the idea of irreconcilable contradictions. There are no such irreconcilable contradictions and therefore there cannot and may not be any unpeaceful state either in general or in particular, outwardly or inwardly. Schleiermacher dealt with the most diverse moral and religious themes from the point of view that the truth lies in the middle, in reconciliation, in the point of no distinction, in the 'simplicity of the mind of Jesus', in 'common feeling', in the 'equalizing common note' between the supposed opposites, and that we must see the relative nature of the opposites, the fact that their quality as opposites is only provisional and capable of being annulled. That is why Schleiermacher does not like the Old Testament—because he saw in the notion of the Law which he thought prevailed there the division between heaven and earth, between grace and sin, which is removed in Christ, and may not be renewed again. That is why he has little liking for the figure of John the Baptist in the New Testament either. 'The one word of peace does in fact contain everything', he once declaimed.[1] The divine Spirit or communion with God or the kingdom of God is, according to his express declaration, the One from which the two proceeded, and into which they must again be converted.

This helps us to understand why Schleiermacher claimed so emphatically that his *Doctrine of Faith* was the first dogmatics at all events of the Prussian *Union*, and why the union between the Reformed Churches and the Lutherans was to him something which was indeed decisively necessary. And his further strongly marked aim over and above this union was the uniting of the orthodox-pietist and rationalist parties, which were coming into ever-sharper conflict in the twenties, within the United Evangelical Church. It was as a result of this tendency that the *Doctrine of Faith* did not take another form which, according to Schleiermacher's explanation, it might have taken,[2] and which might have decisively increased its influence and usefulness to the Church. The *Doctrine of Faith* is divided, as we know, into a first part, consisting of the generally religious premises (the Christian ones included, it is true) and a second specifically Christian (Christological-soteriological) part. Schleiermacher pondered the idea of reversing this relationship, of moving the first part, which at least approximated to a natural theology, and upon which the eye of the reader must first alight, to the end, as a kind of epilogue, as a definite *a posteriori*. He did not do this partly in order not to lend his support to the 'forcing out from our church membership' of those worthy men who are called rationalists, and he did not want to do this 'for natural fear that the little boat in which we are all sailing might capsize'.[3] He thought that he was thereby serving peace and by doing this was also serving the Church and God himself.

What Schleiermacher calls peace in his sermons and in church politics, however, coincides in content with the ultimate and highest principle, both in form and in content, of his philosophic teaching. This teaching is characterized by a method of division and unification of all principles. He carries it through by dealing with subject and object, knowledge and being, reason and nature, ethics and physics, speculative and empirical knowledge, and everywhere the transitions,

[1] *Sermons*, III, 468.　　[2] *Open Letter to Lücke*, Mul., 46.　　[3] Ibid., 44.

in contrast to those of Hegel's dialectic, are flowing from the one opposite to the other, and are quantitative. The truth—once again in contrast to Hegel—is not to be found in some definable third thing, but in the indefinable centre between the first and the second, at the point where peace reigns, a point to which from all sides only approximations are possible. In feeling and—for figurative thought and speech, which is of course inadequate—out of feeling, peace exists also between the ultimate and highest contradiction, that between the infinite and therefore identical being and knowledge of God and our finite and therefore divided, non-identical being and knowledge. World-wisdom and world do not, it is true, coincide in an absolute knowledge, as they do with Hegel, but Schleiermacher does in fact have his dialectic, as knowledge of a unity which can be felt, i.e. of the presence of God felt in human awareness. Seen from this aspect the principle of the centre is at once identical with the strongest and most decisive lever of Schleiermacher's apologetics. The Moravian and Romantic was bound to have recourse to this kind of apologetics and to no other!

From here we can also gain an insight into the essential content of the two *loci classici* in Schleiermacher's theological doctrine of principles: the second *Address* on religion and Paragraphs 3 and 4 of the *Doctrine of Faith*. In the second *Address* religion is described as the moment of the unity of intuition and feeling, which takes place beyond all thought and action. Intuition is the receptive, and feeling the spontaneous side of the act of awareness, in which man in his finite quality comes to partake, as Schleiermacher put it at this time, of the infinite quality of the universe. Intuition and feeling is the opposition of that which affects religiously, and the state of being affected religiously. The overcoming of this opposition, the One in the middle of these two, is the esential nature of religion. 'Intuition without feeling is nothing . . . feeling without intuition is likewise nothing: both are only anything if and because they are originally one and undivided.'[1] Paragraphs 3 and 4 of the *Doctrine of Faith* state, however, that: 'The piety which is the basis of all church communions (and which is therefore common to them all, and underlies all expressions of piety, no matter how diverse these may be) is, looked at purely in itself, neither a piece of knowledge nor an action, but a determination of feeling or of immediate self-awareness. It is that determination by virtue of which man is aware of his own self as utterly dependent or—what comes to the same thing—as in connexion with God.'

What Schleiermacher expressed in the *Address* by means of the dual

[1] *Addresses*, pp. 72f.

concept of intuition and feeling he characterizes here by means of the
concept of feeling, which has now been widened and comprises the
moment of intuition, in which that which affects, that which explains
the origin of man's utter dependence is already posited. Because
feeling in itself is the victorious centre between knowledge and action,
because, in contrast to these functions, it is itself the true self-awareness and by virtue of this fact alone is at least the subjective representative of truth; again, because feeling as pious feeling is man's feeling of
utter dependence, i.e. the feeling of his connexion with God, Schleiermacher's theology is the theology of feeling, or to put it more exactly,
the theology of pious feeling, or the theology of awareness, or to put it
more exactly, the theology of pious self-awareness. That is why Schleiermacher in 1832 found that the text of St John, 1.51: 'Hereafter ye shall
see heaven open, and the angels of God ascending and descending upon
the Son of man' was expressly affirmed 'by the most perfect and blissful
experience of a faithful spirit', for which there is no longer any division
between heaven and earth.[1] Piety does not only seek, does not only
hope, does not only expect, does not only worship, but is this centre,
this peace which passeth all understanding. That is why for Schleiermacher proclaiming God means proclaiming one's own piety, that is
why for him preaching consists essentially of a self-imparting by the
preacher.

And since what is to be proclaimed here is indeed a determination,
but a determination of feeling, Schleiermacher gives to the Word, and
with the Word, to intellectual truth, only a position of secondary importance. The tenets of the Christian faith are simply only 'conceptions
of states of mind of Christian piety, represented in speech'.[2] The tenets
are only derivatives of the original thing, the inner state.[3] The divine
is ineffable. Talk about religion will one day be succeeded by 'the
soft silence of holy virgins'.[4] Of the three modes of speech, the poetical, the oratorical and the didactic, the poetical is the highest;
and what is higher than all of them together, and better, is music.
'Singing piety is the piety which ascends most directly and most
gloriously to heaven.'[5] Thus theology, if only because it is merely the
human word, and only, of all its forms, the didactic human word, is
free, capable of transformation, and relatively non-binding—not bound
in respect to its subject. That is why Schleiermacher finds it possible
to adapt his theology so carefully to the educated awareness of his time,
without worrying too much or nearly so much about whether his

---

[1] *Sermons*, III, 167f.   [2] *Doctrine of Faith*, para. 15.   [3] *Open Letter to Lücke*, Mul., 34.
[4] *Addresses*, 9f.   [5] *Christmas Celebration*, Phil. Libr., Vol. 117, p. 23.

theology was doing justice to its subject, to Christianity. That is why for him dogmatics is nothing more nor less than the 'representation of the opinion of the Church',[1] a branch of the church lore of the present, paraphrasing historically and empirically in systematic order the reality of the pronouncements, which are possible and necessary at the time, of the spirit affected by the Christian religion.

Truth in the strictly intellectual, expressible sense, which is because of these very qualities only the provisional truth, remains the concern of philosophy; truth in the ultimate, decisive, but also ineffable sense is reserved for mute feeling, the feeling which in the best event sings, and only as a last resort, and then inadequately, speaks. Schleiermacher's real and serious opinion was that all theological pronouncements were strictly theological to the extent that they were intended and meant to be received as pronouncements of religious feeling, referring to this feeling itself and to nothing else. Or, to put it negatively, that they declined in theological severity in proportion as they referred— as pronouncements upon some human knowledge or action—simultaneously to the objects of human knowledge or action. It is precisely as they enter upon the field of what is objective and to that extent expressible, that they become, according to Schleiermacher, potentially inadequate, as it were, by having lost their sure footing, the centre which represents the peaceful, ineffable truth.

This fear of objective and expressible pronouncements which are made inadequate by these very qualities, a fear which was determined by the Romantic principle of the centre, now provides the basis for a special methodic teaching in the *Doctrine of the Faith*, which is typical of Schleiermacher's theology as few other things are. I refer to the teaching of the three forms of dogmatic tenets. These, according to para. 30 of the *Doctrine of Faith*, can either be conceived of as descriptions of human states of mind or as notions of divine qualities or ways of behaving, or as pronouncements about certain ways in which the world is constituted. The feeling of utter dependence is never present in itself and isolated. It is present as real awareness filling out time, and always in such a way that it is linked with a time-filling, sensory form of self-awareness. Thus in the first place every formula for the feeling of utter dependence as such must at the same time be a formula for a certain state of self-awareness, a certain human state of mind. Every such sensory form of self-awareness must, however, be made to refer to a certain form of the world, such as typifies this form, this time-factor of self-awareness; i.e. it must be made to refer to something outside

[1] *Doctrine of Faith*, para. 19, suppl.

self-awareness, to a certain form of the not-self. Thus in the second place every formula for the feeling of utter dependence which is real in this sensory form can at the same time be a formula for the world, as it is real in this particular modification. And now the feeling of utter dependence is not what it is in and of itself, for God too is posited in self-awareness: thus the formula concerning the feeling of utter dependence can at the same time be understood as a formula for God himself. To express it more simply, and in a concentrated form, in a little variation on the theme of pious self-awareness: from intellectual reflection upon pious *self*-awareness there emerge the statements concerning the pious state of mind as such and in itself. From reflection upon pious self-*awareness* there emerge the statements about the world. From reflections upon *pious* self-awareness emerge statements about God. The form of the first group of statements, which always form the first section, the actual corpus of the exposition, in the individual sub-divisions of the *Doctrine of Faith*, Schleiermacher calls the dogmatic basic form, because their content necessarily rests upon pure self-experience, whereas the content of the statements about the world and God could in themselves always be understood either in the scientific sense or as an expression of metaphysical speculation. For this reason these latter statements must show that they are true theological statements by referring back to the first form of statements, i.e. that they can ultimately likewise be understood as pure pronouncements upon the religious state of mind and for this reason also, looked at according to their form, they are called tenets of the dogmatic subsidiary forms. The groups of statements upon the qualities of God and features of the world which come within these subsidiary forms always form the second and third sections in the individual sub-divisions of the *Doctrine of Faith*. If it were intended to present the content of the *Doctrine of Faith* in the form of a table, then, taking the longitudinal section of the whole, these second and third sections would have to be placed to left and right on either side of their respective first sections. This method means that the doctrine of God, for instance, extends throughout the whole work and is only finished when the book is finished. In the section on 'The way the world is constituted in relation to redemption' the entire doctrine of election, of the Holy Spirit, of the Church and the whole of eschatology is dealt with.

These are just some of the singular features this method involves. It must, however, be said that as a method it accords very well with the intention and spirit of the whole book. And Schleiermacher, without actually achieving this, wanted to advance even further in this direction. When he began to busy himself with the new edition in 1829 he considered the possibility, as is shown by para. 30 of the second edition and above all by the second open letter to Lücke, of cutting out the two subsidiary forms in favour of the main form, because they were 'superfluous really, in the strict sense'.[1] That, he expressly states, would be dogmatics in the peculiar form it had fashioned for itself in him.[2] He had, however, not done this, he says, in order to preserve, for one thing, the 'historical attitude' and 'church character' of his work, and further in order not to let slip the possibility of a critique and reduction of the doctrine of God, cosmology and anthropology as contained in the old dogmatics. These are reasons which cannot be described as very weighty or very much a question of principle. Schleiermacher takes leave of these unexecuted thoughts with a reminiscence taken, this time, from the Old Testament, that of the dying Moses' sight of the land of Canaan. 'I rejoice at least', he concludes in writing to Lücke, 'in the conviction that I have seen from afar at least the form for a freer and livelier way of treating our teaching of faith.'[3] This future ideal way of treatment, this Canaan, would thus consist in the disappearance of even the semblance of the idea that the subject of dogmatics was anything else but human states of mind. This semblance has not entirely disappeared in the form in which Schleiermacher left his work. But even so Schleiermacher approached very near to his ideal, and the fact that we know from his own pen what his true intentions were, may console us in some measure for the imperfection of what he actually achieved.

V. In conclusion let us enquire about the objective basic motifs of content in Schleiermacher's theology. We have called it a theology of feeling, of awareness. Thus we have already named one of these motifs of content, and indeed the one which is the original, primary and characteristic motif of content of this theology, and we have elucidated it in the foregoing.

The great formal principle of Schleiermacher's theology is at the same time its material principle. Christian pious self-awareness contemplates and describes itself: that is in principle the be-all and end-all of this theology. But what is this Christian pious self-awareness? The principle of mediation we have discussed already hints that the definition of Schleiermacher's theology as the theology of feeling or awareness cannot in any case imply that the formal and material principle of this theology is human feeling or awareness in such a way that this

[1] Mul., 47f.   [2] Ibid., 49.   [3] Ibid., 51.

feeling is understood as an indivisible unity. For it is a certain feeling, the feeling of piety, which is referred to. Feeling or awareness is here the centre in such a way that it distinguishes itself from another feeling or awareness outside it, in such a way that it shares its own unity voluntarily, as it were, with this other feeling or awareness, that it allows itself to oppose this other feeling or awareness in relative tension and is what it is only in the mediation between itself and the other feeling or awareness, and not in a pure identity with itself. This must in fact be so, if only as the result of the premises of Schleiermacher's dialectic, according to which there is no pure identity in finite self-awareness. And Schleiermacher was after all a Christian theologian to the extent that it was clear to him, and remained clear to him, that theology must in some sense have two motifs of content, that it must speak of God *and* man, of man *and* God. As has now become plain, man, human self-awareness, determined namely as pious self-awareness, was doubtless for Schleiermacher the central subject of his theological thought. In the very places where the theology of the Reformation had said 'the Gospel' or 'the Word of God' or 'Christ' Schleiermacher, three hundred years after the Reformation, now says, religion or piety. But Reformers did not neglect to split as it were their theological centre and to oppose it by something relatively different from it. They power-fully confronted the Word of God with the human correlate of faith, even though this correlate had its basis entirely in the Word of God, and was created and sustained by the Word of God. And in a similar way Schleiermacher's theology, too, is not centred in one point, in the sense that in that case it would not be aware of any other motif. Since by birth and upbringing he thinks in terms of man, just as the Re-formers had thought in terms of God, this second motif with him must manifestly be identical with, or be the same in intention, as that which was primarily for them: God, Christ, revelation or what you will.

It is noteworthy that, by acknowledging the dualism of two basic theological motifs, Schleiermacher, in principle, enters into the course of Trinitarian theological thinking together with the Reformers. Even if he does not go beyond this, the fact must not be overlooked in the assessment of his undertaking. Trinitarian thinking compels theology—even a theology which cannot perhaps do much directly with the idea of the Trinity—to be completely in earnest about the thought of God in at least two places: first, at the point where it is a question of God's action in regard to man, and, secondly, at the point where it is a question of man's action in regard to God. It is aware of God as the Word of the Father which is spoken to man and as the Spirit of the Father and of the

Word which enables man to hear the Word. It cannot seek to have merely one centre, one subject, just because its subject is God. To the extent that it sought to resolve itself into a mere teaching of God's action in regard to man, into a pure teaching of the Word, it would become metaphysics. And to the extent that it sought to resolve itself into a teaching of man's action in regard to God, into a pure teaching of the Spirit, it would become mysticism. The one, however, would be just as little a pure teaching of the Word of God, as the other would be a pure teaching of the Spirit of God. A pure teaching of the Word will take into account the Holy Spirit as the divine reality in which the Word is heard, just as a pure teaching of the Spirit of the Son will take into account the Word of God as the divine reality in which the Word is given to us. It was with this thought in mind that the Reformers propagated the teaching of the Word of God in its correlation with faith as the work of the Holy Spirit in man.

Schleiermacher reversed the order of this thought. What interests him is the question of man's action in regard to God. We must not condemn him for this out of hand. If we call to mind the entire situation of theology in the modern world then we shall find it understandable that it fastened upon the point which had come to the centre of the entire thought of modern man. This point was simply man himself. This shifting of interest did not necessarily have to mean man without God, man in his own world. It could also mean man in the presence of God, his action over against God's action. A genuine, proper theology could be built up from such a starting-point. We may ask the question whether it was a good thing that Schleiermacher adapted himself to the trend of the time in this way and took up his position at the spot where he was invited to do so by the prevalence of the Copernican world-picture, by its execution during the Enlightenment, by Kant, by Goethe, by Romanticism, and by Hegel.

There was in fact no need for the Copernican conception of the universe to acquire the significance of a command that theology should in future be anthropocentric theology. It might perhaps have been both more spirited and wiser to take up and carry through the Reformed theology of the Word more than ever at this time, in instructive opposition to the trend of the age. For indeed this Reformed theology had not been founded upon and conditioned by the Ptolemaic conception of the universe and, as a pure theology of the Word, it offered opportunity enough to do justice to the tendency of the age by an honest doctrine of the Holy Spirit and of faith. There was ambiguity in the fact that theology took the trend of the times as a command which must be followed as a matter of course, and in its inability to do justice to the tendency of the age other than by becoming anthropocentric in accordance with the changed picture of the universe. The suspicion arises whether this does not betray the fact that theology forgot its own theme over against all world-views. But this reversal of theology's way of looking at things was not necessarily bound to mean that theology was now no longer theology, or had even become the enemy of true theology. Again, a genuine, proper theology could be built up from such a starting-point. Theology could remain true to its own theme while it went with the times and thus completed this reversal. What Schleiermacher constructed by means of his theology of awareness by planting himself in the centre which for the Reformers had been a subsidiary centre, *could* be the pure theology of the Holy Spirit; the teaching of man brought face to face with God by God, of man granted grace by grace. If it was this, then as a theology it was just as much justified as the theology which was orientated in the opposite direction, the theocentric, Reformed theology. The fact that Schleiermacher intended it as such (even if he did not perhaps execute it in this way) is revealed by the fact that he is very much aware of a second centre beside his original one, and seeks to grant it its full validity. In doing so he enters in principle into the course of Trinitarian thinking. The only question can now be, whether he will be in a position, in Trinitarian terms, to recognize and ensure as much validity for the divinity of the *Logos*, which forms for him this second centre, as for the divinity of the Holy Spirit, which is his actual centre or rather is apparently meant by what he presents as his actual centre. Will this show if it is not only intended to be, but if it is in truth the *divinity* of the Holy Spirit which forms this actual centre of his? Reformation theology, starting in reverse fashion, from the *Logos*, passes this test: as a theology of the Word it is at once a theology of the Holy Spirit to such a degree that it can largely be understood as a theology of faith too, and it is this very fact which proves that it is the divine Word that forms its true centre. Will Schleiermacher's theology also pass this test, thus proving that for all the great reversal which is its starting-point, as compared with Reformed theology, its proceedings are theologically unexceptionable? Here we must make two preliminary points:

1. The task of taking into account this second motif and making it valid, which Schleiermacher does not wish to avoid, is an unmistakable source of embarrassment and care to him and something he finds particularly strenuous. The car must certainly continue to run, and it

does in fact do so where in this theology and proclamation it is a question of speaking of Christ, of divine action as such, of the Word, and of the objective moment of salvation. But—to speak in the technical terms of the motor-car—from time to time the second, hill-climbing gear has to be engaged. This is betrayed to the layman as well because of the increased noise, suggesting a greater strain, coming from the dialectic mechanism.

In some way or other, for instance, it emerges from the *Christmas Celebration* of 1805 that in fact Christ is, and is intended to remain, the subject of the celebration of Christmas. The exaltation of the religious disposition, which is there in the first place, certain and blessed in itself, is never questioned in the slightest. But at the same time this other motif, after having been questioned at the outset, must first be worked out and established by means of difficult considerations which encounter all sorts of significant doubts. Similarly in the *Addresses* and in the *Doctrine of Faith* and the sermons there can be no mistaking that for Schleiermacher the theologian, the historical element in religion, the objective motif, the Lord Jesus, is a problem child, one which certainly must be brought to honour, and which is somehow brought to honour—but which is still a problem child. Schleiermacher, the apologist, is forced to go to considerable trouble to understand and present this on the one hand in such a form that it is as far as possible safeguarded from the objections of modern awareness, thinking in anthropocentric terms. He has to work on the image of Christ provided by the biblical and dogmatic tradition like a sculptor working a block of marble, in order to produce the statue, the particular Christ who might be considered adequate from this point of view. And he has to go to similar trouble to show that seen from the basic fact of pious feeling the figure, now made unassailable, which is the product of his Christology is really important and necessary; and that we should not, as might be thought, be just as well-off without it. He succeeds in both things, both in working out a tolerably modernized Christology, and in showing, in tolerably convincing fashion, that this Christology is indispensable. He does not succeed without sometimes resorting to artifice. He does not succeed consistently nor perhaps in a way which is ultimately convincing and worthy of credence. But all the same, he succeeds somehow. It is just that it was a piece of extremely hard labour in apologetics—and this is a shadow which remains come what may—which was necessary to bring about this success.

This cannot be said of the Reformation in regard to its subsidiary centre. It would be absurd to say of Luther's doctrine of faith that it had in itself cost him a particular dialectic exertion. From the outset his teaching of the Word is so constituted that he can and must speak with an inner objective necessity not only of Christ but of faith too. With Luther the divinity of the *Logos* demands in the most direct way possible the divinity of the Spirit. The relationship between the two motifs is open, self-evident, and alive, although as with Schleiermacher there is a difference of emphasis, in that here it is the first one which forms the centre-point. Luther certainly did not speak as an apologist of what for him was the second motif. He neither needed to model the concept of faith to comply with a certain world view, nor did he need first to work out the indispensable nature of this concept. The concept of faith, rather, is already posited, both in its content and in its range, in and with his conception of the Word, and all his theological labour could only be devoted to showing this right, which stood firm from the outset and inwardly, and the self-evident dignity of what for him was the second motif. It is impossible, *mutatis mutandis*, to say this of Schleiermacher's theology. Whatever else we may think about it, it is impossible to dispute the fact that it is a product of art. This fact alone is sufficient to cause us at least to wonder whether in his theology the divinity of the *Logos* is pre-supposed as unequivocally as the Reformers posited the divinity of the Spirit, and whether, if this was not the case, the *divinity* of the Spirit which seemingly formed the centre of his theology was really the divinity of the *Holy* Spirit.

2. To overcome the difficulties with which he was faced by his acknowledgment in principle of the second motif Schleiermacher used the principle of mediation, which we have already considered as the most significant formal motif of his theology. But why is it so difficult for him to acknowledge and ensure the validity of this second motif? Because apparently it did not escape him that the first and the second motifs were, in the Reformed theology at all events, related to each other in such a way, and were opposed to each other in such strict distinction, as the Incarnation of the Word and the pouring out of the Holy Spirit are, or, to go still higher, as the second and third persons of the Godhead as such oppose each other. In this opposition both were strictly characterized as moments of the divine revelation and protected, each by its correlation with the other, from being confused with a mode of human cognition. Schleiermacher could not acquiesce in this opposition, because it was not his intention at all strictly to characterize these two moments as revelation, nor to protect them from being confused with a mode of human cognition. As an apologist he was bound to be interested in understanding revelation not strictly as

revelation, but in such a way that it might also be comprehensible as a mode of human cognition. As an apologist he was thus bound to look upon this opposition as an inconvenience, and to look for a means of overcoming it. And the means he found was this principle of mediation.

The efficacy of this principle is at once shown by the fact that Schleiermacher presents as the theme of theology, as seen from the anthropocentric point of view, not the outpouring of the Holy Spirit— this might in itself have been possible—but religious consciousness as such. Faith understood in this way, not as God's revelation, but as man's experience, allowed, nay demanded, that the second objective moment should be understood accordingly, i.e. not presupposing a strict opposition to the first, and not as a correlate to the concept of the Holy Spirit, as understood in the Trinitarian sense, but as a correlate to this human experience. It was in accordance with the line of thought pursued by Kant and Lessing that Schleiermacher allowed his first moment, as the psychological one, to be opposed by his second moment as the historical one. Historical knowledge, too, is a mode of human cognition, even if it is a different one from that of psychological knowledge. Between these two motifs mediation is possible. Seeing them together cannot be altogether out of the question. The great difficulty Schleiermacher had in acknowledging and explaining his second motif was determined by the old teaching of the *divinity* of the Logos and of the Spirit. After he had mastered this teaching by interpreting it in the relationship of the historical to the psychological, there then remained the smaller difficulty of bringing these two things into connexion with one another, that is to say of overcoming Lessing's big ditch, and showing in opposition to Kant that the historical element in Christianity was more than a temporal vehicle of timeless reasonable truth. Because of his principle of mediation, he was able to show this better than Herder had attempted before him. For basically it is a question of nothing but carrying out Herder's programme. In carrying out this programme, in demonstrating that faith and Christ, equated with experience and history, are the foci of an ellipse, Schleiermacher turns the Christian relationship of man with God into an apparent human possibility. It is apparent because a mode of human cognition corresponds to it on both sides, because these two modes can be brought into a peaceful, mediating relationship, and because they were thus treated by Schleiermacher.

They are not in fact related in this way in the theology of the Reformation, and they are not subjected to such an interpretation there. The sole mediation which enters into consideration there is the recognition of the Father in the Son through the Spirit in the strict irreducible opposition of these 'persons' in the Godhead. This mediation cannot be made comprehensible as a mode of human cognition. It is unusable in apologetics. But the question is whether the theological concern can be preserved, other than at the expense of the interest of apologetics. And conversely the question must be asked whether with Schleiermacher the concern of apologetics has not been preserved at the expense of that of theology. The fact that Schleiermacher's theology was anthropocentric is not in itself a sufficient justification for this question, let alone that this fact should be made the subject of a reproach. What certainly does make this question necessary is the way Schleiermacher immunized the concept of revelation, as he has done by this interpretation, and the way in which he made possible for himself the mediation between his anthropological centre and the other, the Christological centre, by means of this interpretation. Let us now try to see in concrete fashion how this came about.

(a) In order to describe the way Schleiermacher understood the relationship between the two motifs we have used the image of the ellipse with its two foci. This image must be supplemented by the further remark that the ellipse tends to become a circle, so that its two foci have the tendency to coincide in one centre-point. But at the same time it is unlikely that this centre-point will lie mid-way between the two foci, since the power of attraction of the first focus is from the outset much stronger than that of the second, and since the second, once the circle has been achieved, might perhaps have vanished altogether, having succumbed entirely to the first. When Schleiermacher speaks of Christ and Christians and their mutual relationship, what he primarily has in mind is neither the one nor the other, but one single concept embracing both, namely the 'composite life', humanity, the history of 'human nature'. In this history it is a question of the 'redemption' of human nature. This redemption, however, is at the same time its fulfilment. It is a question of the furtherance of its 'higher life', of its gradual ascent from the sensory to the spiritual state, from a dim to a powerful consciousness of God. To this extent it is a question of its approach to the way in which man was originally determined, which was thrown into question by sin. Piety is the condition of being involved in this approach. And if this approach is that which is brought about by Christ then the condition of Christian piety is that of complete piety in as much as the approach which is brought about by Christ is

the most complete of all. For the dignity of Christ consists in a consciousness of God which is utterly powerful, which precludes all sin,
and which is posited together with Christ's self-consciousness. The
statement that religious consciousness is Christian consciousness is as
much as to say that it refers to Christ, which in turn is as much as to
say that what is real in Christ in its original and perfect form ('arche-
types'), is likewise gradually imparted to this consciousness. That is
redemption through Christ. Redemption is the higher human life of
the Christian, which did not have its beginning with the creation, nor
in Adam, but perfecting and crowning creation, first in Christ, and
which now also reaches the Christian as an impulse, as movement, as
the life of the spirit of Christ in his Church.

That Schleiermacher put the historical element before the psychological at first seems plain: the first influences and the second is
influenced. But this does not prevent Schleiermacher from summarizing
the whole—inevitably disconcerting us at the first glance—in the title
'Concerning the state of the Christian, in so far as he is aware of the
divine grace', as if Christology for all that were merely a smaller circle
within the greater one described as 'the state of the Christian', etc. Is it
not so? Does Christ mean significantly more to Schleiermacher than
a special and admittedly most important way of more nearly determining the state of the Christian? Schleiermacher himself does not seem
to think it a vain question to ask whether the exaltation of life, as the
process in which we are involved, might not be primary, and the figure
of Christ merely the symbol, the reflex, projected back into history, of
this original light. This is asserted without contradiction by one of
the speakers in the *Christmas Celebration*. Nor does the other question
which was also raised in the *Christmas Celebration* seem a vain one. I refer
to the one as being whether the figure of Christ is anything but the
historical point of departure, discovered in retrospect, of that unity of
the human and the divine, such as comes about in the self-consciousness of humanity as such. If this putting Christ before Christians is to
stand (and at all events Schleiermacher declares this to be his intention),
then according to the way he approaches the problem these questions
must surely be asked and left open. This giving of precedence, and
together with it the distinction of the two motifs, is relative. The
distinction is made, but as soon as the point is reached where the
relationship between the two distinguished motifs is to be represented,
it becomes plain that their distinction is conceived as a fluid one. It
is fluid within the composite phenomenon of the higher life inaugurated
by Christ. But this is in process of developing within ourselves, within

the composite phenomenon of the single effect of Christ, which embraces his effect just as much as our being affected. Where the one begins and the other leaves off is something as difficult to determine as the question of where with Novalis, art begins and philosophy leaves off, where religion begins and where love leaves off. Redemption, according to para. 11, 2 of the *Doctrine of Faith*, is, passively, man's transition from the bad state of restricted activity of the higher self-consciousness to the better one of a relative liberation; actively it is the aid given to him to this end by another.

This 'transition' and this 'aid' can in fact be distinguished only relatively the one from the other. Even if Schleiermacher, too, finds that there exists between them an opposition as between what is and what should be, between receiving and giving, between the continuation and the beginning, the imitation and the prototype, the general and the particular, we do not lose sight for an instant of the fact that these antitheses are mediated: that they are mediated by means of their belonging together in the comprehensible composite phenomenon of the higher life. At some point or other they must coincide. And it is only with the prospect of this final coincidence and from this point of no distinction that they are distinguished at all. It is this which justifies our speaking of the mystic element in Schleiermacher. It also makes it fitting for us to recall in this context Schleiermacher's proximity to Hegel. His placing of things in opposition is as seriously meant as Eckhart's distinction between God and the soul, as Hegel's distinction between thesis and anti-thesis. It is meant as seriously as any opposition can be meant whose elimination is pre-supposed and which is therefore bound to come about. Anyone who is in a position to focus Christ and the Christian together, as a composite phenomenon, manifestly knows of a third thing above both, and will thus be capable of distinguishing between them in this manner, only relatively; and putting one before the other is bound to remain questionable in principle, even if he wishes to do so and does in fact do so.

(*b*) According to Schleiermacher Christ is the Revealer and Redeemer in so far as he effects the higher life. It is this idea of effecting the higher life which we must now investigate. In it Christ, as the cause, is obviously distinguished from the higher life in us, as the effect. The 'higher life' means: the development of our existence, and—since our existence significantly comes about in our consciousness of our existence, or self-consciousness, our self-consciousness, however, being significantly determined as pious self-consciousness—the development of our piety. In so far Christ should be the cause of our piety. Piety, according to Schleiermacher's general definition, is nothing but the feeling of an effect, the feeling of utter dependence. Consciousness of this utter dependence of ours is the same thing as consciousness of our connexion with God. According to para. 4 of the *Doctrine of Faith* man knows that in respect to the world he is relatively free and relatively dependent. If in this relative freedom and dependence in respect to the world he feels that he is at the same time utterly dependent upon something else, which is not the world, then he is pious; he is aware of his connexion with God. The other thing, the Whence of our being, in respect to which we feel that we are utterly dependent, is God. But we cannot actually say 'in respect to which', since feeling, in contrast to knowledge and action, has not anything standing in opposition to it, has not any object. It is only in the feeling of his effect that God is given to us as a cause, and not in any other way. If he were given to us in some other way, if he were given to us in some way as an object, then a counter-effect on our part would come about too, in respect of him, so that there would be freedom and not utter dependence. We should then not be dealing with God, but with the world. God, therefore, is not given to us as an object. God signifies rather one of several factors shaping man's feeling, and it is this factor upon which we 'throw back' its being determined as pious feeling. The consciousness of God thus remains 'shut up' in feeling, so that the expression of the idea 'God' cannot signify anything else but the expression of feeling concerning itself, the most immediate self-reflection. And this quality of God as not being given as an object, to represent the Whence of our being is, according to Schleiermacher's express declaration, identical with God's 'original revelation'. With the utter dependence of his being, which pertains to man as it does to everything which is in being, he is also given, as a man, immediate self-consciousness, which is engaged in the process of becoming awareness of God; he is thus given God, and his piety is only the advance of this process which is peculiar to his human existence as such.

This determination of God's quality as the cause, as seen within the general conception of religion previously posited seems to present Christology with the following dilemma. *Either* Schleiermacher's view of the matter allows and demands that we should substitute Christ in the very place where he was speaking of God. This would then decide the fact that 'Christ' is not to be understood as an objective quantity, but only as this factor which also determines feeling itself, as the Whence of our existence that cannot be distinguished from our feeling itself. For as an objective quantity Christ could not be that upon which we are utterly dependent, and thus could not be God. Hence he can only be this other thing in our feeling itself, upon which we 'throw back' its determination as pious feeling. Thus in speaking of him we are speaking immediately of our feeling itself. Thus he is identical with this quality God has of being given, by virtue of which self-consciousness quite naturally becomes consciousness of God. And he is identical with this original revelation of God, which precedes all history, and is given with our existence itself. It would therefore be impossible to speak of a distinction between him and pious feeling as the self-consciousness which becomes consciousness of God, especially if his divinity were to be treated seriously. *Or* on the other hand Schleiermacher's view allows and demands that we should at all events understand Christ as an objective quantity, and thus distinguish him from pious feeling as such; that we should not equate him with the timeless original revelation, but grant him his historical individuality and think of him in this individuality as a temporal point of reference for pious feeling. This, however, directly implies that he is part of the world, i.e. that he is of the quintessence of all that in relation to which we have relative freedom, and upon which, therefore, we are only relatively dependent. This is to deny the only thing which, according to Schleiermacher's way of thinking, could be his Godhead—for all that, within the world, this figure might represent a highest point, a point, perhaps, of unique excellence, significance and effect he is in this case the climax, the possibly incommensurable climax of the divine power in mankind as such, and hence the stimulator, the possibly incommensurable stimulator of the divine power in all others. His ability to stimulate and the others' ability to be stimulated is then, however, not seated in himself, but in the hidden higher thing, in the consciousness and possession of God, as the bearer of which he would ultimately, even if in a particularly distinguished way, be aligned with everyone else.

Schleiermacher did not opt for the first, but for the second of these possibilities. He renounced the idea of a purely speculative Christology, but precisely in so doing, according to the premises of his conception of religion, he was bound to renounce the idea of the Deity of Christ or, to put it differently, to understand the Deity of Christ as the incomparable climax and decisive stimulator within the composite life of humanity. And it was not possible to arrive at an unequivocal opposition of Christ and Christians from this angle either. The antithesis between the two is seen through even before it is elaborated, and cannot be a final one. The first thing, and therefore the final thing too is the unity between the two, and the point at which this unity can be perceived is not by any means Christ, but the Christian, the view of Christ being in principle a view back towards him.

We are bound to ask a question concerning the entire concept of Christ's 'effecting', of the relationship of cause and effect, which Schleiermacher first called upon in order to describe the relationship between God and man in general, and then the relationship between Christ and the Christian. The question is whether this concept, in view of its certain naturalism, is not already right from the outset a symbol for the fact that, according to the premise of his principle of mediation, Schleiermacher, while he wanted to accord precedence to the first of these two factors, and asserted that this precedence existed, was in fact incapable of putting this idea into effect with anything like an ultimate seriousness of intention.

(*c*) This distinction of Christ above Christians is that of the 'original fact' of the whole of Christianity, of the 'archetypal image', as Schleiermacher was also fond of saying. Christ is the principle of individuation of this religion. He is that power, formed in a certain way, which, thought of as determining and forming, makes this religion precisely what it is. For as Schleiermacher already said in the *Addresses*, feeling is not without intuition. It is not without the stimulation provided by a certain something which affects religiously, by the action of which there comes about a certain state of being affected religiously. Outside of this correlation no religion exists. According to Schleiermacher there is no religion in itself, no natural religion. Or to put it more exactly: natural religion, that original state of being pious, which coincides with the original divine revelation, is for ever real only in a definite, concrete and temporal way. It is in the Finite, in this or the other concrete, temporal intuition that the Infinite for ever reveals itself. There can be no original divine revelation without the temporal exponent of historical revelation. Religion begins with an incomprehensible fact, with something worthy of thought, with a single, isolated intuition in the sphere of nature, of history or of society, or also in the sphere of a man's own inner life. Religion is always real as positive religion. It is only when one settles in one such form of central intuition that one acquires a fixed address and active citizen rights in the religious world. But this world is 'a perfect republic', in so far as none of the forms of central intuition which are possible in it excludes in principle even one of the others which are possible in it, and in so far, rather, as innumerable intuitions of different kinds, and therefore determinations of feeling, have their right, equal in principle, to exist beside and after each other, as the 'glorious branches into which the heavenly tree of the priestly art has distributed its crown and top'. The one thing which reveals itself in all of them admittedly has its reality only in each individual one, in this or that positive religion. But because it is the individual one each is not for that reason the only one, since it has its truth only in the one thing which is also real in all the other individual religions.

It is thus, according to para. 10 of the *Doctrine of Faith*, that the impulse proceeding from Christ imparts to Christianity colour and tone, historical breadth and the possibility for its existence. Religion in this determined impulse is real as Christian religion. But its truth, its content, is none the less nothing but the feeling of utter dependence, at its highest level, in its stamp as awareness of redemption. Revelation, i.e. here Christ, is the individualizing element in this religion, and to this extent the effective, realizing element. It has nothing to do with the antithesis between things true and false. All, and no, revelation is true. Revelation is the excitement of feeling in an individual, which, moving, conveys itself to others and thus allows a development from the religious individual to a religious type, a religious species, a religious community, a Church. In the case of the Christian religion this dominating individual, who impresses himself upon all others and is effective in the after-effects of his spirit, is Christ. That was what Schleiermacher meant when he defended the 'high arbitrariness' of Christianity against the attacks of Schelling. He fought against the same opponent in the natural religion of the Enlightenment: Christianity is not a universal religion of reason, it is positive, revelatory religion. But its positive quality, its character as revelation, is exhausted in the individuality it receives from the manifestation of Christ and his after-effects. Christ is the archetypal image, the original source, the original fact. These things mean that he is the historical beginning of this religion, this Church, and as such he is the beginning which is decisive for every age. Christ as the archetypal image is primal, productive, singular, just as in other fields, that, however, of religion included, every original image or archetype is primal, productive and singular. There is no doubt that Schleiermacher sought to assert something like the absoluteness of Christianity, and continually asserted it. Strangely enough it was in the pulpit particularly that the problem again and again crossed his path: why Christ in particular? Why can we not manage without him? Why can we not manage with someone else? Perhaps with someone else who is yet to come? The answer consists in the constantly repeated protestation that everything we have of higher life we have from him.

There can be no doubt about the personal sincerity of this assertion. But it is just this which is in question—whether this assertion can be considered as objectively valid, whether the strength of this assertion can be some other strength beside that of the asserting believer himself, or of the composite life of the community of the Christian Church, from out of whose heritage the preaching believer speaks. Schleiermacher does not seem to be able to say that there is an eternal significance of Christ, an absoluteness of Christianity. At the back of even his most forceful protestations, unrevoked, and irrevocable, unless he is to abandon his basic premise, there stands the fact he established in the *Addresses* that the basic outlook of every religion is in itself eternal, since it forms a supplementary part of the infinite whole of religion in general in which all things must be eternal. The sincerity and strength of the distinction which pious feeling is inclined and determined until further notice to accord to Christ in relation to itself stands and falls with the sincerity and strength of pious feeling itself. The original fact of Christ and the fact of my Christianity are links in a chain, and the relationship of mutual determination which links in a chain necessarily have makes it plainly impossible to assume that the effect they have on one another cannot in principle be reversed. From this angle, too, the way Schleiermacher approaches his task makes it necessary for us to content ourselves with a distinction and an according of precedence which is relative, fluid, and challengeable in principle. The posing of the question of truth can at every instant become a danger to this distinction.

To summarize: Schleiermacher's Christology has as its summit the indication of a quantitative superiority, dignity and significance in Christ as opposed to our own Christianity. This is as much as to say that just because the point with Christ is that he has only an incomparably greater quantity of that which we see in ourselves as our Christianity, this indication is ultimately linked with the assertion, the self-assertion, of our own Christianity. The two foci of the ellipse draw relentlessly closer to one another, and how is the dissolution and disappearance of the objective moment in the subjective to be prevented? *The Word is not so assured here in its independence in respect to faith as should be the case if this theology of faith were a true theology of the Holy Spirit.* In a proper theology of the Holy Spirit there could be no question of dissolving the Word. Here, quite seriously, there is a question of such a dissolution. The only thing which prevents it is Schleiermacher's good will in not allowing things to develop so far. This good will must once again be formally acknowledged, but that in no way alters the fact that we feel ourselves here in all seriousness threatened by this dissolution. Thus it seems necessary for us after all to begin to consider whether what has happened here is that it is not the Holy Spirit, but, as Schleiermacher claims, merely man's religious consciousness which has after all become the theme of theology. In some depth of his mind Schleiermacher must have intended otherwise. This different intention must then have become submerged in the stormy need of the apologist to make plain the working of the Holy Spirit in the familiar form of religious consciousness. And when he had done this the only thing left for him to do was to equate the objective moment, the Word, with the form, likewise familiar, of that which is historically effective and original, thus arriving at the relative opposition with which he could do justice to modern cultural consciousness, but possibly not to Christianity.

Not in explanation, but in order to illustrate this situation, I should like to recall in conclusion yet another correspondence in Schleiermacher's theology, the execution of which raises doubts similar to those which have just forced themselves upon us. I refer to his teaching of sin and grace. What about this antithesis, forming as it does the theme, and providing the principle according to which the second part of the *Doctrine of Faith* is divided? According to the way Schleiermacher himself explains it sin and grace are comprised together in the one outer bracket of the consciousness of redemption: sin as the restricted awareness of the higher life, as the absence of ease in originating pious moments of life, as the non-domination of the feeling of utter dependence—and grace as the ease with which we are capable of reading into the various sensory stimuli of self-consciousness consciousness of God; consciousness of sin being at the same time that of a human deed, and consciousness of grace being at the same time that of a divine impartation. There is no true Christian consciousness in which these two states would not be contained, in the relationship of a More and Less, and thus once again in a quantitative relationship, and indeed in 'fluid differentiation'. Schleiermacher does not consider an objectless, absolute relationship with God, either in the negative or the positive sense, as a possibility that need be taken seriously into account. Our pious self-consciousness simply sways between these two extremes, sharing the inequalities (of development and restriction, pleasure and pain) of temporal life. The Christian is always aware of sin *and* grace both in and with one another. That means that with Schleiermacher there can be no question of man's knowing that he is earnestly adjudged a sinner, and equally earnestly ultimately pardoned.

And this, together with the absence of the vision of man which Luther and Calvin had in the teaching that man was in himself completely sinful and in Christ completely righteous, probably helps to explain the fact that we cannot reckon, in Schleiermacher, with an ultimate opposition between God and man, between Christ and the Christian.

The question as to how it was that Schleiermacher himself was not alarmed by this result, and how he could think—as he did in fact think —that he was not destroying Reformation theology, but taking it up and continuing it in a way suited to his time; how he failed to notice that his result challenged the decisive premise of all Christian theology in a way which had not been known, perhaps, since the days of the ancient Gnostics—this question presents us with a mystery which cannot be solved. We can only establish that the classic representation which the Christian doctrine found in the great moment when the spirit of the eighteenth century was fulfilled and overcome resulted in the development of an obscurity in its very statement, in the opposition of God and man, an obscurity within which every identifiable sign points to the fact that here man has alone remained master of the field to the extent that he alone is the subject, and Christ has become his predicate. The only consolation we can draw from this discovery is that this cannot be what the Christian Church intends, and therefore could not be what Schleiermacher intended either. The consolation we draw at this point, a point decisive in the history of recent theology, is however provided by what is truly a maxim of faith and not a maxim of historical knowledge. That which is historically knowable would leave us here ultimately without comfort.

12

WEGSCHEIDER

In the year 1815, that is, sixteen years after Schleiermacher's *Addresses*, there appeared a *Dogmatics*, written in Latin, which so met the needs and the attitudes of unknown masses of theological readers that (in strong contrast to Schleiermacher's *Doctrine of Faith*) it appeared in a second edition two years later; by 1844 it was in its eighth edition. The author was three years younger than Schleiermacher (1771-1849) and survived him by fifteen years, so he at least belonged to the same generation and time as Schleiermacher. Whereas Schleiermacher asked questions, he edified. Whereas Schleiermacher was praised, he was read. Whereas Schleiermacher's theology was representative of a whole period, in that in its day it interested and captivated the élite of the pastorate, this theology had a widespread influence at the same time, and reached the masses of citizens and peasants through the pulpits of countless villages and small towns. If one could investigate the religious geology of the non-theologians of North and Central Germany, one would hardly find even a narrow vein of Schleiermacher; not too far down, however, one would come up against a broad stratum deriving from the spirit of this *Dogmatics*. The book I mean is the *Institutiones theologiae christianae dogmaticae* of Julius August Ludwig Wegscheider, professor in Halle from 1810 to 1849.

Alongside General Superintendent Bretschneider of Gotha, but more consistently and unequivocally than he, Wegscheider was a representative of 'rationalism' in theology. In the nineteenth century, rationalism simply means a theology which is resolved to accept the directives of Kant's philosophy of religion in the matter of the place of reason in religion, and to allow their validity without enquiring too closely—without enquiring too closely, that is, into the concept of reason that is presupposed. With Schleiermacher, we have made the acquaintance of a theology which refused the description 'rationalist' in that it did not take over unquestioningly the concept of reason presupposed by Kant, but expanded it in such a way as to embrace in principle the particularity of experience and of history. We could see that it was the same concept of reason from the apologetic approach of Schleiermacher's theology, from the unmistakable dominance of the psychological over the historical, from the uncertain position that was finally accorded to history, even here. Now, of course, the *religious* man had become the measure of all things, but in so far as the religious man was seen and understood on the basis of a pattern of general human culture which gave his religion a subordinate place, even if the pattern was wider than that of Kant, even here the human Logos, a human reason, albeit understood more richly and more profoundly, was made the final criterion.

Wegscheider's *Dogmatics* were a catastrophically retrograde step in comparison to Schleiermacher. If we look back at the themes in Schleiermacher's theology that we discussed, we may, of course, also say of Wegscheider that there are indications that he wanted to be a *Christian theologian*; secondly, however, he wanted at all costs to be a *modern man*, and because he, too, was not altogether clear about the relationship between these two tendencies, thirdly, he also wanted to be an *apologist* and to interpret Christianity in such a way that it never came in conflict with the modern consciousness. But where in the fourth place we had to speak of Schleiermacher's *principle of mediation*, in Wegscheider a great gap yawns. For him, the concern expressed by Herder in relationship to Kant was no concern. He had not gone through the Community of Brethren, Romanticism or even post-Kantian philosophy—other than as an astonished onlooker. He understood nothing of art on the one side nor of philosophical speculation on the other, and a considerable wave of the religious movement does not seem to have penetrated his solid countenance. He had no imagination and therefore no feeling—would be the verdict in the light of Schleiermacher's *Addresses*, which went past him without leaving any impression.

It is clear that on these presuppositions he could have only a much more modest horizon and apparatus for establishing and developing the essential themes of his theology. We would only have to go on to say that consequently he had to be a worse theologian than Schleiermacher if we were to apply to him Schleiermacher's presupposition that theology is the religious man's description of himself, and as such is directed to the religious and spiritual riches of such a man. The undeniable weaknesses in Wegscheider's horizon and apparatus could, on other presuppositions, have been turned to advantage. However, since Schleiermacher's conception of theology represented perhaps

the most profound formula for rationalism, and since Wegscheider's
own programme ended, in a more meagre way, with the religious
man's account of himself, the latter's contribution inevitably has to be
judged to be incomparably worse alongside that of Schleiermacher. As
a result, its sole merit was that it brought out what could be achieved
on the same presupposition in the least favourable circumstances: the
ribs, as it were, that were left once one stripped away from the
Schleiermacherian body the ripe flesh with which it was clothed. For
this judgment I can turn for support to Schleiermacher's pupil Gass,
who in more than one place welcomed Wegscheider's results, and only
regretted the way in which they had been reached.[1] Wegscheider is—
and one does him no dishonour in saying as much—a theological
Philistine of a kind that hardly ever reappeared again among the
leading theologians, with one exception, a man to whom I shall not
apply publicly such a blatant epithet. That is not to say that there is
a veritable abyss between Schleiermacher and him. One cannot doubt
for a moment that Schleiermacher advocated his cause in an incomparably better way. But it is the merit of this theological Philistine
that he showed the minimal content of the cause in blunt words and
thus at any rate contributed to sharpening the questions it raised.

Wegscheider understands the *systema Rationalismi*, which he embraces
without batting an eyelid, as the *purior religionis doctrinae typus*, based on
itself, which is to be derived from those passages of Holy Scripture
which correspond with the laws of reason planted by God himself in
the human spirit. By virtue of the guidance of divine providence,
working in conjunction with human knowledge, today, in the year
1815, we live in an *aevum cultius*, compared with all previous periods.
The fruit of this progress is insight into the absolute validity of the
recta or *sana ratio*, i.e. the unity of the laws of human thought and will
that correspond to the laws of nature. The integrating element of this
reason is an *idea religionis*, a *fides rationalis*, in comparison with which
all other kinds of belief are to be rejected as either mysticism or tradi-
tionalism, unless they have a merely exoteric preparatory significance.
Theology has to recognize and accept the fruit of this progress without
qualification. Yet it cannot either suppress or take away the light in
which other scholars rejoice. It cannot hope to make credible to the
homo cultior of the present a doctrine that contradicts the decrees of
sana ratio. Public worship has to be guided by the religion of its age,
and the religion of the day is at all events one which is in conformity

[1] W. Gass, *Die Geschichte der protestantischen Dogmatik* IV, 1867, 460, 468f.

with *sana ratio*. Therefore it can only know of a natural, i.e. reasonable revelation, which is identical with what is given to reason. Where it is not to be rejected, all positive religion simply consists in the fact that men of extraordinary religious knowledge have drawn others after them by virtue of divine providence. Such founders of religion, e.g. Christ, are worthy of belief and reverence, but only in so far as they proclaimed the pure and unalterable faith in reason in a particularly lofty and impressive way. Anything in their teaching or in that of their successors which goes beyond this is now to be rejected as ancient myth, temporally conditioned divine accommodation or speculative addition. According to Wegscheider, the establishing of this norm is nothing other than a carrying through of the Reformation. That is why he dedicated the second edition of his *Institutiones*, which appeared in the jubilee year 1817, again without batting an eyelid, to that 'pious man' Martin Luther.

Dogmatics has three tasks: discovering the origin of dogmas, giving accounts of the dogmas themselves, and criticism of the dogmas. The decisive task of present dogmatics is the third. It has no intention, say, of avoiding the *fundamentum biblicum*. The Bible is not to be paraphrased, but to be understood historically, grammatically, and with a critical eye to its content. The degree to which it is a foundation—and the same holds true of the confessional writings—depends on the degree to which it corresponds with reason. God has given us reason for this purpose, and the Reformers and Jesus himself summon us to draw this dividing line through the Bible. We are to distinguish between those passages of Scripture in which reason can be recognized, *quae intellectu faciles ad edocendas et tranquillandas animas optime conveniunt*—from the divine accommodations, human misunderstandings and myths that the Bible also contains. Why the Bible in particular? Why the Christian religion? Because as a result of the divine guidance of the human race this corresponds in its pure form, especially in the figure of Jesus, most exactly with the demand of the reason given by God. These are the principles on which Wegscheider works.

I shall illustrate their scope from some examples in his special dogmatics. Wegscheider betrays his Lutheran origin in that he has at the heart of his dogmatics a fundamental principle which recapitulates the content of Christianity. This principle is not the doctrine of atonement or salvation that derives from the apostles, but the teaching given by Jesus himself, *that is revealed through him in such a way that all men can reach eternal life through divine knowledge.*

The *trinitarian concept of God* has to be modified to the effect that we have to reverence God as the Father, and Jesus as the divinely approved ambassador in whom the wisdom and power of God were supremely efficacious. We are to follow and serve him zealously as an outstanding pattern of a holy life, as one who is himself the radiance of the Godhead. Finally, the Holy Spirit is the divine working by which God stimulates and supports our wisdom and virtue by the institution of the Christian religion *salva tamen hominis libertate*, to whom we are to surrender ourselves with reasonable zeal.

Man is really *in the image of God*, in that the human spirit is like the spirit of God; the likeness is potentially his own from the beginning, and is to be realized by him in the course of his life. His ascent, however, is hampered by the constantly lurking, overpowering tendency to *sin*. Sin is free transgression of the commandment, to be explained by the overwhelming dominance of the senses over reason and by a lack of proper instruction and upbringing. It may not be said that man is born a sinner. This doctrine is incompatible with the goodness, wisdom and righteousness of God, is unknown to Jesus himself, and conflicts with pedagogical experience. It is to be reduced to an indication of the power of heredity, of the natural weakness of the unformed reason, of the influence of environment, upbringing, example and moral custom. Sin can and should be overcome by man.

Wegscheider deals with *Christology* in the following way: Jesus of Nazareth, to whom his followers gave the name Christ, merits the highest reverence among the wise men who by God's providence have gained great renown among their contemporaries and posterity as teachers and lawgivers. In a way that can easily be understood, particularly in psychological terms, but against his own wishes, the *doctrina Jesu* increasingly became a *doctrina de Jesu*, *a* teaching about his person that aroused dispute and confusion. A critical examination shows that he was a man of the highest gifts, especially religious gifts, who by teaching and by example proclaimed a purified Mosaic religion. As a result, he was crucified by his foolish people, was taken down from the cross by his disciples apparently dead, appeared among his followers again on the third day, confirmed to them once again his intention to found a new religion, and then disappeared, never to be seen again. What is left of the doctrine of an incarnation of God that took place in him, a myth that is also widespread elsewhere, is that we recognize as divine the principle which was at work in his life and the guidance which he may be seen to have been given. The whole of the Church's teaching about his person, on the other hand, must be abandoned as ethically fruitless and contrary to reason, unless it is replaced by the statement that in him we have to reverence and imitate the prototype of the man who is to be filled with true religion and virtue.

The *forgiveness of sins* to be obtained through him may never amount to a destruction of the exact and strict proportion between human virtue and vice and divine reward and punishment. Rather, with an increase in virtue and the knowledge of God, trust and hope are restored to man. In relation to his moral worth, the sinner is excused his previous sins, but in such a way that, depending on the severity of his guilt, each man must be content with a lesser degree of temporal and eternal blessedness. Any other conception of forgiveness would sever the nerve of his zeal for virtue. There can be no talk of a vicarious satisfaction of Christ, since it is contrary to reason and morality. His death is to be celebrated as a symbol of the inauguration of the new religion brought about by the death of the founder and to this degree as a symbol of the love of God for man. It is to be proclaimed as a summons to the sinner to improve himself as rapidly as possible. The only meaning that can be given to grace is that God is not only the Creator and Sustainer of the spiritual powers of mankind and their Lawgiver, but also the origin of the Christian religion and its salutary effect, so that the concept of grace can be reduced to a general concept of a particular providence, or—as the natural capacities and impulses of man cannot be denied in this respect—a particular divine concursus. The concept of *justification* as it was held by the Reformers obviously derived *e notionibus certis aevi incultioris anthropomorphisticis* and is to be associated with the simple truth that man is pleasing to God and worthy of blessedness, which is why he must seriously concern himself with turning to God, not through individual works and merits but *sola fide*.

Baptism cannot, of course, be given other than moral significance, so that there can be no dispensing with confirmation, which is to be celebrated *summa cum gravitate et severitate*. In the *eucharist*—once again a Lutheran reminiscence—we receive *in, sub et cum pane et vino* the whole Christ, in so far as he obliges us to follow his example in all that is true and noble, if need be to death. The *Church* exists only *in concreto* as a *societas singularis* of men who acknowledge a particular Christian type of teaching. It is better, and therefore more worth toleration and support by the state, the more it represents the *purior doctrinae typus*, obeys the laws of the state and corresponds to its wishes. Frederick the Great is quoted with approval: '*Le gouvernement laisse à un chacun la liberté d'aller au ciel par quel chemin il lui plaît. Qu'il soit bon citoyen, c'est tout ce qu'on lui demande. Le faux zèle est un tyran, qui dépeuple les*

provinces, la tolérance est une tendre mère qui les rend florissantes.' The multiplicity of churches does not do away with the moral unity among their
members, and this very idea of tolerance is one of the foremost
acquisitions of modern times.

Finally, Wegscheider's *eschatology* consists, positively, in the doctrine
of the immortality of the soul, defended as a principle capable of being
proved by reason: after the death of the body, the spirit lives on into
eternity and enjoys in the beyond the lot that is the right reward of
its conduct. On the other hand, the doctrine of the resurrection is
seen as a Zoroastrian, Jewish myth which is contrary to reason; that
of the return of Christ as a misunderstood symbol; and that of the
judgment of the world as a superfluous doublet to the divine decision
that is made upon each individual immediately after death. Blessedness and damnation, finally, are spiritual conditions in which perhaps
some change is to be expected, and in which in any case there will be
differences of degree even among the blessed ones, which have been
conditioned by their life in this world.

This is a theology of pure rationalism. It is superfluous to put the
necessary question and exclamation marks to illuminate this view. It
is said of this rationalism that at the very time of its appearance it was
made obsolete by Schleiermacher and Hegel on the one side, and by
newly aroused Pietism and biblicism on the other. In fact, it was
rarely at that time (and not at all later) that men wished to make
profession of *sana ratio* so straightforwardly and openly. Under the
influence of Schleiermacher, Hegel and the Revival, it was impossible
to deny that a meaningful interpretation of Christianity required a
wider horizon and a richer apparatus than this. On entering the great
heritage of those alongside whom the brave Wegscheider had lived as
a poor man, people found it easy to go beyond him and his like and
to treat his *Institutiones* as a wonderful museum-piece.

It must, however, be emphasized once again that what is to be said
about the horizon and the apparatus of a theology cannot be the last
word that is to be said about it as theology. The question arises with
Schleiermacher himself, and still more with his followers, above all in
the light of the neo-Kantian reaction associated with the name of
Albrecht Ritschl, with which Schleiermacher's original presuppositions
emerged once again, whether, when all the powder smoke had blown
away, what the newer theologians had to say in the last resort, when
they wanted to speak quite simply and directly, went so very far beyond what Wegscheider had said, both axiomatically and theoretically. One may in no event overlook the fact that his proximity to Kant

gives him the protection of a certain respectability, to which many
of those who dissociated themselves from the Kantian directives without adequate discussion and without radical opposition could not lay
claim. Perhaps it would have been better for men to laugh less at his
poverty and to think of his theology, not without fear and sympathy,
more as the terrifying example of a way which was at the least very
similar to their own. Perhaps in the end no man has occasion to laugh,
even today. Let anyone who does not know the theological Philistine
whose all too honest, all too unproblematical and undemonic countenance looks on us here with terrifying effect, yet with honour—*n.b.*,
who does not recognize this face from the unguarded moments of his
own theological reflection—let him dare to cast the first stone.

13

DE WETTE

In contrast to the robust confidence of Wegscheider, in which we have just been delighting, and also in contrast to the harmony of the scholarly personality of Schleiermacher, we now have to do with a spirit who found it difficult to reconcile within himself the conflict between the different tendencies by which the theology of the time was moved. His tomb bears the statement that in his person the earnestness of the truth of scholarship and the profundity of the truth of faith complemented each other to the best effect. One of his closest friends, Daniel Schenkel, was responsible for putting it there; another, Karl Rudolf Hagenbach, was responsible for adding an equally reverential question mark. De Wette was a noble melancholic. We have no need to point to the conflict that is to be found in his theology, as it was plainly there for his contemporaries to see. He hid it neither from himself nor from others. His mentor in the philosophy of religion was Johann Friedrich Fries, behind whom in turn stood F. H. Jacobi, who thought that he should and could enlarge the Kantian critique of reason by a philosophical doctrine of faith, and who is the author of the notorious statement in which he describes himself as a man who is a Christian by disposition and a pagan by understanding. If one interprets this phrase, with K. R. Hagenbach, to mean 'A rationalist in understanding, a mystic or Pietist by disposition', one has a formula which will serve as the aptest general description of de Wette's theology. We shall have to consider the possibility of this synthesis when we come later to talk of the pietistic theology of the period.

Wilhelm Martin Leberecht de Wette was born in 1780. At the Weimar *gymnasium* he was a pupil of Herder and listened to his sermons. From 1805 to 1807 he was a lecturer in Jena, from 1807 to 1810 a professor in Heidelberg. With Neander and Schleiermacher he made up the newly-founded theological faculty in Berlin from 1810 to 1819. Because of his part in a letter to the mother of Kotzebue's murderer, Sand, he was dismissed in 1819 and spent three years teaching privately in Weimar. He was just on the point of accepting a pastorate in Brunswick when in 1822 he was called to Basle. The real and joyful mutual recognition of de Wette and the theological genius of this particular city and university that necessarily followed will be clear to anyone who knows both de Wette and Basle. The call had to come and had to be accepted. He became a citizen of Basle, reorganized the faculty there and was acknowledged its head, and died, much lamented and generally respected, in 1849. The most important of his countless writings for understanding his life-work are, alongside a series on theology and the exegesis of Old and New Testaments, his *Lehrbuch der christlicher Dogmatik* (Textbook of Christian Dogmatics) (1813 and 1816); the novel *Theodor oder des Zweiflers Weihe* (Theodore, or the Doubter's Consecration) (1822); *Das Wesen des christlichen Glaubens vom Standpunkt des christlichen Glaubens dargestellt* (The Essence of Christian Faith presented from the Standpoint of Christian Faith) (1846); and three *Darstellungen der theologischen Ethik* (Presentations of Theological Ethics) (1819, 1823 and 1833).

Three elements are significant for a picture of de Wette's theological character:

1. It was his purpose, following in the footsteps of Fries, to improve Kant, to understand philosophy and therefore also theology primarily as *anthropology*. Rational man occupies the central point of interest rather than reason as such, and as a consequence the way becomes open for a greater stress than is to be found in Kant himself on the unavoidable need for cognition of the ideas that are inaccessible to knowledge as such because of the limitation and the mere phenomenality of knowledge. The presence of a capacity for reason distinct from the understanding and the will, but equally necessary, has to be asserted: the capacity for *awareness* of the eternal being of things in *feeling*, for rational faith in the *soul, freedom, God*. As *moral* faith it is, beyond all knowledge, a feeling of *values*; as *aesthetic* faith in the unity, the beauty, the purposefulness of being, it is a *religious* feeling: devoted cheerfulness, holy sorrow, and finally prayer and worship. 'All the contradictions of science and of life are resolved into harmony in the triad of these moods of feeling' (*Dogm.* I, 19). As the religious *view of the world* expresses this feeling in the form of dogmas, symbols and myths, it becomes the object of theology as *the critical science of the pure form of expression*. Dogmatics is 'a presentation of Christianity (as this particular religious view of the world) from the perspective of an intelligent conviction relative to the development of a time' (*Dogm.* I, 39).

2. Alongside F. C. Baur, de Wette is the *historical* theologian of this generation, with a quite different independent interest in this side of the task from that which is to be credited, say, to Schleiermacher. He combines the historical and grammatical schooling which, as presented by Semler and the rest of the so-called neology of the eighteenth century, was also the presupposition of rationalists like Wegscheider, with Herder's suggestion, a question that had completely escaped Wegscheider, that the multiplicity and peculiarity of historical life was the real concern of the method. Working with greater philological exactness than Herder, he was at the same time freer with the contrast of 'historical' and 'unhistorical' in respect of the object of historical science. His concept of religion, so close to that of aesthetics, enabled him to find revelation even where he could not find it with certainty as a rationalistic historian. The Pentateuch, for example, loses nothing, but even gains, when it is understood as a theocratic epic which derives from the religious and patriotic enthusiasm of a later time of oppression. Job is a Hebrew tragedy. The significance of the prophets and their predictions is to be sought in their relationship to their own time. The central problem in the New Testament is that of the oral tradition which preceded the writings, which not only passed on material but also reshaped it and gave it new forms. De Wette shares a predilection for the Gospel of John with Herder and Schleiermacher, Fichte and Schelling. In the historical-theological sphere he was consistent, and even terrifyingly modern for free-thinking contemporaries. Wellhausen later praised him as a 'clever fellow' whose writings already contained everything that he himself had done in the Old Testament field. The fundamental openness to the subject-matter, bound up in his writings with the most radical historical criticism, also extends to the history of Christian dogma. 'My philosophy allows me to recognize the system of our Church as being fundamentally right, and there is no main dogma to which I could not subscribe, in its true spiritual meaning, with complete conviction' (*Dogm.* II, x).

3. De Wette as a theologian was explicitly oriented towards the *Church*. If his friend Lücke is right, it was the sermons by Schleiermacher that he heard in Berlin which aroused him in this respect. He practised his anthropological dogmatics and his critical biblical scholarship not in the service of an uninterested and presuppositionless science, but in the service of the Church. Not only could he subscribe to traditional dogma, but in 1825 he subscribed to it in the form of the Basle Confession of 1536. He read not only systematic and exegetical

but also practical theology (not without urgent commendation of the importance of the liturgy), was a member of the Basle Church Council and, like Schleiermacher, preached often, in the academic style of a professor, but from an inner concern, zealously and carefully. In this way he was the outward embodiment of the personal union of modern philosophy, historical-critical learning and sensitivity and good church piety, particularly desirable in Basle, but also impressive elsewhere. It is part of the general excellence of this man that the problems of his concerns nevertheless come to light so often, in an instructive way.

First, let us consider de Wette's principles of doctrine. In his view, even dogmatics is 'critical anthropology', and its task, as we have already heard, is the discovery of the spiritual truth of religious symbolic language by means of abstraction and systematization, the application of which, however, must not lead to the destruction of the symbols themselves. By setting himself in the community of faith the theologian, first of all confessing his personal belief, has an objective content for his doctrine of faith. The doctrine itself is eirenic, in so far as it derives all possible oppositions in the interpretation of the symbols from an indubitable common factor, and apologetic, in that this common factor is contained in germ and unconsciously in the needs and dispositions of the human temperament itself. Since the *capacity on which faith is grounded* is set above the understanding and the will of man, but at the same time always presupposes these two, faith, in contrast to all orthodox and rationalistic intellectualism, is to be understood both as an attitude and as 'the *power* that fills and moves the entire temperament'. How was this capacity established? It happens in this way. As the *understanding* investigates nature and history, it comes up against the idea of the real, the total, the unconditioned, the necessary, which is its unattainable goal and its impassable limit. The same thing happens to the *will* in respect of the idea of a perfect moral development or a kingdom of God. To reach and touch this limit as such is *presentiment*. Going beyond it is achieved by virtue of the capacity of *feeling*, which is an integral part of reason, and the act of feeling as such is *faith*. 'The supreme truth has its place where reason unconsciously loses itself in the eternal life of the Spirit, where inspiration, self-denial, devotion prevail, and all reflection and sophistry cease.' It is a matter of the capacity for an 'inner view', but an inner view which has the complete certainty of objective experience and which represents the simultaneous practical and theoretical involvement of man. Philosophy can establish this contact with God in feeling with the understanding and for the understanding, but it cannot arouse it or replace it. The realization of the contact and thus, too, the realization of the knowledge of ideas and with them the realization of morality come about only through inspiration and revelation—only 'in Christ'. Christ is the revelation of life which, while not being for everyone to affirm in faith, is in itself necessary for reason in respect of the above-mentioned capacity and the need based on it. If it can only be *believed*, because it consists in facts that are only evident inwardly, it *can* at least be believed on the basis of that capacity and that need. In this way de Wette feels that he can reconcile not only rationalism and supernaturalism, but also Pelagianism and Augustinianism, purely historical criticism and devotional consideration of Holy Scripture, as opposites which point beyond each other. 'Thus mysticism, noble mysticism, is the middle term between the two equally important views which mutually seek and find each other.'

In the case of de Wette, a more instructive course than the enumeration of detail is to look at the whole of his dogmatic and ethical system as it is presented in his last works. His *Dogmatics* falls quite naturally into two large parts: 'The original, but destroyed union of man with God', and 'The union of man with God restored by Christ'. It is understandable that more weight falls in the first part on the original presence of this union and in the closing chapter on the need and possibility of its restoration than is to be found in the intermediate considerations about the disruption that has taken place. The significance of sin is no more catastrophic here than it is in Schleiermacher. Accordingly, in the second part the new creation is described—and here Herder comes into his own—as pure humanity. Humanity is inward piety which carries within itself the consciousness of personal worth, presents itself in moral community and is in essence as much faith directed towards the beyond as it is creative love. The historical person of Jesus forms its beginning and centre. The crown of the content of Christian faith is the doctrine of the divine rule over the world, the divine properties and the divine Trinity. Here de Wette recognized in the *Father* the transcendent God of Judaism and rationalism, who in Christ is yet understood as all-loving and gracious and is therefore the consummation of all faith in God. He sees the *Son* as being immanent in the world, realizing salvation and appearing in history in human form. Finally, in the *Holy Spirit* God unites himself with the individual *qua* individual, becoming flesh in us ourselves. In exact correspondence to this trinitarian doctrine, de Wette's ethics comprise a *general* moral doctrime, in which the *moral disposition* and the need of human nature are set over against their consummation and satisfaction in the Christian *revelation*; the giving of the Christian moral law is presented as being made up of the two. Next follows the history of Christian moral teaching, and the third part is made up of special moral teaching with particular applications and a closing chapter on moral pedagogy and asceticism.

When we survey the whole of this theological aim and accomplishment, the first thing to strike us is de Wette's express declaration that essentially he is following the same goal as Schleiermacher (*Dogm.* I, iv). He obviously affirms the 'all is yours', in a somewhat obscure relationship to 'and you are Christ's', so that he is obviously devoted to the ideal of humanity and thinks within its framework, taking *sana ratio* as his foundation. However, like Schleiermacher he is more urgently concerned with the character and independence of Christian religious knowledge than is Wegscheider; like Schleiermacher, he is more clearly aware than Wegscheider that if theology is to be grounded in *ratio* there needs to be at the least an exact delimitation of this presupposition: a place must be marked out and delimited within man's inner life and consciousness that is peculiar to theology, and the subject matter of theology must be exactly specified. Here, however, de Wette has now come closer to Wegscheider than to Schleiermacher, in that he too completely lacks a speculative background to the foundation of religion, an analogy to Schleiermacher's principle of mediation, so that the *theoretical* character of this foundation, which is also, of course, the heart of the matter in Schleiermacher, stands out much more sharply. In the case of de Wette, as opposed to that of Schleiermacher, one cannot doubt for a moment that it is really the act of feeling, and only that, which is the basis of his theology. Whereas this heart of the matter must always first be worked out in the case of Schleiermacher, with de Wette it is manifestly and unequivocally plain. He is an honest Kantian who must seek a religious capacity or, as it was termed later, a religious *a priori*, to progress from *credere* to *intelligere*; he could and would be a theologian of revelation only if and when he could present revelation as a realization of this capacity. In the earlier, more radical stage of the development of his thought which was later abandoned, he could formulate his intention in a letter to Fries, dated 1811, in this way: 'I want to demonstrate the religious ideas in the Bible and thus, so to speak, set up the basic norm of Christianity. I want to show up the dogmas, however, as nothing, by means of philosophical criticism. In this I am pointing the way towards the continuation of Christianity; I am a prince of the Church, as Schleiermacher says. (Read his *Encyclopedia* and tell me what you think of it.) Will you promise me this princely crown? If my view of the continuation of Christianity is wrong, there can be no more Christianity' (Gass IV, 522). In the open way in which he proceeds from this starting point de Wette is without doubt a rationalist, but in the first place he is a more critical, in the second a more historically educated, and in the third a more religiously inclined rationalist than Wegscheider. In his simultaneous and equally vigorous application of the Kantian limit, of historical thinking and the concerns of the Church, he anticipated in a remarkable way the aims and achievements of Herrmann on the one hand and Troeltsch on the other, in their different, but equally rationalistic ways.

This very *honesty* with which de Wette wanted to combine philosophical and historical rationalism on the one hand and faithfulness to revelation on the other, the greater clarity for which Lücke praised him in comparison to Schleiermacher, now also sheds light on the question why he did not have a greater influence in comparison with Schleiermacher and why his following was so small that when his approach was taken up again much later, hardly anyone remembered the beginnings he had made. Two answers can be given to the question.

1. His theology was faced with a dilemma, as even his contemporaries could see. Somewhere in this theology there is obviously a leap, the success of which must seem problematical: from reason to revelation; from possibility, from human need to Christ. Of course de Wette denied this leap, or at least made it into quite a harmless step. He not only sought, but soon satisfied himself that he had found the feeling for God, the capacity for Christ in reason itself. But he knew and could not conceal that a boundary has been crossed once the act of feeling has been described as knowledge of God, as faith in Christ. Once the original windowlessness of reason and the original otherness of the world of ideas have been seen, it is impossible wholly to forget them in the course of de Wette's account. Must the formula of possibility and reality in which he felt that he had comprehended opposition and transition not be referred *either* to an imprisonment of anthropology and anthropological dogmatics in a mere question confronting a gaping nothingness *or* to the collapse of the anthropological pattern, the emergence of a divine answer independent of any human elation or despair, as the basis of the question? Where criticism is directed to theology and theology to criticism, is there any way of avoiding this

dilemma? Is there a third solution? De Wette thought so, but in all honesty he could not conceal the fact that at heart he was no more satisfied with his solution than were his contemporaries. So some time had to elapse before theology found itself, in the second half of the century and under the influence of the Kant renewal, once again in this uncomfortable position.

2. De Wette resolved to escape this dilemma. The consequence was that, like Schleiermacher, he exposed the question mark, which had necessarily to be removed from both the left and the right hand side. Thus: there is a religious *a priori*, reason *has* a window, and standing beneath this window man can believe. For him, everything depended on this *potential belief*. It was the common factor around which he wanted to unite the Christian churches and sects. It was the basis on which he hoped to enter into apologetic discussion with those outside. Christ and Christian dogma, in its good sense, enter theology as its fulfilment. Yet its content, only completed and realized, is also the content of the entity 'Christ', the content of redemption. It is both what is original and what is to be restored. It is faith in God the Father, which faith in the Son and the Spirit ultimately have to serve.

At this point two suspicions must inevitably be roused. First, there is the question whether at this point too much is not asked of human reason. May not this organ, supposedly with a capacity for God, into which, according to de Wette's account, the Christian proclamation need only stream, merely be a postulate and in no way a necessary datum of the capacity for transcendental apperception, like the theoretical and the practical *a priori*? Or, if a third capacity of reason is to be involved, may not de Wette have unwittingly confused aesthetic feeling and its power of judgment? Any way, can the philosopher whom the theologian de Wette believes will find and reverently acknowledge the possibility of God in feeling be called anything but Ludwig Feuerbach? Then there is another question, whether the Christian revelation is really so suited to enter the carefully-prepared vessel of the ideas of the reality and totality of the kingdom of God, etc., immanent in human consciousness? Is it suited to satisfy a human condition and a human need, as the climax of a movement that begins from men? Can even the meaning of the human words in the Bible and the human words of Christian dogma rightly be comprehended under the perspective of a symbolic, pictorial language of human inspiration, self-denial and worship? All these questions could and can be asked from the side of the Church that de Wette so unquestioningly and so joyfully affirmed, and we can understand the lesser joy which he in fact encountered on the orthodox side, even if the 'ortho-doxy' of the nineteenth century did not perhaps have all that much to hold against him in principle.

I agree with Rudolf Otto, though in rather a different way, in his view that de Wette has wrongly been overshadowed by Schleiermacher in the history of modern theology. More than a *tertium comparationis* may justify the rather bold statement that de Wette is related to Fries as Bultmann to Heidegger. The remark may also be a hint that his figure has real interest, even today.

14

MARHEINEKE

WE shall treat Philipp Konrad Marheineke, a professional colleague of Schleiermacher in Berlin from 1811 to 1846, as the type of representative of *speculative* dogmatics in the period of the refoundation of Protestant theology. Instead of him we might have chosen his older friend, Karl Daub of Heidelberg. Daub may not have excelled Marheineke in spirit and vitality, but his originality on the one hand, and the numerous fluctuations of his philosophical rather than his theological position on the other, cause his picture to flicker and make him interesting as an individual rather than instructive for the historical context which concerns us here. Marheineke, no less profound, but much more consistent, is suited to our purpose because he left his *Dogmatics* in two versions, the first of which, dated 1819, shows him on his own characteristic way, which hindsight shows us to be the way to Hegel, while the second, dated 1827, unequivocally proves itself to be the *Dogmatics* of an orthodox Hegelian. Both books are entitled *Grundlehren der christlichen Dogmatik* (Basic Teachings of Christian Dogmatics), but the second bears a small addition which is nonetheless decisive, and tells us everything: . . . *als Wissenschaft* (as Science). As we hold these two stages of his career together, we shall not fail to see the good points and the less good points of speculative dogmatics.

The speculative dogmatic theologians of those decades and later do not usually enjoy a good reputation in the history of Protestant theology. They have usually had to bear something of the odium that attaches to their philosophical master Hegel, yet without being given their share of the understanding and forgiveness which men have not felt able to refuse their contemporary Ferdinand Christian Baur because of his historical insights and achievements. The charge that was at least there to be laid against a de Wette or even a Schleiermacher, and which was occasionally actually framed at least by one or two malcontents, was at an early stage clearly made against these so-called right-wing Hegelians, the twofold charge that they had betrayed

Christianity as naïvely to philosophy as philosophy to Christianity. One has only to read the first pages of David Friedrich Strauss's *Doctrine of Faith*, where the author makes fun of these men in an unrestrained sequence of malicious remarks. This happened as early as 1840. But it is all too easy to dismiss or to mock or to maintain a sad silence over these men from an imaginary height above their errors. One should use the adjective 'tragic' only rarely. It is not always appropriate where something sad happens, but only when the concepts of greatness, guilt and decline are in place. It is in place with the right-wing Hegelians. Marheineke is a tragic figure. His contemporaries had different views about his personality. Tholuck was indebted to him for one of his various awakenings. The younger Gass praised him as an admirable character, clothed particularly in the eventide of his life with greater openness from a gentler disposition. But he seems to have made life quite bitter for his colleague Schleiermacher. And the verdicts of students in particular on his self-importance and his obstinacy are quite devastating. All this need not mean that he is not to be taken seriously. A respectable man who has read him will not, at any rate, have to chide or to laugh, but will have to sympathize with his historical portrait in fear and trembling.

Marheineke should not be regarded from the start as being on the same line as Hegel. Of course, he entered on this line, but one has to consider whether that does not have a significance quite peculiar to him and whether in his association with Hegel he did not intend and stress a quite definite element in his philosophy. Marheineke is the first of the theologians whom we are considering who gives the impression that he not only thought *also* as a theologian, with true and honest conviction, but thought as a theologian first and foremost. Schleiermacher becomes pathetic when he feels himself slighted as an educated man by a bad theology, and he seems to have regarded education as such as the final standard by which the quality of a theology is to be judged. In Marheineke, as in Daub, one senses the presence of a theological centre and therefore a theological depth to thought. This without doubt has its shadowy side. There is less humanity to marvel at than in Schleiermacher and de Wette. Marheineke was an outspoken polemist. He stood in the most vigorous antithesis, not just to this or that learned opinion of another professor, but to the theological spirit of the whole of his age. He did not want to join in. He stood with a minority opposition. He looked for something more than what was valid for his time, and thought that he could already see it. So in his writings there is a sharp blast against both the old, naïve rationalists and the newer Kantian philosophers; against the supranaturalists who hover between faith and reason; and also, above all, against Schleiermacher's basis for religion. At any rate, the protest movement that he represents attracts attention. What is the reason for it? It is too hasty a judgment to say that here is the arrogance of a philosophical gnostic who knows better than everyone else. Of course, there seems to be something of that from the beginning. It is as though as a philosopher he was not satisfied with the philosophical presuppositions of earlier and later theology, and against it, especially since he had found his repose in Hegel, felt that he could produce the one true philosophy.

There is, however, another element, unmistakable with Daub and unmistakable also with Marheineke, who stands apart from his friend in his thorough preoccupation with Augustine, with Luther, with the Confessional writings (he also wrote a *Symbolics* and a three-volume *History of the Reformation*), which underlies his *Dogmatics*. The impeccable testimony of Schleiermacher's pupil Gass (IV, 486, 495) confirms the impression: it is at any rate also a faith nourished on and oriented by the monuments of the Church's past that is set against the spirit of the time in his writings. This seems to be the starting-point of his thought, whatever philosophical tenets may have accompanied it, when in the first version of his *Dogmatics* he turns Schleiermacher's formula of the *revelation of God in the consciousness* upside down and declares the principle of his own *Dogmatics* to be the *revelation of God which has its norm in Scripture and its rule in the confession of the Church*. Religion, the knowledge of God, rest on divine communication. But this communication is not an individual manifestation of the idea of religion, but is bound up with its absolute content. Consciousness of God is a *product* and not the root of the idea of God. It can only be an organ of Christian expression when what is needful is *spoken to it* authoritatively. It does not have an independent language of its own. Accordingly, the pattern by which Marheineke deals with dogmatics is that of trinitarian doctrine. God himself is and remains the subject and the measure of dogmatic reflection, and neither anthropology nor soteriology can have independent significance alongside this centre. There can therefore be no question of a historical consideration and examination of revelation. Dogmatics begins and ends with the *acknowledgment* of the divine Logos revealed in Christ. There is no difference between the denial of this Logos and the denial of God. It is not possible, however, to discover and to establish the truth of this divine Logos in some way from the needs of human nature. Rather, human nature is only truly there when the divine Logos has assumed it.

This old or, as Gass said, antique basis for theology, going back to the patristic period, was and remained Marheineke's theological concern. One can derive even the content of the second version of his *Dogmatics* from this concern. Even in theology, especially in theology— and this is what evidently led him to Hegel and kept him with Hegel— he was concerned with knowing the truth. In this formal decision he believed that he was taking up the justifiable concern of theological rationalism. So he could not content himself with a supranaturalistic conviction and belief, still less with the transference of the truth to a feeling that could neither hear nor speak. Marheineke, too, knew that religion is life, but he did not want the fact to be ignored that it is life in the *truth*. Not without some anger, he wanted this primal note to be heard again over against Schleiermacher. However, the truth he meant was divine truth, and therefore—at this point he turns away even from rationalism—not the truth of human reason, not abstract rational truth vacantly confronting its object, but concrete, fulfilled truth, containing its object in itself or being in its object, a knowledge that is no less the knowledge of truth by being the knowledge of faith. God is the truth without which the human spirit finds it impossible to have rest in religion, for which it can only long, which it has to know: God, as he is beyond the opposition of thought and being, doing away with the opposition in himself, is God, '*the objective power which dominates life*' (1827, §§ 5; 20). Now the truth of God is the truth revealed by God. Faith is faith in authority. Man does not invent or discover religion; he can only assimilate it afterwards (§ 32), he can only bring it forth in his thought *tanquam in speculo* by virtue of his being in the image of God, and above all by the position of God in reason appointed by revelation (§§ 24-5). 'God is not manifest in the human spirit through these, but through himself, and thus he is also manifest to the human spirit. As reason, this is caught up into him.This is the hardest thing which the science asks of anyone who commits himself to it, that the pure substance should show itself as subject, that he and his spirit should subject themselves to the divine and hand themselves over to it' (§ 115).

This was Marheineke's peculiarity, or rather a characteristic that he had in common with Daub, which he thought he could find again in Hegel. He stressed the fact in his opinion that Hegel's philosophy was the ground on which a dogmatics with this orientation could now exist 'as a science'. But one must first consider his undertaking and try to evaluate it for what it is. He did not begin, but ended with Hegel. He thought that he could not do justice to his theological concern in any better way than by developing it, presenting it and defending it by means of Hegelian dialectic. The question here is whether at this point he did not put himself at fault. However, even if the answer were in the affirmative, one would have at all events to speak of his tragic fault, for there can be no doubt as to the magnitude of his undertaking in itself, quite apart from this complication, no matter how one regards it. With what he described, appropriately enough, as the revelation of God, Marheineke ventured to think again in a theological category which the eighteenth century, supernaturalists as well as rationalists, had quite naïvely forgotten. Kant, of course, was aware of it, but only to keep it at arm's length with that gesture 'God help me!', or to thrust it at theologians in such a way that they inevitably had to and did lose all pleasure in regarding it seriously. It was a category which Schleiermacher, aware of the much better thing that he could contribute as a foundation for religion, seems never to have considered seriously except in caricatures that were rapidly disposed of. Finally, it was never seen and applied so clearly and thoroughly by the theologians of the Revival and the biblicists, whose intentions were so close to those of Marheineke. Yet Marheineke not only knew of this basic category, but resolutely ventured to take it seriously in his *Dogmatics*, not only at a decisive point, but all the way through. His obstinacy towards the spirit of his time would be a noteworthy phenomenon even if his later attachment to Hegel did not lead one to ask in retrospect whether even at the beginning there must not have been considerable philosophical ballast on the theological aim; even if the effect of his theology was merely to contribute a considerable enrichment of the theological problems of his time and not a decisive breakthrough; even if one were to conclude that with this obstinacy he was treading an impossible and unattractive way which could be regarded as an interruption to the development pioneered by Schleiermacher which would fortunately soon be remedied. It is at least instructive that in the middle of this age these thoughts were thought and thrown into the debate not by one of the many outsiders that there were at the time, but in the closest proximity to Hegelian thought, which so uniquely satisfied the desires of the time. The concept 'speculative theology' can indeed also mean that theology, seeing and expressing itself *tanquam in speculo*, has the task of meditating on what has already been thought by God in his word to man. At any rate, this was Marheineke's intention. But in this sense the church fathers and the Reformers were also speculative theologians.

The second version of Marheineke's *Dogmatics* shows us, of course, that speculative dogmatics can also mean something very different. It now shows us the theologian fully clothed in Saul's armour, in the armour of Hegelian philosophy. We must, therefore, go on to ask what that means in principle. The decisive question will obviously be whether Marheineke will be in a position to assign his theological principle a place in philosophical dialectic, without endangering or even perhaps giving up either Hegelian dialectic or the principle. We may say straight away that Hegel himself, who was still alive to see this *Dogmatics*, was quite in agreement with such an application of his thought to theology or with such a theological version of his teaching, albeit in contrast to all the left wing of his pupils. Be that as it may, the only question that interests us is what might become of the principle if the Hegelian substructure to this theology was in order. We must immediately be struck by the fact that the concept of the revelation of God still plays its particularly important part, though it seems to be dominated by a higher concept, in that the dominant concept which appears right at the beginning of the book is now that of the *Spirit*, namely the Spirit of the Christian Church. This Spirit has knowledge of religion and to this extent knowledge of the truth, which is reproduced by dogmatics as science. It is itself the concept, i.e. *the union of revelation and the thought of the human spirit,* and the Church and the theologian have it explicitly as this concept. Revelation, as the essence of religion, means that human thought is 'caught up' into the thinking in which God thinks of himself (§ 21); it means that man comes to reason (§ 22), that human thought corresponds with the divine being (§§ 28-9). Schleiermacher, the rationalists and the supra-naturalists are to be rejected because they know religion, caught in their isolation, in their inner opposition that should be removed by revelation, partly as feeling and partly as no more than critical or dogmatic thinking. In the concept, in the very essence of religion, the dreary separation of object and knowledge is transcended, faith is taken up into knowledge and 'God is known by man as he knows himself' (§ 69). Only the pride and vain glory of the human spirit which recognizes only itself, instead of being caught up into God, can want to have it otherwise (§ 75). For the free divine spirit, which in the concept is the subject of theological knowledge, even reason and tradition are one. If reason has its reality in history, history has its truth in reason (§§ 113, 114). So the knowledge of God (both objective and subjective genitives) is not brought about by man losing himself mystically in God, but in the form of a repetition, an analysis of the content of faith in the teaching of the Bible and the Church, an analysis which in its result is identical with revelation (§ 116).

In this way Marheineke thinks that he can elevate his second version of the *Dogmatics*, founded on the principle of revelation, to the status of a science. In fact, it has now become a science in the Hegelian sense. The question is, however, whether it did not hand over its right as firstborn rather too cheaply for this mess of pottage, whether it has not ceased to be a dogmatics founded on the principle of revelation, which is what Marheineke still asserted.

The Spirit, or the concept, which has now become the subject and the criterion of the *Dogmatics*, is manifestly to the same degree the Spirit or concept of God and man. It is the Spirit or concept of God: so much, of course, the Christian theologian Marheineke asserts, and one has to believe that he means what he says. It is of man: the Hegelian philosopher Marheineke also has to assert that, for his dogmatics is elevated to a science by virtue of the fact that the contrast between God and man is taken up into the synthesis of thought and being. The question is whether, once they stand in this context, his remarks about revelation have not lost the content that they were originally intended to have. Has not revelation now become merely an element of a process beyond which the higher element of a revelation is the authentic element, a process whose subject can at any time be regarded as man quite as much as God? Is there a possibility of distinguishing the incarnation of God, into which revelation has dissolved itself, from some unheard-of divination of man? Precisely by virtue of this incorporation of even revelation into a superior synthesis that can be achieved by human thought, does not an *eritis sicut Deus* ring out which cannot have such force in Schleiermacher, the rationalists and supranaturalists, precisely because they do not know this category? Does not the Spirit, whose triumph is now to consist in the fact that it is the theologian's own spirit, bring about the replacement of God by theology, the Church and in the last resort history? One can only ask. One can only assert the ambivalence of the result obtained by Marheineke.

One will, however, be cautious in asking if one remembers that there is considerable similarity in method between this result and Luther's eucharistic teaching and Christology. Anyone who censures Hegel and Marheineke for their theology of identity should be careful that he does not involve Luther. Historical reflection cannot establish whether Christian belief can exist with this theology of identity. But the question remains, and stands out all the more sharply in the light of the first beginnings that Marheineke made. Ambivalence is certainly to be detected. The rise of a Hegelian left wing shows that it was also possible to understand Hegel in a very different way. It was not necessary to incorporate the concept of a revelation into this system in such a way that it really represented the revelation of God and excluded all Titanism. Still more was it unnecessary to find concrete evidence of the revelation in the Bible and the history of the Christian Church. The right-wing Hegelians can only have been convinced that this must have been the case; they cannot have been certain on the basis of the concept in the way of scholarship. To make its relationship to the Christian tradition clearer, indeed to make the understanding of such an element as revelation possible in the first place, and hence necessary and credible, it was necessary to ground the revelation of God as such more clearly, more one-sidedly in the concept presupposed and to distinguish it from a synthesis that was to be achieved by human thought.

The content of Marheineke's specific dogmatics, too, is really ambivalent in this second version. No Trinity is recognized apart from the world. The world for him is God in his being outside himself, in his objectification; it is one and the same as the Son of God. The Holy Spirit is humanity as it has returned to God in the Church. God is the being of man and man is the reality of God. This reality undergoes a process which is at the same time the process of man and the process of God, his becoming eternally subjective in man. As in Hegel, evil is part of the life of the process; immortality is eternal life in this world and the resurrection is the Spirit's freeing of itself. All this is more than ambivalent. It is not putting it too strongly if one talks of a catastrophe. However, one should not forget Marheineke's original derivation: the disaster, if one has to call it such, that came upon him was that in the last resort he was unable to give a theological form to the theological content that he had in mind, but thought that he could do it still better with the aid of philosophy. That he chose this particular philosophy is surely not his decisive mistake.

15

BAUR

AMONG those who are less well disposed towards him, the general consensus about this man, who has been celebrated as the greatest theologian since Schleiermacher, is that he dealt with the history of Christianity by means of Hegelian dialectic along the lines of Marheineke's work as a dogmatic theologian. This view of Baur is as false and as correct as is the corresponding view of Marheineke. It is false in that Baur, too, was not of Hegelian derivation, but had his theological concerns, which he attempted to bring to bear, long before he made the acquaintance of Hegel. It is correct, in that like Marheineke he in fact discovered in Hegelian philosophy the instrument that seemed incomparably apt for his purpose. This relationship is clearer with him than with Marheineke, because he survived the hey-day of Hegelianism much longer than the latter, so that in his old age he had to learn once again at least partially to renounce Hegelian categories, and his contemporaries, for whom Hegelianism had already become a historical phenomenon, at any rate had occasion to separate to some degree the form from the content in their assessment of Baur's concerns and achievements. Although in the decisive period of his activity he made it easy for them finally to take offence at this form and in view of its dated appearance to regard his concern as over and done with, we at any rate will not treat him so lightly in this respect.

Ferdinand Christian Baur, a son of Württemberg, which has proved so fertile theologically, was born in 1792 and worked for nine years at the convent school of Blaubeuren, where he was the teacher of David Friedrich Strauss and Friedrich Theodor Vischer. From 1826 until his death in 1860, he was at the University of Tübingen. Around his work, which found literary expression in a great series of monographs and extended treatments of New Testament theology, the history of dogma and church history, there developed a theological movement which was named by friends and foes the (younger) Tübingen school or even, emphatically, the 'critical' school. Eduard

Zeller, Albert Schwegler, Karl Holsten, Adolf Hilgenfeld are the most brilliant names among the theological historians who belonged to it; in the wider sense there were also Adolf Hausrath, Heinrich Julius Holtzmann, Otto Pfleiderer and Carl Weizsäcker, not to forget the great apostates, Albrecht Ritschl and Franz Overbeck. That this school dissolved even during the lifetime of its master under the mocking laughter of its opponents and that today every last trace of it has been scattered (H. Lüdemann!) does not tell in the least against its significance. Although the particular historical form of its method, together with its most important results, may have vanished, one might say that like an association which has fulfilled the purpose for which it was founded, it might finally dissolve with all honour because the substance of its concern, which in the last resort was not bound up with its method, found a home even among its opponents, because this substance of their concern has become and remained until now the common property of all modern theology. Nor do matters end there. It might also be added that without the question by which Ferdinand Christian Baur was moved, a Christian theology which to some extent understands and grasps its theme is quite inconceivable. Suggestions made today, that Baur is 'obsolete', are far too premature, and of the problem with which he was concerned it might be said that it can never be abandoned. Baur posed a fundamental theological question which can never be evaded, whatever one may think of it.

Baur's problem is what he termed the writing of church history. Of course, the history of the Church has often been written, in whole or in part, since the time of Eusebius. Baur devoted a book of his own to a description of these attempts, of theological historiography, *Die Epochen der kirchlichen Geschichtsschreibung* (1852), but he had to begin by remarking that the method of this theological discipline as such had not been made the object of particular investigation up to his own time. People thought they knew what they were at when they considered history and wrote history as theologians, and they thought they knew how to do it. Baur, however, was the first to put both these things in question. He revealed the inadequacies of previous aims in this field and the way in which they had been carried out, and thought that he could provide an answer of his own. Theology has always been done and always will be done in a discussion between the Church's present and its past. But how does this discussion take place, and in what perspective? How can the past come at all into the field of view of the present, so that the discussion can take place, as it must, legitimately;

so that the past appears in its reality and not as its own ghost, or as our own imaginings in the present? How is it, for example, that we can now really talk about F. C. Baur and are in a position to take up a position towards him? How can we avoid being occupied with merely a shadow of him or a product of our own imagination? If it is essential for theology really to carry on a conversation with the Church of the past, and not a pseudo-conversation, then the question raised here is clearly an essential one.

Baur was not originally the 'critical theologian', that title for which he achieved fame and notoriety. Or rather, historically his criticism had its roots in what was apparently not an entirely critical direction, namely the so-called supranaturalism of the eighteenth century as it was represented during his time as a student by Gottlob Christian Storr and the younger Bengel. This was a school which thought that it could affirm and defend, if not orthodox dogma as such, at least a system of revealed truths derived from the Bible, over against the anthropological subjectivism of the rationalists and even Kant. Baur had in common with these historians a lifelong interest in objective theological truth. As a historian he was by no means satisfied with a merely empirical, pragmatic consideration and presentation of history, which he thought was to be found among the older men at Tübingen and the supranaturalists. The main thrust of his polemic, however, was directed against the rationalist historians of the century which immediately preceded him, the best of whom seemed to him to be Mosheim, Semler and Planck. The fault that he found with them was not the fault that Herder found, that they did not adequately express historical life—in his view even Herder would have been an empiricist. It was rather that, like the ancient and medieval chroniclers, they were content with incoherent reports of facts, that they summed up the facts in the light of perspectives that could never lay claim to objectivity, among which historical truth was either not to be seen at all, or was only inadequately visible. One man quite arbitrarily made remarkable personalities as such the object of his interest, another political circumstances, another the particular cultural significance of church history; again, one would make an abstract concept of reason and another the vague freedom of the individual over against society the criterion of his judgment and thus of his presentation. Baur found grounds for objecting to such an unprincipled, arbitrary approach, partly distorted by the material and partly distorting the material, even among the best-known church historians of his own time: Gieseler, Hase, Neander. A history of dogma like that of Harnack would have been condemned irretrievably by Baur's judgment that the criterion of the 'gospel of Jesus' as Harnack understood it, the message of God the Father, the infinite worth of the human soul and the love of the brethren, represented a pragmatism that was an inadequate touchstone for judging the depths and the riches of history. Harnack in fact quite deliberately went back beyond Baur to the method of the eighteenth century.

Now alongside this empirically pragmatic historiography, Baur saw another historiography at work, above all in the much earlier period, which he could not approve of any further. He called it *dualistic* historiography, which understands history under some perspective as the scene of final decisions, a scene on which now God, now the devil appears. This happens when Eusebius thinks that he can draw the line from the incarnation of Christ through the glorious suffering of the martyrs to Constantine's Christian state church as the line of the victory of light. It happens when later ancient church historians take as their guiding line the victory of orthodoxy over heresy. It happens when the Magdeburg Centuriators of the Reformation period see Christ and the Roman Antichrist struggling with one another in history. It happens when Baronius offers the Catholic counterpart to this Protestant achievement. It happens when Gottfried Arnold takes the Donatist view that the theme of church history is the triumphant suffering of the little flock under the assaults of the clergy of the great Church, so fatal at all times. And it is clear that any resolute pragmatism, in so far as it ventures to make its criteria absolute, similarly is to be included in this dualistic type, whereas on the other hand the affinity of this dualistic approach to history with a rationalistic pragmatism can never remain completely hidden. Baur did not censure these earlier historians for thinking that they knew too much with their confrontations between God and the devil; his charge was the same as the one he made against the empiricists and pragmatists, that they knew too little about the one thing, the totality, that one must know if one is to have an objective view of history, to know the truth and to see reality.

Against these two methods Baur raised the by no means ungrounded objection that neither had really shown full awareness of the real subject-matter of church history, the former because it had no concept of a cause, an objective, a theme of history, and therefore could not see the wood for the trees; the latter, because while it had this concept, it immediately stunted it and limited it by antithesis, and a dualistic objective is no objective at all.

Leaving aside the answer which Baur himself gave to the question what was to be put in place of these two rejected methods, it must be said that the voicing of criticism of these two methods, of suspicions about them, is in itself a decisive step. Baur certainly made it plain to everyone who wanted to occupy himself with the history of the Church and thus to come to know it, to the consciousness of every theologian, that they had to ask the very real question whether they did justice to the subject-matter of history merely to relate it, perhaps very exactly, perhaps very faithfully, perhaps very vividly and in a lively fashion, as had been done, or alternatively to depict the history of the kingdom of God in its struggle against the world outside and within the Church. Once this question has been put plainly, can one really still be an uncritical theologian, a theologian operating with one of the two methods or even with both alternatively? Can one get round Baur's question by the objection that he himself, as is well known, put forward as an answer an unacceptable Hegelian solution? Is not the historical derivation of Baur's hesitations from supranaturalistic biblicism, questionable as this may always have been, a sign that his origins at any rate are not from thinking outside the Church, that his criticism, too, was genuinely theological?

To formulate his own solution Baur in fact took refuge in Hegel, just as Marheineke, in his attempt at a valid concept of revelation, presented his dogmatics in the newer and finer raiment of Hegelianism. As with Marheineke, the burning question with Baur is whether this support that is sought and found in philosophy may not obscure his theological concern as such beyond redemption. Perhaps, too, there is another question, whether, if Baur thought that he had to grasp at this support, his may really have been understood and thought to have been a genuine theological concern at an earlier stage. A much-quoted word of Baur from his first full-length work runs: 'Without philosophy, history for me remains dead and dumb.' Without philosophy, i.e. for the Hegelians, without knowledge of the Idea whose manifestation is history, whose manifold yet intrinsically necessary and unitary self-movement from its foundation to its questioning to its higher unity represents history. In positive terms, critical method means *speculative* method, knowledge of history as a process of the Idea of history. 'Or should there still be any doubt as to whether the history of the Christian church is the movement of the Idea of the church, and therefore consists of something more than a succession of changes following one another at random? If it is right to speak of an Idea of the church, then that Idea, like any other, must possess within itself the living impulse to go out from itself and to become actualized in a series of manifestations that can only be regarded as various aspects of the relation that exists generally between the Idea and its manifestation.'[1] The Idea of the Church! By this can be meant God, Christ, the Holy Spirit. Of course, Baur would say to us. What else could be meant? Let us listen to him once again in his own words, a significant passage from the introduction to his *Lehrbuch zur Dogmengeschichte* (Handbook on the History of Dogma): 'The method of the history of dogma can only be the objective one of the subject-matter itself; one can only involve oneself in the course of the development that the dogma has undergone in its immanent movement and follow it, in order to under-stand—because nothing here is merely chance and arbitrary, one moment is continually the necessary presupposition of the other and all together as the unity of their concept. It is therefore dogma itself which is involved with itself in this process, which in it is related only to itself in order, by producing its content from itself and subjecting itself to itself, to come to consciousness of itself. One might equally well say that the whole course of the history of dogma is the ongoing process of the thinking consciousness with dogma, and any significant change that enters into the history of dogma is merely another attitude of the consciousness of the subject to the objectivity of the dogma. The only reason why the one can be said as well as the other and why both are true in the same way is, however, that on both sides it is the same essence of the Spirit that effects this process in itself. If on the one hand it is dogma that proceeds out of itself and becomes objective to itself in order to disclose itself to the subjective consciousness and in it first to come to its true existence, so on the other hand, it is the subjective consciousness itself that seeks to take up dogma into itself and become one with it, and this is only possible on the presupposition that dogma and the consciousness standing over against it are related to each other like the objective and subjective side of the same Spirit that is identical with itself. Within these two sides the whole movement of dogma takes its course as the unending work of the Spirit that struggles within itself, striving for the freedom of its self-consciousness in the absolute content of dogma.'

In applying this method Baur, to mention some of his most important historical results, saw in Christianity the higher union of paganism and Judaism; he regarded primitive Christianity from the perspective of an opposition between a Jewish-Christian-Petrine Christianity and a

[1] 'The Epochs of Church Historiography', in Peter C. Hodgson, *Ferdinand Christian Baur on the Writing of Church History*, 1968, 244.

Gentile-Christian-Pauline Christianity, both of which are transcended in a Johannine Christianity; he understood Galatians as the thesis, Corinthians as the antithesis and Romans as the synthesis; starting from the Gospel of John as the synthesis, among the Gospels he saw the Jewish-Christian Matthew (as the earliest Gospel) and the Gentile-Christian Luke as the oppositions that were overcome in this synthesis, while Mark was an earlier form of the Johannine unity; church history he divided into the period before the Reformation as the time of affirmation and the period after the Reformation as the negative time of the Church losing itself in the world—the third, higher time of the Church he evidently believed to have dawned in the present.

Revolt against this method and its results could not but come and did not fail to come. Of course, it might be easier to challenge the results than the method and still easier to contradict the method than to take up the concern in a really better way than the one heralded here, however perverse the method and results might be. It might be said that the Hegelian philosophy to which Baur adhered was already played out and obsolete during his lifetime. That, however, need not tell in the least against its truth, and the substance of Baur's concerns and achievements in no way stands and falls with the substance of his philosophy. It might be objected that Baur constructed his history according to a pattern imported from outside, indeed that he fabricated it. But it should at all events be noted that Baur was a thorough and exact scholar and not a poetic historian. A man who was to be found at his desk all his life, summer and winter, from four in the morning, does not at any rate look like one who is in a position to improvise history because he is in possession of Hegel's third act. Only God knows whether Baur found his historical lines *a priori* or *a posteriori*. One should also be careful with the other common charge, that he did not pay sufficient attention to the concrete reality of history, and above all the great variety of individuals or personalities. Hase already took him up on this point, and it is here that the breach came between him and his pupil Albrecht Ritschl. But one ought to listen to what Baur has to say about the question of personalities in history. 'What empty names would all those important people of history be if their supreme interest for us were not that we saw in them the reflection of an Idea that stands over them and gives them life, in which they them-selves have the fixed resting point of their historical existence?'[1] Hase's Romantic view of history and Ritschl's historical positivism and voluntarism perhaps do not represent more than a return to the

[2] F. C. Baur, *Die Tübinger Schule und ihre Stellung zur Gegenwart*, 1859, 8.

phenomenalism that Baur had good reasons for abandoning. And if, finally, Baur is attacked by a renascent supranaturalism, by the whole right wing of contemporary and later theology, with the question what place he retains for revelation and miracle, a counter-question might be posed: might not the concept of revelation that was then envisaged itself be no more than an element in the overreaching concept of the Idea of history, so that those who had parted company with Baur and argued against him were merely lacking in courage and consistency? There are only two sides from which Baur can really be challenged. One is the standpoint of Franz Overbeck, who took up a position over against all previous writing of church history, even that of Baur, with his programme for a profane church history, i.e. one that was fundamentally uninterested in Christianity. It would have had to depict the whole phenomenon only in the strangeness that it must have had for the good Europeans of the nineteenth century: monasticism as the last great attempt to establish the immense Christian impossibility in ongo'ng Western history, which was increasingly alienating itself from original Christianity. Overbeck laid against Baur, acidly and maliciously and wanting to know more than one man can know of another, the charge that he had not described Christian history but with a stiff neck had described his own present.[1]

The other effective challenge could not come from any supranaturalism but only from a historical theology that was resolved not to take the step over which Baur was agreed with old and new supranaturalists alike: the identification of the Spirit that knows and rules history with man's own spirit that considers history. This would be a theology which would believe this spirit to be the Spirit of God and therefore would think that it did not have it. Such a historical theology would then in no way subordinate church history to a general concept of history in order to prove its belief and its churchliness. It would put itself not in a place above the Church, but really in the matter itself, i.e. not on the throne of God or in the idea of humanity but in the concrete obedience of the Church. Furthermore, it would not do away with the difference between the history of dogma and biblical theology, as Baur did, and as has happened—as the substance of his method— in recent theology. Without any other weapon than that of historical criticism, and without neglecting this weapon, it would know that in all circumstances, however historical and critical the reading, the Bible must be read with faith and the documents of the history of the Church and of dogma with love; that in the one God speaks to us in

[3] F. Overbeck, *Christentum und Kultur*, 1919, 180f.

the Prophets and the Apostles, and in the other in the voices of the Fathers; that in the Bible history is to be understood as an answer, but in the history of the Church, of dogma and of theology it is to be understood as a question; that the Bible is the criterion of all learning, that in the others, positive or negative learning is to be sought. In both places it would have to make its way between a pragmatism that wants too little and a dualism that wants too much. In faith and in love it would have to observe the barriers which separate the men who understand history from God as the judge and guardian of history.

From this standpoint Baur might be asked, without any thought of knowing better, but also without any superficiality, how he thought the Idea of history differs from the concept of God on the basis of the characteristics that he provides. What is history? Baur replies: 'History is the eternally clear mirror in which the Spirit regards itself, contemplates its own picture, in order to be what it is for itself, for its own consciousness and to know of itself as the motive force for what has happened in history.'[4] 'Really?', one might ask. If the history of the Church were such a history, in which *God* speaks in the neighbour and God speaks in the *neighbour*, is the history of the Church, too, to be understood and presented as such self-contemplation?

[4] F. C. Baur, *Lehrbuch der christliche Dogmengeschichte*, 1847, 59.

16

THOLUCK

'JESUS CHRIST, the same yesterday and today and for ever!—When the sacred flame of faith gleamed only faintly below the cloudy mass of false belief, when the sleep of death embraced the community of God and Rome's rulers laughed at the field of bodies on which they trampled down the life that they should have cherished, there resounded from the mouth of him who is yesterday and today: "Awake, thou that sleepest!", and—the great giant's body arose from its long sleep and felt new power go through its veins and a breath from beyond in its stilled heart. The Church of Christ had overcome the first death and had tasted the first resurrection.—And after three centuries judgment had once again broken in on the earth. Life was volatilized into a concept, the spirit into a breath of wind. With veiled countenances the disciples fled from the despised cross and with mocking laughter the Prince of Darkness cried his ὁ Πᾶν τετέλεσται over all the earth. The fields sighed for rain and the deer longed for fresh springs of water. And he who is today and yesterday said, "Death, where is thy sting? Grave, where is thy victory? Jerusalem! Lift up your eyes and look around, all these multitudes come to you. As I live, says the Lord, you shall be adorned with all these as with a necklace, and you will lay them round you like a bride, for your dead shall live! And the Church of Christ had overcome the second death and celebrated the second resurrection. Who would deny that we live in this resurrection time? A struggle of spirits has begun in the religious sphere such as there has perhaps never been since the days of the Reformation . . .'

So begins the preface to the first edition of Tholuck's famous book *Guido und Julius. Die Lehre von der Sünde und vom Versöhner oder Die wahre Weihe des Zweiflers* (Guido and Julius. The Doctrine of Sin and of the Reconciler, or, The True Consecration of the Doubter, 1823). The passage quoted shows how the Revival movement at the beginning of the nineteenth century understood recent church history and the place that it assigned to itself in it—it too, as one can see, was in its way convinced that the present was a good time, one of the best of all times. Of course, this Revival movement influenced other spheres of church life: preaching, the ethos of the Church, church politics, church activity more than theology. In theology its influence was indirect rather than direct. The various shades of confessional Lutheran theology as represented by Julius Müller and Richard Rothe, the theology of the biblicists, was stimulated and enriched by it, but the distinctive form of these types did not derive from it. The one man, Tholuck, was and remained a pure theologian of the Revival, and there was no one beside him; and if the impact of the Revival movement is important enough for the whole of the theological problematic of the nineteenth century to deserve our attention here, we must keep to this one man. Though this confronts us with a difficult task! For precisely as a pure theologian of the Revival, he stands out above others to whom one can give this name in that one can hardly say much about his theology other than that he did it as a revived and a reviving man. Tholuck possessed an imposing array of learning, especially in oriental studies. He wrote several New Testament commentaries and a number of studies on the early history of rationalism. He distinguished himself by making the chief works of Calvin available again in cheap editions, with the support of a rich Englishman. He did not acquire a great, even internationally renowned name, however, as a result of these things, but because in a way that impressed many of his contemporaries he was professor and consistory councillor in Halle from 1826-77, first the young Tholuck and then the old Tholuck. The man who as a *Privatdozent* in Berlin had written the famous book about sin and the reconciler was found by countless theological students in Halle to be a Christian soul whose pastoral care they received. At any rate, they believed in the fullest trust that this was the case. After his death a monument was erected to him, as to all the more or less significant representatives of this movement, in the form of a great two-volume biography (by Leopold Witte).

From it we learn the following facts. Born in 1799, the son of a small tradesman in Breslau, Tholuck originally wanted to become a goldsmith and then, following an extraordinary gift for languages, an orientalist. However, as a student in Berlin, through the prelate von Dietz and especially through the pious Baron von Kottwitz, he found himself in the sphere of the new Pietist movement. As a young theologian he was impressed not so much by Schleiermacher as by Marheineke, and in 1820 (against Schleiermacher's objections, but under the protection of the minister von Altenstein) became *Privatdozent* in Berlin. As early as 1823 he became *extraordinarius* professor, and in 1826 (the very year in which F. C. Baur went to Tübingen), through the influence of the pietistic orthodox party of Hengstenberg's *Evangelische Kirchenzeitung*, which had meanwhile increased, he became *ordinarius* professor in Halle: he was appointed there as a corrective to Wegscheider and the equally rationalist Old Testament scholar Gesenius. One sees in him a remarkable spirit (still following the biography) comprising a thoroughly mundane and modern versatility on the one hand and a profound melancholy, continually struggling with ideas of suicide, on the other. One notes that this structure and its symptoms are characteristically determined by the powerful religious impact of 1817, but in no way changed by it. One marvels at his great capacity for fostering friendships and other personal relationships. One comes to know him, driven on all his life by a strange unrest, as an indefatigable traveller, journeying for his own enjoyment, to visit like-minded men, and most often, to preach. Then again he is the father of the Halle students, a man who must have been capable of combining drollness with edification in an unforgettable way. One is somewhat astonished at the outward success of a career for the accomplishment of which vigorous striving, the help of powerful friends and the often-invoked 'will of the Lord' must have been in remarkable competition. One is astonished, too, that the biographer has nothing to note of historical significance from the last thirty-seven years of his life (II, 392), and then to come upon the account of the golden jubilee of his doctorate, celebrated in 1870. Its procession of pupils and friends, the 'countless host of disciples', is compared with the 'little community of 1820', and it is said to have been a 'triumph of the new life that has made its way through our Church for half a century', a picture which should be entitled 'the victory of faith' (II, 492).

The victory of faith? Yes, if the incontestable victory of the pious man Tholuck, his obvious establishment and assertion of himself in this world was itself the victory of faith. There is hardly the affirmation, development and proclamation of an original theological programme to be seen here alongside the existence and influence of the theological personality. With Tholuck—and this is the only conclusion to be drawn from the actions presented in this biography—theological concern is in the most marked way concern with oneself, and theological presentation is self-presentation. Furthermore, anyone who wants to concern themselves with him must necessarily, above all, concern themselves with *him*. From this fact alone we can see that he, and with him the revivalist theology of his time, does not at any rate fall outside the framework of the theological problems of his time, but on the contrary has roots in the centre that was fixed for it by Schleiermacher. The religious individual cannot be more important, all the rest cannot be more shapeless, biography cannot replace theology more emphatically, the Christian cause cannot be more thoroughly taken up into the person of the Christian man, than was the case with Tholuck. Tholuck was a pure, typical theologian of the Revival; its character does not emerge so plainly with Hofmann, with Rothe, with Beck and with the others who are usually named in this context as it does with Tholuck. All these were emphatically different from, and more than revivalist theologians, whereas Tholuck was that and only that. But in so far as they were *also* that, the characteristics evident in Tholuck were also their characteristics, characteristics of the whole impact that the Revival gave to the history of theology. That it is said of a whole series of other nineteenth-century theologians (from J. T. Beck to Wilhelm Herrmann) that they had to be seen and heard and known personally if they were to be understood, is part of the effect that the Revival had on theology. And for that reason Tholuck's figure is interesting in respect of the question what significance the Revival movement might or might not have for the theology of the time.

What does Revival mean? And what is revivalist theology? If we want to address this question to the work, both classical and enthralling in its own way, of the twenty-four-year-old Tholuck, we will do best to compare him a little with Schleiermacher. Above all, we shall notice that in his early writings Schleiermacher seems wooden, artificial, theoretical alongside the *Addresses*, which pour out in inexhaustible cascades: this time they are not addresses about religion but beyond question addresses *from* religion. It is not meant to be a value judgment if we say that in respect of the central concept of his theology, the much-cited 'feeling', Schleiermacher is related to Tholuck as a painted flower to a real one or a game with matches to a conflagration. In the one place there is careful, perceptive teaching about feeling; in the other the reckless, stormy, one-sided language of feeling itself. In the one place there is the theoretical academic and historical understanding of religious experience, in the other religious experience as event and as circumstance. 'Guido!', calls the one letter-writer in Tholuck: 'Guido, there is one truth, which is not there for speculation but for enjoyment. This you are told by someone who has enjoyed it' (p. 8). 'The history of the war of the human heart', the 'poetry of the personal God through

lessons of the heart' (pp. 19f.) is to be found here. Schiller seems to
have written *Der Taucher* in order to do the following service: 'Do you
want the picture of my inner life? It boils and seethes and bubbles
and hisses like water mingling with fire; the steaming spray spurts up
to heaven and flood presses on flood endlessly, but—an arm and a
gleaming neck are bare, and he is there, swinging the goblet in his
left hand with a joyful wave' (p. 26). It is experience and still more
experience that speaks here, in a way which seems unattractive, urgent,
all too strident, if not tasteless, alongside Schleiermacher's theology of
experience. Behind it one can unquestionably hear the beat of the
often-mentioned 'heart', and through it, if one does not shrink, one
can feel oneself addressed in the heart, where one merely breaks one's
head on Schleiermacher. In Tholuck we have real personal excitement; not the concept, but the unmastered event of the arousal of the
centre of consciousness and life that lies beyond all understanding and
intentionality. As Tholuck is fond of saying, we are dealing with the
'immediate'.

At this point, however, he parallels not only Schleiermacher and
de Wette, but ultimately also the Hegelians, in regarding this event
as identical with the encounter of man with *God* and therefore in
regarding the centre of life and consciousness, man's heart, as being
capable of such an encounter. 'The spirit *qua* spirit has, at the heart
of all its manifestations, an immediate being, given outwardly from
within, the life in God (or God's life in it) that makes the spirit the
spirit. All expressions of the spirit will only be understood if they are
taken back to this root. In it they all have their unity. From this one
source flow, as different manifestations, mediate reflective thought and
the resolve that is directed towards action' (pp. 151f.). Tholuck brings
forward as a witness to these statements Plato with his teaching of
holy μανία, of θεῖος ἐνθουσιασμός, and without the slightest qualification sets Schleiermacher's *Addresses* beside him. He also finds that
the New Testament teaches a 'disposition of the inner nature towards
Christian truth which consists in the life of the original ἀλήθεια in man,
(p. 165). That man understands the Christian truth shows that he was
originally related to it. 'Now that in man which God wants, when it
feels itself attracted by its kindred spirit, which comes to it from the
Christian revelation, will be filled with self-surrendering love towards
that to which it is akin, the more the consciousness of this affinity
increases. Each time it will penetrate further, and therefore more, into
that same thing, and seek to understand it, but this understanding
will be nothing other than an appropriation of the beloved object,

THOLUCK 513

a transition into it. In fact, what is happening here is precisely what is happening in any act of the living understanding' (p. 159). In view of the last sentence, it may be difficult to mistake the connexion of these considerations with the epistemological and speculative efforts of contemporary theologians who were not involved in the Revival. I shall go on to quote a sermon outline of 1860, in which the following may be read: (1) One does not come to Christ by disputation and reflection, but through a feeling of the heart; (2) Not so much through a dark feeling in the heart as through a tug of the heart; (3) Not so much through a tug of the heart that comes from the heart as through a tug that is the voice of God the Father in the heart; (4) Not so much through the clarity of the voice of God that speaks in the heart as through the faithfulness with which we hear it (*Sermons*, 1860, p. 246). Note the crowning return to the subject in the last statement, the religious psychological circle that is described here! Schleiermacher would hardly have found anything to object to in this disposition.

Tholuck's writing of 1823 found considerable approval among those affected by the movement throughout Germany and beyond, and made no small contribution towards extending this movement. There were, of course, no lack of objectors from the representatives of this movement, and their objections were directed, apart from some concessions to biblical criticism, which Tholuck had allowed himself in his book, against the remarkable doctrine of 'the immediate' as the bridge between reason and revelation. 'My dear, dear Professor,' wrote one man to him, 'you don't come out straight enough here with Galilean talk. You should have drawn a straight line between faith and mere rational assent . . . you should have said that faith in Christ our saviour is purely and simply a gift of God; I need not quote you the passages where that stands out clearly enough. I would just like to say this to you. You are not quite correct in the dogma of the Holy Spirit who is the sole teacher and converter to Christ. That is why you so over-estimate small things' (Witte, I, 328f.). As a consequence of this criticism, not only Tholuck, but the Revival movement as a whole, should have grown beyond itself into insights which would have made it something rather different from what it became. But the genius of the Revival movement was on the side of Tholuck and not on that of this sympathetic critic, and this genius was closer to the Idealist spirit of the time than he himself and others, especially later, were ready to admit. Revival was called, and was, revival of the stimulus, and the stimulus was the stimulus of the Christian heart. The book about sin and the reconciler, indeed the whole of the Revival movement, is concerned with the dialectic of the heart's experiences, with the wonder of the Christian man, as an individual and in community with others. All this was not in principle outside the field of vision of even a Schleiermacher. One can certainly not seek the significance of Tholuck and revivalist theology in general in the transcending of the knowledge of Idealist theology by a knowledge which was in principle of a different kind. Nor, of course, can one look for it in an independent and powerful development of this knowledge: Tholuck's doctrine of reason and revelation can only be described as the work of a dilettante compared with the foundations laid by Schleiermacher, de Wette and Marheineke, and it does not lay claim to being of particular interest even on the level on which Tholuck concerned himself with it.

Instead, the Revival in theology of which Tholuck was the representative contributed two other things.

1. It brought to mind that the content of all theological statements is at least also conditioned by a particular human situation to which they are directed. There are no general theological truths; there are only truths which are truths in the mouth of the man who utters them in a particular situation, in that they bear witness and give a foundation to knowledge in his mouth and in this situation. The theology of the Revival did not present this insight—one might even call it the insight into the existential determination of the content of all theological statements—in the form of another doctrine of *theological principles*, but in the form of the fact of the *man* who was more deeply disturbed and more powerfully moved by religion than the rationalists, than Schleiermacher and de Wette, and even the Hegelians. In so doing, its primary effect was to emphasize in a purely practical way the basic methodological thesis of the prevailing theology of religion as a concern of the human spirit. At the same time, however, it also recognized itself again, theoretically, in Schleiermacher's account of the nature of religion. When it spoke theoretically, it put itself on the ground of this prevailing theology. The question, therefore, is whether it understood better than the prevailing theology that the particular situation of man by which the truth-content of theological statements is conditioned is not given into his own hand, so that it can be only the situation of faith, and of faith as a work of the Holy Spirit. Especially if one notes the unheard-of way in which revivalist theology led men to occupy themselves with themselves, to rotate themselves, to

take an important, indeed tragic, view of themselves, the question
arises whether this is not even to be regarded as the topmost summit
of modern theological anthropology.

On the other hand, it should be remembered that the Revival
brought the man with religious concerns and troubles into the foreground in a way which had not been foreseen by the prevailing theology, which felt that it must protect itself against such a development
with a degree of anxiety, as the example of Schleiermacher himself
shows—to say nothing of the prominent repudiation of Goethe.
Idealism, for its part, did not want to recognize itself in *this* possibility.
The boundary of humanity was without doubt once again threatened
by this figure of the pious man. So strange and astounding did these
spirits with their reports from the interior of the pious man's disposition
seem, that the doubt could arise whether the reports only came from
this interior, as they purported to, whether they did well to appeal,
on the basis of the dominant theology, to their experience instead of
to faith, and whether they were not to be understood, contrary to their
own pretentions, not as messengers of their experience of the heart
but as witnesses to Christ, despite all the foolishness following on such
a description. It is undeniable that this is the way in which they were
largely regarded. The theology of the nineteenth century wore a more
serious face than that of the eighteenth. And if one asks why, one factor
that must surely be taken into account is the *pectus facit theologum* that
revivalist theology once again introduced into the debate, despite the
ambiguity of the phrase. Revivalist theology gave such powerful expression to it that the phrase, despite all its ambiguity, pointed beyond
itself. The category of the holy, which was to be detected in the
tumultuous outpourings of these theologians, could become a reference
to the Christian idea of God, and it cannot be mistaken that this in
fact largely became the case.

2. That revivalist theology, despite the way in which it was bound
up with the presuppositions of its time, at least gave a signal, is confirmed by the fact that it introduced once again to the periphery, to
the consciousness of the time, a particular piece of Christian knowledge
that had been forgotten by the eighteenth century and that had not
emerged into the light even with Schleiermacher. 'The third chapter
of Genesis and the seventh chapter of Romans are the two pillars on
which the structure of living Christianity rests; they are the two narrow
gates through which man enters life.—*Descendite ut ascendatis!*' (*Guido
und Julius*, 22). Significantly enough, this last quotation of Tholuck's
comes from Augustine. But it is Paul and also Luther who seem to

be brought here from the depths to the heights, as though by an earthquake. That revivalist theology was in fact—as far as one can speak of facts where it is concerned—repristination, restoration, re-establishment, if not of all, at least of some of the decisive ideas of that particular apostle and that particular church father may indicate that the emotional arousal did not lack the knowledge of what is more than arousal, even if it did not achieve a fundamental theological knowledge in its area. Tholuck said, once again, that it was important 'to descend into the deep horrors of one's own breast' (p. 26) and to see 'that we are truly all very evil' (p. 27); to recognize the wound for what it is and for the size that it is (p. 20); to see selfishness as the worm that feeds on each man's inner life and to see as the originator of this evil not an evil principle, much less God, but oneself; to see oneself, consequently, as being inescapably guilty and as lost through guilt (pp. 18f.). Yet it was not so much the way in which the feelings were aroused so strongly as the simple yet momentous truth that was recognized in this emotion which had such a powerful effect in the Revival. A second element is the word of the rebirth of the sinner through the love of God that has appeared in redemp-tion, which, once it has found man, no longer lets him go; to which man is to cling in ever deeper recognition of sin, but also in allowing the life and suffering of the Lord so to speak to become a personalized conscience (p. 75). He may and should consider the certainty of his salvation which lies outside him and above him in the counsel of God (pp. 84f.); he may and should allow himself to be rekindled in every cold moment of life by faith in the mercy that is outside us and above us (p. 86). Those who truly receive grace are those 'who always go about with the noose round their necks, who are ashamed of grace, and fear that they may forget their origin' (p. 87). Their sanctification is a daily prayer for forgiveness, since even the sanctified man remains man (p. 95).

I have deliberately composed my report from those passages in which the emergence of a line from Paul can be unambiguously seen in Tholuck. There are enough other ambiguous or unambiguous pas-sages which point in another direction. It is obvious that the Pelagian-ism of the eighteenth century, its great confidence in the good nucleus in man and the Augustinian conception of infused grace, the old primal evil of Pietism, are here seen and overcome only partially. Quite remarkably, astonishingly clear insights are accompanied by all kinds of Christian communal enthusiasm and ultimately with a pernicious deathbed Romanticism. It is evident that no new insights have been had in the fundamental theological approach, that despite all its excellent individual details, the whole of this doctrine of sin and grace comes under the common denominator of what is still ultimately a human possibility, that instead of a history of the acts of God it becomes a history of the human heart, brilliant and impressive, and attractive in its way, but at the same time also relative and human—all too human. When one sees this anthropological captivity one sees how it could and had to come about that the Revival meant a great deal for the Church, but not more. It achieved great, suspiciously great, ecclesiastical success; it won its supporters high office, honour and influence. It stimulated the Church to mission at home and abroad, and it gave preaching new intensity and weight. But it cannot really be said to have been a second resurrection of the Church; it was not even remotely comparable with the Reformation. In the sphere of theology, at any rate, it did not become fruitful by being able to create a new contemporary meaning for the doctrine of justification, of faith, of the Word of God, to which it appealed loudly and honourably enough. Tholuck had nothing even approximately equivalent to what a Schleiermacher or an F. C. Baur could offer, quite apart from everything else because the encounter he made was not so dangerous, because while he clearly wanted to say something different from the prevailing theology, yet in the last resort he said the same thing, but with much less of a cutting edge and much less consistently, and thus inevitably came off second-best. That has been the fate of the whole of the conservative theology that has followed in the wake of the Revival, from the nineteenth century to our own day. It was too near to its supposed opponents for it to be able to overcome them inwardly, and as a result it also had to remain externally subject to them all that time.

Nevertheless, it remains true that revivalist theology rediscovered the idea of free grace for sinners, even if it did not follow it through completely, and whether with understanding or not, it led the century on a way that it could no longer completely forget. Tholuck is a remarkable figure. But his merit is so significant that one—who knows? —must ask in conclusion whether he who, compared with others alongside him to the right and the left, was a man without features, a number without a particular unit value, was not in the end a sort of postman like the Wandsbeck messengers (to which he was so fond of referring, after Luther), a messenger worth as much as ten others. There are situations when a postman's visit is much preferable to all other visits, however much more value they may have in themselves. The theology of the nineteenth century may have been in a similar situation. But strictly speaking we cannot talk of merit in history. So we can content outselves with stating that this is what Tholuck's function was.

17

MENKEN

GOTTFRIED Menken's name is not to be found in the accounts of the history of modern theology known to me. The reason for this is probably that the authors of these accounts were and are as a rule university professors, who as such had a certain tendency to regard as historically significant in this sphere only those with the same status as themselves. All his life Menken was 'only' a pastor, though as a writer he was a very fertile and widely read pastor. He is also easy to overlook because he stands apart in a degree of solitude: a local minister in Bremen without any recognizable connexion with the great decisions which shaped the history of the theology of the nineteenth century and without a recognizable school or the like attached to him. Yet anyone who overlooks him here overlooks something extremely important. Menken is a very necessary figure in his place. He was the independent representative in the nineteenth century of a type that otherwise we see only in connexion with other types, above all with the Revival: he was a representative of so-called biblicism. Menken is often mentioned in connexion with the Revival. But he had already had his decisive say long before there had been a Frau von Krüdener or a Baron von Kottwitz—at least for church history. What lives and abides in him is flesh of the flesh and spirit of the spirit of the eighteenth-century biblical scholarship and biblical piety native to the lower Rhine and South Germany, which was thoroughgoing, yet thoroughly non-academic and often anti-academic. The Revival soon made an alliance with this type. If one wants to see it in its original form, if one wants to understand the relatively independent position taken up by a Hofmann and a Beck, and later by a Cremer, a Kähler or a Schlatter over against Pietism, one must come to know Menken. As with the rationalists Wegscheider and Bretschneider, it is of course the eighteenth century that still stubbornly speaks here at the beginning of the nineteenth century and its characteristic tendencies. But one must know that such a development also took place from this side, if one is to have a correct view of the theology of the nineteenth century. In what follows I shall quote: 1. the 'new edition' of Dr G. Menken's *Writings* (*Schriften* I-VII) that appeared in Bremen in 1858f.; 2. the *Life and Work of Dr G. Menken* by C. H. Gildemeister, Bremen 1861 (*Leben* I and II); and 3. the *Letters of Dr G. Menken to H. N. Achelis*, Bremen 1859 (*Briefe*).

Menken was an exact 'contemporary' of Schleiermacher: he was born in the same year, 1768, and died in 1831, three years before Schleiermacher. Like him, he waged a war on two fronts against the Enlightenment and orthodoxy. He went beyond Schleiermacher in the sharpness of his polemic on both sides. But he delivered this polemic without any positive sympathy for Schleiermacher and the other philo-sophically-motivated participants in the same dispute. Schleiermacher spoke by no means disrespectfully of Menken, whereas Menken in-exorably wrote on a sermon of Schleiermacher's, which came to him in a book club portfolio: 'Do you betray the Son of Man with a kiss?' (*Leben* II, 148). In the writings of Fichte he sensed 'the soliloquy of Satan, when he feels himself eternally damned in the lowest, darkest depths of the abyss and in defiance of God renounces all blessedness, gnashes his teeth and denies that there is blessedness in the whole universe, and then again demonstrates that he alone is blessed, for he alone is independent of God' (*Briefe*, p. 113). But even Kant, for him, was only the consummation of the Enlightenment (*Leben* I, 170; *Briefe*, 48). In the strivings of the age of Goethe and Hegel he seems only to have seen the old enemy in a new form, without regarding a deeper acquaintance with this new form as necessary. The Enlighten-ment, against which he fought all this life, was the old neology, which had been seen and struggled against by Lavater, Jung-Stilling, Hamann, Matthias Claudius, and before them by Bengel and Oetinger. But even the orthodoxy against which he fought existed in his time for the most part only in books. So Menken was one of those theologians whom one easily overlooks because at the climax of their life one sees them discussing and fighting with the ghosts of the living opponents of their early and formative years, ghosts which may seem to younger contemporaries, who never knew them when they were alive, like mere Aunt Sallies set up for the lusty polemist. We have experienced some-thing similar in modern times in the case of Wilhelm Herrmann and Hermann Lüdemann. One can only issue a warning against taking a man less seriously because of this characteristic. Original men, living in a rich thought-world of their own, are often a little indifferent to the question of the topicality of their frontiers, but that does not mean that they cannot clarify in a significant and instructive way their yes or no to the opponents that they have chosen arbitrarily or by chance. This is perhaps a more important and more correct yes or no, and it is perhaps more instructive and more significant than many of those uttered on all too topical issues.

Menken's opposition to the Enlightenment differs from that of Romanticism, Idealism and the Revival, and from that of Goethe, Hegel and Schleiermacher, above all in the fact that there can be no question with him of any triumph that has already been achieved over his opponents, of an inner victory. Even in his old age, Menken still regarded the Enlightenment as the spirit of the time, which was to be taken completely seriously because it was gaining the upper hand and determining the overwhelming majority in the Church and in the world. He opposed it with the fury of those who have been put in the minority, not understanding it in a thoughtful way, but with extreme resentment. The confirmation classes which the young Menken received at the home of the preacher Runge in Bremen came to an unedifying conclusion when the pupil tore up the instruction of his teacher and threw the paper under a commode in the man's own house (*Leben* I, 9). He 'despises' and 'hates' the Enlightenment (*Schriften* IV, v). He is 'disgusted' above all with its moralism, which he sees as nothing but the art 'of wallowing around in filth and mire with moderation and regularity, without hating the filth and mire, without wanting to get out of it—without being disgusted at such a worm's existence.' 'What good is your morality to the man whose breast is filled with the sense of eternity, who hungers and thirsts, pines and fades away, until he finds an eternal, an infinite—eternal life, eternal love—God?' (*Leben* II, 18f.). Better to have sermons on vaccination, fruit-growing and potato-planting than moral preaching, because as suppression of the Gospel this amounts to poison (*Schriften* VI, 214). 'I regard it as my duty almost to preach against morality and to warn people of it, and to show more and more clearly that morality and Christianity are two different things' (*Briefe*, 106). And if we hear from the rationalists that tolerance is the supreme achievement of the new Christian age, we hear from Menken: 'Cursed be the shameful tolerance to which it matters nothing whether a man blasphemes God or hallows his name! From now on I shall practise only intolerance; I will blot out from my heart the shameful generosity towards people who despise God and attempt to fill it with hate, with true, earnest hate, against those who hate God or the word of God—which is the same thing' (*Leben* I, 80).

Menken's feelings were as passionate as this. But there is a certain element of chance in the fact that it is the Enlightenment of the century against which he speaks. He could later be more tranquil about these things without saying anything different. The position that underlies his wrath would have led him into a similar battle, *mutatis mutandis*, in any century. Christianity is more precious to him as an alien, isolated entity in the world. He is 'disgusted' at the Enlightenment because it does not understand this, because it does not take part in the battle of Christianity against the world which is a necessary part of its being. 'Christianity is such an original, unique thing, so contrary to all man's usual thinking, so irreconcilable with certain concepts and feelings which we have taken in with our mother's milk and which we do not want to abandon, that there is always a secret doubt in our heart, that we always fear that we may fall short. It is a dangerous business. . . . And so we build a Christianity, a structure for eternity, on loose sand' (*Leben* I, 65). This 'we' is not to be understood rhetorically. In the last resort Menken is not fighting against himself, and in himself against man as he always is, when he is fighting against the Enlightenment. We have a letter of his written in 1797 to a young cousin who wanted to study theology and whom he is warning against this very desire: 'All those who wish for divine life in Christ Jesus must suffer persecution; how much more will that *not* be the case for the Christian preacher of the nineteenth century!' (*Leben* I, 278). For his part, Menken wants to consider 'political existence' as a Christian and as a theologian soberly and without illusion. He only wants to seek Christianity 'in a few unknown cottages and hearts'. He accepts the possibility that he will not be able to communicate his concepts and truths to the world. He sees centuries between him and his native world. He knows 'a weariness of the soul, that one would rather do anything but preach' (*Leben* I, 157). One can see that there is a contrast for him here which only in the last resort found its paradigm in his opposition to the Enlightenment. Menken seems more resigned, more gloomy, more pessimistic than Schleiermacher, the Hegelians, the men of the Revival. But if there were perhaps psychological reasons for this attitude, it also seems to be grounded in principle in another, special knowledge of Christianity.

Let us listen to him, in order to understand him further and then to approach the other antithesis that he presents, first of all as he talks about what the office of preaching means to him. It is not, as one might expect, the content of the task given with this office; it is not his understanding of the substance of Christianity, that necessarily forces the theologian Menken into his isolation. He was not, say, a preacher of a particularly sharp concept of the physical or ethical transcendence of God, of the strictness of the divine law or of the profundity of human sin. In all these things he is, rather, in remarkable proximity to his contemporaries. In the central question of reconciliation he was, following Samuel Collenbusch, a zealous proponent of a theological position that through its philanthropic mildness distinguished itself advantageously from the harshness of the Catholic and Protestant scholastic tradition. Its content coincided remarkably with the humane tendencies of the age. In his view of a bliss graded according to worth and merit he is closest to Wegscheider and other cruder believing rationalists; he also teaches that obvious semi-Pelagianism which seemed and remained no less obvious to Goethe than it did to a Spalding or a Jerusalem. In Menken's favourite and principal doctrine of the kingdom of God there is hardly anything to be found that should have inevitably driven him to his combative attitude, his martyr's mood. This is rather to be understood from the perspective of a quite definite *principle of form* which from the start was normative in his understanding of his task as a preacher. This principle of form was *biblicism*. Menken had preached even while at the *gymnasium* in Bremen, and laments were made even about this preaching gymnasiast that 'he only wanted to draw his Christianity out of the Bible' (*Leben* II, 7). This is immediately followed by the report (*Leben* I, 21f.) that as a student at Jena, after a brief spell of astonishment about the 'abomination of the idolatry of philosophy' which he found set up in the theological faculty, he soon resolved 'to give up the exegetical lectures once and for all' and to apply himself to private study of the Bible. 'My reading is very limited and yet very extensive; it begins with Moses and ends with John. I read and study the Bible and that alone.' He makes the resolve to be 'a holy idiot' rather than to begin again in another direction (*Leben* I, 22). The temptation with which he had to struggle at the beginning, though surely without too much difficulty, was mysticism. He thrust it aside. Anyone who knows Scripture and human needs will not build his faith 'on anything but history' (*Leben I*, 24). The Bible is history—that is the approach to it which Menken begins and maintains. Yet *Die Religion in Geschichte und Gegenwart* is quite right in saying that he read the Bible 'completely without the stratum of historical differentiation' (IV, 267). In his old age, Menken wrote: 'I am quite indifferent whether the facts and stories on which Christianity is based took place nineteen centuries or nineteen days ago; every day I sit at the apostles' feet and allow them to tell me everything' (*Leben* II, 115). Hence the formal principle of the task of preaching: 'Christianity has no priests, needs no priestly state and authorizes no special priestly state. It has only teachers, and has these only in a very narrow, very definite sense; they are not teachers of any self-chosen science and knowledge, but only teachers of itself, its substance, its history, its feasts (the facts and happenings on which these feasts are based), and exponents of its Holy Scriptures. That is what preachers are to be.' If they are anything else, they are so 'only through unfaithfulness to the holy duty that they have taken up and of which they have been relieved neither by God nor by the state' (*Schriften* IV, 280f.). Menken was in no way interested in the confessions, but it is unmistakable that with these remarks he was re-establishing a fundamental principle specifically of the Reformed tradition. This gives rise to four qualifications and closer definitions, all in their way significant for the isolation and combative attitude which he thought to be essential to the task of theology.

1. A methodological principle for the form of the sermon: 'It is not commensurate with the truth to read something into a text. It is contrary to the truth to attach something to a text . . . I believe that Satan will have achieved a master stroke against the kingdom of God on earth if he succeeds in suppressing the old analytical biblical method and introducing the synthetic method. For when people began to use the word of God as a treasure-chest of sayings, did not allow the text to serve as a motto, and instead of expounding a word of God to the people spoke about some general, poor theme that floated about in the air, this removed all the value from preaching.' Preaching simply means interpreting Scripture (*Leben* I, 210f.; cf. *Schriften* V, vii). 'Any human testimony to the truth deserves this name and consideration and has real value and reliability only to the degree to which it draws on this divine testimony and is based on it, is completely and utterly analogous to the same and synonymous with it' (*Schriften* II, vi).

2. A curtailment of the usual content of preaching: alongside the proclamation of the biblical word of God, other elements have no place in the sermon because *per se* they can only be error and apostasy. There is in fact no natural religion which could be regarded as the presupposition and groundwork of revealed religion. The human race was never left to its own speculation. It was never without revelation, without a positive word from God (*Schriften* VI, 76f.; VII, 322). All other supposed human knowledge of God could and can only be

apostate knowledge. For that reason preaching can and may have no other content than the historical revelation of God.

3. An extension of the usual content of preaching: if Menken is an avowed opponent of every combination of philosophy and theology he is also, taking up the legacy of the Reformed tradition, a decisive advocate of the constitutive significance of the Old Testament. 'Salvation comes from the Jews.' 'No new covenant is conceivable without an old covenant which is made obsolete by the new. A Gospel of fulfilment cannot be without a preceding testament of promise' (*Schriften* VII, 323f.). 'The New Testament without the Old is like a building without a foundation, like the fragmentary second part of a history whose first part has been lost . . . like the beautiful and full peroration of a speech whose first part has been lost, which fills the whole soul but does not still it; leaving behind sorrow in the burning desire to find the first part again, from which alone could proceed such a discourse, more divine than human, which now does not, alas, wholly convince, does not wholly satisfy, because it is torn and incomplete and therefore incomprehensible' (*Schriften* V, vi). 'The history of the Israelites is indisputably the main theme of the whole Bible, the type of the upbringing of human race . . . The history of Israel is the history of the universe, of mankind and of the individual.' So the young Menken had written, and in his old age he still wrote: 'The writings of the Old Testament contain the completest proof for the existence of God: they prove the existence of God in the only possible way that it can be proved—by facts' (*Leben* I, 25; *Schriften* VII, 324).

4. An assertion of the freedom of preaching over against the Church: one of the most explicit formal features of Menken's theology is its explicit anti-confessionalism. He wanted to be a palaeologist as well as a neologist! Unmistakably he approaches the word 'Church' as only he can: he is concerned with 'Christianity', with the 'truth', with the 'substance', with the 'kingdom of God', and *not* with the Church —an antithesis which becomes characteristic of the whole biblicist line down to its last representatives like Johannes Müller and Hermann Kutter. For: 'Where is the Church? Is it in the East or in the West? Does it assemble under the pastoral staff of the ecumenical patriarch in Constantinople or round the triple crown of the papacy in Rome? Did it vanish . . . long centuries ago with the early Syrian Christians in the interior of Southern India or with the Waldensians in the valleys of Piedmont? Did it express itself in the communion of the Holy Spirit unerringly and decisively for all times at Augsburg, or at the Council of Trent or at the National Synod of Dordrecht? Or

has the *idea fidei fratrum* first and foremost produced the true and perfect idea of Christian truth and doctrine in most recent times? (*Schriften*
VII, 238). Menken thinks that he should make use of the right to
criticize dogma that is in fact provided for in the Reformed confession
(but is there reserved for the Church as such). He is concerned 'neither
with old nor with new, neither with defence nor with attack, neither
with harmony with the dogmatics of some church party nor with
orthodoxy nor heresy, but purely with true Bible teaching' (*Schriften*
VII, 256). New?, he cries to those who suspect him of novelty. 'New?—
and what you offer to me as old is only revered by you as such because
it is in a sixteenth-century catechism from the Pfalz or Saxony, or
because an archbishop of Canterbury in the eleventh century or a
bishop of Hippo in the fifth century thought and regarded matters
in this particular way . . . I am not concerned to discover how Ursinus
or Luther or Anselm or Augustine or Irenaeus thought of things and
defined them and expressed them. They and their definitions are too
new; I want the old, the original, the only thing that is valid—Holy
Scripture itself.' The Church is not the 'eternally chaste possessor and
protector of the divine'. All too often its teaching has been under the
influence of 'a philosophy of the time or a theology of the church fathers
to which superstitious reverence has been paid' (*Schriften* VII, 264).
The Bible alone is the sure starting point because it is God's word and
scripture. 'The symbolic books, on the other hand, are a human matter
which, if they are not to be and to become papistical, must necessarily
remain subjected to human testing and investigation' (*Schriften* VII,
245). In using this freedom, Menken does not shrink, for instance,
from saying of the much-honoured basic text of the German Reformed
Church, during an elaboration of his doctrine of the atonement, 'that
it is perhaps the most thoughtless thing that a Christian pen ever
wrote down when the Heidelberg catechism, in saucy presumption,
ventures to say that our Lord bore the wrath of God in his body and
soul throughout all his life' (*Schriften* VI, 176). He also found 'other
exaggerated and presumptuous statements' in this book, which seemed
to him to be extremely suspicious because of its Caesaro-papistical
origin and because of the youth of its author (*Schriften* VI, 248ff.).

On this last point it is unmistakable that Menken, even from the
point of view of his formal principle, was at least on one side completely
a child of his time, towards which he felt so isolated. Here there evidently opened a door through which he was connected with the spirit
of the time that he hated so much. Who would not expect to find
behind that argument 'Where is the Church . . .?', if it were presented

to us anonymously and out of context, a man of the Enlightenment, perhaps from the school of Semler? Who would not think of Schleiermacher in the triumphant 'neither orthodoxy nor heterodoxy'! With the reference to the influence of the philosophy of the time on dogma, who would not think backwards to Mosheim and forwards to Harnack and Loofs? We must evidently ask whether in Menken it is not the Bible, read with a highly personal view which by-passes exegetical study and interpreted in an extremely arbitrary way, which is made a principle of theology (and at precisely the same point) in the way as happens elsewhere with reason, feeling or experience, with the equally arbitrary qualification that the historical relativism which is so freely applied to dogma may not be applied to the Bible introduced and interpreted in this way. The way in which Menken autocratically thinks that a man in his own time can make direct contact with the Bible, by-passing the Church of his day and the whole of the earlier Church—something that was alien even to the Reformation!—unites him, unites the whole of modern biblicism and by and large the whole of the 'positive' theology of the nineteenth century, very clearly with the theology from which it wishes to distinguish itself, as a theology of faith in revelation. The expression applied in rebuke to the young Menken, 'He was infatuated with a desire to draw his Christianity from the Bible' corresponds to an impression from which one is not entirely free even with the later biblicists: under the slogan 'The Bible and only the Bible', there was found room for what was perhaps a very pious, but by virtue of its impudence a very modern approach to a matter which, if theologians were to do it justice, should not be dealt with in this particular way. Dogma might represent a corrective which should not simply be passed over unscathed, as happened here. Menken seems to have done too much in the direction of that disrespect and impiety that was so markedly active in his youth, only then to fall victim all the more certainly in this arrogance to absolute dependence—not on Church and dogma, but on certain principles of interpretation of his master Collenbusch and thus once again on the spirit of the time. This is what always happens to those who all too consistently and all too absolutely want to have the Bible and only the Bible as their master. In this form, too, absolutism is the decisive characteristic of the spirit and the system of the eighteenth century that comes to a climax in the Enlightenment.

This is one side of the matter which should not be concealed. We need waste no words over the other, the significance of the renewal of the old Reformed principle of Scripture that takes place with

Menken. Among the many things with which people were 'infatuated' at the end of the eighteenth century and the beginning of the nineteenth, this concern of Menken's was perhaps the most promising and came closest to the point at which all infatuation has an end.

The promising side of the biblicist principle makes itself clear in the content of Menken's theology and preaching. First of all a general comment may be made: in Menken one can study, for example, what it means if the Old Testament is really allowed to speak in theology on the same level as the New: how much more severe, manly, strict, pertinent and at the same time humble even the New Testament proclamation becomes in this context. One can study in Menken how the 'reflecting on the law day and night' that is characteristic of biblicism gives the thought, the attitude, the diction and the expression of the theologian a savour, a power, a mystery that will be sought in vain in those who are not concerned in this direction. This short poem, quickly sketched out by the young Menken on a journey (*Leben* I, 148), gives some idea of this:

> So shall I follow where the Father's hand
> directs me, and so graciously prepares
> both joy and sorrow. I shall go with trust,
> with childlike, joyful confidence and hope,
> although my eyes may not discern the path.
> Like Moses I shall be, as though I saw
> him whom I do not see. O, let me feel
> the comfort of thy presence and thy strength,
> filling my soul and quieting my distress.
> I call to thee—be gracious, Lord, and hear.
> In mercy thou hast said 'Seek ye my face'.
> Turn not away thy countenance from me.

This is obviously not Enlightenment, Idealism, Romanticism, Pietism or even orthodoxy; it is a piety and an approach that is relatively independently oriented on the Bible.

But let us return to the matter in hand. Menken seeks and finds in the Bible a totality, 'the system of Scripture' (*Schriften* VI, 196), its organism, as Beck will say later. 'The Bible is not a dogmatics, an account of different teachings composed in chapters and in paragraphs . . . it is rather a historical, harmonious whole' (*Schriften* VIII, 88). Menken at one point compares it with the seamless robe of Christ: looking at individual points one sees stones of stumbling, 'but the more one looks upon the whole, the more it becomes the foundation and

the corner-stone of truth and the rock of salvation' (*Leben* II, 136).
But what is this 'totality' of Scripture? Menken stresses very strongly,
and again in a modern way: it is not a doctrine. 'I do not believe
that it can be said that any doctrine improves, but faith in the truth,
which is always bound up with a view of the facts, with an impression
of the facts, does improve. Christianity is not a doctrine, but a fact,
a divine institution. I will not be redeemed by faith in the fact, much
less by a doctrine of it, necessary as both these things are, but by the
fact itself' (*Briefe*, 125). Now this fact is 'the one thing that unites all
the details of the Bible in a whole, explains them, discloses them,
defends them, reconciles them, authenticates them and seals them—
the kingdom of God.' In the despised grain of mustard seed, in the
servant-form of the cross and the crown of thorns, in the most ignominious self-emptying—the kingdom of heaven (*Schriften* VII, 294).
'The scriptural doctrine "of the kingdom of God" is the main concern
of the whole Bible' (*Schriften* VII, 55). It should not be confused with
the Gospel, doctrine, religion, news, morality (*Schriften* VII, 56). Not
even—as we have already heard—with a Church. For it is more than
all this. Nor is it to be called just a spiritual realm. 'O you cold, gloomy
Sadduceeism, I do not want your merely spiritual heaven!' (*Schriften*
VII, 59). 'Christ is a physical king as much as he is a moral king.
And as certainly as Christ is spirit, life, the power and wisdom of
God, so certainly is he corporeal; so certainly does the power and
wisdom of God which makes up his person have its being in an organic
body. Things are as certainly visible in him as they are invisible.
Moral power of physical—what is it? can it be?' (*Schriften* VII, 60).
The kingdom of God is a theocracy stretching over the entire universe
(*Briefe*, 35), an institution whose 'aim is the furthering of the greatest
possible blessedness of the whole reasonable creation and especially
also the redemption, blessing and glorification of the whole human
race' (*Schriften* VI, 180; VII, 58). Things are to become 'other and
better' on earth. This expectation is as old as humanity, but humanity
has forgotten that its basis is the word of God. 'Other and better'; not
for the sake of man but for the sake of the glory of God, not by man but
through God himself: 'Heaven and earth are waiting for the theodicy
from the hand of the one who made heaven and earth.' God is now dis-
honoured and shamed by this world. 'How could a soul in which the
love of God is poured out through the Holy Spirit find rest before it saw
God glorified in his creation and God's creation blessed in God? God
preserve us from the common view that things are so right on earth
that there is no need to have them different or better, as from eternal

damnation itself. May he teach us to believe, to hope, to long for, to love, to endure, to hate the evil and love the good. May his name be hallowed and his kingdom come on earth as in heaven!' (*Schriften* VII, 108). 'If the Bible misleads us in what it tells us about the kingdom of Jesus Christ it deceives us in everything that it says about him and about God. If we are to be Christians for this life alone and not to hope for the new heaven and the new earth in which righteousness will dwell, where there will be no more death, no more suffering and no more crying, we are the most wretched of all men. Let us throw the New Testament into the fire, brothers!' (*Schriften* VII, 54f.). 'Man's existence is only a true life when he who is made for eternal things and yet is enclosed in a transitory being . . . has before his eyes a goal that goes far beyond corruptible nature into eternity, and is eternally on the way to a goal in which he can abide' (*Schriften* VI, 409). And this is what is given to him in Christ, whose death is a procession of triumph and victory over conquered Satan and his princes, a sign and standard of salvation, redemption and life (*Schriften* VI, 410).

Without doubt, important things are said here which contrast most favourably not only with Idealist theology but also with the Revival and with old orthodoxy, indeed even with the Reformers themselves. Good exegesis has rediscovered them and they have been powerfully expressed and proclaimed again. At one point Menken says very rightly that to say something new to young and old one need only speak of these things simply and in a lively way in accordance with Scripture (*Briefe*, 35). Christ the real victor, the real king and therefore Christ our real hope; the second petition of the Lord's Prayer understood in a real way such as it not to be found even with Luther (because of excessive caution towards chiliasm!)—this booty obtained from a bold foray on the Bible evidently justifies the foray, for all the doubtful elements which are to be found surrounding it. Are there not sentences here that Leonhard Ragaz could have written? Here was surely more than the repristination to be found in Tholuck and his friends; here was discovery, indeed independent rediscovery, of an original and necessary biblical insight that even the Reformation did not have.

We should not maintain silence about the reverse side of the matter: the consequence was that Menken said these new things without being concerned about the old, that he lacked an ear for certain things that he should have allowed himself to be told by, say, 'a sixteenth-century catechism from the Pfalz or Saxony'. In wanting to assert and to present the 'whole' of the Bible completely on his own initiative he robbed himself of an assurance of which his teaching of the real kingdom of God and real hope, admirable as they were in themselves, was very much in need. It cannot be denied that in the last resort he failed to see the *eschatological* character of this reality discovered in the Bible quite as much as Schleiermacher, when he wanted to depict the reality of the new life in the individual and in the community. The danger, the ambivalence of unrestrained talk of history, institution, facts; the possibility that on this line biblicism might also become a pacemaker for historicism, which is what he wanted to fight against; the critical significance of the saying 'My kingdom is not of this world'—all this escaped Menken. He did not see—and here he was not and did not remain the only one—that salvation history does not tolerate the introduction of a synchronistic historical table, which is what he attempted (*Schriften* VI, 134f.). He did not see its hiddenness and therefore its potential stature. In fact he dissolved the indispensable concept of the omnipresence of God in favour of the concrete 'Here is Jehovah' (*Schriften* VI, 45). And he evidently reinterpreted the concept of the holiness of God in an arbitrary way—anticipating Ritschl—into that of 'condescending love' (*Schriften* VI, 46). He obviously found all too quickly in the people of God on earth 'the most admirable and most exalted of all creatures' (*Schriften* VI, 79, 80, 184), 'venerable men, holy men' (*Leben* I, 173), indeed 'divine men' (*Schriften* VI, x), the 'chief persons in the world' (*Schriften* I, 145), and therefore, for example, in the Beatitudes of the Sermon on the Mount 'instruction in the many special qualities and excellences which are required of man if he is to have a part in these blessings' (*Schriften* I, 136). All too clearly he could say: 'Faith is *not* a gift of God. Faith is the supremely good attitude of man that is due to God and the only means of knowledge and communion with God' (*Leben* II, 43). And 'this faith is only complete where, for the sake of the promised reward, for the eternal, heavenly things, a man pursues holiness' (*Schriften* VI, 217). Menken comes down directly on the side of Wegscheider in his declaration that God's righteousness consists in the impartiality of his love, by virtue of which he deals with no creature from arbitrary favour or disapproval, so that each possesses as much blessedness and glory as he is worth, and stands in the place where he must stand if the supreme blessedness of the 'whole' is be furthered (*Schriften* VI, 180). This is matched by his statement that Christ proved himself the worthiest in the entire universe by his supreme obedience on the path of test ng and by his good conduct. His 'inner excellence' has brought justification for the whole race which will become ours on condition of faith and sanctification. There can be no question of his bearing vicariously the punishment of the wrath of God (*Schriften* VI, 181f., 190f.), so that justification is in fact dissolved into the sanctification that is to be inaugurated by Christ and consummated on earth (*Schriften* VI, 183f., 223).

What has become of the justification for the protest against the confusion of Christianity and morality? In the light of this Christology and doctrine of redemption Menken, at any rate, had no occasion to chide Schleiermacher for his Judas' kiss, for here his thoughts are all too similar to those of Schleiermacher, however different the way by which he has arrived at them. It also must be remembered that Menken allowed himself to be directed by his legitimate concern for the reality of the divine on a way that unmistakably leads from theology to theosophy. It is not just that the world of good and evil spirits and its relation to the human world and to the divine control over the world is a positive article of faith that is inseparable from the concept of divine monarchy. He also teaches expressly that man even now has a twofold body, an earthly one and a heavenly one (*Schriften* VI, 70), and in addition to that there is also a corporeality of God. 'My friend, my wife, my heaven, my God must be corporeal and personal—or my whole being must be otherwise; for as things now are, I would have to commit a murder if I were to separate spirit and body, inward and outward sense' (*Leben* I, 104). In all this, boundaries are evidently overrun which would have been better preserved by careful consideration of the contribution made by the Church's dogmatics, without doing damage to the newly-discovered doctrine of the kingdom and to truly biblical realism. Eschatology without careful consideration of Anselm's *quanti ponderis sit peccatum*, eschatology without attention to the Reformers' *iustificatio impii* is no eschatology, however real and comforting it may seem. The whole principle of biblicism only becomes weighty and true when through respecting dogma it is removed from its fatal proximity to other modern titanisms. The Church is wholly under the Scriptures. It is wholly the Church only as it hears Scripture. Menken understood that. But the Scripture can be heard only in the Church, and not in the empty room of man's own invention. Menken does not seem to have understood that. He is one of those German Reformed theologians for whom the mystery of electing grace, vouchsafed in a particularly special way to the Reformed Church, was not a living truth. Understood as a living truth it would have disclosed him and the Church and the biblicists in all their limitations. But to understand it as a living truth, he would have had to understand these limitations, would have had to know what the Church is.—When we note these weak points in Menken's theology we should not fail to recognize the almost prophetic significance both of its formal principle and of its actual content in the reverence which Menken's whole figure undeniably compels. But it is the tragedy of Menken and of the nineteenth century that the contribution he made towards a theology of faith in revelation for his century was characterized later more by its doubtful than by its promising side.

We have now made the acquaintance of a whole series of more modern theologians born in the eighteenth century and largely brought up and educated in it. With them we have seen the most important problems and themes that presented themselves to the nineteenth century. We shall see how homogeneous the presuppositions were and at the same time how fruitful was the stimulus that Protestant theology had once again received, when in the continuation of our account we survey a second series of figures whom we shall find in different ways occupied with repeating, correcting, developing the basis that had already been established. With one exception these are people who were born in the first decade of the nineteenth century. This is not meant to be the expression of a value judgment that we are dealing with a second generation. Those who continued the work of building were in part more significant and more influential than those who laid the foundations. For the latter only remains the praise—but it does remain —that they were the first to strike out on certain ways.

18

FEUERBACH

FEUERBACH was an outsider; not a theologian, but a philosopher engaging in theology. There are few philosophers who have not at some time and in some way engaged in theology. But Feuerbach, the philosopher, engaged in nothing but theology. 'Strictly speaking, all my writings have only one aim, one sole motivation, and one sole theme. This theme is religion and theology and everything connected with it', he once said. His love seems to have been an unhappy one, for in effect what he practised was anti-theology. But he practised it so knowledgeably, and with such relevance to the theological situation of his age, throwing such clear light upon it, and, moreover, in a way so interesting in itself, that we must allow him to speak together with the theologians.

Ludwig Feuerbach was born in Landshut in 1804, studied under Daub and Hegel, became a *Privatdozent* (unsalaried lecturer) at the University of Erlangen in 1828, and died near Nuremberg in 1872 as a private scholar. Of his numerous writings the most important are: *Das Wesen des Christentums* (The Essence of Christianity) (1841) and *Das Wesen der Religion* (The Essence of Religion) (1851). His aim was a simple, but big one: he sought to take Schleiermacher and Hegel seriously, completely seriously, at the point where they concurred in asserting the non-objective quality of God. He wanted, that is, to turn theology, which itself seemed half-inclined towards the same goal, completely and finally into anthropology; to turn the lovers of God into lovers of men, the worshippers into workers, the candidates for the life to come into students of the present life, the Christians into complete men; he wanted to turn away from heaven towards the earth, from faith towards love, from Christ towards ourselves, from all, but really all, supernaturalism towards real life.

In his eyes even Kant, Fichte and Hegel are still supernaturalists, to the extent that they are seeking the divine Being in reason, separately from man. The true man is not the man sundered from nature, abstracted from the world of the senses, but the man who is identical

with the totality of his body. It is man in this sense whom Feuerbach
would like to assist in acquiring his birthright. He does not want to
think as a thinker, but to think, as he expressly says, in 'existence', i.e.
as the living, actual being which he finds present, as himself, in the
world, and co-existing with it. Only the distinction of I and Thou is
real. And it is precisely in the experienced unity of this distinction that
man's essence is to be found. The concept of the object is nothing else
but the concept of an objective I, and thus of a Thou. By the consciousness of the Thou I become conscious of the world, and with the
world, of myself. And this consciousness is imparted by means of the
senses; truth, reality, the world of the senses, and humanity are
identical concepts. The secret of being is the secret of love in the most
comprehensive meaning of the word; which means that ultimately
head, heart and stomach jointly seek and find one object. With this
premise as his starting-point Feuerbach sets out to transform the
theologians into anthropologists—but this time in earnest.

Feuerbach does not deny either God or theology. In denying the
existence of an abstract divine Being, divorced from nature and man,
he is merely affirming God's nature as man's true nature. And in
denying a false theology distinguishing theological and anthropological
tenets, he is merely affirming anthropology as the true theology. The
weight of Feuerbach's feeling is positive. He, too, is singing his *Magni-
ficat*. He affirms, loves and praises man and his will for life, the will
revealed in the needs, desires and ideals which prompt man to rise
above his dependence, his limited and threatened state, to distinguish
between the valuable and the worthless, to struggle for what is valuable, and against what is worthless. And he affirms, loves and praises
man's tendency to make absolute the reason, necessity and right of this
will for life of his, and thus to become religious in the most diverse
ways. Feuerbach would wish us only to perceive and acknowledge that
the name of 'God', in which all man's highest, worthiest and most
beloved names are concentrated, actually first sprang from the human
heart, and that religion is thus in the deepest sense concerned with man
himself; he would have us perceive and acknowledge that with God it
is a question of man's own will for life, and not of a second, different
thing in opposition to it. 'God, as the quintessence of all realities or
perfections, is nothing else but the quintessence, comprehensively
summarized for the assistance of the limited individual, of the qualities
of the human species, scattered among men, and manifesting themselves in the course of world history.' The interest I feel in God's
existence is one with the interest I feel in my own existence, and indeed

in my own everlasting existence, and this latter interest is fulfilled in
the consciousness of the species, the consciousness to which I exalt
myself in positing God as existing. God is my hidden, assured existence
as a member of the human species. There is no quality or capacity
attributed by theological dogmatics to God, which would not be better,
or more simply conceived of as a quality and capacity of the human
species, of man as such, which I have occasion in varying degrees to
affirm, to aim at, and to believe in in my concrete existence as a man.
Theology itself in fact admits in Christology that God is entirely
human. He is human—and this is the true Christ—in the consciousness
of the species, in which we actually partake together of redemption,
peace and fellowship. The Word of God should be understood as the
divinity of the human word, in so far as it is a true word, a self-imparting of the I to the Thou, and thus man's essential nature, and hence
again the essence of God himself. Baptism and Holy Communion, in
which Feuerbach took an especial interest, are manifestly a ceremonial
recognition of the divinity and healing power of nature, the divinity of
the objects of the pleasure of the senses. And thus the Holy Spirit is
the personification of religion itself, the groaning of the creature, the
religious feeling's mirrored self. In short: Why search afar? Behold,
the good things lie at hand! What man, contradicting and doing
violence to himself a thousand times, seeks in and from a divine object—
these things are his own predicates, or alternatively those of his species.

That is the liberating truth Feuerbach seeks to express, at a time
when, as he never tires of stressing, this truth has long since shown
itself to be self-evident, through the actual historical course which
religion, the Church, and theology have taken. 'Theology has long
since become anthropology'—from the moment when Protestantism
itself, and Luther in particular, ceased to be interested in what God is in
himself and became emphatically interested in what God is for man.
Theology's course of development has irresistibly proceeded in such a
way that man has come more and more to renounce God, in proportion as he has come to proclaim himself. And it is an open secret that
Christianity in its theological form has long since disappeared, not only
from the sphere of reason, but also from the actual life of mankind; and
that man's awakened self-consciousness has meant that Christianity in
this form is no longer taken seriously. Religion exists. Religion is possible and necessary. But it is man who is the beginning, the middle and
the end of religion—man and man alone.

Whatever else it may imply, this anti-theology of Feuerbach represents a question; a question put by him to the theology of his time, and

perhaps not only in his time. In our previous discussions we have seen how theology was influenced by the belief in humanity which was developing in opposition to it and suffered itself to be driven into the corner of apologetics. We saw that its whole problem had become how to make religion, revelation and the relationship with God something which could also be understood as a necessary predicate of man, or at any rate how to demonstrate that man had a potentiality, a capacity, for these things. To Feuerbach at all events the meaning of the question is whether the theologian, when he thus formulates the problem, is not after all affirming the thing in which the ascent of humanity seems to culminate in any case, namely man's apotheosis. It was in this sense that, making up his mind quickly and fully approving of it, he wanted to understand and adopt the true aim of that theology. If theology was to be understood in that sense, he wanted to be a theologian himself.

Was he in fact completely in the wrong? Had not the theologians themselves tended to work in this same direction before him? We are reminded of Schleiermacher's doctrine of the relationship between God and pious excitement, which, as he expresses it, is manifestly not one which has lost all the characteristics of an encounter. We are reminded further of Schleiermacher's doctrine of the three dogmatic forms, of which the second and third, the utterances concerning God and the world, might just as well have been left out; and we are reminded of the same author's Christology and doctrine of atonement, seemingly projected back from the personal experience of the human subject. We think too of de Wette, who had already caused the word 'anthropology' to be pronounced and adopted as a slogan within theological circles themselves. We think of Hegel and his disciples, and of the might they bestow upon the human mind in its dialectic self-movement; a might which eventually and finally prevails over God too, and his revelation. We think of Tholuck, with his proclamation that it was the 'heart' which was the seat of divine wisdom in man. The question arises whether Feuerbach does not represent the point of intersection where all these lines converge, little as this may have been the intention of their originators; the question whether, taking into account the premises established at that time, the drawing of this unwelcome conclusion could effectively be avoided; the question whether the theologians themselves could at least protest to this anti-theologian that he had mistaken their intentions, and that they were seeking something else.

But it is not only in the relevance of what he said for his own time that Feuerbach is interesting. The question he represents becomes acute whenever incautious use is made in theology of mystical ideas,

of the union of God and man; in fact, whenever these ideas are used
other than in an eschatologically ensured connexion. And there is
something here which should give us Protestant theologians special
food for thought. Feuerbach preferred to call to witness for his interpretation of Christianity, not his theological contemporaries, but
Luther of all people. First he called to witness Luther's concept of
faith, in which faith had acquired the nature of a divine hypothesis,
and might upon occasion be called the 'creator of the Godhead' in us.
Secondly, and chiefly, he called upon Luther's Christology and doctrine
of the Lord's Supper. Luther taught, with the over-emphasis of genius,
that the Godhead should not be sought in heaven but on earth, in the
man Jesus, and then again that Christ's nature as the God-Man should
substantially be sought in the sacred elements of Holy Communion.
And Lutheran orthodoxy has cast this inspired doctrine into the dogma
of the *communicatio idiomatum in genere majestatico*, according to which the
predicates of the divine glory, omnipotence, omnipresence, eternity,
etc., are to be attributed to the humanity, as such and *in abstracto*, of
Jesus; and this it has expressly called the 'apotheosis' of Christ's
humanity. In principle this clearly meant that the higher and lower
positions, those of God and man, could be reversed. And what the
theologians of old had seen as being right for the person of Christ was
now, to more modern and even less restrained speculating minds,
capable of seeming proper for man in general. German theology had
for centuries guarded itself perhaps all too rigidly against the Calvinist
corrective, so that it was bound to become uncertain now whether the
relationship with God had really in principle to be thought of as
irreversible. Hegel, as we saw, emphatically declared that he was a
good Lutheran, and so did Feuerbach, in his own way and upon his
own level. In the light of Feuerbach's interpretation of Luther, we must
ask whether it may not be advisable for us to reflect, as regards the
non-reversibility of the relationship with God, upon some things which
Luther, in establishing his doctrine, seems to have neglected to ponder.
And today especially it should certainly be useful for us at least to be
aware that the doctrine of I and Thou was put forward as early as
1840 in the strongest possible form, with Luther as its authority, as the
true *via regia* of faith and revelation. But it was put forward, be it noted,
with this particular interpretation.

The question raised by Feuerbach further becomes acute at the
point where it is opposed to all spiritualist understanding of Christianity. The very thing which might at first sight seem to be the weakness of Feuerbach's position, namely its sensory and natural quality,

might at any rate be also its particular strength. In speaking of man's reality as consisting in the unity of head, heart and stomach, Feuerbach is obviously concerned with the same ideas as Menken. It was man's existence, and indeed, as he stressed with passionate exaggeration, man's sensory existence, which interested him. He sought to have God's Beyond transposed into this human life. This might have been a denial of God's Beyond and thus a denial of God himself. But a denial or neglect of the relationship of God's Beyond with human life might also signify a denial of God; it is precisely a one-sided idealism and spiritualism which might cause us in a particularly dangerous way to suspect that the teaching of God is a human illusion. The question arises whether it might not in fact be this whole man, soul and body, of whom Feuerbach clearly sought to speak, who really corresponds to God. The question arises whether Feuerbach, with his protest, might not after all have upon his side the radical Easter belief, the belief in the resurrection of the flesh, which prevailed in early Christendom and still exists today in the Eastern Churches. One thing is certain here: the fact that a common concern unites him with J. T. Beck and the two Blumhardts, and with the theology typical of Württemberg as a whole. It is doubtful whether we can answer Feuerbach, who might upon this point also be in the stronger Christian position, if we fail to take this concern fully into account. Perhaps, to serve as a basis whereby a standpoint inwardly superior to Feuerbach's illusionism might be gained, a very real faith in resurrection corresponding to a real faith in God is necessary.

Feuerbach's doctrine was possible because there were several things which he failed to see, just like his contemporaries and opponents in theology. It was impossible for his contemporaries at any rate to point out his mistakes to him. It would have been possible to object, in terms just as basic and sweeping as those Feuerbach himself used in speaking of man and his existence, that 'man's essential being', the 'consciousness of the species' which he made the measure of all things and in which he thought he saw man's true divinity, might be a supernatural fiction in exactly the same way as Hegel's concept of reason, or any other abstraction. This objection was in fact raised by Max Stirner, a Hegelian living at the same time as Feuerbach, and tending even further to the left than Feuerbach himself. The true man, if he is to be thought of in completely existentialist terms, should surely be individual man. Like all the theologians of his time, Feuerbach discussed man in general, and in attributing divinity to him in his sense had in fact not said anything about man as he is in reality. And Feuerbach's tendency to make the two largely interchangeable, so that he speaks of individual man as if he were man in general, and thus dares to attribute divinity to the individual, is evidently connected with the fact that he does not seem sincerely and earnestly to have taken cognizance either of the wickedness of the individual, or of the fact that this individual must surely die. If he had been truly aware of this, then he might perhaps have seen the fictitious nature of this concept of generalized man. He would then perhaps have refrained from identifying God with man, the real man, that is, who remains when the element of abstraction has been stripped from him. But the theology of the time was not so fully aware of the individual, or of wickedness or death, that it could instruct Feuerbach upon these points. Its own hypotheses about the relationship with God were themselves too little affected by them. In this way they were similar to Feuerbach's, and upon this common ground his rivals could not defeat him. That was why the theology of his time found it ultimately possible to preserve itself in face of him, as it had preserved itself in face of D. F. Strauss, without summoning an energetic cry of 'God preserve us!'

19

STRAUSS

D. F. STRAUSS was born at Ludwigsburg in Württemberg on 27th January 1808, and studied in Tübingen under the Supranaturalists, Steudel and Bengel (grandson of the famous Johann Albrecht of the same name), and under F. Chr. Baur, who was active there from 1826 onwards. He was also taught by Eschenmayer, the mystic and mantic scholar. His studies in theology and philosophy led him 'from the steppes of Kant and his expounders to the more succulent pastures of natural philosophy',[1] to a highly personal union, that is, of the influences of Jakob Böhme, Schelling and Justinus Kerner (the author of the *Seherin von Prevorst* (Wise Woman of Prevorst)); then on to Schleiermacher and thence to his temporary goal, which he found in Hegel. In 1835 and 1836, repeating his course at Tübingen, he wrote his *Leben Jesu, kritisch bearbeitet* (Life of Jesus, a Critical Treatment), a work which made him at once and for many years to come the most famous theologian in Germany and ensured that he would never in his life be considered for any post in the church or in the academic world. In the following years he published a series of polemics in which he sought to defend what he had written and yet was able to give it a milder tone. His appointment as professor of theology in Zürich in 1839 came to nothing owing to the opposition of the conservative element there. Zürich was forced to pension him off. At this he completed his denial of the Bible, Church and dogma, in the two-volume work *Die christliche Glaubenslehre in ihrer geschichtlichen Entwicklung und in ihrem Kampf mit der modernen Wissenschaft* (The Christian Doctrine of Faith in its Historical Development and in its Conflict with Modern Science, 1840-1), and disappeared for a while from the theological arena, becoming a freelance journalist. This was the time of his unhappy marriage, which ended in separation after four years, to the famous Bohemian singer Agnes Schebest, whose excessive jealousy made his life a misery. The memory of this marriage inflicted upon Strauss a melancholy he was never able to shake off again. Thus it was that his attempt, in 1848, to

[1] *Gesammelte Schrifte* (Collected Works), 1876, I, p. 125.

enter politics brought him more grief than joy. In 1864 he felt compelled to enter into the theological discussion once more, which had
taken a new turn through the intervention of the Tübingen school, and
wrote a second *Leben Jesu* (Life of Jesus), this time intended 'for the
German people'. In 1865, with *Die Halben und die Ganzen* (The Halves
and the Wholes) he attacked Schenkel's *Life of Jesus* and the liberal
theology of the Protestant League; during the Franco-Prussian war he
conducted a celebrated patriotic correspondence with his French
counterpart, Ernest Renan, and concluded his theological writings
with *Der alte und der neue Glaube* (The Old and the New Faith), in 1872,
a work whose almost unanimous rejection in every camp embittered
the last days of his life, following as it did upon a long period of loneliness. He died in his native Ludwigsburg on 8th February, 1874.

We shall first attempt to draw a general picture of his theological
character. Afterwards we shall turn our attention to the practical
problem which will remain unforgettably connected with his name, and
which he was the first to bring to the notice of theology with axiomatic
distinctness, especially in his first *Life of Jesus*—an achievement parallel
to that of Feuerbach concerning the problem of religion—I mean the
problem of God's revelation in history.

'Strauss must be loved in order to be understood', Albert Schweitzer
has said.[1] As things stand, however, this can only mean that we must
feel sympathy for him. Strauss is not a tragic figure. We must have
sympathy for him chiefly because those things in his life which involuntarily give rise to honest regret in the beholder are unconnected
with any great and albeit perhaps guilty aims and since they are rather
more accidental in their nature than necessary, more trivial than
daemonic, more liable to evoke head-shakings than fear, and because
the sympathy without which we cannot in fact understand him, can
scarcely ever be mixed with admiration for the way in which he
suffered, since this once again evokes yet more pity for him, rather
than any respect.

But of course: sympathy here, particularly, cannot by any means
mean the pity of the objective observer. It may well be that in David
Friedrich Strauss, just because there was no tragic quality in him, a
secret ailment of the whole of modern theology is focused and represented in a special way, so that it was not without justice that he was
probably the best-known and most influential theologian of the
nineteenth century, in non-theological and non-church circles. We may
reflect upon the great practical problem he raised, which caused him to

[1] *Geschichte der Leben-Jesu-Forschung* (The Quest of the Historical Jesus), 1926, p. 69.

be so violently rejected, and think how he was in fact unable to find an effective counter to this rejection; we may observe him in the grief and loneliness which was brought upon him on the one hand by the truth he unwillingly represented, and on the other by the insufficiency and lack of fertility of his zeal for truth. Observing these things we involuntarily see not only him, but in a certain aspect the typical theologian of the century, so that we are not then content, like Hausrath, to establish that Strauss was 'essentially a pathological figure'.[1]

Strauss's most significant achievement lies in the historical sphere. It cannot be said that he was a historian in the sense that F. Chr. Baur was, nor one of such standing. He found it possible to write, as early as 7th April, 1837: 'I am beginning to find the manner of pure science a dry one. I was not really meant to be a scholar; I am much too dependent upon mood, and far too self-occupied.' Over and over again he made similar statements about himself. The discovery in historical method he undoubtedly made in his first Life of Jesus he hit upon more by chance than anything. This is shown by the fact that he did not abide by it, in its most decisive feature, in the second, in 1864, and indeed rather found means to adapt his method, in this very decisive feature, to the criticism that had been noised in respect of the first Life of Jesus. How did this come about? 'The mood was no longer there, in which I had written the book originally.'[2] The other, smaller historical works mostly biographical in content which we have from Strauss are not governed by the spirit of cohesive historical research either, or by an actual feeling for the past. In presenting Hutten or Voltaire, Frischlin or Schubert, he was much more concerned, once again upon his own confession, with the dream-image of his own existence than with the historical material as such. 'I am not a historian; with me everything has proceeded from dogmatic (or rather anti-dogmatic) concerns.'[3] The hero of a Strauss biography 'had to show intellectual interests, had to have intellectual accomplishments which could be pointed out, and indeed in a direction related to mine; he had to be facing the light, and freedom; an enemy of despots and the priesthood'.[4] Thus his serious attempt to write a biography of Luther was also bound to come to grief simply because he could not but consider Luther's concept of faith as 'something purely irrational, and indeed horrible'.[5] 'A man

---

[1] D. Fr. Strauss und die Theologie seiner Zeit (D. Fr. Strauss and the Theology of his Time), 1876, Vol. 2, p. 390.
[2] Collected Works, I, p. 6.   [3] Letter of 22nd July, 1846.
[4] Collected Works, I, p. 31.   [5] Letter of 24th December, 1857.

in whom everything proceeds from the consciousness that he and all men are in themselves utterly depraved, and subject to eternal damnation, from which they can be redeemed only by the blood of Christ and their belief in its power—a man with this consciousness as his core is so alien, so incomprehensible to me, that I could never choose him as the hero of a biography. No matter what other qualities I might love and admire in him, this inmost consciousness of his is so repugnant to me that there could never be any question of the sympathy existing between him and myself which is indispensable between the biographer and his hero.'[1] Speaking in this way he had in fact, with hostile acumen, seen in Luther what the historians as a rule either cannot or will not see, but he was not himself a historian.

Strauss has been called a speculative mind. This is only true if we look upon Strauss not so much as one who thinks as one who broods, with a passionate, shrewd, and skilful, co-ordinating brooding. Upon points of detail Strauss was without doubt clever, amazingly clear-sighted, stimulating and often amusing in description and debate. What he completely lacked was the 'thinker's' ability to build up consecutively, to construct, to synthesize.

In this respect he failed in a way which was nothing short of disastrous no less than three times in his life. Each time it was when writing one of his three most important works. The first time was on the occasion of his first *Life of Jesus*. This work, faithful to the Hegelian tradition, was really only intended as a critical analysis of the naïve conception of Christ, as furnished by tradition, to be followed by a speculative reconstruction of Christology as the true turning-point of the book. The first part of the programme, the antithesis, was meticulously executed. What was to be the actual positive achievement, however, the very part which Strauss, according to a letter of the 6th February, 1832, considered, strangely enough, to be the easiest, remained unwritten, apart from the often-quoted allusions to it in the final section of the second volume. The same thing happened again in 1840-1 in his *Doctrine of Faith*. What was intended and promised in the polemics preceding it was a positive representation of dogma following a critical reduction of dogmatics, a dogma conclusively intellectualized by speculation, but justified too by this process, in the manner, perhaps, in which A. E. Biedermann later did it in the third part of his dogmatics. All Strauss was able to do, was to steer the ship of dogmatics carefully on to the rocks of a somewhat facile confrontation with Spinoza's and Hegel's philosophy and have it founder there

[1] *Collected Works*, I, p. 41.

with all hands. The 1,400 pages of this second work were not followed by a positive second part either. The same inability to keep to a system was shown yet again in 1872 in *The Old and the New Faith*, in which Strauss finally achieved an exposition of the new faith, but in the form of a journalistic conglomeration of a little Darwin, a little Goethe, a little Lessing, a little art criticism, and a great deal of anonymous, flatly bourgeois morality so incoherent that one would suppose its author to have been forsaken by any idea of the form, even, of the art of philosophy. It was indeed too easy for Nietzsche, in the well-known, devastating first part of his *Unzeitgemässe Betrachtungen* (Untimely Observations), to bring about the old man's literary and philosophical demise, a few weeks before the latter met his physical end. Certainly there can be few who have thought more, more industriously, and more existentially than Strauss in their lives; but even more certainly he was not a thinker.

Furthermore, Strauss has been represented as the quasi-daemonic type of cold, dry, intellectual logic, particularly by his opponents, and he has been made the object of a horrified amazement. And he himself, in fact, seems to have thought that his strength lay in this direction. He imagined he had discovered in himself the gift of 'dialectic thought', as a substitute for the creative imagination which he lacked.[1] When he went on his first train-journey (between Heidelberg and Mannheim) in 1841, he had, according to a letter of 24th May, 1841, 'no fear, but the feeling that the governing principle of such inventions was most closely related to my own . . . this abstraction, this tearing-away of the individual by a universal might, such as occurs with these colossal, gigantic machines is exactly the same principle which we represent in the study of knowledge'.

We can certainly gain the impression that here is a logic proceeding, as it were, on rails, by consulting any piece of Strauss's work; the great declaration of bankruptcy of *The Christian Doctrine of Faith*, for instance. But if we look at his life-work as a whole, we find the term 'spiral', which Hausrath used to describe it, too suggestive of a unity. At this time it was Feuerbach who was characterized by the intellectual logic of the things he wanted, and not Strauss, who wrote of himself on the 17th March, 1838, that 'every six years or so an old scholar dies off in me'. Strauss was clever, but not clever as F. Chr. Baur, who was able to lay hold of an idea, and pursue it singly in perhaps very varied form. Strauss was clever, rather, in a very illogical fashion, first in one way, and then in another, just as the cleverness happened to come as a

[1] *Collected Works*, I, p. 12.

result of all kinds of determining factors which were of an outer rather than an inner nature. At the time when he was becoming a Hegelian, for example, he was able to preach in a faultlessly orthodox way and unobjectionably and successfully answer a prize question of the faculty of Catholic Theology of Tübingen, mark you, upon the resurrection of the flesh. 'With complete conviction I proved the resurrection of the dead by exegesis and natural philosophy, and as I made the last point it was clear to me that there was nothing in it at all.'[1] Between 1836 and 1840, in consideration of his outer situation too, he was prepared to make concessions, and to compromise about his *Life of Jesus*, the effects of which had surprised him himself. Then contrariwise in 1840, in anger about his experiences at the hands of the people of Zürich, he notoriously performed a reduction of the *Doctrine of Faith*, instead of a reconstruction, and in the same mood also took back his concessions concerning the *Life of Jesus*. Then as a private author he advocated a liberal Church and theology once again, in spite of his book of 1840-1. This in no way prevented him from attacking the Liberals from the rear in the sixties, once again chiefly because he had been personally disillusioned. This was precisely the most difficult time that liberalism had in church politics. It did not prevent him from playing off Hengstenberg against Schenkel, and thinking that this very work (*The Halves and the Wholes*) was 'the best I have ever written in polemics'.[2] On top of all this he finally, after forty years as an idealist, fell among the materialists 'like Karl Moor among the robbers' (Hausrath), and indeed among the scientific materialists, and of these among the Darwinists, of all people. Arrived at this point Strauss, the pupil of Hegel, was finally unable to recall any argument against man's origin with the apes. Thus, with the best will in the world, we cannot say that Strauss's life-work has a particular tendency or character. The tendency it does have is to take the line of the most obvious, of least resistance, of finding the easiest opportunity for striking out at theology or the Church, and justifying again and again the writer's own departure from their murky kingdom. One's final impression—which is Hausrath's too, who was very well disposed to him—does little to bear out convincingly Strauss's realism. It is that, deprived of his grounds for feeling ill-used and given a respectable professorship somewhere, like all the others he would have been capable of different achievements in questions of decisive importance, and certainly of taking another ultimate course. In these circumstances it is impossible for us to admire him as the champion of intellectual logic.

[1] Letter of 8th February, 1838.   [2] *Collected Works*, I, p. 62.

STRAUSS 547

And only now in fact do we come to the most important point. Strauss offered to his time the sight of the theologian who has become an unbeliever, for all to behold and without denying it. From 1839, at the latest, he wrathfully and zealously stood in opposition not only to the Church, but to God himself, like Michael Kohlhaas going to law, finally continuing to fight his case as an outlaw, having made of this dispute his life's profession. And contending even beyond the grave, he forbade any participation by a clergyman at his funeral already ten years before the event.[1] The denial he gave, as for instance in his *Doctrine of Faith*, is truly a very angry one. 'I have encircled and assaulted theism from every side, and bested the language of pantheism from an open position', he triumphs in a letter of 27th February, 1840. The chapter on the Church concludes with the frank declaration[2] that theology today could only still be productive by carrying out the task of destruction. Its task at the present time was to demolish a building which no longer fitted in with the architectural plan for the new world, and to demolish it in such a way that, even if it was not brought down upon the heads of its inhabitants, their gradual departure would be in part awaited, and in part accelerated. The study of theology, once the path to the ministry, was now the best way to become unfit for it. For as dogma was the outlook upon life of an idiot consciousness, theology being however the knowledge of this consciousness, this knowledge had at the present time become so critically penetrating, owing to the influence of philosophy, that anyone arriving at such a science would of necessity abandon that of which it is a science, namely the outlook upon life of an idiot consciousness. We should soon be reaching the state where the only people who could still be considered for the office of clergymen would be religious idiots and those theologically self-taught, those speaking and presiding at pietist gatherings.

'The religious chord in him gave forth no sound', Hausrath laments, and considers it to be Strauss's greatest failing that he simply did not understand that religion was not a matter for thought, but for feeling: 'a way of sensing God, and tuning oneself to the world'.[3] If it had been a matter of feeling, sense and mood he would inevitably have been the most faithful theologian, for with these things he was richly endowed, indeed to the point of over-sensibility. If this had been in question, then we might still have held it to his credit that in the time before he became critical, at the end of the twenties, he too experienced a revival —it was, after all, not for nothing that he lived at the same time as

[1] Letter of 22nd May, 1863.   [2] Vol. 2, p. 624.   [3] Op. cit., I, p. 6; II, p. 391.

Ludwig Hofacker, Albert Knapp and the other fathers of Württemberg
neo-pietism—and sang of it in a poem, the last verse of which runs:

> Yes, be Thou sun, and I the tree,
> But hopeful gazing up to Thee;
> Be Thou the streamlet on the lea,
> And I the grass-blade close to Thee;
> O let me ne'er be rich and mine
> But only, Jesus, poor and Thine![1]

We should be deceiving ourselves if the many angry words which
Strauss put on paper about the Church and theology and everything
that has to do with them were to tempt us to think straightaway of
those souls which, according to the Calvinist doctrine of predestination,
are hardened from eternity. Strauss did make such a markedly anti-
Christian impression upon not a few of his contemporaries. Above all
he himself continually flirted with his unbelief in such a way that we
cannot help taking the phenomenon into account. But I strongly
advise anyone who today is still perhaps tempted to behold in him
something like the spirit which constantly denies, to read his *The Old and
the New Faiih*. For the impression this work gives is that this heretic and
unbeliever, who appears to be so dreadful, is in fact basically nothing
but a Central European rejoicing in his learning, but not, unfortunately, quite content with himself and the world about him. The hell
which quite properly seems to contain him is more like a 'home,
sweet home' or *Gartenlaube*[2] than an inferno such as Dante or the
cheerful Angelus Silesius saw and described. The book has four
parts:

1. Are we still Christians?—Answer: No, because first it is no longer
necessary for us to be Christians, and secondly, it does not suit us any
more.

2. Are we still religious? Answer: 'Yes or No, according to what you
mean by religion.' And yet Yes, in so far as, in spite of Schopenhauer,
we are happy in a feeling of dependence upon the All, for which in the
face of such pessimists, we demand most decidedly the same piety as the
pious man of former times demanded for his God. 'Our feeling for
the All reacts, if it is done injury, in absolutely religious fashion'[3]—after
all, then: Yes!

3. What is our conception of the world? Answer: We arrive at it by
a free interpretation of Kant-Laplace, Lamarck, Darwin, Haeckel—

---

[1] 1827 or 1828, *Collected Works*, XII, p. 96.
[2] *Lit.*: arbour; title of a once popular illustrated German family magazine (Tr.).
[3] *Collected Works*, VI, p. 97.

i.e. as infinite, animated matter, engaged in an ascent to ever higher forms.

4. How do we order our lives? Answer: In determining ourselves in accordance with the idea of the species! This is then elucidated by a loosely-linked series of observations on the necessity of monogamy, but also on the right to divorce, on the justification for war and capital punishment, on the excellence of the feeling of nationalism as compared with all cosmopolitanism, on the rights of the monarchy and nobility (although the author himself is proud that he is a bourgeois), on the dangers of a social democracy, on the sanctity of private property, and on the necessity for a corresponding limitation of the right of universal suffrage. All this is well in keeping with the fact that Strauss was so deeply shocked by the revolution of 1848, almost before it was there, as only a good Conservative could be at that time, and that he expressly yearned for 'the old police state';[1] further, that when, like Christoph Blumhardt fifty years later, he had, paradoxically, become a member of the Württemberg Parliament, he spoke, upon the occasion of the shooting of Robert Blum, emphatically against a demonstration of that parliament in his favour, and, finally, that he openly declared[2] that he would rather be governèd in the Russian than in the democratic manner. In conclusion there is a description of how those for whom the book is supposed to have been written spend their Sunday, as distinct from those who profess the old faith: they do this with political discussions, and then with studies in history and natural science, with edification from *Hermann and Dorothea*, and finally with performances of works by Haydn, Mozart and Beethoven. 'A stimulant to mind and spirit, humour and imagination, such as leaves nothing to be desired. Thus we live, thus we pass blissfully upon our way!'[3]

Strauss, we tell ourselves on reading this, was not the Antichrist by any means. And almost the last thing there is to be said about the non-tragic quality of his general attitude—and this is just what evokes our sympathy—is that he did not even have the qualifications and the stature of a true evil heretic. It is that the result of all his negations was by no means an appalling Promethean uproar, but for all his attempted flat denials of God always only this self-conscious intellectual bourgeois quality, which was always morose, without the slightest notion of all the true heights and depths of life, the bourgeois quality in its specific national German form at the sunset hour of the age of Goethe, upon which Nietzsche then poured such cruel scorn as the embodiment of

[1] Letter of 13th April, 1848.   [2] Letter of 26th February, 1852.
[3] *Collected Works*, VI, pp. 198f.

the 'philistine of culture'. I quote in conclusion two very good speci-
mens of Strauss's poetry:

> I longed to travel; now I do not leave,
> And yet I do not know, if I shall stay.
> Certain it is that here's a foreign land:
> And where my true one is, I cannot say.
> I think I once had children, two, and dear;
> But yet I know not if it was a dream.
> A wife I spurned, if love to hatred turned,
> A hatred turned to love, I do not know.
> Books I used to write, or so they say—
> If they speak truth, or mock, I cannot tell.
> I hear, an unbeliever I am called:
> I know not if I am not rather pious.
> The thought of death has never caused me fear:
> I know not if I am not long since dead.[1]

> He to whom I thus lament
> Knows that I am not lamenting;
> She to whom I thus comment,
> Knows that I am not near fainting.
> Like a light we fade today,
> As a glow that dies;
> Slowly we are borne away,
> As a sound that flies.
> May this final flicker,
> May this sound but be
> Pure and clear for ever
> However weak it be.[2]

We certainly cannot read these poems without a sense of sympathy
for a fellow human being. It must and may, however, be said that this
is not the speech of the Antichrist; nor of Prometheus; nor of any true,
perilous spirit of rebellion. It can in fact only be the speech, always a
little haughty, and always a bit disillusioned, of the true nineteenth
century. And if there are those who are perhaps inclined to admire and
praise the 'truthfulness' of such language, and that of Strauss's language
altogether, then they should at all events grant that Albert Schweitzer[3]
was right in describing it as an 'uncreative truthfulness'.

If that were all there is to say about Strauss then the question, the
admittedly serious question, with which we should have to take leave of
him, could only be the one to which we have already alluded: whether
it was not that with him something was nakedly revealed to the light

---

[1] 1848, Collected Works, XII, p. 64; for orginal, cf. Appendix, p. 421.
[2] 29th December, 1873, Collected Works, XII, p. 226; for original, cf. Appendix, p. 422.
[3] Op. cit., p. 78.

which remained more or less hidden in those more brilliant and more fortunate figures—or those, rather, who did not lay themselves open so much as he did, who were his close neighbours in theology and, further, whether the common hidden element in all nineteenth-century theology which became manifest with Strauss was not so much a particular sin of wickedness, but just one of an extraordinary weakness?

But this does not conclude our discussion of Strauss and his significance for the theology of more recent times. We turn our attention now —and here our task becomes more difficult—to the author of the *Life of Jesus*.

First, as a general appraisal of this work, I shall relate some of the characteristic things which Strauss said in the second book with this title, the *Life of Jesus* of 1864. Paragraphs 33 and 34 are concerned with 'the religious consciousness of Jesus'. Jesus's religious consciousness, Strauss begins, must have been there first, as the original thing, his consciousness that he was the Messiah being the form this religious consciousness only subsequently took. According to the meaning of the Gospel according to St John, which could not be explained away, Jesus considered himself as the personal divine Word of the Creator, which had been with God from eternity, which then became man for a while, for the sake of redemption, and then afterwards returned to God. We cannot possibly suppose that Jesus really did this. For first, in the accredited story no example of such a consciousness is known to us. But if we were to meet a man with such consciousness, we should take him to be a half-wit or a deceiver. Jesus as described by St John, with his 'he that seeth me seeth him that sent me', and 'I and my Father are one', must inevitably be as contemptible to us as Louis XIV with his, 'I am the state'. The finer a man's religious sense is, the less he will be able to forget, for all the liveliness of his feelings, that in the equation between his human self-awareness and his awareness of God there is always an indivisible remainder. Thus we can do nothing with the speeches of the Christ of the Fourth Gospel. 'A Jesus who takes it upon himself to say such things does not exist as an object of historical study.' Things are different if we take the Synoptic Gospels as our guide. Here we learn, from the Sermon on the Mount, particularly, that Jesus saw in him whom he felt and conceived as God, and described as the 'heavenly Father', 'indiscriminate goodness'. This indiscriminate goodness was manifestly the basic mood of his own nature. He was aware of his similarity with God in having such goodness, and transferred it to God as the basic determining feature of the divine nature as well. If men are the children of this God, then they are brothers to one another, and to this extent Jesus's consciousness may also be described as a human mood of love transcending all the hindrances and limitations of human life, a mood which then gave rise to an inner feeling of happiness, compared with which all outward joy and suffering was deprived of its meaning. Serene and cheerful, unbroken, and acting as the result of the delight and joyousness of a beautiful nature, Jesus had, 'to use the poet's words, absorbed the Deity into his will', thus uniting in himself the best of the Hellenic and of the Mosaic heritage. This harmonious composure of mind certainly did not come about in Jesus without violent exertion, but it certainly came about (as distinct from Paul, Augustine and Luther) without an inner struggle. He appears as a fundamentally beautiful nature, whose only development comes from within, which only needed to grow ever more clearly conscious of itself and to become ever firmer in itself, but which did not need to turn back and—apart from isolated waverings and errors, and the necessity for a progressive, earnest endeavour for self-vanquishment and renunciation—begin any other life. This, according to the Strauss of 1864, was Jesus's religious consciousness, as it historically really was, according to the Synoptic Gospels. With regard to the Messianic form of this consciousness, too, which for all this cannot be removed from the Synoptics, Strauss was able to judge at this time with understanding mildness: 'Did Jesus believe that he would come again in the clouds of the heavens? . . . Are we not thinking too much in western fashion, if we cannot conceive of the conjunction of such an idea with great wisdom in an Oriental?'[1] What points of view such deliberations might eventually have stimulated even in respect of the Christology of St John's Gospel!

Let us follow this with what Strauss finds to say in the final paragraphs, Nos. 99 and 100, of the same work, about the significance of this Jesus for us. Our historical information concerning him is incomplete and uncertain. It is out of the question that faith and salvation can depend on things only the smallest part of which are not in doubt. And, in any case, it is a matter of principle that there should be no such dependence. 'Just as certainly as the destiny of man is a universal one and accessible to all, so the conditions upon which it is to be achieved . . . must be accorded to every man'; the perception of the goal must 'not only be an accidental one, a historical perception coming from without, but a necessary perception of reason, which each man can find in himself'. The distinguishing of the historical from the ideal

[1] Letter of 9th November, 1862.

Christ, i.e. the original image of man as he should be, which resides in human reason, and the transference of the faith which saves from the first to the second figure, is the imperative result of the more recent development of mind. It is 'the continued development of the religion of Christ to a religion of humanity, towards which all the nobler endeavour of our time is directed'.

This does not imply that this original image, the ideal Christ, could be present in us to the same extent, if a historical Christ had never lived and exercised his influence. The idea of human perfection, like other ideas, is at first given to man only as a disposition, which is then gradually developed in its actual form. It is those who variously advance the human ideal, among whom Christ in every case pre-dominates, who serve the development of this disposition. 'He intro-duced features into this ideal which were previously lacking, or which had remained undeveloped, curbed others which opposed its universal validity, and by the religious form he gave it he bestowed upon it a higher consecration; by its embodiment in his own person, a most lively warmth.' Even if he was not the first or the last of his kind, and even if important aspects of the human ideal, e.g. regard for the family, the state, and art, are missing from his shaping of it, yet all the features with which it would be desirable to supplement this ideal can be added to his version of it in the happiest manner, 'if only we have once understood that Jesus's version is itself a human achievement, and thus something which is as in need of development as it is capable of it'. On the other hand, to conceive of Christ as the God-man can only hinder us in thus making fruitful his moral and religious greatness. The purpose of critical research into his life is therefore the removal of all that which makes of him a more than human being. This is something which is a well-meant and at first perhaps beneficial illusion, but which, in the long run, is harmful, and nowadays quite destructive. Critical research must also aim at the restoration of the picture of the historical Jesus in his simple, human features, in so far as this can still be accom-plished; and, for the good of their souls, the direction of men to the ideal Christ, this pattern of moral perfection. Concerning this pattern the historical Jesus has indeed thrown light on several salient features, but as a disposition it just as surely belongs to the universal heritage of our species, as its further development and completion can only be the task and work of humanity as a whole. This, then, according to the Strauss of 1864, is the significance of Jesus for us.

To summarize: in 1864 Strauss thought that there was a historical core to the 'life of Jesus', which was shrouded in a veil of myth. With

John it was a thick veil, with the Synoptics not so thick, but on the whole it was not impenetrable. It was difficult but not quite impossible to distinguish the core as such. This core consists in a human personality which made actual to a high degree the religious disposition, and to this extent the disposition of man as such. Together with others of its kind this personality should be assessed by us not, indeed, as the basis, in the strict sense, for our achievement of our human destiny, but certainly as the means towards this end.

If Strauss had said this in his first and famous *Life of Jesus* in 1835-6, it would definitely not have become famous, and it would not have cost its author his place at the university. As something which at that time could be regarded as having the attraction of a certain harmless novelty it would have brought him to the heaven of a university post in the usual way; and nothing would have been known of the great vexation which the name D. F. Strauss symbolizes in theology to this very day. In contrast to the first, Strauss's second *Life of Jesus* became neither infamous nor famous. It might perhaps have got him his desired chair at the eleventh hour, as the document of a definite, but none the less only mildly sinning common or garden liberalism, which had, in the meantime, long become the common cry, if the stir which the famously infamous book of 1835-6 had caused had not still lingered on and blinded the people of the time to the fact that the true offending element of the first book, that of its method, had to all intents and purposes been removed in the second. For in principle and in method this second book was in fact a *Life of Jesus* of the kind any number of others have written both before and after him.

The historical element in Christianity, that is, concretely, Christ-ology, had admittedly given the founders of the theology of more recent times some trouble. But they had all managed to cope with it in one way or another. Quite naïvely they thought man could be conscious and possessed of religion, of the consciousness of God, the experience of transcendence, the Christian quality within himself, as something which was there and given, something which could be joyfully reckoned with. They thought man could be conscious and possessed of the historical basis for religion in the same way, no matter whether one understood it like Schleiermacher, more as a historical beginning, or, like Marheineke, more as a metaphysical origin, or lastly, like Tholuck and Menken—the 'Positives' of that time—more as the supernatural divine imparting of religion. They used history just as unquestioningly as they used psychology. They were unquestioning in their belief that it was possible truly to assume in individual man something like, for example, the feeling of utter dependence, with God as the content of its object. On the other hand they were unquestioning in their belief that somewhere in the related whole of man's history there might be something like a perfect archetypal image of this, man's own possession, something given, to which—in accordance with the correlation between Christ and faith handed down by the Church— the thing given within man himself could equally calmly and surely be referred back. The Romanticism and the rationalism which allowed the men of this age to discover the presence of God's miraculous quality in their hearts, or God's reason in their heads, also enabled them to assume that this miracle or reason very probably had its absolute place in history too, and to state, 'in accordance with church tradition, that this place was in Jesus of Nazareth. The age which could not produce and consume enough biographies and auto- biographies to the glorification of that which the man of that time found within himself—this same age inevitably hit upon the idea of a *Life of Jesus*, and put it into effect, both before and after Strauss, with the daring peculiar to it for such undertakings in the most varied forms; and always with the assumption that the one was as possible as the other. In detail, it was possible to proceed in varied ways with this: it was possible to read and evaluate the sources in the naïvely historical or in the critically historical manner. If the latter method was chosen, as Schleiermacher and Hase did, one could give preference to the Gospel according to St John at the expense of the Synoptics. Or one could reverse this relationship as gradually became the accepted method after Bretschneider's *Probabilia* of 1820. Then again it was possible to accord the rank of the oldest reporter among the Synoptics to Matthew, as Strauss did in 1864 and as F. Chr. Baur too wanted to do, or it was possible, as came to be the vogue at about the same time, to join the 'lions of St Mark', with or without assuming the existence of a source of sayings supplementing his Gospel. Or, like Eichhorn, one could think of an original Gospel which had been lost, or, as in Schleier- macher's theory of diegesis, which is once again becoming interesting today, of a great number of anecdotes and gnomic sayings circulating singly as representing the New Testament in its original form.

Further, it was possible to conceive of the relationship between the reports and the events reported, particularly as regards their largely miraculous nature, in such a way that one attempted to interpret them in some manner, i.e. to explain them as things which really happened. This could be done by juggling away the supernatural element in the reports as misunderstanding of all previous exegesis, or as a misunderstanding of the reporters himself, thus evolving a life of Christ which could be concurred in even if one's name happened to be Wegscheider (this was done in classic fashion, for the rationalists, by Paulus of Heidelberg). Or one could take refuge (this was the course of the so-called supranaturalists, also that of Tholuck and Neander) in the allusion to all kinds of as yet unknown forces of nature, to the hastening of natural processes, and above all to a dominion, incalculable in its effects, of mind over matter, as providing the explanation—a solution which was assured of great interest and applause in those decades, when magnetism, occultism, and everything connected with them were the subject of a deep fascination. One could also proceed by mediating or combining these two methods. Schleiermacher, for instance, had a foot in both camps, being a supranaturalist as far as all the miracles of healing were concerned, and a rationalist, for example, in the question of Jesus's resurrection, which he fairly openly explained as an awakening from a deep coma, in the pulpit too.

Finally, since in those decades the words 'poetry' and 'poetic' also had a quite individual and, indeed, a good sound, one could bring in the concept of myth, the idea that a story did not really happen, but was invented to illustrate a religious truth. The concept of myth was introduced at about this time by de Wette, at first for research into the Old Testament. It was, however, ventured upon only hesitantly, and applied only to the stories of the childhood of Jesus and of his resurrection—and then only by a few. It was possible to concede that the historical events might largely be surrounded, and perhaps permeated to their very core by such myth, without being deceived that between the cloud at the foot and the cloud at the summit of the mountain there was yet a great deal of the mountain visible in between, a lot of material which was no doubt historical, or which could at least be interpreted historically by either of these two methods. And then again differences were possible in the evaluation of the life of Jesus established in this way. It was possible to evolve a figure very similar to the God-man of the old dogmatics, and to which his soteriological predicates could be transferred with relative ease; the only difference was that the attempt was now made to understand this figure quite decisively as a divinely powerful one in the history of the world and of mankind as such. With Wegscheider, it was possible to revere in him the *doctor divinus* of the truth of reason common to all men, or with Schleiermacher, the productive archetypal image of one's own experience or that of the Christian Church, or, as we have just heard in discussing the Strauss of 1864, the religious genius, to whom one could then perhaps again ascribe, in retrospect, some of the predicates of the God-man. It was possible to present and illuminate the once-for-all-ness and necessity of the revelation which came about in none other than this Jesus—once again with variations in strength, and by the use of various arguments.

All these possible methods of writing a Life of Jesus are in part strikingly divergent, but there are five points which are agreed upon in all of them:

1. As faith has its reality in the immanence of human consciousness, so its correlation to Christ is a connexion within the immanence of history. As we have faith in the same way as we have other capacities or experiences, so we have Christ in the same way, in principle, as we have other people.

2. We have Christ as a person of a distant by-gone time, in so far as we have 'sources' of his life. For the Gospels are sources. They were written as such, or it is as such that they interest us; at any rate it is as sources that we now use them. We can employ them as sources in the same way—even if perhaps we subject them to the same provisos—as someone interested in the history of the kings of Rome would employ the books of Livy.

3. We are seeking the historical Jesus—for we want to have him historically, as we have other historical personages. He can be distinguished from the sources (or how else, indeed, could they be sources?). He can be recognized according to the sources, from the sources, and upon the basis of the sources as he lived and as he was, at a certain time and in a certain place. He can be perceived as clearly or as dimly as we can perceive his contemporary, the emperor Tiberius. He stands and becomes visible behind the sources: in such a way, in fact, that historically it is not merely Matthew or John whom we have, but in truth Jesus, as 'the historical core' of what they have imparted.

4. Jesus is a human personage who is in principle accessible to historical knowledge in precisely the same measure as Tiberius is accessible to it. The way in which he was conscious of himself is a form of self-consciousness which is at least conceivable, which is possible—perhaps not quite in the way in which John presents it, but at any rate in the way in which it is shown in the much more innocuous Sermon on the Mount—but who knows, the positive theologians say, perhaps as depicted by John too!

We can, as has been shown, in some way come to terms with his miracles, with virgin birth and resurrection, divesting them of the true miraculous character by describing them as misunderstandings, hidden secrets of nature, or as myth; or by somewhat enlarging *ad hoc* the concept of what is historical, calling historically real something one would never otherwise be prepared to call historically possible. In one way or the other: by regarding the miracle as a frame from which the content can be distinguished. The content, however, is the man Jesus, who was certainly a religious genius, and as such an extraordinary, an astonishing man, a man to be adored, but one who, like all men, is accessible to our understanding, and comprehensible as an object of historical knowledge. Let us constantly remind ourselves: if something like the feeling of utter dependence can find a place in the picture we form of ourselves, then why cannot someone like Jesus Christ also find a place in our picture of history? It will be a Jesus reduced in stature and hammered into shape, perhaps, a Jesus who is perhaps a trifle groomed, domesticated and made practicable when compared with all the strange things which are said of him in the texts, even in the 'Life of Jesus' versions of positive theology. But it is precisely in this way that he will find a place there, even if only just so that a historically immanent connexion between him and our faith becomes possible in principle.

5. As a personage who is so possible and comprehensible historically Jesus in fact is of the highest value for us, as can once again be established historically. He is then a central person, or the central person, the man who was perfect to the extent that we can call him a revealer of God, and indeed the chief revealer, as Strauss too concedes in 1864, from among all those whom people believe they can thus designate apart from him.

These then are the common assumptions for modern research into the life of Jesus. Strauss's *Life of Jesus* of 1864 no longer diverged from them; as far as they were concerned it no longer offended. For in it Strauss found a way of coping with the problem of Christology which was no better and no worse than that of any of the others. That was why it was not the famous Life of Jesus. That was why, although it could not further its author's reputation with the public and with the authorities, it did it no more damage either. That is why its only significance for the history of theology is that it helps, by contrast, to illustrate what the name of D. F. Strauss really stands for. Let us turn our attention now to the author of the first *Life of Jesus* of 1835-6. The name of D. F. Strauss stands for no more and no less than the breaking-up of this concerted body of opinion about research into the life of Jesus, the protest against its method, the declaration that its entire undertaking was impossible to execute. This is important enough to warrant a point by point demonstration with reference to the five headings we have just drawn up.

1. In 1835 Strauss demands from the biographer of Jesus, as his first duty, an observation and thinking which is without premises—which is not, that is, burdened in advance by faith. If he really wants to write a biography of Jesus, if he wants to have Jesus as we can have other men, then he has to choose not faith, but an observation and thinking which has no interest in faith. For we cannot expect to find what we believe, as such, in history. And that which we wish to seek in history must as such be accessible to this disinterested observation and thinking. By making this distinction Strauss challenged from the outset the historical immanence of the connexion between Christ and faith. It is now a question of whether the object of faith on the one side, and that of observation and thinking on the other, will prove to be one and the same.

2. In 1835, condemned by every New Testament scholar who followed him, Strauss does not begin with a critique of the sources as such, by establishing the order of precedence of the four Gospels, or their dependence upon one another, or with hypotheses concerning original pre-manuscript sources or some such thing, as in fact as a historian it was his duty to do, and has been done universally since. Even afterwards he accorded the labours his colleagues directed to this end little more than an ironical scepticism. He himself mentions[1] that it was only seven years after his book appeared that he had the idea of pasting together a synopsis according to Luther's translation! For him John and Mark and 1 Corinthians 15 are all equally damned in advance when judged by the canon of critical historical thinking with which he approaches them, and which can be roughly formulated in the following questions: To what extent can what is recounted be reconciled with the logical, historical and physiological law, otherwise known and valid, governing all events? To what extent can parallel reports really be reconciled with one another in what concerns time and place, the number and names of the participants in what is reported, in that which concerns the circumstances and material for these affairs themselves? And then, above all: To what extent does the poetical character of a representation or its content as far as it is contained also in other sources (e.g. in the Old Testament or in pagan saga and myth) make its historical nature not unlikely? We can imagine what the answer is: Upon all points, so to speak, the form of the New Testament narrative is not that of a historical report, but simply that

[1] Letter of 27th January, 1843.

of a myth. So strong is Strauss's impression of the particular nature of these sources that he makes their disqualification as historical sources the starting-point for his method. And all he has to say about them, simply as regards their content, without testing them further as historical sources—is that none of them, with the exception of scattered remnants, stands firm before this canon, that they cannot derive from eye-witnesses and thus cannot come from the apostles, unless we care to regard them as deceivers.

3. It is for this very reason—and this was the chief thing which made Strauss's first *Life of Jesus* so celebrated and notorious—that he not only does not discover a 'historical core' to the life of Jesus, but does not even begin to enquire after it. He does not deny that a historical core is a possibility, as Bruno Bauer did later, and as Kalthoff and Artur Drews have done in our century. But neither does he assert and demonstrate a historical core to the life of Jesus. Strauss is not interested in it. His work is purely critical. He is only concerned with showing the presence and origin of myth, whatever might be 'behind' it. That is what went home to the hearers of 1835 and had an effect in all directions. Here as well it was only that something was being challenged. But it was challenged comprehensively and thoroughly: where was the possibility of a method which made the historical correlate of faith uncertain in the same way as Feuerbach's psychology of religion made its metaphysical correlate uncertain. The supporting staff—from this aspect, history—could also be a reed to pierce the hand. That is why the Strauss of 1835 had everyone against him: from Hengstenberg to de Wette, who had yet himself admitted the enemy, the concept of myth, at least into the forecourt, into scientific research into the Old Testament. That is why the cry could now be heard even from those who were supposedly orthodox: Better Paulus the rationalist than Strauss the explainer of myth! Paulus, even if his interpretation did make things a trifle shabby, at least let everything stand as historical, whereas Strauss made everything, without exception, historically uncertain.

4. Strauss, as may be easily understood, did not go to any trouble, either, to work out a character picture of Jesus. He was lacking in the vision which perceives, to use Weinel's words[1] 'that what truly gives human history its greatness, worth and power is the great personality of genius'. He had not yet read any Carlyle! Does not the problem of personality interest him at all? This can scarcely be maintained of a man who afterwards, as a historian, preferred to occupy himself in the

[1] *Jesus im 19 Jahrhundert* (Jesus in the Nineteenth Century), p. 42.

biographical field. Or perhaps he is not interested in the person of Jesus? Or is he perhaps hampered by the fact that the Evangelists themselves are much more interested in something quite different from the actual character of Jesus, these miracles, for·instance, which are the cause of so much offence? So that he thinks, perhaps, that he has no material for such a picture? Suffice it to say that the picture is not drawn. The very cause, that is to say, for the sake of which the other researchers into the life of Jesus, before and after Strauss, marched out with sword and lance, is neglected. Jesus should be accessible, understandable as a man, so that we could 'have' him, as we have other men. But Strauss's lack of concern and his silence upon this point made it seem as if Jesus were inaccessible and incomprehensible as a man, and as if we might not, therefore, be able thus to have him.

5. The Strauss of 1835 also quarrelled with the view that it was possible, with the instruments of observation and thinking, to ascribe to this historical phenomenon in particular, to Jesus of Nazareth, a qualified highest value, a unique and absolute quality. The final section of his second volume (1836), in which he expresses himself upon this point, is so important for the history of theology, that here we should allow him to speak for himself a little: 'If reality is ascribed to the idea of the unity of divine and human nature, is this as much as to say that it must once have become real in one individual, as it was never again either before or since? This is by no means the way in which the idea realizes itself, pouring out its whole abundance upon one example and begrudging itself to all others. Rather it likes to unfold its wealth in a diversity of examples which complement each other, in the interchange of individualities one in decline, the other rising.' Humanity is the absolute, the true content of Christology. This content has been made to be attached to the person and history of an individual only, but this has been done for the subjective reason, first, that this individual, by his personality and the things which happened to him, became the occasion for the lifting of this content into the universal consciousness, and, secondly, that the intellectual level of the world of former times, and of a nation at any time, is only capable of contemplating the idea of humanity in the concrete figure of an individual. . . . The knowledge we have acquired in our age, however, can no longer suppress the awareness that the connexion with an individual is but the form of this teaching relating to a certain time and a certain people.'

The positive element in Strauss's position, which becomes visible in the fifth point, could and still can be disconcerting, and yet it cannot be overlooked that its negative side had enough weight behind it to lay the axe at the root of the naïveté with which the rest of theology at that time thought it could master revelation in the same way as history in general is mastered. Something absolute as a part of world and of human history as such is a sword of lath. Strauss's book made this very plain and well understood, and those who read it were shaken to the core, for it was precisely upon the card of history that they had staked no less than half their means, the other half being on that of religious consciousness. The situation was such that in running away from Feuerbach they ran straight into the arms of Strauss. And if they managed somehow to escape Strauss they were still not free of Feuerbach. That was the deeply disturbing feature of the state of theological discussion a hundred years ago: the deeply disturbing background to the history of theology in all the ensuing decades. Strauss is also similar to Feuerbach in that he was equally devoid of humour, and similarly incapable of criticizing his basic positive outlook, whereby his negations might first have acquired theological content. But unfortunately Strauss was unlike Feuerbach in that he was uncertain of his case in expressing these epoch-making negations. He was in fact not certain of his case in principle.

When the storm of hostile reviews and works against his first *Life of Jesus* set in, Strauss at once (in his smaller pieces of this time and above all in the third edition of the book in 1838) began to retreat in the direction of the position in which we have found him in the *Life of Jesus* of 1864. He does indeed hurl himself in his polemics, with all the power of his pungent pen, upon weaker opponents like Steudel, his former teacher at Tübingen, and grinds them to powder, but cannot avoid making important concessions to more serious representatives of the official theology, like Ullmann, Neander, and Tholuck. They relate particularly to the fifth point of the series we drew up. Strauss now suddenly recalls the saying of Hegel: 'In the forefront of all actions there stands an individual' and concedes:

1. That religion belongs to an incomparably higher sphere of human intellectual activity than science, art, etc., and that the man who has achieved the highest in this sphere therefore does not stand upon the same plane as the others, but has a claim to stand at the centre-point of the circle, in the closest proximity to the source itself;

2. That a higher realization of the religious idea than Jesus cannot historically be demonstrated;

3. That the union of the human individual with God in his immediate self-consciousness, and therefore God's becoming man in this

individual, is not philosophically impossible, and that its reality is only a historical question.[1]

In conjunction with this he is now also prepared—in 1864, impressed particularly by the works of F. Chr. Baur, he did not go so far again—to listen to a discussion concerning the genuineness and credibility of the Gospel according to St John. 'We have no way of knowing whether a mind of the religious fervour of Jesus might not have been able in the reflex of the imagination to form the communion with God, of which he was aware, into a recollection of a former dwelling with God.[2] 'I would not venture to assert that there is anything in the sayings in John which would decisively resist explanation partly as the result of John's personality, and partly from the fact that he wrote the Gospel at a very advanced age.'[3] The same weakening of the historical canon makes its effects felt as regards the question of miracles. Renewing his earlier interest in natural philosophy Strauss now finds all kinds of things historically possible which three years previously had only seemed comprehensible to him as myth. And it is in the Gospel of St John, of all things, that he too now thinks he can demonstrate a historical core, which afterwards split up into the three-fold synoptic account. He also does not now scorn the harmonizing of the Gospels quite so much, which three years before he had so sharply proscribed. And, in a free version of Schleiermacher we are tempted to say, he now defines Christ along the lines that he was 'the man in whose self-consciousness the union of the human and the divine first appeared with an energy which thrust back to the infinitesimal minimum within the whole range of his mind and life all restraint upon this union; who to this extent stands unique and unrivalled in world history. This does not mean that the religious consciousness which was first achieved and expressed by him should be allowed to withhold itself in detail from purification and further development in the progressive advance of the human spirit.'[4]

We must be clear about the significance of the fact that Strauss's negotiations with Zürich and the disaster which befell him there came about just at this period when his critique was engaged in this backward movement! Influenced by these events, and embittered by the fact that in spite of his concessions he was still not trusted (far from it indeed, for Tholuck, for instance, was now quite openly triumphant that the critic's once pure, clear voice was beginning to break, so that the distinct 'No' was now a quavering upon 'Yes and No') he then

[1] Hausrath, I, 304f. and 324.   [2] *Life of Jesus*, third ed., Vol. I, p. 539.
[3] Op. cit., p. 741.   [4] Op. cit., p. 778.

ab irato not only wrote his *Doctrine of Faith,* but undertook a *restitutio ad integrum* in the next editions of the *Life of Jesus.* He has done himself an injustice, he has ground flaws into the blade of his own trusty sword, he now confesses in the fourth edition, and he restores the critical attitude of the first and second!

It is all the stranger that in spite of this we should meet him again, in 1864, at the spot where we did meet him: upon the broad highway of research into the life of Jesus, engaged in an attempt to extract a historical core from the shell of the sources.

And now the strangest thing of all. When he saw that this new course was making just as little impression upon the theological profession and the Church as that of 1838-9, he followed up his second retreat, in *The Old and the New Faith* of 1872 in which a section is also devoted to the life of Jesus, by a third advance. Here the true meaning, apparently, of the first and second advances too comes to light trivially but with a clarity which does not leave anything to be desired. As a historical man was Jesus such that he still determines our religious feeling? the old man now asks. He answers 'No', for we know too little which is reliable about him! 'Anyone who has once been made a god has irrevocably lost his human quality. It is an empty illusion to imagine that accounts of a life which, like our Gospels, apply to a supernatural being, can ever provide, by any process whatsoever, material for a natural, consistent and harmonious picture of a man or of a life.' 'All the efforts of the most recent authors of works on the "Life of Jesus", however much they may lay claim to show by means of our scriptural sources a human development, an arrival and growth of insight and a gradual widening of comprehension in Jesus, show themselves by the absence of any supporting reference in the records . . . to be pieces of apologetic artifice devoid of any historical value.'[1] If there is anything historical at all to be taken from the Gospels, then it is the fact that Jesus, a mere man, expected to appear in the clouds of the heavens in the very near future, in inauguration of the kingdom of the Messiah proclaimed by him. It was this which made the decisive impression upon his disciples, and not any sermon upon pureness of heart or the love of God or our neighbours. According to our concepts he was a noble spiritual fanatic whom we do not seek to choose as the guide of our lives since he could only lead us astray, just as it was only the manufacture of the idea of the resurrection of the slain master which saved his work at that time: a 'humbug of world-historical proportions',[2] which did at all events bear witness to the strength and

[1] *Collected Works*, VI, pp. 50f.   [2] Op. cit., p. 45.

persistence of the impression he made upon his followers. By what means? By the irrational and fantastic quality of his own nature, and of his own ideas, about which, incidentally, he perhaps had doubts at the end. In face of these we must indeed mourn him, with regard to his end, for the sake of the excellent qualities of his heart and striving. But we cannot escape the judgment that 'such a fanatical expectation only gets its just deserts if it comes to grief by ending in failure'.[1]

Who should seek to decide which was the genuine Strauss: the Strauss of the two retreats or the Strauss of the three advances? The naïve and a trifle boring liberal Strauss, who can however be talked to, or Strauss the savagely angry critic, who refuses to negotiate? One thing is certain. The unmistakable feebleness of the first figure only serves to throw into high relief the strength with which the second confronted theology with a series of questions upon which, just as with Feuerbach's questions, it has not, right down to the present day, perhaps, adequately declared itself.

Once again we formulate them, in five points:

1. Is it not a fact that if we conceive of the Christian faith as a relation which is historically immanent, thereby making faith a matter of history, we destroy it as faith?

2. Is it not a fact that the New Testament records are useless as 'sources' of a pragmatically comprehensible picture of a man and of a life? For it is from the very first word that they seek to be something quite different, namely testimonies to a 'superhuman being', corresponding feature by feature to the prophecies of the Old Testament, a being whose image must defy all historical reconstruction.

3. Is it not a fact that a 'historical Jesus' established behind the so-called sources, and therefore quite independently of the witness of the New Testament, can only be comprehended as such if we remove those predicates of his which are essential to this witness: his consciousness of himself as the Messiah of Israel and as God's eternal Son, his proclamation of the kingdom of God and expectation that he would come again, and his resurrection from the dead? Is it not a fact that the sentimental, moralizing description of character which is indispensable to the establishment of this figure has nothing at all to do with the faith of the Apostles?

4. Is it not a fact that according to the representation in the Gospels the so-called personality of Jesus is so indissolubly linked with these predicates that the historian aiming at a Life of Jesus cannot escape a fatal dilemma? He has either to undertake this erasure of the predicates

[1] Op. cit., p. 51.

and give a moralizing interpretation, or, like Strauss, he has to conceive of Jesus as a noble spiritual fanatic. He must do this unless he prefers to call a halt at the Early Church in Palestine as the last historically accessible date, and apply the concept of myth to everything or nearly everything lying beyond it—in which case he must at least take into account the possibility that Jesus never lived as Drews' thesis did.

5. Is it not a fact that the goal of historical research can at best only be a historical Christ and that this implies a Christ who as a revealer of God can only be a relative Christ? Is it not a fact that such a Christ can only be a helper of those in need, who as such requires all sorts of associates, and figures to supplement him, who at best could only be related to a real, eternal revelation to mankind as a most high and perhaps ultimate symbol is related to the thing itself, who could on no account be the Word that became flesh, executing God's judgment upon us and challenging us ourselves to make a decision?

This is what D. F. Strauss asked theology, just as Feuerbach asked it whether the Godhead man sought and thought he had found in his consciousness was anything but man's shadow as it was projected upon the plane of the idea of the Infinite.

Strauss was no great theologian. It is precisely when we take him seriously, that is when we hold him to his attitude in the first *Life of Jesus*, the *Doctrine of Faith*, and *The Old and the New Faith*, that we are still bound to conclude that his theology ultimately only consisted in the fact that he saw through a bad solution of the problem of theology, gave up any further attempt to improve upon it, abandoned the theme of theology, and departed from the field of action. 'The only aim of all my theological writing was to free me from the black folds of the cassock; and in this it succeeded perfectly.'[1] Blessed with a little impudence, any child can do the same, and we really have no occasion to worship such people as great theologians. The strangest thing of all is that this rather cheap 'freeing from the folds' was never so successful that Strauss at any time really had any peace from theology, that he never really managed to put it behind him as something completely settled. The problem he had so ostentatiously abandoned pursued him to the last like a fate: and the more intensively it followed him the less he knew what to do about it. It was as if this problem had an interest in him. He repaid this interest by meeting it coldly, unreceptively and helplessly in some way, but he could not, after all, detach himself from it and he continually became excited about it. He was continually impelled to react—always differently and always unsuitably—but still

[1] Letter of 1st October, 1843.

to react. He could only suffer from it. That was his misfortune. And that, negatively, it is true, might be described as his greatness in theology. It might have been better if many theologians, positively greater ones, both of his time and of other times, had suffered at least a little more from the problem of theology. The fact that Strauss, for all his determination to shake it off, in fact stood so passively and helplessly before it, reveals in a unique way the urgency of this problem, and this is after all some justification for this man, a justification which is not quite so obvious for many who were more energetic in their approach to the problem.

In conclusion, may I present yet another argument in apology for Strauss? I am not unaware of its personal nature, but for the sake of completeness I cannot hold it back. I am in fact not quite certain that Nietzsche's invectives have really said all there is to be said upon the subject, not even in respect to the Gartenlaube[1] into which Strauss finally fled, and in which he was probably at bottom most intimately at home. It seems worth remembering that in the midst of the calamitous song of praise which Strauss dedicated to 'culture' he again and again avows, in a variety of ways, 'that for our age the music of Mozart occupies the same position as Goethe does in poetry. He is ὁ πάνυ, the universal genius. Next to him the best of the others only distinguish themselves by the fact that in them this or that single quality of mind or aspect of art has been further developed, but just for that reason developed one-sidedly.'[2] Anyone who has understood that can be pardoned much tastelessness and much childishly critical theology too. In this poor Strauss really seems to have chosen the better part, as against Nietzsche, who, as is well known, was the helpless slave of the dreadful Wagner at the time of his great deriding of Strauss.

Be this as it may. It is simply the case that together with Feuerbach, Strauss is the theologian who was most significant for the situation of theology in the time after Schleiermacher's death. It is a fact that he and no other man has the merit of having put this question, the historical one, that is, to theology, with such a grasp of the basic issue. Since then theology has talked round it in many and various ways; which was, rather, evidence of the fact that it had not heard his question. Many people have not been able to overcome Strauss to this day; they have simply by-passed him, and to this very day are continually saying things which, if Strauss cannot be overcome, should no longer be said.

I should now like to adapt the words of Albert Schweitzer, quoted

[1] *Lit.*: arbour; title of a once popular illustrated German family magazine. (Tr.)
[2] Letter of 5th March, 1868.

at the beginning, as follows: One must love the question Strauss raised, in order to understand it. It has been loved only by a few; most people have feared it. To this extent the name of Strauss together with the name of Feuerbach signifies the bad conscience of the theology of more recent times. To this extent Strauss was perhaps not so very wrong in calling his first *Life of Jesus*[1] an 'inspired book'. And to this extent the fact that they did not make him a professor of theology, but self-righteously, and with an all-too-easy mind, banished him *extra muros*, was all things considered scandalous. I imply by this that Alexander Schweizer, at all events—I name him in particular as one of the positively 'great' theologians of that time—did not have the inner right to oppose Strauss's appointment to Zürich in 1839. Proper theology begins just at the point where the difficulties disclosed by Strauss and Feuerbach are seen and then laughed at. Thus such men and their questions are 'loved'! Alexander Schweizer and his kind neither saw these difficulties, nor were they capable of this laughter. In such a situation, however, Strauss could not and must not be pensioned off.

[1] *Collected Works*, I, p. 4.

20

SCHWEIZER

ALEXANDER Schweizer, from a distinguished Zurich family of theologians, was born in 1808 and, after staying for several years in Germany, where he studied particularly under Schleiermacher, became a *Privatdozent* in 1834. He was made *extraordinarius* professor in 1835 and *ordinarius* professor in 1850, remaining in Zurich to the end of his life. In addition, from 1844 to 1871 he also held a pastorate at the Grossmünster; he belonged to the Zurich Church Council from 1849 to 1872. He died in 1888.

He was the type of theologian who approved of the union between traditional Christianity and modern culture, who thought of nothing but maintaining and continuing this union. He no more thought of leaving the Church than of disputing with the consciousness of his time; for him there was complete and perfect harmony, indeed unity, between the content of the thought of the Church, properly understood, and that of modern thought. In other words, he was a mediating theologian. As such he could perhaps flourish only in Switzerland and specially in the church of Zwingli, in East Switzerland, though at the same time he is typical of a particular theological stratum running through all non-German Protestantism. It is as a type representing this basic attitude that Schweizer must be discussed.

His primary theological concern, apparently completely oriented to history, was the presentation of orthodox dogmatics, especially of the Reformed observance. In 1844 and 1847 he published *Die Glaubenslehre der evangelischen reformierten Kirche* (The Doctrine of Faith of the Protestant Reformed Church) and in 1854-6 *Die protestantischen Centraldogmen in ihrer Entwicklung innerhalb der reformierten Kirche* (The Central Protestant Dogmas as developed within the Reformed Church), each work in two large volumes. Karl Hase embarked on a similar undertaking in his *Hutterus redivivus*, as did Frank of Erlangen in his *Theologie der Konkordienformel* (Theology of the Formula of Concord), with reference to the dogmatics of Lutheran orthodoxy. But Schweizer is not concerned to repristinate the old dogma as is Hase γυμναστικῶς and Frank δογματικῶς. Again, one might take as an analogy the unrolling of the old doctrine in the *Glaubenslehre* of Strauss, though with the proviso that unlike Strauss, Schweizer was not concerned with the negation and dissolution of dogma. What, then, was his concern? His third great work, *Die christliche Glaubenslehre nach protestantischen Grundsätzen* (The Christian Doctrine of Faith on Protestant Principles) (1864-9), gives the answer: he is concerned to demonstrate the agreement between the orthodox past, taken as a preliminary historical stage, and the freethinking present, as the next stage in the total theological process. Repristination along the lines of Hase and Frank, and dissolution, as we find it in Strauss, are both equally impossible for Schweizer, because in him they form a single, eirenic whole: the central dogmas of the orthodox past are also the central dogmas of the freethinking present. If one pursues their history in the past, the criticism which produces their authentic content refashioned in the form necessary for us today follows of its own accord. So Schweizer is in the position of being able to present the basic features of his own *Doctrine of Faith* in the same way in which he had presented early Reformed dogmatics twenty years earlier. Even in their details, his own statements seem to be nothing but the consistent and purified development and consummation of early Reformed dogmatics, once his historical account of this orthodoxy and its inner questions and struggles has shown where these statements, drawing the provisional conclusion, are to begin. He argues for a Union Protestantism, once he has established that this had already been the ultimate tendency of Reformed orthodoxy, in which the true substance of Lutheranism was best carried on, and whose apparently most irreconcilable culminations can very well be united with their Lutheran counterparts, at least in a retrospective view. He recognizes the central teaching of Christianity in the doctrine of the almighty providence and rule of God, or subjectively in the feeling of absolute dependence, once he has discovered that the central dogmas of earlier Protestantism, grasped particularly well by Reformed orthodoxy, had grouped themselves around this very idea. He rejects verbal inspiration, the immanent Trinity, the divinity of Christ, Anselm's doctrine of the atonement, once the history of dogma has shown him that even in earlier days all this belonged to those elements of Christianity that are temporally conditioned and one-sided, having their place among the unrevised remnants of mediaeval error, the abandonment of which can be commensurate with Christianity's innermost intentions. In this way it is possible for

Schweizer, with up-to-the-minute modernity and unconventionality, to put himself reverently in the shades of Zwingli and Calvin, in the context of the whole theological tradition—no mention of heteronomy, no mention either of unbroken autonomy. Today Schweizer would doubtless have called it 'theonomy'.

As a result, even his apologetic concern is much more tireless, much freer, even, than that of Schleiermacher. Mediation between traditional Christianity and the modern consciousness, which for Schleiermacher was still an action and a wearisome action at that, has for Schweizer already become a completed event, a condition. He has a good consciousness about his doings, even down to the innermost recess. He is already *standing* in the middle. This is what a theology of mediation is. This is what makes it different from Schleiermacher and his questing spirit. Schweizer, Schleiermacher's most faithful pupil and the only one really to have made a name for himself alongside Twesten, made the small but significant correction or interpretation of his master's fundamental teaching by wanting to find the source of the doctrine of faith in the Christian *experience* of the contemporary *Church*. He does not want Schleiermacher to be understood in the sense of the feeling of the individual. Faith comes from hearing and seeing, it is an assent to the Church's experiences of life. From the start it belongs to the Church. Nor does Schweizer want to keep to the wordless immediacy of feeling as its authentic form—here he is emphatically not a Romantic, in contrast to Schleiermacher. Feeling first becomes experience, Christian experience, in being directed towards teaching and action. As such, 'as the current teaching, conceptions, attitudes and customs' of the Christian, it is the subject-matter of the doctrine of faith. Each doctrinal statement is valid to the degree that it 'can express living piety without involving itself in contradictions partly with itself and partly with our knowledge of the world' (*Glaubeslehre* I, §12). It should be noted that, according to Schweizer, internal contradictions and contradictions with our knowledge of the world bring to an end the concept of the 'expression of living piety'. A statement which contained such contradictions would not be a statement of living, *present* piety. For 'the doctrine of faith has to depict really credible faith, the faith that is believed, the faith of the present, the Christian truth as it expresses itself in us and lives in us'. Schweizer wants to make a fundamental break with methods of reproducing the faith of the fathers. Our faith is *our* faith, different from that of our fathers, in that the Protestant Church has been led to our standpoint by providential guidance. The whole development of the Church is 'a progression to

ever purer faith and a constant shedding of superstitious admixtures'.
Ecclesia semper reformari debet (I, §15). Not unbelief, but belief and
thoroughgoing investigation of the Scriptures has led to our altered
attitude towards earlier dogmatics. It is, in short, a 'fruit of more correct knowledge' (I, §13-14). And if we now ask how and where our
faith (that is, really credible faith and faith that can be believed) may
be recognizable as the providentially ordained stage of progress of the
present Church, Schweizer answers without delay, 'in Schleiermacher's
Doctrine of Faith'. The Church of the present has understood itself here,
not of course in the theological details, but in the method. 'From this
stage of development, as it has taken place and as it is expected, we
consider the faith of our Protestant Church, no matter how many have
a quite different conception of the present period' (I, §20). Now the
present consciousness of faith, understood in this way, contains the
truth of the Bible, the symbols of the Church, the theological tradition,
and even more: the elements of truth of the Enlightenment, of modern
culture and philosophy. These have entered into faith and continue
in faith, and to that extent faith is simply the subjective appropriation
of something that presents itself objectively, that can only become the
substance of the doctrine of faith if it is appropriated subjectively, if
it enters into faith and is contained in it (I, §17). The doctrine of faith
must therefore refuse to be grounded directly on dogma or the Bible,
just as it must refuse to be grounded directly on reason (I, 13-15).
It draws the material to be known 'from life itself' (I, §10).These are
glad tidings of Schweizer's fundamental doctrines, and the one who
proclaims them is concerned to do justice to and to help to establish
the validity of all previous wise thoughts. This doctrine of faith has
only the following presuppositions: (1) faith in a providence that is
also active in the history of theology, working in such a way that the
highest stage of theological progress reached at any time for the
moment represents *per se* theological truth; (2) the capacity to see past
history striving with teleological certainty towards this present moment;
(3) the self-confidence which puts the believing thinker in the position
of entering upon this moment as the instrument of the will of providence, certain that it is his own *Kairos*. The classical mediator has
all these presuppositions; for that reason he has all the needs of
apologetic behind him; he draws from life itself. He looks after
Christian concerns not as an anxious advocate, but as a cheerful
and superior major domo. He is as certain of his power over himself
as he is certain of himself, and he is quite extraordinarily certain of
himself.

From this point Schweizer becomes quite automatically the critic of all theological extremes. In 1839 he was among the opponents to the call of D. F. Strauss to Zurich. Equally as a matter of course he kept clear of all influences from the Revival and from theologies of repristination. It is not that he was not wise enough to consider seriously the extremes on the left wing and on the right. He may have been quite acute in passing by the possibility of a restoration of the old strict orthodoxy of Dordrecht and the possibility of a world-citizenship that shed Christianity altogether. There are two evident reasons which restrained him from the extremes.

1. The mediating theologian is the born surveyor of the world, who can put everything neatly in its place. Schweizer's predilection for the *locus de providentia* is no coincidence. His spirit contemplates, to use Gellert's words, with praise and thanksgiving the disposition of all things in order. But even according to Gellert, all this is to take place only in eternity. However, the mediating theologian has taken Schleiermacher's 'be eternal in every moment' seriously, and so he is protected from all extravagances. This may be the place to consider Schweizer's philosophical and dogmatic system. The former may be summed up in the statement that Protestantism is the realization of the pure essence of Christianity (I, §39), just as Christianity is in turn the realization of the pure essence of religion (I, §34), a relationship which expresses itself in time as the ongoing process of the history of religion, in such a way, however, that each later (and therefore higher) stage takes up into itself in purified form all the earlier (and therefore lower) stages. Thus Protestantism is at the same time Christianity pure and simple, and Christianity is religion pure and simple. If religion in general is the interiorization of the dependence of the finite on the infinite, as Christianity it is a complete religion of redemption, and as Protestantism, finally, a liberation of religion from all traditional appurtenances, in particular from all paganism and Judaism; here the struggle against paganism is the special charisma of Reformed Protestantism and the struggle against Judaism the special charisma of Lutheran Protestantism. The dogmatic system is then developed in a similar way. Christian faith contains a religious faith which can already be reached without Christian experience, but which is only consummated in that experience (I, §54). Here a distinction must be made in turn between the manifestation of God, his properties that can already be recognized here in the natural world, and the dependence of that world on him and the same circle of revelation in the higher moral world (I, §59). If this general faith, which, like earlier natural theology

is to be incorporated into dogmatics (I, §23), is a purely negative presupposition (as a religion of the law) and yet a positive preparation
(as a preliminary stage of the religion of redemption) (I, §94), then
the kingdom of God or the life of salvation only appears when the
religious consciousness has been trained to specifically Christian belief.
Here the economy of the Father represents the cause of salvation itself,
the economy of the Son its realization in principle, and the economy
of the Spirit its actual realization.

In Schweizer's philosophy of religion, then, as in his dogmatics, we
encounter a system of concentric circles. We need only stand in the
centre for all conflicts between philosophy and revelation, reason and
history to be removed; but if we stand in the centre we also necessarily
miss all the exaggerations that bring about discord. Seductively attractive possibilities open up here: a real theological heaven on earth, in
which one is in all seriousness reminded of the masterpiece of mediaeval
wisdom, the system of St Thomas Aquinas, that similarly reconciles
nature and grace, Christianity and antiquity. If this had been Schleiermacher's purpose, we would have to say that he had been surpassed
in consistency and clarity of form by his pupil. If Schweizer is to be
unfavourably compared with his teacher, it could only be because with
him, precisely because of this consistency and clarity of form, one sees
a question mark set over Schleiermacher's intentions even more plainly
than in the case of Schleiermacher himself. Is standing in that prominent centre-point, that consciousness of *Kairos*, that thinking in the name
of divine providence, a human possibility at all? Or may not standing
in this place and thinking from this place prove, in a completely unromantic light, in the soberness of Zurich (which is the presupposition
and the basis of action here), a splendid illusion or figment of the
imagination?

2. The mediating theologian is a man who thinks practically and
tactically. He is by nature unfavourably disposed towards the extremes,
towards a Strauss or a Tholuck, because in the most particular sense
he thinks ecclesiastically. He answers questions about the substance of
dogmatics by pointing to what was really credible and what was really
believed in such and such a year. He answers the question of the truth
and its criteria by showing that whatever tradition and reason now
present as the truth is implicitly contained in the confession of such
and such a year. The *status quo*, understood properly, is thus the
measure of all things. The mediating theologian is quite unaware of
the pressure to move forwards from it; he is a *beatus possidens* and as
such a born churchman, Dostoievsky's Grand Inquisitor transposed

into Protestantism. If we are bold, unflinching Protestants, purifying ourselves with increasing energy from paganism and Judaism, then all is well; that means that we are also implicitly Christians and religious men. There can now be no question of moving forwards; it is a matter of continuing as we are, of asking how the little ship of the Protestant Church can steer a little further through the billowing waves of the time, between Roman superstition and modern unbelief. Extremes, extremes of piety or impiety, can only disrupt this business. In this respect, nothing is more significant in Schweizer than the battle against the *concept of miracle* that he carries on at all stages of his system. There can be no miracles, whether natural, or moral, or even the miracle of the kingdom of God. Miracle is in truth the divine causality, or the dependence of the world on God at every stage. Alongside this there is nothing new. For the same reason Schweizer fights against all radical theology 'with weapons of righteousness on the right hand and on the left', as the motto of the *Kirchenblatt für die reformierte Schweiz* proclaimed from that time down to the beginning of the century. Radical theology of the right wing or the left comes too near to God who bears witness to himself in the *Kairos* properly understood, in the *status quo* that has now been reached. He has long ago told us all that we need to know, so that we can go forward only with tiny steps into the unforeseeable future without being able to expect anything new. Once reason, Bible and dogma have had their say, anything else would be a painful disruption and therefore one to be averted. For this attitude, a struggle against the extremes becomes virtually an end in itself. The miracle of the omnipotence of God or the miracle of the theology of mediation makes all lesser miracles impossible.

This is one aspect that—as one may say in all truth—opens up a great abyss. The 'eternal covenant' of which Schleiermacher once spoke is here evidently formulated, paragraphed, sealed and placed in the archives. And so it seemed. Schweizer was a pious, wise and learned man. But the fruits of his theology are without question tedious, at any rate for dogmatics. The result of his work was obviously that there could no longer be serious, burning, fundamental problems in theology. One can understand from this why from the middle of the century onwards all the more lively spirits among the theologians increasingly began to turn from dogmatics to historical questions. How could it seem worth while to them to spend a lifetime taking part in that further process of refinement in which, according to Schweizer and the rest of the theology of mediation, alone the future of a fundamental academic concern for Christianity could lie? Does it not seem as though at this point dogmatic scholarship, after the rich food of the excitements and stimuli of the beginning of the century, or perhaps even drugged by them, wanted to fall into a kind of winter sleep? When one realizes that from a formal, academic point of view Schweizer's theology represents a climax, one of the few culminations of systematic theology since Schleiermacher, and when one also remembers that it was representative of a whole style of liberal theology, then here is certainly a symptom worth pondering, especially in view of the theological character of the whole century. If anyone wanted to despair at newer theology, he should not so much despair at Feuerbach and Strauss, but at Alexander Schweizer, who had settled all the problems. Theology could not die from the acute questions posed by these outsiders. But would it not inevitably die in the purity which triumphed here? Theology thinks that in fact it did not die then. If we ventured to set ourselves on that lofty watchtower from which Schweizer thought that he could speak, we might perhaps say that the winter sleep on which theology now entered served by God's providence at that moment to preserve it. But as we are not in a position to put ourselves there, we can only assert that the course of modern theology begun by Schweizer came to an end without offering a possibility for further thought about it. The only possibilities offered here are either to remain stationary or to turn round and go in the other direction.

21

DORNER

HERE for the first time we have to deal with a theologian who, while standing amidst the problems of the nineteenth century, points beyond them in his contribution to theological method and poses new questions to us by the new answers that he gives. Dorner was able to combine Hegel and Schleiermacher: that in itself distinguishes him from both figures and still more from Schweizer on the one hand, and from Marheineke on the other, and also, of course, makes him in a twofold degree a man of his time. But the basis for this combination in Dorner is an unmistakable, independent theological interest that can find rest neither in the speculation of the subjective side nor in that of the objective side, as it was practised in the two schools. With Schweizer, Dorner wants to affirm faith, and with Marheineke, revelation, without allowing now the one and now the other to issue in a human possibility. It is an interest that goes beyond the human possibility of religion, beyond the correlation of self-awareness and history, albeit in relationship to it, and again wants to reckon seriously with God as the ground of revelation and faith.

Dorner remains a child of his time in that he, too, pursues his concern in the form of a speculation about God that goes far beyond those of Schleiermacher and Hegel. This tends once again to make the theological character of his undertaking ambiguous, and even in detailed points it proved to be a significant source of error. At any rate, it had the significance of obscuring, indeed concealing, the trend of Dorner's concern from his contemporaries. From our present position we might say that Dorner attempted a breakthrough in principle, but ultimately proved unsuccessful. His contemporaries failed to recognize the new element, the attempt at a breakthrough as such, and only saw the failure, i.e. the fact of one of those powerful half-dogmatic, half-philosophical systems which arose one after the other in the first half of the century, for which men in the second half of the century, now uninterested in principles and seeking renown in history, had no interest. When Dorner's principal systematic work appeared, he had been anticipated by six years by Albrecht Ritschl, thirteen years his junior, whose work on *Justification and Reconciliation*, free of metaphysics, did more justice to the change in the times, so that from the start Dorner's book had to fight against a prejudiced view that it was old-fashioned and out-of-date. It did not establish itself, and the name of Dorner, whose learning and powers of thought were so often revered, became covered with a thick layer of dust soon after his death. Perhaps the time will still come when it is recognized that he did not deserve such a fate. Let us attempt to see what might have been seen here.

Isaak August Dorner, also from Württemberg, was born in 1809 and in 1834 studied at the Tübingen *Stift*, at the same time as Strauss. His career took him to a variety of places, so that in 1838 we find him *extraordinarius* professor in Tübingen, in 1839 *ordinarius* professor in Kiel, in 1844 in Königsburg, in 1847 in Bonn, in 1853 in Göttingen and finally in 1862 in Berlin, where he died in 1884. He, too, combined theological teaching with a variety of other activities and finally, as Prussian Chief Church Councillor, he was responsible for the direction of the Church. He, too, first produced two large historical works: *Die Entwicklungsgeschichte der Lehre von der Person Christi* (The History of the Development of the Doctrine of the Person of Christ) (1839-40) and the *Geschichte der protestantische Theologie besonders in Deutschland* (History of Protestant Theology, especially in Germany) (1867), which is mentioned in the introduction. His own dogmatics, the voluminous *System der christlichen Glaubenslehre* (System of the Christian Doctrine of Faith), first appeared in 1879-80 and his *Ethics* appeared posthumously in 1888. His son was August Dorner, who made something of a name for himself in his day, particularly as a philosopher of religion in Königsberg.

Dorner entitled his main work *The Christian Doctrine of Faith*, and the title of its introduction, 'Pisteology', strengthens the impression that we are in the vicinity of Schleiermacher. But with Dorner all three terms must be taken equally seriously: Christian, doctrine, faith. *Faith*, he wrote as early as 1856, recognizes itself as a 'mere *point of communication* through which the knowledge and love of God in which he reveals himself become human knowledge both of man's own redemption and of God and his love' (*Schriften*, 32). Just as there can be no philosophy as a science of the truth of thought without the presupposition of thought in a particularly pure form, so too there can

be no science of the truth of faith without the presupposition of that
form of faith in which that point of communication is really present,
in which religious certainty is to be had (*Schriften*, 78; *Doctrine* I, 16f.).
Hence the Christian doctrine of faith and, as an introduction to it, a
special pisteology. Even this foundation for the starting-point that
Dorner has in common with Schleiermacher shows that *duo cum faciunt
idem, non est idem*. With Schleiermacher there can be no question of a
real starting point from faith. But there can be with Dorner. For him,
religious certainty is not identical with the foundation of Christianity
on itself; it is only the presupposition for scientific knowledge of it
(*Doctrine* I, 146). Knowledge of the truth is materially independent
of experience, of one's own subjectivity as the medium of this knowledge (*Doctrine* I, 150f.). Truth is the foundation of faith and not *vice
versa*, and faith recognizes this foundation as being based on itself
(*Doctrine* I, 162). Dorner refers to Paul and John in distinguishing
gnosis from *pistis* as the latter's particular act, 'the gift of insight into
the truth as such and into its consequences', an insight which, while
not complete, but partial, in an image, in a mirror, nevertheless really
comes about. This *gnosis* is the presupposition of theology without
theology thereby leaving the sphere of faith. As the *gnosis* of faith it is
and remains distinct from all natural theology (*Doctrine* I, 152f.). So
faith is not a real principle, a *principium essendi*, but only a *principium
cognoscendi* or *medians*. The *principium essendi* is God in Christ through
the Holy Spirit. And even as the *principium cognoscendi*, faith is only the
principium cognoscendi subjectivum to which must be added the *principium
cognoscendi objectivum* in the form of authentic testimony of Christ, Holy
Scripture (*Doctrine* I, 157).

In addition to the concept of faith, Dorner is also, unlike Schleiermacher, independently and positively interested in the concept of
doctrine, and above all in the *entity* that is the concern of the *cognoscere*
of the doctrine of faith, in what is specifically *Christian*, which is identical
with the divine Trinity. Dorner declared that Schleiermacher's 'immortal service' was that he had restored to faith the position that it ought
to have in Protestant theology. But he regretted that Schleiermacher,
like Melanchthon before him, had assigned an insignificant, indeed
negative place to the doctrine of the Trinity, without which there
could be no doctrine of justification. If the independence or even the
existence of the religious object is misunderstood, or ignored, how can
faith be evangelical, justificatory, the confidence in God in Christ, in
the all-sufficient power of salvation that rests objectively and immovably
alone in him? Must that not divert attention to the soul, to the ego,

to a principle of holiness and blessing which is immanent either in the ego or in the community as such? And with this do we not reach that self-redemption against which the Reformation itself fought? Do we not reach an apotheosis of the members of the Church? Is the continued work of the exalted Christ not transformed into a mere historical effect? Is this not confidence in the divine powers at work in humanity (*Schriften*, 30f.)?

These are Dorner's *material* objections to Schleiermacher. And with them he combines his criticisms of Schleiermacher's *method*: Dorner praises Schleiermacher for having resisted with victorious success the supranaturalist error, that men come to faith through knowledge. But he censures him because in contradiction to the *credo ut intelligam* in the motto of his *Doctrine of Faith* he could bring about indifference to objective truth and knowledge of that truth, because the believing knowledge dealt with in his writings is only a knowledge of the pious man about himself, about his own status. But if there is no objective knowledge, how can piety be distinguished from chance and arbitrariness (*Doctrine* I, 4f.)? The human personality is one element, in that it is pious and thinks. Piety cannot be content with agreeing with the Bible and dogma, nor can it retreat into being its own basis (*Doctrine* I, 23, 153, 156). It cannot and will not remain alone and isolated. God and consciousness of him belong to the religious process, not by conclusions from a causal argument, but immediately. 'At one and the same time we recognize Christ as the one endowed with redeeming power and ourselves as his redeemed, as the objects of his love. (*Doctrine* I, 160f.).

The positive content of Dorner's pisteology is as follows. Clearly following Hegel, he distinguishes three stages of belief:

1. There is a certainty of faith that propagates itself through the Christianity of families and peoples, the certainty of the common faith of the Christian Church: it cannot be denied-an important pedagogical significance, but it can become dangerous if it suppresses the subjective religious personality and taints the purity of objective truth. It can end in a breach, whether this be apostasy from Christianity or a Reformation-like retreat beyond tradition to the Bible. Even this, however, is not to go beyond the stage of historical belief. There remains a disturbance in the subject, as well as from the perspective of the object, which has a necessary ground, which must break out sooner or later (*Doctrine* I, 65f., 76f., 95f.).

2. By nature, now, the subject that goes astray in historical faith, yet longs after its own certainty, tends to turn to the spiritual, ideal,

eternal side of faith: from the chance truths of history, however useful they may be in pedagogy or as symbols, to the eternal truths of reason. The more consistently this happens, the more surely faith ceases to be faith whose object, although ideal, is also real and thus is in no way identical with those eternal truths (*Doctrine* I, 100f.). Utterly and completely taken up into Idealist philosophy, it can only end in scepticism (I, 106f.).

3. The third stage is reached when theoretical doubt becomes practical, doubt in Christianity becomes the doubt of the subject in himself, in his own excellence and purity, when he recognizes the impossibility of giving himself indulgence. The transition from this, authentic, religious doubt, to religious certainty is godly grief, or the repentance that brings no regret (II Cor. 7.10). If the religious impulse, once awakened, does not persist in its subjectivity; if it does not want to feed on itself and consume itself in itself; if it is not merely directed towards an eternal godlike being, but to God's being (insofar as that is also a principle of action), to a word of God that has become a historical power and manifested itself in time, then the *Church*, i.e. the Christian community, can give it an impression of the real force and trustworthiness of Christianity. The *Holy Scriptures*, above all of the New Testament, i.e. the total testimony of the primitive Church to Christ, can present it with Christ's picture; the *sacrament*, finally, can communicate the divine pronouncement, the divine verdict that the love of God and the right to be a child of God apply to it indeed. Now if the subject understands and affirms the salvation prepared in this way, not arbitrarily, but also not sluggishly, in confidence, in the consciousness of its duty not to lose confidence, hearkening to the Father's movement towards the Son—then receptivity and grace in the innermost centre of personality together strike a 'renewing spark of life—'and the one who is grasped by the grace that descends on him has now become one who grasps, indeed a possessor'. Standing in time, the believer knows that he is in eternal life, united with the centre of all truth in heaven and on earth; now he has the religious certainty of Christian salvation, the *fides divina*, in which there takes place a συμμαρτυρία of the awareness of self and the awareness of God, in which a new awareness of self and of God is secretly planted, indeed in which a marriage of man with God in the Holy Spirit takes place (*Doctrine* I, 127f., 143; *Schriften*, 68).—So there is this third and highest form of faith, and the Christian doctrine of faith is to deal with its truth, i.e. with its knowledge of God and man.

I need not stress how closely Dorner agrees with Schleiermacher in this last train of thought. And not only with Schleiermacher, but with Hegel and the whole of his time. It is clear how the eschatological notion of being a child of God is now bent round again and made into a synthesis by means of which the antithesis in ourselves between the empirically historical and ideal faith is bridged. This contrasts with the other possible synthesis, by means of which the relationship of faith to its object might emphatically be reserved for God himself and for God alone, and thus be characterized as the synthesis of faith. The assertion of a receptivity in man, the Catholic-type conception of the *gratia preveniens* which runs alongside this receptivity, the mystical culmination of this pisteology, are all elements of a speculative basic approach which can even be seen here, in Dorner. But the difference between Dorner and his time is far more important than any agreement. His *gnosis* is at any rate at heart a twofold one, and of the two constitutive elements, the objective and the subjective, the objective is by far the predominant one. The attempts made later by Erich Schäder with his programme of a theocentric theology had long been realized by Dorner in an impressive way, and even Schäder did not manage to get beyond the barrier that Dorner encountered, that idealistically mystic synthesis at the point where one would expect to hear of faith and of God, or of Christ and only of Christ. The tendency of Dorner's principles—and this is where they are new in comparison with Schleiermacher and Hegel—is that they go against the spirit and the taste of his time by making a distinction within the unity of the two factors and by stressing the priority of the objective factor. It was a quite astonishing venture when Dorner undertook, in his doctrine of the relativity of both empirical history and idealistic faith, to bracket off both Schleiermacher and Hegel, in their entirety, as the first two stages of his pisteology, and treat them as thesis and antithesis. He then had real Christian faith beginning on the one hand with the doubt of the subject in itself, with godly grief, and on the other hand with the Word of God that encountered it, with Scripture, Church and sacrament. With the decisive appearance of these two factors, the circle of problems in which more recent theology moved and felt that it should and could only move, was for a moment broken. Here there emerged the possibility of a real question from man and a real answer from God, in such a way that the answer from God was evidently intended to become the object of a Christian *gnosis*, the theme of theology. Intended—for the doctrine of the 'renewing spark of light', in which Dorner's pisteology eventually culminated, did not in the end allow this conclusion. But that does not mean that we can overlook the fact that for the first time something new presented itself here.

We can look at this new element from the other side if we consider Dorner's great treatise *Das Prinzip unserer Kirche nach dem inneren Verhältnis der materialen und formalen Seite desselben zu einander* (The Principle of our Church according to the Inner Relationship of the Material and Formal Side of the Same to One Another) (1841). The question discussed here is one that aroused much attention in the forties and fifties and concerns the fundamental principles of Protestantism: the *doctrine of justification* and the *scriptural principle*. In this writing, so characteristic of his early days, Dorner wants to show that these two principles and only these two principles are involved, that they form a unity between themselves within which each has an independent significance, and that it is particularly urgent to revalue the second, formal, objective element in a completely different way. In a manner that is very characteristic of his approach, he sets the usual more or less radical battle against the so-called dead letter of historical authority in parallel to the antinomianism of the sixteenth century, which wanted to be content with justification without works (*Schriften*, 70f.), as though a love could be the love of God that justifies men. Thus even a faith that is certain of itself, whether it claims to be faith in the Logos, in the incarnation of the Logos, or in the eternal, ideal Christ, is ultimately empty (p. 73). It can be demonstrated from the nature of faith that as a material principle of Christianity faith must always be accompanied by a relatively independent, objective pure account of Christianity as a formal principle, in such a form that it may have itself and be faith. Just as human awareness of self and personality only arises with the distinction of subject and object, I and Thou, and just as Idealism dissolves when in its strictest form it becomes acosmism, so there may be no acosmism of faith (p. 85), no negation of Christian objectivity, of the world of Christian realities (i.e. the Christian truths that are at the same time facts). No one is born as a new man without being born into a Christian objectivity or without Christian objectivity being born in him, as a member (p. 87), and faith can never, even after its origin—it must constantly reproduce itself—dispense with this objectivity (p. 89). The fact that there are false objectivities does not prove that there cannot be a true objectivity: this is what faith, together with its content, claims to be. But if faith by nature goes together with Christian objectivity (p. 89), it must be that in understanding, wonder, love and even reverence it acknowledges this as something higher, loftier, greater, more divine, inwardly more perfect than it is itself, as a norm. Note the comparatives! One might perhaps term them qualified comparatives, which could well be in place in so far as faith, Christian subjectivity, in fact finds itself on the same level as Christian objectivity and on this common level there must be a relationship of subordination, a relationship of law and obedience (p. 91). In the last resort Christian objectivity is identical with Christ himself: he is the formal principle. Dorner now wants to protect himself from putting a λόγος ἄσαρκος in place of the real Logos that came in the flesh. Even in his continuing influence, in his actuality, Christ is inward *and* outward, ideal *and* historic (pp. 107f.). So Dorner stesses the 'flesh of Christ', the bridge on which he is recognized as the God-man, and in which faith has its abiding object (p. 111). Now if the Church is to be considered to be such a bridge for the whole period of Christ's continuing work, we must go on to add that what is meant is the original Church, the Church in which the whole of Christian faith of all times agreed has to recognize itself again, by which it has agreed to direct itself, in the establishment and continuation of the New Testament canon (p. 112). 'We hear in the Scriptures the spirit-filled choir of Apostles transposed into our own time, and we know that we are acknowledged by them to stand in their faith, outside which there can be no Christian (faith)' (p. 116). In them we hear 'the words of the Lord himself ring out, and it seems as though the separation brought about by time and space is overcome by Scripture. Christ's historical manifestation is brought into the eternal now and is set before us' (p. 116). Really? Yes, for Dorner argues: 'The first member of the generation after Christ must have borne what is objectively Christian within himself, otherwise Christianity would not have come into the world. But it did come into the world. So that first member must certainly have had what is originally Christian' (p. 117). There can evidently be no third principle alongside these two, faith and the Word given to it (p. 100). Anything more than this can only be a reference to the Holy Spirit, 'whose office it is to give each of the two sides of the principle the force of relative independence and thereby maintain the difference without which neither of the two would be what it is. At the same time, however, the Spirit only bestows power on each of the two by uniting it and joining it with the other. Thus the Holy Spirit performs only the same office in the economic Trinity that he performs in the immanent Trinity, where he is equally the distinguishing and the unifying principle. But his office in the world is the transfiguration of Christ, which consists in making the world the kingdom of God with the Church as its centre, and making both of these the representative portrayal of the indissoluble union of the inward or merely subjective and the externally objective, the ideal and the historic, the divine and the human, which was primally brought about in Christ' (p. 99).

Dorner's limitation also appears in this train of thought. The bracketing off of Schleiermacher's and Hegel's approaches at this point rightly becomes in practice the bracketing off of historical authority and faith. But it now happens that secretly not only the concept of historical authority, but the concept of the Word, indeed expressly of Christ himself, is bracketted off, so that Christ and faith are ultimately subordinated to the concept of the Holy Spirit. The same thing has evidently happened as what we see in the doctrine of the 'renewing spark of life', and the impression is given that the Holy Spirit is to be understood as none other than this renewing spark of life in us. Quite apart from the fact that *this* stress on the Holy Spirit means no more and no less than that he is characterized as the real God over against the Father and the Son, stress on him in this context and at this point must indicate that the theological questions and answers have come to rest in a mystical point of unity that lies within ourselves. Except that here, too, one should not overlook the dualism of Word and faith maintained within the bracket and the preponderance of the Word in this dualism. In Dorner's work there can be no question of the dissolution of the Word in faith (in contrast to Schleiermacher) or of the dissolution of faith in a general Logos-knowledge (in contrast to Hegel). The Word that has become flesh in Christ and has been made concrete in Scripture is characterized as the Word given to faith, which is followed by faith, which is the basis for faith—and not *vice versa*. In this relationship and in the proportions with which it is presented, there appears with Dorner a theology which again sets out to be knowledge of God. That should not be forgotten, however much Dorner himself concealed it by his speculation on the spirit, rooted in mysticism.

Another indication that a new element has appeared with Dorner is that in his writings, as opposed to those of Schweizer, there are again theological problems, there is a concrete theological situation with concrete needs, hopes and concerns. Dorner is certainly a child of his time in wanting to model German theology principally on the Apostle who in the early Church was called above all others 'the theologian': John, who, 'taught by God and knowing God in Christ, had the charisma by virtue of which all is known in one' (*Schriften*, 13). But unlike Schweizer, with this wish Dorner deliberately looks into the future. He is not concerned, say, because of the modern unbelief that surrounds the Church and theology. Nor is he concerned with the ultimately rather tedious resentment against Catholicism and orthodoxy which usually forms the inevitable correlate to such anxiety. His hesitations, like his proposals, come from within. Above all, he asserts that Protestant theology is still only at the beginning, in the years of its youth, but that now the critical moment has come when it must lose what it has if it is not in a position to gain more than it had through the development of what it does have. Above all, Dorner concurs with the verdict of old Oetinger, that Protestant theology, especially in Germany, has remained too much a mere ordinance of salvation; salvation has been conceived too much, albeit inwardly, in this-worldly terms, through faith which is certain of the blessedness of the soul and the consummation of the person. *Eschatology* came to grief even at the time of the Reformation (pp. 15f.), and as a result it was all the easier in the period that followed for Pietism and orthodoxy, like Gnosticism and Montanism in the early Church—both unfruitful and both ultimately suffering from the same ill—to separate. It was all the easier, too, for an abstract religious and equally abstract secular this-wordliness to dominate the field. Dorner therefore finds the true descendant of the principle of the Reformation and at the same time the new impulse for theological knowledge in the eighteenth century (like Menken before him) in Johann Albrecht Bengel, who set the 'prophetic word of God' over against the self-satisfied inwardness of orthodoxy and Pietism. Eschatology must free the way of Protestant thinking for history and for ethics; it must make it impossible for this thinking to remain sunk in the self-contemplation of faith (p. 207). Moreover, eschatology is the primitive religious form of becoming aware of the unversality and absoluteness of Christianity. Eschatology must be a special help in dogmatics 'by means of which a true, living understanding of Christ's majesty may be achieved. Whereas, if we were limited to its effects hitherto, if we only wanted to recognize it from the excellence of ourselves or others, or from the glory and splendour of a particular church, it would be concealed rather than revealed' (p. 21). Finally, eschatology must give true Christian realism its due: the revelation of the inward in the outward, but also the ethical character of the union of the Christian spirit with nature, and hence the necessary restraint against over-hasty external assimilation to this world, an admonition to remember the changeableness and mutability of all possible ethical statements, a reminder of the Apostle's 'have as though we had not' which must stand over them all, and finally of the virtue of hope, which above all 'in the sphere of the Church' can serve as a wholesome safeguard against a desire for false and over-hasty accounts and anticipations of the consummation in arbitrary flights of the imagination, as against innumerable phantoms, occasions of wasted energy, false confidence in transitory forms and the factions that follow from all this (p. 23). True eschatology will 'destroy the vanity of being finished at some point with the development that has to be undergone and reapply to the living idea of the Church and the kingdom of God the love which is only kindled by the prototype. In this way it will sustain the true Church in living, rejuvenating progress' (p. 23). But at the same time as this glance forwards, and in the closest connexion with it, Dorner now equally earnestly requires a glance backwards, at the presuppositions of justifying faith in the objective doctrines of God's being, person and Trinity, of the person and work of Christ, which has only just been touched on by the Reformation (as was the case with eschatology) and since Pietism has been allowed to lie fallow, in a certain position of honour, but without being assimilated. The progress made by the theology of the Reformation in anthropology and soteriology fell short of any further recognition of objective dogmas, and so later developments increasingly lacked the right equilibrium. 'The trend in the Reformation towards the salvation of the personality, without the objective counterbalance of other doctrines, was exposed at an increasingly rapid rate to those subjectivistic aberrations which shake off all objective elements, and in so doing became falsified' (p. 25). 'The problem is to take up again the treatment of those doctrines from the stage of Protestantism, as being the highest standpoint so far reached, and not merely attach them externally to the evangelical principle and its stage of consciousness, whether as products of philosophical speculation or as the results of church work in past centuries or as the mere findings of scriptural doctrine' (p. 31). It should not seem as though God were merely there to pour out blessings on man and make himself a means for man. The process of love that goes out from God would not reach its goal if it were only forward-moving, if God wanted to be loved by us only in humanity, this extended self of our ego, and if the circle of love were not also able to close by love returning to its source. It would be egotistical if we saw only ourselves as God's purpose, and did not want to think and desire further. The revelation of the love of God demands that through it, as in a mirror, we recognize God himself, recognize what God is in himself and as he wants to be both known and loved, because he is truth and love (pp. 32f.).

22

MÜLLER

JULIUS Müller, a Silesian, born in 1801, came to Berlin as a student with the Revival movement. In 1825 he became a pastor in his homeland, where he made a name for himself, in contrast to his later attitude, as an opponent of the Union politics of the Prussian government. He became a university preacher in 1831 and in 1832 a *Privatdozent* in Göttingen, *ordinarius* professor in Marburg in 1835 and in Halle in 1839 (where he managed to be appointed in succession to Ullmann against the candidacy of F. C. Baur, though not without worldly-wise intrigues from Tholuck against the faculty and the Minister). He died there in 1878.

Our concern with this theologian in the present context is not because of his general theological position and attitude. It can be distinguished from that, say, of Alexander Schweizer only through a rather greater openness on the conservative and pietistic side, without approaching him in clarity and consistency. Its starting point is also 'the present consciousness of the Church in its living members, in which it has certainly not been abandoned by the Spirit which founded it' (*Doctrine of Sin* I, 1). He, too, wants to derive this consciousness from revelation. He, too, understands this consciousness as the source of an academic presentation of Christian doctrine. He, too, wants to reconcile religion and speculation in the form of a theistic philosophy on which dogmatics has to construct itself, He, too, was (or at least became) an ardent advocate of Union, about the 'divine right' of which he wrote a special work in 1854. Since we have already made the acquaintance of this type to some degree, it would not be worth spending time on Müller for the reasons so far given. Bu this one great book, his monograph *Die christliche Lehre von der Sünde* (The Christian Doctrine of Sin), which appeared between 1838 and 1844, compels our attention. Not so much the result of this book as the concern that underlies it. This concern makes Müller, like Isaak August Dorner, an interesting representative of the unrest with which this generation took over the heritage of Schleiermacher, all the more interesting because this unrest makes itself felt only at one point (though at this point it really does become visible!), while everywhere else and in the last resort even at this point the manner of the man was and remained that of his time, quite unaffected by originality. With him, too, we have to talk of a breakthrough that ground to a halt, of a new element that flashed out like a meteor, only to vanish again later. Julius Müller did not penetrate as far as wide-ranging, general insights like Dorner's dialectic of object and subject, but in compensation, at the one point with which he was concerned he saw more widely and profoundly, and opened up more radical perspectives even than Dorner. Like Dorner, he, too, is concerned to criticize the Christian monism in which ultimately we found all the people we have considered here to agree, with a criticism of the view of God and man, of subject and object, that sees them together, indeed in one, and on that basis believes that it can overcome the problem of theology all along the line. At a single point Müller used twelve hundred pages to show where this Christian monism must cease to be either monism or Christian, at an 'incomprehensible' point on the human side, which is not in any way and in any circumstances compatible with God. This one point which Müller saw and attacked was the problem of sin. Of course Tholuck, and indeed the Revival, had already spoken in earnest tones about sin. Julius Müller was not aroused in his youth to no effect by Tholuck, who was only two years his senior. But in academic theology it was Müller, and not Tholuck, who countered contemporary enthusiasm over 'comprehension' with the assertion that the word 'sin' in the midst of Christian self-awareness might designate something which can be met only with the 'comprehension of incomprehensibility' (II, 232). 'Comprehension of incomprehensibility'—that might mean the distintegration of the syntheses of both Schleiermacher and Hegel. Müller did not bring that about. He wanted to comprehend the incomprehensible well enough for the incomprehensibility to be refuted and done away with even here, so that the syntheses of Schleiermacher and Hegel could ultimately be restored. But this result, the positive culmination of Müller's doctrine of sin, should not conceal from us the fact that the insight and purpose here could have meant a disintegration of these syntheses and hence the beginning of a new trend in theological questions and answers. The significant part of Müller's contribution is to be found in the first volume of his work, and it is to an analysis of that that we now turn.

Müller agrees with Schleiermacher that everything in Christianity rests on the great opposition of sin and redemption. But, he says, if that is so, then 'religious dread' of sin cannot be annihilated by a 'purely speculative, conceptual recognition of it' (I, pp. vif.); the split in our life introduced by sin cannot be dealt with 'by the well-known dialectic of immediacy and mediation', for which the split becomes an unavoidable, indeed ultimately a divinely necessary transition (I, pp. viif.). 'To want to know evil *a priori* is in fact to do away with the concept of evil' (I, 24). Evil is 'a shadow of the night that darkens every area of human life, that we see constantly swallowing up even its brightest, lightest forms' (I, 32). We cannot not think about it and we cannot master it by thinking of it. In contrast to all ills that are not proof against a union with our disposition, evil is 'that which is simply alien and contradictory to our being, with the existence of which no higher standpoint of reflection and no more developed knowledge is reconcilable' (I, 34f.).

What is the *nature* of sin? Müller first answers this question by defining sin as dissociation from the law (I, 53), and therefore as disobedience towards God who is the originator of the law, as a breach of the covenant (I, 117), and thus as completely selfish isolation of the creature from God as his Creator (I, 180, 192). It is worldly delight (I, 213), from which issue lying, arrogance and hate (I, 220f.), which makes its disruptive effect felt even in the sphere of knowledge (I, 252f.). But sin is essentially guilt, i.e. it is caused by the subject and it is a responsible and punishable action (I, 263f.). Moreover, it is guilt towards God. The position in which man finds himself as a sinner may in no way be understood as a result of the divine order (I, 293f.). God judges and God punishes and, still more, God redeems; he forgives sins on the basis of the reconciliation of the sinner. Thus sin is excluded from divine causality (I, 342f., 343f.). Thus sin enters our consciousness and becomes a fact of our experience in this context and in no other (I, 367). From this point Müller proceeds to an impressive discussion of the various answers to the question of the origin of sin and marks out the following areas:

1. Evil can be understood as *metaphysical incompleteness*, as a deficiency in man as a created being. Should man not be regarded, following Leibnitz, as an asymptote of Godhead, and sin as his eternally not-yet-having-reached, part of his concept as man? (I, 376). This would be conceivable if there were only sins of weakness, if evil did not encounter us in most cases in the form of a heightened energy of willing and thinking (I, 379f.). But this theory cannot explain the positive

opposition of evil to good as it corresponds to the real content of the Christian moral consciousness (I, 385).

2. Nor is *sensuality* the essence and the source of sin. This second explanation only indicates the drive to self-righteousness rooted in the depths of selfishness: sin is to be removed from man's authentic ego and transferred outside him; it is to be made into a smut that has merely dropped on to man, which prevents the true, supposedly pure form of the inner life from shining through and muddies its appearance. The heart itself is to be protected against accusations. We ourselves are not evil. We suffer evil. But all this means that the nature of man, which in itself is guiltless, sensual, is calumniated and man is already presupposed to be godless, instead of the principle of sin being sought in alienation from God, the true wretchedness of which man necessarily conceals from himself in this way (I, 427f.), a course which he cannot, incidentally, attribute to Kánt (I, 460f.).

3. The third doctrine of sin contested by Müller is that of *Schleiermacher*. He finds the fundamental error here in the fact that Schleiermacher sees the relationship between created and uncreated personality only as absolute dependence and therefore the relationship between uncreated and created personality only as one of absolute causality. So the dilemma arises: either there is real opposition between God and evil—in which case evil must be envisaged as having been ordained and brought forth by God. Or, evil must be excluded from divine causality, in which case it is to be understood only as mere negation (I, 483). Schleiermacher has combined these two equally intolerable possibilities by explaining evil as the power of sensual nature that constrains the spirit and yet conditions the liveliness of its development, to this degree being a power that is willed and brought about by God. As the author of redemption, God is the author also of the sin that makes redemption necessary (I, 487). We are guilty only in our own consciousness, not before God and not in the divine judgment (I, 489). Sin becomes identical with the consciousness of sin (I, 477) as the counter-working of the element of the eternal self-consciousness that constrains the spirit (I, 481). (At this point it is not clear how such a constraint of the feeling of absolute dependence can come about only in the consciousness; whether for Schleiermacher sin is not, strictly speaking, an impossibility (I, 480f.).) This is an indication, Müller thinks, that we should not abide by the consciousness that is given to us of sin as our own act and guilt as turning away from God, and should not long to climb on our own shoulders and look beyond ourselves (I, 493).

4. Müller paid particular attention to the view that sin is to be explained from the way in which the whole of life is *conditioned by opposites*. People point to the concrete concept of the individual as multiplicity combined in the innermost unity. By virtue of the polarity that is essential to all that is finite, each element requires its opposite and together with this some mediation. The opposition of good and evil seems to be nothing else but the antithetical relationship which emerges at the supreme climax of the finite, being known to us, in the spiritual life of man, in the greatest acuteness and tension, and which in this form apparently excludes all mediation. But only apparently. For a scientific consideration cannot call a halt even with this opposition. Without weakness, struggle and passion, it is said, moral Idealism is an empty, tedious abstraction, a Chinese painting without shade and therefore, essentially, without light. Man only becomes conscious of good by looking in the mirror of evil. Human life acquires content, significance and character only in moving between the poles of yes and no, love and hate, altruism and egoism, in the mixture of good and evil. Müller believes that this theory reaches its culmination in the doctrine of Hegel (I, 495f.), that the unity of animal innocence from which man begins must be sublimated in its spiritlessness by division, in order to find itself again in higher immediacy. Müller has two objections to make to this: 1. There is no need for evil in order that the moral life of the spirit should in fact be communicated through opposition. This it is in itself and in accordance with original divine ordinance. Individuality in fact has an antithetical character. But the antithesis of good and evil is to be differentiated sharply from this normal, divinely-ordained antithesis. In a certain way evil may in fact be a means to good, so that Christian poetry can venture to say:

O certe necessarium Adae peccatum,
quod Christi morte deletum est!
O felix culpa, quae talem ac tantum
meruit habere redemptorem!

However, that does not do away with the strict and sober Christian view that evil is not so much the antithesis as the adversary of good. One may find sin in the finest accord with the perfection of this present world, but sin is never in any way a condition of the fulfilment of the kingdom of God in another world. That is the end of sin (I, 512f.). 2. Of course, the whole present form of our being is so conditioned by sin that we are not in a position to envisage a pure and untroubled development of human life. But it does not follow from that

that sin must be regarded as a necessity. Though sin may belong as a rule to the real life that we know, it is alien to the original ordinance of God that the path to a deeper independent knowledge of the truth should go by the way of the overcoming of thousandfold error; that for example the most brilliant individuals win through to their goal for the most part only by considerable vacillation and the most serious error; that the history of our race is by and large a history of battle and destruction; that we have to be told about the impermanence of all earthly things above all by war. Ultimately, rather, it is the case that sin obscures the characteristic features of life and does not bring them to light, constrains and does not further the revelation of its primal form, even in earthly life (I, 521f.). Finally, it is to be said against Hegel that there cannot be a metaphysical necessity for evil as 'that which should not be', because the conscience can only deny the persistence of evil as long as and in so far as it does not know of another, more persistent no against its happening. The devil has no sense of humour, and does not allow man to understand evil only as a point of transition, as though it were not *evil* (I, 544f.).

5. In the last place Müller now rejects even the *dualistic* explanation of evil, according to which it is supposed to be a second absolute, a second substance over against God. In that case its significance is not ethical, but physical. Man falls victim to it through natural necessity and therefore he must be freed from it by a natural process. God himself would be given a destiny by a fundamental being originally independent of him and opposed to him. Good is certainly quite independent of evil. But evil is already dependent on good in that it only comes into existence at all as an opposite to good. So we are not dealing with a one-sided, irreversible relationship of dependence. If we wish to ascribe absolute being to evil we may no longer understand it as what should not be—and this is true both in respect to dualism and in respect to Hegelian monism. So it reveals itself to us not only as emptiness and nothingness, but as something fearful and gruesome, as a rushing river of thousandfold torment, because the good from which it turns is not only reality but ethical goodness, personality, love. If evil is to realize itself it must always attach itself in some way to the good, make use of it. It has no intrinsic power to produce and to shape. It does not venture to be itself, it is caught up in a restless flight from itself and conceals itself hypocritically behind all kinds of appearances of good. In the end it betrays the dependent character of its existence by finding itself in a dichotomy not only with good, but even with itself; its two fundamental trends, to arrogance and to

the predominance of sensual delight in incessant war, stand side by side. As alienation from God it achieves what it strives for, and in so doing finds its punishment and its downfall (I, 559f.).

The contribution of the first volume of Müller's monograph may be summed up as follows: in the analysis of the Christian consciousness which he has undertaken in company with the rest of the theology of his time, Müller has had his attention drawn to the element of human sin in such a way that he cannot avoid the perplexity it causes by any of the means customary in his time. He will accept neither that it is given as such with man's creaturely existence, nor that it is especially determined by the tangible physical components of this existence. He cannot see it with Schleiermacher as a mere constraint, nor with Hegel as a necessary antithesis to good, nor, finally, can he remain content with the dualistic conception of a substantiality of evil. He stands perplexed before a reality and has to reject as unsatisfactory, one after the other, all attempts to explain how it can be possible, to understand it systematically. Will he stop there? In that case, the concept of sin must become a theological concept in a quite different sense of the word 'theology' from that accepted by all his contemporaries. In that case, sin for him can only exist as an underivable qualification of man by God's revelation. But if that is so, God's revelation itself must become a reality which is withdrawn from the circle of systematically comprehensible possibilities, which must be seen as a reality *of God*, and which can be understood only in this light, without corresponding in any way to a human possibility. It was not out of the question that by his understanding of sin Müller arrived at an understanding of the distinction between God and man that went far beyond that of Dorner in consistency and significance. Dorner's doctrine of sin had remained completely caught in the realm of the attempt made by Schleiermacher and Hegel to incorporate evil into a metaphysic of the good as a constraint and a necessary antithesis. This may also explain why Dorner could ultimately sublimate his attempt, which had such a different character, in the mystical culmination of his pisteology. Müller's insight into the helplessness of all attempts at a theodicy of sin could have led to the point where this mystical culmination became impossible for theology, and thus have forced it to take a quite different methodological track: if there is no possibility of incorporating evil into the system, then this is also an impossibility as far as the 'renewing spark of life' is concerned. In that case, a doctrine of the Holy Spirit must appear at this point which leaves no doubt that the Holy Spirit and our own religious spirit are and remain two different things. In that case, beyond the Word and faith there would remain only the incomprehensible synthesis in God himself; the establishment of theology as an analysis of Christian self-consciousness would have become an impossibility. But even with Julius Müller, this point of thoroughgoing renewal was not reached, not because in the last resort he did not refrain from wanting to give an answer to the question of the possibility of sin and thus implicitly an answer to the question of the possibility of the good, of grace, of revelation and ultimately of God himself. So let us also give a short account of the content of the second volume of his work.

Müller finds the principle, the possibility of evil in the freedom of the human will for self-decision (II, 1f.). Freedom means 'also to be able to be otherwise' (II, 32). It is, of course, impossible to demonstrate such a decision on the part of the will as the beginning of moral development (II, 96), unless we resolve—and this is the point at which Müller's attempt at an explanation begins—to transcend the region of temporality and to seek the place of this decision beyond earthly life. Müller begins from the concept of personality. God's personality is not like human personality in being conditioned by the way in which the ego distinguishes itself from others (II, 160f.); it is conditioned absolutely by the inner infinity of the determination of his being. His freedom, his aseity, is the principle of that infinity (II, 169) and at the same time also the principle of the existence of creation, of another being by virtue of his love, of creaturely personality which by nature is endowed with freedom of the will (II, 178f.). Unlike God, man cannot see good in himself in a quite original and independent way, and therefore he does not have it as his own being. He can only be good in relationship to the God who determines him in his existence. Alongside this possibility, that man should be good, there is also the possibility of evil, of apostasy from God. Now Müller wants to locate the place where the decision about these two possibilities is made in a 'sphere of timelessness', since it cannot be demonstrated anywhere in time. This sphere is not to be confused with eternity; it is a 'kingdom of the intelligible', understood not as a higher ideal being of the soul, but as a 'tranquil, timeless, shadowy realm, as it were the mother's womb, in which the embryos of all personal beings, lie hidden', 'the simple undetermined beginnings of our being, which lie beyond its concrete content' (II, 206f.). In this way evil, incomprehensible in its reality, is comprehended in its possibility (II, 219f.). It is impossible to avoid the assumption of a divine self-limitation which 'allows' this

(II, 272f.); it may not be termed impossible, as this would contradict the concept of the omnipotence and the love of God (II, 261f.). Sin is really a universal fact in human experience, experience both of oneself and of others (II, 309f.). And it is a corruption of human nature itself (II, 349f.). Augustine's dogma of original sin leaves unresolved the contradiction between this universality and naturalness of sin on the one hand and the personal guilt of the individual on the other (II, 495). So even from here there arises the concept of a sinfulness which has its basis beyond our temporal and individual existence, as it was conceived of even by Origen. The contradiction vanishes 'when each man who in this earthly, temporal life seems imprisoned in sin has, in his primal state outside time, turned his will from the divine light to the darkness of the self that is sunk into itself' (II, 496f.). Thence man comes into the world, not incapable of being redeemed, but in a dichotomy with himself, in that strangely mixed, vacillating state of the natural man (II, 507f.). We are really bound by the fact that our will is by nature inwardly broken, split off from itself, and no moral development of man can do away with this perversion of the basic relationship. The perverted original decision is the persistent dark foundation of the human consciousness, even if God now takes it up and restores it to fellowship with himself by free grace through reconciliation and redemption in Christ. Even when this has been accomplished, those who are hallowed will always be the ransomed of the Lord: they will not be innocent, without any awareness of sin, but will be the redeemed, who know that their guilt is covered by forgiveness (II, 509f.).

We can break off here. Müller's positive doctrine of sin is one theory alongside others, and it would probably turn out that measured by his own criticism it is no better than any other, in that he evidently undertakes to climb on his own shoulders and look out beyond himself. For looking out on a timeless primal state manifestly means looking out beyond oneself. Or does it not? Be this as it may, the significance of Müller rests on the fact that he made clear that this looking out is prohibited to theology, a contribution which cannot have been sufficiently noted.

23

ROTHE

Two things have to be said about Richard Rothe: in an extraordinary way he is a case in himself, and in an extraordinary way he is a paradigm for the theological concern of the whole century. Where does this man belong? His general tendency to put Christian doctrine in the context of comprehensive speculation on God and the world doubtless puts him among the followers of Schleiermacher and Hegel, and particularly in the mediating group that we have come to know through representatives like Schweizer, Dorner and Müller. But one can immediately go wrong in a classification of this kind if one thinks on the one hand of the quite unmodern supranaturalism which marked out Rothe from his teachers and his contemporaries. Unlike any of them, Rothe was a fiery adept of the Revival movement, and unlike any of them he was a lifelong Pietist. Theosophy in the old, primeval sense of the term seems to have revived in him, and in addition he appears as a monk, a saint. His biographer Hausrath reports in amazement that one never seemed to meet him when he was not in secret conversation with an invisible power and reality; on one bright day during his lifetime he is said to have appeared to one of his pupils 'in a transfigured form', a miracle that certainly would not have happened to a pupil of Alexander Schweizer. 'He was different from everyone else that we knew. What the others talked about in an edifying way, he represented in his person' (Hausrath II, 564f.). But with this classification one could also go wrong in the opposite direction. It could also be said that Rothe was more modern than all the rest put together. Troeltsch saw his own concern anticipated in Rothe rather than in Schweizer. He was a remarkable supranaturalist in every way, who was an opponent of seventeenth-century orthodoxy with a passion that almost put him alongside David Friedrich Strauss, but he could hardly do anything with Reformation theology either. His was a remarkable Pietism which without any breach, without any Lucifer-like fall, could quite gently and naturally discover its identity with a *Kultur* Protestantism;

which—as Schleiermacher always kept wanting to say in two words
—in a word simply undertook to identify Christianity and true
worldliness, Church and state. Here was a Pietism in which one can
see heralded the monergism of the kingdom of God as Hermann Kutter
saw it, lay-Christian activism as understood by Leonhard Ragaz, and
the religious Socialism of our day. Here, too, was a remarkable theosophy—at least if one measured it by Oetinger, at whose feet Rothe
claimed to have set—which set out to subordinate completely biblical
exegesis with the certitude with which Rothe expressed himself[1] to
an anterior metaphysics, a theosophy which thoroughly deserved to
have as its author Rittelmeyer's Christian community and to honour
him as one of its first church fathers. Rothe was indeed a case by himself. But he was this by being 'a compendium of all the religious and
theological tendencies of the time' (Heckel); his originality had at
the same time an average significance unlike any other, so that an
abbreviated account of the nature and purpose of nineteenth-century
theology might well take the form of an account of this one Richard
Rothe himself.

Richard Rothe was born in Posen in 1799. He grew up in Breslau
in a home whose piety can be described in Stephan's term as 'noble
rationalism'. He was first alienated from it by his acquaintance with
Romanticism, above all in the person of Novalis, to whom he remained
faithful in a quite special way until his old age. From 1817 to 1819 he
studied in Heidelberg at the feet of Hegel and Daub, and from 1819
to 1812 in Berlin. In the preaching seminary at Wittenberg he then
came under the influence of the director there, Heubner, Baron von
Kottwitz, Tholuck, and his fellow-student Ewald Rudolf Stier, and
made the acquaintance of Pietism. From 1824 to 1828 he was embassy
preacher in Rome, where he struck up a friendship with the ambassador, Josias von Bunsen, who was extremely interested in the history
of theology. In this direction he discovered a new side of his own personality. In 1828 he himself became director of the Wittenberg
seminary and in 1837 published his first book, *Die Anfänge der christlichen
Kirche und ihre Verfassung* (The Beginnings of the Christian Church and
its Constitution). Here we already find the idea of the issuing of the
Church in the state, which was so characteristic of him. In the same
year he became professor and director of the seminary at Heidelberg.
In 1845 he published the first volume of his chief work, *Theologische
Ethik*, which for him also includes dogmatics. From 1849 to 1854 we

[1] K. A. Auberlen, *Oetinger*, p. xx.

find him in Bonn, but he gladly returned from there to his Heidelberg.
In 1863 the important work *Zur Dogmatik* appeared (three articles on
the concepts of dogmatics, revelation and Holy Scripture). In his old
age he began to take a lively part in the church politics of Baden and
indeed of all Germany, and to the astonishment of all—though one
must say in a completely consistent development—became one of the
founders of the German Protestant alliance. In 1867 he died, greatly
mourned, leaving grateful friends in every camp, but hardly any real
followers.

Rothe's theology is not to be sought, say, in his posthumously
published *Dogmatics*. For him dogmatics (*Zur Dogmatik*, 14) is merely
the historical and critical 'account' of the teaching that is publicly
recognized in a particular church community; it is the presentation
and assessment of the dogmas which another fundamental theological
discipline has as its presupposition. This fundamental discipline is what
Rothe calls speculative theology, *philosophia sacra*, or even explicitly
theosophy. What does that mean? Rothe answers: a scientific system
which, unlike philosophy, does not understand God from the world
but the world from God, 'a system of truly reborn, strict knowledge,
not by virtue of the natural spirit of man but by virtue of the holy
spirit of God'.[1] For philosophy, God, as ultimate cause, remains incomprehensible. But in addition to the human understanding in itself
itself there is also the *speculative capacity* of the spiritual man that is
matured in the moral process. Speculation as thinking from the totality,
simply as unitary thinking, becomes possible to the degree that the
individual is already taken up into the spirit. The system of Rothe's
theosophy is built up on three decisive presuppositions: (1) Reality,
the world, is simply the outward realization of the divine Idea; (2) The
Idea of God, together with the world, is also to be found in man as a
microcosm; (3) In that case, the Idea of God can be developed from
the human spirit *a priori*, through self-reflection by means of pure
thought. True thought that is capable of such an achievement is pure
thought that takes place with the eyes shut, that removes itself from
the attractions of the empirical world. 'In the realm of learning I
openly confess that I belong to the school of dreamers, but at
the same time I warn everyone against thinking that dreaming is
easy work.' Reason bears the system of the thinking of all being in
its bosom and brings it forth into the light of day by virtue of its
thought.

[1] Auberlen, op. cit., p. xvi. What follows is based on Hausrath II, pp. 85f.

God is Spirit conscious of itself and therefore person—absolute person. Now in that God thinks of himself, in accordance with the law of contradiction he also thinks of his contradictory opposite, a being which is not everything that he is. So creation is an absolutely necessary act of God. To comprehend himself as a person, God must think his *non-ego* and presuppose it in his thought. Consequently the world, like God himself, is without a beginning. God and the world are correlates. There is no world without God. The imperfections of the world are based on the fact that the *non-ego*, creation *per se*, is an opposite to God. But the creative activity of God, his expression of himself, continues in a series of stages of development. By virtue of this, the incompleteness of creation is caught up in a constant upward process. Herein lies the justification of God with regard to the deficiency of his creation: finite spirits find themselves in a provisional condition, in constant progression from separation from God to nearness to God. Now these spirits are so created by God that they have their being through God, but their characteristics through themselves. The substance of the soul or spirit goes forward by an act of the creature's own will. So the spirit is a product of a moral process of development which is brought about in the creature by the resolve of its own will. The I is an action produced by the reciprocal influence of consciousness and activity.The unity of the two is personality. Unlike other animals, man is a personal animal who simultaneously and actively distinguishes himself from his perception of the object by being one with it. By thinking, the human I attacts the other element, the real, to itself and appropriates it. And that is man's task, to 'transubstantiate' the material, natural substratum of his character. The animal process of life is to become a moral one. By virtue of its self-awareness, its capacity for distinction and its freedom of choice, the I builds itself a spiritual body from the material life that determines it. Now if the right moral standing rests on the right idea of man, this in turn rests on the right idea of God. No morality, therefore, is conceivable which is not at the same time piety. God needs the personal creature as co-operative causality and places that task in his hand. 'We are God's fellow workers', and are so within the course of the totality of all happening. From the first exercising of reason, the gravitation of the material masses, the development of nature progresses to the chemical process and to living vegetation, and the first goal of creation is reached in humanization, which completes the spiritualization of matter by the transition to the moral process. This produces a reason that is aware of itself, takes all being into its consciousness and subjects it to man. Now the creation of man is by no means finished and complete at the beginning. Hence follows the necessity and the inevitability of man's passage through sin. It is part of the concept of creation, properly understood, that the personal creature still stands immediately under the dominion of matter and can only master it by struggle and work. The goal of its life is the organization of matter by the spirit, the union of spirit and nature, and to this degree the conquest of sin.

Now on the basis of these presuppositions, the *doctrine of values* in Rothe's ethics first deals with man's self-spiritualization, with the origin of an organism with a spiritual soul that becomes the substratum of eternal life, the inner man that renews itself from day to day. This inner man arises when we impose the stamp of our will on the material man and so develop the spiritual man. The embodiment of all demands to be made on man towards this end is the unconditional surrender of oneself to God in the form of a morally well-filled life. Love for God proves itself in our collaboration with the moral purpose of the world, an activity for which man is free and towards which he is in a position to direct himself. Now the place where this moral process is furthered is the moral community: artistic, academic, commercial, civic, public life; the community of piety, marriage and the family. Man sins primarily because he is a personal animal, made unclean and intermingled with matter. But he is not to affirm this material principle of his own accord, to allow it to run its course unhindered, deliberately to fall out from the movement upwards towards the spirit. If he does that, he does personal sin. Thus the basic form of sin is the sin of sensuality, which is originally the sin of self-seeking. The antidote to the guidance of providence is the wickedness that follows sin, which therefore, like evil, belongs completely to the development of the perfection of the world. There is no original *status integritatis*. As part of a material world, the creature necessarily carries within itself an element of opposition to the purely spiritual God. God could only hinder the outbreak of this evil by refusing the creature freedom and personality, but this would make the good impossible. God has appointed evil, but as something that sublimates itself. Rothe makes that clear by means of the world of demons (resuscitated individuals, according to his interpretation of this concept) who in Hades weave a new body for themselves out of the fine elements of nature that they retain though this body can only be doomed to destruction. Thus Rothe's hell, as might be expected, has only a transitory character. As one can see, the critical analyses of the first volume of Müller's *Doctrine of Sin* made no impression on Rothe.

If we survey what has been said so far, we might ask what room there might be for Christology, indeed for something like reconciliation or redemption, and what form it might take, alongside or in this great natural process which at its climax turns into morality or self-spiritualization. And in fact even admirers of Rothe like Holtzmann and Hausrath felt that despite the attention that Rothe had paid to it, this complex of concepts ultimately formed an alien body in his thought-world. But let us listen to his own view. The miracle of spiritualized humanity is a matter of its own free self-determination. But for this there is needed a perfect man who corresponds with his concept, who is exempted from corruption and therefore theonomic, a man born of a virgin, who sets the task of other men before their eyes as an example, completes fully the spiritual appropriation of the material nature of man and in his transsubstantiated body emerges from the grave, gives all others a guarantee of their own transfiguration and thus is author of a new, normal development that leads to its goal. This man permeated with the spirit is the redeemer or the Christ, the second Adam, the miracle of the creation of the free grace of God for whom the first, incomplete creation was ordained from the beginning. His life work is the foundation of a holy family which continues his redeeming work. From this circle, which continually expands its historical influence, a new religious and moral development comes about which will finally reach the goal originally appointed, of a spiritualized humanity. According to Rothe, revelation means the setting in motion of natural psychical powers of the human consciousness of God by God himself, in a way that is to be compared with the playing of the organ. This happens on the one hand through evident events of history (manifestation), and on the other through corresponding inner illumination (inspiration) (*Zur Dogmatik*, 59f.). Both elements coincide in Christ as the Revealer. He is redeemer in that he communicates his being to an increasing number of men. He is reconciler in that because of him God can forgive sin even before it has been completely sublimated, since the achievement of the divinely appointed goal is guaranteed in him. Rothe, too, thinks that he can make a special appeal for his doctrine to the Gospel of John.

Rothe's *doctrine of virtue* is now built up on this doctrine of values. On the basis of the presuppositions that we have seen, virtue is evidently that determination of the individual by means of which he is involved in the constant appropriation of material nature to human personality, that is, in the constant spiritualization of the natural man. Vice, by contrast, is nothing positive, but consists of distortions and deformities. A real kingdom of evil is thus inconceivable. But how does virtue come about? One would expect it to be a normal result of the moral process accelerated by the pattern and surety of Christ. But here Rothe surprises us for a second time by introducing a supra-naturalist alien body, in that he has rebirth and conversion, like the appearance of the Redeemer earlier, grounded in a special, immediate miraculous working of God, in an *influxus Dei physicus* that is described in thoroughly monergistic terms. Spiritualization is accomplished in the individual thus converted by the increasingly intensive indwelling of the Holy Spirit (that is, the spiritualized Ch.ist) within him as it takes form in him. This is a process which is depicted in the sacraments (in the mysteries, as Rothe likes to say, following the usage of the early Church).

Thirdly, the *doctrine of duties* now arises on the basis of the doctrine of virtues. Normal progress requires a rule which is universal and objective, the idea of a lawgiver who stands above the process. Now if the real moral normalization of sinful man only comes about by virtue of redemption, the revelation of Jesus must be identical with the revelation of the law. At this point we have the development of Rothe's famous teaching about Church and state. The idea of God concealed in revelation enters the universal consciousness of man and in this way the objective forms of human existence, here to become nature (*Zur Dogmatik*, 77). Christianity is a spiritual power that permeates all the pores of the world and all the spheres of the spirit and dominates them. It is Christ who is really active here. For that reason Christianity is by necessity constantly different, it is involved in a progressive transformation. The last and authentic goal of Christ's activity was and is—not a Christian Church, but a Christian world, and particularly a Christian state as an all-embracing moral organization of the world. The morality embodied in the state is in itself human, and thus includes the religious element. The consummate state cannot be conceived of as being other than religious. So the idea of the kingdom of God is realized not in the narrow social form of the Church but in the consummate state. Augustine already termed this kingdom a *civitas Dei*, a city of God, not a Church of God. The Church is a community with a religious goal. But it can be meaningfully closed off only so long and in so far as the natural community of life has closed itself off from piety. For that reason, in its isolation the Church is not an original form of human existence. Christ willed it only as a means of preparing for the transformation of the world. He did not found it; what he founded was the kingdom of God. It is important to see that the Church is a historical factor working to bring to maturity the fruit of the kingdom of God, with whose appearance it will reach its end. The general rule can be established that the nearer a point lies in history after Christ to the origin of the Christian life, the more strongly will movement predominate in it on the side of the life of the Church; similarly, the nearer it lies to the consummation of the Christian life, the more strongly will movement predominate in it on the side of the life of the world. The time when the Church will be able to disappear completely still lies in the distant future, but the turning-point of the decisive shift of emphasis in favour of the world and the state already lies behind us. This turning point is the Reformation. At that time there developed the bourgeois moralistic ground on which the religious life that the Church was no longer able to sustain began to settle. Since then this shift has continued in increasing proportion. Awareness of it is Rothe's characteristic awareness of the *Kairos*. It can be seen increasingly clearly that the Church performs its service, but that its hour has struck. The offshoots capable of growth which Christianity still produces flourish on worldly soil, and not that of the Church. Now Christianity will move in this direction. It will trans-substantiate itself into secular history, a proof that the immeasurable historical influence exerted by Christ is now present in still greater proportions than before. But for that very reason the solution today must be: not more, but less Church! For 'what other human work in Christian history will man be able to carry out which is more congenial and sympathetic to the sense of the Lord Jesus and a more appropriate means for him to purify our sinful race for the moral state after which it strives, if not the state? The moral community, the modern state, has done more to bring man to a condition befitting the will of Christ than all the churches of Jerusalem or Rome or Wittenberg or Geneva. That is a historical fact. I will not be put off with empty phrases!' Live only for the strivings that modern times call human, both in the direction of your own person and in the direction of the race as a whole; but at the same time take up the tasks to which you devote yourself in the light that has streamed out from Christ! Know with utter certainty that in all this you are doing nothing less than Christ's own work and are working to build up his kingdom! That will be the best way of confessing Christ. Even when there is no knowledge that our culture is a child of Protestantism, when there is no explicit con-fession of Christ, there is an 'unconscious Christianity' (as the sum of good properties which are present in today's generation) that has grown up in a Christian culture, as a gift and legacy of the Christian past. This unconscious Christianity is worth more than many forms of conscious Christianity. They are also Christians who do not give themselves that name, in that they stand in a continuation of the work of Christ. Christ himself would recognize the defence of his cause more in secular negotiations of parliaments, the concerns of state and society, than in the discussions of synods about dogma, liturgy and church constitutions. So we should stop troubling our really cultured contemporaries with the Church and cease to attempt to persuade them to express some enthusiasm for it, which cannot truly be theirs. They have quite rightly recognized that the special existence of the religious community only has a transitory character. So Rothe can finally exclaim: The chief task of believers today must be to free Christ from the Church! The widespread anguish about the apparently so confused and uncomfortable state of the Church will vanish once it has been understood as a condition that is as necessary as it is hopeless. The fall of the Church, about which believers lament so loudly, is not worth the tears. What it means is that men are becoming independent, that the old form is breaking up and is joyfully hastening towards its dissolution in the state.

The following eschatological ideas, once again in the most surprising way, form the crown of Rothe's system: To complete the rebirth of the spiritual organism that is developing here some further work of some kind is needed in the Beyond, in a kingdom of the dead in which the individual either purifies himself and becomes a light-being or perseveres in his rejection of God and becomes demonic. The return of Christ brings the exclusion and the annihilation of the demons, and then there dawns his kingdom on earth, the thousand-year kingdom, after which there will once again be a transformation and spiritualization, this time even of those who are perfected. All matter will now be destroyed because the earth itself will now become heaven, as a new creation proceeds from the burnt-out ashes of the old world. Rothe himself says of this end-point, although it may seem to have been conceived in a supranaturalistic way, that the continuity of creation remains undisrupted. What we have here is a development of the creature brought about by God himself. The creation is creation only in so far as there is no lack of a mediating link in the chain of many-layered creaturely being, only in so far as the creative activity of God can be seen as an uninterrupted chain of development at each of its stages.

What have we been listening to? Theology as a solemn renewal of the Gnosticism of the second century and implicitly a little of all the heterodoxies that have become acute in the course of the history of dogma? Or theology as a solemn self-dissolution? Any way, as with Alexander Schweizer, we have arrived at an end-point, not to say a cul-de-sac, on the line of the theological possibilities opened up at the beginning of the century. The lively and profound reflections of Rothe, with all their riches, did not produce a theological school any more than did the sober and tedious thoughts of Schweizer. Perhaps in each case this was because here one could only stand in admiration or despairingly seek one's salvation in flight.

24

HOFMANN

Johann Christian Konrad (von) Hofmann was born in Nuremberg in 1810 and first studied in Erlangen, where he was particularly influenced by Johann Christian Krafft, Reformed pastor and later professor, and Karl Georg von Raumer, naturalist, pedagogue and patriot. In Berlin he was powerfully attracted, not by Schleiermacher, Hegel or Hengstenberg, but by the historian Leopold von Ranke, so powerfully, that for a moment he thought of devoting himself entirely to history and politics. In 1832 he became a *gymnasium* teacher, in 1835 a tutor, in 1838 a *Privatdozent*, in 1841 *extraordinarius* professor at Erlangen, and in 1842 *ordinarius* professor at Rostock. He was called back to Erlangen, quite against his own inclination, in 1845, and there with Thomasius, Zezschwitz, H. Schmid, Theodosius Harnack and Frank he was instrumental in bringing about the rise of a theology that represented a mild yet powerful union of Schleiermacher, Revival theology, confessionalism and biblicism, a treasure in which the faculty there delighted for many decades and which earned it the name of the Erlangen school. Hofmann's publications include: *Weissagung und Erfüllung im Alten und im Neuen Testament* (Prophecy and Fulfilment in the Old and New Testament) (1841-4), *Der Schriftbeweis* (The Proof from Scripture) (1852-5), the posthumously edited *Theologische Ethik* (1878), *Encyklopädie der Theologie* (1879) and *Biblische Hermeneutik* (1880), and finally *Die heilige Schrift neuen Testamentes zusammenhangend untersucht* (A Comprehensive Investigation of the Holy Scriptures of the New Testament) (1862-78), a great design for a combination of individual commentaries, biblical history, biblical theology, introduction and translation, which remained a torso despite posthumous expansions.

Hofmann was an uncommonly active and many-sided man, in practice much more of a *Kultur* Protestant than Richard Rothe, though with one important exception, that he seems to have had no aptitude for or interest in philosophy, though being wide open for anything to do with history and literature. He was a sociable person, an eager speaker, writer and deputy, prominent in political activity (n.b. in a progressive direction), and also concerned with the inner mission and foreign mission. Though he had no lack of theological opponents, especially from the right wing, the side of a more acute confessionalism, he could ward them off with an energy which seemed to increase rather than decrease in his old age. On the attack, for instance against liberal-theological historians but also against Ultramontanism, he could wield a sharp sword, and clearly did not dislike having to fight a war on two fronts, which is what Menken had also had to do. So his life was unusually rich and eventful. He died in 1877, still speaking Hebrew in his last feverish delirium. 'His name will retain its splendour', wrote Kattenbusch of him. The older generation in Protestant Bavaria still holds him in special honour today as their church father, and in fact we do find here one of the most impressive figures of the history of the theology of our time, despite all the problems that we come up against.

Anyone who opens the works of Hofmann will not have to thumb through many pages before he keeps coming across the key-word that is more significant for the purpose of his theology than any other. This is the word 'fact'. The conviction from which Hofmann always starts and to which he always returns is that Christianity is fact—it is certainly also teaching, but it is not only or even primarily teaching: above all it is fact. Not the fact of a particular conception of divine things or a divine figure or a peculiar moral disposition of man, but a fact of which I am as certain as the fact that I am: the fact of the relationship between God and man that is communicated in Christ, that is realized in him, in which he stands, that he bears in his person (*Ethics*, 14f.). Hofmann goes on to elaborate this 'fact of Christianity' by saying that the relationship between God and humanity is realized in the person of the supramundane Christ and is witnessed to and confirmed within the world by means of the visible Church, in which Christ himself is active (*Enc.*, 10). Thus the Church, its confession and its doctrine, is the medium for, the reflection or the expression of, the fact of Christianity or of Christ himself. 'We recognize this Christianity again in that of the Lutheran confession' (*Proof* I, 8). This Platonizing term 'recognize again' evidently indicates that the confession or the Church is thought of as being different from the fact or Christianity; it also indicates that with Hofmann we are no less clearly in the footsteps of *Schleiermacher* than in a context of mediation theology. Also faithful to Schleiermacher is the presupposition that the Christian as such finds himself in a relationship to God which is given with his very

life, quite apart from his being a Christian, a relationship which precedes all special 'experience' and all individual developments in life.
As a result of sin this is expressed only as false religion and is therefore
set over against the fact of Christianity, which is the realization of the
truth of religion (*Enc.*, 14f.). Consequently the task of theology is the
scientific recognition and expression of this fact of Christianity as the
realization of the truth of religion (*Enc.*, 17; *Ethics*, 14). Hofmann did
not doubt for a moment, just like Schleiermacher, that this fact could
be a possible subject for knowledge and description. 'Nothing is closer
to me than the fact that I am a Christian. That fact lies closer to me
than the fact that I am a man' (*Ethics*, 16). The fact does not lie in
any way outside the one who has to give scientific expression to it,
but is an independent possession within him (*Proof* I, 8; *Enc.*, 20). Thus
what is to be known and expressed is neither the content of the Bible
nor that of a church confession nor even—and this is where he begins
to differ from Schleiermacher—a doctrine that is held at a certain
time in the Church, not even as qualified by the individual characteristics by which everything is shaped in the theologian concerned (*Proof*
I, 8, 11). On the contrary—and here again he differs from Schleiermacher—I have to exclude every individual element that may be
attached to the fact of Christianity on my side. This fact is concerned
with the relationship of God to me in so far as I am man, and not
this man; it is concerned with the relationship of God to humanity,
in which I share as being part of humanity (*Ethics*, 16f.). Once again,
Schleiermacher's formula, 'the description of the pious Christian
disposition', is inadequate, as it cannot ignore the character of the
Christian (*Enc.*, 51); it can only deal with the objective fact of the independent relationship to God in Christ in this individual (*Proof*, I, 11).
Whereas to the philosopher as such his subject-matter, humanity,
must ultimately remain a riddle in the face of which he can only end
with a question, the theologian begins with an answer, in that he sees
in himself humanity in Christ having come to its consummation (*Proof*
I, 15; *Enc.*, 21). Therefore (and to this extent) theology—and now
Hofmann seems to have gone far beyond Schleiermacher in his own
direction—is simply the Christian's knowledge and account of himself
and nothing else. 'Theology is a free science only when what makes
the Christian a Christian, his independent relationship to God, makes
the theologian a theologian with a scientific knowledge and account
of himself, when I, the Christian, am the innermost material for the
discipline that I, the theologian, pursue'. Of course I am what I am
as a Christian only in the community, as the result of church activity.

But not only is it always the present Christ whose activity serves the community and its activity; in addition, that relationship to God, once I have a share in it, has begun an independent existence in me which is not dependent on the Church or even on Scripture, and which does not have the real guarantee of its truth, in one or the other, but rests in itself and is immediately certain truth, supported and guaranteed by the Spirit of God that dwells within me (*Proof* I, 9-11). 'I, the Christian, am the subject-matter of knowledge for myself, the theologian' (*Ethics*, 17).

It is certainly remarkable and instructive that perhaps the greatest conservative theologian of our period should at the same time have been the one who drew the consequences of Schleiermacher's standpoint in terms of the purely individualistic determination of theology more sharply, at least in theory, than any liberal—and as a result could be praised by Wilhelm Herrmann as 'one of the greatest pioneers of the Reformation' because his method was less determined by ecclesiastical considerations than was that of Schleiermacher and because it demonstrated emphatically that Christian faith must go its own way if it is to make clear the doctrine that is valid for it.[1] Of course Hofmann elaborated his thought in this direction: it is to be presupposed that the theologian is a member of the Church (*Enc.*, 21; *Ethics*, 21). Only in this way can the Christianity that he describes be not only a form of Christianity, his Christianity, but *Christianity* (*Proof* I, 8). Where things go right, Scripture and the Church must present us with precisely what we discover from ourselves (*Proof* I, 11). But what the Church and Scripture essentially are must already have been shown in a systematic way, that is by introspection. For 'true knowledge of a thing does not come about through history. The only question is whether the result of historical investigation accords with that which is achieved in a systematic way' (*Enc.*, 26). Thus 'Scriptural proof' can and should only serve to show that the right facts have rightly been arrived at by introspection (*Proof* I, 15f.). 'The basis of Christianity is not really the history of Christ and his Apostles. Christianity is based primarily on the present Christ, who has as his presupposition the historical Christ, and points back to this historical presupposition of his presence' (*Enc.*, 28). So scriptural proof consists in giving this retrospective proof: a man confirms and possibly also corrects the knowledge that he has obtained from himself as a Christian by the Bible. The justification for systematic theology is that Christianity is a personal affair; but Christianity is equally an affair of the

[1] W. Herrmann, *Die Kultur der Gegenwart*, 1906, 608.

community, and so systematic theology must be joined by historical activity, and the testimony of the Church and of Scripture must be heard (*Enc.*, 33). Thus Hofmann finally arrives at a threefold existence of Christianity: 1. in the rebirth of the Christian; 2. in the history of the Church; 3. in Holy Scripture; of these one must always preserve us from misinterpreting the others. Still, according to Hofmann's clear statements, the starting point and the normative source remains the first of the three, the fact of a man's own rebirth. From this the theologian derives the 'doctrinal whole', the fact that is to be demonstrated by scriptural proof and later discussed and illuminated by the Bible and church history. Only then, later, does it become scriptural knowledge of the Church—a relationship in which one can hardly fail to be reminded, *mutatis mutandis*, of Schleiermacher's doctrine of the three fundamental dogmatic forms.

Now if this is the case, we are confronted in Hofmann with a riddle that hardly admits of solution. One would expect a theologian who sees things in this way to have devoted all his interest and concern to the task of constructing a dogmatics based on that fact of rebirth as the authentic source of theology; one would expect him to have produced a *Doctrine of Faith* that went even beyond Schleiermacher in the direction of individualism; one would expect that he would have sought his problems in the direct of the life-work of Wilhelm Herrmann and would at best have been occupied only incidentally with the secondary task of scriptural proof and proof from the Church. But this expectation would be incorrect. In fact, what interested Hofmann was scriptural proof and only that. In the great work that bears this title he devoted twenty pages to the obtaining of the 'doctrinal whole' from the experience of rebirth and almost sixteen hundred to the demonstration that this was in accordance with Scripture. He became quite infuriated when the public with stubborn one-sidedness were interested in what was to be proved rather than the proof itself (*Schützschriften* I, 1). When he himself had devoted all his attention to the essence, manner and accomplishment of the proof! The rest of his main literary works confirm this unexpected declaration; he did not produce a dogmatics, but for the most part exegesis and yet more exegesis. But how is all this to be explained? In the context of the presupposition which Hofmann himself provided the answer must be: he did not see his life's work in what according to his own declaration was the chief task and the real substance of theology. He occupied himself with what according to his own declaration was in principle the subordinate work of στωρεῖν, particularly with regard to the Bible. Thus his life-work ought to be understood as one gigantic *parergon* to what, according to his own declaration, made up the real task of theology. If this conception, according to which Hofmann will have spent all his life consciously and deliberately so to speak only in subsidiary work, is held to be psychologically impossible; if one cannot avoid the impression that Hofmann felt that his scriptural work was the real and principal theological task, then all that is left is the assumption that his declarations of principle, however earnestly they were intended in their context and however significant they were for the character of his whole concern, did not have for him the weight that one might assign to them if one were determining what his purpose was in the usual and certainly justified way of going by what the man himself said. In that case one would have to ask whether in these declarations Hofmann was not on the one hand pursuing a definite apologetic goal to which he could only do justice by his theory, and on the other hand expressing himself with desirable openness about the attitude and method with which he approached Scripture, the sense in which he was a biblicist—without imagining that the statements themselves outlined a programme. In other words, he did not allow them to prevent him from following his own programme, secured by his apologetic and merely characterized by the method. But his programme *was* biblicist: to derive, depict and develop the theology that he thought he had found in the Bible and not, therefore, in his own experience. The reference to his own experience is an apologetic mask, in which the modern biblicist justifies himself to the spirit of the time. At the same time it is a confession that his biblicism does not exclude but includes the high competence and bold autocracy of the modern thinker, that this biblicism is a conscious and powerful, completely contemporary mastery of the Bible. Nevertheless, it is the Bible that interests this theologian and not his reborn existence, as should be really the case according to his own declarations: the Bible, which those declarations characterize as *his* Bible, but still the Bible. That Hofmann, breaking through his programmatic declarations by his real programme, lived for this interest is, despite the limitations of his course of action, his real significance in the history of recent theology.

No one needs proof for this conception of the man once he has seen the 'doctrinal whole' which Hofmann the theologian claims to have discovered in Hofmann the Christian. The relevant, relatively short passages in Hofmann's *Proof from Scripture* and *Encyclopedia* may perhaps be counted among the most remarkable documents in the whole history of theology (*Proof* I, 35f.; *Enc.*, 38f.). The Trinity of God, but also the facts that 'there is a history' into which God enters without infringing that Trinity; that our race derives from a human couple and that alongside it there is an angelic world; the Babylonian separation of the peoples because of sin and the choice of the one people Israel by the grace of God; the basic features of the history of Israel; the appearance of Jesus; the split between Israel and the Church; the formation of a New Testament canon and the reception of the Old Testament—all this is said to be quite as much the content of the Christian experience of rebirth as sin, the testimony of God to himself in Christ, and justifying faith. And if one finds it illuminating that Hofmann the Christian should have taught Hofmann the theologian that man achieves rebirth through Church, word and sacrament; should also have taught him the fundamental disposition of the man who is reborn, one will certainly find it astounding that on the basis of the statements of the same authority there can be a Christian affirmation of the family, or private property, of patriotism, of riches and of the position of one's own state in the world. Once again one is astonished at the breadth of the concept of experience when one sees that from it can also be derived the eschatological prospect of struggle for selection within the Church, the return of the Jews to Palestine and a much more extensive history of the end corresponding with the visions in the Revelation of John, up to and including the continued existence of the godless in damnation for eternity. It is a banal question but one that cannot be avoided, whether something has not happened here which according to the programme should only happen later, whether Hofmann the Christian, who claims to know all this, is not already Hofmann the theologian, who knows the history of the Bible and the Church, indeed Hofmann the man of culture and the politician of modern Germany, whose scriptural proof can only be a detailed repetition and development of what he has drawn himself, not from himself but rather as raw material, rough-hewn, from the book of history, which really should only be opened at a later stage.

This seems to suggest a second point: Hofmann the Christian, who has clearly already been reading in this book, has also already been the pupil of *Ranke*, full of burning interest to understand Christianity 'historically', that is, in the context of a chain of events which, it is thought, can be viewed as a whole and can be understood and mastered spiritually. In this way Christianity can be made possible for Hofmann himself and his contemporaries. Of course he understands Christianity as a special history which is mysteriously embedded in secular history and which mysteriously embraces it, as salvation history. In the perspective of F. C. Baur this is a pattern for a mythological dualism. Yet in that this or that is important to him above all as history, as the history in which he finds himself as a reborn Christian, he is in principle no less a modern man than Baur, and in the confidence with which he lays hold of this history he is no less a modern Christian and theologian. The view has been expressed that Hofmann's conception is to be regarded as a legacy by means of Vitringa, Bengel, Menken and Krafft from none other than Johannes Cocceius, of such critical importance for the history of Reformed theology. It is hard to find historical proof for such a supposition. In that case, though, it would be something else to reflect on that Lutheran theology, which regarded Hofmann as one of the most prominent fathers of modern Lutheranism, should have been blessed and equipped by him with this most questionable result of old Reformed doctrine, the doctrine of the affinity between the ideas of predestination and providence, and that this should have been made into a Christian philosophy of history (*Ethics*, 20).

Be this as it may, there is no mistaking the peculiarity in Hofmann's proof from Scripture: that what is supposedly to provide the proof, Scripture, is in reality what is also to be proved. Or, to put it the other way round, what is supposed to be proved, the content of Christian experience, has also to provide the proof in the form of a scriptural proof which is in effect no more than a further expansion of the circle of Christian experience. His scriptural proof suffers from the fact that it is only an extended proof from experience and his proof from experience from the fact that it is itself already a proof from Scripture. With Hofmann, the historian and exegete has occasion to lament the subjectivistic entries in the book of history, and the systematic theologian who wants to observe Hofmann's injunctions has occasion to regret the objectivistic entries in the book of experience. This twofold *petitio principii* is not safeguarded and shown to be necessary on either side, say by the assertion of the trinitarian relationship of Word and Spirit, but designates as subject of the whole proof man; Christian man, but nevertheless the man who wants now to be master of himself, now to be master of his history. In view of this inner vitiation of Hofmann's theology one can only point out yet again that his interest in the two factors, knowledge of experience and knowledge of Scripture, was an unequal one. He pursued it with the instruments and interests of an extreme Schleiermacherian and thought that as a Schleiermacherian he could establish its character as a science. But the discipline he was engaged in was scriptural. And since he pursued this discipline with great acuteness (his exegesis is well worth studying, even now) in a sphere that he shared with others, he in practice (as did Dorner theoretically) heightened the unrest in this sphere, the un-Schleiermacherian opposition of subject and object, the remembrance that man, even reborn man, is not alone, but has in God a powerful and ultimately unavoidable point of encounter. The biblicism of Erlangen theology did not burst the bounds of the prevailing method. To celebrate it again and again as the emergence of a fundamentally new attitude, or as a revival of the old theological position of the Reformers, is to construct a false picture of history. But it did contribute towards sustaining and continuing within this framework the theological movement that we saw to be threatened with paralysis in the case of Schweizer and with convulsive cramps in the case of Rothe.

25

BECK

JOHANN Tobias Beck was born in 1804 at Balingen in Württemberg. He studied exclusively in Tübingen and (here we are reminded of Menken!) for the most part without even hearing the professors there, much less accepting anything from them (Riggenbach, 31). Two months after his examination in 1827 he was already a pastor in the farming village of Waldthann. After very energetic activity, mostly concerned with moral improvement, he left this congregation because he was not given his rights over the deliveries of wood that were his due before God and man, and in 1829 became city pastor and director of the *gymnasium* at Mergentheim. His first literary works derive from this time. They attracted the attention of wider circles to him, and in 1836 he became *extraordinarius* professor in Basle (whither he was called by the Society for the Furthering of the Knowledge of Christian Theology and Christian Life). He made friends there with de Wette, but had a serious disagreement with the leaders of the Basle Mission because of what they regarded as a quite unacceptable Festival Sermon that was delivered in 1838. In 1843 he became *ordinarius* professor in Tübingen on the proposal of F. C. Baur. He had the best personal relationships both with Baur and his successor Weizsäcker, while the official circles of the Church and of Pietism in Württemberg and in the rest of Germany constantly had fresh occasion for greeting him with a wonderment that sprang more from respect than from love. This did not prevent Tübingen from having a power of attraction that reached far beyond the borders of Germany, so that it could to some degree be measured alongside Erlangen and Halle. Beck had many pupils, but founded no school. Had he wanted to, he could not have done so. Had he been able, he would not have wanted to. Both must be said. Among his writings, special mention should be made of the following: *Einleitung in das System der christlichen Lehre* (An Introduction to the System of Christian Doctrine) (1838), *Die christlichen Lehrwissenschaft nach den biblischen Urkunden* (Christian

Doctrine according to the Biblical Evidence) (1841), *Die christliche Liebeslehre* (The Christian Doctrine of Love) (1872-4), and *Christliche Reden* (Christian Discourses) (1834-70). He died in 1878.

From this information alone one can guess what must be said first. J. T. Beck was a kind of natural event in the midst of the civilization and more or less real culture of more recent Protestant theology. Here, more than with any of the men we have met so far, one is tempted simply to call a halt, along with countless contemporaries of Beck, before the original, religious, man of power who encounters us with unrepeatable individuality on almost every line. I mention only a few of the most attractive features which make him an unforgettable figure, even for a posterity that can know him only from his writing: 1. The unshakeable, wrathfully strict *fear of God* and the honesty which was the essence of his being and which expressed itself in a combination of New Testament religion and Old Testament ethics, an incomparable certainty of himself and his subject, which were brought into play when solving or even dismissing his own problems and those of others. 2. A supreme *independence* from both revolutionary and reactionary methods in theology which, once he had achieved it and sustained it, allowed him to keep emerging with his yes and his no at places where no one had expected him. 3. The marvellous *coherence* of a pattern of thought in which he himself was both confessor and professor, in the evolution of which his own speculations and a wealth of biblical elements in fact form a whole that can hardly be dissolved, to which one cannot deny parabolic significance in the best sense of the word. 4. Last and not least, what Weizsäcker in his speech delivered at Beck's grave rather euphemistically entitled the 'purifying and judging' side of his activity: I mean the peppery yet enlivening polemic, to be distinguished from the eruptions of a volcano by its uninterrupted flow, which Beck directed from the stately pulpit which he erected and took over: against modern culture and its sciences, above all against its theology, and even more sharply against modern Christianity, and particularly—with a disproportionate emphasis on the right rather than the left wing—against hierarchical bureaucratic ecclesiasticism; against Pietism both quietist and activist; against the mission to the heathen which for him had almost come to be the great Christian idol of the time; against Christian Romanticism and against all Christian scheming and plotting and deceit; against all open or concealed Christian imperialism in the English style or all national and patriotic Christianity in the German style. What he said in this connexion, above all in his famous *Expauken*, and in his letters, but partly also in official documents (as for instance in his letter of rejection to the leaders of the Basle Mission) exceeds anything that was said by opponents of the Church at that time both in its insight into the destruction of Israel and in its never-failing powers of expression. Here there is a direct link with Kierkegaard, and indeed with Kierkegaard of the last years, who was the only distinguished theologian of the time of whom Beck had a good opinion and who for him was one of the few righteous men 'who looked beyond the transitory horizon of the Church, the mission and other communities to the horizon of the kingdom of God and bore witness from his watchtower'.[1] It is impossible to understand Beck's theology if one acts, like most of Beck's followers and those stimulated by him, who nourished themselves on Beck's piety (as did even the two Blumhardts), and gladly delighted in his biblicism, only to direct the water that they felt streaming from there as quickly as possible back to the mill, though they were warned urgently enough against the danger of doing this in Tübingen. Without the background of this accusation and prophecy for the Church against the Church, Beck is not Beck, and surely one of the chief reasons why he never exerted a wide influence afterwards is that he could never transfer a breath of it even to his pupils, that people thought they could follow him into what seemed to be such a fruitful position without seeing that it could only be and remain fruitful because it was a position of opposition. To follow him meant, not least, to take up this opposition. But such a course was never pursued.

However, let us allow Beck to plead his own case, by listening to a concentrate extract from his first fundamental work, *An Introduction to the System of Christian Doctrine or a Propaedeutic Development of the Science of Christian Teaching* (1838).

Beck's science of Christian teaching is also meant—despite the loaded word—to be *gnosis*, believing *gnosis*. In contrast to all speculative *gnosis*, but in accord with natural science, it is the reproduction of a given, namely of the biblical revelation of truth, a reproduction which still makes a complete claim on reason, on the thinking spirit. *Negligentiae mihi videtur, si, postquam confirmati sumus in fide, non studemus, quod credimus intelligere* (Anselm) (pp. 2f.). By faith, the first basic element of this *gnosis*, is to be understood 'the substance of Christian teaching that has entered into man as a spiritual property and has become dynamically immanent in him'. I must have it myself, yet it

[1] J. T. Beck, *Gedanken* I, 1858 (³1876), 158.

leads an independent life, and this life is revelation, secret divine wisdom, which fills the knowledge, feeling and action of man at the foundation of these functions, though it really has its place in the centre of conscience as the central point from which our life is directly determined by God; it is the primal sense of and the primal impulse to truth; it is the new, the spiritual man (pp. 8f.). The attitude of our thought to faith must not be passive, but receptive; it is to grasp that by which it is grasped, though it is to be sustained and determined completely by faith itself in such a way that by faith it becomes a new spirit. And it is clear that my reason can only reproduce as much genuinely Christian content as faith produces in it (pp. 17f.). Produces! Faith is essentially an infinite spiritual economy of life to which our natural thought-patterns have to be subjected, which extends them beyond their normal limitations. It is a system of infinite life, in principle perfect, which gradually reveals itself in finitude, yet which implicitly bears its whole content within itself at every stage. For that reason, thought must constantly extend beyond the subjective content of faith, must draw on the primal spiritual product of faith, the canon of revelation. It must be genetic, i.e. a thought that pursues the genesis of faith. The revelation of faith is a tree of life which is meant to be searched by the *gnosis* of faith throughout its growth, from root to crown (pp. 22f.). According to the 'real genetic method', the name Beck chooses to apply to his approach in contrast to the speculative approach of Hegel and the reflective approach of Schleiermacher, the system of the doctrinal concept must be a reproduction in thought of the system of the life of faith (pp. 33f.), just as natural science simply has to reproduce the system of nature. It is not the concept that has to work on and define the subject matter, but *vice versa*. But the concept has to surrender itself to this determination freely, deliberately, and in accordance with the laws of its inner nature. It is neither author nor builder nor supplier of material for the system, but the living collaborator of faith in belief in God's grace (pp. 39f.). Consequently it is clear that there cannot be a separation between dogmatics and ethics: theology has to accomplish scientifically what revelation has accomplished in reality: the unity of the doctrines of faith and morals (pp. 43f.). Similarly, it is clear that theological investigation may not for a moment leave the ground of revelation; it may not be philosophical (p. 48). So it may not start either from a previously purified view of religion (p. 50) or from the secondary and ambivalent element of immediate self-consciousness (pp. 50f.), as is to be said with Hegel against Schleiermacher, nor again may it start from feeling as an individual factor of life of the soul (pp. 56f.). It must start from the true genesis of religion, from its reality, the essence of which is faith (pp. 61f.), which according to Hebrews 11.1 (ὑπόστασις καὶ ἔλεγχος) is at the same time the the supratemporal world dwelling within man and the revelation that disciplines him and subjects him (pp. 63f.). This faith was originally 'woven into' the human organism by divine revelation and in all circumstances is preserved in it (p. 72). Revelation and religion are one in origin, a unity of which man can be as certain as of his own being. If a new revelation at any time follows this original revelation, it cannot conflict with reason but only with irrationality. False religion or unbelief consists in the fact that the implanting of the supramundane or the divine in man, once begun, is not maintained or carried through by him (p. 91). Unbelief is inconsistency, which has its origin in an anti-religious principle dwelling within man, in sin (pp. 94f.). Immediately, however, it establishes a positive community of man with ungodly spirits (p. 105) and therefore expresses itself in the multiplicity of religions with their falsely divinizing symbols and their falsely humanizing myths (p. 109). Faith, on the other hand, is inability to believe that it is possible that what is good and true is a mixture of divinization and humanization (p. 114). Accordingly each special revelation of the truth legitimates itself primarily by its relationship to the universal basic revelation as the renewed beginning of the life of that original religion of faith in a more definite expression and consummation of it (p. 117). Once again the principle of the origin of such a special revelation, i.e. such a strengthening of the revelation that man already knows, can only be the divine witness (p. 118). It will oppose historic and positive irreligion equally historically and positively (p. 119). So the Old Testament is a historically positive organ of revelation built into the basic revelation, which marks itself off from false religions and is itself in progressive movement (pp. 120f.). In the school of this revelation faith first takes the form of faithfulness to elective grace, to heartfelt knowledge of the self, world and God, to a confident and certain longing, searching and striving for the better thing that is to come (p. 132). All this until the time was fulfilled for the revelation of the divine power of love proceeding from the spirit and the reality of the revelation that had already been given, the overflowing of the divine grace by virtue of which the divine life is implanted in the world as a reality, by virtue of which God was essentially in Christ instead of all mere receivers of revelation (pp. 140f.). Here is the restoration of the original image of God, the consummation of the primal revelation, the completion of the eternal divine prothesis of revelation, related to which and incorporated in which all earlier revelation, together with the Christian revelation, forms a living system of revelation, a living kingdom of truth (p. 145). As a revelation of doctrine, salvation and the kingdom (the three offices of Christ), the Christian revelation is the beginning of the consummation, i.e. the beginning of the essentially complete revelation that is still to come (pp. 146f.). Its content is a concrete, historical account of the God who bears witness to himself in grace, who gathers up believers into the body of Christ as a form of education for the coming kingdom of God (pp. 148f.). Its decisive effect on believers is the 'formation' of Christ as the Lord in them. As the initiator of faith, Christ brings about the purificatory justification in which the opposition between the subject and the object of faith is transcended, and as the perfecter of faith he brings about the transformatory justification in which an ever more inward union of subject and object is achieved. Thus in the union of Christ's initiation and perfection faith is righteousness itself, the constant sanctification by God of the spirit, the body and the soul (pp. 152f.). Now as the culmination of the whole organism of revelation the Christian revelation is planted not only in the whole life of the individual but also in the historical life of man, indeed even in natural life, so that the whole of earthly life can become a model and a copy of heavenly life in which the Christian revelation has its final goal, into which it grows by virtue of its own development, without the addition of a new revelation (p. 160). A characteristic of the divine activity of revelation is thus a combination of what is new with already existing good and divine elements in such a way as to bring about a blessing on creation. For that very reason it is grounded in man apodeictically, by means of an experience, which is accessible to everyone (pp. 161f.). But as the revelation is not a fortuitously limited event of ordinary historical life, but sets out to propagate itself in untainted objectivity, its nature requires as a force and means for propagation the word of the canonical Scripture that is born from it (pp. 209f.). By virtue of the pisteo-dynamic, charismatic, apocalyptic *theopneustia* (pp. 235f.), the biblical writers receive the spirit of revelation that embraces the whole of their activity and makes their word the Word of God (p. 240). By virtue of the same process each individual book of the Bible is the originally true account of a particular stage of revelation and activity of the Spirit, and the Bible as a whole is the originally true image of the organism of the truth of revelation itself (p. 256). That this is the case, i.e. that Scripture proves its own significance, can be recognized by means of a

pneumatic criticism and exegesis of the Bible (pp. 360f.), the meaning
of which cannot, of course, be that Scripture must first be spiritualized
by the exegete; rather, the *pneuma* is the spirit of the Scripture itself,
the spirit of the faith that alone can expound the Scriptures. Scripture,
of course, has not only this spirit, but a body and a soul, a human
exterior, which becomes the object of grammatical-historical exegesis,
and a human inwardness, which becomes the object of psychological
exegesis. But an exegesis that wanted to stop at one or the other
would be anthropological and not psychological. It is important to
ascend to the pneuma, without allowing oneself to go wrong by supposing that this emerges directly in a literary-historical or a psychological context (p. 275). Pneumatic exegesis must take up learned
exegesis in the narrower sense into itself (p. 280). Its canon and at
the same time the criterion to which it subjects even learned, historical-
grammatical and psychological exegesis will be a twofold one: it will
be concerned for a genetic understanding of the whole Bible (pp.
281f.), and it will never engage in exegesis without application (pp.
287f.). Let us conclude with a dictum in which Beck distinguished
himself vividly enough from all non-pneumatic exegetes, and in
which of course the hermeneutist Beck himself threatens to become a
biblical writer: 'The eye of the wise sees what is there, but the brain
of the idle man invents hypotheses' (p. 292).

We need not waste words in stressing the originality, coherence
and paraenetic force of this theology. If one asks how it came about
that it did not have the influence on its time that one might expect
from its properties, if its author in the last resort appears as a lone
figure in the history of theology, in the same way as Richard Rothe,
we should not content ourselves by stating, as was said above, that
to follow this man resolutely would have meant a place in the opposition not only in theology but above all within the Church and
within Christianity, a position to which hardly anyone would really
have felt adequate in the middle and during the second half of the
nineteenth century, though without this Beck's *gnosis* inevitably had
to remain one *gnosis* among others. In addition, we should remember
the mixed influence, which was also quite penetrating, that Beck
doubtless quietly exerted on countless pastors and also on the history
of theology through the life-work of men like Kähler and Schlatter
and my own father Fritz Barth. But we cannot stop there. Least of
all can we stop at an evaluation of Beck as a sort of misunderstood
prophet, for whom his time had no attention, although the same

things might be said of him in this respect that were said of his compatriot J. A. Dorner. Rather, in addition to all this we must also say
that the theology of Beck, in a definite and by no means incidental
way, resembled that of Hofmann in being insufficiently alien, all too
contemporary, so that it did not stand out as decisively from the
work of other theologians as its author felt it did and thought it should.
Earlier, in the cases of Menken and Hofmann, we had to ask whether
'biblicism' was and could be sufficiently different from the other -isms
of more recent theology. Its affinity—in the case of Menken to the
brilliant individualism of the end of the eighteenth century and in
the case of Hofmann to Romantic historicism—at least cannot be
denied. So, too, with Beck, there is an affinity to Romantic naturalism.
That the truth of revelation must form an 'organism', a 'tree of life'
with root and crown, and that the genetic method must be the real
one—this and the whole burdening of the matter with such conceptuality was not taken by Beck from the Bible. Rather, here was
a currently favourite scheme with a certain stratum of the educated
people of the time by means of which Beck approached the Bible,
just as others approached it in their own way. On the very first pages
of the book discussed here he finds the parallel between theology and
natural science to consist in the fact that each is the account of some
thing 'given'; he calls faith a substance which enters into man and
becomes his possession; like a good scientist, he sees continuity everywhere, between God and man, between the new revelation and the
basic revelation that has already been given and is inalienable,
between purifying and renewing justification, between the *regnum
gratiae* and its consummation in this world. All this shows that the
affinity is not only external, not only one of conceptuality, but completely normative for the content of his supposedly purely biblical
theology. Despite all the polemic against Schleiermacher and Hegel,
despite the unmistakable differences from these masters of the century,
despite the biblical power and flavour that cannot be mistaken, is the
world of those masters, in which faith—and with it revelation—is a
given and its life is an integral development of this given—really
transcended? Is it not simply enriched by another variant? There
were contemporaries who charged Beck with simply presenting in his
doctrine of justification the Catholic doctrine of the Council of Trent.
That verdict may be too summary, but it is unmistakable that with
Beck we are nearer to Andreas Osiander than to Calvin. And if it is
the case, then at this decisive point Beck is not very uncontemporary.
He was too much in tune with the times for his call 'Back to the

Bible!' to have seemed very revolutionary. Others before him and after him found this in the Bible. So we cannot be surprised that in the last resort, in his limitations and his promise, we see this earnest, powerful and venerable manifestation, alongside Menken and Dorner surely one of the most noteworthy figures in our account so far, in the same series as the rest.

26

VILMAR

IF in J. T. Beck we have met a theologian who made it easy for many contemporaries and those who came after them to pass by him with a pardoning laugh because of the originality with which he posed and resolved problems, his lack of concern for what his time considered to be a good academic tone and the rashness of his polemic, in Vilmar we have a berserk figure of whom all this is true to a heightened degree. The sheer astonishment and indeed indignation with which virtually all the rest of German theology reacted to his pronouncements stands over against the honour that he enjoyed—and to a degree still enjoys—in certain circles of the church in his homeland of Hessen. It needs considerable good will to read him quietly as a theologian and not be captured by the persuasive effect of his language. And it needs a great deal of good will to accept what he considered to be his concern as a fitting part of the history of theology as an academic discipline, even if it had a place within the complex of the problems of the time, filled a gap and thus made his name revered. Although he was a professor of theology, Vilmar without doubt did not have what might be called academic distinction: with him we find ourselves in the atmosphere of an excited and perhaps rather disturbed pastors' conference. That need not mean that the theology he represents must be necessarily bad or even insignificant, but one must acclimatize oneself to it on coming from academic theological discussion, and one cannot say that Vilmar makes this acclimatization easy. Even within this framework Vilmar's discourse is marked out by an extraordinary hard-headedness and narrow-mindedness which makes it easy to turn away from him offended. In more than one respect, Vilmar is the type of the zealous pastor who has always known what he wanted so well that he has never really considered anything else, say the problems with which his contemporaries are battling, and has never accepted them as his own need. It is very easy for such a person to be consistent and weighty because he is incapable, or has made himself incapable, of really taking other views into account, much less of thinking carefully through them. For example, Vilmar feels strongly called to sweep out the Calvinistic leaven that has been present in Hessen for quite some time. But it does not trouble him to quote Calvin's main work as the *Institutiones religionis Christianae*, which, he says, appeared anonymously in 1536 (*Dogm.* I, 79), and it seems to me to be very doubtful whether he ever looked into this book. The reader learns that Thomas Aquinas was murdered in 1274 by Charles of Anjou, and is only told one thing about his work: 'He is indefatigable in distinguishing, to the point where the matter is quite forgotten in the treatment of its parts' (p. 78). Vilmar did not argue with his contemporaries, even with Schleiermacher, in anything other than crude slogans. In presenting his own work he dealt so arbitrarily with history and adopted such an opinionated manner that one is tempted to deal with him as he dealt with so many others, namely by letting him speak and then go his way. Nevertheless, despite everything, in being a complete outsider Vilmar gave sharp definition to a concern the emergence of which forms part of the picture of the academic theology of his day, precisely because in certain respects it points beyond his day. Perhaps it was essential that the opposition which Vilmar wanted to raise and the matter he wanted to present had to be brought about in this somewhat unattractive form.

August Friedrich Christian Vilmar was born in 1800 at Solz in Kurhessen. He studied in Marburg, and in 1824 became rector of the city school at Rothenburg. In 1827 he went to be teacher at the *gymnasium* in Hersfeld, and in 1833 became director of the *gymnasium* in Marburg. As a council deputy he also did considerable services for the schools of Hessen. In 1851 he became administrator for the general superintendent's office at Kassel. Although during the years of revolution, as an intimate of the controversial minister Hassenpflug, he maintained and gave expression to a strictly conservative political attitude, he was not confirmed as general superintendent by the Crown Prince in 1855, because at the same time he had made a name for himself in church politics as being a vigorous opponent of the *summus episcopus* of the district. Instead of this he was transferred as a professor of theology to Marburg, where he exerted a strong influence on the theological students as a passionate protagonist for a specifically Hessian Lutheranism, living in some tension with the rest of the faculty. The year 1866 brought to him, the resolute particularist and advocate of a Greater Germany, not only the destruction of the independence of his fatherland of Hesse but also the end of his political ideals; with almost religious grief and anger he saw it as a 'glaring breach of the two tables of the law'. He died in 1868, perhaps the only theologian of his century who was loved and honoured by as many people for being a man of God as he was hated for being a tyrannical obscurantist. He left no theological school behind him. On the other hand, his approach lived on into the very recent past in a characteristic and noteworthy way in the small Hessian *Renitenz* Church, which at the time of the *Kulturkampf* resisted incorporation into the Prussian Union and from then on continued its peculiar existence with all the good and less good properties of an *ecclesia pressa*. Vilmar's *Geschichte der deutschen Nationalliteratur* (History of German National Literature), first published in 1845 and then printed in many editions down to our own century, is widely known even in non-theological circles. His theological programme is contained in his polemical writing *Die Theologie der Tatsachen wider die Theologie der Rhetorik* (The Theology of Facts against the Theology of Rhetoric) (1854), which verges on, or perhaps goes beyond, the limits of a pamphlet. Also to be mentioned are his *Pastoraltheologische Blätter* (Notes on Pastoral Theology) (1861-4) and two posthumous works, *Die Lehre vom geistlichen Amt* (The Doctrine of the Ordained Ministry) (1870) and his *Dogmatik* (1874).

According to Vilmar, Schleiermacher's *Doctrine of Faith* 'was a very brilliant attempt to combine pantheism and Christianity'. 'To return to Schleiermacher now or to expect help from him is either myopia or ill-will.' Yet by going back to the person of Christ, Schleiermacher pioneered the way back to faith. Many people, taught by their experiences of the wars of liberation and the general trend away from rationalism, trod the same path and recognized 'that the complete truth to which they were now beginning to return had long been present to them within Christianity, indeed in the Church, in whose teaching they found once again their own beginnings in Christian knowledge and life, only complete, so that they had to recognize that they themselves were neophytes and had to learn from the Church to attach themselves completely to the Church, because it alone completely corresponded to their experiences' (*Dogm.* I, 86f.). Had theology trod this way from Christ to the faith of the Church, all would have been well. But this did not happen: 'Most people did not think it necessary to enter into a discussion with real life, or, what amounts to the same thing, with the Church' (*Dogm.* I, 87). Vilmar feels that he must also press this charge explicitly against the biblicists Hofmann and Beck. A dogmatics which draws biblical doctrinal material afresh from Holy Scripture without considering the experiences of the Church is nothing but the result of the subjective experience of the dogmatic theologian. It is often simply the result of his studies, indeed simply the result of his views and for the most part the result of the culture prevailing at the time: he erects and directs a system and digests the biblical material in accordance with it. There can at best be a chance contact between this procedure and what he, Vilmar, desires (*Dogm.* I, 66). But what is it that he desires? Vilmar begins very energetically with the postulate that theology should release itself above all from the claim to be a science. It is not a science, at least in the modern sense of the term. For a science in the modern sense is concerned with the accurate observation of individual facts, the classification of results and then with progress from there to new observations with new results. It goes from the part to the member, from the member to the whole. This is so with natural sciences, with medicine, with modern linguistics. But it is not what happens in law and theology. The application of such a method to theology leads straight to the atheology of Strauss and Feuerbach. Theological knowledge rests on life in the totality of divine revelations and from there descends to the members and the parts (*Theology of Facts*, 12f.; *Dogm.* I, 35f.). It would be rather different if science were to be understood in the old sense as ἐπιστήμη, *doctrina*; in that case *doctrina* would need to be coupled immediately with *disciplina* (*Dogm.* I, 3). For 'theological knowledge, and above all dogmatics, is not exclusively at the service of aceticism, nor is it speculation in the tranquillity of so to speak a monastic life; it is at the service of the divinely ordained direction of the Church, the divinely ordained sacred ministry, and can only be completely evaluated from that standpoint. The knowledge which pertains to the ordained ministry is an energetic knowledge that proceeds from itself, guides the community and leads it towards its goal. It therefore surveys the whole course and way of the Church backwards and forwards; it is a knowledge that belongs to the χάρισμα κυβερνήσεως' (*Dogm.* I, 60). 'Theology has to exercise the office of a pastor in such a way as to guide the rising generation so that it can become a generation of faithful pastors who are in a position to keep the sheep together, go after them, seek them and find them again. It has to bring up pastors' (*Facts*, 5). Hence there is an essential connexion between theology and the Church. 'Anyone who has not directed his attention exclusively towards bringing up pastors is not a teacher of theology' (*Facts*, 6).

Theology is intended for the Church; it belongs to it, that is, it directly serves the teaching office of the Church (*Dogm.* I, 89). When it moves away—and this is the burden of Vilmar's charge against more recent theology—from the sphere of the Church, it no longer serves salvation, but the idle curiosity of the individual. It should realize that as part of the preparation for the ordained ministry it has a relationship like that of a school to real life. It should therefore be told: *Non scholae, sed vitae discimus*. 'The life of the Church stands over and above dogmatics' (*Dogm.* I, 59). Its task is that of preserving the substance of salvation contained in Holy Scripture and handing it on to the future servants of the Church in such a way that they find themselves in possession of this matter, completely, without deficiency, certainly, and as easily as possible (*Facts*, 16). 'Theology is the most unconditional antithesis of egoism, of introverted selfishness, of all esoteric. The knowledge of God which calls itself theology is at the same time talk of God. And talk of God goes out into the world, into the life of man. The theologian serves real life' (*Facts*, 5). In this way a theology of facts differentiates itself from a mere theology of rhetoric, which only knows of a Jesus Christ who once was, and not of a Jesus Christ who is still near and present in person today; which teaches his resurrection without comprehending and making clear the ongoing influence of this fact on the present moment; which has a doctrine of the Holy Spirit, but does not know and confess the Holy Spirit himself (*Facts*, 10); which occupies itself with laughable critical-grammatical artifices in studying the Bible (*Facts*, 14); which is always researching when it is a matter of faithfulness and experience (*Facts*, 16); which is occupied in quite useless controversy with 'every young philosopher, genuine or spurious' (*Facts*, 18); which is at every moment in the position of surprising the public with something new, which elevates 'absence of presuppositions' to a principle and in this way achieves nothing but 'the destruction of theology, the annihilation of faith, enmity against Christ and separation from God and from the soul that needs and is capable of its own redemption' (*Facts*, 20). This culminates in the great dialectical peace-negotiations between God and the devil over the right formula which can be used to talk of salvation in such a way that the fact of salvation is left out of account and eventually, once all extreme formulas are laid aside, becomes irrelevant (*Facts*, 22). In contrast to this, in theological lecture-rooms the talk should be 'of the fearful earnestness with which each young man who visits the room will look on the real life that faces him', 'of the seriousness of the judgment with which the pastorate looks into

the eyes of the young theologian' (*Facts*, 6). One might call this concrete relationship of theology not only to the Church in general but
also to the pastorate in particular the fundamental principle of Vilmar's
own theology. From this point three perspectives, or special doctrines,
appear, which he believes to be decisive.

1. We have already heard that theology has to preserve and trans-
mit the substance of salvation that the Church receives. Consequently
it may not present itself as the result of the experience of an individual
in the Church, much less as the result of his speculation; it is itself
the Church's confession (*Facts*, 35). Now a confession of the Church
is the result of what has been experienced and undergone by the
Church as a whole, expressed in a definitive form for its time (*Facts*,
72). So theology is a compilation of the Church's experience of the
acts of God in Jesus Christ up till now. By its teaching the Church
provides an answer to the deeds of its Lord, or rather, it answers his
questions to the Church, whether it has understood and accepted his
gifts of eternal mercy, has woven them into its own life and thus preserved the word of his patience (*Facts*, 35). Here Vilmar takes up a
theory first put forward by T. Kliefoth, according to which each
period of the history of dogma has in a providential way had its own
curriculum to pursue, the result of which has been taken over into the
Church's treasury and there stored. So, for example, the Reformation
doctrine of justification by faith appears as a new experience of faith
which forms the culmination of all previous experience and emerges
from that experience not with the necessity of a logical conclusion but
as a fact (*Facts*, 41). According to Vilmar, the further experiences
lying immediately before us relate to the nature of the Church and to
the last things (*Dogm.* I, 8). Thus from a historical point of view it is
no whim but a necessity of the particular *Kairos* when Vilmar makes
the concept of the Church his central concept. From this general view
there follows the more specific course theology is to take: it has to make
known and to present to the future pastors of the Church a compilation of the different teaching experiences of the Church, the way in
which they have followed on from each other, the path that the Church
has taken towards knowledge of the kingdom. It has to put them in
a position where they can protect the flock from the errors that have
already entered into the Church and have been rejected by it (*Dogm.*
I, 60).

2. For that very reason, because theology is essentially concerned
with the endowment and the task of the Church, its teaching must
be essentially reference to experience, an indication of the divine facts.

Teachers may not be just teachers, nor may their audience be merely audience and pupils; the former must be *masters* so that the latter can be *disciples*. And the masters must themselves have experienced and been through the divine facts, they must themselves have fought the battles, done the work, solved the tasks; they must introduce their disciples to these experiences and encounters by the power of the Holy Spirit (*Facts*, 9). It cannot be that theology thinks it can know of and talk about its subject-matter on the presupposition that this subject-matter is remote from it, that it can take a bird's-eye view, or at least contemplate it from a safe hiding-place: the nations may be fighting against each other in distant Turkey, but not next door (*Facts*, 37). 'If a man is going to teach rightly and to protect souls properly, he must have seen (seen with physical eyes: I mean it quite literally) the devil gnashing his teeth from the depths and have felt his power against a poor soul; he must have heard his blasphemy, and especially his mocking laugh, from the abyss. Who can testify to this now? Who can come forward as a true teacher in Christ's place with such an experience, with the victory of the Crucified One on his lips and in his eyes?' (*Facts*, 39f.).

3. This same relationship of theology to the Church, and particularly to the pastorate, taken in connexion with that realism of Vilmar which we have just mentioned, now produces—and this is the characteristic feature of his special dogmatics—an astonishing doctrine of the ordained ministry, sharply in contrast to that of the Reformed tradition. It is essentially the same doctrine that was put forward at the time by other outspoken Lutheran confessionalists like Kliefoth, Harless, Löhe, Delitzsch and others. With Vilmar, however, it has a special significance because of its connexion with the general complex of questions that he wants theology to pursue. For him the Church is no mere community, but an institution, an ordinance, an objective foundation that produces community (*Facts*, 48). Κοινωνία, *communio sanctorum*, does not mean community, but denotes 'a relationship among the members of the Church which is communicated through a relationship of these members in Christ' (*Dogm*. II, 206). The Church is a continuation of the being and activity of Jesus Christ, an expansion of his person, represented in a community of men called to redemption. Christ is not to be called the author or founder of the Church. That is not Christ, but the apostle Peter. Rather, 'The true presence of the Holy Spirit and the true divine and human presence of Christ is the Church' (*Dogm*. II, 183). And now this institution with which our salvation is bound up does not exist without certain persons by

whom it is transmitted. The word is bound up with the proclamation, the sacraments are bound up with their administration. This transmission through persons precedes the existence of the Church as a community (*Dogm.* II, 272). The faith and blessedness of the community, i.e. the continued existence of the Church, is bound up with the presence of the ministry. The community is formed and sustained by the *ministerium ecclesiasticum.* It has nothing, possesses nothing, gives itself nothing of the salvation it transmits; it acts only as a recipient (*Dogm.* II, 275). On the other hand, the laying on of hands, through which it propagates the ordained ministry from person to person, gives the Holy Spirit in all reality as the transmission of the direct mandate of Christ, gives the possibility not only of proclaiming the forgiveness of sins but of bringing it about, indeed gives the possibility of performing the actions of Christ in his place as his own (*Dogm.* II, 277). 'Which ministry is directly and immediately his ministry; it can only be his ministry in the most direct way, because the truth proceeds only from this ministry, and by it alone is the way shown, by it alone does the light shine on the community' (*Facts*, 87). No mention that, say, the community itself provides itself with this ministry, that *its* power and strength, *its* commission and mandate are exercised in the pastorate. Rather, it wants to know whether the minister has the right and the power to forgive sins, a question which is answered by the doctrine of the 'immediate divine *potestas*' of the ministry (*Facts*, 95). Is the Holy Spirit, the Lord Christ, personally, physically present among us? Or are there merely forces, influences of the spirit of Christ? Yes or no? *Hic Rhodus, hic salta!* (*Dogm.* II, 281). In the ordained ministry Christ is the judge of all the world, and the masses are judged, as according to Matt. 16 and 25, in accordance with their attitude to the holders of this ministry, to the servants of the Lord (*Dogm.* II, 322). Vilmar is aware that he is saying something strange in this theory. 'The world will accept a God in the beyond, the distant, long-dead Christ, the phantom of the Holy Spirit; but as soon as this God enters this world, as soon as the dead Christ wants to show himself alive and present and even ruling in the real world, as soon as the phantasmagorical Holy Spirit wants to come very perceptibly into reality and judge this reality—the powers of the flesh rise up: the plebeian masses of all kinds raise a unanimous, inarticulate cry of rage and the *sansculottes* of the salons, the smoking dens and of theology call day by day to the sweet crowd: hierarchy—papacy—catholicizing—prelacy—Trent—deep Middle Ages—thick darkness—servitude of the spirit—inquisition—burning at the stake! And with the repetition of

these words there immediately begins the thousand-voiced charivari.'
'The very first of these cries belongs *only* to the crowd!' retorts Vilmar.

With all respect to the way in which he ventured to give offence, it was perhaps not only the Holy Spirit which secured him this kind of answer. In stressing the relationship between theology and the pastorate, Vilmar said something new to his time, and that meant an action whose influence was not reduced by the impetuosity with which it was accomplished. We do, however, have to recognize a narrowness in the one-sided way in which Vilmar derived the essence of theology from this relationship and in which he overlooked the fact that theology, like every discipline, is not only teaching but *research* and teaching. This narrowness is clearly a reaction and as such is bound up with a questionable and rightly questioned one-sidedness. But even given the significance of the way in which Vilmar shed light through his view of the inner course of the Church, of the way in which all theological statements are related to experience and, finally, of the singular task of the *ministerium verbi divini*, we may not overlook the fact that all of this happened with him in a way which all too clearly bears within itself the traces of the spirit of the time against which he fought, for it to be evaluated or even taken over as a new approach. Incautious wonderers be warned! In his doctrine of the Church we are instinctively reminded of the connexion between modern theology and the Hegelian philosophy of history that can also be seen in Hofmann. In Vilmar's doctrine of experience, despite all its crudeness, it is impossible to mistake a connexion with Schleiermacher, whom Vilmar rejected so vehemently. And finally, in Vilmar's doctrine of the ordained ministry one need only look back for a moment to Feuerbach to be clear about the extent to which he is playing with fire, albeit in the supreme euphoria of faith.

27

KOHLBRÜGGE

KOHLBRÜGGE is not even mentioned by name in any of the books
on the history of theology known to me.[1] He was in fact unknown
to the academic theology of his time, and even today one will meet
countless well-read theologians who are not aware of their ignorance
here. The fact that Kohlbrügge, too, was a pastor, and the already-
mentioned custom of professors of theology only to occupy themselves
with their peers, offers some explanation here, but does not explain
everything. There are unexpressed but very influential disparagements
in the history of theology, and in one of them is involved the name
of Kohlbrügge, because of the matter that he represents. For the
theology of his time, which is still largely the theology of our time,
Kohlbrügge inevitably represented a much greater stumbling-block
than the more clamorous Vilmar. He represented a matter which could
only come under consideration once a beginning had been made on
the revision of principles, once a discussion had begun not only on
the Enlightenment but on the basis of the Enlightenment, the pietistic
understanding of the Reformation. The starting point was not the
Enlightenment, as it was for Ritschl later, but the Reformation itself.
That was Kohlbrügge's concern. He did not join Schleiermacher and
his followers in a concern to reconcile the Christian experience of man's
self and history with modern thought, nor did he join with the theologians of the Revival, the biblicists and the confessionalists who wanted
to defend and exploit the Christian experience of man's self and history over against modern thought. He raised the question whether
the Christian experience of man's self and history could be a useful
object in discussion about Christianity. For him, in contrast to the
opinio communis current from Hegel to Vilmar, Christianity was identical
with free, continually free grace, over against all Christian experience
of man's self and history. In the light of grace he regarded Christian
experience of man's self and history as nothing but sin, and wanted

[1] With the exception of two footnotes in H. Stephan (1938!).

to know only the faith of the sinner who lives solely from faith. This presupposition was so alien, not only in the world of Schleiermacher and Hegel but in the Protestant world as it developed from about 1700; it is so alien still, that one must employ neither the foolishness nor the wickedness of his contemporaries as an explanation of that tacit disparagement, as an explanation of why at first Kohlbrügge simply could not be understood. In the first place Kohlbrügge is outwardly similar to a Julius Müller and a Vilmar in that he focussed sharply on a particular *locus* of dogmatics and illuminated the whole in its light. The difference is that this particular *locus* chosen by Kohlbrügge was by chance the *locus classicus* of the Lutheran and Calvinist Reformation, that as a result Kohlbrügge had hit on the central problem of all Protestantism. The impulse to renewal given by this position was so significant that it either would have had to have catastrophic effects or remain largely meaningless—meaningless because it would have been humanly impossible to correct all the books that would have had to be corrected as a result. In addition— we have noticed the same thing with Menken, Dorner and Beck— he was completely a child of his time in the way in which he presented and defended his thesis, not standing out so distinctly from his surroundings that all who were of good will must have seen and heard. So he forms as it were an island, inundated at first, made up of another view of the problem, past which his own time and the time that followed inevitably rushed, caught up as they were in developing their own problems. That today we can see it again may be a sign that the floods of those days are now sinking. But one cannot be surprised that it is still invisible to all those for whom the sinking of the floods has not yet become an event. For those for whom this event is an event, it will be impossible to miss Kohlbrügge as an important historical figure.

Hermann Friedrich Kohlbrügge, on his father's side descended from a German Lutheran family, was born in Amsterdam in 1803; his mother tongue was Dutch. He spent his youth partly working in his father's soap factory and partly as a theological and philosophical teacher. The year 1826 brought him a conversion experience as a result of the death of his father, by which his obligations were discharged, in which the saying in Isa. 54.10 ('The mountains shall depart . . .') became important to him. In 1827 he became auxiliary preacher to the Lutheran congregation in Amsterdam, but after only three months he was dismissed as the result of a bitter dogmatic conflict with the rationalist chief minister, in which he was the attacking party. During a period of sickness he underwent a second inner crisis in which it became clear to him that the grace that does not depart from us is a gift without a gift in return, free grace. He obtained a doctorate in the University of Utrecht in 1829 with a dissertation on Psalm 45, was made economically independent by a rich marriage, and immersed himself in the history and doctrine of the Reformed Church, with the result that in 1830 he applied to join the Reformed Church of the district. This attempt was, however, rejected by the church authorities, among whom there was a rationalist party, and so to begin with he was exiled and left homeless between the two churches. In 1833 he came for the first time to Elberfeld, the 'city that stands on a hill', as used to be said in respect of the degree of spiritual success in the Wuppertal of the time. He preached there to great crowds until a prohibition issued from Berlin in view of the striking content of these sermons spoilt his career here also. He returned home and for ten years lived as a private teacher in Utrecht. When an independent 'Dutch Reformed Church' (which still exists today) with an independent constitution, attached in its organization to the Church in Holland, was formed in Elberfeld with the assent of Frederick William IV, subsequent to the Union, Kohlbrügge received a call to it in 1845. There he ended his life in 1875, after a ministry of thirty years. No further writing of even approximately academic character came from his pen after his dissertation, despite the specifically academic interests that he never gave up. His literary remains consist essentially of countless sermons produced individually and in series, of which for example the *Twenty Sermons delivered in the Year 1846*, with which he introduced himself to Elberfeld, deserve mention. Kohlbrügge left behind a numerically small but quite notable theological school in the Reformed circles of Germany, Holland, Switzerland and America, which did not lack some degree of academic representation. Names to be mentioned are Johannes Wichelhaus, *extraordinarius* professor in Halle, a sharp opponent of Tholuck and Müller, who died in 1858; Kohlbrügge's son-in-law Eduard Böhl, *ordinarius* professor in Vienna, the composer of a Reformed dogmatics, who died in 1903; and Adolf Zahn, finally a Reformed pastor in Stuttgart, who died in 1900. In what follows we shall keep to the account of Kohlbrügge's main thoughts in the *Erlauternden und befestigenden Fragen und Antworten zu dem Heidelberger Katechismus* (Explanatory and Didactic Questions and Answers on the Heidelberg Catechism).

I know—everyone must know this, that I am such a sinner that God cannot have dealings with me and must eternally cast me away from his holy countenance. But that is my sin: all the thoughts and endeavours of my heart and all the considerations of my understanding, according to which I always will otherwise than what God wills. Whatever he says I interpret in a perverse way, whatever he orders and disposes rightly I disrupt and derange, whatever he has made truly and well I distort; I never understand him in his righteousness and goodness as I should, but nurse evil thoughts about him; I remain attached to what is visible; I struggle against his eternal wisdom; I have made and continually make myself totally unfit for his good law and his holy commandment. In short, I can do nothing and will do nothing, although the purpose is with me (*Questions and Answers*, 10f.). No matter how often I take the law in hand, I shame it, instead of using it to overcome even one evil thought in my heart (p. 18). My corruption is nothing alien to me, a passion or the like that I could overcome. I am fundamentally corrupt and good for nothing (p. 23); I am lost, however brave, however pious, however upright I may be (p. 25). I must know all this. If I did not know it, I would seek consolation in my repentance and my penitence. in my improved moral way of life or in the works of my piety, in my conversion and in the way in which God guides me in my temptations and in my tribulation, in my cries for grace and forgiveness and in the promises that I make to myself in my struggle against and apparent overcoming of sin. In that case I would fall victim to security, self-confidence and despair, for all this cannot answer against the remembrance of even a single sin (pp. 12f.). The law is given to us to convict us at a stroke of hate against God and our neighbours, to cause us to seek the good where it is to be found despite our uselessness, but in no case and in no sense within ourselves (pp. 19, 26). Only two of the six hundred thousand who came out of Egypt reached Canaan in the Promised Land. Who were they? Joshua and Caleb. And what do these names mean? One who saves and a dog (p. 29). One who saves? Yes, I have the word and deed of my God, otherwise I have nothing. Without me, indeed against my will he has saved me according to the counsel of his well-pleasing in Christ Jesus. He has found nothing in me but sin. In him I find only mercy (p. 13), mercy in accordance with his law, for otherwise it would not be God's mercy, mercy not without satisfaction, but mercy (pp. 30f.). For in the days of his flesh our Lord went in our person, in the person of the sinner (p. 35), and died the death cursed by God, on the cross. For the high God has always wanted to come down to men on earth, so it befits men to remain on the ground, to live from the word, from the grace, from faith; but man does not want to do that: he wants always to go higher when he can. In this way he is put to shame and the curse strikes him. For thus says God: beware that you do not go up on the mountain! So it is an urge of the flesh that despises God when a man wants to ascend to God through his own power and wisdom and righteousness: he remains hanging between earth and heaven. For this our sin, which incurs the penalty of death, our Lord died by hanging between heaven and earth, with hands and feet nailed fast, that is, as one who could not bring anything to pass (pp. 93f.). According to God's righteous and irrevocable utterance our death is an eternal death. If grace is to prevail, if the righteousness of God is to be preserved, God's truth to remain untarnished, this death has to be overcome; but it could only be overcome and was only overcome by the death of the son of God (p. 94). In this way is described the Archimedean point on which the earth is moved, from which we are given life by God, where man, his will and his action, his appropriation and his realization, are left completely out of account. For no man can be saved when he wants to be. That depends solely on God's will and mercy (p. 46). If we look steadfastly at the way in which we deserve damnation, at our complete helplessness, at the sovereignty and freedom of God who does not respect persons, and at the blood of the Lamb that takes away the sins of the world (p. 49), then we shall cast ourselves into the hands of this our sovereign God for better or worse with the petition: 'Turn thou me and I shall be turned!' We shall cast off all presumption to our own righteousness and seek our certain and eternal comfort in the doctrine of the eternal free election by grace, by virtue of which God could even leave us in the damnation that we have deserved (p. 48).

Now this freedom and sovereignty of God denotes not only the beginning, but also the continuation and consummation of his relationship to his own. He is always and in every respect the Lord, not only the source but also the place and the embodiment of all good, whose own we can boast that we are. I am righteous before God in Christ. Accordingly I am not righteous in myself or through myself or through my works (p. 125). Even those who are born again have a tendency to all evil (p. 126). Those who believe know neither *before* Christ nor *after* him that they have done a single good work (p. 156). To believe means to reply yes with a cry of grief, of need and of joy to the question of the great God: Do you think that I have done this for you and in your place through my anointed? It is to say

Amen to the fact that God has shown us our blessedness outside us and without us in Christ; it is to regard God as an honest man, to rely on his word, his promise, his Lamb (p. 129). It is to direct one's eyes and heart as a godless sinner towards God and to have the saviour as the true creator of one's soul (p. 130). This faith is the embodiment of all good works. How do you have a good conscience? I have it when I look on Christ as on my sin and my righteousness. A good conscience is had through the resurrection of Christ from the dead. What does killing the works of the flesh through the spirit mean? It means standing by the word of the Lord Jesus, 'My grace is sufficient for you', without any excitement, resistance or excuse (p. 96). What is the right use of the gifts of the Holy Spirit? When one knows that one does not have gifts but knows that one has a gracious God (p. 117). Kohlbrügge once wrote to his pupil Wichelhaus: 'I know well what you mean when you write that you became a theologian as a result of many battles, but don't let on to yourself that you regard yourself as a theologian . . . My dear John, I know the important posts that you hold; but stop keeping something from yourself!'[1]. What is the mark of the true Church? That it keeps Christ as its head. That it knows no other head, that it allows itself to be directed and ruled only by the word of Christ . . . that it is a poor and meagre people reckoned as nothing in the Christian world (*Questions*, 114). Which is the most grateful of God's creatures? The dog. In what, then, should your gratitude consist? I should keep close to grace, like a dog to its master, and continually turn to this grace for grace and thus remain and persevere in the redemption by which I am freely redeemed. The dog crawls most humbly to its master when it is beaten by him. He is grateful to God who acknowledges that it is impossible for him ever to be grateful to God; he takes the cup of blessing and drinks it, praises the Lord that his goodness washes over us powerfully like a stream. He does not know that he is grateful. He accuses himself of being ungrateful. He cannot, however, assure the devil, sin, death and the world that the Lord is not his God and saviour, who redeems him from blood-guilt and saves him from death (p. 151). It is clear that Kohlbrügge has a very different understanding of the 'new man' from, say, Richard Rothe. If the old man is Adam and what we have become, what we think, do and plan with Adam, the new man is simply Christ and what we have become in and with Christ (p. 154). Idolatry means to leave grace and pursue another sanctification than that which is in the blood of Christ (p. 165). On the other hand,

[1] *Briefe*, ed. J. J. Langen, 1911, pp. 71f.

perfection is to be found in the gracious reckoning of the righteousness of Christ according to the testimony of a good conscience in the
Holy Spirit, in turning the eyes to the purifying blood of Christ (p.
207). And that is the grace of the Holy Spirit: every day it makes us
more blessed in revealing to us our uselessness and complete nullity,
and the love, all-sufficiency, might and power of the Lord Jesus (p.
209). Of course, nothing is accomplished with too-easy talk of faith,
helplessness and grace. We have to see that for our part we cannot
remain in our sins (p. 14). On the other side, we have to see that the
believer is empty in and for himself and receives everything only
through prayer that the enemy does not swallow him up, that death
and sin do not choke him (p. 215). But what does the upright man
do about prayer? He prays without ceasing, but he does not know
that he does it: rather, he accuses himself for doing so little, indeed
nothing, for not even being able to pray. Wherever life is, there is
a continual sighing for light and air, there is hidden a cry, a groaning,
a questioning, a worshipping, a jubilation, an entering into the presence of God, in dumb talk, but day and night aloud in the heart.
Can one pray without sinful thoughts? No, but we are not for that
reason to cease from prayer (pp. 215f.). Thus prayer, and in the end
only prayer, is life, the beginnings of heaven (p. 220). 'So when I
die—but I shall no longer die—and someone finds my skull, this skull
will still preach to him: I have no eyes, but yet I see him; I have
no brain, no understanding, and yet I comprehend him; I have no
lips, and yet I kiss him. I have no tongue, and yet I praise him with
all of you who call upon his name. I am a hard skull, but I am nevertheless completely softened and melted in his love; I lie here outside
on God's earth, but inwardly I am in paradise! All suffering is forgotten! This his great love has done for us, as he bore his cross for us
and went out to Golgotha. Amen' (*Passion Sermons*, 173f.).

What has been said may be sufficient to substantiate the assertion
made at the beginning: a tone is perceived and taken up here which
was not perceived or taken up in such a way from Hegel to Vilmar—
indeed from the time of Leibnitz to our day. This tone was identical
with the tone with which at any rate the Reformers continually began.
It does not fit at all well, not only to the way in which the Enlightenment was completed and overcome from Hegel to Vilmar, but also
to the presupposition of the Enlightenment that had been taken over
unseen from Hegel to Vilmar, namely the Augustinian presupposition
that the work of Christ and of the Holy Spirit can be detected in man

and that Christianity is essentially to be understood from this ascertainable divine working. This note thus raised with unprecedented radicalism the question whether a completely new beginning was not needed for treatments of the theological problem. Kohlbrügge introduced the theology of the Reformation on to the scene again more powerfully than anyone before him or after him in the nineteenth century, and in so doing reminded Protestantism of its origin, its nature. His return to this theology can be advantageously distinguished from, say, Tholuck's undertaking in the same direction: 1. The dogma of the Reformation is renewed integrally at its most difficult point: the lack of freedom of the will, double predestination and forensic justification are not swept out of the way. 2. It was a timely renewal, in that it directed these principles of the Reformation in an appropriate way against the Augustinian Christianity that was spreading once again in the shadow of the Reformation, and in accordance with the altered situation gave them a much sharper point than did the Reformers themselves.

We should not, however, ignore Kohlbrügge's limitations. At one all-important point he certainly reached Calvin's profundity in the inexorability of his understanding of grace as free and abidingly free. Indeed, with his precision that excluded all misunderstanding, he even went beyond Calvin. Yet Calvin on the whole understood the problem of the relationship between God and man in a different way from Kohlbrügge—and rather better. Kohlbrügge seems to have thought that he could embrace Christian truth in a single principle and thus comprehend it systematically. In this even he is a modern theologian. Calvin saw problems where Kohlbrügge (and this was the weakness in his strength) saw nothing but his single problem. For Calvin, nature does not vanish alongside grace, and for him, more clearly than for Kohlbrügge, there arises beyond nature and grace, creation and reconciliation, redemption, the still eternity of the *vita futura* as the solution of the riddle that here and now we live as those who die; that we die, and behold we live. For him, obedience does not vanish in faith, the grace of sanctification in the grace of justification. For him the law remains important as the correlate of the Gospel, as the meaningful word of God to the man who lives in the world. For him the task of the Church to proclaim the glory of God on earth in the utter damnedness of everything earthly, including its own being, does not fade away; it remains even in the Church's existence as the community of sinners who have been cast down to the ground and raised again. In Calvin, the dog, to take up that vivid image once again, does not only crawl humbly to his master, but he can and must jump up, bark, hunt, grab and bite when his master whistles and commands (without at the same time ceasing to be Caleb the dog). This is not to say that all this really vanishes with Kohlbrügge, but rather that the danger of its disappearance threatens —and it is undeniable that this occasionally happened very obviously with pupils of Kohlbrügge. Where one hears only one word, or almost only one word, in Kohlbrügge, one regularly hears two words in Calvin. With Calvin there is a meaningful distinction and a careful dialectical relationship, in which freer course is given to the word of God.

And with this we come to the second point. We can say of Kohlbrügge's attitude to the Bible the same thing that we can say of the biblicists Menken, Hofmann and Beck. Kohlbrügge takes his stand on a strict, not organic but (if you like) mechanical doctrine of inspiration. What is Holy Scripture? Answer: completely and utterly God's word, from the first verse of the first book of Moses to the last verse of the Revelation of John (*Questions*, 3). But again, as an exegete of the Bible Calvin is without doubt less cramped, freer, more open, less burdened by presuppositions than Kohlbrügge, with whom one never gets away from the impression that because the Bible had a violent effect on him, he was all too capable of doing violence to the Bible. From Romans to the book of Esther it bears witness and must bear witness to its own doctrine of grace. And if a passage comes up that is difficult to interpret at first glance, like Hebrews 12.14: Follow after peace with all men and the sanctification, etc., Kohlbrügge does not fail to make the holy text unmistakable by translating it: Follow . . . the sanctification (namely being made holy) without which no one will see the Lord (*Twenty Sermons*, 160). Kohlbrügge's insight into the sovereignty and freedom of God must have allowed him, one would have thought, to forego this kind of thing and quietly to acknowledge the question mark set by the Bible against any human theory, even his own or that of the Reformers. In that case his effect as an original sectarian would have been less than it was, and his influence as a teacher of the Church, which is what he really was, would have been greater. But to advance these qualifications is not meant to reduce the impression made by his thesis and the way in which it is presented. In not one of the theologians discussed here have we been tempted to criticize him by the standards of a Reformer. It is a sign of the greatness of Kohlbrügge that in his case such a course is unavoidable.

28

BLUMHARDT

To discuss this man in a history of theology might seem a questionable undertaking both with regard to the concept of theology and with regard to Blumhardt himself. Unlike Menken, Vilmar and Kohlbrügge, Blumhardt never had any intention of taking part in the theoretical work of the Church. Even as a practical man he was more a pastor than a preacher. And even as a pastor he attached remarkably little importance to theological correctness. What, then, is he doing among the horde of well-armed men that we are discussing here? One can indeed protest with Ragaz against putting Blumhardt, the man of God, who was not to be studied but only to be experienced, among the men of the synagogue and treating him as a theologian. However, against this second objection it should be remembered that Blumhardt's biographer, Friedrich Zündel, who perhaps stood closer than anyone to him during his lifetime, did not feel restrained by any pious feelings towards him from presenting what he had received from him (I am thinking of Zündel's well-known books about Jesus and the Apostolic Age) in the form of fundamental theological reflection. In his biography he speaks explicitly of a 'theology' of Blumhardt (p. 284), and devotes a chapter to presenting it in detail. What could be received from Blumhardt, no matter how primitive the form in which he himself might have offered it, is at any rate also knowledge, and in substance is original and important enough to give us cause not to leave empty the place which is now marked by his name in the picture of the theological knowledge of the time. As for the objection based on the concept of theology, it might be retorted that academic theology has its limitations with regard to history and substance where it has to be unacademic if it is not to become immaterial. Unacademic, that is, not only in the sense of being uninterested in the disputation between theology and philosophy, but also in the sense of being uninterested in the development and fixation of theological theory as such. Theology is concerned with a subject about which theories can be made on the basis of its revelation of itself, but not otherwise. This limitation to the possibility of theorizing must become visible in theology itself by theology not taking up too rigid an academic position. Theology must not be pedantically exact down to the last detail and at any price, but must also tolerate alongside itself the free, relaxed character of the knowledge and discourse of a Blumhardt. Indeed, it can incorporate him within the framework of its own work. All too often decisive things have been recognized and stated precisely at these boundaries of theology as a discipline. So the unacademic garb which Blumhardt wore with honour to a greater degree than any other is not refused a place here on any theoretical principle either. We may listen, too, to what this completely unarmed warrior knew and had to say.

The life of Blumhardt must partially be regarded also as a portrayal of the theological matter with which we are concerned here. Johann Christoph Blumhardt was born in Stuttgart in 1805. In 1825 he went to the Tübingen *Stft*, where three such different types as Wilhelm Hofmann (later Basle mission inspector, professor at Tübingen and Berlin court preacher), the poet Eduard Mörike and D. F. Strauss were his friends, but where he also belonged to the group of revivalist students centring on Ludwig Hofacker. After a brief curacy in Dürrmenz, in 1830 he was called to the Basle mission house as a teacher. In 1837 he became curate in Iptingen; in 1838 (following Christian Gottlob Barth, a man who was uncannily active in every kind of work for the kingdom of God) he became pastor at Möttlingen by Calw. After several years of comparatively unsatisfying activity in this community he reached the year 1842-3 and the events which later played a decisive role in his life and teaching under the name 'the struggle'. This was a pastoral struggle waged by Blumhardt against the psychosomatic illness of a girl in his congregation, Gottliebin Dittus, which was entered on and carried through by Blumhardt on the presumption that hers was a case of demon possession on the analogy of the well-known New Testament narratives. He believed that in the face of the magnitude, fearfulness and reality of this distress only Jesus himself could prove the saviour through his direct action, and not he, Blumhardt, the pastor. And unless his word and faith in him were not true, Jesus *must be* the redeemer. The end of the struggle was the complete healing of the girl. Jesus *was* the conqueror. For Blumhardt in the midst of Pietism this breakthrough represented a quite unpietistic discovery and recognition. The contrast was not between Jesus and the unconverted heart of man, but between Jesus and the real power of darkness, in which man finds himself. This was what the struggle was about, and it was here that Jesus proved victorious. These events were followed in 1844—a second turning point for Blumhardt—by a general revival movement in the congregation at Möttlingen and far beyond. The healing of Gottliebin Dittus, which was followed by countless other striking events of this nature, had for both pastor and congregation the significance of a sign in the synoptic sense of the word. From it was aroused and seen once again the reality and concreteness of the power to forgive sins contained in the imminent approach of the kingdom of God. Unbidden, but irresistibly, people came to him to confess what they had to confess, and he for his part saw himself compelled, unsought, unasked, governed by no preconceived theory, to absolve them in the name of God with a quite unpietistic objectivity (Zündel, 174). That was the time when that poetically weak but deeply-felt verse arose to accompany the whole Blumhardt movement:

> Jesus wears the glorious crown,
> Triumphs over all his foes;
> Jesus conquers; all the world
> Now his domination knows.
> Jesus comes with victor's might,
> Leads from darkness into light.

Now every Sunday Möttlingen became a place of pilgrimage sought out by crowds from far and near, 'a community gleaming in its first love'. But a further new insight had already burst upon its leader. Again in good New Testament fashion—but now, so to speak, comes the turn from the Synoptic Gospels to Paul—he sees all these experiences only as a down-payment, as a pledge of the Spirit, as a breath of spring before an all-embracing revelation of grace. 'I will pour out my Spirit upon *all* flesh!' Blumhardt does not see the fulfilment of this promise either in his Möttlingen congregation or in the Revival movement as a whole. He looks beyond the human conditioning of all that has so far been achieved, all that can be achieved on present presuppositions. His thoughts and prayers go beyond the present. If Jesus is coming again—and it must be that he is near—he must be preceded by a new time of grace, by a new outpouring of the Holy Spirit. The locomotive has broken loose from the train. Now it is stuck on the track. It must reverse and be hitched up again; then it will go forward. The broken thread of the first Christian age must be picked up again, from above, but not without preparedness and openness from below.

So Blumhardt diverges from the way of Pietism at a second point and now does it decisively. He becomes a theologian of hope. The Möttlingen movement declined again, as happened everywhere with the Revival movement; it became a great holy memory, a memorial to the acts of God, from which the way now had to lead forward. This development could not surprise Blumhardt. It could not be a deadly blow to him as it was to so many men of the Revival movement in their old age, sinking them in deep resignation. Blumhardt sought and found another area to work in. In 1852 he acquired Bad Boll at Göppingen which he made into a sanctuary for the oppressed and at the same time a starting point for his extended lecture-tours, adopting a twofold perspective: the present help and grace of God in the individual and the promise of an imminent appearance of his glory to all the world. His insight did not develop further from this point. His son Christoph, who developed Bad Boll after the death of his father, must of course be discussed in detail later, in another context. The 'history of the house', as Zündel tells it in his book, is theologically a history, moving through all sorts of crises, of that twofold insight, of the ἀπαρχή that is certainly and surely given in the shadow of the greater fullness of the revelation of grace in the end-time, that has not yet come about, and that in itself is only the herald of the manifestation of the kingdom of God. One thing more, though, should be said, that Blumhardt had quite a specific expectation of seeing the dawn of this time of grace in person, did not really reckon with the possibility of his own death, and therefore met it when it came in 1880—again quite unpietistically—as an alien, abnormal, remarkable occurrence. Blumhardt produced 'Letters from Bad Boll' in 1873-7 and again in 1879-81. His remarks were arranged and published in a collection occupying a series of volumes by his son. I shall attempt to sum up his thought in the following points.

1. Blumhardt once wrote: 'I did not reach my notion of hope by grubbing around *systematically*, sitting thoughtfully behind a desk. So I am surprised by many thoughts which are put to me and do not know how to answer them. I think that my dear friends who are aroused by my thoughts should themselves consider how it might be without making me a teacher in everything, for that is certainly not my desire' (*Glaubensfragen*, 52). This remark can be taken as a confession of Blumhardt's inability, as a result of personal and historical

circumstances, to work out a theoretical theological system, but it should not raise any objections against the content of his ideas. In any event, however, one cannot pay too much attention to the hint given here in connexion with questions about his theology. If one keeps to the exact words of Blumhardt's remarks, takes them as parts of a developed and worked-out system and follows through their immediate or subsequent consequences, instead of reflecting on them in excitement, the result is confusion. One lands oneself in every possible absurdity. As they stand, they abound with the most naïve collection of impossibilities, old and new. One can only understand them if one understands how, to a greater degree than is necessary in any kind of theological statement, their truth-content breaks into pieces in being applied to the subject-matter with which they are concerned. Neither individually nor in a system do they make sense unless sense is sought in the direction in which they are aimed.

2. We do best to begin immediately from Blumhardt's most scandalous notions, notions about which those who stood nearest to him often kept quiet or which they treated as something of which they should be ashamed. We have already heard how Blumhardt regarded the dawn of a historical period of grace preceding the *return of Christ* as being imminent, so definitely, that in old age, at the beginning of each year, he would say with increasing excitement: 'This year might . . .' There is a credible tradition that at Bad Boll a coach was kept ready, year in, year out, with all its equipment, ready to begin the journey to the Holy Land to meet the returning Christ, if need be. As we have said, Blumhardt did not reckon that he would die, but thought that like a second Simeon and as more than a Simeon he would be able to see the Lord with his physical eyes. It is certainly astonishing that a man who shared his basic education in Swabia with David Friedrich Strauss should have cherished and put forward such an idea. But Blumhardt posed to his contemporaries the counter-question, whether the real life of man and the Gospel of Christ were such that this question could be avoided. We must understand Blumhardt primarily in the light of this counter-question. He saw the tension, the glaring contradiction between the magnitude of human need and the magnitude of the divine promise so intensively in such real terms, that he looked not only for a notional resolution of this opposition but for a real one, and looked for it from day to day. So we must first talk of his realization of this antithesis.

3. Even before the events at Möttlingen, unlike his pietistic friend and predecessor in office, C. G. Barth, he was concerned even as a

pastor—particularly as a pastor—to keep the real life of men in mind, to instal the holy not in a holy place, but in everyday reality. Personally he was the opposite of a melancholic and a pessimist, but in an exceptional way he was a bearer of other peoples' burdens, with all his pores open for the sighing of the creatures around him. Thus he saw in real human life, as it encountered him in every single instance of his pastoral work, a drop of a particular wave in the sea of suffering, which, together with human sin but no less fearfully real, and therefore contrary to God, characterizes and determines this life of man (Zündel, 244). 'Is what we know and see to go on for eternity? Must not all the trafficking in which men engage with each other one day cease?' (Zündel, 303). What he is referring to is not the subjective problem of suffering but the objective problem, the problem of Job as it is universally understood. In the state in which we find ourselves is there not too much that objectively does not belong, too much radical purposelessness, too much Satanic darkness, for one to be able to answer the problem of theodicy with the usual talk about blessing, about the divine will and the divine disposition of suffering? (Z, 244). At this point Blumhardt's attitude is quite primitive and straightforward: the Christian answer to the objective phenomenon of suffering is rejection, protest, an angry No. With Blumhardt, though, this rests on a different view and knowledge of reality from usual, even from the usual Christian view. At first one can only ask whether suffering can be avoided. Now Blumhardt cannot even pass over the one fallen among murderers. Nor can he help himself with the problem by which he is confronted even through help. Blumhardt tried to help and did help, but beyond him burned the riddle of suffering. It occupied his thought, and forced him emphatically away from the usual theological solutions and answers.

4. Yet the starting point of his thought is now not human need but the divine *promise*. Much more real to him than the reality of darkness in which he sees men suffering is the other reality, that Jesus has come to seek and to save what is lost. His rejection, his protest, his angry No comes not primarily from the standpoint of the suffering man but from here. Because the suffering of man derives from sin it is something that does not belong, something that ought not to be from God's point of view. The name of Jesus represents God's necessity, power, reaction against this element that does not belong. And for that reason, we, too, cannot be indifferent to it, cannot stand over against it passively. It is not that we can avert it, but we would expect and ask Jesus to avert it if he is what he is and our faith in him is as it

should be. The appearance of Jesus raises not only a question of attitude but a question of power, to which we must react. In this sense, at the climax of his struggle over Gottliebin Dittus, Blumhardt cried: 'Put your hands together and pray: Lord Jesus, help me! We have seen for long enough what the devil does, now let us see what the Lord Jesus can do!' (Z, 114, 133, 141). So in the first place it is not the eschatological Jesus, the one who is to come, from whom Blumhardt begins, but the present, living Jesus, of whom Pietism could say so much and yet, in Blumhardt's view, so little. He felt that there was lacking in the pietistic Jesus that unwillingness of the real Jesus at the tomb of Lazarus (Z, 284), the will of the real Jesus to help and to prevail, as he saw it. Once again, the question here is: can one in fact avoid Blumhardt's insight and knowledge? Is it a tolerable theological notion that two thousand years ago the glory of God was proclaimed over the darkness by signs and wonders, while today patient resignation in the power of darkness is to be the last word? For Blumhardt this was intolerable. Jesus Christ the same yesterday and today. So he takes up the struggle with need in the name of Jesus.

5. We have a false picture of Blumhardt if we regard him as a quietist eschatologist who 'waited' for the miraculous kingdom to come with folded hands. On the contrary, he often talked about the *participation of man* in this struggle occupying heaven and earth in a way on which Kohlbrügge on the one hand and Feuerbach on the other would cast serious doubt. 'In the last resort, so much redemption is or is not projected into human life as there is or is not faith and wishing in faith on the part of humanity' (Z, 115). Looking back on his battle he could say, 'At that time the Saviour stood at the door and knocked, and I opened to him' (Z, 116). 'It is much easier to live resigned to the will of God than to push away the reins which hold up God's help' (Z, 218). 'What God promises always depends more or less for its fulfilment on man's free will, whether he really desires the promise or not' (Z, 265). Such statements may show that it was a God who laid a claim on man, of whom Blumhardt believed that he could expect great, new help, but—and this must be said against what might sound like Pelagianism in this statement: it was a God who claims man for himself, for faith, for crying and calling after him. In fact we find ourselves somewhere beyond the opposition of quietism and activism. This is the point from which Blumhardt became a pastor.

6. The concept of *pastoral care* is, of course, too narrow for Blumhardt's intention and achievement in Möttlingen and in Boll. He was

primarily and above all concerned with the whole man, with the healing of body and soul. So the forgiveness of sins and the healing of sickness always went side by side in his activity, in such a way that the relationship of men, the whole man to God, was made the decisive question. His approach thus differed from that of modern scientism, which is notoriously concerned not with the glory of God but with the soundness of man. But he also differed from the usual attitude of the Church and of Pietism, which wanted to extend the question of God only to the soul, the conscience, the interior of man. To this degree, Blumhardt's thought is Eastern-Christian and not Western, in that the affliction of φθορά is not disregarded beside the guilt of ἁμαρτία. In either case the name of Jesus is the word that brings the solution. I need not say how far we find ourselves here from the consciousness theology of the century. For this attitude alone, however unacademically it may have been expressed, Blumhardt would deserve a place in the history of more recent theology.

7. One cannot have a fuller part in present Christian experience than Blumhardt wanted. Moreover, the accusation that he occasionally laid against the Church was not that it neglected eschatology and hope but that it did not do what could be done today in the name of Jesus. 'The harvest is ripe, the reapers are there, but they hesitate to bring home the harvest' (Z, 176). At the end of his forties, however, a wider, loftier view increasingly reaches beyond the present and his own present experiences. Here an antithesis of concepts becomes particularly important, between the individual thing or the 'individual', the individual Christian, and the whole, the kingdom of God that embraces the whole of creation. This is the problem with all the grace, help, liberation and redemption that may be given to us: it always concerns only a few. The question over which the normal pastor thinks he can and should reassure himself, 'What will become of everything, of humanity, of the world', troubles Blumhardt perpetually and above all. What is the minority that can be reached by the Church, the Revival, by mission, etc., in comparison to the infinitely many whose need cries out to heaven? The Christian should venture to pray 'Deliver me from my adversary', not only for himself but for humanity (Z, 242). Zündel writes that Blumhardt 'was and remained poor and cried to God for all. He simply could not understand people who contented themselves or even vaunted themselves with a "Praise God, I am, I have, or we are, we have!" ' (Z, 247). According to Blumhardt it is a 'petty view' to treat Christianity as the private concern of every individual. Even the salvation of the individual is bound up with the

innermost content of the whole of human history, with the consummation of the victory grounded in Christ's redemptive death and resurrection. 'Yes, dear Christian, make sure that you die saved! But the Lord Jesus wants more. He wants not only my redemption and yours, but the redemption of all the world. He wants to finish off the evil that dominates in the world and make the whole world free that occupies itself in sheer godlessness' (Z, 302). In the finest church hymns there was too much talk of 'I' for Blumhardt, nor could he stand the way in which they closed with dying, as though that could be taken for granted (Z, 360). He also felt that he had to raise the same objection against the theology of his compatriot J. T. Beck. In this urge for the objectivity (which is what was his primary concern) not only of the origin but also of the goal and realization of redemption, Blumhardt now develops his 'notions of hope' in his own characteristic way.

8. On the basis of Scripture he expects above all a new *outpouring of the Holy Spirit*. 'I feel that things cannot continue in this sorry way. The first gifts and powers, O, they should come again, and I believe that the dear Saviour is only waiting for us to ask him for them again' (Z, 155). So he wrote during the time of his first love in Möttlingen. He cannot understand how one can say 'There is a Holy Spirit', without being able to say where. Where is the Spirit of truth that guides into all truth? Where is the other Comforter, the personal element from God which is to represent Christians and remain with those who have him? Where is the spirit of gentleness and humility? Where is he? Who has him? Or are these words of the Lord only phrases and manners of speaking which in reality are to be taken in an entirely different way? (Z, 253). No, the one who can say 'The Holy Spirit is there', 'The Church has him', and so on, is speaking from a system, from a basic notion which has no support in Scripture, much less from experience. 'We will have to understand the Holy Spirit in a quite different way. He is not something given that continues to work eternally' (*Glaubensfrage*, 50). Indeed Scripture speaks explicitly of repeated outpourings of the Spirit, not of a provision given once and for all (*Glaubensfrage*, 53). Blumhardt thinks that he can recognize such an outpouring of the Spirit in the Reformation. But now we stand in a time that is empty of the Spirit and can only, indeed must, pray to the Lord that he will take up what he has begun and continue it until it is given everywhere (*Glaubensfrage*, 52). 'If what was begun by the Reformation and later came to a standstill is to flow again— as it must, unless the future of the Lord is to become void of meaning—

it must happen that the stream is poured out again from above and flows down as it were with what came in the period of the Reformation, thus setting this in motion again. Indeed that is what I wish. I will testify as long as I live, and my last breath shall be the prayer, "Lord, give thy stream of the spirit and of grace, that the whole world may be aroused by it" ' (Z, 276).

9. In connexion with this Blumhardt expects the dawn of a *new time of grace* on the earth. One cannot refrain from bestowing on Blumhardt the heretical name of a chiliast—if that really is a heresy. 'Anyone who cannot believe in a great redemption which the Lord will bring about even before his coming to judgment does not, I would say, believe in the sense of Jesus' (Z, 317). The gifts of the Holy Spirit must —and this is his view—be effective in the breadth and the width. The forgiveness of sins must penetrate to all. The prophecies—those of Deutero-Isaiah were particularly important to Blumhardt—must be fulfilled. Then comes the end, the return of the Lord for judgment, which will not be an execution but a restoration (Z, 464). For: 'Do not believe that the Saviour will come to be the great head-lopper' (Z, 238). There is a certain weakness and indeterminacy in this last notion of the return of the Lord himself, in contrast to the blessings that precede him. Blumhardt did not take the last step that should have been taken, the clear subordination of the penultimate things to the last things. Perhaps he did not recognize as such the eschatological principle of the Christian objectivity that he so powerfully affirmed, and confused the resurrection of the dead and eternal life with the thousand-year kingdom. As a result his expectation of the dawn of this kingdom, at first sight so baroque, seems to fit all too well into the nineteenth century, even perhaps to resemble the views of Schleiermacher and Rothe.

Let this be recognized as the tribute that in the last even he owed to the spirit of his time. Within this limitation there remains his contribution, that with stammering tongue, but audibly to those who had ears to hear, he raised a whole series of questions once again that had to break through this limitation, and indeed the limitations of both liberal and pietistic theology. He raised the question of theodicy, of the universality of revelation and grace, of the practical significance of the New Testament miracles, of the unity of soul and body, of the real power of reconciliation, of the character and presence of the Holy Spirit and the reality of Christian hope. Academic theology made things too easy for itself by overlooking these questions because Blumhardt raised them and answered them only in a pastoral way, and not academically. The moment had to come and did come which brought the insight that there was something decisive to be learnt here—for academic theology.

29

RITSCHL

IT has been said of Ritschl that in the history of theology since Schleiermacher he is the only one who, in the true sense, has given birth to an epoch. This is not true because all the strivings proceeding from Schleiermacher, who was, despite all argument, the only one who really gave rise to an epoch, continued on their way in a very significant fashion beside Ritschl, and were even more than ever taken up again after him. As has already been said, Schleiermacher's influence was incomparably stronger in 1910 than in 1830, and one does not have to be a prophet to observe that if the older age of theology were to remain master of the field today, or conquer it anew, then it would do so under the banner of Schleiermacher, or perhaps of Hegel, and on no account under that of Ritschl. Ritschl has the significance of an episode in more recent theology, and not, indeed not, that of an epoch. If it were possible for us to continue our account in the way in which it has been presented up to now, then we should have to depict Ritschl amid his contemporaries and opponents to left and right: Luthardt, Frank and von Oettingen on the one side, and Biedermann and Lipsius on the other. We should, however, also have to point out, in the figure of Lagarde, who also belonged to this generation, the turn events took immediately after Ritschl, and which brought everything once again on to the course characterized by the name of Schleiermacher. We should then have to discuss the theologians born from the eighteen-thirties to the eighteen-fifties, that is to say, Overbeck, Pfleiderer, and Lüdemann on the one hand, and Cremer, Kähler, Schlatter, Ihmels and Seeberg on the other, who in the main only managed to speak, or were only heard, after Ritschl's death; and we should have to show that Ritschl's followers, Schultz, Herrmann, Kaftan, Haering, Kirn, Kattenbusch, Harnack, Rade and others, who were also of this time, did not dominate the picture quite so completely, even towards the end of the century, as the historians of Ritschl's school would have us believe. And we should then have to study the complete return to the main tendency which Ritschl forsook, in those who were born in the sixties and seventies, who were the men of the day in 1910, and still are in part today, men like the band of historians led by Troeltsch; namely Gunkel, J. Weiss, Bousset, Heitmüller, Wernle, and further the similarly orientated systematic scholars Otto and Wobbermin, men who are opposed from the right by E. Schaeder and C. Stange, a generation in which people like Johannes Müller and Rittelmeyer, Kutter and Ragaz could not be overlooked either. In the development thus hinted at the school of Ritschl played the undoubtedly important *rôle* of a reaction. It is thus, however, and not as the beginning of a new epoch, that it distinguishes itself from the flood of events and personalities, and that we are thinking of its leader as we bring this account to its provisional close.

The practical significance of this reaction is as follows. Ritschl rejected all the previous attempts to overcome the Enlightenment which were centrally determined by the tendency of Romanticism. Instead he energetically seized upon the theoretical and practical philosophy of the Enlightenment in its perfected form. That is, he went back to Kant, but Kant quite definitely interpreted as an antimetaphysical moralist, by means of whom he thought he could understand Christianity as that which grandly and inevitably made possible, or realized, a practical ideal of life. In this his abandoning of all knowledge which could not be rendered comprehensible within this framework is seen properly as the characteristic thing about his theology, provided we hold up beside it the positive determination with which on the one hand he apprehends and affirms this practical ideal of life as such, and with which on the other he makes the interpretation of Christianity, the Bible and particularly the Reformation, serve the founding and strengthening of this ideal. We must not allow ourselves to be blinded by sight of the extensive material Ritschl drew from the Bible and the history of dogma to the fact that this, and ultimately this alone, was his chief concern. Nobody either before or since Ritschl, perhaps—Wegscheider was the one exception—has expressed the view as clearly as he, that modern man wishes above all to live in the best sense according to reason, and that the significance of Christianity for him can only be a great confirmation and strengthening of this very endeavour. One could of course ask whether this will, soberly and honestly expressed by Ritschl, was not universally present, somewhere in the background of the theology of the whole century, except in certain outsiders, and whether all else was not more like an artificial fog surrounding this will than actually another will. We can ask whether the entire theological movement of the century resulted not at all in an overcoming of the Enlightenment, of its decisive interest of man in himself, but in its fulfilment.

But even if we understand it in this way we should still have to admit that the production of this artificial fog on the part of others had at least betrayed people's disquiet who for all that did not in fact want to admit that this will is the truth or, at least, that it is the whole truth. Ritschl, on the other hand, feels no trace of this disquiet. He stands with incredible clearness and firmness (truly with both feet) upon the ground of his 'ideal of life', the very epitome of the national-liberal German bourgeois of the age of Bismarck. That distinguishes him from those who went before him and from those who came after him. The passion with which he was attacked both from left and right is quite understandable—this self-assurance of modern man was not to everyone's taste, even between 1860 and 1890—and quite understandable too was the fact that he and his school could not long sustain themselves, once the jubilation over Columbus's trick with the egg had died away.

And yet perhaps the views of those who stood to left and right of Ritschl, who went before and came after him, were not basically very different from his. It was not hypocrisy, but this deeply-rooted disquiet which caused everyone before him and after him, and those on his left and right, to agree in the conviction that these views could not at any rate be expressed in this way. The plan for the overcoming of the Enlightenment had to be taken up again, after it had been postponed for a while, while theologians were blinded by Ritschl's simplification. The plan had to be taken up again with the risk that they would have to link up once again with Romanticism, and that they might perhaps not be able to find any better guidance from this source than the first generations of the century had done, with the risk that, far from managing this better, they might manage things even worse than their predecessors. It was Ritschl's great merit that with his reaction he showed that it was possible to abandon the Schleiermacher-Hegel approach, and he thus for a moment clearly illuminated the point of departure for the complete development, the perfected Enlightenment; though he then showed in effect that if theology did not wish to place itself in far too exposed a position, it could only employ the Schleiermacher-Hegel approach upon the basis of this point of departure; that a different approach would make necessary the choice of another point of departure, that it would, in fact make necessary a true overcoming of the Enlightenment. To this extent Ritschl is not at all a bad person with whom to conclude our account.

Albrecht Benjamin Ritschl was born in Berlin in 1822, and went to the universities of Bonn, Halle, Berlin, Heidelberg and Tübingen. First, at Tübingen he became a historian in the manner of Baur. In 1846 he qualified as a lecturer at the University of Bonn. The second edition of his book *Entstehung der altkatholischen Kirche* (The Origin of the Old Catholic Church) in 1856 brought him into conflict with Baur. He became an associate professor in 1852, a full professor in 1859, and was transferred as a systematic theologian to Göttingen in 1864, where from the end of the seventies onwards he was the head of the school bearing his name. He died in 1889. Chief consideration must be given to his two works, *Rechtfertigung und Versöhnung* (Justification and Reconciliation), 1870-4, and *Geschichte des Pietismus* (The History of Pietism), 1880-6. He set down his thoughts in condensed form in his *Unterricht in der christlichen Religion* (Instruction in the Christian Religion), 1875, in the lecture *Die Christliche Vollkommenheit* (Christian Perfection), 1874, and in the treatise *Theologie und Metaphysik* (Theology and Metaphysics), 1881, all of which appeared in several editions.

In order to understand Ritschl we must lay the emphasis upon the final word of the title of his chief work, *Justification and Reconciliation*. With Ritschl reconciliation, to put it baldly, means the realized ideal of human life. It is the intended result of justification (*Instruction*, para. 46). All Ritschl's thinking springs from this result. It is this result and this result alone in which he is interested. Completed reconciliation consists in God's confronting the believer as his Father and justifying him in his child-like feeling of utter trust,[1] giving him spiritual dominion over the world and engaging him in the work in the kingdom of God. This state is the state of Christian perfection. Religiously it consists in faith in divine providence, in humility, in patience and in prayer; morally it consists in activity in one's profession and in the development of personal virtue. In it 'the individual person acquires the value of a complete whole, which is superior . . . to the value of the entire world'.[2] In Christian perfection a man's life becomes a life-work accompanied by a justified sense of one's own work.[3] His perfection perpetually includes within itself an insight into a certain imperfection, but he may in principle 'be comforted' about this, since will and action would not be possible if his imperfection were the final word that could be said of him.[4] The quintessence of the task imposed upon man, which at the same time is his highest good and his own final

---

[1] *Instruction*, para. 46. [2] Ibid., para. 59.
[3] *Christian Perfection*, p. 13. [4] Ibid., p. 1.

aim, is the kingdom of God, in which the love of one's neighbour is activated.[1]

But the kingdom of God can only be lived for within the communities which have been naturally determined, particularly in the regular working activity of one's moral profession, and not outside them,[2] so that loyalty to one's profession is at once the true fulfilment of the model of Christ.[3] Where there is no reconciliation in this sense, as the realization of the ideal of life, or where reconciliation in this sense is not activated, there is no justification either. Ritschl finds he can express this, somewhat in the Pelagian manner, by calling man's conscious activity in reconciliation, and therefore in the kingdom of God and therefore in his profession, the 'condition' for the forgiveness of sins.[4] Or he can put it in an Augustinian way too, by simply equating the effect of grace and the impulse to corresponding self-activity; good conduct and the effect of grace.[5] But on no account may the balance for imperfection of moral conduct be sought in the certainty of justification or of the forgiveness of sins, but only in the resolve and implementation of a greater endeavour to improve,[6] whereas the meaning of the forgiveness of sins and of justification is entirely and alone that of placing man in the position where this activity is possible and demanded. There must not therefore be any thinking or any action which is not directly, perfectly or imperfectly activity in the kingdom of God and thus activity in one's profession and the development of virtue. There must not be any action directed towards God which by-passes this activity.

It was from this standpoint that Ritschl became the ferocious opponent of Pietism—which he accused of returning to the tendency of monasticism—and the opponent of all metaphysics in theology, which instead of holding solely to the effects of God which can be experienced, seeks to hold also, or indeed predominantly, to a God in himself. Again, it was from this standpoint that Ritschl became the opponent of mysticism as a religiosity which overleaps the will of God and of man. Christianity is an outlook upon life and it is morality, but in no way is it an immediate relationship with God. Roman Catholicism and every form of Anabaptists' faith is dispatched at one blow by virtue of the fact that they think they know of a Christianity, and perhaps indeed of a more perfect Christianity beside that provided by the consciousness and realization in the moral sphere of the fact that we are children of God.

---

[1] *Instruction*, paras. 5f.   [2] Ibid., paras. 27f.   [3] Ibid., para. 56.   [4] Ibid., paras. 45f.
[5] *Justification and Reconciliation*, III, para. 36; *Instruction*, paras. 39 and 55.
[6] *Instruction*, para. 46.

According to Ritschl there should strictly speaking not be any Sunday, and no eternity either, or at any rate no silent eternity, and he did in fact define God's eternity as the constancy of God's will for the creation and maintenance of his Church, overcoming the barrier of time.[1]

Justification is related to reconciliation, thus understood, as the great guarantee and realization, apprehended in faith, of this ideal of life. Reconciliation is event in the Christian Church as in the communion of the faithful, and faith is, simply, faith in the divine justification which in principle turns man from a sinner into a non-sinner.[2] Sin is deed and only deed. It is man's deed, performed in opposition to the action taking place in the Kingdom of God. In content it is selfishness, or a seeking after things which are of an inferior rank—i.e. an upsetting of the scale of things.[3] In form it is enmity to God, and lack of reverence and trust.[4] Its consequence is a reduction of the right to be a child of God, and, in conjunction with this, man's subjection to the evil as a restriction of his freedom in achieving his life's goal.[5] In origin it is ignorance,[6] which is strengthened by the existence of a realm of sin, i.e. by the mutual effect of the sinful conduct of all men upon one another, which with Ritschl takes the place of original sin.[7] Justification does not mean the removal of the power of sin dominating the individual—this must be combated and removed by the decision of the individual will, a process for which religious redemption can only pave the way. Justification rather means forgiveness.

In this sense Ritschl understood and affirmed the Reformation doctrine of justification as forensic. The intercourse between God and man, terminated by sin, is resumed by God. Upon the basis of the conditions he has to fulfil man may, unhindered by guilt or the feeling of guilt, join in the building of the Kingdom of God as something which is his own final goal.[8] This forgiveness of God's and this permission granted to man which is based upon it are the particular possession of the Christian Church. In justification God assigns man his place in his Kingdom, in spite of man's sin and upon condition that he should now desist from it. In so doing he makes him into a Christian. And everything there is to be said about God, according to Ritschl, is comprised simply in the statement that God wants, creates and maintains the Church in which this possession is to be received, in which, that is, men are admitted to the Kingdom of God with this intention and in

[1] *Justification and Reconciliation*, III, para. 37; *Instruction*, para. 14.
[2] *Instruction*, paras. 26 and 35.   [3] *Justification and Reconciliation*, III, p. 317.
[4] Ibid., III, para. 40.   [5] Ibid., para. 42.
[6] Ibid., para. 43.   [7] Ibid., para. 41.   [8] *Instruction*, paras. 44f.

this manner; that is, in which they are called to be active in this kingdom. God is love. That is, he did not have to make man's true goal
into his own goal, but, as he is love, he has this goal originally as his
own.[1] God—with regard to the fact that God's kingdom is indeed
nothing else but man's own goal—God is 'the power which man
worships because it upholds his spiritual sense of his own worth against
the restrictions imposed upon it by nature'.[2] His omnipotence is his
'care and presence of grace for pious men'.[3] His righteousness is the
logical manner in which he leads them to salvation.[4] His personality
gives evidence of the value which religion attributes to the spiritual
life of man.[5] Similarly God's creation of the world has of course taken
place solely for the sake of the Kingdom of God, i.e. for the sake of
men's own goal, and is to be understood only in this sense. And
the idea of a wrath of God, and indeed even of a holiness of God
which should be distinguished from his righteousness, would manifestly
imply a negation of his love and thus of man's own goal, and is therefore to be regarded as an idea which was already vanishing in the Old
Testament, but which in the New Testament can only be maintained
eschatologically, that is, only as a description of God's attitude towards
the unjust.[6]

What distinguishes Christianity from every other religion is that it
answers the question all religions ask. Man knows himself as part of the
world and at the same time he is predisposed to spiritual personality.
How can he then establish the claim to dominion over the world which
is based upon this predisposition, against the limitation imposed upon
him by the world?[7] How can we, by appropriating the divine life,
make assured the value of our spiritual life within its limiting involvement with nature or in the world?[8] That is the meaning of an apologetics
of Christianity: to demonstrate this significance of Christianity for the
realization of the ideal of human life—to demonstrate that the Christian
idea of God is the first to offer the necessary connexion of ideas between
our outlook upon life, which is dependent upon the perception of
nature with all its limitations, and our necessary moral self-judgment,
and that therefore to this extent it fills a gap which philosophy leaves
open, and must of necessity leave open.[9]

But the knowledge of God as the God of love, and thus as the God
who forgives sins, who removes our natural limitations, who admits

---

[1] *Justification and Reconciliation*, III, p. 259.   [2] *Theology and Metaphysics*, p. 11.
[3] *Instruction*, para. 15.   [4] Ibid., para. 16.
[5] *Justification and Reconciliation*, III, p. 173.   [6] Ibid., II, paras. 12-15 and 16f.
[7] *Instruction*, para. 8.   [8] Ibid., para. 59.
[9] *Justification and Reconciliation*, III, para. 27; *Instruction*, para. 29.

us into his kingdom and makes us his children, free, but also bound in duty to him—this knowledge comes about in the form of a judgment which is completely different from all the judgments of science in the form, namely, of a value judgment. A value judgment is a judgment in which a certain aspect of being is expressed concerning a certain object of human experience with regard to the value, i.e. the practical significance, which it has for man, a certain aspect of being which, apart from this practical significance, could not be expressed concerning the object. Now the object of human experience which has for man the value of Godhead, and concerning which, therefore, in a certain sense we can venture to pronounce: 'He is God'—this object, and therefore the occasion for the knowledge of God as the God of love, is the historical phenomenon Jesus of Nazareth. Jesus, in himself being in surpassing fashion the bearer of grace as well as of dominion over the world,[1] is the archetypal image of the humanity which is to be united in the kingdom of God[2] and his vocation is simply to reveal the God who is love. In so far as he exercises this vocation upon us, or in so far as we experience and evaluate his historical existence as an action revealing God, he is himself God. It is not through a command, and not through directly divine authority, but as a prophet: through his morally effective sayings and as priest: by the way in which his action is ready to serve, that he exercises the *munus regium* as God and substantiates to us his divine right of dominion. He realizes his own goal which is identical with God's own goal, which, once again, is identical with our own goal. It is in the recognition and expression of this connexion that this decisive value-judgment, which provides the basis for Christian theology as such, comes about; we obtain justification, that is, we obtain admission to the kingdom of God, that is, we obtain the realization of our own purpose of life in no other way but through Jesus in his Church; and thus and in this sense we have God in Christ.

The rounded, transparent and compact quality of this train of thought makes it very understandable that Ritschl should have found followers and support. The reasons why he could not establish himself have already been alluded to and need not be repeated. There were very real reasons why all his contemporaries, apart from the adherents to his school, and the history of theology after him showed themselves to be governed by the determination not to allow his words to hold sway as the final and characteristic words of the entire age, no matter how genuine and impressive they might be in their own way.

[1] *Instruction*, para. 24.   [2] Ibid., para. 22.

INDEX OF NAMES

Achelis, H. N., 520
D'Alembert, Jean Lerond, 176, 183
v. Altenstein, Karl, 510
Aner, Karl, 163, 164, 165, 168, 169,
170, 173
Angelus Silesius, 548
Annoni, Hieronymus, 111
Anselm of Canterbury, 526, 532, 570,
618
Aristotle, 241, 251
Arndt, Ernst Moritz, 438
v. Arnim, Bettina, 430
Arnold, Gottfried, 59, 152, 241, 502
Athanasius, 108, 130
Auberlen, Karl August, 599
Augustine, 17, 108, 130, 132, 140,
164, 165, 209, 282, 301, 346, 493,
515, 526, 552, 596, 603
Augustus the Strong, 44, 86, 127

Bach, J. S., 69, 70, 71, 72, 73
Bahrdt, K. F., 122, *168–9*, 170, 171
Baronius, Caesar, 502
Barth, C. G., 644, 647
Barth, Fritz, 622
Basedow, J. B., 33, 60, 62
Bauer, Bruno, 560
Baumgarten, Jakob, *160–1*, 162, 165,
172
Baur, F. C., 85, 387, 483, 484, 491,
499–507, 510, 517, 541, 542, 545,
555, 563, 588, 614, 616, 657
Bayle, Pierre, 35, 160, 179
Beaumont, Christoph de, 205, 207,
213
Beck, J. T., 122, 511, 519, 528, 539,
616–24, 625, 628, 635, 642, 651

Beethoven, Ludwig van, 69, 72, 178,
549
Bengel, Ernst Gottlieb, 501, 541
Bengel, J. A., 40, 118, 122, 134, 520,
586, 614
Biedermann, Aloys Emanuel, 385,
544, 654
Bismarck, Otto von, 439, 656
Blum, Robert, 549
Blumhardt, Christoph, 539, 618, 646
Blumhardt, Johann Christoph, 539,
618, *643–53*
Böhl, Eduard, 636
Böhme, Jakob, 541
Böhme, Justus Henning, 86
Bölsche, Wilhelm, 344, 346
Bossuet, Jacques Benigne, 36
Bousset, Wilhelm, 655
Breitinger, J. J., 68
Brentano, Clemens, 344
Bretschneider, Karl Gottlieb, 426, 474,
519, 555
Brockes, Barthold Hinrich, 159
Brunner, Emil, 21, 28, 426, 428, 436
Buddeus, J. F., 138, *141–4*, 151, 156,
158, 163, 164
Buffon, George Louis Leclerc de, 179
Bultmann, Rudolf, 490
Bunsen, Josias v., 598
Bunyan, John, 38

Cagliostro, Alex v., 35
Calvin, Jean, 108, 129, 137, 150, 165,
183, 189, 303, 428, 429, 432, 571,
623, 626, 641, 642
Canz, Israel Gottlieb, 160, 165
Cardanus, Hermann, 241

Carlyle, Thomas, 335, 560
Carpov, Jakob, 160, 165
Casanova, Giacomo, 35
Chamette, 41
Charles of Anjou, 626
Charpentier, Julie, 359
Cicero, 76, 77
Claudius, Matthias, 271, 520
Clement XIV, 87
Cocceius, J., 614
Cochleus, J., 241, 242
Colbert, J. B., 46
Collenbusch, Samuel, 523, 527
Columbus, Christopher, 38, 656
Cook, James, 36
Copernicus, Nicolaus, 37, 38, 167, 270
Cremer, H., 519, 654

Dante, Alighieri, 548
Darwin, Charles, 545, 548
Daub, Karl, 426, 491, 492. 493, 494,
    534, 598
Davel, J. D. A., 119
Delitzsch, F., 631
Descartes, René, 241, 384, 409
Dessau, Leopold von, 41
Diderot, Denis, 176, 179, 180
Diederichs, Eugen, 342
Dilthey, Wilhelm, 430
Dippel, J. K., 111
Dittus, Gottliebin, 644, 645, 649
Dorner, Isaak August, 24, 307, 316,
    330, 577-87, 588, 589, 594, 597,
    623, 624, 635
Dostoievsky, F. M., 574
Drews, Arthur, 560, 566
Durante, Francesco, 177

Eberhard Ludwig of Bavaria, 44
Eckhart, Meister, 466
Edelmann, J. C., 111
Eichendorff, Joseph v., 344, 348
Eichhorn, J. G., 555
Elert, Werner, 21
Epictetus, 77
Epicurus, 77
d'Epinay, Louise, 183
Erasmus, Desiderius, 145
Ernesti, J. A., 165, 171

Eschenmayer, Karl August, 541
Euclid, 252
Euler, Leonhard, 36, 47
Eusebius, 500, 502

Fahrenheit, Gabriel D., 41
Fénelon, François, 36, 61
Feuerbach, Ludwig, 11, 489, 534-40,
    542, 545, 562, 565, 566, 568, 576,
    628, 633
Fichte, J. G., 253, 350, 359. 384, 393,
    394, 396, 438, 443, 484, 520, 534
Francke, A. H., 60, 61, 103
Frank, H. R., 20, 23, 28, 569, 570,
    607, 654
Franklin, Benjamin, 252
Frederick the Great, 34, 35, 36, 45,
    46, 47, 64, 69, 70, 87, 90, 116, 124,
    127, 149, 207, 209, 234, 235, 425,
    479
Frederick William I of Prussia, 45, 46,
    61, 87
Frederick William II of Prussia, 61, 87
Frederick William IV of Prussia, 342,
    636
Fries, J. F., 306, 482, 483, 487, 490
Frischlin, Nikodemus, 543

Galilei, Galileo, 37, 38
Galvani, Luigi, 41
Ganganelli (Clement XIV), 87
Gass, Wilhelm, 24, 142, 152, 158, 160,
    162, 165, 170, 171, 425, 476, 488,
    492, 493, 494
Gellert, C. F., 38, 77, 112, 127, 135, 573
Gesenius, Wilhelm, 510
Gesner, Matthias, 60
Gieseler, J. K. L., 501
Gildemeister, C. H., 520
Gluck, Christoph Willibald v., 69, 73
Goethe, J. W. v., 11, 34, 35, 36. 38,
    41, 46, 55, 65, 66, 68, 72, 77, 88,
    113, 123, 128, 131, 132, 133, 137,
    162, 166, 167, 168, 174, 176, 178,
    179, 215, 216, 221, 225, 229, 230,
    231, 233, 235, 266, 267, 294, 318,
    327, 328, 341, 342, 356, 404, 405,
    410, 438, 459, 515 520, 521, 545,
    549

Goetz, Walter, 36
Goeze, Melchior, 234, 242, 245, 250, 255
Gottsched, J. C., 33, 67, 68, 235
Grimm, Melchior, 179, 183
Grützmacher, Richard, 25
Gunkel, Hermann, 655
Guyon, Jeanne Marie de, 36, 103

Haeckel, Ernst, 342, 548
Haering, Theodor v., 654
Hagenbach, Karl Rudolf, 482
Hahn, P. M., 40
Haller, Albrecht v. 35
Hamann, J. G., 271, 318, 520
Handel, G. F., 69, 73
Harless, Adolf v., 631
Harms, Klaus, 346
Harnack, Adolf v., 25, 170, 336, 387, 501, 502, 527, 654
Harnack, Theodosius, 607
Hase, Karl, 501, 505, 556, 569, 570
Hassenpflug, Hans Daniel Ludwig Friedrich, 626
Hausrath, Adolf, 19, 500, 543, 545, 546, 547, 597, 599, 602
Haydn, Joseph, 69, 73, 549
Heckel, Theodor, 598
Hegel, Georg Wilhelm Friedrich, 176, 267, 341, 342, *384–421*, 426, 434, 438, 447, 448, 449, 451, 453, 459, 466, 480, 491, 492, 493, 494, 495, 496, 498, 503, 505, 520, 521, 534, 537, 538, 539, 541, 544, 546, 562, 577, 580, 582, 585, 589, 592, 593, 594, 597, 598, 607, 619, 623, 634, 635, 640, 654, 656
Heidegger, Martin, 490
Heitmüller, Wilhelm, 655
Hengstenberg, Ernst Wilhelm, 510, 546, 560, 607
Herder, J. G., 88, 166, 169, 266, 267, 281, 294, *313–40*, 343, 344, 345, 347, 389, 392, 394, 410, 427, 451, 463, 475, 482, 484, 501
Herrmann, Wilhelm, 20, 307, 308, 343, 346, 488, 511, 520, 610, 611, 654
Heubner, H. L., 598

Hilary, 151
Hilgenfeld, Adolf, 500
Hiller, P. F., 111
Hinneberg, Paul, 526
Hobbes, Thomas, 53, 54, 86, 188, 191
Hodgson, Peter C., 504
Hofacker, Ludwig, 345, 547, 644
Hoffmann, Heinrich, 34, 57, 58, 84, 163
Hofmann, J. C. K., 511, *607–15*, 623, 628, 633, 642
Hofmann, W., 644
Holbach, Dietrich, 179
Hölderlin, Friedrich, 451
Holl, Karl, 22, 301
Hollaz, David, 142
Holsten, Karl, 500
Holtzmann, H. J., 500, 602
Homer, 334
Hooke, Robert, 41
Horace, 334
d'Houdetot, Sophie, 183, 185
Huber, Marie, 122
Hume, David, 176, 209, 218, 269
Hutten, Ulrich v., 543

Ihmels, Ludwig, 654
Irenaeus, 164, 165, 526

Jacobi, Friedrich Heinrich, 235, 238, 271, 306, 482
Jerusalem, J. F. W., 97, 127, 165, *167–8*, 169, 170, 523
Jommelli, Niccolo, 177
Joris, David, 145
Joseph II of Austria, 36, 40, 41, 46, 47, 61, 88
Joseph Emmerich of Mainz, 46
Jung-Stilling, J. H., 118, 300, 309, 520

Kaftan, Julius, 387, 656
Kähler, Martin, 519, 622, 654
Kalthoff, Albert, 560
Kamnitzer, Ernst, 345
Kant, Immanuel, 34, 38, 47, 144, 174, 220, 223, *266–312*, 313, 314, 315, 316, 317, 318, 322, 326, 328, 330, 331, 332, 333, 334, 338, 339, 341, 342, 343, 344, 345, 347, 385, 389,

Kant, Immanuel—*continued*
　393, 394, 396, 397, 409, 410, 417,
　427, 434, 459, 463, 474, 480, 483,
　489, 495, 501, 520, 534, 548, 591,
　655
Karl Alexander of Württemberg, 44
Karl August of Saxe-Weimar, 46, 88
Karl Eugen of Württemberg, 44
Karl Theodor of Bavaria, 44
Karl Wilhelm Ferdinand of Bruns-
　wick, 167
Kattenbusch, Ferdinand, 24, 608, 654
Keith, Jakob v., 207
Kempis, Thomas à, 140
Kerner, Justinus, 541
Kierkegaard, Sören, 34, 400, 618
Kirn, Otto, 654
Kliefoth, Theodor, 630, 631
Klopstock, Friedrich Gottlieb, 68, 166
Knapp, Albert, 548
Kohlbrügge, H. F., *634-42*, 643, 649
König, J. F., 161
Korff, H. A., 34
Kottwitz, Hans Ernst v., 509, 519, 598
Kotzebue, August v., 482
Krafft, J. C., 607, 614
Krüdener, Barbara Juliane v., 519
Kühn, Sophie v., 359, 361, 366
Kutter, Hermann, 525, 598, 655

Lagarde, Paul Anton de, 654
Lamrck, Jean Baptiste de, 548
Lange, Joachim, 141
Laplace, Pierre Simon, 271, 548
Lasson, Georg, 385
Lavater, J. C., 133, 271, 520
Leibnitz, Gottfried Wilhelm, 34, 35,
　37, 77, 78, 79, 85, 89, 102, 113, 119,
　135, 157, 165, 241, 318, 394, 590,
　640
Leo, Leonardo, 177
Leopold of Dessau, 41
Lessing, Gotthold Ephraim, 26, 34,
　46, 47, 68, 137, 144, 167, 174, *234-*
　65, 266, 267, 289, 315, 317, 327,
　331, 332, 333, 334, 344, 385, 389,
　392, 394, 409, 412, 427, 433, 463,
　545
Le Vasseur, Thérèse, 179, 209, 218

Lipsius, Richard Adelbert, 654
Livy, 557
Locke, John, 54
Löhe, Wilhelm, 631
Loofs, Friedrich, 527
Löscher, Valentin Ernst, 139-41, 143,
　158
Louis XIV of France, 36, 41, 42, 43,
　44, 45, 46, 49, 59, 67, 77, 87, 176,
　551
Louis XV of France, 44, 177
Louis XVI of France, 49
Lücke, Friedrich, 440, 445, 457, 484,
　488
Lüdemann, Hermann, 500, 520, 654
Ludwig IX of Hesse, 44
Lülmann, Christian, 426
Luthardt, Christoph Ernst, 654
Luther, Martin, 15, 17, 22, 24, 69,
　103, 108, 129, 132, 137, 140, 151,
　165, 167, 245. 254, 303, 325, 327,
　416, 428, 429, 432, 461, 462, 476,
　493, 497, 515, 517, 536, 538, 543,
　544, 552, 559
Lutz, Samuel, 103, 132

Mackintosh, H. R., 11
Malesherbes, Chrétien Guillaume de,
　179
Marheineke, Philipp Konrad, 307,
　426, *491-8*, 499, 503, 509, 514, 554,
　577
Martensen, Hans Larsen, 578
Max Emanuel of Bavaria, 44
Melanchthon, Philipp, 76, 579
Mendelssohn, Felix, 178
Mendelssohn, Moses, 235, 238
Menken, Gottfried, 11, *519-33*, 539,
　554, 608, 614, 616, 623, 624, 635,
　642, 643
Michaelis, J. D., 165, *171-2*
Michelet, Karl Ludwig, 385
Miller, Johann Peter, 153
Milton, John, 38
Montagu, Lady, 41
Montesquieu, Charles, 40
Montgolfier, brothers, 41
Montmollin, F. G. de, 208
Mörike, Eduard, 644

Mosheim, J. L. v., 86, *152–6*, 501, 527

Mozart, Wolfgang Amadeus, 34, 46, 63, 64, 70, 73, 178, 269, 365, 549, 567

Mulert, Hermann, 440

Müller, Johannes, 525, 655

Müller, Julius, 8, 509, *588–96*, 597, 601, 635, 636

Münscher, Wilhelm, 168

Muralt, Ludwig v., 111

Naumann, Friedrich, 342

Neander, August, 425, 482, 501, 556, 562

Neuser, Adam, 241

Newton, Isaac, 241

Nicolai, Friedrich, 33, 34, 165, 166, 244

Nietzsche, Friedrich, 137, 145, 342, 545, 546, 567

Nitzsch, Karl Immanuel, 425

Nollet, 252

Novalis, Friedrich v. Hardenberg, 34, *341–83*, 389, 392, 427, 451, 466, 598

Odenwald, Theodor, 22

Oecolampadius, Johannes, 145

Oetinger, F. C., 40, 118, 122, 520, 586, 598

Oettingen, Alexander v., 654

Origen, 596

Osiander, Andreas, 623

Osterwald, Jean Frédéric, *147–9*

Otto, Rudolf, 490, 655

Overbeck, Franz, 23, 145, 387, 500, 506, 654

Papin, Denis, 41

Paulsen, Friedrich, 387

Paulus, H. E. G., 556, 560

Pergolesi, Giovanni Battista, 177

Peter the Great, 39, 88

Petitpierre, Ferdinand Olivier, 149

Pfaff, Christoph Matthias, 86, 138, *143–4*, 153

Pfleiderer, Otto, 500, 654

Philip of Orleans, 44

Philippine Charlotte of Brunswick, 168

Planck, Gottlieb Jakob, 501

Plato, 40, 241, 334, 429, 434, 512

Plessing, Friedrich, 216

Plutarch, 76, 77, 178

Pope, Alexander, 40

Priestley, Joseph, 41

Przywara, Erich, 21

Pufendorf, Samuel v., 86

Quenstedt, Johann Andreas, 130, 160, 161

Rade, Martin, 654

Ragaz, Leonhard, 530, 598, 655

Ranke, Leopold v., 607

Raumer, Karl Georg v., 607

Reimarus, Elise, 238

Reimarus, Hermann Samuel, 235, 238, 239, 242, 243, 248, 249, 252

Renan, Ernest, 542

Richelieu, Armand Jean du Plessis, 43

Riggenbach, Christoph Johannes, 616

Ritschl, Albrecht Benjamin, 22, 24, 25, 27, 28, 85, 107, 137, 306, 307, 341, 343, 387, 426, 439, 480, 500, 505, 531, 577, 634, *654–61*

Rittelmeyer, Friedrich, 598, 655

Rock, J. F., 118, 119

Röller, Traugott Günther, 96, 97, 103

Rothe, Richard, 19, 509, 511, *597–606*, 607, 615, 622, 639, 652

Rousseau, Jean-Jacques, 11, 34, 149, *174–233*, 234, 235, 236, 238, 262, 266, 267, 270, 281, 293, 316, 317, 344, 433

Runge, Conrad Heinrich, 521

Sand, Karl Ludwig, 482

Sander, F., 28

Schaeder, Erich, 20, 582, 655

Scharnhorst, G. J. D., 438

Schebest, Agnes, 541

Schelling, F. W. J. v., 392, 396, 397, 404, 443, 447, 448, 449, 451, 484, 541

Schenkel, Daniel, 482, 542, 546

Schiller, Friedrich v., 216, 512

Schlatter, Adolf, 519, 622, 654

Schlegel, Friedrich, 344

Schleiermacher, F. E. D., 11, 15, 17, 18, 22, 23, 24, 25, 26, 27, 28, 99, 160, 166, 169, 173, 174, 178, 267, 306, 308, 316, 328, 339, 342, 343, 344, 345, 347, 348, 361, 387, 392, 410, 411, 414, 417, 421, *425-73*, 474, 475, 476, 480, 482, 484, 486, 487, 488, 489, 490, 491, 492, 493, 494, 495, 496, 497, 499, 509, 511, 512, 513, 514, 515, 517, 520, 521, 522, 527, 531, 532, 534, 537, 541, 554, 555, 556, 563, 567, 569, 571, 572, 574, 575, 576, 577, 578, 579, 580, 582, 585, 589, 591, 594, 597, 598, 607, 608, 609, 610, 611, 614, 619, 623, 626, 627, 633, 634, 635, 652, 654, 656

Schmid, Heinrich, 607

Scholz, Heinrich, 427

Schopenhauer, Arthur, 539

Schubert, Franz, 69, 178, 543

Schulz, David, 88, 654

Schumann, Friedrich Karl, 21

Schwegler, Albert, 500

Schweitzer, Albert, 542, 550, 567

Schweizer, Alexander, 425, 568, 569-76, 577, 585, 588, 597, 606, 615

Seeberg, Reinhold, 22, 654

Semler, J. S., 160, 162, 165, *169-71*, 172, 235, 484, 501, 527

Seneca, 77, 293

Shaftesbury, Anthony Ashley Cooper, Lord, 38

Shakespeare, William, 236

Socrates, 40, 204, 219, 241

Sophia Charlotte of Prussia, 78

Sophocles, 236, 334

Spalding, J. J., 95, 97, 165, *172*, 523

Spemann, Franz, 25

Spener, Philipp Jakob, 103, 128, 141

Spinoza, Benedictus de, 131, 235, 318, 394, 544

Stange, Karl, 655

Stein, Charlotte v., 38

Stephan, Horst, 11, 12, 34, 84, 163, 319, 634

Steudel, J. C. F., 541, 562

Stier, Ewald Rudolf, 598

Stirner, Max, 539

Stolzenburg, Arnold F., 138

Storr, Gottlob Christian, 501

Strauss, David Friedrich, 11, 426, 492, 499, 540, *541-68*, 570, 573, 574, 576, 597, 628, 644, 647

Swedenborg, Emanuel, 35

Sydow, Karl Leopold Adolf, 430

Tauler, Johannes, 140

Tersteegen, Gerhard, 36, 103, 115, 118, 127

Tertullian, 164, 165

Thaer, Albrecht, 239

Tholuck, Friedrich August, 160, 492, *508-18*, 537, 554, 556, 562, 563, 574, 588, 589, 598, 636, 641

Thomas Aquinas, 17, 156, 157, 384, 389, 396, 574, 626

Thomasius, 26, 29, 86, 607

Tiberius, Emperor, 557

Tieck, Ludwig, 344

Tillich, Paul, 9

Töllner, J. G., 172-3

Tolstoy, Leo, 342

Troeltsch, Ernst, 20, 22, 84, 126, 163, 307, 308, 316, 341, 342, 343, 347, 361, 488, 597, 655

Turrettini, Franz, 129

Turrettini, Jean Alphonse, 129, 149-51, 207, 208

Twesten, August, 425, 571

Ullmann, Karl, 562, 588

Ursinus, Zacharias, 526

Viktoria, Luise Adelgunde, 67

Vilmar, August Friedrich Christian, 26, 29, *625-33*, 634, 635, 640, 643

Vischer, Friedrich Theodor, 499

Vitringa, Campegius, 614

Voltaire, Francois Marie Aroult de, 34, 36, 59, 69, 124, 134, 176, 179, 182, 183, 208, 218, 235, 543

Vorländer, Karl, 300

Vulpius, Christiane, 179

Wackenroder, Wilhelm Heinrich, 345

Wagner, Richard, 69, 342, 567
Walch, C. W. F., 152
Walch, Johann, Georg, 147, 151–2, 153
Warens, Françoise Louise de, 178, 179, 181, 184, 209, 215, 224
Watt, James, 41
Wegscheider, Julius August Ludwig, 27, 306, 308, *474–81*, 482, 484, 487, 510, 519, 523, 531, 556, 655
Weinel, Heinrich, 560
Weiss, Johannes, 655
Weizsäcker, Carl, 500, 616, 617
Wellhausen, Julius, 484
Werenfels, Samuel, 129, 144–7
Wernle, Paul, 84, 111, 147, 159, 163, 187, 655
Wette, Wilhelm Leberecht de, 306, 316, *482–90*, 491, 492, 512, 514, 537, 556, 560, 616

Wettstein, Johann Jakob, 146
Wichelhaus, Johannes, 636, 639
Wilhelm II, German Emperor, 387
Witte, Leopold, 509, 513
Wobbermin, Georg, 22, 343, 655
Wolff, Christian, 33, 34, 87, 131, 137, 143, 144, *156–60*, 161, 162, 165, 277, 394
Wöllner, J. C., 87, 170

Zahn, Adolf, 636
Zeller, Eduard, 500
Zeno, 77
Zezschwitz, Gerhard v., 607
Zinzendorf, Nikolaus Ludwig, Graf v., 35, 66, 103, 115, 122, 132, 133, 137, 146
Zündel, Friedrich, 643, 646
Zwingli, Ulrich, 569, 571